HARDNESS of HEART HARDNESS of LIFE

The STAIN of HUMAN INFANTICIDE

LARRY S. MILNER
MD, JD, MLS

Mazo Publishers

Hardness of Heart, Hardness of Life: the Stain of Human Infanticide

ISBN 978-1-956381-405

infanticide@ameritech.net

Published by

Mazo Publishers
www.mazopublishers.com
Email: mazopublishers@gmail.com

Front Cover:
Abraham Offering Up His Son Isaac, Genesis 22

5432

This book is dedicated to my three daughters:

Kimberly Beth, Wendy Lynn, and Jodi Allison.

With each day of research, and with every page of agonized text in the preparation of this book, I realized more and more how love can overcome even the most primitive impulse of a parent to harm their offspring.

I hope that the findings contained herein will extend this realization to parents, and future parents, all over the world.

Contents

About The Author

Dr. Larry S. Milner, MD, JD, MLS is a board-certified physician in Internal Medicine, Hematology and Oncology, as well as an attorney. He received his medical training at the University of Illinois, Massachusetts General Hospital, University of Pennsylvania Hospital, and the National Institutes of Health. He trained at Loyola Law School in Chicago, and has a Master of Liberal Studies degree from Lake Forest College.

In addition to being the author of *Hardness of Heart, Hardness of Life: the Stain of Human Infanticide,* for which he is an expert in the field of infanticide, Dr. Milner is also a recognized historian with expertise in Hebraic, Greek, and Egyptian cultures.

He is the author of *Shattered Faith: The Life of Abraham; Shattered Trust: The Life of Moses; Moses' And Muhammad's Contribution To Monotheism; Hebraic Influences On Greek Philosophy And Mysticism: The Legacy Of Isaiah's Anointing Of King Cyrus II Of Persia; Hebraic Influences On Greek Civilization: Was Achilles a Jew?*; *Legacy Of The Burning Bush: A Kabbalistic Interpretation of the Hebrew Exodus; Tainted Hands: An Encounter With The Mosaic Code*; *Your Name Is Achilles: Son Of Daniel; The Sun Shone Only In Goshen: The Effect Of The Exodus On Akhenaten In Egypt* and *Shattered Dreams*.

Dr. Milner and his wife, Marlene, divide their time between Lincolnshire, Illinois and Boynton Beach, Florida. They have three daughters, Kimberly Seiden, Wendy LaVarre, and Jodi Morton, and wonderful grandchildren.

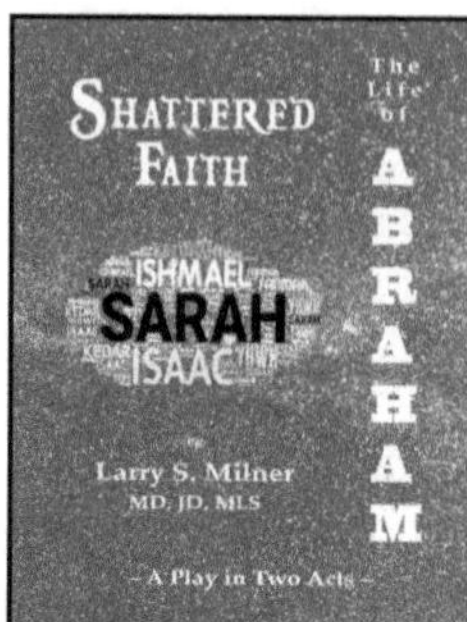

Shattered Faith:
The Life of Abraham

Shattered Trust:
The Life of Moses

Hebraic Influences On
Greek Civilization

Tainted Hands: An
Encounter With The
Mosaic Code

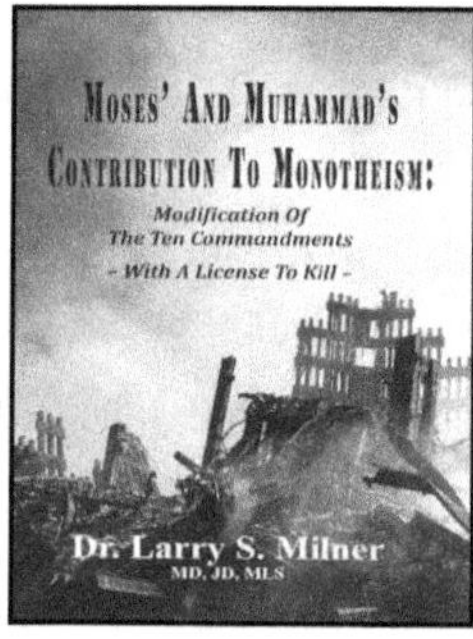

Moses' And Muhammad's
Contribution To
Monotheism

Hebraic Influences On
Greek Philosophy
And Mysticism

Legacy Of
The Burning Bush

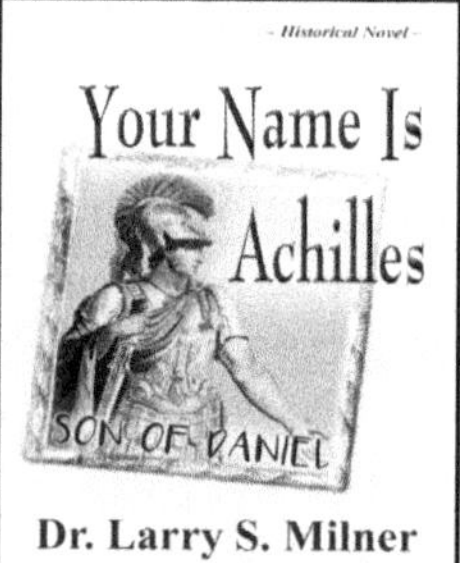

Your Name Is Achilles:
Son Of Daniel

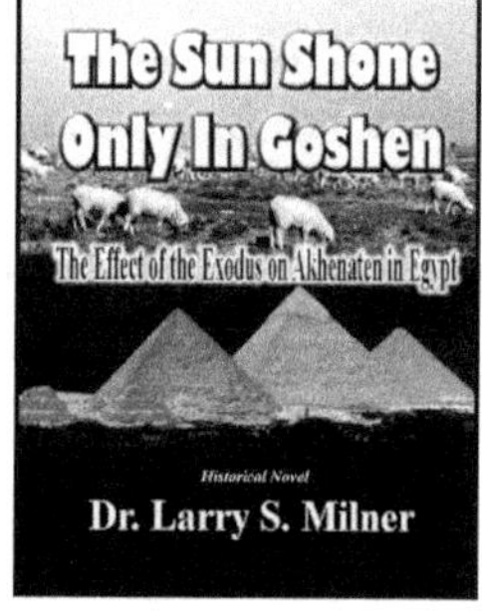

The Sun Shone
Only In Goshen

Other Books

by

Dr. Larry S. Milner

Shattered Dreams

HARDNESS of HEART HARDNESS of LIFE

The STAIN of HUMAN INFANTICIDE

INTRODUCTION

> "Infanticide has been practiced on every continent and by people on every level of cultural complexity, from hunters and gatherers to high civilizations, including our own ancestors. Rather than being an exception, then, it has been the rule."[1]

In 1978, Laila Williamson, an anthropologist with the American Museum of Natural History, summarized the data she had collected on the presence of infanticide from a variety of sources in the scientific, and historical, literature by bluntly concluding that murdering one's own child was a common human trait. Although verification of each event was not always possible within each civilization studied, the information she gathered clearly showed that the problem was of protean proportion and not simply dismissible as an accidental aberration. Much of the evidence she cited came from the work of Divale and Harris who performed demographic analysis of 561 local band and village populations from 112 different societies. They found that in an ethnographic census of 393 populations, 179 practiced infanticide commonly, 29 occasionally, and 94 on an isolated basis.[2] Only 91, or 23%, did not show any evidence of an accepted custom of infanticide.

Many observers of human behavior have brushed this incontrovertible evidence aside, and continued to view the killing of children by parents as a desultory footnote in the history of mankind.[3] After all, how likely is it, the argument goes, that a review of mostly tribal populations can be expanded to a generalization on the entire human race? These are "savages" from the wild; they have little in common with the rest of our modern civilization.

To some degree, this brusque dismissal appears to have a modicum of legitimate critique. If the problem of infanticide is truly this widespread – if the history of mankind has indeed been peppered with the constant killing of children by their biologic parents – why has there been so little overt reaction among either governmental, religious, or academic sources? Surely the presence of this much killing, if indeed it had occurred, should provoke a response at least equal to that which has transpired with respect to the morality, or legality, of abortion. Nothing short of mayhem has developed over the argument of when life begins, and whether the fetus has an independent right to life. Should there not have been as equally intense outrage over murdering a child once it was born, if indeed the crime is that common?

The logical response to this query is obvious – yes. But whatever the reasons for the lack of societal outrage, the historical evidence of infanticide clearly supports Williamson's conclusion. In the words of Lloyd DeMause:

> All families once practiced infanticide. All states trace their origin to child sacrifice. All religions began with the mutilation and murder of children.[4]

Where then do we find a rationale for this social commentary vacuum? One possible explanation could be that the claimed frequency of such a detestable parental act is simply not believed. Most people find it difficult to accept that anyone, except the most severely mentally disturbed felon, would kill their own child. In fact, the report of such a crime in the newspaper generally appears on the front page, with pictures of the accused parent boldly displayed, so unusual and shocking are the details to the average reader.

And even when stories are proven true, just how much depravity can the public absorb? There are many problems in the world today: hunger, pollution, war and crime. Newborns die everywhere from a variety of nutritional or medical problems; we are inundated with the statistics of famine, of genocide, of man's utter disregard for the sanctity of life. Just how important can the loss of a single infant be to the community-at-large?

People can accept just so much negative news before the source is turned off; the newborn is a good place to start. This is known not only to newspaper reporters, but also to scientists seeking research grants or academic support. Investigation into the widespread killing of children by their parents is not high on the public relations list of most universities. Robert Weir wrote that "infanticide has been tolerated by the great majority if not all of the world's societies."[5] While harming a helpless child may induce instant sympathy, the incident is unfortunately soon forgotten. Newborns do not have an equal legal status to that of an older child or adult, and generally there are few individuals outside of the family circle to come to their aide.

The informational gap on this subject is incredibly wide. Scholarly works, as well as the lay press, show a rarity of comment that indicates how often historians miss the human factor in studying past civilizations. As for the research into general human behavior, infanticide has been almost totally ignored. When acts of child-murder are referenced at all, they generally are passed off as some quirk or defective apparatus of an unusual place or time. Look in the index of almost any major social treatise and you will find only a rare reference to the presence of infanticide.

But the fact of the matter is that infanticide is not an isolated phenomenon and cannot be explained by some aberrant, sociopathic excuse. From sacrificial killings meant to appease the wrath of gods, to the abandonment of bastard newborns in an attempt to hide from shame, human beings have slaughtered their offspring with no less frequency than they have murdered in the pursuit of war and oppression. The shear numbers are staggering. In every era, in every country, some degree of infanticide has been found. While certain societies have noted only sporadic cases, others reveal that 10-50% of all newborns have been killed either at birth, or soon thereafter. And for the most part, these killings have proceeded with either the direct participation, or the permission, of the child's parent and societal legal codes.

Of course, this does not negate the role of criminal activity. Infanticide has indeed been due to psychopathic behavior, or even temporary insanity, which makes the actions of the guilty party excusable under most legal systems. But the killings are so pervasive among disparate groups of man that an explanation must be sought not in human behavioral pathology, but in the very genetic nature of our species itself. Along with billions of other traits, inherited from one generation to the next, has come a tendency to eliminate our own children when some type of self-survival impulse is ignited.

Such a negative connotation to the nature of man does not sit well with modern beliefs. We have come to think of ourselves in humanistic tones which frames us in the benevolent image of a man-made God: an "Imago Dei", capable of rational thought and moral action. In the first chapter of the Bible we read that "God created man in his image."[6] Humankind has accepted this pronouncement as evidence that they are blessed in a manner unlike every other living creature. But our factual behavior, at least with respect to the prevalence of infanticide, does not seem to support such a self-serving hypothesis.

In this book, without judging whether our actions are good or evil, or whether they reflect the words of a higher Deity, I intend to show that the frequency of infanticide is so prodigious that it must be assessed as indicative of "normal" behavior. While it may not be the type of behavior we are used to seeing as "humane," it nevertheless must be reinterpreted in light of this undeniable common prevalence. Every society has had its criminals who have acted outside both the moral and legal code, but the majority of documented infanticides reveals that the parent has acted in an understandable, and often forgivable, way. Most readers would respond to this statement with disbelief because they do not see such criminal propensity within themselves, or their close circle of family and friends. However, it is also a fortunate fact that most citizens of the Western World have never been faced with the need to consider an infanticidal option for any of the reasons that are discussed later in this book. In the words of a very old proverb, it is very hard to walk in another man's shoes, and it is not a fair judgment to vow that you would be willing to exchange your own life for that of your child when the occasion is likely never to arise.

This brings us to the very core of why it is so difficult to analyze the basis for our actions in the complicated society we live in today. Before we can truly comprehend the reason why an individual responds to a particular stressful situation, we must first understand the instincts which guide our basic biologic drives. Much of our behavior is reflexual rather than learned; the genetic material guiding our response has survived, to some degree, within our own chromosomes from prehistoric ancestors. While this conduct, over time, can be modified to some extent, we are nevertheless a product of our nature and are limited by self-serving, self-preserving genes.

Such pagan shortcomings do not sit well with many modern humanists who would like to believe that man is capable of always acting in a moral, ethical, "humane" way. They find no limitation to the benevolent potential of the human species; evil is a preventable commodity as long as society makes the right choices. But such an ideal assessment is only possible when seen through modern methods of environmental control.

The twentieth century has completely isolated us from our true biological beginnings. Our way of life demonstrates how totally our dominion over the earth is now almost complete. In only 7000 years, a mere blink of the eye in the evolution of our species, we have gone from domestication of plant and animal life to a state where we not only farm the commodities we desire, we are now able to modify that life to our liking with gene-splicing technology. Mountain ranges, which once stood as proud and inviolate structures leading to the legendary feats of Hannibal, are now pocked with tunnels, electric lines and ski lifts to satisfy the recreational desires of the masses. The deepest ocean floor, imagined with intensity by Jules Verne, is crisscrossed with telephone cables; the heavens, which have mesmerized man from the very moment his eyes could look up at the sky, now abound with satellites and man-made debris.

Our ability to rapidly change an environment that took millions of years to form is frightening. We seem to be intent on a rapid pace of progress driven by an insatiable quest for knowledge and reward. It is not only greed which fuels this drive, it is the belief that scientific advancement is synonymous with "good for mankind." And in this venue we ravage the forests, pollute the seas, and fill the air with toxic wastes that affect every living species on earth.

This general indifference to the physical environment of our planet has carried over to our interpersonal relationships with our fellow human beings as well. It has been relatively easy for historians to portray the human species as a violent race, capable of ruthless behavior from an anthropologic perspective. Our intense desire for domination over neighboring populations has characterized every society of mankind. While one can usually find improvement in thought and design throughout every gathering studied, there is usually an affiliated spillage of blood as well.

The history of the Golden Age of Greece is not confined to Socratic discussions and the rise of a democratic spirit, it is deluged with the bloody wars so descriptively portrayed in the heroic tales of Homer and the chronicles of Herodotus. The Romans were famous for their architectural advances, and for legal systems which form the ethical basis of our modern age, but their conquests of other nations entailed so much mutilation and devastation that the Roman populace would eventually take pleasure in watching human slaughter continue in their amphitheaters as entertainment and sport. The Egyptians, Sumerians and Assyrians may have left us a legacy of language and astronomic expanse, but the bloody battles they waged throughout the cradle of civilization is punctuated with chilling tales of torture and death. In the words of Anthony Storr: "The somber fact is that we are the cruellest and most ruthless species that has ever walked the earth."[7]

Much of this callous destruction of life has been excused as killing with a necessary, social purpose in sight: Crusades designed to follow the commands of God; border skirmishes and world wars to free those enslaved by a tyrannical regime; covert actions of a democratic society to protect the rest of the free world from mayhem caused by rebellious fanatics. Ibn Khaldun, the fourteenth century Arab scholar, believed that these wars were:

> Something natural among human beings. No nation and no race is free from it.[8]

But even if one accepts such a pessimistic and unitarian attitude toward killings condoned by the fervor of nationalistic spirit, is it possible to use a similar explanation for the frequently encountered killing of a child by its own parent? Where can national safety and concern be hidden within such a seemingly brutal act? It might not surprise some skeptics that people view those of another color or race with caution and fear; hatred has always driven part of our social behavior. But what could possibly cause one to turn against his own offspring? Surely the inherent love of a parent for their child would be expected to countermand such a horrific impulse. And most evolutionary models of social motives do predict that genetic relationships will be associated with a mitigation of violent conflicts.[9]

If not only from a moral or religious base, then from a scientific, evolutionary approach, the survival of our species would seem to demand that such a protective trait be securely in place. How could our race replicate itself unless such desires force the parent to rear the majority of its young? Insects, who rely on thousands of eggs being dispersed at one time, can survive on the statistical reliance that some offspring will live; but with the ability to average only one birth a year, Homo sapiens cannot depend on numbers for equal assurance.

And so there must be some natural impulse which has evolved over the eons of time that encourages man to protect his young. One can see evidence of this throughout the animal kingdom. As the miracle of birth expels the helpless, totally dependent fetus into the world, almost every species shows some innate impulse to begin the nurturing process without being shown what methodology to use. Parents immediately tend to the neonate in an effective manner that is genetically determined. The mother or father almost never abandons the brood for self-centered reasons, but remains nearby to protect the young from predators and to provide nutrition until the infants are capable of surviving on their own. This instinct – "acquired through the process of natural selection because it has a tendency to preserve the next generation and thereby the species," – is everywhere to be found.[10] If such a trait was not inherent, there would be little chance that the fragile young newborns could survive the rigors of early life.

So it is with human beings as well. Our desire to procreate appears to be uniformly present and is culturally displaced in only rare exceptions, as among the ancient Roman nobility and certain American Indian cultures.[11] Aristotle noted that men, like other plants and animals, "have a natural desire to leave behind them an image of themselves."[12] In most societies, childless marriages and barren women were objects of pity or scorn.[13] Under the *Code of Jewish Law*, for example, an Orthodox Jewish husband had to divorce a woman who was unable to bear a child after ten years of marriage.[14] And the most serious violation of Confucian ideology is to not have children under the principle of filial piety.[15]

The Greeks and Romans even imbued their gods with such yearnings for fertility. Pluto, the lord of the underworld, complained bitterly to his brother Jove about his childless and unwed state, and even threatened war if he was not allotted a son. He spoke of his loneliness in an impassioned plea:

> And shall I in this empty palace, sans joy, sans fame, know no child's love to still instant care? I will not brook so dull a life.[16]

The first monotheistic God, as referenced in the Old Testament, made it a positive command to have children. Noah was told: "Be fertile, then, and increase, abound on earth and subdue it."[17] According to the *Talmud*, life was incomplete if this directive was not followed:

> A man without children is as if he were dead.[18]

> A man without children is like a piece of wood, which though kindled does not burn or give out light.[19]

In the early Irish poem, "Childless", the reasoning for despair was clear:

> There is no hell, no lasting torment,
> But to be childless at the end,
> A naked stone in grassy places,
> A man that leaves no love behind.[20]

Along with this protean desire to have children came an innate impulse to nurture them as well. Xenophon, the fifth century B.C. Athenian historian, explained that men had an inborn desire to beget children, and that mothers would naturally be desirous of rearing their babies.[21] Plutarch, in the first century A.D., noted that despite the pain of childbirth, "nature leads the mother to not neglect or avoid her child."[22] Epictetus, a contemporary of Plutarch, agreed that "once a child is born it is no longer in our power not to love it or to care for it."[23]

Western religious teachings were similarly supportive. Isaiah, the Old Testament prophet, assured the people of Israel that the Lord would not forsake them because, as any parent, He could not turn His back on them: "Does a woman forget her nursling, and have no compassion on the child of her womb?"[24] Children, the *Psalms* proclaimed, were a gift from God: "They are His reward."[25] St. Augustine, the most respected of the Church Fathers, in the fourth century A.D. wrote how mothers nursed their children under the direction of God: "For they, by an instinctive affection, were anxious to give me what Thou gavest them."[26]

It is this necessary function of child-rearing that likely formed the very basis for how most human beings have chosen to live – within a family unit. Surveys of almost every known human society have shown the nuclear family as the critical recognizable unit.[27] Rousseau called the family "the oldest of all societies, and the only natural one."[28]

In the most primitive tribes that have been studied in modern times, social groupings primarily revolved around this biological family unit.[29] The male was generally the dominant head, although some societies developed matrilineal structures. In this latter arrangement, the maternal uncle actually had more authority over the children than the father.[30] Female dominance was quite rare, however, and polygyny, or the marriage of one man with more than one wife, was one hundred forty-one times more common than polyandry, where a woman had more than one husband.[31]

For the most part, marriage, or the union of a male and female, was the basic model for family procreation. The function of the father was generally to support and protect the wife and children; the wives would perform household duties and were responsible for raising the children.[32] Those males that did not marry were generally looked on as unnatural or were ridiculed.[33] So important was procreation that in many tribes the marriage did not actually take full effect until a child was born.[34] In ancient Egypt, for example, there was an initial one year "trial marriage" in order to determine first if the wife could become pregnant.[35] After that, the marriage could become a permanent bond.

As civilization advanced, the status of the family remained the most prominent social source of strength. Aristotle, who based his philosophy on logic and reason, called the family an "association established by nature for the supply of men's everyday wants."[36] And one of these supplies remained a steady source of heirs for both the satisfaction of the parent, and of the state as well. In numbers came strength, and defense against outside predators required a constant supply of healthy warrior men. In ancient Sparta, to encourage the having of children, fathers of three children were excused from military service, and the father of four did not have to pay taxes.[37]

This time-tested desire for children has become so ingrained in our present assessment of normal human behavior that negative or depressive reactions to the thought of parenthood has been considered by some psychiatrists as an abnormal state caused by problems in the person's own upbringing.[38] It is obvious, then, that if our society may see the parent who questions even the desire to have children as defective or strange, it will usually automatically label one with the thought of committing infanticide as schizophrenic or psychopathic.[39] Dr. Marcia Angell, in a 1983 editorial against the rigid restrictions on allowing handicapped newborns to die, reasoned that "probably most parents would give their lives for their children; the circumstances in which parents would prefer death to survival for their child must be extraordinary indeed."[40] Rather than considering the possibility that the parent was under a transient abnormality, as might be expected in other types of capital crimes, or that the homicide could possibly have a defense of justification, the perpetrator of infanticide has often been segregated as a special type of personality disorder.[41] In medieval England, when the secular courts began to prosecute for the crime of infanticide, the defense of insanity was almost always raised, and was almost always successful as well.[42] A jury of one's peers could not imagine a "sane" person capable of such depravity.

It is easy to understand the reasoning behind this conclusion. Most parents genuinely believe that if they were ever faced with the frightening prospect that their child could be injured, they would risk their own life rather than let their children suffer harm. No matter how much they may love another unrelated human being, a child was a product of their own being – a genetic part of their very soul. No love could be as intense, or self-sacrificing, as that between a parent and a child.

But how prevalent is this natural bond which unites a parent to its biologic offspring? Herodotus, in his epic *History*, related how Darius, the Great Persian King, had arrested Intaphrenes and his entire family and charged them all with being enemies of the state. Such a crime usually led to immediate execution, but the beautiful wife of Intaphrenes begged Darius for mercy and the king relented, offering to spare her own life and that of one other family member. The woman chose her brother with the explanation that she could always marry a second time, and thereby have more children, but she would never again be able to have another brother.[43] She allowed her children to die, but only so that another loved one, a brother even more dear, could survive. Was her decision pathologic or insane?

Evidence of other rational excuses for allowing one's child to die may be observed on sociological grounds. Thomas Malthus, in his *First Essay on the Principle of Population* in 1798 A.D., postulated that there were two laws fixed by nature: food was a necessary ingredient to the existence of man, and passion between the sexes would constantly result in the accumulation of excess members of the race.[44] This meant that the population would increase unchecked in a geometrical ratio, while the necessary subsistence to feed the inhabitants increased in only an arithmetical ratio.[45] The result was a constant tendency of animate life to expand beyond the available nourishment supply. If the food reserve to a community was already strained to the limit, and a newborn infant was allowed to live, it meant that the death of some other family member from starvation was more likely to occur.[46] Was it pathologic or insane to then bury the baby at birth and allow the mother to return to her life-saving labor?

But even without these questions of loyalty to others within the family or caste, there is another justification which is clearly present in all human beings, save the pious martyr: the instinctual drive for self-survival. As much as we might strive to develop a human moral code that will put the welfare of all individuals on an even footing, the human organism will usually put its own safety above all else when threatened with mortal danger, even above that of its own offspring. As Tolstoy emphasized:

> Man lives only for his own happiness – for his own good. If he does not feel a desire for his own welfare he no longer feels himself to be alive.[47]

Part of this self-survival involves seeing a child as a potential adversary in competition for limited assets. While offspring are usually the means to "genetic posterity," the conflict between them "is an endemic feature of sexually reproducing organisms because the allocation of resources and efforts that would maximize a parent's genetic posterity seldom matches that which would maximize a particular offsprings."[48] In other words, while children provide the means by which a family is assured continuation of its genetic heritage, individual members may find alternate goals which are in conflict with the common good.

This brief excursion into some of the reasons which explain why a parent might kill a child does not validate the act of infanticide, but it does help to elucidate it without resorting to a psychiatric or psychopathic diagnosis. It is this concept of excusable homicide that I believe explicates the majority of instances of child-murder throughout the evolution of our modern civilization. In this book I will analyze the historical evidence for infanticide from the viewpoint of many perspectives: religious, legal, scientific and social. I am not going to include any extensive discussion of abortion since, although technically a form of infanticide according to those who believe life begins at conception, the ethical and emotional arguments over this topic cover too great an expanse. I am also not going to discuss the killing of children by other family relatives, such as siblings. The parent-child relationship is closer, and more unique, than any other intra-familial bond, and generally does not involve the emotion of jealousy which plays such a large role with siblings.

Finally, I am going to restrict my analysis to the factual killing of children and not diffused behavior. In 1972, a seminar for playwrights and psychologists was held to explore the present day problems of filicide and infanticide. Emanuel Schwartz outlined the literary evidence in which parents seem to maim and murder their children:

> We see filicidal themes in various forms of behavior, from traditionally accepted practices like circumcision to acts of gross mutilation; from parental disinvolvement to outright abandonment; from mistreatment to battering; from military conscription to murder.[49]

In this book I will not deal with wishes; such an approach would take us too far afield.

It may seem to be a strange arena where you try and understand how an individual can take his or her own child and strangle it to death. Yet, the importance of understanding the reasons for infanticide is borne out by its mathematical proportions. Since man first appeared on earth about 600,000 years ago, it has been calculated that about 77 billion human babies have been born.[50] If estimates of infanticide of 5-10% are true, then up to seven billion children have been killed by their parents, a figure which should suffice as one of incredible importance.[51]

Julian Huxley called evolution "an enormous number of blind alleys, with a very occasional path of progress."[52] It remains to be determined whether we are a benefit to the world at large, or a blind alley; whether the killing of children is a madness of a sick mind, or the product of a race that puts survival of the fittest above protection of the few. In other words, can we agree with Tylor's dictum that "infanticide arises from hardness of life rather than hardness of heart."[53]

If we are to make the determination fairly we must remember the story as told by Max Black:

> A philosopher once said to a fish, "The purpose of life is to reason and become wise." The fish answered, "The purpose of life is to swim and catch flies." The philosopher muttered, "Poor fish." Back came a whisper, "Poor philosopher."[54]

Endnotes

1 . Williamson, "Infanticide: An Anthropological Analysis," 61.
2 . Divale & Harris, "Population, Warfare, & the Male Supremacist Complex," 525.
3 . "Infanticide is everywhere an uncommon event and tends to be poorly documented." Hrdy, "Fitness Tradeoffs in the History and Evolution of Delegated Mothering with Special Reference to Wet-Nursing, Abandonment and Infanticide," 431.
4 . DeMause, "The History of Child Assault," 1. Mays concludes that infanticide has "been shown to be practiced in human societies on every continent and at every level of social complexity from hunter-gatherers to urban societies." Mays, "Infanticide in Roman Britain," 883.
5 . Weir, Selective Nontreatment of Handicapped Newborns: Moral Dilemmas in Neonatal Medicine, 4.
6 . Genesis 1:27. The Anchor Bible, 4.
7 . Bloch, So The Witch Won't Eat Me, 109.
8 . Khaldun, The Muqaddimah, 223.
9 . Daly & Wilson, "Evolutionary Social Psychology and Family Homicide," 519.
10 . Westermarck, A Short History of Marriage, 5.
11 . Aptekar, Anjea: Infanticide, Abortion & Contraception in Savage Society, 49, 52.
12 . Aristotle, Politics, I.2.1252a, 1128.
13 . Williamson, "Infanticide: An Anthropological Analysis," 63.
14 . Code of Jewish Law, 145.4, Volume IV, 7.
15 . Qiu, "Morality in Flux: Medical Ethics Dilemmas in the People's Republic of China," 17.
16 . Claudian, The Rape of Proserpine, I.109-111, Volume II, 301.
17 . Genesis 9:7. The Anchor Bible, 57.
18 . Nedarim, 64. Talmudic Anthology, 70.
19 . Zohar, i.187a. Ibid. 124.
20 . O'Connor, The Fountain of Magic, 38.
21 . Xenophon, Memorabilia, I.IV.7, 57.
22 . Plutarch, "On Affection for Offspring," 4.496, Moralia, Volume VI, 351.
23 . Epictetus, The Discourses, I.XXIII.5, Volume 1, 149-151.
24 . Isaiah 49:15. The Anchor Bible, 110.
25 . Psalms 127:3. The Living Bible, 495.
26 . St. Augustine, Confessions, I.VI, 6.
27 . Homans, The Human Group, 190.
28 . Rousseau, The Social Contract, I.2, 50.
29 . Oliver, The Pacific Islands, 31.
30 . Westermarck, A Short History of Marriage, 21.
31 . Divale & Harris, "Population, Warfare, & the Male Supremacist Complex," 523.
32 . Westermarck, A Short History of Marriage, 23.
33 . Ibid., 31.
34 . Westrup, Introduction to Early Roman Law, Volume I, 29.
35 . Ibid., 30.
36 . Aristotle, Politics, I.2.1252b, 1128.
37 . Balsdon, Roman Women, 191.
38 . Zilboorg, "Depressive Reactions Related to Parenthood," 927.
39 . Browne & Palmer, "A Preliminary Study of Schizophrenic Women Who Murdered Their Children," 75.

40 . Angell, "Handicapped Children: Baby Doe & Uncle Sam," 660.
41 . Harder, "The Psychopathology of Infanticide," 244.
42 . Damme, "Infanticide: the Worth of an Infant Under Law," 9.
43 . Herodotus, The History, 3.119, 262.
44 . Malthus, "An Essay on the Principle of Population, As it Affects the Future Improvement of Society with Remarks on the Speculations of Mr. Godwin, M. Condorcet, and Other Writers (1798)," I, On Population, 8.
45 . Ibid., 9.
46 . Aptekar, Anjea: Infanticide, Abortion & Contraception in Savage Society, 56.
47 . Leo Tolstoy, "On Life,", I, On Life & Essays on Religion, 16.
48 . Outlining the theory of R. L. Trivers. Daly & Wilson, "Evolutionary Social Psychology and Family Homicide," 521.
49 . Schwartz, "Child Murder Today," 360.
50 . Desmond, "How Many People Have Ever Lived on Earth," 44-45.
51 . DeMause estimated that one-half of all children born in antiquity were killed, one-third in the medieval period and one percent in the eighteenth century. DeMause, "The History of Child Assault," 2.
52 . Huxley, Man in the Modern World, 13.
53 . Todd, The Primitive Family as an Educational Agency, 128.
54 . Moorhead, The Meaning of Life, 24.

CHAPTER I

HISTORICAL BACKGROUND – ANTIQUITY

> "To the shame of civilization it must be avowed that not a State has yet advanced to that degree of progress under which child-murder may be said to be a very uncommon crime."[1]

This 1861 British editorial in the widely read, and well-respected, medical journal *Lancet* was part of a growing contemporary debate in England over what should be done to try and reduce the shameful frequency of infanticide that was spreading throughout the country. While various experts from a variety of disciplines castigated the conditions which allowed such heinous crimes to exist, they also pointed out that the problem was not unique to the British Isles in the nineteenth century. Throughout the history of the civilized world, from the Golden Age of Greece to the splendor of the Persian Empire, the killing of children was a vice that had pervaded almost every society of mankind.

In the next few chapters, I am going to present this world-wide history of infanticide from a chronological standpoint. The chapters which follow will then deal with the motives which undermine the crime, irrespective of the perspective of time. Before proceeding, however, it is necessary to clarify a few descriptive terms. The killing of one human being by another has been subdivided into many categories, dependent upon the status of perpetrator and victim. While the title of this book uses the term "infanticide" to refer to the murder of a child by its parent, this usage is not entirely accurate. The term "infanticide," in common application, denotes the killing of an infant soon after its birth.[2] There has not, however, been universal agreement on restricting the use of the word to only a narrow age range of young victims. Social anthropologists have simply defined infanticide as the killing of a "newborn child" by their parents or with their consent.[3] Ethnographers have found that referring to it as the "deliberate killing of a child in its infancy, up to two years of age, covers the majority of cases."[4] In the nineteenth century it was common to refer to infanticide as the killing of an infant at any age from birth to childhood.[5]

With such imprecise terminology, it is not surprising that some countries have restricted the legal usage of the term to more definite circumstances. In Canada, for example, infanticide occurs when a "female person" causes the death of her newly born child "if at the time of the act or omission she is not fully recovered from the effects of giving birth to the child and by reason thereof or of the effect of lactation consequent on the birth her mind is then disturbed."[6] In Britain, infanticide includes the killing of infants up to twelve months of age, again only by mothers.[7] If a child is destroyed before it is capable of independent existence of its mother, the offence is then referred to as "child destruction."[8] In Denmark, infanticide is a medico-legal term that designates the killing of a child by its mother while the killing of a newborn by the father is "wilful murder."[9]

The killing of a son or daughter of any age is also referred to as "filicide."[10] "Neonaticide" has been recommended to refer to the killing of a newborn under twenty-four hours of age.[11] "Pedocide" has been used at times to denote the killing of any child,[12] or the killing of a child between the age of one and sixteen years.[13] Adelson defined post-infancy "pedicide" as the killing of a child who has emerged from infancy but not yet attained the age of fifteen years.[14] The word "libericide" is also rarely used to denote the killing of an older child.[15] "Progenicide" has been suggested for any act that is carried out in accord with cultural norms and functions selectively to reduce the probability of survival of offspring of a person or group.[16]

For the purposes of this book, the term infanticide will be used to cover instances of child-murder without differentiation as to gender of the killer or age of the victim.

A. Prehistoric Times

According to Dr. John Lightfoot, a seventeenth century A.D. biblical scholar and vice chancellor of Cambridge University: "Man was created by the Trinity on the 26th of October, 4004 B.C. at 9 o'clock in the morning."[17] This analysis, based upon biblical reports, would account for the presence of man on earth for almost six thousand years.

Needless to say, the accuracy of this particular estimate has been seriously questioned. Scientists now believe, according to fossil records, that the family of man has likely been around for over two to three million years, with the evolution into modern Homo sapiens occurring somewhere around 100,000 years ago.[18] Where the biblical reference is simple and replete, the species Homo sapiens, of the genus Homo, of the family Hominidae, of the superfamily Hominoidea, of the suborder Anthropoidea, of the order Primates, of the cohort Unguiculata, of the infraclass Eutheria, of the class Mammalia, of the phylum Chordata, of the kingdom Animalia is more complex.[19]

Let us stay, for the moment, with the more classical, scientific view. From geologic records, the universe is estimated to be around fifteen billion years old. The earth, as a planetary structure, is thought to be over four billion years old, with almost ninety percent of this time lost in what is called the Precambrian period. No evidence of fossil life on earth is found until that of plant remains in the Paleozoic Era (Lower Paleolithic Age) from about 590 Myr (590 million years) to 248 Myr. The geologic eras which follow are the Mesozoic Era (Middle Paleolithic Age) from 248 Myr to 65 Myr, and the Cenozoic Era (Upper Paleolithic Age) from 65 Myr to around 8,000 B.C.[20]

The evolution of man during this period of time can be discerned through reconstruction of various fossilized remains. Mammals first appeared in the Mesozoic Era about 165 million years ago. Primates, the order which includes the species of human beings, arose about forty million years ago during the Cenozoic Era.[21] The precursor of the ape family, *Aegyptopithecus*, developed during the Miocene Epoch, from about 24 Myr to 5 Myr,[22] and one of the earliest recognizable precursors of man within this grouping, *Ramapithecus*, lived around 15 Myr.[23]

The formation of the actual family of modern man, *Homindae*, occurred during the Pliocene epoch which lasted until about 1.8 Myr. At the end of this period the first true hominids, sufficiently human to go by the name of Homo, emerged.[24] The first hominids are now dated to around 4.5 Myr, while the earliest members of the genus *Homo* likely evolved from its more apelike predecessor, *Australopithecus*, around 2.5 Myr.[25] One of these creatures, *Homo habilis*, was an ape that walked upright around 2.5 Myr and then developed by 1.5 Myr into *Homo erectus*, the first member of the *Homo* line to move out of Africa.[26] This species included the Java man and Pekin man. The *Australopithecus* genus, discovered in South Africa, was a similar hominid that developed around the same period of time.

The Pliocene Epoch ended, and the Pleistocene began, as ice started to spread and cover a large part of the northern hemisphere.[27] During this period of time, about 200,000 to 400,000 years ago, *Homo sapiens* finally begun to appear and thrive. Neanderthal remains clearly identify social groupings of men, and corroborate the use of primitive tools, and even artistic renderings, that are consistent with a quite advanced cooperative gathering.

Why is all this dry archaeologic information necessary to relate as we begin to dissect out the history of infanticide? It is simply to recognize that our modern genetic heritage did not commence when Columbus discovered America. Despite the rapid advances made in our understanding of the physical and social sciences, our basic nature has been affected by more than a few hundred years of growth. These ancient ancestors can provide clues as to why we react to stress the way we do, and whether those methods are reasonable or aberrant.

While scientists generally agree over the basic evolution of man in the fossil record, we still know little of how these early humans actually lived. It appears obvious that this was an age that required incredible fortitude to survive, and it seems reasonable to assume that emphasis was placed on physical strength, rather than philosophical convictions, to aid in food gathering and defense. Ethical tenets were likely few in number, and superstition guided placation of whatever supernatural forces, or deities, did exist. The value of a helpless newborn's life in this uncertain environment was not very great, and little time could be wasted in protecting those who could not contribute to the welfare of the social group.

While the premise of our modern age has generally been to consider infants to have natural rights equal to those of adults, early man was faced with survival limitations that required a more harsh and realistic view. It was an existence that truly fit the premise of "survival of the fittest" and, in the words of J. M. Rist: "It was almost universally held in antiquity that a child has no intrinsic right to life in virtue of being born.[28] If there were means available to allow for survival, so be it. If not, then life must go on and society did not find the killing of a neonate a criminal act.

Passive death of newborns from neglect by parents who were busy with other tasks must have been prominent, in addition to direct elimination of unwanted births. The primary motive for these killings was the difficulty in rearing children while living the harsh reality of a hunter-gatherer life. The food supply was not only unpredictable, it was mobile. If a family was to maintain a proper habitat near the traveling herd, they had to be able to move quickly whenever the need arose. It was especially difficult to care for a newborn infant during these periods of rapid change. A mother who was feeding one child at her breast could not afford to wean the infant until it was three or four years old and, therefore, any other babies born during this interval would have to be abandoned.

Williamson estimated that during this period of time, infanticide rates of 15-20% were prevalent.[29] Birdsell gives a somewhat higher rate, ranging from 15-50% of the total number of births. He believed that "systematic infanticide has been a necessary procedure for spacing human children" which persisted until the development of advanced agriculture.[30] Neel, using the present day Yanomama Indians as a model of how life was likely to have been in prehistoric times, estimated that the infanticide rate was 15-20%.[31] He cautioned against moralizing about this large figure, since the rate might seem excessive to our modern concepts. He added that:

> Accepting the general harshness of the milieu in which primitive man functioned, I find it increasingly difficult to see in the recent reproductive history of the civilized world a greater respect for the quality of human existence than was manifested by our remote "primitive" ancestors.[32]

If our forefathers had to practice infanticide, it was because of the hardness of their life, rather than the hardness of their heart.[33] It was not anger that led them to strangle or expose their children, it was the only way they could assure that the other members of a family could survive.

The aborigines of Australia manifest a lifestyle that also approximates this earlier prehistoric era. The Australoids are hunter-gatherers who rely on healthy women to help in the search for food. Mothers can carry only one suckling child with them during their travels in the bush, and children born during the time an older sibling needs care are generally killed.[34] In addition, during periods of drought and famine, younger children are often not provided enough food to maintain their life, or are eaten in order to provide nourishment to older siblings and parents.[35] Reports on the incidence of infanticide in these Australian tribes have ranged as high as 30% of all live-births.[36]

While the usual picture of life in the Stone Age is generally portrayed as a very harsh existence, some researchers have found indications that the travail may have been less bitter. Marvin Harris believed that Paleolithic hunters enjoyed relatively high standards of comfort and security, and were generally well nourished. However he noted that this was only due to a low population density – between 1600 and 20,00 human beings in all of France during the Stone Age – and that infanticide had to be used to maintain these minimal numbers.[37] He estimated that from 23-50% of children had to be removed at birth in order to preserve the 0.001% population growth that was present at that time.[38]

In addition to the natural stresses that were placed upon their lives, these early human beings also killed some of their children because of superstition and religious rites. There is a great deal of archaeologic evidence that sacrifices occurred to a variety of gods and goddesses during this era. Lubbock described archaeologic remains which included burnt bones indicating the practice of infanticide in pagan Britain.[39] At Ofnethohlen, in Germany, a mass burial from about 20,000 B.C. showed thirty-three skulls of which twenty were children showing signs which suggested some type of sacrifice.[40] In the great bas-relief from Laussel, France, where drawings dating back to the Paleolithic era can be found, the figure of a menstruating goddess holding her menstrual blood horn can be seen which has signs indicating she is to be placated by the sacrifice of human infants.[41]

While these data are obviously contrived from sketchy information, it is easy to understand why parents needed assistance from supernatural sources. As one searches the animal kingdom for variations in pre-pubertal growth, the human species is unique in the long interval between fertilization and puberty. No other animal spends so much time in maturing to full adulthood, and although this likely aids the development of certain positive human attributes, a very large burden is placed on the human mother for the feeding and safekeeping of her child. During the first four or five years of life, a single child would ultimately control most of the available time a female had for rearing during the pre-agricultural era. No matter how much the parents may have wished to raise two children simultaneously, their way of life made such a desire prohibitive.

Much of this dependency changed when the ability to provide adequate food in a specific geographical area became widely available. With the development of effective agricultural techniques, communities of many families were formed which would assure mutual assistance to aide in the rearing of children. This arose independently in three areas of the world: the fertile crescent area in the eastern Mediterranean region around the valleys of the Tigris and Euphrates rivers; a second center in China; and a third in Central America.[42] The more popular scientific determination of when these farming communities were established was somewhere around 8500 B.C.[43] There were signs of agricultural workings as early as 7000 B.C. in Mesopotamia, and 5000 B.C. in Egypt.[44]

As agriculture became more prominent, food became more plentiful.[45] Around 3000 B.C., with the development of the harder and more durable bronze alloy of copper and tin, it became possible to develop very extensive societies with weaponry that enabled land already tilled to be defended, and additional acres acquired.[46] Man was now beginning to tear away from the restraints placed upon him by his natural environment.

Along with the security from a more stable food supply, however, came the threat of an even more ominous disaster – famine. While certain years brought an abundance of food, others seemed to be even worse than before. A large crop harvest would initially promote the feeding of larger numbers of people, and as a result there were fewer deaths and an increased population density. But the uncertainty of each years harvest would put these survivors at even greater risk in the future. If food was scarce at any particular time, it was, by necessity, the welfare of the adults which came first. Without proper manpower to both harvest, and defend, the food supply, all the citizens in a gathering would be in danger of losing their lives. Following adults, the older children were cared for next as they provided necessary assistance in the harvesting of food. The youngest children were provided for only if there was surplus food. At the bottom of the list, helpless and unable to offer material help, came the newborns. When times of stress appeared, they were routinely thrown into rivers, flung into trenches, and exposed on every hill and roadside, "a prey for birds, food for wild beasts to rend."[47]

But it was not only the precarious nature of their day-to-day life which led our ancestors to commit infanticide, it was also superstition and fear. The gods of Paleolithic times "did not exist to be loved, but to be placated," usually by the sacrifice of animals, but also of humans as well.[48] Life was not sacrosanct in those distant times, and the power of the gods had to be assuaged.

The early pagan gods were ornery and not only quick to kill humankind, but also their own. In the Akkadian creation epic of Mesopotamia, from the early second millennium B.C., the story was told of the gods Apsu and Mummu-Tiamat who begot the next generation of gods. The clamor of these children infuriated Apsu, who found the noise loathsome. He vowed to destroy them so "that quiet may be restored."[49] His wife admonished this coarse response and demanded that the children be treated with kindness for although "their ways indeed are most troublesome" we should still attend them amiably.[50]

Male gods, however, continued to shun paternal control. In the Zoroastrian mythology, the first human couple grew from the seed of Gayomart. When offspring appeared, the parents devoured the children rather than raise them. Finally, the Wise Lord took away the sweetness of children and then Mashye and Mashyane gave birth to the human race.[51] A similar fable was seen in the Greek legend of Zeus and Cronos, described in more detail in a later chapter. Cronos swallowed each of his children as they were born, and only the cunning action of Rhea, the mother, saved Zeus from certain destruction.

We therefore find that the earliest religions included gods who treated their offspring, not with love and kindness, but with jealousy and fear. Children could encompass an image of danger, and it was necessary, at times, to destroy them if survival of the parent was threatened. This lesson, according to the historical record, was not lost upon subsequent mortal believers.

B. Ancient Greece

While the valley of the Tigris and Euphrates rivers have historically been identified as the location of the origin of the Garden of Eden, and the resultant birth of mankind, Western civilization looks more to the Golden Age of Greece for the cultural beginnings of "modern" civilization. In those heroic days, when gods and men performed the deeds which were to become models of courageous behavior for centuries afterward, we uncover the first concrete evidence of infanticide that was socially accepted at the time.

Archaeologic support for the presence of man on the Greek mainland dates back to the sixth or seventh millennium B.C., during the Mesolithic period, and in Crete to about the fourth millennium B.C., during the Neolithic Period.[52] It is generally believed that the first Greek speaking, Indo-European tribes began to appear in mainland Greece about 1900 B.C., at the beginning of the Middle Bronze Age.[53]

The first civilization which appears to have widely flourished in the area surrounding the Aegean Sea was that of the Minoans in Crete. This kingdom, where the legendary Minotaur resided, was ruled by king Minos and became a vast regional power before suddenly disappearing in a violent destruction around 1400 B.C. It was followed on the Greek mainland by the Myceneans whose military general, Agamemnon, was famous as the leader of the Greeks during the Trojan War. The Myceneans reached the height of their power around 1600 B.C. and then, as the Minoans before them, seemed to abruptly disappear around 1200 B.C.

Traditional Greek history dates from 776 B.C., the year the quadrennial Olympic games in honor of Zeus were said to be founded, and the date which provided a calendar for future events.[54] It was during this classical Hellenic era that we see the first widespread documentation of infanticide within large populations of otherwise sophisticated, and educationally advanced, peoples. That the Greeks practiced the exposure of at least some of their children is generally accepted.[55] Although Isocrates, writing in 342 B.C., said that the Athenians were not guilty of exposure or infanticide, his view is in the extreme minority.[56] The popular view, as W. K. Lacey aptly summarized, was that: "There can be no doubt whatever that the exposure of surplus children was practiced through antiquity."[57] The only significant disagreement among historians is on the extent of the practice.[58]

Parental control of the Greek father over the life of his child was absolute. As early as the sixth century B.C., the Cretan Law Code of Gortyn verified the extent of this authority. If a wife was separated from her husband and bore a child, she would bring it to her husband in the presence of three witnesses. If the husband should not receive it then "the child shall be in the mother's power either to rear or expose."[59] It was the father who ultimately directed whether his child would live or die.

This extreme power was typical of the general format of parental authority in most ancient societies throughout the world. Newborns did not automatically become part of a family simply by being born; they rather were admitted only if the father desired to keep the child and undertake the tribulation of rearing it to adulthood. Solon, who lived from 640-560 B.C., was a statesman who laid the constitutional foundations of Athenian democracy. While generally seen as a legal reformer, he nevertheless agreed that the Athenian father had the legal right to slay his own child.[60] Aristotle described this control over children as similar to that of a king over his subjects. It was not dependent upon constitutional laws, like the power which a Greek husband had over his wife, but was rather part of the rational process which nature gave to men in order to assure the family would remain strong.[61] To the Greeks, a strong state could only be assured by strong heads of strong families, and the husband stood at the front of this paternalistic line.

If the Athenian father desired to keep his newborn infant, he would formally acknowledge the child as his own at the *dekate* on the tenth day after birth.[62] If the child was unwanted, it was not usually killed outright but was rather exposed under legal sanction.[63] This power of the Greek father resided whether the child was that of his wife, or of some slave or concubine. The Roman father had less authority in this regard, and could only control the fate of his legitimate children.[64] A child could not be exposed after the *Amphidromia*, a family ceremony where the child was carried around the hearth by the nurse and given a name.[65]

In addition to choosing whether the newborn should live or die, the Athenian father could also have his child killed as punishment for various crimes. *An Ethiopian Romance*, the third century A.D. novel by Heliodorus, describes how a father brought a charge of assault against his son in Athens. Although he eventually allowed the assembly to decide the choice of punishment, he told how "the law permits me to execute him with my own hand."[66]

While any child could theoretically be done away with under this theory of law, the majority of newborns that were killed by Greek parents were either deformed, illegitimate, or born to parents who could not afford to raise them.[67] Despite the fact that the Homeric Greeks were usually described as wealthy, the average Athenian family lived on a day-to-day basis, hoping that there would be adequate amounts of food to maintain their sustenance. There were times when another mouth could simply not be fed and the newborn would be exposed with little social pressure or threats of criminal misconduct.

There were also instances where the Greeks were not as compassionate with their children as one might have expected from a society that gave rise to the principles of democracy and the pride of friendship. They had opened the eyes of the world to the rights of free speech and the privilege of voting for one's leaders, but their behavior did not always follow the sweetness of their voice. Polybius, in his *Histories*, explained that the low birth rate in Greece during the second century B.C. was not due to war, or epidemics, but rather to the fact that: "Men had fallen into such a state of pretentiousness, avarice and indolence that they did not wish to marry, or if they married to rear the children born to them, or at most as a rule but one or two of them."[68] It seems that the Greek male looked more to the pleasures of the present, than to the responsibilities of the future.

Such attributes, which seem so degrading to us today, were not considered unusual at the time. Even the Greek gods acted in similar ways which indicated that the moral examples of the deity were not necessarily being disobeyed. The liturgy of Greek religion is literally filled with episodes of incest and infanticide. If even a god acted in such a way, how could anyone complain when a mortal followed the superior model?

According to Greek mythology, Cronos (Saturn), the first powerful God who ruled the Heavens above, was warned by Gaia and Ouranos that some day he would be defeated by one of his own sons.[69] In a fashion that was to become commonplace among gods and kings alike when such portents were given, Cronos decided to eliminate his destined fate by killing his children at birth. In this way no son would ever be allowed to live to an age to harm him. As his fertile wife Rhea then delivered a baby, year after year, he "gulped down" each one as if they were a pitted olive.[70] In almost endless grief, Rhea gave birth to Hestia, Demeter, Hera, Pluto and Poseidon and then watched as Cronos swallowed each one immediately after they were born.[71] Finally, Rhea developed a plan to save her next child from destruction. She decided that immediately after birth she would substitute a huge stone in swaddling clothes for the real child, and then give it to Cronos to swallow. When her next baby son, Zeus, was born, the ruse worked and Cronos swallowed the stone and was satiated with the belief that the baby was destroyed. Zeus was then secretly sent to Ida to be raised away from his father's sight. In order to drown out his cries, which would have warned Cronos of the subterfuge, the Curetes and Corybantes beat on their shields and helmets to make noise.[72] Zeus was saved, but his father was to pay dearly for the rescue.

The foundation for future animosity between Greek parent and child was clearly set within the legends of their gods. When Zeus was grown, he returned to defeat his father and imprison him in an underground cave, proving the feared prophecy true. Little wonder then that a young Greek father might have second thoughts over the wisdom of raising a son which the seers have warned of possible trouble. Future myths of gods, and stories of mortals, would carry on this same infanticidal theme pointing out how one's progeny could become one's heirs if they were not carefully watched and controlled.

The Greeks may have learned some impious lessons from the life styles of their gods, but they also had to face the reality of an extremely hard life here on earth. Estimates of infant mortality in Greek society, from non-criminal causes, ran as high as 30-40%.[73] Even the most devoted and caring parent lost young children to medical illness and accidental death, and a stoic attitude about the frailty of one's offspring was a necessity. "Parents who lose children must be satisfied with the cold comfort that they can have new ones," was an attitude that was prevalent.[74] When you learned to live with this much death, the disappearance of a neighbor's newborn child was not an event of great social concern.

As an adjunct to this cold reality, there was little societal gain from allowing a disabled child, who could not ever fare for itself, to live forever dependent on the benevolent care of others. From the earliest legal codes in Greece, the lives of such infants were not protected under the law, and in some cases they were actually encouraged to be killed. Plutarch related that the law of Lycurgus in Sparta reasoned that the life "of that which nature had not well equipped at the very beginning for health and strength, was no advantage either to itself or the state."[75] And where there was no advantage in the ancient world, there was no protection. The Greeks used infanticide to rectify the mistakes of Nature and were thereby saved from problems of defective heredity.[76]

Much of this tolerance toward infanticide was reflected in the writings of the Greek philosophers and playwrights. Plato, the student of Socrates and teacher of Aristotle, wrote of Grecian life around the middle of the fourth century B.C. His *Discourses* are often cited as evidence for the frequent occurrence of infanticide during that era, but his treatises must be interpreted cautiously for they show great variation and often refer to the "ideal," rather than the "real," state of affairs.

Plato has been cited, for example, as justifying the use of infanticide to limit the size of the state.[77] However, in *Laws* he actually suggested that measures may have to be taken in order to keep the number of households in the state at 5040, and that there are measures available to check propagation beyond that critical level. While discussing the use of exposure, he also noted that one method would be to send out colonies of people that seem suitable to outside lands.[78] This ancient device of colonization had long been used by a number of countries to control their population growth, and did not require the purposeful elimination of any offspring. It would be wrong to look at only one section of his work without reference to the entirety.

There are, nevertheless, many notations in the works of Plato to show at least a fundamental acceptance of the use of exposure, or infanticide, under certain circumstances. Plato was well aware of the serious burden which could be placed on society by unlimited increases in the size of the population. More than two millennium before Malthus outlined how populations grew geometrically, and the food supply only arithmetically, Plato showed an understanding of this problem in *The Republic*. If the population increased beyond a desired amount, he warned, the lives of all citizens would be endangered.[79] The State should instead preserve an equitable balance by assuring that the suitable number of inhabitants would be maintained. How this would occur was not discussed in that particular passage, but disposal of neonates would have been an acceptable option.

Plato was also concerned that the population be primarily sustained by healthy children. He wrote in *The Republic* that in the ideal commonwealth the procreation of children would be similar to the raising of horses or dogs: "There is a need for the best men to have intercourse as often as possible with the best women, and the reverse for the ordinary men with the most ordinary women; and the offspring of the former must be reared but not that of the others if the flock is going to be of the most eminent quality."[80] With ethnic cleansing still present in our modern age, it should not surprise us that even the Golden Age of Greece looked with favor on only a few of its citizens. While Plato may have realized the pragmatic and political value of philosophical tenets, he clearly retained a segregational attitude about the value of individual life.

Plato concurred that parents retained extreme authority over the lives of their children, but there was evidence in some of his works that such parental control was not without some limitation. In *Laws*, he explained that if a parent killed a child in a fit of rage, there was the need for purification and exile for three years and then the wife and husband must be separated and never again have a child.[81] It was the anger, rather than a reasoned decision to dispose of an offspring, that appears to have been the issue here so that the parent's power was subject to some scrutiny when rational thought was interrupted by irrational behavior.

Aristotle, the pupil of Plato and tutor of Alexander the Great, also clearly accepted the concept of infanticide for certain select situations. He steadfastly agreed with the disposal of deformed infants at birth. In *Politics* he stated directly: "Let there be a law that no deformed child shall live."[82] If the need to control the numbers of children who were born was because of excess population, however, he argued for the use of abortion rather than exposure after birth.[83] Aristotle's philosophical principle of reasoned action and natural law did not require heroic efforts to keep infants alive when there was little chance of independent existence.

In Sparta, one of the stronger independent Greek states, a more socialistic approach to family life was taken. Where Athens became the model of democracy, Sparta promoted the importance of the state over that of the individual. Lycurgus, the lawgiver of Sparta, was well aware of the inherent power of the Athenian father, but found this to be in conflict with the primary needs of the state. He believed that the father did not have the power to dispose of the child as he wished, because children were seen as the property of the whole commonwealth and not only the parents.[84] It was therefore up to the government to decide whether a particular infant should live or die, and not the biologic father. If the authorities felt that the infant would be of value, then it would be proper for them to demand that the child be raised. This decision was made at the *Lesche* where the elders would carefully view a child brought to them by the father. If they found it well-built and sturdy, they would order it reared. If the infant was ill-born and deformed, however, they would order it brought to the *Apothetae*, a chasm at the foot of Mount Taygetus, where it was abandoned or thrown off a cliff.[85] Sparta was known for its athletic and disciplined youth; there was no place among them for the sick or infirm. Infanticide offered a solution to their eugenic concerns by eliminating the unfit at birth.[86]

This rigorous approach toward the ideal Spartan state carried on in the disciplining of Spartan children as well. Even at a young age, the child was expected to endure whippings and regimented control in order to assure that they developed the strength to survive the rigors of life on their own. This led to the modern day usage of the word "spartan" to mean a life without frills and unnecessary comfort. At times, it led to no life at all.

Of all the Greek states, some have postulated that only Thebes did not reveal any evidence of infanticide.[87] C. W. Westrup, however, pointed out that Thebes had to forbid exposure by threatening the punishment of pain. If anyone wanted to get rid of a child for economic reasons, they were "allowed to hand it over to a magistrate who then awarded it as a slave to the first bidder."[88] This obviously was in response to episodes of exposure which were occurring at the time, and would tend to disprove their prior claims of innocence.

C. Roman Empire

The first settlements of early Italians in the Tiber Valley occurred around the first millennium B.C., and culminated with the mythical founding of Rome by Romulus in the second year of the seventh Olympiad, at about 751 B.C.[89] After the death of Romulus, Rome was ruled by kings until 510 B.C. when Tarquin, the seventh and last king, was expelled for tyranny. A Republic was then set up and one of the first acts to follow was the writing of the Twelve Tables (Lex Duodecim Tabularum), the famous document which initiated the development of Roman Law. It was this legal system, more than any other, that formed the underlying principles of law in most Western countries today.

The traditional account of the genesis of the Twelve Tables is that three commissioners were sent from Rome to the Greek states in order to collect what was deemed useful in their various legal systems. They returned in 452 B.C. and ten decemvirs, or magistrates, were then given one year to frame a body of laws for the newly formed Republic. At first they made ten tables, and then added two more the following year. The laws were approved by the senate and then engraved on columns in the most conspicuous part of the Forum.[90] The populace was summoned to read them, and to be responsible for knowing, and following, the agreed upon decrees in their everyday lives.[91]

These tablets were held in strict regard by the Roman people. In 44 B.C., Cicero lamented how he was required, as a child, to learn all the laws but that nowadays no one bothered to do the same. Tacitus admired the Twelve Tables and regretted that they were "the last specimen of equitable legislation."[92] To a man, every Roman author for centuries thereafter only referred to these principles with honor and respect.

And while the hallowed chambers of law courts today still resound with references of respect to this famous collection of legal standards, within the body of the revered document lay the authority for a Roman father to decide the life or death of his child from birth. The Twelve Tables clearly directed this intent: "Let a father have the power of life and death over his legitimate children, and let him sell them when he pleases."[93] With respect to abnormal infants, the directive for eugenic action was more explicit: "If a father has a child born, which is monstrously deformed, let him kill him immediately."[94] If a Roman father wished to expose his child at birth, he had the authority of statutory law to do so. The Romans considered many of these abnormal births as evil portents, and thought that the disaster could be prevented by killing the child. The birth of a hermaphrodite was included in this category.[95]

This prerogative of the Roman father, known as the "patriae potestas," contained the ultimate power of life and death over legitimate offspring and was conferred upon him with the sanction of a lex regia.[96] The privilege was extended only to the man, and if a mother killed her child, she could be found guilty of the even more severe crime of parricide. The punishment for this crime was like no other, and consisted of being "sewed up in a sack with a dog, a cock, a viper, and an ape, and enclosed in this horrible prison he is to be, according to the nature of the place, thrown into the sea, or into a river."[97] Despite this terrible threat, many women obviously disposed of their newborns as reflected by the Roman playwright, Plautus, who had the courtesan Phronesium explain why she needed to pretend to a Babylonian soldier that she gave birth to his child: "If I let this child of ours live and bring it up, he'll give me all of his property."[98]

How could the Roman father be given such unbridled authority? As with the Greeks, life was not an easy one for the average Roman citizen who faced the possibility of death from many causes every day. Medicine was in its infancy, wars were rampant, and food was often scarce. Bruce Frier estimated that only 49% of Roman children saw their fifth birthday.[99] Inscriptions on Roman tombs indicate that at least one-third of the population was dead by age ten years, and the average life expectancy was age twenty-two years for men and twenty for women.[100] While this applied great pressure against population growth on society as a whole, a man's tenuous domain remained of primary concern.

The usual method of disposing of unwanted infants was abandonment at birth.[101] Most historians agree that the extent of exposure among the Romans was very prevalent.[102] William Graham Sumner found that "exceptions to the practice of these vices are noteworthy phenomenon."[103] It affected every class of person and the Romans even regarded it "remarkable that other nations did not expose children."[104] John Boswell, the Yale historian, estimated that the rate of abandonment at Rome during the first three centuries of the Christian era was about 20-40% of all children born.[105] He nevertheless believed that most of these cases were not instances of malevolence, but involved the expectation that the child would be picked up by some other person and saved by "the kindness of strangers." To Boswell, this was preferable to actually killing the infant outright at birth.[106]

The expectation that the exposed baby could live and be raised by another family, was certainly one reason why the Romans frequently utilized abandonment as the preferred means to eliminate an unwanted newborn. The possibility of such an event was engraved in the very history of the founding of Rome itself. According to legend, Rome was established by twin boys, Romulus and Remus, who had been ordered exposed at their birth "in accordance with an ancestral custom."[107]

From that time forward, exposure was a prominent feature of Roman life. Virgil, writing of his visit to the underworld in the Aenead, recorded his untoward reaction to the numbers of newborns he found wallowing in the depths of Hell: "Here voices and loud lamentations echo: the souls of infants weeping at the very first threshold – torn away by the black day, deprived of their sweet life, ripped from the breast, plunged into bitter death."[108] It is hard not to shudder with the intensity of Virgil's indignation at the gruesome event he witnessed. Lucian, in "Voyage to the Lower World," told how the invoice of new arrivals listed three hundred babies, "including those that were exposed."[109] According to literary sources, Roman Purgatory was no stranger to innocent newborn babes.

The Roman father's authority to decide whether his children lived began even before the baby was born. When a woman became pregnant, she had to notify her husband within thirty days of diagnosing her condition. Once this was done: "If he does not send people to watch and examine her and does not state before witnesses that she is not pregnant by him, he will be forced to recognize the child when it is born."[110] This meant that a father could not later claim that an infant was illegitimate, and refuse to be responsible for its care, if he did not do so when first notified by the prospective mother.

While the Roman father was not legally required to raise any of his offspring, there was an encouragement from the time of Augustus to produce heirs and increase the privileged class.[111] Since so many children failed to reach the age of majority, there were often times when heirs would have to be sought through adoption or other artificial means. This practice was particularly common among the ruling class. In 9 A.D., Augustus introduced various reforms which would penalize the unmarried male and encourage the raising of children.[112] While lessening the exposure of well-to-do infants, this action likely increased the abandonment by poorer parents who rightfully expected that there was a better chance that their child might be adopted by wealthy families looking to take advantage of these economic benefits. If a young married woman of means did not want to undergo the rigors, and real danger, of pregnancy, she could always send her servant to find an exposed child and begin a family with ease.

In the early years of the Roman Republic, the unwanted newborns were often brought to a column near the Velabrum – the traditional location for exposure. They were left on display in the open for speculators who sometimes took them to sell as prostitutes or slaves.[113] Sextus Pompeius Festus referred to the columns in the market place as *lactaria* or "nursing columns," because people would bring their nursing infants there to be deposited.[114] Boswell believed that most children left at these settings were found promptly and reared by others.[115]

Because of his unique power of *patriae potestas*, the Roman father could easily choose the type of child he wished to keep. As with the Greeks, the Romans put a premium on healthy male heirs; others were not treated as kindly. Romulus was said to have formulated the nature of this practice when he "obliged the inhabitants to bring up all their male children and the first born of the females, and forbade them to destroy any children under three years of age unless they were maimed or monstrous from their very birth."[116] He added the requirement that before the child was destroyed it should be sanctioned by five nearby related neighbors.[117] It is questionable whether this latter addendum was put into practice by the populace.[118]

Soranus, the eminent Greek physician who practiced in Rome during the second century A.D., discussed at length the appropriate treatment of the newborn infant during that period of time. He noted that Hippocrates refused to give women abortives because "it is the specific task of medicine to guard and preserve what has been engendered by nature."[119] He mentioned, however, that not all physicians during that era agreed with this restriction, and in his treatise he discussed the various methods which a woman might use to help induce an abortion.[120]

In his section "On the Care of the Newborn," Soranus included a discussion on "How to Recognize the Newborn that is Worth Rearing":

> Now the midwife, having received the newborn, should first put it upon the earth, having examined beforehand whether the infant is

> male or female, and should make an announcement by signs as is the custom of women. She should also consider whether it is worth rearing or not. And the infant which is suited by nature for rearing will be distinguished by the fact that its mother has spent the period of pregnancy in good health, for conditions which require medical care, especially those of the body, also harm the fetus and enfeeble the foundations of its life.[121]

Despite his clear moral acceptance of disposing of unsatisfactory infants at birth, Soranus remains today the acknowledged founder of the specialty of Obstetrics and Gynecology. Modern practitioners may debate whether physicians should serve as executioners for the state when the death penalty has been imposed on a convicted felon, or whether physicians should morally perform abortions when it is the choice of a woman not to give birth, or whether euthanasia is appropriate on a terminal cancer patient, but it is unlikely that many physicians in Roman times were dissuaded from following the precepts of Soranus because of similar ethical concerns.

Although the Romans were heavily involved in the exposure of their own children, they nevertheless attempted to combat the rising numbers of Christian converts by charges that children were being killed in various sacrificial rites. Minucius answered these charges by noting that it was the practice of the Romans "to expose your very own children to birds and wild beasts, or at times to smother and strangle them."[122] While expounding on how the Christian God would never accept the killing of a human in this manner, he pointed out that it was the Roman deities, and especially Saturn, who would devour their children.[123]

But the complacency of the Roman hierarchy to infanticide began to change around the time of Christ. Epictetus, born in 50 A.D., asked that since "sheep and wolves do not abandon their offspring, how can we?"[124] Ovid, in the poem "Heroides," dolefully questioned the exposure of the bastard child of Canace by her father. "What crime could the babe commit," he appealed, "with so few hours of life?"[125]

As poets and philosophers progressively highlighted the immorality of infanticide, legislators and emperors began to modify the legal right of a father to harm his child at will. In 52 B.C., the lex *Pomepeia de Parricidiis* held that if a man "hastens on the fate of an ascendant or a son, or in any way attempts anything included under the designation parricidium, he shall be punished with the penalty of parricidium."[126] Prior to this time, Roman women could be convicted of killing their child, since the *patriae potestas* was restricted to men, but now the process was extended for murder to the father as well. Ulpian, a Roman jurist from 211-222 A.D., had indicated that "a father cannot kill his son without giving him a hearing but must accuse him before the prefect or provincial governor."[127] In addition, in the views of Paul, a person who abandoned a child was equated with one who smothered it to death.[128]

There was also a progressive attempt to encourage the raising of offspring, instead of abandoning them, by providing monetary assistance to families in need. Pliny the Younger, in the second century A.D., recorded how laws were passed to encourage the rearing of children "by high rewards and comparable penalties."[129] This referred to the efforts of Augustus to encourage marriage and raising of families by laying heavy disabilities on unmarried men and extending special privileges to fathers of three children in the Lex Papia-Poppaea of 9 A.D.[130] Pliny then praised the Emperor Trajan, who reigned from 98-117 A.D., for "you are a prince whose reign makes it both pleasure and profit to rear children."[131] He added that the safety of the country from outside marauders was also a necessary concern for "there is indeed great encouragement to have children in the promise of allowances and donations, but greater still when there is hope of security and freedom from fear."[132] When the fate of the entire populace was at stake, the life of even a newborn child needed protection.

Emperor Constantine the Great, the first Christian ruler, commanded that the public had to maintain the children of those who were unable to provide for them in order to prevent the murder, or exposure, of infants due to poverty. In 315 A.D. he ordered relief be given to those who claimed they were unable to pay these costs.[133] This program was similar to what later would become foundling hospitals in the Middle Ages, and was comprised into the Theodosian Code, although it was rejected in Justinian's collection.[134] This legislation was not very effective, however, for in 329 A.D., Constantine allowed parents to once again sell children if there were insufficient means to care for them.[135]

Although some attempts were made to pay parents to keep children alive to replenish the diminishing Roman population in the two centuries following Augustus,[136] the law did not clearly change until the statement in a letter from Emperor Constantine to Varinus, Viceregent of Africa on the 11th of the Kalends of Dec, 319 A.D., that "if anyone should hasten the end of either of his parents, his son, (or) his daughter," he shall suffer the penalty of parricide.[137] While mentioned earlier as a possible punishment for women who killed their children, this ruling broadly extended the force of the law. It is generally referred to as the moment when the Roman Empire finally outlawed exposure and infanticide as criminal acts.

D. Persian Empire

Arabia is a primary geological formation of southwest Asia that extends for about one million square miles. From the third millennium B.C. onwards, the peoples of this region pushed northward under the pressures of drought and famine, and took over control of the lands they entered. In Sumeria, they became the Babylonians; in Syria and Phoenicia they evolved as Canaanites, Hebrews and Arameans.[138] They were called Semitic people because of their language and were thought to have descended from Shem, the eldest son of Noah. Their religion was generally of the primitive type, and deities associated with the natural surroundings were frequently worshiped. These gods were charged with the power to compel the service of man, and failure to appease them could result in tragedy and death.[139]

Persia, or the area now known as Iran, was populated around the middle of the sixth century B.C. from a clan of the Hakhamanish who spoke an Indo-European dialect and overthrew the native dynasty of the Susa. Soon thereafter, Cyrus came to power and greatly expanded the boundaries of what would then be known as the Persian Empire.[140]

As we have seen with the founding of Rome by Romulus and Remus, Cyrus was also the victim of a forced exposure. He was the son of Mandane, the daughter of king Astyages. Before his birth, Astyages dreamt of a vine that grew from Mandane and covered all of Asia after her marriage to Cambyses. He asked an oracle of the meaning of this dream and was told that the child of Mandane would eventually rule in his place.[141] When Cyrus was born, Astyages took note of this prophecy and ordered his servant Harpagus to kill the infant by exposure. Harpagus then directed Mitradates, a slave, to expose the boy but when Mitradates took the infant into the woods, he became too compassionate to perform the deed and instead raised Cyrus as his own son.[142] When Cyrus was grown, he overthrew Astyages and became the ruler of Persia. Once again, as had happened with Cronus, a portentous dream proved true despite attempts to escape the Fates by the commission of infanticide.

The Persian kings demanded much devotion from their followers, and the safety of the country was often put above the welfare of one's own child. Herodotus related how Xeres praised his commander Boges who was under an intense siege in Eion by the Greek general, Cimon. When the food in the town had run out, Boges scattered the gold and silver and then "piled up a great pyre and slew and cast into the fire his children and wife and concubines and servants."[143] Before Cimon could enter the town and capture him, Boges threw himself on the pyre as well. The willingness of the Persians to lay down their life in the service of their revered ruler was legendary, even in the days before Islam.

But the most enduring memory of infants killed in this part of the world was the beastly record of widespread female infanticide. The

Persian hierarchy was dominated by males, as was much of the world at that time, and a preference for sons reached lethal proportions. Before the time of Mohammed it was not unusual for daughters to be buried alive, either immediately after birth or later in childhood.[144] The problem was not restricted to one specific area but was common all over Arabia.[145] A common proverb held that it was a "generous deed to bury a female child."[146] Avner Giladi concluded that: "The practice of infanticide was deeply rooted among the inhabitants of Arabian peninsula in pre-Islamic times for ritual purposes, social reasons (females) and economic and demographic reasons."[147]

There was also disposal of children who were deformed or unable to be maintained at birth.[148] While the customs were generally followed with little restraint, it was said that the only occasion on which Othman ever shed a tear was when his little daughter, who he was burying alive, wiped the dust of the grave earth from his beard.[149] In the chapter which follows, the effect of Islam on this custom will be further amplified.

Endnotes

1 "Infanticide," Lancet 2 (1861): 314.
2 Usually for the purpose of concealing its birth. Campbell v. People, 159 Ill 9, 42 NE 123, 127 (1895).
3 Williams, "The Legal Evaluation of Infanticide," 115.
4 Williamson, "Infanticide: An Anthropological Analysis," 62.
5 Mapes, "Infanticide – The Slaughter of the Innocents," 741.
6 Criminal Code of Canada, 1985, Section 216.
7 Forbes, "Deadly Parents: Child Homicide in Eighteenth- and Nineteenth-Century England," 175. Some authors continue to use the term infanticide for killings up to one year of age. Montag & Montag, "Infanticide, A Historical Perspective," 368.
8 Halsbury's Laws of England, 1176, 628.
9 Harder, "The Psychopathology of Infanticide," 196.
10 Oxford English Dictionary, Volume IV, 213. This term does not appear in legal literature.
11 Resnick, "Child Murder by Parents: A Psychiatric Review of Filicide," 325.
12 Adelson, "Slaughter of the Innocents," 1349.
13 Marzuk, Tardiff, & Hirsch, "The Epidemiology of Murder-Suicide," 3181.
14 Adelson, "Pedicide Revisited," 17.
15 Harder, "The Psychopathology of Infanticide," 196.
16 McKee, "Sex Differentials in Survivorship and the Customary Treatment of Infants and Children," 91.
17 Lull, "The Antiquity of Man," 1.
18 Garrett, "Where Did We Come From?," 436.
19 Buettner-Janusch, Origins of Man, 4-5.
20 Gribbin & Gribbin, Children of the Ice, 9.
21 Clark & Piggott, Prehistoric Societies, 28.
22 Gribbin & Gribbin, Children of the Ice, 62, 69-71.
23 Jordan, The Face of the Past, 13.
24 Gribbin & Gribbin, Children of the Ice, 76.
25 Gore, "The Dawn of Humans, Expanding Worlds," 86.
26 Ibid., 83, 100.
27 Ibid., 99.
28 Amundsen, "Medicine and the Birth of Defective Children," 7.
29 Williamson, "Infanticide: An Anthropological Analysis," 66.
30 Birdsell, "Some Predictions for the Pleistocene Based on Equilibrium Systems Among Recent Hunter Gatherers," 239.
31 Neel, "Lessons From a `Primitive' People," 816.
32 Ibid.
33 Reference made by Tyler. See Todd, The Primitive Family as an Educational Agency, 128.
34 Hippler, "Culture and Personality Perspective of the Yolngu of Northeastern Arnhem Land: Part I – Early Socialization," 227.
35 Roheim, "The Western Tribes of Central Australia: Childhood," 199.
36 Cowlishaw, "Infanticide in Aboriginal Australia," 263.
37 Harris, Cannibals & Kings, The Origins of Cultures, 10.
38 Ibid., 15.
39 Lubbock, Pre-Historic Times, 176.

40 Davies, Human Sacrifice, 32.
41 DeMause, "The Fetal Origins of History," 34.
42 Gribbin & Gribbin, Children of the Ice, 123-124.
43 The Age of God-Kings, 9-10.
44 Ibid., 46.
45 Ibid., 12.
46 Ibid., 153.
47 Euripides, Ion, 503-504, 205.
48 McCully, "Archetypal Psychology As A Key For Understanding Prehistoric Art Forms," 529.
49 "Akkadian Creation Epic," Ancient Near Eastern Texts, I.37-40, 61.
50 Ibid., I.46.
51 Hinnells, Persian Mythology, 63.
52 Marinatos, Crete & Mycenae, 14.
53 Mylonas, Mycenae & the Mycenaean Age, 3.
54 Hale, The Horizon Book of Ancient Greece, 116.
55 Golden, "Demography and the Exposure of Girls at Athens," 316.
56 Isocrates, Panathenaicus, 122-123, Volume II, 449.
57 Lacey, The Family in Classical Greece, 164.
58 Bolkestein, "The Exposure of Children at Athens," 222.
59 The Law Code of Gortyn, Column III.49, 41.
60 Epiricus, Outlines of Pyrrhonism, III.211, 467. This was also confirmed by Hermogenes Rhetor. See Boswell, The Kindness of Strangers, footnote 15, 60.
61 Aristotle, Politics, I.1259b.1-3, 1143.
62 In Theaetetus, Socrates analogizes this rite to Theaetetus in order to test whether his conclusion that knowledge is perception is correct: "Now that he is born, we must run round the hearth with him, and see if he is worth rearing." Plato, Theaetetus, Volume II, 163.
63 MacDowell, The Law in Classical Athens, 91.
64 Harrison, The Law of Athens, 71.
65 Williams, "The Legal Evaluation of Infanticide," 116.
66 Heliodorus, An Ethiopian Romance, I, 13.
67 Lacey, The Family in Classical Greece, 165.
68 Polybius, The Histories, XXXVI.17.7, Volume VI, 385.
69 Hesiod, Theogony, 464-465, 24.
70 Ibid., 467, 24.
71 Apollodorus, Library, 1.1.5-6, Volume 1, 7.
72 Ovid, Fast I, IV.210, 203.
73 Golden, Children and Childhood in Classical Athens, 83.
74 Ibid.
75 Plutarch, Lives, "Lycurgus," XVI.2, Volume I, 255.
76 Roper, "Ancient Eugenics," 384.
77 Cameron, "The Exposure of Children And Greek Ethics," 108.
78 Plato, Laws, V.740E, Volume I, 367.
79 Plato, The Republic, 372bc, 49.
80 Ibid., 459de, 138.
81 Plato, Laws, IX.868CD, Volume II, 249.
82 Aristotle, Politics, VII.1335b, 1302
83 Ibid.

84 Plutarch, Lives, "Lycurgus,"
85 Ibid., XVI.1, 255.
86 Roper, "Ancient Eugenics," 391.
87 Lacey, The Family in Classical Greece, 231.
88 Westrup, Introduction to Early Roman Law, Volume I, 251.
89 Cicero, De Re Publica, II.X.18, 127.
90 Lobingier, The Evolution of the Roman Law, 66.
91 Livy, History of Rome, III.XXXIV.6, 113.
92 Tacitus, Annals, III.27, 116.
93 Justinian, The Institutes, Table IV.I, Appendix I, 592.
94 Ibid., Table IV.III, 592.
95 Warkany, "Congenital Malformations in the Past," 86.
96 Radin, "The Exposure of Infants in Roman Law and Practice," 338.
97 This law was passed in the consulship of Pompeius, 52 B.C., and was borrowed from the Twelve Tables. Justinian, The Institutes, IV.XVIII.6., 506.
98 Plautus, Truculentus, II.IV.399, Volume II, 109.
99 Wiedemann, Adults and Children in the Roman Empire, 16.
100 Ibid., 15.
101 Kathryn Moseley, "The History of Infanticide in Western Society," 349.
102 Cameron, "The Exposure of Children And Greek Ethics," 105-106.
103 Werner, The Unmarried Mother in German Literature, 18.
104 Boswell, The Kindness of Strangers, 134.
105 Ibid., 135.
106 Ibid., 136.
107 Strabo, The Geography, 5.3.2, Volume II, 381.
108 Virgil, Aenead, VI.562-566, 153.
109 Lucian, "Voyage to the Lower World," The Works of Lucian of Samosata, Volume I, 232.
110 Justinian, Digest, 25.III.12, Volume II, 737.
111 Boswell, The Kindness of Strangers, 58.
112 Balsdon, Life and Leisure in Ancient Rome, 82.
113 Ford, "The Emergence of the Child as a Legal Entity," 395.
114 Boswell, The Kindness of Strangers, 110.
115 Boswell, "Exposition and Oblation: The Abandonment of Children and the Ancient and Medieval Family," 15.
116 Dionysius, Roman Antiquities, II.XV.2, Volume I, 355.
117 Westrup, Introduction to Early Roman Law, Volume I, 255.
118 Gardner, Women in Roman Law & Society, 156.
119 Soranus, Gynecology, I.XIX.60, 63.
120 Ibid., I.XIX.61, 64-65.
121 Ibid., II.VI.10, 79-80.
122 Minucius, The Octavius, 30.2, 107.
123 Ibid., 30.3, 108.
124 Epictetus, The Discourses, I.XXIII.7, Volume 1, 151.
125 Ovid, Heroides, 107-108, 141.
126 Hunter, Roman Law, 903.
127 Justinian, Digest, 48.VIII.2, Lex Cornelia, Volume IV, 819.
128 Ibid., 25.III.4, Volume II, 738.
129 Lex Iulia de martandis ordinibus in 18 B.C. and Lex papia Poppaea in 9 A.D. Pliny, Panegyricus, 26.6-7, Volume II, 381.

130 Bennett, "The Exposure of Infants in Ancient Rome," 347.
131 Pliny, Panegyricus, 27.1, Volume II, 381.
132 Ibid.
133 Balsdon, Life and Leisure in Ancient Rome, 88.
134 Blackstone, Commentaries on the Laws of England, Book the First, Section Four, I.2, Volume I, 131.
135 Balsdon, Life and Leisure in Ancient Rome, 88.
136 deMause, The History of Childhood, 28.
137 Justinian, The Code of Justinian, IX.XVII, Volume 15, 31.
138 Brockelmann, History of the Islamic Peoples, 1-2.
139 Ibid., 8.
140 Hackin, Huart, Linossier, De Wilman-Grabowska, Marchal, Maspero & Eliseev, Asiatic Mythology, 35.
141 Herodotus, The History, I.108, Volume I, 141.
142 Ibid., I.108-110.
143 Ibid., VII.107, Volume III, 411-413.
144 Hastings, Encyclopedia of Religion & Ethics, Volume I, 4.
145 Pakrasi, Female Infanticide in India, 16.
146 Westermarck, The Origin and Development of the Moral Ideas, Volume I, 406.
147 Giladi, "Some Observations on Infanticide in Medieval Muslim Society," 187.
148 Ryan, "Child Murder In Its Sanitary and Social Bearings," 4.
149 Koran, footnote 2, 204.

CHAPTER II

HISTORICAL BACKGROUND – THE INFLUX OF RELIGION

> "Here is my final conclusion, fear God and obey his commandments, for this is the entire duty of man. For God will judge us for everything we do, including every hidden thing, good or bad."[1]

As we have seen, the Golden Age of Greece may have witnessed the birth of grand philosophical and cultural advancements that spread slowly to encompass much of the world, but it did little to protect the lives of its vulnerable children who were born to the renowned citizenry. Treated as chattel, the newborn infant often faced a life in antiquity that was more a cacophony of abuse than a harmony of tender care. Parents were not subject to legal requisites in their care of children, and if the value of infant life was ever to be equated with that of a healthy adult, a more potent caution than societal mores and taboos would have to be found. A satisfactory solution was eventually to be uncovered in religion's threat of an eternal afterlife of pain in Hell.

As reflected in the biblical passage from *Ecclesiastes* above, crime could possibly be hidden from secular authorities with appropriate stealth and camouflage, but one could never escape punishment in the final judgment of the All-knowing, Almighty Lord. Abraham, the grand biblical Patriarch, fathered the development of three major religions – Christianity, Judaism, and Islam – and each one utilized the threat of everlasting torture to foster moral behavior in their frightened adherents. As Ezekiel was to warn the Jews who turned away from God's commandments, and worshiped false idols, that their corpses will be set in front of those idols, and:

> Your survivors will think of me among the nations where they are held captive, how I was grieved at their whoring heart that turned away from me, and at their eyes that whored after their idols; they will loathe themselves for the evil things they did, their abominations of every sort. And they shall realize that not for nothing did I, YWYH, declare that I would do this evil to them.[2]

While the methodology may have been crude, these great creeds of life finally provided the newborn infant with some modicum of protection. As the progeny of God Himself, rather than the property of a mortal parent, the life of a child was considered equally valuable to that of an adult; if infants were not properly cared for, the fury of the Almighty would be forthcoming. It was wrath, rather than warmth, which assured appropriate behavior in the frightened, pious subjects.

While ardent faith in the Divine Being has certainly been an integral part of every religious belief throughout recorded history, the key word describing long term success has definitely been "fear." Cicero, writing a few decades before the birth of Christ, clearly recognized the effectiveness of this awesome power and posited that the basis for the success of religion was not only worship of the gods, but also the provocation of intense fear.[3] Mortal tyrants had only the warning of pain and suffering here on earth to demand obedience from their loyal subjects, but religions threatened an eternity of damnation if the commandments of their particular deity were not followed.

In this role of fearful overseer, judge, executioner and king, God has usually been identified as a "Father" in his dealings with mortal man. Sir Thomas More described how the Utopians believed that there was a:

> Certain single divinity, unknown, eternal, boundless, inexplicable, beyond the understanding of the human mind, diffused through the whole of this universe in virtue, not bulk. They call him "the father."[4]

So it was with the descendants of Abraham as well. Devout Jews, Christians and Muslims accepted this authority of God and instilled obedience with images of fear. Moses told the people of Israel that God was a "devouring fire, a jealous God."[5] The message was clear, if you did not follow His laws, you would be destroyed. The warning from *Ecclesiastes* showed that you cannot hide your actions from God: "For where a man goes is plainly visible to the Lord, And all his paths are under observation."[6]

Tertullian, one of the early Christian Church fathers, cautioned that the soul of man knows the Lord and "if it knows Him, it certainly fears Him."[7] The true believer must follow the teachings of God not only from inner faith and understanding, but also from fear of retribution if the commandments of God were disobeyed. We may have been given the gift of rational thought and free choice as part of our rational being, but as Erasmus explained, Christ the king "has told us clearly that he who does not stand for Him stands against Him."[8]

And for rebellious behavior which arose despite the warnings, punishment was varied, but severe. The classical secular retribution in antiquity was a "life for life, eye for eye, tooth for tooth, hand for hand, foot for foot."[9] But for religious crimes, even after death the disbeliever continued to be punished in Hell for all eternity. If this prospect was not enough to demand obedience, there was the additional threat of danger to future generations: "When I punish people for their sins, the punishment continues upon the children, grandchildren, and great-grandchildren of those who hate me."[10]

Many hesitant followers were clearly afraid to take a chance that such warnings were false or misplaced. They obeyed the litany of rules which were promulgated by the mortal messengers of God, and prayed for mercy and forgiveness when some weakness caused them to stray. Others, believing that the institution of the Church was of human, and not supernatural, origin were clearly upset at the dogma which was preached. Thomas Paine, writing in *The Age of Reason* in 1794 A.D., admonished those that attempted to enslave the free will of man: "All national institutions of churches, whether Jewish, Christian, or Turkish appear to me no other than human inventions set up to terrify and enslave mankind, and to monopolize power and profit."[11] The Church was omnipotent, not by the designation of a Supreme Being, but rather by the same machinations used by tyrants to enslave their own, and other populations, by military force.

These remarks of Paine, like so many other free-thinking critics, may have made for widely read treatises among intellectual minds, but they did not stem the tide of religious growth. A clear belief that all human beings were children of God, and that human life was not to be taken without authority of the Lord, became accepted as if it was a natural consequence of evolutionary growth. Contrary actions were animalistic or barbarian; the concept of *patriae potestas* as an inherent right of a parent was dead.

This development had inevitable consequences, most of which were beneficial to the survival of children. Prohibition of infanticide and abortion was a feature of Judaeo-Christian morals from the very start. It followed closely upon the apocalyptic traditions of the pagan Orphic tradition.[12] The concept of divinely sanctioned inviolability of life held that every human being was born with certain inalienable rights, the chief of which was the right to live, and that man was created in the image of God – "Image Dei."[13] It was immoral to kill another human being, even if it was only a helpless newborn, because each life was a reflection of the Almighty God. In the words of Pseudo-Phycylides: "A woman should not destroy the unborn babe in her belly, nor after its birth throw it before the dogs and the vultures as a prey."[14]

Although the Old Testament never actually forbade the practice of infanticide directly, the religious interpretations which followed were based upon monetary punishment inflicted upon anyone who caused a miscarriage of a pregnant woman: "If two men are fighting, and in the process hurt a pregnant woman so that she has a miscarriage, but she lives, then the man who injured her shall be fined whatever amount the woman's husband shall demand, and as the judges approve."[15]

A similar fine was seen in the Code of Hammurabi from about 2250 B.C. If a miscarriage occurred, a fine of ten shekels of silver was levied, while if the woman died, the daughter of the offender was put to death.[16] The Middle Assyrian Laws, from about 1300 B.C., held that if a man struck a pregnant woman, and caused the loss of the fetus, then "he shall pay two talents thirty minas of lead; they shall flog him fifty (times) with staves (and) he shall do the work of the king for one full month."[17] In another section, punishment would include the loss of life.[18] The Hittite Laws also declared a fine for causing a miscarriage with ten shekels of silver to be paid if it was in the tenth month, and five shekels if the pregnancy was in the fifth month.[19]

Just because the teachings of religious leaders in general prohibited the practice of infanticide, however, it did not mean that followers were always uniformly obedient. The Bible is replete with instances of infanticide that brought down intense castigation and warnings of retribution from the prophets, and for centuries thereafter church leaders and writers were faced with the need to continue forbidding, and forewarning, of the deviant practice.

A. Judaism

The precepts of Judaism are contained in the Torah, or Pentateuch, the first five books of the Old Testament. According to tradition, these writings were made by Moses who, just before the Israelites crossed the Jordan River into the Promised Land, "wrote out the laws he had already delivered to the people and gave them to the priests, the sons of Levi, who carried the Ark containing the Ten Commandments of the Lord."[20]

Biblical scholars, however, beginning with the work of Spinoza in the seventeenth century A.D., have determined that the Torah was actually written not by Moses but by a number of other sources known as J (Yahwist), E (Elohist), P (Priestly), D (Deuteronomy), and R (Redactors).[21] These conclusions have been based on detailed analysis of linguistic characteristics and historical facts.

Whether the Torah is the work of one or many authors, however, its moral lessons have clearly guided the lives of not only Jews, but much of the Western World. Blaise Pascal, the seventeenth century natural philosopher and mathematician who was not a Jew himself, believed that this piece of work was one of the most important to all mankind. He noted that: "The law by which this people is governed is at once the oldest law in the world, the most perfect, and the only one which has been continuously observed in any state."[22] He added: "I find it strange that the first law in the world should also happen to be the most perfect."[23]

In addition to the lessons of Torah scripture, Jewish law is also composed of the writings and teachings of several learned rabbis. This collection, known as the *Talmud*, was produced in the aftermath of the Roman destruction of the Jerusalem Temple in 70 A.D., and is composed of the Mishnah, a code of law compiled by Rabbi Judah ha-Nasi, and the Gemara, the record of the extensive discussions over the meaning of the Mishnah which took place in rabbinic academies. The time between the completion of the Mishnah, and the completion of the Palestinian *Talmud* was about two centuries.[24] Many other scholars, or Tannaim, had written discussions about the meaning of Scripture, but none achieved the degree of authority of R. Judah.[25] There are two versions of the *Talmud*, one the product of scholars in Babylon, and the other from Palestine.[26] Although clearly diverse in many aspects, the two treatises are very similar in form and content due to the interchange of opinions and ideas which transpired during their preparation by emissaries sent between Babylon and Palestine.[27] Their area of greatest divergence is in the matter of civil law.[28] Where Palestine had become a primarily agricultural society, Babylonia underwent an expansion of commercial trade.[29] Many of the severe criminal codes of the Bible were interpreted more leniently in later times in accordance with the humaneness of Pharisaic Judaism.[30]

For the most part, all of these sources declare that Judaism is a pro-natal tradition which proclaims the messianic notion that someday a child will be born that will enrich and save the human family.[31] This faith in a future Savior, rather than the Jesus Christ proclaimed by those Jews who converted to Christianity, gives each new life a precious and divine potential which dictates that no life may be taken by purposeful human action since it could never be known if the loss would be that of the Savior himself. How can any murder be excused when the very future of all of mankind could depend on the life of that one single soul? Every Jew was therefore instructed to rear his family as if the Deliverer might spring from their own seed.

Maimonides, the renowned twelfth century A.D. Jewish philosopher and physician, pointed out that a single man was first created in *Genesis*, "to teach us that if any man destroys a single life in the world, scripture imputes it to him as though he had destroyed the whole world."[32] Each life, each spark of being, was a gift of God and only the Holy Father could extinguish its flame.

The teachings of Judaism contrasted with that of classical Greco-Roman thought in ascribing to life a divine origin, not just for its heroes, but for all of mankind. Without having to fable a sexual event between a mortal and a God, the concept of the essence of every human being have a soul from the Lord was unique to Jewish thought. The Greeks and Romans defined the qualities of personhood on judicial grounds, the Jews left the designation to God.[33]

As a by-product of this reverence for life, directives against murder were repeated in many sections of the Old Testament.[34] The prohibition was even extended to cases where one's own life was in mortal danger, and murder of another human being was the only pathway to safety.[35] The rabbis reasoned that it would be better to die, and then live in the eternity of time with the good grace of God, then extend your life on earth by committing a forbidden sin.

These precepts against murder, however, extended only to life after completion of the birth process. The fetus under orthodox Jewish law was not considered a person until it was fully born. While it was clear that God was directly responsible for the fetus developing in the womb, intrauterine life was not equated with a living human being.[36] The Sages interpreted the Biblical teachings to mean that the commandment to not kill another person could not be construed to mean a fetus.[37] If the life of a mother was endangered by hard labor, the fetus could be "cut up" while still inside the womb; but if "the greater part of it was already born," then it was not permissible to sacrifice the infant in order to save the mother's life.[38] The rationale was that "the claim of one life cannot override the claim of another life."[39] Under orthodox views, the commandment to not kill existed even if the birth was a creature with a double back or a double spine. If it was an actual birth, and not a miscarriage, "it has the status of a person and killing it would be considered infanticide which is prohibited."[40]

For the Jew who dared to disregard these warnings – beware. If one did not act properly, and did commit murder, the punishment was that determined by the Biblical adage a "life for life, eye for eye, tooth for tooth, hand for hand, foot for foot."[41] This meant that anyone found guilty of murder must die according to the law of talion.[42] In addition, no ransom could be accepted in order to spare the penalty.[43] The only instance where execution might not be mandatory was where the victim was a newborn infant. While the newborn was placed on an equal footing with an adult in terms of its right to life, there were some differences which reflected the view of many other contemporary cultures. The actual status of becoming a true person, or "nefesh," did not occur under Jewish law until thirty days of age. It was therefore generally not considered appropriate to require the death penalty for killing a child under the age of thirty days.[44]

As a result of this unique respect for human life, infanticide, which was widely practiced in pagan society, was "simply unknown both as a phenomenon in Jewish history and as a distinct rubric in Jewish law."[45] Many authors of that era remarked on this unusual behavior. Tacitus recorded that the Jews "regard it as a crime to kill any late-born children."[46] Strabo noted that the Egyptians and the Jews rear every child that is born and that this custom was "jealously observed."[47] Diodorus of Sicily also distinguished the Egyptians and the Jews from the rest of the Greco-Roman world by their devotion to raising all of their children.[48] The Bible would support the notion that Egyptians would raise all children once they were born, for when the Pharaoh had directed the Egyptian midwives, Shiphrah and Puah, to slay all the newborn male Hebrew children, the women returned and explained that they failed because the Hebrew mothers "have their babies so quickly that we can't get there in time."[49] This implied that while a newborn might possibly be disposed of during the birth process itself, once the baby was witnessed and accepted, it's removal would be considered an unlawful murder.

That so many contemporaries found it unique that the Jewish people did not practice infanticide did not mean that no individual Jew ever did away with their children. It seems certain, however, that Jewish society, as a whole, did not condone the practice. Jewish writers of the time voiced strict commandments against infanticide as a reflection of this unique characteristic. In the *Wisdom of Solomon*, the Canaanites were said to be hateful "for their loathsome practices, acts of sorcery and licentious mystery rites; ruthless slayers of their children, and entrail-devouring banqueters of human flesh."[50]

Philo, the eminent Jewish philosopher who was born around 20 B.C., was one of the first commentators to speak out clearly against infanticide. Although direct references in the biblical text never specifically mentioned the act of infanticide, Philo interpreted the teachings of Moses as forbidding the practice.[51] This seemed reasonable to him "since the displeasure of the law is not concerned with ages but with a breach of faith to the race," and so the prohibition of murder, within the context of the Biblical text, should include all living beings.[52] Denouncing the exposure of children as a form of murder, he refused to segregate an infant because of its newly born status.

Josephus, the Jewish historian and contemporary of Philo, also condemned the practice of infanticide. He presumed that Jewish Law required all offspring to be reared, because God had enjoined the Jewish people: "To bring up all our offspring, and forbids women to cause abortion of what is begotten, or to destroy it afterward; and if any woman appears to have so done, she will be a murderer of her child."[53] It would be an anathema because "she destroys a soul and diminishes the race."[54] Josephus was not critical, however, of the biblical punishment of stoning a child to death if that child was rebellious to his parents.[55]

Not only were Jews forbidden the killing of children, but the Torah demanded that there was an extra duty for them to have offspring, if capable. The duty of procreation is called the "first mitzvah" of the Torah and was based mostly on instructions the Lord gave to Noah and Jacob.[56] The chosen people would need to expand their numbers if they were to populate the earth, and this required more than a subtle suggestion. The *Talmud* directed that "he who does not engage in procreation is as if he committed murder."[57] The Mishnah agreed that "a man may not desist from the duty of procreation unless he already has children."[58] The Halakhah, as well, followed the teaching of Hillel in that the obligation was not discharged until the birth of at least one son and one daughter – when the couple "replaces itself."[59] Maimonides acknowledged that while the mitzvah of "*p'ru ur'vu*" may be fulfilled in this way, the Rabbis advised: "not to desist from procreation while he yet has strength."[60]

Even the spilling of sperm as a means of contraception was not allowed, and such an act was considered equal to homicide since from every seed a person could have been born.[61] Sigmund Freud, in explaining a dream to a man where withdrawal during intercourse was used to prevent pregnancy, said: "It gave you reassurance that you had not procreated a child, or, what amounts to the same thing, that you had killed a child."[62]

In fact, if a man was to make himself a eunuch "let such be driven away, as if they had killed their children," for they could no longer procure them.[63]

But despite this extensive encouragement to reproduce, and then raise children without harm, the Old Testament does contain references to infanticide which are allowable under the Law. The frequency of these events have been disputed but James George Frazer believed that the ancient Hebrews sacrificed their first-born children frequently.[64] This view was based on a literal translation of the commandment of God given in the book of *Exodus*: "The first-born of thy sons shalt thou give unto Me."[65] From this sentence, Frazer implied that the killing of children was a common event, and reflected similar practices in other Semitic races like the Carthaginians, Phoenicians, Canaanites, Moabites, and Sepharvites.[66] A passage in *Ezekiel* would tend to support his assertion:

> I let them adopt customs and laws which were worthless. Through the keeping of them they could not attain life. In the hope that they would draw back in horror, and know that I alone am God, I let them pollute themselves with the very gifts I gave them. They burnt their firstborn children as offerings to their gods![67]

Most modern interpretations, however, do not follow Frazer's view. The majority contend that the consecration to God of the first-born male does not mean an actual sacrifice, but rather a figurative devotional event when it references human beings. The Lord instructed the Jewish people that they may purchase the first-born of the animals back from the Lord but they "*must* (italics mine) buy back your firstborn sons."[68] The animals were to be sacrificed but the children redeemed.[69] While there are a number of occurrences of sacrificial infanticide which are well documented within the biblical text, they refer to the actions of a specific individual rather than the entire population.

One area of killing which was clearly authorized for all Jews within the text of the Old Testament was the punishment of a "rebellious child." Biblical law was very harsh in this regard, and parents were given the authority, and even the directive, to raise their children to follow the teachings of the Lord. This requirement was important "for the death of the wicked benefits themselves (in that they sin no more) and the world."[70] If a child was not directed towards living a pious life, his evil habits would ultimately lead to sin.

The warnings to follow these precepts were clearly expressed in numerous sections of the Bible:

> One who curses his father and his mother – His lamp will go out in the darkness of night.[71]
>
> Anyone who reviles or curses his mother or father shall surely be put to death;[72]
>
> Anyone who curses his father or mother shall surely be put to death – for he has cursed his own flesh and blood.[73]
>
> Anyone who strikes his father or mother shall surely be put to death.[74]

But despite these clear premonitions, parents could not take the law into their own hands. If they felt that their "stubborn or rebellious child" did not obey them, despite being punished, they were directed to:

> Take him before the elders of the city and declare, "this son of ours is stubborn and rebellious and won't obey; he is a worthless drunkard." Then the men of the city shall stone him to death.[75]

The punishment was intended only for sons and did not allow for execution of daughters. In addition, it was in effect only during the time that the young boy "produces two hairs until he grows a beard right around," meaning the hairs of the genitals and not of the face.[76] Death would not be an appropriate punishment for the very young, or the mature adult. As might be expected, this aspect of Jewish Law was very controversial and seldom followed.

Other areas of documented infanticide among the early Israelites occurred during famines that were brought on, according to the prophets, as punishment for the sins of the people against the Lord. Forewarnings of such events can be found in many biblical sections. Moses told the people of Israel, before they crossed the Jordan River into the Promised Land, that if they did not obey all the commandments of the Lord, curses would fall upon them: "You will even eat the flesh of your own sons and daughters in the terrible days of siege that lie ahead."[77] And to emphasize this even more Moses continued:

> The most tender and delicate woman among you – the one who would not so much as touch her feet to the ground – will refuse to share with her beloved husband, son and daughter. She will hide from them the afterbirth and the new baby she has borne, so that she herself can eat them.[78]

The warning by Moses is repeated elsewhere, that if the Israelites did not obey, "you shall eat your own sons and daughters."[79]

A similar warning was given by Ezekiel, who prophesied in Babylonia around 593 B.C. Because the people had rebelled against the judgments of the Lord, and became more wicked than other nations, the anger of God would be vented and: "Surely parents will eat children in your midst, and children shall eat their parents."[80] Jeremiah, as well, told how the Ben-Hinnom Valley would be no longer called Topheth but "The Valley of Slaughter", for "I will see to it that your enemies lay siege to the city until all food is gone, and those trapped inside begin to eat their own children and friends."[81] The Topheth was an area just south of Jerusalem where a cult of child sacrifice was entrenched.[82]

These forebodings came true, according to the biblical text, during a siege in Samaria by King Ben-hadad of Syria, when the king of Israel was asked by a woman to help with the deadly famine that was killing the people of the town. She proposed that they eat his son one day and her's the next as there was no other source of food. The king agreed and then boiled his son for them to eat.[83] The next day he directed her to kill her son, as she had promised, but the woman now refused to follow his command and hid the boy away.[84]

This brazen act was not often repeated, however, and other mothers allowed their offspring to be eaten as food. During one famine in Jerusalem, the hunger was so great that:

> With their own hands the kindly women cooked their children. This was the food they had, when my people was ruined.[85]

In addition to actions initiated by want of food, there were also numerous recordings of children being killed during sacrificial rites. The most famous of these was a sacrifice begun, but never completed. This was, of course, the willingness of Abraham to offer up his only legitimate son, Isaac, when commanded to do so by the voice of the Lord. This event, which is discussed more thoroughly in the Chapter on Sacrifice, has been the hallmark of faith in the justice of the Almighty God for both Jews and Christians alike. The story is meant to remind all the faithful of the extent to which a pious man must go in his devotion to the wishes of the Almighty God.

But where Abraham was checked by the angel of the Lord before the deadly knife could be thrust into Isaac's body, some Israelites did not abort their sacrificial rites. Ahaz, the king of Judah who ruled for sixteen years in Jerusalem from about 743-727 B.C., was a very wicked leader according to the rabbinic tradition. He did not follow in the ways of king David, but rather made offerings to various deities and idols. He even "passed his son through fire, imitating the abominations of the nations whom YHWH dispossessed before the Israelites."[86]

Another Judah king, Manasseh, was also guilty of a similar offense. He reigned from 687-642 B.C., and restored the pagan cults of Baal and Asherah. It is said that: "He made his sons to pass through the fire in the valley of Ben-Hinnom, practiced soothsaying, divination, and sorcery, and dealt in necromancy and familiar spirits."[87]

Other references to impious actions on the parts of the Israelites, which were threatened to incur the wrath of God, were recorded in various writings by the Prophets. These are covered more extensively in the Chapter on Sacrifice. But one particularly controversial sacrifice concerned Jephthah, a warrior from Gilead appointed by the Israelites to command their army against the Ammonites. Jephthah vowed to the Lord that if He would help him to victory then: "Anything coming out the doors of my house to meet me, when I return with victory from the Ammonites, shall belong to Yahweh; I will offer it up as a burnt offering."[88] Upon his return home, Jephthah expected some animal to appear so he could guarantee his promise, but instead his only child, a daughter, ran out to greet him. When he recognized who it was, he tore his clothes and knew that he had made a vow to the Lord that he could not take back.[89] He was forced to give up his daughter's life in order to save his solemn word, for an oath to God superseded even the life of his very own child.

In addition to Old Testament sources, there are references to infanticide in other writings. The Third Book of the *Sibylline Oracles* is believed to be of Jewish origin, and tells how the people have wandered from the path of the Immortal God. But a warning is put forth to change "entirely the thought in thy heart," and "thine own offspring rear and do not murder."[90]

Although the practice of exposure was much rarer among the Jews than other peoples in antiquity, there were still instances of child abandonment, the most prominent being the voluntary expulsion of Hagar and Ishmael by Abraham, and the forced riverside abandonment of the infant Moses in Egypt. But although the numbers of fabled exposures are small, actual cases must be greater since the *Talmud* includes children who were abandoned as one of the ten genealogic classes which endured the Babylonian Exile. The *Talmud* explained that the survivors could be categorized as: priests, levites, Israelites, Halalim, proselytes, freedmen, mamzerim, nethinim, shetuki, and foundlings.[91] The foundlings, or Asufi, were those who were gathered from the street "and knows neither his father nor his mother."[92] The cases were obviously numerous as there is extensive discussion on how to determine whether a child was to be considered legitimate, despite being abandoned. Such a holding, for example, would be made when "he has been massaged with oil, fully powdered, has beads on him, wears a tablet with an inscription or an amulet."[93] Although there is little information available on how many children were actually subject to this analysis, most historians believe that the majority of cases were due to economic distress and poverty.

Like other races, Jews were also not immune from actions based on vanity, revenge, or self-survival. The *Talmud* included a ruling by Mar, son of R. Ashi, that a mother was forbidden from remarriage if her child died because it was possible that she killed it "so as to be in a position to marry."[94] A story was told that such a case actually occurred where a mother had strangled her child in order to remarry. But the incident was not felt to be proof of the supposition for such a woman would have to be an imbecile as it "is not likely that sane women would strangle their children."[95] As today, the ancient Hebrews found it inconceivable that infanticide and sanity could exist together in the mind of a Jew.

B. Christianity

Christianity, as a philosophical extension of Judaism embracing the same basic tenets of the Old Testament, held infanticide to be against the teachings of God and Jesus Christ.[96] But the early Church Fathers went beyond the limitations of the Talmud and insisted that all human life was inviolable, even the killing of newborns and fetuses. This was truly a new concept for where Judaism retained the definition of "life" as being after the birth process, Christianity extended this protection to the fetus within the mother's womb.

Despite this unique humanistic theologic position, early Christians were often accused by the Romans of incredible atrocities, including that of infanticide. The Church was charged with initiating new recruits by covering "a young baby with flour and then inflict(ing) blows on it and then lick(ing) the blood with thirsty lips."[97] The Romans denounced their claims of innocence and piety as reprehensible lies, and insisted that the Christians were nothing more than a dangerous, malignant sect of renegades.

Today we find such claims little more than a specious smokescreen by an Empire desperately trying to maintain its power base. But similarities to other pagan rites were indeed visible within the sacraments of the Christian Church, and there was much food-for-thought among the Roman censures at the time. The crucifixion of the Son, Jesus Christ, was not only permitted by the Father, but even offered willingly in order to atone for the sins of mankind. Such behavior was not uncommon in many pagan societies, and the ingestion of wafer and wine, representing the body and blood of Christ, evoked images which could support claims of cannibalism.

For the next few centuries, Christian Apologists were busy trying to answer these slanderous accusations to the satisfaction of their new converts. Mostly they pointed to their deep respect of human life to denounce any possible acceptance of infanticidal deeds. Tertullian, in the second century A.D., related in his *Apology* how the Christians "are accused of having sworn to murder babies and to eat them."[98] Such a declaration was ridiculous, he argued, for not only is murder forbidden by us, once and for all, but: We are not permitted to destroy even the fetus in the womb.[99] The logic, of course, was simple: "No life, not even the very spark of life after conception, could be taken by one who claimed to be a Christian.

In *Embassy for the Christians*, also written near the end of the second century, Athenogoras argued passionately that the Christians were innocent of the charges brought against them. His reasoning was that:

> The same man cannot regard that which a woman carries in her womb as a living creature, and therefore as an object of value to God, and then go about to slay the creature that has come forth to the light of day. The same man cannot forbid the exposure of children, equating such exposure with child murder, and then slay a child that has found one to bring it up.[100]

Minucius Felix, the third century A.D. African Apologist, replied that the only person capable of believing the stories of Christians draining a baby's blood "is one who is capable of actually perpetrating it."[101] It was the Romans who knew so much about the atrocities of infanticide because of their obvious guilt, and not the blameless followers of Christ; it was absurd to suggest that Christians could possibly condone the murder of innocent children.

These Apologists could point to a number of sources to back-up their assertions. The prohibition of infanticide was a prominent feature of many early Christian teachings. While much is still in dispute about the origin of some of these works, two of them have almost identical warnings to not commit infanticide. The *Didache*, or "Teachings of the Apostles", written around 60-160 A.D., stated that: "Thou shalt not murder a child by abortion, nor shalt thou kill it when it is born."[102] Although some believe the *Didache* to be a composite work, rather than that of a single author, it was viewed by many of the early Church Fathers as equivalent to Scripture.[103]

Another treatise, the *Epistle of Barnabas*, was thought to be written by the man who was the apostle and companion of St. Paul. It was dated from around 79-130 A.D., and stated an almost identical command as the *Didache*: "Thou shalt not murder a child by abortion, nor again shalt thou kill it when it is born."[104]

This clear commandment against infanticide reappeared under different authorship for many centuries. In the 8th Book of the *Apostolic Constitution*, which was supposedly handed down from the Apostles by S. Clement, the Bishop of Rome in about 350 A.D., Peter himself was said to have commanded that: Thou shalt not cause abortion, nor after the child is born shalt thou kill it.[105] Over and over again, this phrase becomes burnt into the catechism of the new converts.

There were also warnings from the Church Fathers about the dangers of exposure which indicated that the practice was still frequent enough to be of significant concern. Saint Justin Martyr, in the second century A.D., wrote that it was wicked to expose children, both boys and girls, for "almost all those who are exposed are raised to prostitution."[106] It was only after this cautionary note that Martyr added that a second reason to not expose an infant was that the child could die and the parent would then be guilty of murder.[107] Lactantius, who published his works around 302-323 A.D., also maintained that it was as wicked to expose newborns as to kill them.[108]

Another reason for the emphasis of the Church against exposing a child at birth was the Christian doctrine that children who died without baptism were doomed to eternal perdition.[109] The rite of baptism exorcized the stain of original sin, and was the only way a parent could protect their child from suffering for all eternity. But the baptismal rite, in addition to expiating sin, also made the priesthood and the entire social community aware of the infant's birth. If an unmarried mother brought her child to the church for baptism, she thereby publicized the bastard delivery which was forbidden under Christian doctrine. Many women therefore opted to secretly expose the child rather than undergo the resultant castigation.

For many centuries, the punishments ordained for abandoning a child reflected this mandate of baptism. The Council of Mentz in 852 A.D. decreed a harsher penalty for a mother who killed her unbaptized child than for one who killed it after baptism.[110] This was seen in many other Middle Age penitentials as well. The problem was not eased until the development of foundling homes which allowed an unmarried woman the ability to bring her child secretly to a location where future care could be provided along with baptismal rites. The Church began to provide some shelter in this regard, in 442 A.D., when the ecclesiastical Councils of Vaison and Arles enjoined the clergy to exhort girls to leave their unwanted infants in niches at the church door rather than expose them in the wild.[111] This helped prevent the death of the infant, and the practice eventually led to the development of foundling homes which spread throughout Europe during the Middle Ages. See the Chapter on Exposure for further discussion of this topic.

The rise of Christianity was concomitant with the fall of the Roman Empire, both from a temporal and geographic perspective. The Romans had earlier began to modify the right of a parent to control the life and death of their children, and in 318 A.D., the Emperor Constantine, who had converted to Christianity in 312 A.D., finally declared that the slaying of a child by a father was not protected by the *patriae potestas* and would be considered a serious crime. By the end of the fourth century A.D., this violation became punishable by death.[112]

As Christianity became ingrained into the fabric of Roman society, the Christian emperors promulgated further protection for the welfare of their children. Valentinian extended parental responsibilities for the care of offspring in 374 A.D. when he became the first emperor to pronounce that parents must support and rear all the children born to them, and that those who abandoned an infant would be subject to a penalty "prescribed by law."[113] It would finally be illegal to expose a child under secular law as well as religious and moral teachings.

For families with the ability and means to raise a child, such a warning likely resulted in a lesser chance of infant abandonment. But for others, especially unmarried young women who could not afford to have a newborn child be ascribed to their care, the added risk of legal punishment was not a significant deterrent. If they were discovered, so be it; their plight was pitiful, but understandable.

Once the tide against social acceptance of infanticide was turned, the Church continued to build walls against its resurgence. In 529 A.D., the emperor Justinian ruled that it was not right that those who abandoned their children, "possibly hoping they would die," should retain legal status and be able to later reclaim them.[114] Anyone who therefore found an abandoned child could claim it has their own without fear that the biological parent would later have a change of mind.

In 588 A.D., the Council of Constantinople finally compared infanticide directly with homicide.[115] After centuries of reprimands and rebukes, the religious ideals of sanctity of life finally began to filter down, in true legal terms, to the newborn infant as well as the adult. Civil and church authorities working together had been able to control the heinous actions of infanticidal parents more than either alone. As the Middle Ages drew near, ambitious plans to eradicate the problem were developed. In 589 A.D., at the Third Council of Toledo in Spain, the clergy asked the civil authorities to enjoin and unite their efforts in order to prevent the crime of infanticide from spreading throughout their land.[116] Canon 17 noted that it had been reported that in certain parts of Spain parents were killing their own children, and in order to respond the judges were commanded "to diligently seek out this horrible crime together with a priest and to forbid it by applied severity."[117] No longer could society, secular or religious, tolerate such impious acts.

But while Christian ethics were clear on how infanticide was to be perceived within the Church itself, there were still mixed signals which an uneducated, and naturally susceptible, populace could find supportive of some of their old habits. The litany of moral dilemmas that the common man faced each day was simply too great to assure that anyone but a saint could follow every one of the commandments. While each devotee might agree with the principal basis for right and wrong, as outlined by the religious writings, it was not as easy to live one's life in absolute acceptance. As John Stuart Mill was later to admit: "It is scarcely too much to say that not one Christian in a thousand guides or tests his individual conduct by reference to those laws."[118] We will see the results of such deviation in the chapters which follow.

C. Islam

In the great trinity of religious beliefs which evolved from the time when Abraham first decided to migrate to the Promised Land, we find that child abandonment, and child sacrifice, played critical roles in the lives of all three progenitors. As Moses, who was exposed soon after birth, survived to become the revered law-giver of the Jews, the progenitor of the Arabs was also exposed by his parents. Where biographical information about the Jewish Patriarchs, or the Christian son of God, Jesus Christ, are built mostly upon faith and writings of uncertain reliability and origin, the life of Mohammed, the founder of Islam, is much more detailed and clear. Written records and historical fact abound, and we can learn from reference, rather than inference, what this remarkable man was like.

Mohammed was born around 570 A.D. in Mecca to the clan of the Banu Hashim. His father, `Abdallah, the son of `Abd-al-Muttalib, died two months before his birth, and his mother, Aminah, died a few years later. Orphaned at a young age, he was raised by his grandfather `Abd-al-Muttalib, and then his uncle Abu Talib.[119] At the age of twenty-five years, he married an older, wealthy widow, named Khadija, and spent the next few years working as a successful merchant. He gradually became more intrigued with the doctrines of religion, however, and began to withdraw for long periods of time into the solitude of Mount Hira to contemplate the meaning of Allah – the Omnipotent Lord. One night, during the month of Ramadan in 610 A.D., he had a vision from the angel Gabriel and from then on began to hear, and record, the word of God. His prophecies and writings, collected over the next twenty years, were finally compiled into the Koran (Qur'an) in 652 A.D., and the essence of a new religion, Islam, was formed.

The followers of Mohammed believed in the One God – Allah – and in total surrender of their entire life on earth to God's will – Islam – after which the religion took its name.[120] The Koran itself was revered as the words of God in direct revelation, which in the words of the fourteenth century A.D. Arab scholar Ibn Khaldun, "requires no outside proof" of its truthfulness.[121] It differed from the Torah and the Gospels in that the Prophet Mohammed received it directly in the words and phrases in which it appeared.[122] As Ibn Khaldun points out:

> God sent our Prophet Mohammad to us, in order to call us to salvation and bliss. He revealed to him His noble book in the clear Arabic language.[123]

While many of the teachings of Allah were easily accepted, there was one area which hit upon ancient mores of dubious concern. The Persian world, even before the time of Mohammed, was a male-dominated society. Females were generally seen as a burden, and it was not unusual for daughters to be killed at birth.[124] Such female infanticide was common all over Arabia during this period of time, and was also prevalent in the Mecca society in which Mohammed grew up.[125] These centuries before Mohammed were later to be referred to as the "Days of Ignorance" in order to point out how their actions were explainable by the lack of direction from Allah.[126]

In general, it was only the newborn infant who was killed, but girls were occasionally spared until the age of six years and then sacrificed in a similar fashion.[127] The religious precepts of Islam, while finding that the killing of infants was generally wrong, did not alter the lesser status of the female population. As the *Koran* stated: "Men are superior to women on account of the qualities with which God hath gifted the one above the other."[128] The *Koran*, for the first time, introduced reforms that included the prohibition of female infanticide.[129] Mohammed outlined this problem in various sections of the Holy book.[130] How will you answer, he asked, "when the female child that had been buried alive shall be asked for what crime she was put to death."[131] While daughters may indeed be less favored under the eyes of

Allah, it was not permissible to take away their lives simply because one desired a son. He reproached the people for their reactions to a daughter's birth:

> And they ascribe daughters unto God! Glory be to Him! But they desire them not for themselves. For when the birth of a daughter is announced to any one of them, dark shadows settle on his face and he is sad. He hideth him from the people because of the ill tidings: shall he keep it with disgrace or bury it in the dust? Are not their judgments wrong?[132]

He also admonished fathers for wanting sons rather than daughters:

> What! hath your Lord prepared sons for you, and taken for himself daughters from among the angels?[133]
>
> God's the kingdom of the Heavens and of the Earth! He createth what He will! and he giveth daughters to whom He will, and sons to whom He will.[134]

One does not question God, one follows the law and gives thanks for any blessed receipts. There were additional warnings to not commit infanticide because of financial despair: "And do not kill your children for fear of poverty; We give them sustenance and yourselves (too); surely to kill them is a great wrong."[135]

Avner Giladi noted that prohibition of infanticide was not only a feature of the *Koran*, but was also a prominent component of the Hadith literature which was created in the first century of Islam.[136] Muslims, like their biblical cousins the Christians and Jews, totally rejected the killing of infant children.

Islam thereby provided an obvious theologic direction to prohibit the practice of infanticide among its converts, but did not change one of the underlying reasons for its utilization – the subservient nature of women when compared to men. As long as sons were more highly desired than daughters, the problem of female infanticide would remain.

D. Hinduism

This chapter would not be complete without at least some reference to one of the most popular religions of the world: Hinduism. Hinduism is not an offshoot of the biblical Patriarch, Abraham, but its origins date back to between 1500-1200 B.C. when the sacred ten books of the *Vedas* were said to have been written. Buddha, or Gautama Siddhartha, a deified religious leader from Asia, was thought to have been born around 563 B.C., and his followers formed the mystical faith of Buddhism. Together, these two beliefs provided the spiritual theology for millions of people in India and throughout the world.

As was evident in many of the creation myths of other ancient peoples, sacrifice played a role in the creation of mankind within this religion as well. In the "The Hymn of Man," from the *Rigveda*, the story was told of Purusha, who had a thousand heads, eyes and feet, and "is all that yet hath been and all that is to be."[137] The Sadhyas and Rishis gods sacrificed Purusha as an offering to create all the creatures of the air, and animals of the land. And from that great sacrifice came the castes of men which included the Brahaman priests from his mouth, the Rajanya kings from his arms, the Vaisya traders from his thighs, and the Sudra laborers from his feet.[138]

Out of this saga of life and death also developed the Hindu belief in reincarnation and the rebirth of man through a series of repetitive lives. While the body itself might pass through the degradation of death, the Hindus believed that the soul would live eternally. In the "Conquest of Death," in the *Katha Upanishad*, it was explained that:

> The Knowing Self is not born, it dies not; it sprang from nothing, nothing sprang from it. The Ancient is unborn, eternal, everlasting; he is not killed, though the body is killed.[139]

A human being therefore need not fear death for "a mortal ripens like corn, like corn he springs up again."[140] Believers were willing to sacrifice all they possessed in order to achieve heavenly reward and eternal peace. Vajasravasa, for example, gave up the life of his only son, Nachiketas, in order to achieve this glorious end, and then, in respect to the loss of the child, named the fire sacrifice rite after the boy.[141]

What might appear to others as an act of callousness, this readiness to sacrifice one's own child, was, in reality, a pious show of devotion, similar to that revealed in the tale of Abraham and Isaac. The *Bhagavad-Gita*, or "Blessed Lord's Song," explained that:

> As man casts off worn-out garments and puts on others which are new, similarly the embodied soul, casting out worn-out bodies, enters into others which are new.[142]

The spirit of man lives on: "It is eternal, all-pervading, unchangeable, immovable, everlasting."[143] Under such a belief it was not necessary to mourn the loss of another person: "For that which is born death is certain, and for the dead birth is certain. Therefore grieve not over that which is unavoidable."[144]

In part, because of this religious belief, and partly because of the many social pressures that preferred the birth of a son to a daughter as well, the history of India was filled with evidence of widespread female infanticide as is discussed in the chapter on Female Infanticide.

Endnotes

1 Ecclesiastes 12:13-14. The Living Bible, 529.
2 Ezekiel 6:9,10. The Anchor Bible 129.
3 Cicero, De Inventione, II.XXII.66, 231.
4 More, Utopia, II.IX, 108.
5 Deuteronomy 4:24. The Living Bible, 153.
6 Proverbs 5:21. The Anchor Bible, 51.
7 Tertullian, "The Testimony of the Soul," Chapter 2, The Fathers of the Church, Volume X, 135.
8 Erasmus, Handbook of the Militant Christian, I.I, 64.
9 Deuteronomy 19:21. The Living Bible, 165.
10 Exodus 20:5. Ibid., 66.
11 Paine, The Age of Reason, I.I, 22.
12 Cameron, "The Exposure of Children And Greek Ethics," 111.
13 Ferngren, "The `Imagio Dei' and the Sanctity of Life: The Origins of an Idea," 23.
14 Pseudo-Phycylides, The Sentences of Pseudo-Phycylides, 184-185, 101.
15 Exodus 21:22. The Living Bible, 67.
16 The Code of Hammurabi, King of Babylon, 209-210, 77.
17 "The Middle Assyrian Laws," A.21, Ancient Near Eastern Texts, 181.
18 Ibid., A.50, 184.
19 "The Hittite Laws," I.17, Ancient Near Eastern Texts, 190.
20 Deuteronomy 31:9. The Living Bible, 175.
21 Genesis, The Anchor Bible, xx-xxi.
22 Pascal, Pensees, 451, 171.
23 Ibid., 454, 177.
24 Ginzberg, On Jewish Law and Lore, 12.
25 Ibid., 9.
26 Hirschfeld, "Tiberias," 48.
27 Ginzberg, On Jewish Law and Lore, 8.
28 Ibid., 14.
29 Ibid., 15.
30 Ibid., 6.
31 Vaux, Birth Ethics, 11.
32 Maimonides, "The Book of Judges," Sanhedrin, Treatise One, 12.3, The Code of Maimonides, Volume III, 35.
33 Ferngren, "The `Imagio Dei' and the Sanctity of Life: The Origins of an Idea," 26.
34 "He who sheds the blood of man, By man shall his blood be shed; For in the image of God was man created." Genesis 9:6. The Anchor Bible, 57. See e.g. Exodus 20:13; Deuteronomy 5:17.
35 You have no right to murder him to save yourself since his life is no less valuable than your own. Pesahim, II, Gemara, 25b, The Babylonian Talmud.
36 Psalms 139:13; Jeremiah 1:5; Isaiah 49:1.
37 Rosner, Studies in Torah Judaism: Modern Medicine and Jewish Law, 63-64.
38 Tohoroth, Oholoth, 7.6, The Babylonian Talmud, 660.
39 Ibid.
40 Rosner, Studies in Torah Judaism: Modern Medicine and Jewish Law, 75.
41 Deuteronomy 19:21. The Living Bible, 165. If there was only injury, the punishment was "to be injured in exactly the same way: fracture for fracture, eye

for eye, tooth for tooth. Whatever anyone does to another shall be done to him." Leviticus 24:19,20, Ibid., 109.

42 Leviticus 24:17-20. Milgrom, "Lex Talionis and the Rabbis," 16.
43 Numbers 35:31.
44 Rosner, Studies in Torah Judaism: Modern Medicine and Jewish Law, 69.
45 Jakobovits, "Jewish Views on Infanticide," 23.
46 Tacitus, The Histories, V.V, Volume II, 183.
47 Strabo, The Geography, 17.2.5, Volume 8, 153.
48 Diodorus, The Library of History, 1.80.3, 40.3.8, Volume I, 275, 285.
49 Exodus 1:19.
50 The Wisdom of Solomon, 12:4-5, 237.
51 Philo, The Special Laws, III.XX.117, Volume VII, 549.
52 Ibid., III.XX.118, 551.
53 Josephus, "Against Apion," II.25, The Works of Flavius Josephus, 597.
54 Josephus, Against Apion, II.202, 373-75.
55 Josephus, "Against Apion," II.28, The Works of Flavius Josephus, 597.
56 Genesis 9:1,7; Genesis 35:11. Feldman, Marital Relations, Birth Control & Abortion in Jewish Law, 46.
57 Ibid.
58 Ibid.
59 Ibid., 48.
60 Ibid., 50.
61 Code of Jewish Law, 151.1, Volume IV, 17. "It is forbidden to discharge semen to no purpose." "It is equivalent to killing a human being." Maimonides, The Book of Holiness, "Forbidden Intercourse," Treatise I, 21.18, 137.
62 Freud, The Interpretation of Dreams, IV, 156.
63 Josephus, "Antiquities," IV.VIII.40, The Works of Flavius Josephus.
64 Frazer, The Dying God, 173.
65 Exodus 22:28b. The Holy Scriptures, 60.
66 Frazer, The Dying God, 178-179.
67 Ezekiel 20:25-26. The Living Bible, 647.
68 Exodus 13:13. Ibid., 59. "You must be prompt in giving me the tithe of your crops and your wine, and the redemption payment for your oldest son." Exodus 22:29. Ibid., 68. "Your sons must all be redeemed." Exodus 34:20. Ibid., 80.
69 For a general discussion see Levenson, The Death and Resurrection of the Beloved Son.
70 Sanhedrin, Mishnah, VIII.72a, The Babylonian Talmud.
71 Proverbs 20:20. The Anchor Bible, 120.
72 Exodus 21:17. The Living Bible, 67.
73 Leviticus 20:9. Ibid., 104.
74 Exodus 21:15. Ibid., 67.
75 Deuteronomy 21:18-21. Ibid., 167.
76 Sanhedrin, Mishnah, VIII.68b.
77 Deuteronomy 28:53. The Living Bible, 172.
78 Deuteronomy 28:56-57. Ibid., 173.
79 Leviticus 26:29. Ibid., 111.
80 Ezekiel 5:10. The Anchor Bible, 100.
81 Jeremiah 19:6,9. The Living Bible, 596.
82 Levenson, The Death and Resurrection of the Beloved Son, 10.

83 2 Kings 6:28.
84 2 Kings 6:29,30.
85 Lamentation 4:10. The Anchor Bible, 76.
86 2 Kings 16:3. The Anchor Bible, 184.
87 2 Chronicles 33:6. The Anchor Bible, 195.
88 Judges 11:31. The Anchor Bible, 206.
89 Judges 11:35. Ibid.
90 Sibylline Oracles, Book III, 948, 951-952.
91 Kiddushin, Mishnah, IV.69a, The Babylonian Talmud.
92 . Ibid.
93 Ibid., Gemara, IV.73b.
94 Kethuboth, Gemara, V.60b, The Babylonian Talmud.
95 Ibid.
96 Not only was Jesus himself a Jew, descended from King David, but so were his Apostles. Paul described himself as "the strictest of Pharisees when it comes to obedience to Jewish laws and customs." Acts 26:5. The Living Bible, 892.
97 Felix, The Octavius, 9.5, 65.
98 Tertullian, "Apology," 7.1, Apologetical Works, The Fathers of the Church, 25.
99 Ibid., 9.8, 31.
100 Athenagoras, Embassy For The Christians, 35, 76.
101 Felix, The Octavius, 30.1, 107.
102 Didache, D.ii.2c, Barnabas, Hermar and the Didache, 109.
103 Chadwick, The Early Church, 46.
104 Epistle of Barnabas, xix.5d, Barnabas, Hermar and the Didache, 112.
105 Ethiopic Text, 4.9-13, Arabic Text, 4.14-15, Saidic Text, 6.14-15, Statutes of the Apostles or Canones Ecclesiastici, 129, 235, 297.
106 Martyr, "The First Apology," 27, Writings, 63.
107 Ibid., 29, 65.
108 Lyman., "Barbarism and Religion: Late Roman and Early Medieval Childhood," 90.
109 Ferngren, "The Status of Defective Newborns from Late Antiquity to the Reformation," 53.
110 Ibid., 54.
111 Robins, The Lost Children, 1.
112 Langer, "Infanticide: A Historical Survey," 355.
113 JC 8.52.2. Boswell, The Kindness of Strangers, 162.
114 JC 18.52(51).3. Ibid., 190.
115 Radbill, "A History of Child Abuse and Infanticide," 177.
116 Ibid.
117 Amundsen, "Visigothic Medical Legislation," 568.
118 Mill, On Liberty, II.970-972, 58.
119 Brockelmann, History of the Islamic Peoples, 13.
120 Ibid., 16.
121 Khaldun, The Muqaddimah, 73.
122 Ibid., 74.
123 Ibid., 354.
124 Hastings, Encyclopedia of Religion & Ethics, Volume I, 4.
125 Waddy, Women in Muslim History, 12.
126 Poetry of the Orient, 4.

127 Smith, Kinship & Marriage in Early Arabia, 293.
128 Koran, IV:38, 415.
129 Mayer, Islam & Human Rights, 110.
130 Infanticide is mentioned if five suras: 81, 17, 16, 6 and 60, the first four of which are in the Meccan period. Giladi, "Some Observations on Infanticide in Medieval Muslim Society," 186.
131 Koran, LXXXI:8-9, 45.
132 Ibid., XVI:60-62, 204.
133 Ibid., XVII:42, 168.
134 Ibid., XLII:48, 274.
135 Ibid., XVII:31.
136 Giladi, "Some Observations on Infanticide in Medieval Muslim Society," 188.
137 Yutang, The Wisdom of China and India, 23.
138 Ibid., 24.
139 Ibid., 46.
140 Ibid., 42.
141 Ibid., 43.
142 "Srimad Bhagavad-Gita," II.22. Ibid., 62.
143 Ibid., II.24, 63.
144 Ibid., II.27

CHAPTER III

HISTORICAL BACKGROUND – MIDDLE AGES

> Exposure in the Middle Ages "was practiced on a gigantic scale with absolute impunity, noticed by writers with most frigid indifference."[1]

The Almighty God may have presaged a better life for children in the future by promising eternal peace and equality in the hereafter for those who followed faithfully His litany of commandments, but it took many years before the plight of children's life here on earth improved. Many centuries would have to pass before significant changes in the behavior of parents towards their offspring would develop as a result of the social acceptance of religious beliefs, and, in the meantime, infanticide would pervade the fabric of every culture of civilized man.

One particular custom which continued with little abatement from the moral teachings of the Church was infant abandonment. Boswell found that exposure appeared in nearly every type of historical document, from law to literature, throughout the Middle Ages.[2] While philosophers preached ethical foundations of Humanism, and the Western clergy threatened eternal perfidy, the population-at-large continued to slaughter their children with little compulsion or guilt.

The historical period commonly known as the Middle Ages extended from the end of the Roman Empire, around 476 A.D. when Germanic tribes began to invade western Europe, to the 1500s when Constantinople fell to the Turks and the Renaissance in Italy began in earnest. Historians viewed this era as a time of superstition, poverty and war; it was also a time, in the words of Michelet, best described as "a thousand years without a bath."[3]

The early Middle Ages were especially characterized by insecurity and social instability resulting from intermittent invasions of armies that ravaged the population without discrimination. As hordes of strange intruders rampaged throughout the Continent, peasants and royalty alike became accustomed to the frailty of life, and the stifling nearness of sudden death. Genghis Kahn alone killed more than four million people during his conquests of the Asian continent.[4] In Europe, raids by Vikings, Germanic tribes, and neighboring fiefdoms traded victories like travels along a Monopoly game board.

And if townsfolk survived the ravages of war, they often succumbed to an ever-present specter of disease. Plague, small pox, and dysentery were relentless killers of all age groups and it is estimated that about 25% of the population of Europe died during the epidemics of 1348-1350 A.D..[5] Bubonic plague – the Black Death – killed almost 33% of the population of Europe between 1346-1352.[6] Healthy adults had to worry more about how they were going to survive the uncertainty of daily life than concern themselves with the future welfare of their progeny. In the *Decameron*, Boccaccio described how fathers and mothers "refused to see and tend their children, as if they had not been theirs."[7]

With such a constant onslaught of mortality, it was very difficult for people to maintain attitudes of fairness and equanimity. The concept of natural natal rights was a philosophical development that simply could not germinate in such an uncertain terrain. That one might have inherent claims to life, liberty, and happiness was no less true in that era than now, but the only adage which was universally apparent was: "Might is Right." Religious leaders might preach of the sanctity of life, and threaten eternal punishment in Hell, but neighboring towns were being sacked, a family down the road was dying of the plague, and everyone you knew was hungry and afraid. As Walter Ullmann succinctly concluded:

> The individual as a being endowed with indigenous, autonomous and independent rights was a thesis for which we shall look in vain in the Middle Ages.[8]

Although it was a tortured life for inhabitants of all ages, this era took its greatest toll on newborns. According to some observers, infanticide was the most common crime in western Europe from the Middle Ages to the end of the eighteenth century.[9] The primary reason for this carnage was the precarious economy caused by the political unrest. A married couple had very limited resources and were forced to face harsh realities when attempting to raise the eight to fifteen children expected to be born to them during their married life.[10] The care and feeding of children was generally the responsibility of the mother, and both single and married women alike found it very difficult to adequately provide for their offspring. If they were left alone in the world, their only viable solution was to abandon any newborn child at birth. Young children were often neglected as the mother attempted to find some means of income to support herself and other family members. As a result, infanticide generally became known as a feminine sin and crime.[11] This was especially true among the poor. Having no birth control except abstinence, and little knowledge of abortion methodology, a destitute mother could little afford to raise every child born to her. Statistics showed that the average number of children recorded for wealthy families was 5.1, while for those with middle income it was 2.9, and among the poor 1.8.[12] There was no evidence that the numbers of pregnancies followed similar lines.

A large part of this problem was due to the frequency of illegitimate births. Bastards have always fared more poorly than their legitimate siblings, and the Middle Ages proved no exception. There were many opportunities for sexual activity outside marriage bonds. Catholic priests were not allowed to marry, but their connubial affairs were nevertheless legendary.[13] In addition, the two hundred years of the Holy Crusades, which were first preached on November 25, 1095 by Pope Urban II at the Council of Clermont, created a constant source of illegitimate pregnancies that spread across the continent. Women served the crusading armies, as well as traveling pilgrims, which "provided a means for satisfying sexual appetites through casual encounters and mercenary arrangements."[14] In the path of war was devastation and havoc, in its wake were women pregnant and alone. Many young maidens were angrily raped because of their identification with the "infidels." Froissart chronicled how the Normans, Picards and Spaniards entered Southampton in England in 1339 and "defiled maidens and enforced wives."[15] In 1358 the common people arose "and forced and ravished ladies and damosels."[16] It was often easier to take one's frustration out on a helpless lass, than a heavily armed soldier.

Others threw caution to the wind and found a way to make a living through voluntary prostitution. Young women would set up tents and supply the men's needs "like tipsy adolescents, making love and selling themselves for gold."[17] After Acre was captured in 1191, "the troops settled down in the city to enjoy many damsels beautiful."[18] "Safe sex" was not yet a priority among military personnel, and many of these women were impregnated with fetuses that were disposed of soon after birth.

Throughout the Middle Ages, there was clear social concern over the likelihood that an unmarried woman would commit infanticide in secret rather than face the shame of a bastard birth. Vincent of Beauvais, in the thirteenth century, wrote that fathers were always worrying of their daughters "suffocating her offspring," and as late as 1527, one priest admitted that "the latrines resound with the cries of children who have been plunged into them."[19] In many countries, unmarried servant women were regularly inspected to see if their breasts had milk.[20] If there were signs of a recent pregnancy, and no baby could be produced, Article 36 of the Constitutio Criminalis Carolina, introduced in the Holy Roman Empire by Charles V in 1532, allowed for torture to discover the cause. In Article 131, if a baby was later found dead, there was a presumption that the woman had murdered the infant.[21] This was written into law as well in France, Sweden, England, Denmark, Scotland, Wurttemberg and Bavaria.[22]

Babies were also killed for superstitious reasons, such as to benefit a sterile woman or cure a disease.[23] Unexplained infant deaths were frequently blamed on witches or Jews. In the Prioress's Tale, Chaucer detailed the supposed killing of a seven-year-old boy: "This cursed Jew him bent and held him fast, and cut his throat, and in a pit him cast."[24] The Jew was eventually found by the townsmen and summarily hung and then torn apart.

Because of the widespread belief that Jews were instrumental in the death of many Christian faithful, they were expelled from many European countries during the medieval era.[25] In fact it was not until the "Papal Protection of the Jews" ruling, by Pope Gregory X in 1272, that this issue began to abate. The Pope outlined the problem at that time:

> Since it happens occasionally that some Christians lose their Christian children, the Jews are accused by their enemies of secretly carrying off and killing these same Christian children and of making sacrifices of the heart and blood of these very children. It happens too, that the parents of these children, or some other Christian enemies of these Jews, secretly hide these very children in order that they may be able to injure these Jews, and in order that they may be able to extort from them a certain amount of money by redeeming them from their straits. We decree therefore that Jews do not have to obey these Christians and that they should not be stirred up.[26]

Witches, or striges, were seen to steal young children and then devour them, or suck their blood. They were usually described as old hags. Lamiae were in the same class and appeared as birds with women's faces.[27] The fear that witches would steal a newborn, and leave a changeling child in its stead, left superstitions that exist even today.[28] This belief began in the pre-Christian era with the Celts, Germans and Slavs and then carried on in the Medieval church.[29] As a response, those women who were charged with witchcraft were quickly killed. According to Howard Williams, these numbers were not small: "By a moderate computation, nine million have been burned or hanged since the establishment of Christianity."[30] Witches were also blamed for attempting to prevent pregnancies and birth. The greatest sexual sin was birth control, and women were accused of sorcery when they told others how not to get pregnant.[31]

To put it quite bluntly, children were simply not felt to be very important, or worthy of undue concern, during the Middle Ages. Phillipe Aries has argued that a major cause of this callous attitude was that medieval society did not recognize childhood as we know it today, and that as soon as the child could do without their mother or nurse, they entered the adult world.[32] Children "were often brutally exploited and subjected to indignities now hard to believe."[33] While parents generally showed indifference to their children, this did not necessarily mean they did not love them: it was simply the only way they knew to deal with the trials of their time.

Awareness of a special nature to childhood did not begin to emerge until the start of the Renaissance when adults began to develop more interest in small children.[34] This was manifested by increasing importance of the conjugal family as a unit of strength.[35] One should remember, however, that it was not until the 1550s that any institutional procedure for sanctioning the marriage bond was available. Until then, marriage was not a civil ceremony, but only a sacrament vaguely under church jurisdiction.[36] In 1563 the Council of Trent decreed that a priest must witness the exchange of consent in order for a marriage to be valid.[37] This was followed by later decrees which formalized the ceremony itself.

While much of the world faced similar problems with instances of infanticide, specific differences were existent, often based on the unique heritage of the particular country. What follows is a general review of what is known about the fatal nature of child care in various nations during the Medieval era, and then during the centuries of the Renaissance.

A. Italy

The wretched condition of infants in Italy during the Middle Ages was typical of much of Europe at that time. The descendants of the Roman Empire, even those who converted to Christianity, were not able to quickly break from their infanticidal ancestry, and many unwanted babies, either because of illegitimacy or poverty, were disposed of promptly after birth. Generally this was accomplished through exposure, and, since the Catholic Church was prominent in Italian society, it was natural that Italy would be one of the first European countries to develop institutions to provide respite care for those who survived.

The first foundling home developed solely for abandoned infants was established in 787 A.D. by Datheus, the archbishop of Milan.[38] The primary purpose of this institution was to protect infants from death by exposure. Instead of forcing a mother to abandon a newborn that could not be cared for, the foundling home would provide a safe haven that would raise the child and keep the name of the mother secret. The concept was very charitable, but it still took many years to gain social acceptance, and it was not until the end of the twelfth century, when Innocent III founded the large hospital of the Santo Spirito in Rome, that real progress in providing long term care for foundlings occurred. The condition of newborns at that time was so bad that Roman women were said to have been seen throwing their children into the Tiber river in the light of day.[39]

The need for some type of assistance to care for abandoned children was eventually accepted throughout the country. In 1294, a communal commission told the Italian government that the asylum of Santa Maria da San Gallo was necessary to avoid the many crimes committed against infants in that area. In Florence, the Misericordia took in abandoned children from the mid-thirteenth century, and the Santa Maria della Scala was founded around the same time.[40] In 1484, the authorities in Florence were warned that infants would be "found dead in the rivers, sewers and ditches" if the foundling homes were closed.[41]

While these hospitals were quite successful in initially saving the lives of abandoned infants by protecting them from exposure to the elements, the mortality rates over the months that followed was incredibly high, and most infants never lived long enough to leave the institution. This was typical not only of the Italian homes, but across Europe as well. At San Gallo, 20% of the infants died within one month of admission, and another 30% succumbed by the age of one year; only 32% lived to age five years. At La Scala, the record was similarly dismal and only 13% reached age six years.[42] From the very inception of social awareness of the problem, attempts to save unwanted children from an early death were met with limited achievement, although it was an admirable effort, given the social conditions of the age.

B. Germany

The ancient Germanic tribes depended heavily on their physical strength to survive and, like the Spartans, demanded an element of fortitude in their offspring. An infant that was either unwanted, or unhealthy, was usually exposed at birth, and little thought was given to considering it a crime. The exposure was often carried out by either placing the child under a tree in the forest, or committing it to the sea in a small boat. St. Goar described how children who could not be raised because of poverty would be exposed "in a certain marble basin designated for this," and if someone wanted a child to raise they would then pick it up as their own.[43]

The Teutons generally followed the Roman pattern of allowing the father to determine whether such a newborn would live or not.[44] If the father did not take up the newborn baby from the floor, where it was laid after birth, the infant was not reared. This was known as "barn er a golfi," and was similar to the Roman practice of "elavatio."[45]

Once the lips of the newborn had been smeared with honey or milk, the child could not then be exposed.[46] The story was told of Liaf Gurga, the mother of Saint Liudger, who was to be put to death by her Frisian parents but was saved when a servant put some "earthly" food in her mouth.[47] Boswell noted that this was not an unusual practice: "It was the custom of the pagans, that if they wished to kill a son or daughter, they would be killed before they had been given any food."[48]

The giving of sustenance implied the development of a bond which secured the child's life. In Northern Germanic law, the baby did not even have to receive actual nourishment. Custom allowed that if only holy water had been applied to the infant's mouth, the baby could not then be exposed.[49]

This custom was so ingrained that it led to standards of medical practice on the part of midwives or physicians. In 1473, Dr. Bartholomaeus Metlinger repeated the recommendation of Constantinus that after a child was born, "the midwife shall cover her finger with rose or honey, put it in the child's mouth in such a manner that it covers the jaws, gums and tongue so that if there is any to be dissolved it will be dissolved."[50] There was little doubt that the origin of this advice was related to the practice of exposure.

In Germany, the medieval mother played a more important role in deciding the fate of her child than in many other European countries. In a number of southern early Germanic tribes the mother, in addition to the father, had the right to expose or kill her newborn child.[51] In the eighth century, Boniface said that when harlots in the Germanic lands gave birth, they generally killed the children rather than leave them in churches.[52] While German tolerance for female wrongdoing was generally harsh, in the ninth century the law of the Frisians exempted mothers who killed their newborns from the normal fines for murder.[53] It was expected that difficult times would generally result in difficult solutions.

The authority of a parent was also not surrendered if a decision to expose a child was made. The fourteenth century Schwabenspiegel Code held that if a parent abandoned a child, and wished later to reclaim it, "they must first repay whatever cost" was incurred.[54] This ancient Roman allowance had long been deserted in Italy, but remained in Germany for a longer period.

Children in Germany, once old enough to be weaned from the mother's breast, were subject to quite harsh punishment at the hands of strict parents. This authoritarian rule, so characteristic of German discipline, would last for many centuries and the reprimands could occasionally result in the death of the child from an angry father's retribution. Children were expected to follow the limitations set upon them, and to do exactly as they were told. They also were expected to refrain from sexual interplay before marriage was arranged with a suitable partner. In the Heimburg story of "A Cruel Father," a man found that his daughter had become the mother of a child during his absence and he scourged her so intensely because of this deed that she died.[55] While invoking some sympathy for the young shamed girl, the tale was indicative of the German intolerance towards immoral practices at that time.

Germany was also not immune to the common superstitions of the medieval mind. Early Germanic folklore from 500-650 A.D. told of lamiae who visited houses in the night and dragged children from their cradles.[56]

German fairy tales, like those of other countries, often left children abandoned in the forest by their parents, or left unprotected to the evil plots of a wicked stepmother or witch.

C. Scandinavia

Today, the region of Northwest Europe occupied by Sweden, Norway, Denmark, Finland and Iceland – Scandinavia – is generally known as a society of liberality and caring concern for the raising of children. Progressive social programs have been implemented to help foster a healthy environment for the young, including illegitimate offspring who are often cared for on an equal basis with their lawful brethren. Ancient Scandinavian customs were not so principled and fair.

An early king of Sweden, Aun (On), initiated the infanticidal trend by sacrificing nine of his sons to Odin at Upsala in order that his own life might be spared.[57] Aun had been told by the god that he could live only as long as he sacrificed one of his sons every ninth year. With the arrival of each appointed day, Aun performed the sacrifice and was thereby able to live and rule for an extended period of time. Even when he was at a very advanced age, and barely able to get out of bed from infirmity, he still desired to offer another son, but the Swedish populace finally rebelled and prevented him from killing another child. He then promptly died.

As throughout much of Europe, it was the father's decision whether to kill a newborn infant or let it live. The ceremony which occasioned this event in early Scandinavia was called "Wasser weihe."[58] Shortly after birth the child was placed on the father's knee, or on the floor before him, and if the judgment was that the child should live, the father would pick the baby up and pour water on his head as a sign of nourishment.[59] If the child was rejected, it would then be exposed to the elements. Once an infant was given baptism or food, as with the German tribes, it was illegal to kill or expose it.[60]

The Viking husband had great power over the welfare of his family, and his decisions were generally final. He had the authority to order a sickly infant put to death, as well as having an adulterous wife killed.[61] The life of a Viking family was harsh, and children who appeared to be weak at birth were not able to be given the extra attention they needed to remain alive: if an infant was deemed not sturdy enough to live, it was exposed to the elements. One method which the Viking father used to determine the survivability of a newborn was to place a spear next to the youngster; if the infant seized the spear it was allowed to live.[62] The Vikings also exposed excess female babies as unnecessary to the future of the tribe.[63]

Even after most of the Scandinavian countries became Christian, exposure of deformed children, or those without financial support, was socially allowed. Generally, the baby was put out in the forest with a piece of pork fat in its mouth.[64] For the most part, this only occurred with unwanted children. Since the general mortality rate for infants during the first year of life in medieval central Scandinavia was about fifty percent, the loss of a youngster was a common event and did not evoke undue concern.[65] Frailty of life was something which the medieval parent understood.

Implied in several passages of the *Icelandic Sagas*, was the power of a father to "ut bera," or expose his child. In *Gunnlaugs Saga*, for example, Thorstein ordered the child which his wife was to bear in his absence to be exposed if it proved to be a girl.[66] There were also decrees that those with few possessions must have their children exposed.[67]

When Icelanders agreed to accept Christianity, it was made a law that everyone in the country should agree to be a practicing Christian.[68] The intent of this change was to include the prohibition of exposing infants at birth, but the Icelanders were not willing to give up their entire social system at once. In *Njal's Saga*, the solution to this dilemma was craftily explained:

> They shall not expose children at birth nor eat horseflesh. The penalty for carrying on these practices openly shall be outlawry, but they shall not be punishable if they are done in private.[69]

One possible reason for retaining the right to expose was the large numbers of illegitimate children born during this era. There was extensive extramarital sexual activity among the population and men had frequent contact with women before, during, and after marriage.[70] Many children were therefore born to unmarried couples, and the strict code of dealing with such bastards, as outlined in the Catholic church, created a confrontational and chaotic social dilemma. By maintaining the right of a father to expose an unwanted child, Icelandic society was able to control the growth of their families with relative ease. Practicality, once again, took precedence over theologic beliefs.

But times did indeed change, and the legal system gradually eroded a father's authority to kill or abandon his newborn infant. Norway was the first country to abolish, by legal code, the right of a father to expose his child.[71] St. Olaf of Norway complained that the Icelanders abandoned their children "like heathens."[72] He imposed a fine for abandoning a healthy child, but did allow the exposure of severely deformed children once they were baptized.[73] His successor, Magnus, dictated that if an exposed child should die, then the parents would be guilty of murder.[74] The subsequent Frostathing Law changed this however, and freeborn Norsemen were again permitted to abandon their children in a public setting.[75]

Around 1262, there was general submission to the Norwegian crown, and governance was regulated by Graga's laws. The Codex Regius of Graga held that: "Every child that is born is to be brought for baptism at the first opportunity, however deformed it may be.[76] This was designed to identify undesired children and prevent their being summarily disposed of in secrecy. The early laws also referred to the woman as a potential killer of newborns and required that at least two other women be present during childbirth to discourage a fatal delivery.[77]

Superstition was as prominent during medieval times in Scandinavia as in other parts of Europe. The Swedish tale from Sodermanland outlined some of the precautions that were taken in order to protect the life of an infant:

> Every intelligent grandmother knows that the fire must not be allowed to go out in a room where there is a child not yet christened; that the water in which the new-born child is washed should not be thrown out; also, that a needle, or some other article of steel must be attached to its bandages. If attention is not paid to these precautions it may happen that the child will be exchanged by the trolls, as once occurred in Bettna many years ago.[78]

If a child was lost, it could easily be explained by supernatural forces rather than the neglect, or the criminal actions, of the parent.

D. England

Emmison related how infanticide "was woefully common" in England during the Middle Ages.[79] Illegitimacy played an important role in this situation, as was borne out by the Essex County records which showed that of the thirty babies killed by their mothers, all but three of the murderers were unmarried.[80] The gruesome autopsies showed that five children were strangled, two smothered, three suffocated, four drowned, three died of broken necks and two babies had their throats cut.[81]

Statistical studies did not always reveal the sinister nature of this behavior, however. Barbara Hanawalt found only two cases of newborn infants being killed among 4,000 homicide cases taken from coroners rolls and jail delivery rolls during the late Middle Ages.[82] She noted, however, that a statute against mothers killing their illegitimate children was not passed until 1623, and since the crime was easily concealed, it was likely that infanticide, in reality, was not rare.[83] The authorities seldom arrested women suspected of this crime and therefore prosecution was infrequent.

It is this type of conflicting statistical evidence that makes it difficult to estimate exactly how common was the practice of infanticide in

England during the Middle Ages. Two English councils in the thirteenth century referred to the practice of exposing children, but did not discuss the frequency.[84] The English jurist Bracton said nothing about the crime, implying to historians that it might therefore be quite rare, but once again such cases often did not reach the judicial stage, and court records cannot be relied upon as an accurate gauge. The Crown did not take over prosecution of infanticide from the Church until the end of the Middle Ages.[85] In the *Mirror of Justices*, a legal treatise written around 1285, the procedural pathway between the two courts was outlined:

> As to an infant who is slain we must distinguish whether he is slain en ventre su mere or after birth, for in the former case there is no homicide, for no one can be adjudged an infant until he has seen in the world so that it may be known whether he is a monster or no; and as to infants slain in their first year, this belongs to the cognisanse of the church.[86]

Josiah Russell examined the sex ratios of heirs from 1250-1348 and 1430-1545 and found that there was a markedly higher male ratio than expected. This led him to conclude that female infanticide existed in significant numbers during this period. He also found an excess of males among the listings of servants and serfs.[87] While suggestive of a bias against female infants, this data is very indirect, and may also have reflected an underlying sexism which often overlooked women in the tabulation of records. Nevertheless, a desire for sons rather than daughters was certainly present in medieval England as it was over much of the world at that time.

One significant factor which hid the real frequency of infanticide was the social acceptance of the death of an infant by "overlaying," a situation where the infant was suffocated by the body of its mother or nurse while being breast-fed in bed.[88] This "accident" was quite common in England and provided an easy route of disposing of an unwanted child. When a mother found her newborn infant dead in bed in the morning, and cried hysterically over the shock of the discovery, the local authorities found little reason to investigate more carefully. It was not even elevated from a venial to a major sin until 1237.[89] Overlaying is discussed more completely in the chapter on Infant Image.

Thomas Hobbes, in his *Elements of Law*, outlined the legal basis for much of early English common law in the Middle Ages. He pointed out that both natural and divine laws were equally important, "for the law of nature, which is also the moral law, is the law of the author of nature, God Almighty."[90] But while the English common law incorporated lofty principles steeped in Christian ethics, elements of Roman law also found favor with judges and legislators. This was especially noteworthy in the attitude that the English parent retained the absolute right to determine the fate of his child. Hobbes accepted that the natural covenants of cohabitation gave parents comprehensive rights over their children and that they:

> May alienate them, that his, assign his or her dominion, by selling or giving them in adoption, or servitude to others; or may pawn them for hostages, kill them for rebellion, or sacrifice them for peace, by the law of nature, when he or she, in his or her conscience, think it to be necessary.[91]

Despite the claims of the Church that children could not be ill-treated since they possessed the essence of Jesus Christ within their young souls, the medieval English courts were not in favor of changing the autocratic authority parents had over the life and death of their children.

E. Ireland

The ancient Irish were said to have sacrificed to the idol Cromm Cruach "the firstling of every issue and the chief scions of every clan" in order to assure a good harvest on Mag Slacht in the County Cavan.[92] Dorson related how:

> To him without glory they would kill their piteous wretched offspring, with much wailing and peril, to pour their blood around Cromm Cruaich. Milk and corn they would ask from him in return for one-third of their healthy issue.[93]

According to myth, Ireland was first peopled by the Formorians, a group of gods that exacted from their worshipers over 60% of the children born each year.[94] St. Patrick, who lived from 389-461 A.D., and who first brought Christianity to the Emerald Isle, was said to have preached against the burning of first-born children at the fair of Taillte.[95] The Irish form of "Celtic" Christianity, like that in Britain, differed to some degree from that of the Roman Church and signs of private baptism continued until at least the twelfth century.[96] The Penitentials which were developed, however, were particularly developed toward repressing what was viewed as "folk-paganism."[97]

Early Medieval Irish tales included a number of episodes of abandonment for various reasons. In many, prophecy and superstition led to the exposure. Others encompassed reasons such as adultery, incest, illegitimacy, and jealousy.[98] Babies were abandoned in the field, hung on crosses, left in baskets, and thrown at churches.[99]

One of the distinguishing features of early Irish law, which helped reduce the need to dispose of unwanted children, were the Brehon laws which included a provision of "fosterage of children" in order to strengthen the cohesion of the Irish tribes.[100] If children were left without parents, or if they were abandoned, the tribe itself agreed to care for the infant. This greatly improved the chance of an exposed child being discovered before it died.

As in other medieval countries, there were accounts of the killing of some children because of their "irregular origin" during the sixth and seventh centuries.[101] This referred to illegitimate children who were a source of shame in Ireland, as they were in other countries with a strong Catholic influence. A number of medieval religious tales referred to this infanticide by unmarried mothers whereby the "child murderess" would only be able to be repented of her sins if she was willing to ask for forgiveness. In the poem, "Sgealta at Mhuire," by Aonghus Fionn O Dalaigh, a young mother cuts her illegitimate infant's throat and her hand is permanently stained by three drops of the child's blood. Not until she confessed her sin in Church was she able to "re-enter God's grace," and clear her hand of the stain.[102] If the murderess remained unrepentant, there were many legends about how her punishment would include banishment by a priest to an afterlife in hell.[103] The modern day Irish continue their strong condemnations of procreation outside the bonds of marriage, and can point to many centuries of such rigid prohibitions.

Irish lore told of a number of men who willingly killed their children for reasons of power or fear. Balor, a robber of Tory Island, was told by a druid that he would be slain by his grandson. To prevent this from happening, he confined his daughter, Ethne, to a watchtower and kept her hidden from all possible suitors. But Mackinealy was able to gain access by stealth and camouflage, and Ethne soon gave birth to three sons. When Balor found out about this development, he ordered all three boys drowned but one fell to safety as they were being carried to the water.[104] Such actions were quite reminiscent of ancient Greek tales.

In similar fashion, Cormac mac Airt abandoned his daughter, Mes Buachalla, after her birth, and Ragallach, king of Connacht, ordered his daughter killed as well.[105] Cu Chulainn was a great warrior who was forced to kill his only son, unknown to him at the time, when each headed opposing armies in battle. Despite the pleadings of his wife, he told how "I would kill him for the honor of Ulster."[106] Such devotion to the state was common during this era, and heroes usually gave their first priority to their country rather than their family.

F. France

Foundling hospitals for abandoned children first appeared in medieval France in the twelfth century, and were initially directed towards preventing the exposure of bastards. The earliest one, the L'Ordre Hospitalier du St. Esprit de Montpellier, was established at Marseilles in 1188.[107] Others would follow, but their success was limited by the very high mortality rates due to insufficient care and epidemics of disease.

In rural areas, there was evidence that females may have been particularly singled out for removal since farming required male heirs to till the land. Emily Coleman studied the polyptych of Saint Germain-des-Pres from the period 810-829 A.D., and found that the sex-ratios of adults ranged from 110.3 to 252.9, rather than the expected 105.[108] This argued for selective female infanticide, much as was seen in English rural counties. Coleman noted that the sex-ratio became lower as the arable land increased, indicating that food shortages may have played a role in this development.[109]

G. Spain

Spain presented one of the more united fronts to combat the spread of infanticide in their land. The Council of Constantinople, in 588 A.D., compared infanticide directly with homicide and set up a formal declaration of the church attitude towards the sanctity of an infant's life.[110] In 589 A.D., the Third Council of Toledo pronounced a combined effort between civil and religious leaders to prevent the crime of infanticide by legislative means.[111] Canon 17 of that meeting noted that parents were killing their own children in certain parts of Spain and in order to deter these misdeeds, judges were commanded "to diligently seek out this horrible crime together with a priest and to forbid it by applied severity."[112]

Other regimes responded in a similar fashion. Under the Visigothic reign of Chindaswinth from 642-653 A.D., the formulation of a new code of laws was begun and completed in 654 A.D. by his son Recceswinth. Lex VII of that code noted:

> Concerning those who kill their own children either already having been born or in utero. There is nothing worse than the depravity of those who, disregarding piety, become murderers of their own children. In as much as it is said that the crime of these has grown to such a degree throughout the provinces of our land that men as well as women are found to be the performers of this heinous action, we therefore, forbidding this dissoluteness, decree that, if a free woman or a female slave murders a son or a daughter which has been born, or, while having it still in utero, either takes a potion to induce abortion, or by any other means whatsoever presumes to destroy her own fetus, after the judge of the province or of the territory learns

> of such a deed, let him not only sentence the performer of this crime to public execution, or if he wishes to preserve her life, let him not hesitate to destroy the vision of her eyes, but also, if it is evident that the woman's husband ordered or permitted such things, let him not be reluctant to subject the same to a similar punishment.[113]

At the time this law was formulated, such severe punishment of both the husband and wife was quite unusual.

The laws of Teruel, during the thirteenth century, forbade the selling of daughters and "any woman who is proven to have abandoned her child shall be punished and constrained to care for the child, according to the law."[114] The Castilian Fuero Real also punished abandonment. If the child was abandoned knowingly, the parent lost all authority and could not reclaim the child in the future. If the abandonment occurred without his knowledge, then the parent could reclaim the child by paying all expenses.[115] If the child died from exposure, then the parent would be liable to a charge of murder similar to the killing of any other person.[116]

While ethically admirable, some of these revisions occurred too quickly for the practical needs of the general populace. The successor code, known as the Siete Partidas, supplanted many of these provisions, and a variety of defenses were allowed in matters pertaining to the care of one's own child. The right of parents to sell children under trying circumstances, for example, was again upheld: "A father who is oppressed with great hunger or such utter poverty that he has no other recourse can sell or pawn his children in order to obtain food."[117] What happened to the child after the sale was not the father's responsibility.

And the honor of the Spanish aristocracy also required, at times, putting the safety of the town above that of individual family members. The man who was chosen to lead the Spanish Armada against the English in 1588 was the Duke of Medina Sidonia, don Alonzo Perez de Guzman el Bueno. The suffix of his name, el Bueno, which meant the Good, dated back to the thirteenth century when a Guzman's son was captured by an enemy besieging the town, and threatened to kill the boy unless the town surrendered. Guzman staunchly refused to give into their demands, and let the boy be murdered; earning the title of the Good for all succeeding generations.[118]

H. Russia

The Middle Ages in Russia began somewhat later than in Europe, extending from the ninth century A.D., when the Age of Faith came to an end, to the eighteenth century, when Russia adopted the secularized culture of Western Europe.[119] The heathen Russians were said to have sacrificed their first-born children to the god Perun.[120] Prince Sviatoslav reigned from 962-971 A.D., and in 978 his younger son Vladimir succeeded after a bloody war for control of the crown. Vladimir encouraged a resurgence of paganism and crowded his castle with idols. One chronicler said that: "The people sacrificed to them, calling them gods, and brought their sons and daughters to sacrifice them to these devils."[121]

Justice could be brought down upon an entire city for such sins, however, and when the city of Novgorod suffered through a severe famine in 1128, "fathers and mothers would give their children as gifts to merchants or put them to death."[122] As a result, it is said that a blight came upon the land in the form of a flood, and many citizens were killed. The situation did not last long, and Russia soon came back into the Christian fold.

In Medieval Russia, like across the European continent, children had no social position and secular laws did not deal with a parent killing his own children.[123] The Vladimir statute listed child-murder as a crime under the jurisdiction of the church, and did not discuss other ramifications.[124] The Iaroslav statute explained that "if a woman conceives a child without a husband or with a husband and later kills it or throws it to the swine or drowns it," then she must be taken to a convent for prosecution.[125] Church law did forbid the crime and set up punishments for those who disobeyed.

The secular authorities eventually included infanticide as a punishable offense, and in the sixteenth century, the Muscovite Sudebnik law code of Ivan IV punished infanticide severely and warned that it could not be considered as merely some type of population control.[126] Once again, it was the death of a bastard child that evoked special concern. In 1649, the Ulozhenie of Tsar Aleksei Mikhailovich called for the death of a woman who killed her illegitimate child, although it only gave a prison sentence for the killing of a legitimate one.[127]

Rural Russian provinces were under less direct control of the central government, and infanticide remained quite prominent. Like most farming communities, when crops were sparse, and there was not enough food to feed the entire family, it was often the newborn who was left to die.

I. China

The Chinese historical tradition is one of the oldest recorded records of mankind. The "Shu-King" documentation began with the government of Yao, 2357 years before the birth of Christ.[128] Children were seen as a great asset to honored family life in this society as parents needed children to care for them as they aged, and to give due honors of burial and pay respects to their memory after death. Since these tasks were primarily performed by sons, the birth of a male child was widely celebrated.

But the Chinese also had a heritage of strict disciplinary control.

Children were not to question the demands of their elders:

> If a son complains of injustice done to him by this father, or a younger brother by an elder, he receives a hundred blows with a bamboo, and is banished for three years, if he is in the right; if not, he is strangled. If a son should raise his hand against his father, he is condemned to have his flesh torn from his body with red-hot pincers.[129]

While children were greatly desired, they were not necessarily seen as having an independent right of existence.

A story was told, in this regard, of Fu Tun who was Chutzu of the Mohists during the fourth century B.C. His son was charged with killing another man but because he was old, Fu Tun was given permission to not punish the son, since the boy would be responsible for caring for his father in the years to come. But Fu Tun replied, despite this offer of clemency, that "he who has killed a man must die," according to the law. He then had his only son executed as punishment for his sin.[130]

Such devotion to honor is characteristic of Eastern behavior, but the Chinese also demonstrated a long history of another, less desirable, trait – female infanticide. Under the Confucian patriarchal order, which dated from the sixth century B.C., daughters were generally fated to leave the natal household and their presence was therefore seen as an expendable luxury. Many families found themselves simply unable to afford such excesses, and this led to the frequent occurrence of female infanticide.[131] Han Fei Tzu, who died in 233 B.C., told how: "As to children, a father and mother when they produce a boy congratulate one another, but when they produce a girl they put it to death."[132]

Power also often overcame filial bonds in Chinese history, as it did in other societies. The Ch'in dynasty lasted from 221-207 B.C. and was characterized by the rule of a brutal king. A short time before his death, he uncovered a fatal intrigue involving his son. To protect himself, he therefore had the young man executed.[133] Wu Zhao, or Empress Wu, smothered her own infant daughter to implicate the Empress of Gaozong, and then when she was in power she disposed of one of her sons, who was the successor to the Prince, and replaced him with a more compliant younger son.[134]

Chinese history also relates that in the state of Khai-muh, it was customary to devour the first-born sons while to the west of Kia-chi or Tonquin, "there was a realm of man-eaters, where the first-born son was, as a rule, chopped into pieces and eaten."[135] There was also evidence of the burying of children beneath the foundations of buildings during the Chou Dynasty, as well as the Shang dynasty (1766-1122 B.C.).[136] Marco Polo, who was the first European to chronicle Chinese customs in the fourteenth century, noted that it was habitual for poor women in the province of Manzi to expose their babies at birth because they had no means of rearing them.[137] Matteo Ricci believed that the pervasiveness of belief in reincarnation also accounted for the great amount of infanticide in China "since the very poor would kill their infants in the hope that they would be reborn soon into a richer family."[138]

Social preference for boys began to enlarge during the Han Dynasty (403-225 B.C.) but during the Sung Dynasty (960-1280 A.D.), female infanticide became a socially acceptable response to the birth of a daughter.[139] In the *Collections* of Su Tung Po it was stated that the common method for disposal at that time was to put the newborn girl into a bucket of cold water, the designation then being referred to as a "water baby."[140] This was especially prevalent in Fukien, Kiangsi, Szechwan, Anhwei, Yunnan and Hakka.[141]

Endnotes

1 Langer, "Infanticide: A Historical Survey," 355-56.
2 Boswell, "Exposition and Oblatio: The Abandonment of Children and the Ancient and Medieval Family," 16.
3 Fremantle, "The Age of Belief," 57.
4 The Mongol Conquests, 20.
5 Russell, "Population in Europe 500-1500," Volume I, 54.
6 The Age of Calamity, 8.
7 Boccaccio, "The First Day," The Decameron, 33.
8 Ullmann, Law & Jurisdiction in the Middle Ages, 37.
9 Werner, The Unmarried Mother in German Literature, 1.
10 Boswell, The Kindness of Strangers, 14.
11 Shahar, Childhood in the Middle Ages, 128.
12 Ibid., 121.
13 Boswell, The Kindness of Strangers, 341.
14 Finucane, Soldiers of the Faith, 179.
15 Froissart, The Chronicles, 37, 22.
16 Ibid., 182, 139.
17 Finucane, Soldiers of the Faith, 180.
18 Ibid.
19 deMause, The History of Childhood, 29.
20 Ransel, Mothers of Misery, 14.
21 Ibid.
22 Ibid., 15.
23 Oates, Child Abuse and Neglect, 42.
24 Geoffrey Chaucer, "The Prioress's Tale," 1760-61, The Canterbury Tales,
25 King Philip Augustus expelled the Jews from France in 1182 A.D., and Ferdinand and Isabella in Spain in 1492 A.D. Marcus, The Jew in the Medieval World, 29, 51.
26 Ross & McLaughlin, The Portable Medieval Reader, 172.
27 Kittredge, Witchcraft in Old and New England, 224.
28 Kenyon, Witches Still Live, 267-269.
29 Shahar, Childhood in the Middle Ages, 132.
30 Williams, The Superstitions of Witchcraft, 5.
31 Barstow, "Witch Hunts: The Sex Factor," 85.
32 For general discussion see Pollock, Forgotten Children.
33 Ibid., 262.
34 Hunt, Parents & Children in History, 34.
35 Ibid., 35-36.
36 Ibid., 60.
37 Ibid., 61.
38 Lyman, "Barbarism and Religion: Late Roman and Early Medieval Childhood," 90.
39 Trexler, "Infanticide in Florence: New Sources & First Results," 99.
40 Boswell, The Kindness of Strangers, 416.
41 Trexler, "Infanticide in Florence: New Sources & First Results," 100.
42 Boswell, The Kindness of Strangers, 421.
43 Ibid., 218.
44 Hastings, Encyclopedia of Religion & Ethics, Volume V, 752.

45 Westrup, Introduction to Early Roman Law, Volume I, 261.
46 Hastings, Encyclopedia of Religion & Ethics, Volume I, 4.
47 Coleman, "Infanticide in the Early Middle Ages," 58.
48 Boswell, The Kindness of Strangers, 211.
49 Westrup, Introduction to Early Roman Law, Volume I, footnote 3, 259.
50 Ruhrah, Pediatrics of the Past, 75.
51 Westrup, Introduction to Early Roman Law, 249.
52 Boswell, The Kindness of Strangers, 210.
53 Ibid., 211.
54 Ibid., 326.
55 Guerber, Legends of the Rhine, 220.
56 Kittredge, Witchcraft in Old and New England, 225.
57 Frazer, The Dying God, 160.
58 Solomon, "History and Demography of Child Abuse," 773.
59 Werner, The Unmarried Mother in German Literature, 21.
60 Ibid.
61 Fury of the Northmen, 15.
62 Werner, The Unmarried Mother in German Literature, 21.
63 Martinson, Growing Up in Norway, 800 to 1990, 27.
64 Hanawalt, The Ties That Bound, 101.
65 Russell, "Population in Europe 500-1500, in The Middle Ages," 45.
66 Westrup, Introduction to Early Roman Law, 249.
67 Coleman, "Infanticide in the Early Middle Ages," 58.
68 Boswell, The Kindness of Strangers, 285.
69 Njal's Saga, 105, 226.
70 Jochens, "The Church & Sexuality in Medieval Iceland," 384.
71 Westrup, Introduction to Early Roman Law, 250.
72 Boswell, The Kindness of Strangers, 291.
73 Ibid., 292.
74 Ibid.
75 Ibid.
76 Dennis, Foote & Perkins, Laws of Early Iceland, 23.
77 Martinson, Growing Up in Norway, 800-1990, 27.
78 Boos, Scandinavian Folk & Fairy Tales, 306.
79 Emmison, Elizabethan Life: Disorder, 156.
80 Ibid., 156-157.
81 Ibid., 157.
82 Hanawalt, "Among the Lower Classes of Late Medieval England," 9.
83 Ibid., 10.
84 Boswell, The Kindness of Strangers, 333.
85 Greenwald & Greenwald, "Medicolegal Progress in Inquests of Felonious Deaths: Westminster, 1761-1866," 239.
86 "Mirror of Justices," IV.XVI, Of The Judgment of Homicide, Volume VII, 139.
87 Damme, "Infanticide: The Worth of an Infant Under Law," 2.
88 Ibid., 3.
89 Greenwald & Greenwald, "Medicolegal Progress in Inquests of Felonious Deaths: Westminster, 1761-1866," 238.
90 Hobbes, The Elements of Law, II.X.7, 149.
91 Ibid., II.IV.8, 105.
92 Frazer, The Dying God, 183.

93 Dorson, Peasant Customs & Savage Myths, Volume I, 351.
94 Davies, Human Sacrifice, 46.
95 Ibid.
96 O'Connor, Child Murderess and Dead Child Traditions, A Comparative Study, 20.
97 Ibid., 21.
98 Boswell, The Kindness of Strangers, 213.
99 Ibid., 214.
100 Robins, The Lost Children, 3.
101 Ibid.
102 O'Connor, Child Murderess and Dead Child Traditions, A Comparative Study, 86-87.
103 Ibid., 90-92.
104 Rees & Rees, Celtic Heritage: Ancient Tradition in Ireland and Wales, 214.
105 Ibid., 220-222.
106 Dillon, Early Irish Literature, 17.
107 McClure, Coram's Children, 5.
108 Coleman, "Infanticide in the Early Middle Ages," 49.
109 Ibid., 43-54.
110 Radbill, "A History of Child Abuse and Infanticide," 177.
111 Ibid.
112 Amundsen, "Visigothic Medical Legislation," 568.
113 Ibid., 568-69.
114 Boswell, The Kindness of Strangers, 327.
115 Ibid.
116 El Fuero de Teruel, 4.23.3. Ibid., 328.
117 El Fuero de Teruel, 4.17.8. Ibid.
118 Howarth, The Voyage of the Armada, 21.
119 Zenkovsky, Medieval Russia's Epics, Chronicles and Tales, 1.
120 Frazer, The Dying God, 183.
121 Light in the East, 123-24.
122 Zenkovsky, Medieval Russia's Epics, Chronicles and Tales, 78.
123 Ransel, Mothers of Misery, 10.
124 Ibid.
125 Ibid., 10-11.
126 Ibid., 11.
127 Ibid., 12.
128 Hegel, The Philosophy of History, 116.
129 Ibid., 128-129.
130 Yu-Lan, A History of Chinese Philosophy, 84.
131 Stacey, Patriarchy and Socialist Revolution in China, 43.
132 Yu-Lan, A History of Chinese Philosophy, 327.
133 Fitzgerald, A Concise History of East Asia.
134 March of Islam,110.
135 Frazer, The Dying God, 180.
136 Davies, Human Sacrifice, 38.
137 Polo, The Travels, 174.
138 Spence, The Memory Palace of Matteo Ricci, 251.
139 Yao, Chinese Women: Past & Present, 75.
140 Ibid., 91.
141 Ibid., 92.

CHAPTER IV

HISTORICAL BACKGROUND – RENAISSANCE

> "Regicides have been quartered, patricides and fratricides have been broken on the wheels, infanticides without number have been decapitated."[1]

As Heinrich Leopold Wagner noted in the above quotation, during the Renaissance era in the German Empire, infanticide began to take its place alongside other grievous crimes as worthy of extreme punishment. But in other parts of the world, apathy to the crime was not uncommon and may have been due, at least in part, to the difficulty in proving that the parent was guilty of murder. The body of an infant was easily hidden from the rest of society, and, as Adelson noted: "It is relatively simple to destroy the life of a child in almost absolute secrecy without the necessity of taking any elaborate precautions to ensure that secrecy."[2] Nevertheless, as social outrage over the plight of children gradually increased, civil authorities eventually began to take a more aggressive stand and demand some type of retribution against the guilty parties.

Where the Middle Ages represented the "Dark Age" in human civilization, the Renaissance has been seen as an awakening from intellectual slumber into the dawn of modern times. Arising in Italy during the 1300s A.D., the reformation gradually spread throughout the rest of Europe over the next few centuries. Artistic and scientific advancements were rapid, but real social progress did not develop until late in the eighteenth century, the period of time commonly known as the Age of Enlightenment.

It was during the Renaissance that society finally began to permanently alter some of the ancient ancestral attitudes that tolerated the parent's right to commit infanticide. There were many reasons for this evolutionary change, but the two most important were the rise of Humanism and the pressure applied by social activists within both the Church and State. In addition, medical advances, and the availability of condensed milk products the year round, lowered the expected mortality rate of newborn infants, and the likelihood that an infant would survive the first few years of life was increased. People began to concentrate not only on the chronologic length of a person's life, but on the quality of that life as well.

Christianity was to witness one of the more radical changes which characterized this reform era. During the centuries of the brutal Holy

Crusades, Saracens and Christians alike were slaughtered in the name of God, and the power of the Pope enlarged throughout the Western World. Following the adage that "power corrupts," excesses and abuses became rampant within the church hierarchy. Claiming that the Pope, based in Rome, was a "foreign" power interfering with their country's autonomy, local priests began to rebel against the authoritarian rule which threatened them with death for heresy. On October 31, 1517 A.D., when the Pope demanded extra donations from the Germanic princes, Martin Luther railed against the pontificating of papal authority by nailing his Ninety-Five Theses to the door of All Saints' Church in Wittenberg. The fatal net which awaited most critics of the Catholic Church was not able to ensnare this radical dissident, and a rather rapid dissolution of Catholic power in the Germanic lands followed.

Soon thereafter, the worldly power of the Pope began to crumble. In 1534, the English Parliament passed the Act of Supremacy which declared the English king, Henry VIII, rather than the Pope as the Supreme Head of the Church of England. John Calvin followed in France with his *Institutes of the Christian Religion* in 1536, and the major political powers in Europe began to separate from a single theologic commander in Rome.

The effect of these changes was to fracture the unified ethical pronouncements of the Catholic Church. No longer would society look to edicts from Rome in order to deal with the problem of infanticide. Legislation of secular governments would become more determinative of the definition of crime than would the interpretation of the word of God by mortal messengers of a particular religious denomination.

The American revolution in 1776, and the French Revolution in 1789, stratified the world even further as principles of democracy drove Western society into the Age of Enlightenment. The rights of infants to life, liberty, and the pursuit of happiness would still take many years to solidify under the protection of the law, but the process had finally begun. Infanticide would not disappear as a common crime under these moral advancements, but no longer would it be excused as a right of a parent under natural law.

A. Italy

With respect to the visual arts, Italy truly provided the garden to which all the world came to view the beauty of what the Renaissance had to offer. The paintings, sculpture and architectural feats were like nothing before, and many historians found the wonderment and advancement of this era unrivaled in human development.

But the Italians spent much more time in admiration of their ideologic, rather than their biologic, offspring. In Florence, where Rafael restored the magnificent Pantheon to its earlier splendor, the numbers of baptized children who were abandoned ranged from a low of 14%, at the opening of the eighteenth century, to a high of 43% in the nineteenth century. In Milan, where people from all corners of the world gathered to hear arias of unmatched beauty at La Scala, the early eighteenth century witnessed an abandonment rate of 16%, and by the end of the era it was 25%.[3]

Foundling hospitals rescued many of these newborns from an immediate death but did little to assure their long-term survival. Throughout Italy, the mortality rate of children confined to such institutions was distressingly high. The supply of wet-nurses to feed the infants was limited, and dry milk was not yet widely available. In Verona, in 1581, there was only one nurse for every nine to ten infants, and in 1601, in Brescia, the records showed that there were many children dying for lack of milk.[4] While money was readily available from wealthy patrons for the Arts, foundling homes gradually had to close for lack of funds and support. And as they did, countless numbers of newborns died because no one was able to care for them.

B. Germany

In Germany, the criminal justice system took a strong early stance against infanticide. The country had a long history of dealing harshly with women who committed the crime, particularly when it involved unmarried girls. Only the mother, by legal definition, could commit infanticide, but if a father killed his child he was tried for murder and subjected to capital punishment.[5] In Nurenberg, from 1513 to 1777, eighty-seven women were executed for committing infanticide, and all but four were unmarried.[6] Prior to 1500, the penalty for those convicted was to be buried alive; shortly later the method was changed to drowning.[7] In 1532 the Constitutio Criminalis Carolina (Caroline Code) was enacted by Emperor Charles V, and it not only was a landmark legislative act against infanticide, abortion, and rape, but in response to its strict moral tone, the number of executions for infanticide rose sharply.[8]

Frederick William I typified the no-nonsense German approach to the crime. In 1720 he reinstated the use of sacking as punishment for the crime whereby the woman was sewn into a sack and then drowned (poena cullei).[9] In 1740, Frederick the Great decreed that this approach should be abolished and that all infanticides should be punished by the milder method of decapitation.[10] He even prohibited penance in the churches in 1746 because he believed that the "punishment of the sins of the flesh and the consequent disgrace gives occasion for infanticide."[11]

King Frederick II, in a letter to Voltaire in 1777, declared that infanticide accounted for more executions in Germany than any other crime.[12] But where the civil authorities were comfortable with the use of capital punishment as the only proper way to prevent future crimes, judges and juries became more sympathetic and frequently avoided the death penalty in favor of a prison sentence.[13]

In addition, the literary elite took a more sympathetic tone as well. The *Sturm und Drang* novelists (c. 1770 A.D.) carried the banner of empathy for these young women with plots that were often the same: the seduction of a young innocent girl who became pregnant by a lover who then left her alone; the resultant anger of middle class family and friends at the shame that resulted; performance of infanticide when the young woman saw nowhere else to turn; and finally, a trial and execution of the girl while the seducer emerged without penalty. According to Ende, men were encountered only as "judges, inquisitors, clergymen, torturers and executioners."[14] This is discussed more thoroughly in the chapter on Shame.

While the intensity of punishment by the authorities finally lessened in the nineteenth century, a general cruelty towards children from strict family discipline remained. The infant mortality in Bavaria was over 57%, while in adjacent countries it was only 15%.[15] Despite the relative equality of both medical and nutritional care available in the German cities and towns, children were likely to die from abuse. In addition, there was an extremely high suicide rate among children which was blamed upon the severe disciplinary codes and punishment for often minor infractions.[16]

Foundling hospitals to care for abandoned children were developed later in Germany than elsewhere in Europe, primarily because of the distractions of war throughout the Holy Roman Empire. The first one was opened in 1761 by Landgrave Frederick II of Hesse-Cassel.[17] Despite evidence that illegitimacy ratios in the eighteenth century were at five percent, there were many arguments against support of such homes because of cost, high infant mortality, lack of maternal love, and the encouragement of sexual intercourse out of wedlock.[18] Ende believes that foundling homes never played a big role in Germany, and that many German mothers killed their newborns by failing to provide adequate nutrition.[19]

An unusual variant of infanticide was also manifest in anecdotal stories of children being buried alive beneath the doorsteps of new buildings in Germany in the sixteenth century, or in the dikes of seventeenth century Oldenberg. This notion developed in certain areas from the superstition that the house would be unsafe unless there was a spirit gestating within to provide supportive strength. A child would then be walled in at the site.[20] Such tales existed among the Celts, Slavs, Teutons and Northmen, and there were accounts of children being sold in order to be built into the castle walls of Henneberg and Liebenstein.[21] The last instance of this horrific practice was recorded in Algiers, when Geronimor of Oran was walled up in the gate Bab-el-Oved in 1569.[22]

C. Scandinavia

While data from this country about the presence of infanticide is somewhat sparse, it was apparent that many children, especially illegitimate offspring, were exposed or killed at birth. Of the 617 executions for murder in Sweden between 1759 and 1778, 217 were for killing a child.[23] Most of the guilty parents were unwed mothers. The frequency in Sweden began to decline in 1910, the last year a woman was executed for infanticide.[24] Capital punishment was not in favor elsewhere in Scandinavia at this time, and in 1778 the king of Sweden declared that no infanticide would be punished by death but rather the mother would be whipped, and then imprisoned, and then each year be publicly exposed and whipped on the anniversary of the crime.[25]

In Denmark, the penal code of 1866 took compassion on the anguish of a bastard birth, and reduced the penalty for infanticide when the mother had an illegitimate child and then killed the infant during, or immediately after, the birth.[26] This was later extended to include all mothers who killed their infant during the period of postpartum depression.

D. England

We have seen that statistical data from England during the Middle Ages was consistent with an infrequent prosecution of infanticide for a variety of reasons. Ex officio Act recordings during the Renaissance, however, showed a number of successful prosecutions for the crime.[27] In the Essex records from the sixteenth century, Emmison found that of thirty cases which were reported, seventeen women were found guilty and five were innocent.[28]

In 1576, the number of documented cases that came to trial showed a sharp rise, due in part to the "kite" case where an exposed infant was killed by a kite bird attack. This case was included by Richard Crompton in a legal manual as standing for the ability to support a charge of homicide when the mother's neglectful action to provide proper care for the infant was the cause of the child's death. There was no need to show premeditation as required in other prosecutions for murder. The note had read: "A Harlot is delivered of an infant which she puts alive in an orchard, and covers with leaves; and a kite strikes at him with its talons, from which the infant shortly dies, and she is arraigned for murder, and is executed."[29]

Public awareness of this crime became so intense that during the seventeenth century infanticide was the most common form of homicide in England. If parents did not murder their unwanted children outright, they often abandoned them to the elements.[30] The English countryside, as well as the streets of London, were littered with sick and malnourished children whose parents simply left them to fare for themselves.

The Renaissance in England was truly a grim era for many children of all ages. From 1500-1800, approximately 25-30% of children whose births were recorded had died before the age of fifteen.[31] Sanitary conditions in London were very poor – it was not until the 1750s that local regulations for sewage disposal were passed – and epidemics of dysentery were common. Many of the citizens were uneducated, destitute, and unable to care for their young. The low expectation of survival, even among children who were well-cared for, helped develop a relative lack of concern for small infants in general.[32] Over one-half of the children in the late eighteenth century died before the age of three years.[33] And the coroner system, which was established in 1194, reached its lowest points of activity in the seventeenth and eighteenth centuries.[34]

John Locke, the seventeenth century English philosopher, found the situation disgraceful. He called the exposure or selling of children "the most shameful action, and most unnatural murder, human Nature is capable of."[35] He pointed out that wild beasts did not expose their children, and it was "the privilege of man alone to act more contrary to nature than the wild and most untamed part of the creation."[36] This was an abysmal state of affairs and something had to be done.

As continued instances of neglect were publicized, and critics became more vocal and intense, the general public became increasingly aware of the frequency of abandonment and concealment throughout the land, especially of unwanted or illegitimate births. Anger over the deplorable situation grew, and to deal with the crime a simple method was chosen – anyone found guilty of concealing a birth would be given the death penalty. Shortly after king Henry II of France decreed that women who concealed the birth of a child would be executed in 1556, King James I did the same in England.[37] In 1623 an "Act to prevent the Destroying and Murthering of Bastard Children" was passed by the English parliament.[38] This so called Stuart Act, or Concealment of Birth statute, had a profound effect on women who attempted to hide their shame through destruction of their newborn child. Chapter 27 of the statute proclaimed that:

> Whereas, many lewd women that have been delivered of bastard children, to avoid their shame, and to escape punishment, do secretly bury or conceal the death of their children . . . they will henceforth be punished by death as in the case of murder.[39]

This harsh law held that any mother who concealed the birth of an illegitimate child was presumed to be guilty of murder if the body of her infant was later discovered. Rather than be presumed innocent of a crime, as was the standard common-law practice in other criminal cases, she had to prove the baby was stillborn or died from natural causes.[40] If the death of a legitimate baby was concealed, no presumption of homicide was made. The problem for the unmarried mother was that it was almost impossible to prove the circumstances of the birth, since there were seldom any witnesses, and medical examination was inexact. Conviction was almost assured once there was a showing of concealment.

While many of these felonies were probably true homicides, there were also times when a mother of a stillborn, or even a sickly child, became so distraught and frightened that she innocently concealed the body, not realizing the fatal extent of her actions. The law proved so discriminatory and abusive, that juries regularly refused to convict mothers that were brought to trial. The law was finally repealed in 1803 by Lord Ellenborough's Offenses Against the Person Act which allowed juries to find for the lesser crime of concealment of birth when factual circumstances were the same.[41] This greatly reduced the number of capital convictions for infanticide and during the mid-nineteenth century, although there were 5000 coroner inquests a year on children under the age of seven years, only thirty-nine women were convicted of child-murder with thirty-four unmarried.[42] This led some critics, like Edwin Lankester, the coroner of Central Middlesex, to claim that 12,000 London mothers murdered their infants without detection.[43]

A more reasonable response to the problem of unwanted births was developed by the creation of London's Foundling Hospital in 1739 by Thomas Coram.[44] Coram was a retired sea captain who was appalled at the prejudicial care of foundlings in London. He realized that much of the problem stemmed from the shame that resulted from believing that "foundling equals bastard . . . and bastard equals disgrace."[45] There was little sympathy for a woman who was felt to have brought the problem upon herself by engaging in illicit sexual activity. But with the numbers of infants now being abandoned and murdered, the real disgrace to Coram was in the lack of civil action and support. Now that the public had become aware of the upsurge in abandoned babies, funds were made available to support an institution to provide for their care.[46] Coram finally obtained a charter to open a foundling hospital on March 22, 1739. By having a place to bring an unwanted infant, rather than drop it into the river or nearby sewer, it was hoped that the frequency of infanticide could be reduced.

While the London Foundling Hospital did provide a much needed shelter where women could bring their children and still retain anonymity, the fate of the infant was still very precarious. The average mortality rate of infants cared for at the hospital was 48-56%, and while this figure was an improvement over most European institutions, a majority of children still died at a very young age.[47]

As the nineteenth century began, little evidence of improved infant welfare was forthcoming. Summarizing the situation of infanticide in England during this time, Sauer noted that:

> "Infanticide was almost generally disapproved of in Britain, but many people regarded it as a lesser offence than murder, in part because less value was placed on an infant's life and in part because women committing this crime were seen as acting under the pressures of poverty and social stigma."[48]

Infants who were unwanted, even when not killed, were disposed of with little regard to their future welfare. Children of poorer families were often given to the workhouse, especially if the mother had died. Child labor laws had not yet been passed, and youngsters toiled long hours without adequate nourishment or medical care. For many, it was a slow path to death.

Charles Dickens, in his 1839 novel Oliver Twist, described the typical fate that awaited such progeny:

> "It did perversely happen in eight and a half cases out of ten, either that it sickened from want and cold, or fell into the fire from neglect, or got half-smothered by accident; in any one of which cases, the miserable little being was usually summoned into another world and there gathered to the fathers which it had never known in this."[49]

In 1845, Disraeli published his novel, Sibyl, in which he pointed out that infanticide was practiced as extensively, and as legally, in England as on the banks of the Ganges.[50] The Dublin Review, in 1858, characterized child-murder in England as "par excellence the greatest social evil of the day."[51] In Regent's Park, infant corpses were often found floating in ornamental ponds on an almost weekly basis.[52]

Statistical tabulations clearly showed the gruesome state of affairs. While children under the age of one comprised 9% of all drownings in England during the period 1853-82, in London the percentage was an incredible 44%.[53] Similarly, suffocation deaths of children under one year of age in London during this time was 82-89%, while in the rest of England it was only 38-77%.[54]

Stories in the *Marylebone Mercury* typified the daily death toll:

> A heavily drugged infant was found in a basket, 26/12/1857; The body of a baby boy was found floating in a waterbutt of a house, 3/9/1859.[55]

Estimates for the number of such occurrences in London alone ranged from 300-1200 per year.[56]

In the 1860's the British press carried frequent reports of the finding of dead infants in parks, under bridges and in ditches and cesspools.[57] By 1862, one of the coroners for Middlesex stated that infanticide had become so commonplace "that the police seemed to think no more of finding a dead child than they did of finding a dead cat or a dead dog."[58] The *Morning Star* in 1863, referred to the system as a "carnival of infant slaughter."[59] In 1865, the *Saturday Review* castigated the offenders as the "foul current of life, running like a pestilential sewer beneath the smooth surface of society."[60]

The gruesome facts were presented so customarily that it became a topic of black humor. A popular ballad in England during this time was that of the "Cruel Mother," illustrating what often was felt to occur after two babies were born:

> Then she cut her top knot from her head,
>   And tied those babies hands and legs.
> She took her pen knife keen and sharp,
>   And pierced those babie's tender hearts.[61]

Such a grisly state of affairs prompted William Burke Ryan, winner of the London Medical Society's Fothergillian Gold Medal for his 1856 essay on infanticide, to make an impassioned assessment of the problem. In characteristic English prose he graphically stated:

> The feeble wail of murdered childhood in its agony assails our ears at every turn, and is borne on every breeze. The sight is horrified as, day after day, the melancholy catalogue of murders meets the view, and we try to turn away the gaze in the hope of some momentary relief. But turn where we may, still are we met by the evidence of a wide spread crime. In the quiet of the bedroom we raise the box-lid, and the skeletons are there. In the calm evening walk we see in the distance the suspicious-looking bundle, and the mangled infant is within. By the canal side, or in the water, we find the dead child. In the solitude of the wood we are horrified by the ghastly sight; and if we betake ourselves to the rapid rail in order to escape the pollution, we find at our journey's end that the smouldering remains of a murdered innocent have been our travelling companion; and that the odour from that unsuspected parcel truly indicates what may be found within.[62]

Dr. Martin, writing in the Edinburgh Medical and Surgical Journal in

1826, was also appalled at the compassion of English juries which acquitted women even when the evidence of murdering their newborn infant was overwhelming. He felt it was time that the increased frequency of this crime led to a more strict and exemplary administration of the law: "The pardonable leniency of judges and juries will be obliged to yield to the higher considerations of the justice that is due to outraged humanity, and the necessity of giving more effectual protection to innocent blood."[63]

Incredible schemes to kill a child were uncovered in stories by the press. One way in which the killings were related to economic gain was a perverse use of expenses under an insurance plan to pay for funerals called "burial societies."[64] These policies would pay a parent for the death of an insured child and the amount that was forthcoming was often considerably more than the cost of the actual burial itself.[65] While a funeral would generally cost between 20-30 shillings, a club would often pay 3-5 pounds in the event of a child's death.[66] Many cases were found where a parent would join several clubs for a single birth, and then murder the infant in order to collect the excess value of the policies. This is discussed further in the Chapter on Money.

Another way which the murder of an infant occurred was through the system of "baby farming," where women who had to work entrusted the care of their infants to hired nurses – baby farmers – who often then put them to sleep with narcotics from which many never awakened.[67] In 1869, a committee appointed by the Council of the Obstetrical Society of London, referred to this problem and reported that desertion of illegitimate children in London was a frequent event. They concluded that the children were left with wet-nurses who disregarded the child and it ultimately died by slow starvation, neglect or the workhouse.[68] This is also discussed further in the Chapter on Money.

Babies were also often killed by overdoses of opiates which were commercially available by a simple over-the-counter purchase throughout much of England. The most popular of these was Godfrey's Cordial, a mixture of opium, treacle, and sassafras which sold 12,000 doses weekly in Coventry alone.[69] It was widely advertised as beneficial for colic, diarrhea, vomiting, hiccough, pleurisy, rheumatism, catarrhs, and cough, and was claimed especially excellent for young children "that are weakly and restless," for it quieted them and thereby gave the parents a respite.[70] Many of the infants who were so becalmed, however, never awoke from their slumber.

Disraeli outlined this dilemma in his novel *Sibyl*. The youth Mick complained there that his mother did little for him "but give me treacle and laudanum when I was a baby to stop my tongue and fill my stomach."[71] Disraeli pointed out that in the hands of a wet-nurse, opiates were often given to keep a young infant quiet and "prepares them for the silence of their impending grave."[72] If they did not die of a cold or fever, they were "dosed with Godfrey's cordial, and died in peace."[73]

Godfrey's cordial, and other commercial "soothers," could be bought without a prescription in the early nineteenth century, along with many other medications that today would be considered as dangerous narcotics. They remained freely available until the Poisons & Pharmacy Act of 1868 limited them to druggists and then in 1920 when the Dangerous Drugs Act required a physician prescription.[74] At the turn of the century an Australian Royal Commission estimated that 15,000 infants each year were killed by proprietary medicines.[75] In addition to opiate mixtures, gin was also used quite frequently to calm a crying child.

One of the first attempts to counteract these problems was the Poor Law Act of 1834. This statute was promoted by those who believed that many of the infants were killed because of poverty. Working mothers could not remain home to care for their children, and therefore many of the infants were either neglected or cared for by inadequate personnel. The bill was designed to reduce the resultant infanticide rate by giving money to mothers so they would not be dependent on fathers who often suggested the crime rather than have to pay for the upkeep.[76] It had little effect, however, on the overall rate of child-murder.

How many children may have actually been abandoned in London will never be known. Between 1856 and 1860, there were approximately 3901 inquests held on children who were found dead under the age of two years, and a high proportion of these victims were deliberately killed.[77] About seventy-eight infants under the age of one year were declared murdered each year in England and Wales from 1852 to 1856, and another 203 from 1862 to 1866.[78] While this group comprised only three percent of the population, they accounted for sixty-one percent of the homicides.[79] Actual criminal indictments for murder, however, were very rare. Despite the large number of suspected infanticides, as when a child was found buried in a garden or abandoned in the field, from 1730-1774, only sixty-one infanticide cases were actually tried at the Old Bailey in London.[80] Of interest, over one-half of those cases involved unmarried servant women.[81] This was particularly common in England during this era, and is discussed in more detail in the chapter on Shame.

As the statistics of infant death continued to deluge the public press, civil and professional outrage began to swell. Infanticide was called in England "the national stigma of an age," and "par excellence the great social evil of our day."[82] According to Lionel Rose, "ignorance and negligence shaded into a conscious death-wish upon the unwanted child."[83]

In 1867, Dr. Curgeven, Dr. Ryan, and a delegation of medical men from the Harveian Society, called on the Home Secretary with recommendations to check this increase in child-murder.[84] Curgenven pointed out that the death rate of children between the ages of 0-5 years was 11% among the well-to-do in London, 35-55% among the urban working class, and 60-90% among illegitimate children.[85] The statistics were astounding and led to only one conclusion: the higher rates were due to child-neglect on the part of the poor. Although one might not be able to avert a sudden act of brutal murder, infanticide by acts of omission were ten times more common than those by commission, and could be prevented by appropriate social action.[86] It was this deficiency which had to be immediately corrected.

In 1870, the Infant Protection Society, which had been founded by Dr. Curgeven, added to the pressure for reform.[87] Parliament finally agreed and set up a committee to study the problem further. In 1872 the English Legislature passed the first Infant Life Protection Act.[88] It had taken almost a century of protest, but effective means to try and curb the killing of large numbers of infants in England was finally begun.

E. Ireland

Very little infanticide was recorded among the Irish during the Renaissance era. Sauer commented on the paradox of this uniqueness:

> "Trodden, persecuted, poverty stricken often to the verge of starvation . . . seldom do they dash from their breasts the innocent babe."[89]

One reason may have been the popular abhorrence of the crime, as explained by Joyce in *Ulysses* where the people used to "drive a stake of wood through his heart in the grave," when someone committed infanticide or suicide.[90] But the fact remained that beneath the surface of awareness, there were still Irish children killed by beleaguered parents.

The response of the civil authorities in Ireland verifies this fact, and shows the degree of frustration which faced many European nations during the Renaissance era. The Counter-Reformation was particularly strong in Ireland, and Catholicism was able to persist, exerting strong pressure to baptize all infants, while England, and other European nations, evolved into concepts which were more reflective of a concentrated Protestant milieu.[91] In the seventeenth century, however, the religious differences were put aside as an Irish Act, of the same nature as the Stuart Act in England, was passed during the reign of Queen Anne. It was an obvious reaction to the killing of bastard children, but, as occurred in England, the Act was eventually repealed when public reaction to its inherent unfairness magnified the plight of innocent women.[92]

The Foundling Hospital and Workhouse of the City of Dublin opened in 1730, and "a revolving basket was placed on the gate of the hospital into which unwanted children could be put anonymously by day or by night."[93] The fate of these urchins was very poor when compared to other institutions in England and Europe. Mortality rates of children left at the hospital between 1750-1759 was 89%.[94] In 1796, rates of as high as 99.6% were documented.[95] The reasons for this extreme death rate were never determined, but the authorities were forced to consider alternate methods in an attempt to improve the quality of care by reducing the number of admissions. In 1815, a decision was made to require the payment of a fee before acceptance into a foundling home. Reports indicated that: "Carriers who, bringing infants from the country and finding no admission because they had not the necessary fee, left the children on the banks of the adjacent canal to die from cold, starvation, and drowning."[96] It appeared that unwanted babies were not worth the pittance of an acceptance fee.

The hospital finally closed in 1830 under pressure from both the economic and moral arenas. But the rate of infanticide only increased as killing the infant took the place of deserting it to the care of a foundling home. Unable to afford to raise an infant because of economic poverty, and trying desperately to avoid the shame and disapproval of the community in which they lived, some Irish mothers saw little choice but to destroy their baby at birth.[97]

F. France

Conditions in France during the seventeenth and eighteenth centuries were similar to other areas of Europe. The death of an infant from all causes was commonplace; infant mortality rates were consistently over twenty-five percent.[98] The birthrate had increased enormously and unemployment, hunger and illness made the populace destitute and unable to care for their children.[99] The result was that while courtly splendor reigned in the gilded halls of Versailles, the streets of French cities witnessed infanticide of unprecedented magnitude.

The monarchy took a very strong stand against the killing of illegitimate children during this era. In 1556, King Henry II decreed the death penalty for women who were convicted of concealing the birth of their child.[100] France was the first country to pass such stringent legislation, and many countries followed their lead. The effect of this law on the prosecution of young, frightened, unmarried women was great, but the reduction in the amount of infanticide was minimal.

In Toulouse in the eighteenth century, the rate of known abandonment of recorded births varied from a mean of 10% in the first half of the century, to 17-25% on the second half.[101] In poor quarters of the city, the rate approached 40%.[102] In Lyons, almost one-third of the children born were abandoned, while in Paris the figure was between 20-30%.[103]

This led to a spectacular rise in the number of foundlings throughout the country. In Paris, 35% of all births in 1770 resulted in abandonment of the newborn.[104] Although local authorities often counted all abandoned children as illegitimate, probably about 60% of the children were in this class.[105] Much of the apathy towards the life of a newborn infant was blamed on a growing indifference to children even in traditional French families. Many youngsters were put out to wet-nurse as the French mother took a dim view of the rigors of breast-feeding. The proportion of deaths among children in Paris who were cared for in this manner reached 77%.[106] In 1811, the problem was so bad that Napoleon decreed that every hospital should be equipped with a turntable (tour) "so that the mother or her agent could place the child on one side, ring a bell, and have a nurse take the child by turning the table, the mother remaining unseen and unquestioned."[107] This was deemed necessary to help reduce the numbers of outright infant-murders.

But again, as elsewhere in Europe, the institutional care did little but delay the date of the child's death. In Paris, from 1771-1773 the mortality rate of foundlings was 70%. From 1773-1777 it was 80%. And as late as the early nineteenth century, as many as 50% of the children were still dying while under institutional care.[108]

Foundling homes in France were not only intended for destitute women who could not afford to care for their children. The artistic elite who could not be bothered with the boredom and inconvenience of raising a child also turned to the foundling homes for a solution to their parental problems. Jean-Jacques Rousseau, who viewed himself as an educated humanist, wrote of the innate benevolence which he felt towards his "fellow-creatures."[109] Yet he fathered five children by various women and had all of them carried to the Foundling Hospital because he refused to provide for their care: "Everything considered I chose the best destination for my children."[110] His indifference to his offspring typified many other intellectuals of his day.

With the gentility uninterested in caring for their offspring, and the poor unable to pay for their support, children in France demanded little societal attention. Jean-Louis Flandrin claimed that infanticide was the principal method of birth control in France as late as the seventeenth century. The Renaissance may have promoted the ideals of liberty, freedom, equality or death, but: "Women pregnant out of wedlock would regularly murder their new-born bastards, and married couples had no compunction about smothering or abandoning unwanted children in hard times."[111]

Despite this unfortunate state of affairs, juries generally were sympathetic to the plight of such women, and were unwilling to find them guilty of murder, knowing that such a decision would lead to the death penalty. The acquittal rates were always higher than for defendants of similar crimes, and by 1913, 57.7% of women who were charged with infanticide were freed, while only 33.6% of those charged with other felonies were acquitted.[112]

G. Russia

The exposure and killing of infants became a matter of governmental concern in Russia during the beginning of the eighteenth century. In 1712, Peter I issued a decree deploring the needless waste of what he called the "children of shame."[113] He ordered that hospitals were to be opened in every province so that mothers of illegitimate children could deposit their offspring and avoid "committing the still greater sin of murder."[114] In 1716, in his military articles, Peter I imposed penalties for the killing of any child, illegitimate or legitimate.[115]

But the Russian father, like the Roman in ancient times, did not want the government telling him how he must deal with an unruly, or unwanted, child. While the motives of Peter I were admirable, his methods were seen as interfering with the right of a father to maintain control over the discipline and raising of his children. As tension developed throughout his realm, Peter I eventually decided that penalties on the parent would not occur if the child died accidently during disciplinary punishment.[116] In this way, it would be difficult to prove actual misbehavior in all but the most egregious cases.

This was, perhaps, a reflection of the stubbornness of the Russian people, rather than the weakness of Peter I. As Rousseau pointed out, "he sought to civilize his subjects when he ought rather to have drilled them."[117] Customs, long held, did not fall away simply because they were shown to be wrong.

The measures which Peter I promoted appeared to have little effect on the overall rate of infant exposure. In 1763, Ivan Betski told of large numbers of children being abandoned in the streets of Moscow. He encouraged Empress Catherine II to establish large foundling homes in Moscow and St. Petersburg where the largest number of abandoned children were found. These institutions, shortly after opening, were soon to handle more children than all of the European countries combined.[118]

Many believed that the motives of Betski were not entirely out of concern for the lives of the children, but rather for the furtherment of some elaborate social experiment. He planned the homes as "laboratories of social engineering with the purpose of creating in them a third estate of enlightened artists and craftspeople."[119] By taking in abandoned children who were then totally under his control, families could be manipulated without concern for the children's future fate since there were no parental obstacles to his design. This utopian design was never completed, however, as the scale of the project expanded rapidly.

The numbers of children that eventually were admitted to these institutions was so great that all of the facilities were soon overwhelmed: "Instead of training a manageable number of already weaned youngsters, the staff had to struggle heroically just to keep a small percentage of babies alive."[120] Milk was scarce, epidemics frequent, and medical care almost non-existent. The mortality rates among the children in Moscow's foundling home reached 90%![121] In St. Petersburg the results were the same. By the 1880s, the foundling home in Moscow was receiving between 16,000-18,000 infants annually, and had to send over 10,000 to the outlying districts for care. The foster families in the villages were able to reduce their mortality rates to about 20-30%.[122]

The failure of the foundling homes in Russia to properly care for their wards was bitterly commented on by Tolstoy in his play, *The Power of Darkness*. As Akulina, an unmarried young girl, was giving birth, Mitrich mentioned that the baby could be sent to the foundling home if she did not prefer to keep it:

> Whoever likes may drop one there, they'l take 'em all. Give 'em as many as you like, they ask no questions, and even pay – if the mother goes in as a wet-nurse. It's easy enough nowadays.[123]

The mother of the girl, however, answered sarcastically: "Go an take it to the Foundlings – it will die just the same."[124] Rather than leave the family with the shame of the publicity entailed with the birth, the mother elected to kill the baby after it was born by burying it in the cellar.

The fear of bringing shame upon the family in Russia, led to many similar infanticides of illegitimate children at birth. As Tolstoy noted, it was easy to dispose of newborns by burying them out of sight in the ground: "Mother earth will not blab to any one: she'll keep it close."[125]

H. Japan

Although not common enough to be considered a custom in Japanese society, instances of infanticide have occurred throughout much of their history. Seniority counts for a great deal in Asian culture, and deference is always given to one's elders.[126] Abandonment of the aged, therefore, is very rare.

But children, although prized in Japan as in China because of family obligations, were nevertheless often left in harm's way. Historical sources have documented the presence of infanticide among a select number of

Japanese societies. In Kyushu, for example, it has been estimated that 40% of newborn infants were killed, while in other areas estimates have ranged as high as 10-25%.[127] The common euphemism which referred to this practice was "mabiki," or "thinning," a term that refers to the farming of rice seedlings where the weaker stalks are disposed of in order to allow the stronger ones more room to grow.[128] The Japanese considered infanticide in this fashion to select out the infants worthy of being reared, much as a "weeding" or "thinning of rice seedlings" was done to keep the quality of the crop high.[129] This term also referred, at times, to the killing of females, or deformed children, when the father desired to raise only healthy sons.[130]

The population of Japan had increased rapidly in the seventeenth century, and then remained stationary from about 1700 to 1852.[131] One of the reasons postulated for this leveling off was that malnutrition and famine were common in the eighteenth century, and both abortion and infanticide were widespread.

In addition, the Kugawa government increased the level of taxation and many poor peasants could not bear the extra burden.[132] Abortions were expensive and risky and were therefore were used sparingly. Infanticide, on the other hand, was quite safe and allowed for manipulation of the sex-ratio to guarantee perpetuation of the patrilineal heritage. The commonly used method was to obstruct the infants nose and mouth with wet paper causing immediate suffocation.[133] This was referred to as "modosu," or returning and unwanted godsend to Heaven.[134]

The Daimyo government repeatedly had to prohibit the practice, and moralists in many cities rallied against it as well.[135] Infants during this time were typically pressed to death and then the bodies thrown into the river covered with straw mats.[136] After the Meiji Restoration, new regulations made mabiki a crime.[137]

Mildred Dickeman theorized that 90% of the peasant population in Japan used infanticide as a method of population limitation when necessary. In addition to selecting out males, it also allowed for the removal of defectives and twins.[138] She estimated that up to 10-25% of children were killed at birth in the Tokugawa era, and that up to 50% of all females were killed.[139]

Even into the late nineteenth and early twentieth centuries, the mabiki policy of the Japanese at times ensured that the local human crop would be controlled by infanticide.[140] Writing of a typical village called "Nakahara," Thomas Smith studied the fertility pattern of the Nobi plain region of Japan from 1717-1830 and determined that infanticide was a commonly used form of family planning.[141] In addition to limiting the number of children, the practice would allow for advantageous distribution of the sexes in children and also allow for spacing of children that would lead to optimum economy.[142]

There had also been stories of illicit sexual behavior among Buddhist priests in Japan, and Francis Xavier in 1549 claimed that monks lived openly with nuns and "if the nun became pregnant she was aborted with drugs, or else the child was killed as soon as it was born."[143]

I. India

In the ancient mythology of Vedic India, there was a story similar to that of the young Greek Phaeton, the son of the Sun, who was allowed to take his father's chariot across the sky and then was killed when the horses went out of control. Ushas, the Dawn, was also allowed to take the car of her father, the Sun, and when it veered off course, she was killed as well.[144]

Both stories portrayed the actions of fathers who knew better than to relent to the pressures of their children, but could not go against promises they had already made.

The ancient Sanskrit literature also preserved remnants of the time when a parent had the right to expose his children at will. In the law book of *Vasistha*, it was stated that "the father and the mother have the power to give, to sell, and to abandon their sons."[145] Where many Western countries restricted the authority to the father alone, Indian customs, though generally favoring the male sex, did allow the mother to have an equal say at birth. The Taittirtya-Samhita said that a girl at birth was to be exposed while a boy was to be lifted up.[146] The preference for sons can be seen far back into the history of Indian thought.

The practice of female infanticide was especially common in India near the end of the eighteenth century. The frequency was due to a number of cultural factors, but one of the prominent reasons was the economic cost of raising, and then marrying, a daughter. The story of the early discoveries of this problem was detailed in a book by Edward Moor, aptly titled *Hindu Infanticide, An Account of the Measures Adopted for Suppressing the Practice of the Systematic Murder by Their Parents of Female Infants; With Incidental Remarks on Other Customs Peculiar to the Natives of India.*[147] The revelations within this book were shocking, not only to the English, but to many Indians as well.

The problem first came to light in 1789 when Mr. Jonathan Duncan wrote to the Governor General of India on the not "unfrequent practice among the tribe of Rajkumar to destroy their daughters, by causing the mothers to refuse them nurture."[148] The British under Lord Lawrence were so outraged by the disclosure that immediate action was taken at the Umritsur durbar in 1853 to oversee the entire social structure of many villages throughout the country. It was agreed that anyone who committed infanticide would be expelled from their caste, and also that moderate marriage expenses would be adopted to lessen the economic burden placed on a family by the birth of a daughter.[149] This issue is discussed in detail in the chapter on Female Infanticide

J. China

Infanticide was practiced throughout Chinese history to eliminate either defective or unhealthy offspring. But it was the killing of daughters at birth that was most associated with Chinese culture from ancient time down to the twentieth century. For the most part, this custom was economically based, as it was in other rural societies where the female child was seen as a serious burden to poor families.[150]

Jesuit missionaries to China in the seventeenth century found thousands of babies, mostly females, thrown on the streets like refuse to be collected each morning and dumped into a huge pit outside the city.[151] Matteo Ricci noted that many of the exposures were covered up by declaring it an act of piety in order that the child could return to a better life by transmigration of the soul.[152] The poor, unable to supply their children with common necessities, would often expose them in the streets of the great cities like Pekin and Canton.[153] Sir George Staunton estimated the number of children annually exposed at Pekin at about 2000.[154] The incidence of infanticide during the Ch'ing Dynasty (1644-1911 A.D.) was so great that it reached epidemic proportions.[155] In 1697, the Kangxi emperor decreed that "the custom of drowning infant girls is to be abolished completely and anyone who disobeys this is to be punished according to the law."[156]

From 1851-1948 studies indicated that almost five percent of all female births ended in infanticide.[157] The mother generally either "placed her head down in a bucket of water, suffocated her, or simply abandoned her to die."[158] With the population of China so large, and the people so poor, the loss of individual infants did not create a social upheaval for reform. This issue is discussed more fully in the chapter on Female Infanticide.

The control of a child's behavior was also very strict among the Chinese. Parents were given great leeway in their disciplinary actions. The Chinese Penal Code declaimed: "If a father, mother, paternal grandfather or grandmother chastises a disobedient child or grandchild in a severe and uncustomary manner so that he or she dies, the party so offending shall be punished with 100 blows."[159]

Despite the lack of prison terms or more serious punishment, even this aspect of the law was practically ignored by the authorities.[160] If a parent did not wish to raise a particular child, there was little attempt on the part of the Chinese legal system to either care for that infant, or force the family to nurture it.

K. Canada

Canada followed similar patterns to England in its response to the growing problem of infanticide. In 1758 and 1792, the Nova Scotia and Prince Edward Island statutes were passed which made the concealing of the death of a newborn infant a crime punishable by death. As was the case with the English statute, if an infant was found to be likely concealed "either by drowning or secret burying thereof, or in any other way," then the mother would be found guilty unless a witness could be found to state the infant was born dead.[161] These statutes were soon extended into Quebec and the Upper Canada regions. The presumption of guilt, in addition to the ability to convict without having to prove the child was born alive, made conviction easier than the previous charge of murder. Like their earlier corollaries in England, the laws applied only to bastard children.[162]

Following the lead of the repeal of the harsh 1623 English concealment statute in 1803, and also with publicity over two cases involving women who were convicted of concealment crimes, the Canadian legislatures began to repeal the statutes in 1810.[163] New concealment statutes were then passed with penalties that included a maximum imprisonment of two years. The restriction of the charge to only illegitimate births was also later removed.[164]

In 1867, the federal government in Canada acquired control over criminal legislation and among the first consolidation of offenses included the crime of infanticide. It allowed for the death penalty if murder could be proven, and a two year imprisonment for concealment. It also allowed prosecution of both legitimate and illegitimate births.[165]

Despite the legal ruminations, the number of women who were ever charged with the crime was small, compared to the numbers of children killed. Eric Jarvis noted that in Toronto, during the decade of the 1860s:

> There were only seven cases where a woman was ever charged with the offence; but the number of dead infants found and examined by the coroner was between fifty and sixty. And these were only the ones that were discovered, possibly a mere fraction of those actually killed.[166]

Most of the women charged with the crime during this era were single and employed as domestic servants. They were commonly exploited sexually by their employer and, as was the case in England, by other male members of the family.[167] A pregnant unmarried woman was an object of scorn: "If she bore an illegitimate child, she would lose her job and be ostracized from society at large."[168] If she gave in to a sudden impulse to dispose of her infant at birth, juries often sympathized with her plight and showed extreme leniency towards those who were charged with the crime. In most cases the woman was set free or given a reduced sentence.[169]

L. United States

The colonists brought infanticide to America from England, and upon their arrival found that it was also practiced by the native Indian population.[170] The Puritans were a god-fearing lot, however, and the general attitude about retribution for those who committed child-murder was rigid and clear: those found guilty of the crime were uniformly punished by death.[171] Life may have been hard, but there was no reason to resort to crimes that the bible had explicitly condemned.

Despite this pious view of strict adherence to biblical law, the Puritans were not gentle when it came to raising their children under Christian principles. Extreme discipline characterized family life in puritanical Colonial America, and parents were given extensive liberty to strictly punish their children, even to the point of death. In 1646 the General Court of Massachusetts Bay had enacted a law where "a stubborn or rebellious son, of sufficient years and understanding," would be brought before the Magistrates in court and "such a son shall be put to death."[172] This referred to a son who was at least sixteen years of age, and who would not obey even after being chastened. Such stringent discipline was consistent with the Old Testament teaching as discussed under Judaic law. "Stubborn Child Laws" were also enacted in Connecticut in 1650, Rhode Island in 1668, and New Hampshire in 1679.[173] The intent to show statutory support of the rights of parents to determine how to raise their children in the New World lasted well into the nineteenth century.

How ingrained was the attitude of rigid parental control over the discipline of children can be evidenced by a comparison to concern over animal welfare. Henry Bergh founded the Society for the Prevention of Cruelty to Animals (SPCA) in 1866.[174] After first completing his campaign to improve the plight of cats and dogs, Burgh brought by special warrant to the Supreme Court of New York, the case of Mary Ellen who claimed that the child's custodians had beaten her cruelly and that she should be brought under the protection of the court.[175] There were no laws protecting children in those years, and the argument was therefore made that Ellen should be removed from her home "on the grounds that she was a member of the animal kingdom and that therefore her case could be included under the laws against animal cruelty."[176] Human children had been placed in the background while the welfare of animals had been argued for in the social arena.

This resultant court action and publicity eventually led to the founding of the Society for the Prevention of Cruelty to Children which was a parallel protection agency to his first endeavor.[177] The New York Society was founded in 1874 and by 1900 there were over 250 societies nationwide.[178] England saw a similar delay until 1884 when the London Society for the Prevention of Cruelty to Children was formed by the Reverend Benjamin Waugh.[179]

Reform may have been protracted, but the change in attitude toward the mistreatment of children was a welcome sight since watch-groups for the welfare of children were much needed in the United States during this era. In ante-bellum Virgina, during the 1850s, the mortality of children under the age of one year of age was 16-20%. While many of these were due to infectious problems, overlaying was stated to be the cause in 4% of the cases.[180] Savitt believes that many of these were actually due to Sudden Infant Death Syndrome (SIDS).[181] Other cases of child neglect were also evident throughout this period of time as well be discussed in the next chapter.

Endnotes

1 Werner, The Unmarried Mother in German Literature, 7.
2 Adelson, "Slaughter of the Innocents," 1348.
3 Boswell, The Kindness of Strangers, 16.
4 Fildes, Breasts, Bottles & Babies, 273-74.
5 Kord, "Women As Children, Women As Childkillers: Poetic Images of Infanticide in Eighteenth-Century Germany," 451.
6 Langer, "Infanticide: A Historical Survey," 356.
7 Ibid.
8 Ober, "Infanticide in Eighteenth-Century England. William Hunter's Contribution to Forensic Problem," 312.
9 Geyer-Kordesch, "Infanticide and Medico-legal Ethics in Eighteenth Century Prussia," 195.
10 Dated 7/31/1740. Werner, The Unmarried Mother in German Literature, 6, 35.
11 On 6/20/1746. Ibid., 35.
12 Ransel, Mothers of Misery, 15.
13 Kord, "Women As Children, Women As Childkillers: Poetic Images of Infanticide in Eighteenth-Century Germany," 451.
14 Ende, "The Psychohistorian's Childhood & the History of Childhood," 177.
15 Ende, "Battering and Neglect: Children in Germany, 1860-1978," footnote 13, 275.
16 Ibid., 258.
17 Ulbricht, "The Debate About Foundling Hospitals in Enlightenment Germany: Infanticide, Illegitimacy, and Infant Mortality Rates," 213.
18 Ibid., 227.
19 Ende, "The Psychohistorian's Childhood and the History of Childhood," 176.
20 Darlington, "Ceremonial Behaviorism," 306.
21 Elworthy, The Evil Eye, 80.
22 Ibid., 81.
23 Martinson, Growing Up In Norway, 800-1990, 31.
24 Sjovall, "History of Abortion and Infanticide in Sweden," 176.
25 Werner, The Unmarried Mother in German Literature, 61.
26 Harder, "The Psychopathology of Infanticide," 219.
27 Helmholz, "Infanticide in the Province of Canterbury During the 15th Century," 379.
28 Emmison, Elizabethan Life: Disorder, 157.
29 Hoffer & Hull, Murdering Mothers: Infanticide in England and New England 1558-1803, 8-9.
30 Lorence, "Parents and Children in Eighteenth Century Europe," 10.
31 Stone, The Family, Sex, and Marriage, in England 1500-1800, 55.
32 Ibid., 66.
33 Greenwald, & Greenwald, Medicolegal Progress in Inquests of Felonious Deaths: Westminster, 1761-1866," 243.
34 Ibid., 195, 197.
35 Locke, Two Treatises of Government, First Treatise, VI.56.4-5, 181.
36 Ibid., VI.56.11-12, 181.
37 Radbill, "A History of Child Abuse and Infanticide," 177.
38 21 Jac. I, c. 27. Damme, "Infanticide: the Worth of an Infant Under Law," 12.

39 Hoffer & Hull, "Murdering Mothers: Infanticide in England and New England 1558-1803," 20.
40 Rose, The Massacre of the Innocents: Infanticide in Britain 1800-1939, 1.
41 43 Geo. III, c. 58. Weir, Selective Nontreatment of Handicapped Newborns: Moral Dilemmas in Neonatal Medicine, 14. Concealment of birth was made a separate substantive offense, as well as an alternative to murder, by the Offences Against the Person Act, 1828 (Eng) Section XIV, and amended by the 1861 Act, s. 60. Lansdowne, "Infanticide: Psychiatrists in the Plea Bargaining Process," 44.
42 Statistics for 1849-1864 A.D. O'Donovan, "The Medicalisation of Infanticide," 261.
43 Higginbotham, "Sin of the Age: Infanticide and Illegitimacy in Victorian London," 319.
44 Sauer, "Infanticide and Abortion in Nineteenth-Century Britain," 81.
45 McClure, Coram's Children, 9.
46 Ibid., 28, 33.
47 Fildes, Breasts, Bottles and Babies, 276.
48 Sauer, "Infanticide and Abortion in Nineteenth-Century Britain," 92.
49 Dickens, Oliver Twist, Chapter 2, 5-6.
50 Disraeli, Sybil, 131.
51 Behlmer, "Deadly Motherhood: Infanticide and Medical Opinion in Mid-Victorian England," 404.
52 Ibid., 405.
53 Forbes, "Deadly Parents: Child Homicide in Eighteenth- and Nineteenth-Century England," 182.
54 Ibid., 184.
55 Rose, The Massacre of the Innocents: Infanticide in Britain 1800-1939, 37.
56 Ibid., 38.
57 Langer, "Infanticide: A Historical Survey," 361.
58 Langer, "Checks on Population Growth: 1750-1850," 97.
59 Greenwald & Greenwald, "Medicolegal Progress in Inquests of Felonious Deaths: Westminster, 1761-1866," 244.
60 "Infanticide," Saturday Review 20 (1865): 162.
61 Bronson, The Traditional Tunes of the Child Ballads, 292.
62 Ryan, Infanticide: Its Law, Prevalence, Prevention and History, 45-46, as quoted by Behlmer, "Deadly Motherhood: Infanticide and Medical Opinion in Mid-Victorian England," 404.
63 Martin, "Editorial," 37.
64 For discussion see Forbes, Deadly Parents: Child Homicide in Eighteenth- and Nineteenth-Century England," 188-199.
65 Ibid., 189.
66 Havard, The Detection of Secret Homicide, 52.
67 Langer, "Checks on Population Growth: 1750-1850," 97.
68 "Report of the Committee Appointed by the Council of the Obstetrical Society, June 2, 1869," 9.
69 Langer, "Infanticide: A Historical Survey," footnote 23, 365.
70 Fildes, Breasts, Bottles & Babies, 237.
71 Disraeli, Sybil, 120.
72 Ibid., 131.
73 Ibid.

74 Rose, The Massacre of the Innocents: Infanticide in Britain 1800-1939, 12.
75 Ibid.
76 Ibid., 25-26.
77 May, "Violence in the Family: An Historical Perspective," 155.
78 Sauer, "Infanticide and Abortion in Nineteenth-Century Britain," 85.
79 Rose, The Massacre of the Innocents: Infanticide in Britain 1800-1939, 8.
80 Malcolmson, "Infanticide in the Eighteenth Century," 191.
81 Ibid., 202.
82 Sauer, "Infanticide and Abortion in Nineteenth-Century Britain," 85.
83 Rose, The Massacre of the Innocents: Infanticide in Britain 1800-1939, 11.
84 Langer, "Infanticide: A Historical Survey," 361.
85 Rose, The Massacre of the Innocents: Infanticide in Britain 1800-1939, 6-7.
86 Sauer, "Infanticide and Abortion in Nineteenth-Century Britain," 86.
87 Langer, "Infanticide: A Historical Survey," 361.
88 Ibid.
89 Sauer, "Infanticide and Abortion in Nineteenth-Century Britain," 89.
90 Joyce, Ulysses, 96.
91 O'Connor, Child Murderess and Dead Child Traditions, A Comparative Study, 22-23.
92 Davies, "Child-Killing in English Law," 312.
93 Robins, The Lost Children, 15.
94 Ibid., 22.
95 Fildes, Breasts, Bottles & Babies, 276.
96 Robins, The Lost Children, 45.
97 Ibid., 155.
98 Badinter, Mother Love, Myth and Reality, 109.
99 Piers, Infanticide, 56.
100 Radbill, "A History of Child Abuse and Infanticide," 177.
101 Boswell, The Kindness of Strangers, 15.
102 Ibid.
103 Ibid.
104 Meyer, "Illegitimates and Foundlings in Pre-Industrial France," table 9.1, 252.
105 Ibid., 253.
106 Ibid., 258.
107 Langer, "Infanticide: A Historical Survey," 358.
108 Fildes, Breasts, Bottles & Babies, 276.
109 Rousseau, Confessions, VIII, 549.
110 Ibid., 551.
111 Blackhouse, "Desperate Women and Compassionate Courts: Infanticide in Nineteenth-Century Canada," 447.
112 Donovan, "Infanticide and the Juries in France," 162.
113 Ransel, Mothers of Misery, 8.
114 PSZ, no. 2467, Jan. 16, 1712. Ibid.
115 PSZ 5, no. 3003, March 22, 1716. Ibid., 17.
116 Ransel, Ibid., 18.
117 Rousseau, The Social Contract, II.8, 90.
118 Ransel, Mothers of Misery, 8.
119 Ibid., 294.
120 Ransel, "Abandoned Children of Imperial Russia: Village Fosterage," 503.

121 Fildes, Breasts, Bottles & Babies, 276.
122 Ransel, "Abandoned Children of Imperial Russia: Village Fosterage," 505.
123 Tolstoy, "The Power of Darkness," IV, The Portable Tolstoy, 799.
124 Ibid., 801.
125 Ibid.
126 Hastings, Encyclopedia of Religion & Ethics, Volume I, 6.
127 Kuhse & Singer, Should the Baby Live?, 106.
128 Dickeman, "Demographic Consequences of Infanticide in Man," 126.
129 Williamson, "Infanticide: An Anthropological Analysis," 64.
130 M'Lennan, Studies in Ancient History, 105.
131 Dickeman, "Demographic Consequences of Infanticide in Man," 126.
132 Kitahara, "Childhood in Japanese Culture," 60.
133 Shiono, Maya, Tabata, Fujiwara, Azumi & Morita, "Medicolegal Aspects of Infanticide in Hokkaido District, Japan," 104.
134 Kaku, "Were Girl Babies Sacrificed to a Folk Superstition in 1966 in Japan?," 392.
135 Smith, Nakahara, 63.
136 Kitahara, "Childhood in Japanese Culture," 61.
137 Kaku, "Were Girl Babies Sacrificed to a Folk Superstition in 1966 in Japan?," 392.
138 Dickeman, "Demographic Consequences of Infanticide in Man," 126.
139 Ibid., 128.
140 Vaux, Birth Ethics, 12.
141 Smith, Nakahara, 58, 61.
142 Ibid., 83.
143 Spence, The Memory Palace of Matteo Ricci, 224.
144 Hackin, Asiatic Mythology, 104.
145 Vasistha, xv.2. Hastings, Encyclopedia of Religion & Ethics, Volume I, 6.
146 Taittirtya-Samhita, VI.5,10,3. Westrup, Introduction to Early Roman Law, Volume I, 253.
147 Moor, Hindu Infanticide, An Account of Measures Adopted for Suppressing the Practice of the Systematic Murder by Their Parents of Female Infants; With Incidental Remarks on Other Customs Peculair to the Natives of India.
148 Letter dated October 2, 1789. Ibid., 4.
149 Encyclopedia Britannica (1881), Volume XIII, 3.
150 Orleans, Every Fifth Child: The Population of China, 36.
151 Langer, "Infanticide: A Historical Survey," 354.
152 Lee, "Female Infanticide in China," 167.
153 Malthus, "An Essay on the Principle of Population, or, A View of Its Past and Present Effects on Human Happiness; with an Inquiry into Our Prospects Respecting the Future Removal or Mitigation of the Evils Which It Occasions (1872)," On Population, I.XII., 216.
154 Ibid., I.XII.
155 Yao, Chinese Women: Past & Present, 93.
156 Lee, "Female Infanticide in China," 167.
157 Eastman, Family, Fields & Ancestors, 21.
158 Ibid.
159 Ta Tsing Leu Lee, sec. cccxix. M'Lennan, Studies in Ancient History, 87.
160 Westermarck, The Origin and Development of the Moral Ideas, Volume I, 393.

161 An Act relating to Treasons and Felonies (1758), 32 Geo. II, c 13, s 5 (N.S.); An Act relating to Treasons and Felonies (1792), 33 Geo. III, c 1, s 5 (P.E.I.). Blackhouse, "Desperate Women and Compassionate Courts: Infanticide in Nineteenth-Century Canada," 449.
162 Ibid., 450.
163 New Brunswick in 1810, Lower Canada in 1812 and Nova Scotia in 1813. Ibid., 454.
164 Ibid.
165 An Act respecting Offences against the Person (1869) 32 & 33 Vict., c 20, s1, 61, 62 (Dominion of Canada). Ibid., 455.
166 Ibid., 456.
167 Ibid., 457.
168 Quoted from Lori Rotenberg. Ibid., 458.
169 Ibid., 448.
170 Hoffer & Hull, Murdering Mothers: Infanticide in England and New England 1558-1803, footnote 1, 33.
171 Ibid., 44.
172 Sutton, "Stubborn Children: Law & the Socialization of Deviance in the Puritan Colonies," 31.
173 Ibid.
174 Williams, "Cruelty and Kindness to Children," Traumatic Abuse and Neglect of Children at Home, 68.
175 Ibid., 71.
176 Radbill, "A History of Child Abuse and Infanticide," 175.
177 Williams, "Cruelty and Kindness to Children," 75.
178 Bremner, Children & Youth in America, A Documentary History, Volume II 1866-1932, 117.
179 Rose, The Massacre of the Innocents: Infanticide in Britain 1800-1939, 151.
180 Savitt, "Smothering & Overlaying of Virginal Slave Children: A Suggested Explanation," 402.
181 Ibid., 400.

CHAPTER V

HISTORICAL BACKGROUND – MODERN TIMES

"In 1966, the United States had 10,920 murders, and one out of every twenty-two was a child killed by a parent."[1]

Despite our predilection for considering modern civilization "advanced," the crime of infanticide has continued to pervade most contemporary cultures. Nevertheless, even though child-murder remains a statistically common crime, there is clear evidence that the social status of children has finally advanced to a level equal to adults. Legal systems now generally hold that the inherent rights of children are not less because of their age, and parents may no longer claim that they have exclusive control over their offspring simply because of biologic creation.

The major difference between the nature of infanticide in the twentieth century, when compared to the rest of recorded history, however, is due to the impact of one modern medical advancement: the widespread availability of safe, and legal, means of abortion. The ability to easily terminate a pregnancy, and thereby eliminate an unwanted child before it is born, has had a profound effect on the prevalence of infanticide. As described in the previous four chapters, the human species has killed almost 10-15% of all children born since the time Homo sapiens evolved. The majority of these murders have been associated with reasons of necessity – at least in the minds of the infanticidal parent – or with untoward reactions against an unwanted birth. With little ability to abort an unwanted pregnancy safely, troubled parents have had little choice but to wait until full-term delivery before disposing of the conception. If the parent had been able to easily eliminate the pregnancy before birth took place, a major reason for the killing would no longer be present.

The figures tell the story quite clearly. Of approximately 6.4 million pregnancies in the United States in 1988, 3.6 million were unintended and therefore subject to dangerous consequences. 1.6 million of those unwanted pregnancies resulted in abortion.[2] In Britain, more than 160,000 legal abortions, or terminations of pregnancy (TOP), were carried out each year during this same period of time.[3] The Family Planning association in Russia says that there are more than three million abortions performed each year, more than double the number of births.[4] In France, there are almost one million abortions each year, equal to the number of births.[5] This means that over five million pregnancies were aborted in the Western world alone each year, and if the births of those children would not have been prevented, it is very likely that many of those infants would have been victims of infanticidal rage.

In many parts of Asia, where population growth has already taxed the limited food supply to the point of famine, the problem is even more acute. The Chinese government noted that in 1991 there were over fourteen million abortions.[6] In India, there are over five million abortions performed each year, and three million of them are by untrained midwives or the mother herself.[7] Recent widespread use of various forms of contraception in Japan has lowered the number of yearly abortions to about 400,000, but three decades ago over one million women had an abortion each year.[8] The Alan Guttmacher Institute estimates that in Brazil, Colombia, Chile, Mexico, Peru and the Dominican Republic, where abortion is banned except for very strict medical conditions, there are about four million clandestine abortions performed each year.[9] While it is obviously difficult to tabulate exact statistics, Population Action International, a nonprofit U.S. based group which advocates universal access to family planning, estimates that there are about fifty million abortions performed worldwide each year.[10]

Morally right or wrong – a case of murder or manifestation of a woman's right to choose – the fact remains that the frequent use of abortion has eased the necessity for killing an infant after its birth. Were it not for abortion, the crime of infanticide would be statistically greater today than in times past.

While there is presently an extensive legal battle being waged over whether abortion can be limited to certain women, with certain requirements of notification, there is general agreement that the termination itself, at least in the first trimester of pregnancy, cannot be totally excluded by defining it as a criminal act. The common law in England has always permitted abortion to be performed before a fetus was thought to be able to survive outside the womb – the time of quickening – and this legal determination was similarly followed in America from its very inception after the American Revolution.[11] During the nineteenth century, various American states began to limit this availability, beginning with Connecticut in 1821, and a great battle ensued over whether it was the right of a woman to terminate her pregnancy, or whether the state could abolish this right altogether. In 1973, the United States Supreme Court, in Roe v Wade, held that women did enjoy such personal freedom to choose whether the pregnancy would be terminated, and that this option was guaranteed by the United States constitution.[12] Since that momentous decision, first-trimester abortion has been judged to be solely within the province of a woman and her physician, although some inroads have recently been made to allow reasonable statutory restrictions.[13]

As long as the availability of legal abortion is not significantly altered, it is likely that the rate of infanticide will remain static in the years to come. If serious limitations to the accessibility of abortion are passed, however, especially to those women who are economically unable to care for additional children, the numbers of unwanted babies which are killed soon after birth are likely to drastically increase. The rate of population growth in the world today is approximately two percent per year, the highest rate in humankind's experience.[14] Unless some way is found to diminish this relentless regeneration, continued pressure to commit infanticide will not abate.

A. Statistical Analysis

Statistically, the United States ranks high on the list of countries whose inhabitants kill their children. For infants under the age of one year, the American homicide rate is eleventh in the world, while for ages one through four years it is first, and for ages five through fourteen years it is fourth.[15] From 1968 to 1975, infanticide of all ages accounted for 3.2% of all reported homicides in the United States.[16] This represents almost 29% of all child-homicides.[17] From 1976-1979, out of every 100,000 live births, 1.3 resulted in neonaticide (murder within the first twenty-four hours of life), 4.3 in infanticide, and 3.5 in child-homicide.[18] These statistics reflect only cases which were proven by legal prosecution, numbers that most experts agree are greatly under-reported when compared to the actual rate in the population-at-large. Abortion may have dampened the frequency of infanticide, but it has not led to its elimination.

The 1980s followed similar trends. Whereby overall homicide rates were decreasing in the United States, the rate at which parents were killing their children was increasing. In 1983, over six hundred children were reported killed by their parents, and from 1982-1987, approximately 1.1% of all homicides were children under the age of one year of age.[19] Sons were killed by parents at a rate 1.3 times that of daughters.[20]

When the homicide of a child was committed by a parent, it was the younger age child who was in the greatest danger of being killed, while if the killer was a non-parent, then the victim was generally older. In Cuyahoga County, Ohio, 71.7% of victims aged 0-4 years were killed by a relative, usually a parent, while at ages 10-14 years the figure was only 13.4%.[21] For neonaticides, 66% were committed by the parent, and for infanticides, 72%.[22] Jason concluded that these figures were probably falsely lowered by the reluctance of coroners to diagnose homicide in infants who were found dead without obvious criminal intent.[23] Either accidental death, or stillbirth was often given as the cause of death in those situations, even though little, or no criminal investigation was first pursued. Adelson concluded in his review of child-homicides that 20% of the victims were battered children.[24]

Other countries show similar characteristics in the nature of child-murder. In Canada, during the years 1964-1968, there were 1,379 homicides reported by the authorities and 114 (8.3%) of these were incidents of child-murder by a parent.[25] In England and Wales, 25% of all homicides were under the age of sixteen years, and 81% of these were children killed by a parent.[26] The greatest risk of homicide occurred in infants with 21% of the victims neonates, and 13% between the age of one day and one month old.[27] Although women commit only 10% of all homicides in England, they were the guilty party 47% of the time when a child was killed.[28]

In Denmark, between 1946 and 1960, of 540 homicides, 49% of the victims were children.[29] The killers were predominately parents who then frequently committed suicide.[30] In Sweden, from 1971 to 1980, the numbers of children annually killed was 0.6 per 100,000, and almost all the cases were products of intra-familial violence.[31] These figures again represent only cases where legal determination of a crime was completed, and do not reflect the actual number of infanticides which were mistaken as accidental or natural deaths. At the Department of Legal Medicine at the Kurume University School of Medicine in Japan, infanticide cases accounted for 7.4% of all judicial autopsies from 1963-1987.[32]

The characterization of the type of parent who is likely to kill their child has changed little over the years. As far back as the Middle Ages, the children of the poor "were by far the most common victims of the parental negligence and despair."[33] Today, infanticide still is most commonly seen in areas of severe poverty.[34] We will see the reasons for this in the chapters which follow.

Another similarity between the past and present is in the sex of the offender. Just as infanticide was described as a crime that was committed by the mother in medieval times, such a likelihood remains true today. Although men are more likely to murder in general, statistical review of prosecutions show that infanticide is usually committed by the mother with the biological father the killer in only a minority of cases.[35] In the seventeenth century, so many women were identified as the culprit that one commentator asked: "What man would eat his child? only women were capable of that."[36]

Sexism aside, in England during the 1960s, the father was the killer in only 15% of the cases.[37] In the United States this figure is about 24%.[38] Jason, however, found a somewhat different trend. He reported that for murders of children over the age of one year in the United States, white fathers were the perpetrator 10% more often than white mothers, and black fathers 50% more than black mothers.[39] When mothers killed their children, the victim was usually a newborn baby or younger infant. Fathers were more likely to kill older children. Multiple parity, and young maternal age are also risk factors.[40] The Bureau of Justice Statistics reported that infants under the age of five years, between 1976-97, were killed equally by mothers and fathers, each totaling 37%.[41]

During the period from 1961-1983, 70% of the Canadian mothers who committed infanticide of children under the age of one year were single, while if the child was over one year of age, 71% of the mothers were married.[42] This shows how illegitimacy remains a major factor today in the high percentage of women who commit infanticide. In addition, almost all of the women who were convicted of the crime in Canada were Caucasian. No Canadian Indian was charged with infanticide during this period and only a very small number were Eskimos.[43]

Other general characteristics of murdering mothers include a low level of education and unemployment. They also tend to be younger than those who perform murders for other reasons.[44] The most common method of killing children over the ages has been head trauma, strangulation and drowning.[45] In Goethe's *Faust*, for example, Gretchen drowned her child in the lake.[46] Most of the murders today are committed with the use of the mother's hands, either by strangulation or physical punishment.[47] This is seen in both America and Canada.[48]

In Denmark, Harder found that when a father killed his child, the act was often followed by the murder of the wife, which was in contrast to infanticide by women.[49] In a study of filicide in Detroit, Myers reported that when the murder was committed by a father it usually was the result of an intense rage reaction and often occurred when the child had misbehaved.[50] A review of the literature by Campion revealed that 44% of filicidal fathers had a diagnosis of psychosis.[51] When found guilty in a court of law, fathers are far more likely to be sentenced to prison for infanticide than mothers who were guilty of the same crime.[52] The sentences, however, are often quite lenient. In one study of twenty-nine cases of fathers who killed their children in London, six were given life imprisonment but the others all had sentences of ten years or less.[53] Between 1979-1986, Funayama described twelve cases of consecutive infanticide in Japan where mothers killed from three to nine of their children.[54] When spousal murder did not accompany the crime, no woman received more than a three year term of penal servitude.[55]

One usually can find other signs of psycho-pathology in the family of parents who kill their children, such as alcoholism and drug abuse or other criminal behavior. In one review of the reported cases in the literature, only 5% of the mothers, and 14% of the fathers, had no psychiatric diagnosis.[56] Other studies have shown that only about 10% seem to have no feature consistent with a psychotic diagnosis.[57] But these features are likely exaggerated as a statistical tabulation since they only include cases that involved legal proceedings where insanity was generally used as a defense to the crime. Under such circumstances, a high percentage of infanticidal parents will show signs and symptoms of mental disease. Like other crimes of passion, child-murder often occurs when the higher controls of reason are lowered, as in a fit of passion or rage.[58] This act of homicide, during an attack of intense anxiety and despair, is sometimes referred to as "raptus melancholicus," and is commonly present in cases that reach legal proceedings.[59] Other features include preceding periods of tension and depression.[60]

A final statistical characteristic points out the difficulty in preventing the crime of infanticide. Even when it is known that a parent has traits which could result in violent action against their child, such information was often not helpful in preventing the act of murder. In one review, fully forty percent of the parents were seen by a psychiatrist shortly before committing their crime.[61] There was no indication during any of those interviews that the child's life was in any immediate danger. In some cases there may be a sexual basis for the killing but this is actually very rare.[62]

B. Child Abuse

Except for famine in the underdeveloped countries of the world, child abuse by parents is the most devastating problem which affects the welfare of children today. Where abortion has eliminated many unwanted children from being born, nothing has so far been effective in reducing the numbers of parents who seriously harm their children, even to the point of death. And this predicament is truly world-wide. In England, studies have shown that by age four years, some type of "smacking" is almost universal.[63] In the United States over 90% of parents have stated that they use physical punishment at some time in their child's life.[64] In Sweden, about 4% of all children are abused at least one time each year by a parent "so severely that they risked being physically injured."[65] Although tribal populations often do not physically abuse their children, 27% of infanticides which occur in nonindustrial societies are due to neglect and abandonment.[66]

Analysis of the details is staggering. In 1975, Gelles found that 1,000,000 American children were kicked, bitten, or punched by their parents, 750,000 were beaten up by their parents, and 50,000 had a gun or knife "used" on them.[67] The figures for 1992, as given by the National Committee for Prevention of Child Abuse, indicated that 25% of the fatal cases had substance abuse as a contributing factor and neglect in 36%. 84% of the children were under the age of five, and 38% of the children were at one time in government children services systems.[68]

Parents frequently offer the excuse that the children are only being disciplined by the beatings, and that their treatment is not abusive.[69] But there are obviously many cases which extend beyond any reasonable attempt to discipline. The degree of damage that these children undergo is often hidden from view, or explained as accidental in origin. In 1946, Caffey drew attention to injuries in infants that he thought could have been secondary to parental neglect or abuse.[70] While creating some stir among social welfare agencies, his discovery did not become well known until Kempe and his colleagues first used the term "battered child syndrome" in 1962 to describe the spectrum of abnormalities which could be seen.[71] In 302 cases which they presented in their initial report, 33 of the children died and 85 suffered permanent brain injury.

Since then, the syndrome of "battered child" has become all too well known. It primarily affects children under the age of three years.[72] A major diagnostic feature is the marked discrepancy between the clinical injuries manifested by the patient, and the story of how the damage occurred, supplied by the parents.[73]

Today, most states have legislative statutes that provide criminal penalties for the physical abuse of children.[74] Under such laws, for corporeal punishment to be used by parents the method must be limited to that necessary to discipline alone and also be reasonable and appropriate to the child's misbehavior.[75] If the state feels that the parents are not providing a safe environment for the child, they may step in under the role of *parens patriae* to protect the child's welfare.[76] This means that the child is taken from the family and placed in a foster home setting. But such facilities are not easy to find, and may not guarantee long term care. This problem is discussed more extensively in the chapter on Punishment.

C. China

At the risk of appearing to be casting stones at one specific country, no discussion of infanticide in modern times would be complete without an awareness of the problems in China where the killing of newborn children, especially females, has reached crisis proportions. The killing of unwanted infants has long been a custom throughout much of the Chinese mainland. While much of the time it involved the disposal of deformed or unhealthy children, it was also used for population control, especially during times of crop failure. According to Orleans: "It was primarily aimed at the female child who, as a consumer, would be a serious burden to the poor family."[77]

The tillage of farmland in China has never been highly efficient. Crop production per acre of land is small, equipment for planting and harvesting rudimentary, and the ability to store and move food to other areas quickly very limited. Frequently, the food harvest can not support the needs of the entire population. Pearl Buck recorded how famine often caused dire consequences. In *Satan Never Sleeps*, Ho-san explained that starving parents: "Left their children on purpose and called them "lost," so that there was one hungry mouth the less when they reaped the few grains left in a harvested field."[78] In Cochin-China, all children born in the first three years of marriage were killed in an attempt to limit the population growth.[79]

From 1851-1948 studies indicated that almost five percent of all female births ended in infanticide.[80] The mother generally either "placed her head down in a bucket of water, suffocated her, or simply abandoned her to die."[81] With the population of China so large, and the people so poor, the loss of individual infants did not create a social upheaval for reform.

After the People's Republic of China was proclaimed at Peking on October 1, 1949, some attempt to alleviate the practice was made by making the social acceptance of the sexes more equal and putting women to work in factories and in the fields. But despite their increased utility, female infanticide continued.[82] In 1943, an official publication of the Nationalist government exhorted the people that "the drowning of girl infants is to be prohibited."[83] It had little effect.

The modern Chinese government has not had much greater success in stemming the killings. According to the Third national census in China, 1,008,175,288 people inhabited the People's Republic of China on July 1, 1982. This was equal to the estimated population of the entire earth in 1850.[84] In 1971, the political leaders of China realized they had to do something to lessen the rate of growth of the population, and endorsed the idea of fertility restraint in the Fourth Five-Year Economic Development Plan that year. The set of guidelines which were developed was that the ideal family should have only two children.[85] By 1978 it was apparent that the program was not working and they then embarked upon the "one child per couple" policy.[86] This policy resulted in a vast increase in female infanticide as families attempted to have their only allotted child be a son. Some local authorities wanted to fine couples up to ten percent of their wages if they insisted on having more than two children, or force the parents to pay back bonuses received when they pledged to have just one child.[87] Utilizing compulsory sterilization, and recommending abortions, did little to stem the practice. The traditional adage, "A daughter is like spilled water," continued to hold as long as young women, once married, went off to live with the family of their husbands.[88]

In 1983, the official Chinese press was reporting an alarming increase in the numbers of drownings, and murders, of infant girls.[89] Disapproving world media coverage followed shortly thereafter, and political leaders, as well as an outraged public, began to pressure Chinese officials so that the policy had to be modified in 1988.[90] In the interim, it is estimated that over a million babies, most of them female, lost their lives.

D. Statutory Law

The first time a father was stated to have committed a punishable offence for killing his child was in 318 A.D. when Constantine, the first Christian Roman emperor, made it a crime.[91] Since then, the legal approach to the definition of infanticide has been to uniformly consider the killing of an infant as a criminal act of homicide, but the method of punishment has segregated into two separate categories in modern times.

English statutory law, which is also followed in Canada and parts of Australia, defines infanticide as the killing of a newborn up to the age of one year old by its mother. The killing of any other age child, by any other defendant, is not infanticide and is treated as a homicide. The United States, and most other countries of the world, consider infanticide as a form of murder and do not restrict its designation as to either age or sex. Both approaches clearly recognize, unlike their ancient counterparts, that infants have a right-to-life that is based, not only in the precepts of morality, but within the very foundations of the law as well.

In addition to protecting the life of a child, the law recognizes that there is a requirement that parents provide a safe environment for their child's growth. Blackstone, writing in 1771, summarized this view when he noted that:

> The duty of parents to provide for the maintenance of their children is a principle of natural law . . . By begetting them therefore, they have entered into a voluntary obligation, to endeavour, as far as in them lies, that the life which they have bestowed shall be supported and preserved.[92]

It is in the details of carrying out this charge that divergence is found.

1. England

Infanticide as a separately defined criminal act first became a specific offense in England under the Infanticide Act of 1922. The Capital Punishment Commission of 1866 had noted that juries regularly refused to convict mothers of manslaughter where death was occasioned by post-natal neglect as insufficient to constitute a menses for the offence, and also that it was "practically impossible" to secure convictions for murder when the crime was infanticide because "lay and professional opinion were out of sympathy with the law which drew no distinction between these and other types of murder."[93] Based on the premise that postnatal mothers were subject to temporary insanity, the Act reduced the punishment of the offence from murder to manslaughter.[94] It stated that:

> Where a woman unlawfully by any direct means intentionally causes the death of her newly born child, but at the time of the act or omission had not fully recovered from the effect of giving birth to such child, and by reason thereof the balance of her mind was disturbed.[95]

This allowed juries to not be dissuaded from finding a women guilty when they were sympathetic with her plight.

Because of vagueness in certain terms of the 1922 Act, in 1938 the Act was modified and stated that:

> Who causes the death of her child under the age of 12 months by wilful act or omission, but at the time of the act or omission the balance of her mind was disturbed by reason of her not having fully recovered from the effect of giving birth to the child or by reasons of the effect of lactation consequent on the birth of the child.[96]

Between 1923-1948, 602 women were tried for infanticide in England and Wales.[97]

While the intent was to consider infanticide primarily within these bounds, if circumstances showed that there were other reasons for the killing, then the prosecution could charge her with murder, rather than with infanticide. Such occurrences were quite rare, and the last woman to be hanged for murdering her own infant in Britain was Rebecca Smith, in Devizes, Wiltshire, in August 1849.[98] She had confessed to killing seven of her eleven children with rat poison and was punished accordingly.

A similar provision was passed in Canada in 1948, using the English act as a model.[99] It also failed to adequately define "newly born" at the outset but was clarified in 1953-54 to mean any child under the age of one year.[100] If found guilty, the mother is liable to imprisonment for five years.[101] If the circumstances of the case warrant it, the accused can be found guilty on a charge of murder or manslaughter.[102]

In Australia, infanticide is a specific homicidal offense in three states: New South Wales, Victoria and Tasmania.[103] New Zealand provides a charge of infanticide for mother who kill their children under the age of ten years if she was not fully responsible due to childbirth and/or lactation.[104] In Hong Kong, the law is similar to that in the United Kingdom.[105]

In Russia, The RCC, Belorussian, Georgian, Armenian and Kazakh criminal codes do not recognize a special crime of infanticide, but the other ten union republics do segregate out the killing of a child by its mother.[106] If the mother fed or cared for the child in anyway, however, it is considered as murder rather than infanticide.

One interesting aspect of the law in England is the gradual reluctance of juries to sentence women to prison even when found guilty of the crime. From 1923-1927, 50% of the women who were sentenced under the Infanticide Act were sent to prison. During the period 1946-1950, this had dropped to 22%, and from 1961-1965, only 1.3% of women who committed the crime of infanticide were sent to prison.[107] During the period from 1982-1985, the combined infanticide and murder charges were sent to prison only 12.8% of the time.[108] Edwards remarked that "while women who commit the crime of infanticide are in the whole treated leniently, mothers who neglect their children are regarded very often as monsters rather than as sick."[109]

There has been a recent attempt to discard the Infanticide Act because of its discriminatory features. Critics argue that cases should be prosecuted as murder so that mothers and fathers would be culpable of similar crimes. Under this method the individual circumstances of post-partum psychosis would become a defense rather than a statutory offence, and the mental condition of the mother would be inquired into at trial rather than be presumed.[110]

2. United States

In America, infanticide is not restricted to a particular age of victim, or sex of offender, although an attempt to raise this issue was introduced in the United States Senate by Senator Presley in 1989.[111] When an American child is killed by its mother, the case is handled as a homicide and in states where the death penalty is legal, it is possible that capital punishment will be applied. In both England and America, infanticide still requires that the child be born alive, so that a stillbirth is not charged as a murder.[112]

Endnotes

1 . Hoover, Uniform Crime Reports – 1966.
2 . Chicago Tribune (June 6, 1993): section 4, 1.
3 . Filshie, "Termination of Pregnancy," 234.
4 . American Medical News (November 20, 1995): 15.
5 . Beauvoir, The Second Sex, 135.
6 . Aird, "China's War on Children," 59.
7 . Hale, "The Brutality of Growth Control," 1A.
8 . WuDunn, "In Japan, A Ritual of Mourning for Abortion," A1.
9 . Dahlburg, "Faith & Practice: A Changing World Puts Abortion in the Spotlight," H1.
10 . Ibid.
11 . Shepler, "The Law of Abortion and Contraception – Past and Present, 52.
12 . Roe v Wade, 410 U.S. 113, 93 S.Ct. 705 (1973).
13 . Shepler, "The Law of Abortion and Contraception – Past and Present," 58-59.
14 . Small, "Contraception: Use and Failure," 89.
15 . Jason, "Child Homicide Spectrum," 578.
16 . Saunders, "Neonaticides Following `Secret' Pregnancies: Seven Case Reports," 370.
17 . Campion, Cravens & Covan, "A Study of Filicidal Men," 1143.
18 . Jason, Gilliland, & Tyler, "Homicide As a Cause of Pediatric Mortality in the United States," 191.
19 . Saunders, "Neonaticides Following `Secret' Pregnancies: Seven Case Reports," 370; Kaye, Borenstein, & Donnelly, "Families, Murder, and Insanity: A Psychiatric Review of Paternal Neonaticide," 134.
20 . Heiger, "Filicide: An Update," 388.
21 . Paulson & Rushforth, "Violent Death in Children in a Metropolitan County: Changing Patterns of Homicide, 1958 to 1982," 1016.
22 . Jason, Gilliland, & Tyler, "Homicide As a Cause of Pediatric Mortality in the United States," 193.
23 . Jason, Carpenter, & Tyler, "Underrecording of Infant Homicide in the United States," 197.
24 . Adelson, "Pedicide Revisited," 22.
25 . Of the children killed, under the age of sixteen, 54% were by a parent. Rodenburg, "Child Murder by Depressed Parents," 43.
26 . d'Orban, "Women Who Kill Their Children," 560.
27 . Marks & Kumar, "Infanticide in England and Wales," 329.
28 . Wilczynski & Morri, "Parents Who Kill Their Children," 32.
29 . Harder, "The Psychopathology of Infanticide," 197.
30 . Ibid., 243.
31 . Somander & Rammer, "Intra- and Extrafamilial Child Homicide in Sweden 1971-1980," 45.
32 . Hara, Inoue, Tsuda & Ito, "A Brief Statistical Survey on Medico-Legal Activities During the Period of Two Decades Four Years," 1.
33 . McLaughlin, "Survivors and Surrogates," 119.
34 . In a study of filicide in New York City in 1968-1969, 70% of the murdered children were from poor areas. Kaplun & Reich, "The Murdered Child and His Killers," 809.

35 . In the New York City study of 1968-1969, the biologic father was implicated in only 10% of cases. Ibid., 810. In England, in 1971, only 15% were men. Scott, "Parents Who Kill Their Children," 120. Except for a few American studies, most cases of infanticide are by mothers. Harder, "The Psychopathology of Infanticide," 197, 223.
36 . Trexler, "Infanticide in Florence: New Sources & First Results," 98.
37 . Heiger, Filicide: An Update," 388.
38 . Ibid., 389.
39 . Jason, Gilliland, & Tyler, "Homicide As a Cause of Pediatric Mortality in the United States," 193.
40 . Cummings, Theis, , & Rivara, "Infant Injury Death in Washington State, 1981 Through 1990," 1022-23.
41 . U.S. Department of Justice, Bureau of Justice Statistics, Homicide Trends in the U.S.. December 11, 1998. <http://www.ojp.usdoj.gov/bjs/homicide/children.htm> (4/25/99).
42 . Silverman & Kennedy, "Women Who Kill Their Children," 120.
43 . Ibid., 119.
44 . Weisheit, "When Mothers Kill Their Children, 439.
45 . Resnick, "Child Murder by Parents: A Psychiatric Review of Filicide," 328. In a study of filicide in Canada from 1964-1968 this held true for mothers, however 65% of the murders by fathers was by shooting. Rodenburg, "Child Murder by Depressed Parents," 44.
46 . Goethe, Faust, I.4508, 160.
47 . Totman, The Murderess: A Psychological Study of Criminal Homicide, 14.
48 . Silverman & Kennedy, "Women Who Kill Their Children," 113.
49 . Harder, "The Psychopathology of Infanticide," 223.
50 . Myers, "Maternal Filicide," 535.
51 . Campion, Cravens & Covan, "A Study of Filicidal Men," 1143.
52 . Kaye, Borenstein & Donnelly, "Families, Murder, and Insanity: A Psychiatric Review of Paternal Neonaticide," 138.
53 . Scott, "Fatal Battered Baby Cases," 204.
54 . Funayama & Sagisaka, "Consecutive Infanticides in Japan," 9.
55 . Ibid., 11.
56 . Resnick, "Child Murder by Parents: A Psychiatric Review of Filicide," 328.
57 . Myers, "The Child Slayer," 212.
58 . Scott, "Parents Who Kill Their Children," 121.
59 . Rodenburg, "Child Murder by Depressed Parents," 45.
60 . McDermaid & Winkler, "Psychopathology of Infanticide," 22.
61 . Resnick, "Child Murder by Parents: A Psychiatric Review of Filicide," 332.
62 . "It is extremely rare for a father to kill a daughter whom he has used as an actual sexual object, whatever her age." Scott, "Parents Who Kill Their Children," 123.
63 . Scott, "The Psychiatrist's Viewpoint," 191.
64 . Steinmetz & Strauss, "The Family as Cradle of Violence," 50.
65 . Somander & Rammer, "Intra- and Extrafamilial Child Homicide in Sweden 1971-1980," 53.
66 . Shalinsky & Glascock, "Killing Infants and the Aged in Nonindustrial Societies: Removing the Liminal," 280.
67 . Williams & Money, Traumatic Abuse and Neglect of Children at Home, 11.
68 . Chicago Tribune (April 7, 1993): section 1, 1.

69 . Wolff, Postcards From the End of the World, 125.
70 . Cameron, Johnson, & Camps, "The Battered Child Syndrome," 4.
71 . Kempe, Silverman, Steele, Droegemueller, & "The Battered-Child Syndrome," 17.
72 . Cameron, Johnson & Camps, "The Battered Child Syndrome," 5.
73 . Ibid., 7.
74 . Horwitz & Davidson, Legal Rights of Children, 267.
75 . Ibid., 269.
76 . Ibid., 264.
77 . Orleans, Every Fifth Child: The Population of China, 36.
78 . Buck, Satan Never Sleeps, 110.
79 . Briffault, The Mothers, Volume II, 27.
80 . Eastman, Family, Fields & Ancestors, 21.
81 . Ibid.
82 . Time, Fall 1990, 36.
83 . Orleans, Every Fifth Child: The Population of China, 36.
84 . Tien, China's Strategic Demographic Initiative, 2.
85 . Ibid., 29.
86 . Ibid., 87-88.
87 . Mathews & Mathews, One Billion, A China Chronicle, 122.
88 . Ibid.
89 . Ibid.
90 . Nation 246 (June 18, 1988): 848.
91 . Ferngren, "The Status of Defective Newborns from Late Antiquity to the Reformation," 47.
92 . Blackstone, Commentaries on the Laws of England, Book the First, 16.I.1, Volume I, 447.
93 . Davies, "Child-Killing in English Law," 317.
94 . Kellett, "Infanticide and Child Destruction – The Historical, Legal and Pathological Aspects," 7.
95 . Infanticide Act (1922). 12 & 13 Geo. 5, Ch. 18. Ibid.
96 . Infanticide Act (1938). 1 & 2 Geo. 6, Ch. 36. Ibid., 9.
97 . Bartholomew & A. Bonnicci, "Infanticide: A Statutory Offence," 1018.
98 . Behlmer, "Deadly Motherhood: Infanticide and Medical Opinion in Mid-Victorian England," 412.
99 . Section 216 of the Criminal Code. Osborne, "The Crime of Infanticide: Throwing Out the Baby with the Bathwater," 48.
100. Ibid., 55.
101. Section 220 of the Criminal Code. Arboleda-Florez, "Infanticide. Some Medicolegal Considerations," 56.
102. Section 538, 2-3 of the Criminal Code. Ibid., 56.
103. Tasmania Criminal Code Act (1924) S. 165 A; New South Wales Crimes Act, 1900; Victoria Crimes Act, 1958. Bartholomew & Bonnicci, "Infanticide: A Statutory Offence," 1019.
104. New Zealand Crimes Act, 1961. Ibid.
105. Cheung, "Maternal Filicide in Hong Kong, 1971-1985," 191.
106. Juviler, "Women & Sex in Soviet Law," Women in Russia, 257.
107. Edwards, "Neither Bad Nor Mad: The Female Violent Offender Reassessed," 82.
108. Mackay, "The Consequences of Killing Very Young Children," 24. During a

similar period, 9% of women and 56% of men were sent to prison for committing homicide. Wilczynski & Morri, "Parents Who Kill Their Children," 34.

109. Edwards, "Neither Bad Nor Mad: The Female Violent Offender Reassessed," 82.
110. Bartholomew & Bonnicci, "Infanticide: A Statutory Offence," 1021.
111. Senate Concurrent Resolution No. 23 introduced by Senator Presley, February 9, 1989. Iffy & Jakobovits, "Infanticide: New Medical Considerations," 269.
112. State v. Winthrop, 43 Iowa 519 (1876); Keeler v. Superior Court of Amador County, 87 CalRptr 481, 470 P2d 617, 621 (1970).

CHAPTER VI

TRIBES

"They must laboriously wring from hostile Nature every mouthful of their sustenance."[1]

"The practice of infanticide is almost universal amongst the tribes in the savage and half-civilized state."[2]

The above quotations highlight the most commonly used adjectives associated with the description of tribal practices in Western literature – hostile and savage. The first characterization is quite accurate, the habitat of most tribes is not an environment free from widespread danger; the second is unfairly colored by our own particular moral judgments and bias which portray an uncivilized people as devoid of moral restraint.

The life of primitive peoples have long fascinated those who are fortunate enough to live in a comfortable, civilized society. The ancient Romans and Greeks wrote vividly of the attributes of such races and referred to them collectively, and disdainfully, as "barbarians." Throughout history, spreading global empires overran these countries and, with little compunction or restraint, either sold the inhabitants into slavery, or destroyed them as if they were wild animals whose presence impeded the flow of economic progress.

Today, we continue to be intrigued by tribal people, captivated by their lifestyles as if they were on exhibition at a zoo. *National Geographic* magazine, one of the most popular and lasting journals of modern times, owes much of its success to this voyeuristic interest. The graphic portrayal of tribal struggles to survive provides a haunting and beautiful view of nature, heightened even more by the ever-present danger of death.

But the true nature of tribal life is not so easily transmitted into picture or print. Every day, these villagers must renew the sustenance of their family with little guarantee that food or shelter will be available when the sun finally sets. Their ability to survive the daily task of food gathering is never assured and depends more on the facts of the world around them then it does on the philosophical meanderings of learned men.[3]

D. Crawford spent many years among primitive tribes in Central Africa, and perhaps understood their austere conditions best when he wrote: "You can lie awake all night pondering pitifully the needs of the land, and during that long vigil hear the snuffles and hoarse cries of a dozen little babies."[4] Signs of the impoverished conditions were everywhere, but to Crawford they appeared most evident on the youngsters who explicitly showed signs of malnourishment: bloated bellies, staring, pale eyes, and skin on their hands which hung like an ill-fitting garment. In the words of Bishop South, these children "are not born into the world, but damned into it."[5]

And in many ways, the totally dependent young are truly damned. It is the harsh reality of primal life which makes the rearing of children especially hazardous, however, and not some principled motive of an impersonal God. Most tribes are highly mobile by necessity, and women cannot afford to slough their day-to-day family duties while caring for a newborn infant. The health of adults must always take priority, even if this puts the life of a child in danger. If there is not enough manpower to gather food and provide protection, the lives of every tribal member will be endangered. As a result, infanticide may become a necessity when certain stressful conditions, like extreme shortage of food, are met. According to Lloyd DeMause, hunter-gatherer tribes are frequently forced into such circumstances, and are thereby "in the infanticidal mode."[6] It is this aspect of their life that has helped formulate the description of their existence as "savage."

But how savage is it to try and maintain the safety, and survival, of the greatest number of people with an act that may only cost the life of a vulnerable newborn? And which is truly more compassionate, ending a life before the misery of pain and starvation takes hold, or watching your child suffer through a slow, agonizing death over the next few months or years?

The population of primitive tribes must stay within a certain numerical range dependent upon the availability of food. Not only must the hunt, or harvest, be successful with respect to availability of provisions, but there must be adequate numbers of healthy adults capable of procuring it in a timely fashion. This theory of "optimum size," according to Wynne-Edwards and Carr-Saunders, will eventually be maintained by a number of methods, of which infanticide is an important element.[7] If the control is not done voluntarily, then famine or drought will assure that the optimum numbers are met.

Estimations indicate that hunter-gatherer tribes can support a population density of about one person for every ten square miles, while settled agricultural communities can support twenty five people to the square mile.[8] Once the limit is reached, there is no where else to obtain enough food. The Polynesians often say that life is "fakatau ki te kai" or "measured according to the food."[9] It is the natural resources, not the parent, that ultimately determines who lives or dies.

Primitive populations, living under this ever-present restriction, often found it necessary to destroy some of their offspring when food was scarce. Edward Westermarck did not find this morally offensive:

> There can be little doubt that this wholesale infanticide is in the main due to the hardships of savage life. The helpless infant may be a great burden to the parents both in times of peace and in times of war.[10]

The adults had to resort to the killing of infants "as a means of saving their lives."[11]

R. Brough Smyth, writing about the aboriginal peoples in Victoria, noted that infanticide was prevalent among the tribal peoples he studied, but that it could be seen in more advanced civilizations as well. The difference, however, was that: "The white mother kills her infant in the vain hope of preserving her social position – high or low – of concealing the error or crime which preceded the birth; the black woman simply, I believe, because she is not capable of supporting her offspring, or in order to render impossible an increase of population which the food-resources of the tribe would be unable to meet."[12] While any death was wrong, the tribal response appeared to have a more legitimate ethical basis.

Charles Darwin accepted this natural response to excess population growth in his equation of the "survival of the fittest." He wrote that infanticide appears to have originated in savages "recognizing the difficulty, or rather the impossibility of supporting all the infants that are born."[13] A mother may have to breast feed an infant for up to three or four years, and yet the usual period of infertility for a breast feeding mother is about one year.[14] This leaves excessive numbers of children to be born without adequate support services. Darwin saw the tribes response as reasonable, but apparently left some of his rigid scientific assessment aside as he looked further into the reasons for its prominence: "But the trouble experienced by the women in rearing children, their consequent loss of beauty, the higher estimation set on them and their happier fate, when few in number, are assigned by the women themselves, and by various observers, as additional motives for infanticide."[15] In other words, it was female vanity which helped fuel the fires of infanticide once they were lit by the need to control population growth. We will see how other anthropologists, all of them in the masculine gender, have pointed to similar theories.

But to accurately determine how common the practice of infanticide is among primitive tribes requires more than isolated case reports. Most studies are comprised only of historical tales or brief investigations as part of a general anthropological survey. There are, however, a number of inquiries which have documented the practice with detailed analysis. James Neel, for example, investigated the Yanomama tribe in Brazil, and determined that primitive peoples spaced their children through intercourse taboos, prolonged lactation, abortion and infanticide so that an effective live-birth occurred every four to five years.[16] If an infant was born before an older child was weaned, infanticide was the result.[17] There was also disposal of deformed children and excess females. Neel estimated that the average incidence of infanticide was about 15-20% of all live-births.[18]

Female infanticide was prevalent in tribal cultures because daughters were seen as not being able to effectively hunt for food and because they were a dangerous temptation to surrounding tribes in search of wives. In addition, if a costly dower had to be given in marriage, parents may have felt that a newborn girl had to be destroyed for purely economic reasons.[19] While most modern ethicists would find these actions reprehensible, Fison and Howitt noted that: "Savages are perfectly logical people in their own way."[20] It was necessary at times to look at the greater good, and not let the birth of an unwanted infant jeopardize the survival of the entire family or tribe. Rather than have to deal with a crisis later in life, they sought to prevent the problem at the very start.

What follows in this chapter is a review of what is known about the practice of infanticide among primitive hunter-gatherer tribes as recorded in diverse literature references. The reliability of each statement is subject to debate, but for the purposes of this section, I will not attempt to outline each imperfection which may exist. The purpose of this method is to provide a reference that points out both the striking similarities, as well as the unique characteristics, which may be found in such disparate cultures.

A. Pacific Islands

There are more than 30,000 islands scattered throughout the Pacific Ocean and most of them are grouped in the southwestern section under the designation Oceania. The three main groups, Melanesia, Micronesia and Polynesia, are thought to have been initially populated by groups of people who migrated from Asia and Indonesia. But from wherever they came, the practice of infanticide among these early inhabitants was universal. There have been so many descriptions of newborn killings in this part of the world that Johannes C. Andersen described the crime as a "necessity rather than a depravity."[21]

1. Melanesia

This group of islands includes Fiji, New Guinea, New Caledonia, New Hebrides and the Solomon Islands.

Williams recorded that among the Vanua Levu tribe in the Fiji islands, some areas had up to one-half of the children killed by infanticide.[22] Many of these infants were female because the tribes were frequently at war with neighbors, and daughters were felt to be useless as warriors by the male elders of the tribe, and would have caused too much trouble to raise.[23] This complaint was found in other Polynesian societies as well, and the typical response was to destroy a certain number of female infants at birth.

The Fiji were otherwise generally loving toward their children, and once an infant was accepted into the family group, it was unlikely to be killed. But there were times when a Fiji family could not support another mouth to feed, either because of limited food supply or maternal unavailability due to other responsibilities. Rather than simply bury or abandon the living newborn, the mother would then gently compress the lips and nostrils until death ensued, quietly murmuring "sleep, my child" as she did.[24] It was a painful, but necessary, part of parental responsibility to protect the welfare of the remaining progeny, and the reality of life often demanded the extremity of death.

In Ugi, in the eastern group of the Solomon Islands, infanticide was so common that it created a prevalent commerce of slaves. It was so customary for tribal members to kill natural-born infants that almost seventy-five percent of the natives had been brought in from adjoining tribes.[25] Some were bought as children from the bush people of the interior, others were stolen from the interior of St. Christoval, and brought in as slaves to "supply the place of the natural offspring killed in infancy."[26] This practice of buying children elsewhere, as opposed to spending valuable time raising your own, was a unique feature of various other tribal societies as well.[27]

It was also common for illegitimate children to be killed at birth on some of the Solomon Islands.[28] In addition, in the Buka Passage, near the northwest Solomon Islands, twins were generally disliked: "There was general agreement that the mother simply neglected to give one or both of them proper attention, with the result that both died."[29]

Magic also plays a role in determining whether a newborn is allowed to survive in many tribal populations, and we find evidence of this in Polynesia as well. In the Solomon Island of San Cristoval the first baby was considered unlucky – "ahubweu" or "gare utaora" – and it was usually buried alive unless the father was a chief, or was rich.[30] This superstition apparently assured that children who followed would be of greater advantage to its parents.

In British New Guinea, infanticide was sometimes resorted to if the father of the child did not want further children at the time. If it was felt necessary to avoid the troubles of child rearing, the newborn was usually strangled at birth. One test to determine the worthiness of a child to live in this area was to take it immediately after birth to the banks of a stream and moisten its lips with water. If the water was not accepted, the baby was thrown away.[31] This resembled some of the rituals which were used in ancient European tribal systems. A daughter, however, was often preserved in this area because of the bridal price that the father would one day receive upon her marriage.[32]

In other New Guinea tribes, daughters were not as favored and were often killed at birth. Some parents complained that:

> Girls don't stay with us when they grow up. They marry and go to other places. They don't become warriors, and they don't stay to look after us in our old age.[33]

It was also common among the aborigines of New Guinea to kill one member if twins were born.[34] But once a child got past the rigors of birth, they were much desired and highly valued.[35] Margaret Mead, in her extensive study of the habits of various New Guinea tribal systems, discussed the importance of sex in determining whether a particular child was allowed to live. The mountain dwelling Arapesh, who were a Papuan speaking people occupying territory on the northwest coast of New Guinea, illustrated one extreme.[36] They preferred raising sons, and at birth the father stood apart to determine whether to keep the newborn child or not. As the sex of the infant was called out, he would either say "wash it," which meant the child lived, or "do not wash it," which meant the infant was left in the basin.[37] If at least one parent did not want the child, the infant would not be permitted to live.[38] This unilateral authority was necessary because it was essential that both parents cooperated in the observance of the various lactation taboos and if one parent failed in this regard, there was potential danger to the entire tribe. No unwanted child was therefore permitted to live.[39] Based on their male preferences, it was often the female that was left to die.

On the other extreme were the Mundugomor who were also Papuan and lived along the Yuat river.[40] They were cannibalistic and the value of female children was greater than that of the male. For this reason, the decision to abandon a child would generally involve the birth of a boy. In addition, the chance of survival increased with the order of birth, so that an older child would always be favored over one that was newly born.[41] If the child survived the delivery, and was not thrown into the river immediately after birth, it was generally not killed afterwards.[42]

There were a number of isolated reports outlining some of the other reasons infants in various areas of New Guinea were killed. Sumner noted that the Papuans on Geelvink Bay practiced infanticide because children were deemed to be a burden to certain parents. "We become tired of them," some complained, "they destroy us."[43] In Dutch New Guinea, the women would not rear more than two or three children each because of the stress on the food supply.[44]

Among the Kai of north-eastern New Guinea, the decision of whether to kill the newborn infant was made by the mother or her sisters, rather than the father.[45] No man had anything to say in the matter.

In the Murray Islands of the Torres Straits all children beyond a prescribed amount were put to death "lest the food supply should become insufficient."[46] On the island of Rook, off the east coast of New Guinea, the natives used to kill every other child, beginning with the first, but would bury them rather than eat the children "as their barbarous neighbors did."[47] There is less information available from some of the other island groups but J. G. Paton wrote that infanticide was systematically practiced in the New Hebrides.[48]

Even today, infanticide still plays a role in some tribes that have been untouched by civilization. In 1983, a previously isolated tribe, the Hagahai, sought medical attention at a mission station and were then studied from a variety of medical and ethnographic standpoints. Jenkins noted that their estimated infant mortality rate of 568:1000 was contributed to by the presence of infanticide.[49]

2. Micronesia

These "little islands" in the northwest Pacific Ocean include the Bonin, Caroline, Gilbert, Mariana, and Marshall islands.

In the Marshall Islands, because of the necessity for population control, there was often a limit to the number of children a man was allowed to raise. Any excess child had to be killed at birth.[50] Little information is available from other Micronesian cultures on the presence of infanticide.

3. Polynesia

These "many islands" lie mostly east of the International Date Line and include the Austral, Cook, Hawaiian, Marquesas, Samoa, New Zealand, Easter, Pitcairn, Tahiti, and Wallis islands.

In pre-modern Polynesian societies, abortion was universal and infanticide quite common.[51] Oliver noted that "the frequent, systematic, and socially sanctioned practice of infanticide" of the Maohi people of Tahiti horrified early European visitors.[52] He estimated that up to one-third of the newborn children in Tahiti were killed, but many considered this figure too high.[53]

Damaged, unhealthy or premature babies were often left to die since there was little else that could be done to save them. Population control, as seen in Micronesia, was also a requisite in this region at times and according to Pae Sao, there were often only two children who were allowed to live, a tenet known as "fai tama fakanamua". Firth noted that: "If another child is born, it is buried in the earth and covered with stones."[54]

Like most societal structures, the Polynesian father was seen as the titular head of the family and controlled whether the newborn child would live or die. Describing an incident of infanticide in the Sandwich Islands, Ellis reported how the offending father was brought before the king who asked: "To whom did the child he has murdered belong?" When the answer was that it was his own son, the king responded: "Neither you nor I have any right to interfere."[55]

In Tikopia, one of the small Polynesian Islands, infanticide was primarily utilized as a means of population control.[56] The small island size required that families keep their numbers moderate in order to prevent strife.[57] If the father decided that a newborn infant should not live, either because of food supply or bastardy, the face of the unwanted child was turned down at birth and allowed to smother.[58]

Ellis remarked that among some of the tribes in the Sandwich Islands, Captain Cook's name for the Hawaiian islands, the people were wanderers and found children a burden which hampered their mobility. They often were unwilling to take the additional labor necessary to raise youngsters and would expose the newborn, regardless of sex, unless there was an immediate need for additional family members. Like many other early Western observers of primitive cultures, William Ellis applied moralistic values in denouncing this practice: "Like other savage nations, they are averse to any more labor than is absolutely necessary."[59] He disdainfully observed that if the child cried more than the mother could bear, "she thrusts a piece of tapa in its mouth and buries the babe."[60] While such a response may have occurred in sporadic cases, it is highly unlikely to have been a societal trait as Ellis implied. In fact, David Stannard claims that most of the data on infanticide in Hawaii are actually only stories which the missionary enterprises concocted so that their continued existence could be assured.[61]

Some degree of infanticide was practiced in all the Hawaiian Islands, except for the higher class of chiefs.[62] It was estimated that two-thirds of the children in the Sandwich Islands were killed.[63] According to Sheldon Dibble, before the influx of Christianity, "infanticide prevailed to an alarming extent."[64] E. S. Handy stated that infanticide was widespread among all the classes on the Sandwich Islands, and that parents would seldom rear more than two or three children during the life of their marriage.[65] "Sometimes they strangle their children," he observed, "but more frequently bury them alive."[66] He found that the practice of child strangling, or "umi keiki," occurred especially when the child was born to a chief or was an outcast.[67] He also believed that the Society Islanders probably practiced infanticide more than any other natives in the Pacific.[68] Like Ellis, Handy felt that idleness was the principal factor in the frequency of infanticide. He said that the parents murdered their children for "the trouble of bringing them up."[69] In essence, they considered their children a burden.[70]

Another aspect of the Hawaiian decision to kill a child was to preserve social status. If a woman of higher rank became pregnant by a commoner, the infant was killed.[71] This utilization of class structure was seen elsewhere in the Polynesian Islands and helped control attempts to reduce the rigid caste system.

Tahiti was one of the areas in Polynesia where the practice of infanticide was quite intense.[72] Douglas Oliver estimated that infanticide killed more of their people than all of the other killings including war and murders. He approximated that almost three-quarters of all infants were destroyed soon after birth.[73] The primary reason for this carnage was population control as they had no other method of contraception.[74]

The usual method of killing the infant in Tahiti was suffocation, strangulation or neck-breaking.[75] The killings usually occurred immediately after birth, but if the infant was able to reach its mothers bosom, it was saved. Ellis remarked how it was indeed a lucky infant who survived in this way: "Instead of a monsters grasp, it received a mother's caresses."[76]

The Arioi women would usually take a piece of cloth dipped in water and apply it to the mouth and nose of the newborn in order to suffocate it quickly.[77] Another popular method was to twist the neck, as if killing a fowl, or use a sharp pointed piece of bamboo or bone, or dashing the infant to the ground.[78] If the infant breathed long enough to open its eyes in some tribes, it was not usually killed as it was then regarded as having its own "iho," or personality, and thereby had a claim on life.[79]

Captain Cook described on his first trip to Tahiti in 1769, a custom among the Arreoys that allowed them to enjoy "free liberty in love" without suffering any of the consequences. When children were born to these unions, they were immediately smothered and there was no attempt to conceal the crime for it was seen as a branch of their freedom.[80] In fact, if a child was allowed to live, the parents were ejected from the association.[81] During Cook's third voyage, the Otaheite were said to have shown how the father was at liberty to kill a child according to his pleasure.[82]

Social caste ranking also played a prominent part in Tahitian life. If the woman was felt to be inferior to the husband, any child of their union was usually killed.[83] Class lines could then be maintained without resorting to endogamy.[84]

In addition to Hawaii and Tahiti, infanticide was also used to establish sharp social class differences in other ancient Polynesian societies. Offspring of socially unequal liaisons were systematically put to death to prevent undesired mixtures.[85] At times, the killing of infants occurred for such trivial reasons as not lying quietly on their backs and thereby interfering with the desired head flattening.[86] The Niueans would often get rid of infants in wartime by throwing them into a ravine.[87]

In Niutao, if a family had more than two children it was common for subsequent births to result in infanticide.[88] In the eastern part of Polynesia, at the time of the European discovery, there was a religious society called Arior who performed a number of bestial ceremonies and were guilty of both infanticide and cannibalism. They were present, as well, in the Tuamotu Islands and the Marquesas Group.[89] Among the Marquesan tribe of ancient Polynesia, Linton explained that infanticide was due to the reluctance of women to endure the difficulties of child rearing.[90]

Polack noted that the islands of New Zealand showed "wholesale destruction of human life" and that jealousy and interminable quarrels of the women in a polygamist household, along with difficulties in procuring sustenance for the child, were the primary reasons.[91] In addition, women often feared for the future of their daughters who were frequently made to suffer from the barbarities of war, in addition to abuse from their husbands.[92] If a mother thought the prospects bad enough, she would kill her newborn rather than subject it to the suffering she herself had gone through.

In 1838, a Maorie chieftain of the Kawia Tribe in New Zealand, told a select committee of the English House of Lords that infanticide was used as a method of population control.[93] It was primarily directed against the female child. Another major reason was that polygamy caused jealousy among the wives who then sought revenge by destroying a child. Before the infant could be killed, it had to be ritually cleansed of its supernaturally determined punitive powers by the process of "Taiki."[94] This was done to assure the safety of the community. By 1840, most of the infanticide had disappeared through the efforts of Christian missionaries.[95]

Infanticide, while common in many Polynesian societies, was apparently unknown among the Samoans,[96] the Semang of the Malay Peninsula,[97] and in Tonga, Mangia and the Easter Islands.[98]

B. Australia

The Australian aborigines are derived from Stone Age men who populated the continent about 20,000-30,000 years ago. From an original population of about 300,000, before the appearance of European settlers in 1788, only about 40,000 aboriginals remain alive today. These Australoids do not practice agriculture or husbandry, and the tribal size depends on the food available within their territory.[99] Their daily life closely approximates that of their Stone Age ancestors.

According to Malinowski: "Infanticide is practiced among all Australian natives."[100] The prevalence has been variable, but Gason found that among the Dieri, nearly thirty percent of the children were destroyed at birth.[101] This figure has been quoted elsewhere as well for other Australian tribes.[102]

Berndt has disputed some of these figures and believes that infanticide was rare except during periods of food shortage.[103] Most investigators, however, have agreed that the majority of tribes utilized infanticide to some degree in order to control the number, and quality, of newborns allowed to survive.

The most common reason for the destruction of infants at birth appears to have been population control. Tribes simply could not support more than a specified number of members, and if excess children were born, they had to be removed or the entire community was in danger. The usual desired number of children was three per family, and this meant that approximately 20-40% of all live-births resulted in infanticide.[104]

Many of the tribes did not equate the killing of an infant with that of an adult. There was a common belief that the spirit of a newborn child who died would soon return to earth to be born again.[105] This rebirth of the spirit did not occur with older children, and it was therefore rare for any child, except the newborn, to be killed.[106] The Arunta, Kaitish, and Unmatjera particularly believed in this doctrine.[107]

During periods of extreme deprivation, cannibalism of children was seen in a number of areas. In certain Australian tribes, infants were fed to their mothers or older siblings during periods of drought and famine.[108] Even during adequate food supply, if an older child was sick or weakly it would sometimes be fed a newborn infant in the belief that curative strength would be transmitted in this process.[109] Generally, an infant would not be eaten after receiving a name.[110]

The major geographic divisions of Australia includes Western Australia, where much of the Great Victoria desert is located, the Northern territory, South Australia, Queensland in the Northeast section of the country, and New South Wales in the Southeast. Tasmania, an island that lies off the coast of New South Wales, will be included in this section.

1. Victoria

Gason noted how the children of the Dieyerie (Dieri) tribe are never beaten and yet: "Notwithstanding this tenderness for their remaining offspring, about thirty per cent are murdered by their mothers at their birth."[111] He found that most of the reasons for the killings were either that the mother was young, and did not want the trouble of rearing the child, or that the children were sickly or deformed. The infants "are generally smothered in sand, or have their brains dashed out by some weapon: the men never interfering, or any of either sex regarding infanticide as a crime."[112]

Similar statistics have been reported for other areas in Victoria. Taplin said that among the Narrinyeri in years past, "one-third of the infants which were born were put to death."[113] This included every child who was born before the preceding child could walk, all deformed children, many illegitimate children, and twins.

Among the Bangerang nation and Kurnai (Gurnai) nation, children born while the mother was still carrying around a baby, which often lasted for up to four years, were usually killed.[114] If too many children were born into a family, the newborn would often be left in camp when the family left for different hunting grounds.[115] The infant was killed either by exposure, strangling, or burying alive, but infanticide was never effected by violence, such as a blow or cut.[116] R. Brough Smyth concluded that: "From the excess of male adults alive, it may fairly be presumed that a by far greater number of girls than of boys are done away with in this manner."[117]

Scarcity of food from drought or other natural hazards often left the Aboriginals hungry to the point of desperation. The newborn was occasionally sacrificed in order to help save the life of an older sibling. In the Wotjobaluk (Wotjo) tribe, a newborn would be killed by striking its head against the shoulder of an elder brother or sister, and then it would be cooked and served to the older sibling as a source of strength.[118] In all the tribes of the Wotjo nation, and also the Tatathi and other tribes of the Murray River frontage, a weak or sickly child would be fed a newborn infant in this manner.[119] There is no evidence that familial cannibalism occurred except in times of extreme nutritional need.

Such activity was also noted among the Lower Murray aboriginals where offspring were often fed to other family members. Peter Beveridge found this practice not only during episodes of drought, or famine, but at other times as well. In his opinion it was "attributable to laziness principally; for if a mother has two children, one two years old, and the other just born, she is sure to destroy the youngest."[120] This interpretation of Aboriginal neglect was not common among other investigators of the area.

2. New South Wales

During Captain Cook's first voyage to New South Wales, Collins described how Co-le-be sucking infants were buried alive in the same grave as their mother if some illness or accident took her life.[121] The reason for this was that the rearing of children was too difficult for other tribal members. In addition, if another child was born before the first one could shift for itself, it was killed because it was impossible to raise both infants at the same time.[122] This decision to kill an infant because the mother could not suckle another child was common in many other Australian tribes as well.[123]

In the River Darling region, children born while the mother was still carrying a baby would usually be destroyed.[124] During periods of drought, newborns were frequently killed in order to save the trouble of having to transport the infant during the long search for water. The decision to kill the child was generally decided by the mother's brother, and was accomplished "by a blow on the back of the head, by strangling with a rope, or choking with sand."[125]

In the lower portions of the Paroo and Warrego rivers, which joined the Darling River, the first-born child was often killed by strangulation since the women usually became pregnant at an early age.[126] Among the Kamilaroi (Gamilaroi) of New South Wales, infanticide was never effected by violence, such as a blow or cut, but rather either by exposure, strangling, or burying alive.[127] If too many children were born into a family, the newborn would be left in the camp when the family migrated.[128]

The Mining in Southeast Australia killed excess babies by starvation. They reasoned that "if their numbers increased too rapidly there would not be enough food for everybody."[129] The infant was therefore not fed, and quickly died without the need for any violent action by the parent.

Among the Tongaranka, or Wanjiwalku, infanticide was practiced because babies were frequently too much trouble to look after, but was not done until the family had three or four children.[130] A number of authors also noted that the first-born child in far western New South Wales was usually killed.[131]

3. Queensland

Among the aborigines in Northern Queensland, the practice of infanticide was common, especially when there was a scarcity of food.[132] Because of their nomadic life, children were a burden and often not regarded with favor.

The tribes about Maryborough would leave a newborn that was unwanted lying on the ground, or wrapped in a sheet of bark, to die of exposure. This would generally occur if the first child was a girl, or if there were other children to be cared for.[133]

Many of the tribes would not allow women to rear children until they reached the age of thirty, and any women bearing infants at an earlier age would have to kill their offspring.[134] Children were also killed if they created much pain for the mother during childbirth.[135]

4. Northern Territory

The Aranda tribes occupied a large area in the Northern territory. Among the Aranda of Central Australia, infanticide was more common among girls than boys, and would also be seen more frequently when there was already an older child being suckled.[136] The method of disposal was usually to choke the infant with sand immediately after it was born.[137] They believed that the first born of twins was an evil demon, called "aldoparinja," and the grandmother after birth would put coal or sand into the newborn infant's mouth or beat it with a stick.[138] If the baby's body was covered with hair, or if it was in any way malformed, it was also killed.[139]

There were also reports of cannibalism among the Aranda, and mothers were said to have eaten their children during droughts, or fed every second child to the preceding one in order to increase its strength.[140] Geza Roheim explained that:

> When the Yumu, Pindupi, Ngali, or Nambutji were hungry, they ate small children with neither ceremonial nor animistic motives. Among the southern tribes, the Matuntara, Mularatara, or Pitjentara, every second child was eaten in the belief that the strength of the first child would be doubled by such a procedure.[141]

Infanticide was also resorted to if there was a need to control the number of children born to a family. If a mother was already suckling one child, and was unable to give food to another, she did not hesitate to immediately kill the newborn.[142] On rare occasions, a child of even a few years of age was killed in order to feed a weaker, but elder, sibling.[143] They believed that the spirit of the dead infant would then return to where it came, and be able to be born again in the future.[144]

Among the Ylongu, an aborigine tribe in the Arnhem Land region, infanticide was stated to be widely practiced.[145] Twin births almost always resulted in at least one of the infants being killed.[146]

5. South Australia

George Taplin selected Narrinyeri as the general name for the people of the lower Murray River and Lake Alexandrina area of South Australia.[147] These tribes usually killed a baby that was born while the mother was still nursing an older child.[148] They also killed all deformed children as soon as they were born.[149] In the Port Lincoln district, children born while the mother was still suckling a baby were destroyed.[150]

A. W. Howitt remarked that among the Kaurna tribe "in hard summers the new-born children were all eaten," as can be inferred by the remarkable gaps that appear in the ages of the children.[151] He did not provide other direct evidence of the practice, however.

Among the Mukjarawaint, or Jaadwa, tribe in Southeast Australia, the grandparents decided whether a child would be killed in order to be eaten during times of need.[152] The Adelaide would frequently put a female newborn to death since they favored having boys.[153]

Gason noted that the Dieyerie would kill all deformed children "in fear of them becoming a burden to the tribe."[154] Among the tribes about Beltana, girls were married at age fourteen, and it was customary to then destroy their first-born child.[155]

6. Central Australia

The Aranda (Arunta) of Central Australia had no modern conception of physical paternity. They believed that pregnancy came from the spirit of a totemic ancestor entering the female, and was not due to any special performance on the part of the father. The man therefore did not regard his child as offspring, but rather as property which was under his control. Infanticide was not common, but did occur at times, more often involving the birth of an unwanted daughter. In addition, if the mother was still suckling another child, the newborn infant was choked to death at birth. Twins were always killed, and a younger child was occasionally sacrificed in order to be fed to an older child who was sickly and in need of strength.[156]

Among the Luritcha tribe of central Australia, young children were occasionally killed and eaten, especially when an older child was in weak health. This was to "give the weak child the strength of the stronger one."[157]

7. Western Australia

Among the Pitjandjara in the western desert of Australia, Yengoyan estimated that 18-20% of the children were killed at birth in order to practice population control.[158]

While no longer being practiced openly, he felt that children who were unwanted received minimal care with the result that within a few months they had died of malnutrition.

8. Tasmania

When Captain Cook visited Tasmania, off the southwest coast of Australia in 1777, the natives, for all intensive purposes, lived similarly to Paleolithic times. Their wooden spears were comparable to Old Stone Age utensils found in England, and their nomadic life resembled their earlier ancestors. Most observers noted that during hard times, the old and infirm were generally left to die and newborn babies were killed.[159]

The colonists of Tasmania regarded the aborigines as a degenerate race, and would kill them as easily as they would a stray animal. In 1847, when only forty survived, they were transferred to a reservation and the last aborigine, the woman Truganina, died in 1876.[160] Information on the habits of the Tasmanians comes mostly from the early explorers who noted their activities in journals based on stories told to them by various inhabitants.

The evidence, though largely unsubstantiated, seems to indicate that infanticide was widely practiced. "Scarcity of food and the cares of maternity" would occasionally lead mothers to kill their newborn children.[161] If a mother died in early infancy, the child was often buried with her.[162] When half-castes were born, they were frequently destroyed.[163]

The Tasmania aborigines used dogs for hunting of wild game. R. H.

Davies indicated that: "Dogs became so extremely valuable to them, that the females have been known to desert their infants for the sake of suckling the puppies."[164] This was confirmed by C. P. T. LaPlace who found that: "Children are abandoned in the middle of the woods, because their father dreads hunger, or prefers to keep the dog which aids him in hunting down the game."[165]

C. North America

The earliest men in North America likely entered from Siberia, across the Bering Strait, which even in modern times represents a distance across water of only fifty-six miles. It was easily navigable by boat, and during the winter could be traversed by walking. While these early inhabitants were primarily of Mongoloid origin, there was likely some early Caucasoid elements as well.[166]

The native North American Indians had a varied cultural system, similar to the country's diverse climate and geographical base. Geographically, they are often referred to as Southwestern, Southeastern, Northeastern, California Basin and Plains Indians. Canadian tribes did not differ significantly from their neighbors and will therefore be included in this section. Eskimos and Mexican tribes will be discussed later in this chapter.

1. Southwest

The Mohave Indians were generally very fond of children, and saw them as a means of insuring tribal continuity.[167] But instances of infanticide were seen in select situations. This was generally limited either to children who were born in wedlock and repudiated by their fathers, or to half-breed infants.[168] The Mohave were a patrilineal organization, and if a father repudiated the child it had no name and could not then lay claim to membership in the tribe. Not all cases of illegitimacy ended in the death of the newborn, however, since the Mohave were often quite willing to adopt the children of unmarried women. But in cases of spite, or if there was unwillingness to accept the burden of rearing the child, then there was immediate disposal.[169] They would bury such an unwanted child as soon as it was born and before it had suckled at the breast.

Half-breeds were generally the result of prostitution and the Mohave had little respect, or liking, for the white race. This led to children being destroyed at birth if they were of mixed blood.[170] The presence of a half-breed child in their midst was seen as a source of danger to the entire community.[171]

The Mohave Indians also believed that many phases of human behavior were patterned upon mythical precedent. There was a story in their tradition that told of the days before agriculture when food was scarce and people died of starvation. A married couple had a child of nursing age, but could not gather enough food with the mother's ability to travel since she was hampered by the need to suckle her child. After much thought, they decided that it would be better for the family if the child was killed, and so they left the child on the high bank of a river and watched as it fell into the rising water and drowned. Soon thereafter they learned to grow watermelons from seeds and "no longer had to kill their children in order to survive."[172] While admitting to the need to sometimes kill a beloved child, the story implied that the act was wrong unless excused by the presence of famine.

Among the Indians north of the Meso-American border, twins were not accepted as normal and one was usually buried, as were deformed children. Cabeza de Vaca also noted the presence of female infanticide among a number of these tribes.[173]

The Mariames of southern Texas used infanticide to kill female infants in order to prevent overpopulation, and also would kill male infants if there were unfavorable dream omens.[174] At times, there was such extensive female infanticide that the young braves had to obtain wives from surrounding ethnic groups.[175]

The Nambe Pueblo Indians of New Mexico were once a stable and thriving population. Although the exact reasons have never been determined, they suddenly began to develop a sharp decline in their numbers, and the tribe never fully recovered from the decimation. Some believe that this reduction was due in great part to infanticide and abortion.[176]

Among the Pimas of Arizona, infanticide occurred primarily because the mother feared being left alone to care for the child if her husband died.[177] As in most tribal cultures, unless there was aide provided by other families, a woman and child left alone had little chance to survive. A young infant was necessarily killed so that the mother could remain viable.

In some of the Indian legends, shame played a role in the causation of infanticide. In the Zuni tale of "The Boy and the Deer," a young daughter of a priest was impregnated by the Sun. When her time was near she went to the water's edge and gave birth to a baby boy. She then gently "dug a hole, put juniper leaves in it and then laid the baby there."[178]

2. Great Basin

The Great Basin region comprised about 400,000 square miles of western North America between the Sierra Nevada and Rocky Mountains. It included all of Nevada and Utah, most of Western Colorado, and portions of Oregon, Idaho, Wyoming, Eastern California and Northern Arizona and New Mexico.[179]

Among the Western Shoshone, who occupied the regions of Death Valley up through central Nevada and into northwest Utah, infanticide of unwanted infants was fairly widespread in the Western part of the territory. The Death Valley and Big Smoky groups also reported the killing of one of a pair of twins.[180]

The Eastern Shoshone, who occupied much of western Wyoming, suffered a shortage of females due to neglect and purposeful female infanticide.[181] The Kawaiisu, of the Sierra Nevada area of California, usually killed one member of a twin and also practiced infanticide for economic and social reasons.[182]

3. California

As the Euro-American exploration spread across California, many Indian women were forced into concubinage. This resulted in the birth of numerous infants of mixed blood. The Indians viewed these offspring as living examples of the shame which was brutally placed on their nation by the white men, and for many years these infants were killed as a means of nonviolent resistance. Every half-breed child born "was secretly strangled and buried."[183]

The Cahto killed deformed children and twins at birth.[184] The Wappo mother could kill any of her unwanted children at birth.[185] The Konkow considered it so unlucky to give birth to twins that, in addition to killing the children, the mother was often killed as well.[186] Among the Maidu, twins were also an evil omen and both were killed. Other tribes would only kill one twin in the belief that they would fight when they grew up.[187]

Among the tribes of Lake Miwok, if a mother died before a baby was weaned, her child was buried with her.[188] The Wintu killed newborns if the mother died in childbirth and buried them together.[189] The Patwin killed any child whose mother died if no one offered to take over its care.[190]

Among the Pomo tribes, infanticide was used as a means of population control. This was relatively easy for them as they did not consider that either the fetus, or the newborn infant, was alive.[191] Population control was also practiced among the Coast Miwok of California where after a woman had three children subsequent offspring would be killed by stepping on a stick placed across the throat of the newborn infant.[192]

The Lower Californians occasionally abandoned or killed a child when food was scarce. Among the Central Californians, female children were often killed at birth.[193] The Central Pomo of Northern California killed most twins, illegitimates and also those infants born above the ideal of two or three children per family.[194]

Longinos Martinez, in 1792, wrote of an unusual belief of the Eastern Coastal Chumash. The women of that tribe believed that unless a primigravida either had an abortion, or the newborn infant did not survive, they would never be able to conceive again. This led to the murder of many first-born babies.[195]

The Tubatulabal practiced infanticide only occasionally and considered the crime a grave moral offense. The transgressor, however, was not usually punished.[196]

4. Northeast

The Indian tribes of the Northeast included those from the great Midwest up through the Great Lakes into the Northeast section of the country.

In the legends of some of the North American tribes, exposure or infanticide played a prominent part in the lives of famous Indians. Among the Iroquois, there was the story of Deganawida, whose divine origin was announced to his grandmother in a prophetic dream.[197] When her unmarried daughter was found to be pregnant, the woman disbelieved the dream and saw the event as a scandal. The daughter denied having relations with a man, but when a baby son was born they carried him to a frozen river, cut a hole in the ice, and thrust the child in the water to drown. The next morning, however, they found the child sleeping alongside them, unharmed. They repeated the process twice more and the baby still survived. They then decided to raise the child who grew to become a famous Indian teacher.

A similar story was told by the Passamaquoddy, an old Indian tribe related to the Abnaki and Penobscot. They recounted how a woman gave birth and then decided to abandon the child. She set the infant adrift in a bark canoe and it floated downstream where it was eventually found unharmed. The young boy was raised to become a famous chief.[198]

The Iroquois were a league of five tribes including the Mohawk, Oneida, Cayuga, Onondaga and Seneca. The women were generally in charge over the children, and the man had no authority over her in this regard. If a mother died, her infant was usually killed and buried with her.[199]

The northern tribes of this region practiced infanticide more commonly than the southern ones.[200] It was usual that a child could only be destroyed up to age one month.[201] After this, accepted reasons for disposal of infants were no longer valid. The Creeks could only put an infant to death during the first month of life if they obtained approval of a close relative.[202] Reasons would include death of the father, ill health of the mother and birth out of wedlock.[203] Among the Iroquois of northern New York, if a mother nursing her child died, the infant was killed.[204]

The Mississippians, who ruled much of central North America from 700 to 1500 A.D., often sacrificed a child or wife for special occasions.[205] Certain tribes were reported to have sacrificed their first-born sons to the Sun.[206]

5. Northwest Coast, Plateau and Mackenzie

The Loucheux, or Kutchins, in Northwest America, practiced female infanticide and the women said this was done in "a desire to spare them the miseries of life."[207] The women were treated as inferiors by the men and performed all of the heavy work. They were "literally beasts of burden to their lords and masters."[208] Infanticide was seen as a merciful prevention of sufferance.

6. Southeast

The Cherokee Indians of the Southeast destroyed any surplus or unwanted babies at birth, but the father would be charged with homicide if he even accidentally killed his older child.[209] Once again, the age of the child determined the right of the parent to decide its survival. The native Indians of Florida were said to have sacrificed their first-born male children.[210]

7. Subarctic Canadians

Among the Western Woods Cree from Northwest Canada, south of the Northwest Territories, one of a pair of twins was immediately killed, usually the girl. The reason given was that women were not able to adequately nurse more than one child, and therefore could not keep both twins alive.[211]

Among the Chipewyan, female infanticide was sometimes practiced.[212] This was also seen among the Dogrib in the Northwest Territory,[213] and the Tutchone of the Southern Yukon territory in the Yukon Plateau.[214]

The Hare, from the Northwest Territories, reported infanticide, and even cannibalism, during severe famines.[215] This also occurred among the Mountain Indians in the Mackenzie Mountains between the Yukon and Northwest Territory.[216] At times the difficulty of supplying clothing led to infanticide, and baby girls were more often the ones killed since they were considered less important.[217]

The Indians of Acadia, in the seventeenth century, often abandoned their children because of the lack of time in order to care for them.[218] Some North American Indians were said to throw the newborn into a pool of water and allowed it to live only if it rose to the surface.[219]

D. Africa

Africa has been reported to have a lower incidence of infanticide than all of the other continents. The reason for this is not known, although one possibility could be the very high infant mortality which ranges from 26-50%.[220] With such a marked limitation in survival of future tribal members, any additional loss through infanticide could quickly lead to disappearance of a tribal bloodline.

But instances of infanticide have nevertheless occurred, often associated with ritual acts and superstitious beliefs. Tribal culture throughout the African continent has had an integral connection with magic, or "Thola." If a newborn infant had an unusual attribute or appearance, for example, it was likely to be regarded as unlucky or evil, and in order to protect the rest of the tribe or family, it was immediately destroyed at birth.[221] There were many different manners in which this could occur.

1. Twins

In many African tribes, the birth of twins was considered an evil omen, and one or both of the infants were killed. Tribes like the Kikuyu practiced ritual murder of twins for religious purposes.[222] The Nama Hottentots of South West Africa would kill one of a pair of twins unless both were boys.[223] Among the Ibo of Nigeria, twins (umu-nabo) were considered evil, and against nature, and were placed in old water pots, buried, and covered with leaves.[224]

Twins were usually killed as well in Arebo,[225] Lake Victoria Nyanza,[226] Tswana,[227] Portuguese East Africa,[228] among the Ilso of Southern Nigeria,[229] and the !Kung Bushmen of the Kalahari Desert that borders Namibia and Botswana.[230] The Hottentots exposed only female twins.[231]

One problem which may have led to this system is the problem of providing adequate nutrition to more than one newborn. Although the !Kung diet is generally adequate under normal circumstances, it is impossible for a woman to produce enough milk for two children at the same time.[232] Such limitation likely fostered the development of magical beliefs that one, or both, of the twins should die.

2. Unusual Births

A common reason for killing a newborn infant was that it had some abnormality which associated it as a witch baby. In Benin, West Africa, this included breech births, births occurring in the eighth month of pregnancy, babies born with teeth, babies who slid on their stomachs at birth, and children whose upper teeth appeared first.[233] Even in modern times, parents would secretly destroy such children despite governmental sanctions if they were caught.[234]

Among the Kuruman, albinos and physically deformed children were put to death.[235] The Wanika killed all children who were misshapen.[236] The Nama Hottentots of South West Africa killed deformed children and those whose mother died in childbirth.[237] The Dahomeans of West Africa drowned abnormal infants at birth.[238] In much of West Africa, deformed children were not considered human and therefore were not buried or destroyed but simply thrown away after birth.[239]

In the Waschamba tribe of East Africa, if a child presented itself feet first in childbirth it was killed.[240] In British East Africa, if a child was born feet first, it was smothered because they believed that otherwise their crops would all "wither up from drought."[241] Similarly in Tswana, a child who was born this way was put to death because they were seen as evil omens – "ditlhodi" – who could bring disaster on their parents.[242] While other cases of infanticide would be punished by tribal courts, this type of killing did not bring action against the parents.

Defective children were also killed by the !Kung Bushmen of the Kalahari Desert that borders Namibia and Botswana,[243] and in Portugese East Africa.[244] On the Zanzibar coast, weak and deformed children were exposed,[245] and the Vadshagga put to death illegitimate children and those whose upper incisors came first.[246] The Fans killed all sickly children.[247] In an island in Lake Victoria Nyanza, if a child cut its upper teeth before the lower they were killed as it was a sign of great disaster.[248] The Ibo destroyed children who pierced the top gum with a tooth before the bottom one – "nwa-eze-enu."[249]

Among the Ibo of Nigeria, if a woman delivered a child before she began her menstrual periods, the infant was termed "ime-ogbi" and was cast away with the designation of a dumb conception.[250] Children who were born before a mother resumed her menstrual periods after a previous birth were also destroyed as a "nwa-aghom", while if a mother died in childbirth, her baby was buried with her.[251] Other reasons for destroying children at birth included not crying vigorously, born with excess toes or fingers, a weak child who could not move well, and a child who was born after the father died (nwa-azu-nkpa).[252]

3. Tribal Customs & Habits

At times from superstition, but also at times from practicality, certain African tribes would practice infanticide for reasons that may be difficult to defend from a moral basis, but were felt necessary enough for generations of members to follow. The Galles, for example, were a mobile robber horde who moved their camp every eight years. Any children born during this time of transfer were exposed because it would be too difficult to carry them along with their other belongings.[253]

The Gagas were said to put all their children to death in order to evade the trouble of rearing them. They would assure continuance of the tribe by stealing boys and girls from neighboring tribes.[254] The frequency of infanticide among the Kuni was so great that every mother in the tribe was reported to have killed at least one child.[255]

In the tribes that lived on the banks of the Omo about Karo, and in the hills to the east in Abyssinia, infanticide generally occurred among the first-born children. The Banna, Bashada and Kerre strangled infants and threw the bodies away for reasons that are not clear.[256] Some say it was an ancestral custom.

In Uganda, the first-born son of a chief or other important person, was strangled by the midwife who then reported it as a still-born. According to Roscoe: "This is done to ensure the life of the father; if he has a son born first he will soon die, and the child inherit all he has."[257] Among the Ganda of Uganda, the first-born child of a chief's wife, if a son, was killed.[258] First-born children were also killed by the Ilso of Southern Nigeria.[259]

The Senjero in eastern Africa sacrificed first-born sons in order to prevent a bad harvest.[260] In Zimbabwe, as late as 1929, a king's daughter had been sacrificed to bring rain.[261] The Rendille, a group of camel herders in the Kenya Highlands, killed boys born on Wednesdays, or those born after the next eldest son was old enough to be circumcised.[262] They needed to limit their numbers in proportion to the numbers of their flock, and thereby used infanticide when the tribe became too congested.[263]

While they did not condone the killing of an illegitimate child, the Tswana considered the action more leniently than if the offspring was legitimate. If the corpse of an infant was found, the Chief would call the unmarried women of the village together in order to test their breasts for milk. If an unmarried woman was found to have been pregnant, she would then be smeared with a mixture of medicines to cause intense pain as expiation for the crime.[264]

Among some of the tribes in southeastern Africa, if a woman's husband was killed in battle and she remarried, the first child she bore had to be put to death. This infant was called "the child of the assegai" and it would bring bad luck on the second spouse if allowed to live.[265]

In Southern Rhodesia, the "Legend of the Sacrifice of the Maiden" told of how the chief priest instructed the king, after a particularly long drought, that a sacrifice of one of the nubile princesses who had not yet slept with a man must be made before rain would reappear.[266] The king, or mambo, searched his daughters and found that all had slept with a man already. The chief priest then said that the eldest of the not yet nubile daughters should be taken to a separate place and kept there until she became mature. Over the next two years, as the tribe waited, many people died as the drought continued. But then the time of puberty came, the maiden was strangled for a sacrifice to the gods, and the rains immediately began to fall and the country was saved.[267]

Arabs of North Africa, and Negroes in Central Africa, have justified the exposure of infants born of incest on the grounds that the child would be "so and so's son and his nephew."[268] This would be a living contradiction that could not be allowed.

There are varying estimates on how extensive these practices throughout the African continent were. Authors like Howell and Lee maintained that it was limited and only occurred in situations like defective births, and on the death of a husband.[269] Others, like Marshall and Schapera, reported that the extent resulted in the removal of as many as one or two out of every three children. This implied an infanticide rate of almost fifty percent.[270]

E. South America

1. Brazil

Nancy Scheper-Hughes, in Death Without Weeping, details the life of modern day Brazilians in the poor north-east section of the country. She relates how the madness of hunger – delirio de fome – had caused one woman to kill her infant son and one year old daughter.[271] When the young woman had been asked why she had committed such a shameless act, her answer was simply: "To stop them from crying for milk."[272] Poverty was something which necessitated a different outlook of life in the rural areas of the country, and mothers had to at times turn away from what might be viewed as a natural motherly bond to nurture a child and allow the principle of "letting go" to determine how they face the impossible task of raising a child they cannot afford.[273] In addition to causing the abandonment of children because of poverty, this often led to infanticide of deformed babies for reasons of social hygiene.[274] The Amazonian Mehinaku Indians felt no residuals of guilt or blame when they had to kill children for these reasons.[275]

Many other researchers have found similar situations in Brazil. Institutional infanticide was identified among the Tapirape of the Brazilian Amazon where there was a rule that no woman should have more than three living children, and no more than two should be of the same sex.[276] Deformed and illegitimate children, and the second of twins were killed by the Witotas of Northwestern Amazonia, beyond the borders of Brazil.[277] They usually were left in the bush to die or submerged in the river.

James Neel reported on studies among the Xavante of the Brazilian Mato Grosso, the Makiritare of southern Venezuela, and the Yanomama of southern Venezuela and northern Brazil.[278] He found that infanticide, along with intercourse taboos and abortion, was used to space the number of children each family desired so that approximately one child was born every four to five years during the childbearing age.[279] The infanticide was directed primarily at infants whose older sibling was not yet thought ready for weaning, usually at three years of age. Deformed infants, those thought to result from extramarital relationships, and females were particularly prone to infanticide.[280]

The Bororos, a southern tribe that was not put under the modern protection of the Villas Boas brothers, killed all children who did not appear healthy at birth.[281] In addition to concern with only raising healthy children, they no longer maintained much desire to bring children into the world since their ancestral life was threatened by modern invasion into their forest space.[282] A few decades ago, the tribe numbered over 5,000 but their numbers have dwindled down to only around 150.

2. Peru

Fr. Xeres had written that the Indians of the Peruvian valleys between San-Miguel and Caxamalca, sacrificed their own children to idols and then spread the blood of the victims on the faces of the idols and the doors of the temples.[283] John Locke noted that in some provinces of Peru, there were "people that begot children on purpose to fatten and eat them" once they reached thirteen years of age.[284] Such accusations have not been verified by other sources, and the Incas dealt with infanticide "despenamiento" by throwing the culprit from a high mountain peak, or lapidation.[285]

The ancient Peruvians put to death feeble, and deformed or defective children.[286] Infants were felt to be more disposable since they were not usually considered as family members. Andean Indians did not accept a child as a permanent member until it survived at least one year. The Amahuaca did not consider children fully human until the age of three years.[287]

A son was occasionally sacrificed by a sick father in Peru if the priest said the man would die unless the gods were appeased. The sacrifice was meant to satisfy the idol devoted to the god so as to save the father's life.[288] A. de Herrera also found evidence that the Indians of the Peruvian valleys between San-Miguel and Caxamalca sacrificed their children to the idols which they held in great veneration.[289]

Even today, there is excessive mortality among the newborn children of the Aymara Indians in Peru. Studies have shown that this is due, in part, to infanticide which results in population checks required because of limitation in farming land.[290] de Meers compared mortality rates of children among two Aymara and three Quecha peasant communities in Southern Peru and found that infant mortality was especially high for infants compared to children.[291] There was also an under-reporting of female deaths with birth order of three or more suggesting that there was either male preferential care or female infanticide.[292]

3. Paraguay

Dobrizhoffer said that the Abipones in Paraguay killed boys at birth more than girls because sons when grown up "are obliged to purchase a wife, whereas daughters at any age to be married may be sold."[293] John Lubbock noted how the Paraguay Indians practiced infanticide as the "rule rather than the exception."[294]

The Lengua-Mascoy did not rank the crime of infanticide as equal to that of murder of a grown child or adult. They generally were very kind to their children, but under unfavorable conditions, like shortage of food, they would dispose of a newborn.[295]

It has been estimated that among the Paraguayan Chaco Indians, one-half of the children that were born were put to death.[296] They simply buried the infant at birth and there was no grieving or funeral rites that followed.[297] Durant claims that the Lenguas Paraguayan Chaco allowed only one child per family per seven years to survive.[298]

Until recently, the Ayoreo of Southwest Bolivia and North Paraguay accepted the practice of infanticide. They generally utilized it for the birth of a deformed child, twins, children born soon after a previous birth, termination of marriages, and births to women too young to accept the responsibilities of motherhood.[299]

4. Mexico

The earliest Aztecs arrived in Mexico in the thirteenth century and founded the city of Tenochtitlan around 1325 A.D. They developed an elaborate ritual around the use of human sacrifice, and children were killed in many ceremonies. Parents were even known to sell some of their children for this purpose.[300] Except for this practice, the Aztecs prohibited infanticide unless there was a twin birth and then only one child was killed.[301]

Many other Mexican tribes have been reported to practice infanticide for a variety of reasons. The Salivas and Manaos generally put malformed children to death believing that the deformity was the work of a demon.[302] Guaycuran women under the age of thirty years killed the majority of their children in an attempt to seek the good will of their husbands. During the long period of suckling, the men were denied marital relations and frequently then married other wives.[303] The Abipones would put to death all but two of the children in a family.[304] In Patagonia, if parents decided not to keep a child it was either strangled or exposed to the dogs.[305]

While not restricted to Mexican culture alone, modern Hispanic populations also retain stories of the legend of La Llorona, or the "Weeping Woman," who supposedly drowned her children and then was doomed for all time to haunt the site of her evil deed.[306] It is used, at times, to frighten young children away from undesired locales such as garbage dumps and dangerous ponds.

5. Upper Amazon

In the upper Amazon, the Ximanas and Cauxanas tribes killed their first-born children while the Lengua Indians put the first-born to death if it was a girl.[307] The Tapirape set a mandatory limit of each family to three children and used infanticide to strictly control that number.[308] The basis for their decision was the relative sparsity of food which would put the rest of the tribe at risk if population growth was not checked.

F. Eskimos

The Eskimo habitat stretches from the west coast of the Bering Straits over Alaska, on through North America, and then to the east coast of Greenland. Throughout this wide expanse, they are faced with the incredibly difficult task of finding sustenance in a frozen environment. Agriculture is obviously not possible, and food must be sought from sources which are scarce and dangerous to find. For the adult male, hunting is a full-time task, and for the female, managing the household under the trying circumstances of the frozen tundra leaves little time for the raising of children. When conditions permit, Eskimos always raise their young with loving care. They are a gentle people by nature, and depend entirely on cooperation with other family members for their very survival. But if circumstances are harsh: "It is then up to each family to decide for itself: are its present resources (both human and material) sufficient to maintain the baby through its nonproductive years?"[309] If resources are found wanting, the baby is killed and there is no legal sanction or social blame.

This attitude is not cold-hearted but rather a reflection of what it takes to survive near the Arctic circle. Because of the nature of their existence, "what chiefly cuts the Eskimos to the heart is to see their children starving."[310] This empathy, along with the need for adults to constantly forage for food, has resulted in a general understanding that children must be sacrificed before the adult.[311] In other lands, it may be possible for neighboring families to take over the raising of orphaned offspring; in the Eskimo environment, such charity is simply not possible. Despite this icy reality, Clark Garber noted with interest that while infanticide was easily accepted by the Eskimo when necessary, there was no evidence of voluntary abortion.[312]

The custom of infanticide, especially of female children, has been documented frequently among the Eskimos of northern Alaska and Canada.[313] Garber reviewed much of the writings in this area and noted that in times of plenty, very few cases of infanticide could be found. During times of famine, however, it was a common occurrence.[314]

Female children were often considered a burden, and the degree of female newborn death created a polyandrous society, at times similar to the Toda's of India.[315] But where the Todas practiced female infanticide for economic reasons, the Eskimos killed their daughters in response to the arduous existence they faced. Dall wrote that the Alaska Eskimos generally felt that they could not support so many daughters and would take the newborn infant out and "stuff its mouth full of grass, and desert it."[316] Likewise, Jackson noted that among the Mahlemute and Yukon Eskimos, female infanticide was common: "Many Indian mothers, to save their daughters from their own wretched lives, take them out into the woods, stuff grass in their mouths, and leave them to die."[317]

One advantage of this destruction of females at birth was the equalization of the sex-ratio in the adult population. Since males were more likely to be killed from accidents during the treacherous hunting for food, an earlier imbalance would be normalized rather than leave the females at a statistical advantage.[318] Estimates for how many females were destroyed at birth have ranged from 15-50%, in the opinion of Joseph Birdsell, to an astounding 80% made by Knud Rasmussen in his history of the Netsilik population from 1922-23.[319] It should be noted that when Schrire and Steiger reviewed the data collected by others on female infanticide, they concluded that the results were more in response to short-lived periods of stress, and did not indicate such high levels of killings over the long run.[320]

Polar Eskimos, the most northern people in the world, greatly desired offspring but the parents were sometimes forced by circumstances to destroy them. This generally happened if the father died, since the widow would not be able to support the child. She would then strangle her small infant if it could not survive on its own. If a mother died, the man generally buried the younger child with his wife.[321] Others would expose the child by throwing it into the sea. They would not bring up offspring who were of no use and could "only help to diminish the common store of sustenance."[322] During periods of famine, the Polar Eskimos often strangled young children under the age of four in order to save them from slow starvation due to the lack of milk and food.[323]

The Caribou Eskimos, a Central Eskimo tribe, were noted to have a predominance of male children and female adults which Birket-Smith blamed on female infanticide and a hazardous male occupation.[324] The Netsilik Eskimos practiced female infanticide to a very high degree. The decision was generally made by the father immediately after birth and was based on his providing capacity. Women were considered less important, since they could not hunt, and if any child was at risk, it was generally the female who was chosen.

Freeman did not accept this practical explanation for the killing of females at birth. He rather felt it was a manifestation of male dominance in Eskimo society and the desire to retain sole control over the female even from the moment of birth.[325] Whatever the true underlying cause, female infanticide disappeared after the general conversion of Eskimos to Christianity in the late 1930s and 1940s.[326]

The Netsilik practiced so much female infanticide that at times they had to emigrate to the neighboring Aivilik in order to find wives.[327] Among the Caribou Eskimos, betrothals were commonly arranged in infancy as the boy's parents sought to ensure a wife for him in view of the shortage of girls due to the prevalence of female infanticide.[328]

Among the Eskimos of Arctic Canada, babies were often set out on the ice to freeze if the father or elder of the tribe decided that there would be a drain on the food supply.[329] No sickly child, or one without a mother, was allowed to live even during normal times.[330]

The Inuit Eskimos of Quebec were noted to practice infanticide, and even cannibalism, during times of famine in the nineteenth century.[331] The Eskimos of Greenland greatly desired children, both male and female, but no deformed child was allowed to live. Allowing a child to be kept alive by extraordinary means would endanger the ability of the others to cope with the environment.[332] At times, they have even been forced to eat the children who have died during severe famines.[333]

The Eskimos of Pelly Bay regularly killed off a proportion of their female babies.[334] In general, one of a set of twins would be killed, and generally it was the girl.[335] Males were the basic food producers, and were likely to be lost by occupational disability and homicide.[336] Girls would often leave the family at the time of marriage, and thereby were seen as more expendable.

Jenness wrote that the Copper River Eskimos were often unwilling to rear their children: "A baby involves much hardship to the mother, especially in the summer when all the household goods are packed on the back . . . Frequently the parents settle the problem by simply suffocating their baby and throwing it away."[337] It should be noted that this cavalier attitude towards children was not recognized by other researchers of Eskimo populations.

Clark Garber noted that the Barrow Eskimos secretly took the lives of their babies, especially girls, and cautioned that a cursory evaluation may miss proof of the crime.[338] He also found that the Innuits and Utes of Alaska preferred drowning and freezing for the destruction of their infants.[339] While economics were a primary reason, "if a child is born physically deformed, it rarely survives the day of its birth."[340]

Infanticide also found it's way into Eskimo folklore. In the folktale of "The Unwanted Child," a mother with seven children found that difficult times did not allow her to have enough food to feed her recently newborn infant. She decided to throw the child into a fjord, and then began to observe all the taboos which were proper to a woman who just had a miscarriage.

This included cutting fat only with her feet, not speaking unless spoken to, and other superstitious practices. The child did not die, however, and came back to cause the death of some of her other children.[341]

G. Miscellaneous Tribes

In Ceylon, infanticide was practiced among the Kandyans and the hill tribes of North Aracan.[342] Among the Veddahs, no man was allowed to have more than three children, and all those born after that were killed.[343] In Tonquin there was a law forbidding the exposure or strangling of children which indicated that it must have been practiced there to some degree.[344] In Kamtschatka, newborns were throttled and thrown to the wild dogs.[345] The Svans would fill the mouth of newborn females with hot ashes.[346] The Siberian Ghiliak had many of their infants killed by infanticide.[347]

The Borans, on the southern border of Abyssinia, would sacrifice their children, and their cattle, to the sky-spirit Wak.[348] In addition, when a man of standing married, he became a Raba, and then had to leave any children that were born to him over the next four to eight years in the bush to die or else an evil calamity would befall him. The Kerre, Banna, and Bashada, three tribes of the Omo River valley to the south of Abyssinia, also strangled their first-born children and threw the bodies away.[349] Captain C. H. Stigand investigated this practice and noted that this included all the people – rich, poor, high and low.[350]

Will Durant states that "the Bondei natives strangled all children who entered the world headfirst; the Kamchadals killed babes born in stormy weather; Madagascar tribes exposed, drowned or buried children who made their debut in March or April, or on a Wednesday or a Friday, or in the last week of the month."[351]

Endnotes

1 . Nansen, Eskimo Life, 4.
2 . Smyth, The Aborigines of Victoria, 51.
3 . Jung, Civilization in Transition, 56.
4 . Crawford, Thinking Black: 22 Years Without a Break in the Long Grass of Central Africa, 144.
5 . Ibid.
6 . DeMause, "The Fetal Origins of History," 30.
7 . Douglas, "Population Control in Primitive Groups," 264.
8 . Wrigley, Population & History, 45.
9 . Firth, Primitive Polynesian Economy, 43.
10 . Westermarck, The Future of Marriage in Western Civilization, 167.
11 . Ibid., 168.
12 . Smyth, The Aborigines of Victoria, 55.
13 . Darwin, The Descent of Man, I.IV, 134.
14 . Lithell, "Breast-Feeding Habits and Their Relation to Infant Mortality and Marital Fertility," 182.
15 . Darwin, The Descent of Man, and Selection in Relation to Sex, II.XX, 364.
16 . Neel, "Lessons From a `Primitive' People," 816.
17 . Ibid.
18 . Ibid.
19 . Fison & Howitt, Kamilaroi & Kurnai, 137.
20 . Ibid., 135.
21 . Andersen, Myths & Legends of the Polynesians, 445.
22 . M'Lennan, Studies in Ancient History, 90-91.
23 . Ibid., 91.
24 . Fison & Howitt, Kamilaroi & Kurnai, 175.
25 . Guppy, The Solomon Islands and Their Natives, 42.
26 . Sumner, Folkways, 317.
27 . Knibbs, The Savage Solomons, 51.
28 . Sumner, Folkways, 317.
29 . Blackwood, Both Sides of Buka Passage, 164.
30 . Frazer, The Golden Bough, Aftermath, 332-333.
31 . Radbill, "Children in a World of Violence: A History of Child Abuse," 4.
32 . Sumner, Folkways, 317.
33 . Langness, "Child Abuse and Cultural Values: The Case of New Guinea," 14-15.
34 . Ibid., 15.
35 . Ibid., 26.
36 . Mead, Male & Female, 416.
37 . Mead, Sex & Temperament in 3 Primitive Societies, 32.
38 . Mead, "The Arapesh of New Guinea," I, 44.
39 . Ibid.
40 . Mead, Male & Female, 420.
41 . Mead, Sex & Temperament in 3 Primitive Societies, 171, 191.
42 . Ibid., 192.
43 . Sumner, Folkways, 270.
44 . Ibid.
45 . Haaland, Primitive Law, 74.

46 . Sumner, Folkways, 317.
47 . Quotation from Father Mazzuconi. Frazer, The Dying God, 180.
48 . M'Lennan, Studies in Ancient History, 97.
49 . Jenkins, "Health in the Early Contact Period: A Contemporary Example From Papua New Guinea," 997.
50 . Briffault, The Mothers, Volume II, 27.
51 . Ritchie & Ritchie, Growing Up in Polynesia, 39.
52 . Oliver, Ancient Tahitian Society, 424.
53 . Ritchie & Ritchie, Growing Up in Polynesia, 41.
54 . Firth, Primitive Polynesian Economy, 44.
55 . Ellis, Polynesian Researches, 327.
56 . Douglas, "Population Control in Primitive Groups," 263.
57 . Wrigley, Population & History, 43.
58 . Firth, We, The Tikopia, 374.
59 . Ellis, Polynesian Researches, 329.
60 . Ibid., 330.
61 . "The missionaries had a major personal stake in their bogus `discovery' of widespread infanticide and other savage traits." Stannard, "Recounting the Fables of Savagery: Native Infanticide and the Function of Political Myth," 413.
62 . Ellis, Polynesian Researches, 327.
63 . Ibid., 328.
64 . Dibble, History & General Views of the Sandwich Islands Mission, 123.
65 . Handy & Pukui, The Polynesian Family System in Ka-'U, Hawaii, 327.
66 . Ibid.
67 . Ibid., 79.
68 . Ibid., 327-328.
69 . Ibid., 329.
70 . Ibid.
71 . Davies, Human Sacrifice, 192.
72 . Ritchie & Ritchie, "Child Rearing and Child Abuse: The Polynesian Context," 189.
73 . Oliver, Ancient Tahitian Society, Volume I, 424.
74 . Ibid., 412.
75 . Ibid., 425.
76 . Referring to a quote of Ellis. Ibid., 426.
77 . Ibid., 425.
78 . Ibid., 426.
79 . Ibid., 63.
80 . Cook, Captain Cook's Journal During His First Voyage Round the World, III, Tahiti, 95.
81 . Avebury, Pre-Historic Times, 467.
82 . Malthus, "An Essay on the Principle of Population, or, a View of Its Past and Present Effects on Human Happiness; With an Inquiry Into Our Prospects Respecting the Future Removal or Mitigation of the Evils Which It Occasions (1872)," On Population, I.V., 178.
83 . Oliver, Ancient Tahitian Society, Volume II, 455.
84 . Goldman, Ancient Polynesian Society, 188.
85 . Ibid., 563.
86 . Ibid.

87 . Ibid.
88 . Gill, Jottings from the Pacific, 17.
89 . Heyerdahl, American Indians in the Pacific, 143.
90 . Goldman, Ancient Polynesian Society, 564.
91 . Polack, Manners & Customs of the New Zealanders, 92.
92 . Ibid., 94.
93 . Hunton, "Maori Abortion Practices in Pre and Early European New Zealand," 568.
94 . Gluckman, "Abortion in the Nineteenth Century Maori: A Historical and Ethnopsychiatric Review," 385.
95 . Ibid.
96 . Murdock, Our Primitive Contemporaries, 67. See e.g. Sumner, Folkways, 317.
97 . Murdock, Our Primitive Contemporaries, 95.
98 . Goldman, Ancient Polynesian Society, 563.
99 . Bergamini, The Land & Wildlife of Australia, 170.
100. Malinowski, The Family Among the Australian Aborigines, 235.
101. Ibid., 236.
102. Cowlishaw, "Infanticide in Aboriginal Australia," 263.
103. Berndt & Berndt, The World of the First Australians, 124.
104. Dickeman, "Demographic Consequences of Infanticide in Man," 121.
105. Spencer & Gillen, The Northern Tribes of Central Australia, 609.
106. Ibid., 608.
107. Malinowski, The Family Among the Australian Aborigines, 216.
108. Roheim, "The Western Tribes of Central Australia: Childhood," 199.
109. Ibid., 200.
110. Ibid.
111. Smyth, The Aborigines of Victoria, 52.
112. Ibid.
113. Ibid.
114. Aptekar, Anjea: Infanticide, Abortion & Contraception in Savage Society, 160.
115. Fison & Howitt, Kamilaroi & Kurnai, 190.
116. Ibid., 175.
117. Smyth, The Aborigines of Victoria, 51.
118. Howitt, The Native Tribes of South-East Australia, 749.
119. Ibid., 750.
120. Smyth, The Aborigines of Victoria, 52.
121. Malthus, "An Essay on the Principle of Population, or, A View of Its Past and Present Effects on Human Happiness; With an Inquiry Into Our Prospects Respecting the Future Removal or Mitigation of the Evils Which it Occasions," On Population, I.III, 170.
122. Ibid.
123. Malinowski, The Family Among the Australian Aborigines, 235.
124. Aptekar, Anjea: Infanticide, Abortion & Contraception in Savage Society, 160.
125. Bonney, "On Some Customs of the Aborigines of the River Darling, New South Wales," 125.
126. Quoting G. Scriviner. Frazer, The Dying God, 180.
127. Fison & Howitt, Kamilaroi & Kurnai, 175.
128. Ibid., 190.
129. Howitt, The Native Tribes of South-East Australia, 748.

130. Ibid., 749.
131. Cowlishaw, "Infanticide in Aboriginal Australia," 266.
132. Lumholtz, Among Cannibals, 134.
133. Howitt, The Native Tribes of South-East Australia, 750.
134. Cowlishaw, "Infanticide in Aboriginal Autstralia," 267.
135. Ibid.
136. Murdock, Our Primitive Contemporaries, 34.
137. Ibid.
138. Roheim, "The Western Tribes of Central Australia: Childhood," 195.
139. Ibid.
140. Ibid., 199.
141. Ibid., 200.
142. Spencer & Gillen, The Arunta, Volume I, 221.
143. Ibid., 40.
144. Ibid., 39.
145. Hippler, "Culture and Personality Perspective of the Yolngu of Northeastern Arnhem Land: Part I – Early Socialization," 227.
146. Ibid.
147. Tindale, Aboriginal Tribes of Australia, 156.
148. Aptekar, Anjea: Infanticide, Abortion & Contraception in Savage Society, 159.
149. Brodsky, "Congenital Abnormalities, Teratology and Embryology: Some Evidence of Primitive Man's Knowledge as Expressed in Art and Lore in Oceania," 419.
150. Aptekar, Anjea: Infanticide, Abortion & Contraception in Savage Society, 160.
151. Howitt, The Native Tribes of South-East Australia, 749.
152. Ibid.
153. Malinowski, The Family Among the Australian Aborigines, 235.
154. Brodsky, "Congenital Abnormalities, Teratology and Embryology: Some Evidence of Primitive Man's Knowledge as Expressed in Art and Lore in Oceania," 419.
155. Frazer, The Dying God, 180.
156. Murdock, Our Primitive Contemporaries, 34.
157. Spencer & Gillen, The Northern Tribes of Central Australia, 475.
158. Yengoyan, "Biological & Demographic Components in Aboriginal Australian Socio-Economic Organization," 88.
159. Quennell & Quennell, Everyday Life in Prehistoric Times, 51-52.
160. Murdock, Our Primitive Contemporaries, 18.
161. Ibid., 8.
162. Ibid., 7.
163. Roth, The Aborigines of Tasmania, 162-63.
164. Ibid., 162.
165. Ibid.
166. Montagu, Man: His First Million Years, 65.
167. Devereux, "Mohave Indian Infanticide," 126.
168. Ibid., 127.
169. Ibid., 128.
170. Ibid., 129.
171. Ibid.
172. Ibid., 133.

173. Griffin, "Southern Periphery: East," 335.
174. Campbell, "Coahuiltecans and Their Neighbors," 351.
175. Ibid., 352.
176. Speirs, "Nambe Pueblo," 318.
177. Westermarck, The Origin and Development of the Moral Ideas, Volume I, 399.
178. Tedlock, Finding the Center, Narrative Poetry of the Zuni Indians,4.
179. D'Azevedo, "Introduction," 1.
180. Thomas, Pendleton, & Cappannari, "Western Shoshone," 270.
181. Shimkin, "Eastern Shoshone," 330.
182. Zigmond, "Kawaiisu," 403.
183. Castillo, "The Impact of Euro-American Exploration & Settlement," 104.
184. Myers, "Cahto," 245.
185. Sawyer, "Wappo," 259.
186. Riddell, "Maidu & Konkow," 381.
187. Heizer, "Natural Forces and Native World View," 652.
188. Callaghan, "Lake Miwok," 267.
189. Lapena, "Wintu," 327.
190. Johnson, "Patwin," 357.
191. Bean & Theodoratus, "Western Pomo and Northeastern Pomo," 295.
192. Kelly, "Coast Miwok," 421.
193. M'Lennan, Studies in Ancient History, 99.
194. Dickeman, "Demographic Consequences of Infanticide in Man," 122-123.
195. Grant, "Eastern Coastal Chumash," 511.
196. Smith, "Tubatulabal," 440.
197. Hewitt, "A Constitutional League of Peace in the Stone Age of America," 537.
198. Edmonds & Clark, Voices of the Winds, 323.
199. Murdock, Our Primitive Contemporaries, 302, 311.
200. Lubbock, Pre-Historic Times, 534.
201. Westermarck, The Origin and Development of the Moral Ideas, Volume I, 404.
202. Sayre & Sayre, "American Children and the `Children of Nature'", 717.
203. Ibid.
204. Murdock, Our Primitive Contemporaries, 311.
205. Fury of the Northmen, 136.
206. Bennett, "The Exposure of Infants in Ancient Rome," 341.
207. Frazer, Totemism & Exogamy, Volume 3, 358.
208. Ibid.
209. Reid, A Law of Blood, 39.
210. Frazer, The Dying God, 184.
211. Smith, "Western Woods Cree," 260.
212. Smith, "Chipewyan," 277.
213. Helm, "Dogrib," 301.
214. McClellan, "Tutchone," 500.
215. Savishinsky & Hara, "Hare," 322.
216. Gillespie, "Mountain Indians," 331.
217. Ibid., 335.
218. Hastings, Encyclopedia of Religion & Ethics, Volume I, 6.
219. Radbill, "Children in a World of Violence: A History of Child Abuse," 5.
220. Williamson, "Infanticide: An Anthropological Analysis," 69-70.
221. M'Lennan, Studies in Ancient History, 94.

222. LeVine & LeVine, "Child Abuse and Neglect in Sub-Saharan Africa," 39.
223. Murdock, Our Primitive Contemporaries, 494.
224. Basden, Niger Ibos, 182.
225. M'Lennan, Studies in Ancient History, 98.
226. Levy-Bruhl, Primitive Mentality, 150.
227. Schapera, A Handbook of Tswana Law and Custom, 261.
228. Maugham, Portugese East Africa: The History, Scenery & Great Game of Manica and Sofala, 271.
229. Frazer, The Golden Bough, 333.
230. Kuhse & Singer, Should the Baby Live?, 101.
231. Sumner, Folkways, 274.
232. Shostak, Nisa, The Life and Words of a !Kung Woman, 66.
233. Sargent, "Born to Die: Witchcraft and Infanticide in Bariba Culture," 80.
234. Ibid., 81.
235. M'Lennan, Studies in Ancient History, 94.
236. Ibid., 98.
237. Murdock, Our Primitive Contemporaries, 494.
238. Ibid., 579.
239. Todd, The Primitive Family as an Educational Agency, 126.
240. Levy-Bruhl, Primitive Mentality, 149.
241. Ibid., 150.
242. Schapera, A Handbook of Tswana Law and Custom, 261.
243. Kuhse & Singer, Should the Baby Live?, 101.
244. Maugham, Portugese East Africa: The History, Scenery & Great Game of Manica and Sofala, 271.
245. Sumner, Folkways, 274.
246. Ibid.
247. M'Lennan, Studies in Ancient History, 98.
248. Levy-Bruhl, Primitive Mentality, 150.
249. Basden, Niger Ibos, 262-63.
250. Ibid., 180.
251. Ibid.
252. Ibid., 180, 184, 262-63.
253. M'Lennan, Studies in Ancient History, 98.
254. Ibid., 94.
255. Miller, The Child in Primitive Society, 37.
256. Stigand, To Abyssinia Through an Unknown Land, 234.
257. Roscoe, "Further Notes on the Manners and Customs of the Baganda," 30.
258. Murdock, Our Primitive Contemporaries, 537.
259. Frazer, The Golden Bough, 333.
260. Frazer, The Dying God, 182.
261. Davies, Human Sacrifice, 143.
262. Douglas, "Population Control in Primitive Groups," 263.
263. Wrigley, Population & History, 43.
264. Schapera, A Handbook of Tswana Law and Custom, 261-62.
265. Frazer, The Dying God, 183.
266. Campbell, The Mythic Image, 428.
267. Ibid., 428-29.
268. Rees & Rees, Celtic Heritage: Ancient Tradition in Ireland and Wales, 235.

269. Dickeman, "Demographic Consequences of Infanticide in Man," 122.
270. Ibid.
271. Scheper-Hughes, Death Without Weeping, The Violence of Everyday Life in Brazil, 129.
272. Ibid., 128.
273. Ibid., 362.
274. Ibid., 376.
275. Ibid., 432.
276. Johnson, "The Socioeconomic Context of Child Abuse and Neglect in Native South America," 63.
277. Murdock, Our Primitive Contemporaries, 463-64.
278. Neel, "Lessons From a `Primitive' People," 815.
279. Ibid., 816.
280. Ibid.
281. Cotlow, The Twilight of the Primitive, 65.
282. Ibid., 65-66.
283. Frazer, The Dying God, 185.
284. Locke, Two Treatises of Government, First Treatise, IV.57.4-5, 182.
285. Drapkin, "Social Reaction to Deviant Behaviour Among the Incas of Peru," 3.
286. M'Lennan, Studies in Ancient History, 102.
287. Scrimshaw, "Infanticide in Human Populations: Societal & Individual Concerns," 441.
288. Frazer, The Dying God, 185.
289. Ibid.
290. de Meer, "Mortality in children among the Aymara Indians of southern Peru," 253.
291. 156.3 for infants and 59.7 for children. de Meer, Brgman & Kushner, "Socio-cultural Determinations of Child Mortality in Southern Peru: Including Some Methodological Considerations," 323.
292. Ibid., 323, 328.
293. M'Lennan, Studies in Ancient History, 104.
294. Lubbock, Pre-Historic Times, 544.
295. Grubb, A Church in the Wilds, 75.
296. Hastings, Encyclopedia of Religion & Ethics, Volume I, 6.
297. Miller, The Child in Primitive Society, 38.
298. Durant, Our Oriental Heritage, 50.
299. Bugos & McCarthy, "Ayoreo Infanticide: A Case Study," 510.
300. Davies, Human Sacrifice, 212.
301. Murdock, Our Primitive Contemporaries, 383.
302. Hastings, Encyclopedia of Religion & Ethics, Volume I, 6.
303. Ibid.
304. Ibid.
305. Ibid.
306. Walraven, "Evidence for a Developing Variant of `La Llorona'," 208.
307. Frazer, The Dying God, 186.
308. Scrimshaw, "Infant Mortality and Behavior in the Regulation of Family Size," 387.
309. Hoebel, The Law of Primitive Man, 74.
310. Nansen, Eskimo Life, 103.

311. Mirsky, "The Eskimo of Greenland," 75.
312. Garber, "Eskimo Infanticide," 101.
313. Balikci, "Female Infanticide on the Arctic Coast," 615.
314. Garber, "Eskimo Infanticide," 98.
315. Lowie, Primitive Society, 48.
316. Garber, "Eskimo Infanticide," 98.
317. Ibid.
318. Schrire & Steiger, "A Matter of Life and Death: An Investigation into the Practice of Female Infanticide in the Arctic," 162.
319. Ibid.
320. Ibid., 179.
321. Murdock, Our Primitive Contemporaries, 211.
322. Nansen, Eskimo Life, 152.
323. Gilberg, "Polar Eskimo," 586.
324. Damas, "Central Eskimo: Introduction," 392.
325. Balikci, "Netsilik," 424.
326. Ibid., 427.
327. Mary-Rousseliere, "Iglulik," 443.
328. Arima, "Caribou Eskimo," 455.
329. Langer, "Infanticide: A Historical Survey," 354.
330. Mirsky, "The Eskimo of Greenland," 75.
331. D'Anglure, "Inuit of Quebec," 480.
332. Mirsky, "The Eskimo of Greenland," 75.
333. Ibid., 72.
334. Douglas, "Population Control in Primitive Groups," 263.
335. Hoebel, The Law of Primitive Man, 75.
336. Ibid.
337. Garber, "Eskimo Infanticide," 98.
338. Ibid.
339. Ibid., 99.
340. Ibid.
341. Millman, A Kayak Full of Ghosts, 52.
342. M'Lennan, Studies in Ancient History, 105.
343. Briffault, The Mothers, Volume II, 27.
344. M'Lennan, Studies in Ancient History, 105.
345. Ibid., 106.
346. Ibid.
347. Wrigley, Population & History, 42.
348. Frazer, The Dying God, 181.
349. Ibid., 181-82.
350. Ibid., 182.
351. Durant, Our Oriental Heritage, 50.

CHAPTER VII

EXPOSURE

> "To kill one's own child is shocking to nature, and must therefore be somewhat unusual; but to turn over the care of him upon others, is very tempting to the natural indolence of mankind."[1]

As David Hume aptly noted in the above quotation, parents have always found it easier to abandon an infant to an uncertain fate, no matter what the likely outcome, than to actually kill the child with their own hands. The reason for this judicious choice of methodology is simple: while our species retains a conscientious abhorrence of murder, it accepts a sentence of negligence, as long as the excuse given is reasonable. If a newborn was abandoned in the wild without any means of nourishment or protection, there was always the chance that it could be found by a passing stranger and rescued before it died. This meant that the parent was not ultimately responsible for the subsequent survival or death since it was nature, or the Fates, which was directing the final outcome. You say that such a claim is not reasonable? Read on.

The mythology of man is replete with stories of infants who have been abandoned in the wild and then reared to adulthood by foster parents. It even includes legends of survival based upon the foster parentage of animals. Shakespeare dramatized this hope in the words of Antigonus who was directed to abandon the bastard child of Leontes in the woods:

> Some powerful spirit instruct the kites and ravens to be thy nurses! Wolves and bears, they say, casting their savageness aside, have done like offices of pity.[2]

Whether such hopes of redemption by animals could be considered a reasonable belief or not, it is nevertheless true that many children have in fact been abandoned, rescued and then brought up either as adopted children, or as servants and laborers.[3] Not all waifs left in the wild have succumbed to starvation or the jaws of a hungry predator.

On the other hand, the mere chance that salvation may follow exposure has not been universally accepted as a reasonable excuse to obviate blame. John Locke described the exposure, or selling of children, as "the most shameful action, and most unnatural murder, humane Nature is capable of."[4] No natural indolence to the care of one's child was found in the animal world, he explained, and no such cruelty could be found even in the dens of lions or the nurseries of wolves. Man alone acted more contrary to nature "than the wild and most untamed part of the creation."[5] While Locke's indignation is the typical, majority view, other commentators have taken a more empathic tone and accepted that there was a moral difference between leaving a child alone in the environment and outright murder. The noted Yale historian, John Boswell, thoroughly discussed this practice during Medieval times, and referred to this rescue of abandoned children as the "Kindness of Strangers." He proclaimed that: "Killing children is, moreover, not only morally different from leaving them in a place where they might be picked up and reared but it has demographic consequences by not reducing population size as much."[6]

Boswell pointed out that society has never developed serious sanctions against the abandonment principle.[7] He concluded that most parents who exposed their children were actually offering the child to others in order to be reared, and did not actually intend the child to die. As evidence of this, he explained how the etymology of the Latin word "expositio" was generally used to imply acts of removal, offering or separation as opposed to harm or risk. The English word "exposition" was closer to the general connotation of "expositio" than was the term "exposure."[8] The word "expositio" itself did not necessarily mean that the child would die but rather that it would be offered to others in order that the infant could be nurtured as their own.[9] He also believed that this was the basis for the use of the word "alumnus," which referred to those children who were abandoned and then brought up in foster homes.[10]

But whether the exposure of a child was intended to give the youngster a better chance at life, or was, in fact, an immediate entrance to death, the practice has been extremely common in nearly all ancient nations.[11] It was utilized not only by the poor, but by the rich; not only by uncivilized tribes, but by nations considered modern and advanced. In every society where some type of infanticide has been found, one sees exposure as a primary element of the crime.

A. Greek and Roman Empires

1. Greek Empire

The Greeks appear to have practiced the exposure of children throughout their entire early history.[12] As early as 600 B.C., The Greek father could legally expose any unwanted child, as evidenced by the rulings of Solon, the Athenian statesman and law-giver. Solon restricted many individual freedoms for the betterment of the state, but he permitted the exposure of children as a sanction of law to an already prevalent custom.[13] The Greek father could expose his infant child whether it was legitimate or not, as opposed to the Roman patriarch who only had control over his legitimate offspring.[14]

The ancient Greeks referred to the newborn as a "brephos," or one not yet a member of the family unit, as opposed to an "oikos," or member of the household.[15] The ceremony of "dekate," or "Amphidromia," where the infant was carried around the hearth and given a proper name, took place on the tenth day of an infant's life. Once this was completed, the Athenian father had formally accepted the child as a member of his family and could no longer expose it without committing a homicide.[16] If the decision was made to abandon the newborn, rather than proceed with the dekate, it was often placed in a pot so that the profession of women who discharged it were called "in-potters."[17]

The custom of exposing certain classes of infants was clearly accepted as a moral practice by the major Greek philosophers. Plato, in the *Republic*, discussed how the children of the good offspring would be brought to nurses and raised, while "those of the worse, and of the others born deformed, they will hide away in an unspeakable and unseen place, as is seemly."[18] Aristotle also believed that it was a proper state function to require that the procreation of offspring be limited.[19] Exposure was not his preferred method of dealing with the problem, but could be resorted to if necessary.

But where Plato and Aristotle, two of the most influential philosophers of their time, accepted exposure under select conditions, other Greek scholars rejected the practice outright. Isocrates, the fifth century B.C. Athenian orator, was outraged at the frequent stories of Greek exposure of newborns and equated abandonment as a crime equal to murder.[20] Epictetus, the Stoic philosopher of the first century A.D., admonished that animals do not abandon their young and therefore humans, who were supposedly a more rational and higher form of life, should not ever expose their children as well.[21]

Greek theater, nevertheless, contained frequent references to the practice of exposure, and many a hero was to find his true parentage only later in life. The most famous of these stories involved Oedipus, the man who was fated to become king by unknowingly killing his father and marrying his own mother. Made renowned as the "Oedipus complex" by Freud, the nature of the events characteristically belong to the penetrating mind of the Greek playwrights.

The fictional story of Oedipus began with a warning to Laius, the king of Thebes, that his wife Jocasta would soon bear him a son who one day would return to kill him and take over his throne. When Oedipus was born, Laius ordered the boy exposed on Mt. Cithaeron in a vain attempt to bypass Fate and prevent the predicted disaster.[22] As was often the case with ancient stories of exposure, Oedipus was saved by a shepherd and given to Polybus, the king of Corinth, to raise. When Oedipus was a young man, he heard the omen that he was destined to kill his father and, thinking that his adopted father was his real father, he left the country in a similar attempt to avoid his destined Fate. On the way to Thebes he met, and killed, his real father in a quarrel and then continued on his journey to Thebes where he unwittingly married his real mother.[23]

The ancient Oedipus legend came from a variety of sources including *Oedipodeia* and the *Thebaid.* Many of the renowned Greek playwrights, including Sophocles, Aeschylus and Euripides, wrote plays about Oedipus, although only the one by Sophocles is extant. Unlike most exposures of the time, however, the ankles of Oedipus were pierced by iron spikes which left him a deformity, or "swollen foot," from which he derived his name.[24] During the Middle Ages, folk-tales resembling the Oedipus story appeared in two forms: Judas, which follows an almost identical path, and Gregory, which often eliminates the element of parricide.[25]

Another Greek literary sequence leading to exposure was manifest in the story of *Ion* by Euripides. The plot involved the sexual union of a god and mortal – something which was quite common during that era – and the resultant pregnancy led to shame and finally exposure of the newborn child. In this particular storyline, Apollo forced himself on Creusa, the lovely daughter of Erechtheus, who later gave birth to a son, Ion. In order to hide her dishonorable act, she brought the infant to the top of a mountain in a wicker cradle, and left him there unprotected at the site where she had lain with the god.[26] Apollo watched this sequence from afar and then directed Hermes to bring the boy back to the oracle at Delphi where he was raised by the prophetess of Apollo to become the guardian of the temple.[27] Years later, Creusa, miserable because she had been unable to bear children with her new husband, traveled to Delphi for advice on why she was barren. When she met Ion, she did not initially recognize him as the infant she had exposed. Eventually she realized his true identity and forswore her love to him, explaining that it was Fate, and not a sinister disposition, which drove her malevolent action.[28] Many a young woman in the Heroic Age of Greece was to claim a similar excuse.

In Menander's *The Arbitration*, exposure among the lower class of citizens, rather than the elite, was depicted. Davus discovered an exposed infant and decided he could not afford to keep the baby. "Where am I go get all that money to spend," he asked himself, and "what do I want with all that worry?"[29] Children were often considered a luxury in those days, and many of the poorer class could simply not support an added expense.

The comedic plays of Aristophanes portrayed exposure of newborns in a lighter tone. In *Thesmophoriazusae*, Mnesilochus reported how a certain woman remained in childbirth for an incredibly long period of ten days. The woman's lover patiently waited for the delivery, and all her friends and neighbors sympathized with her prolonged painful state. In reality, her pregnancy was a hoax and the delay involved the time necessary for her servant to go and find a baby left exposed in a basket to pretend was her own.[30]

2. Roman Empire

Historians generally accept that exposure was very prevalent during the centuries of the Roman Empire.[31] It affected every class of person, and was so ingrained throughout Roman society that many regarded it as "remarkable that other nations did not expose children."[32] Boswell estimated that the rate of abandonment at Rome during the first three centuries of the Christian era was about 20-40%.[33] Bennett argued that actual exposure in Rome was rare in the early Empire, but that definite cases did appear near the end of the republic.[34] While scholars continue to debate the extent of the problem even today, all agree that the Roman populace accepted the practice readily.

The prevalence of infant exposure in this era was due to many factors, but a callous attitude toward the welfare of the very young infant, coupled with the financial burden of its care, was likely the commonest reason. There was no easy, or effective, means to prevent pregnancy, and so poor families continued to have children until their resources were totally depleted.[35] This was especially true in the provinces, where unstable economic circumstances led to an even greater chance of poverty and famine. Not only were there additional expenses for food and health care after the birth of a child, but the ability of the mother to continue her daily necessary chores was impeded. As the capacity to adequately feed every additional child diminished, the need for abandonment of the newborn increased.[36] Social acceptance of this fact was a practical response to a harsh reality.

The abandoned Roman infant was often placed in a conspicuous locale, and anyone who wanted to raise the foundling could then claim it at as his own. Boswell argued that this was the case in the majority of exposures, and that it was preferable to a parent actually killing the child.[37] By exposing the child, the parents would not have to resort to infanticide and could thereby relieve themselves of socially unacceptable responsibility.

There were many stories of such abandoned infants being raised to adulthood, although verification is obviously very difficult. Juvenal sarcastically wrote that infants abandoned beside cesspools "meet our need for pontiffs and priests with bodies that falsely bear the name of Scauri."[38] It may very well be that some foundlings thrived in later life, but it is likely that the majority died on the very spot they were laid. Given the extreme dependence of the human newborn for careful nurture and sustenance, it seems improbable that infants left alone at such an early stage of life could survive for very long while exposed to the elements.

At the time, the loss of these newborns was not totally ignored. Lucian, in *Voyage to the Lower World*, told of how an invoice of new arrivals contained three hundred babies "including those that were exposed."[39] Dante, also confined to Purgatory the "souls of babes whom death bit off in their first innocence, before baptism washed them of their taint of earth."[40]

Despite our present-day revulsion toward exposure, the Romans could look to their earliest beginnings and find that exposure was sanctioned by law. Romulus, the very founder of the city who had been abandoned as a child himself, permitted the exposure of deformed children. According to Dionysius, a parent was empowered to expose maimed or monstrous infants "provided they first show them to their five nearest neighbors and these also approved."[41] Another edict forbade the exposing of children after they were three years old.[42] If they did not comply with this requirement, they could be penalized one-half of their fortune. While these details of the law under Romulus survive only in references made by later commentators, there is no reason to believe they were not readily accepted by the populace.

The Twelve Tables, which was the first codification of Roman Law from the fifth century B.C., did not allow for the murder of a child once born, but it did not object to its being left to die without nourishment. This was seen as a morally neutral act since "the infant had not yet begun to participate in the life of its social group."[43] That death was almost certain to occur if the baby was not quickly discovered did not make it ethically unacceptable.

The right of ordering the exposure of a newborn child rested solely with the Roman father, and the mother could not legally abandon her child. The infant was not automatically born into a family relationship and the *patria potestas* gave the father the option to refuse to accept any child he so desired.[44] Although foundlings were assumed to be of slave status, it was also legally possible to expose a freeborn child.[45] If the father elected to abandon such an offspring, he also retained the right to later reclaim the infant as long as he paid the cost of rearing.[46] The Theodosian Code clearly explained the process of recovery: "Such claimant shall provide another of the same kind or shall pay a price which can be adequate."[47] This was generally known as the right of the paterfamilias, and was the ruling of Alexander Severus as late as 224 A.D.[48] Gellius, the second century Roman author, while abhorring the practice of abortion, did not disapprove of abandonment under these terms.[49] This would later change under the rulings of emperors in the Christian Era.

In the early years of the Roman Republic, the children were usually brought to the traditional spot for exposure: a column near the Velabrum where they were left on display for speculators who often took them to sell as slaves or prostitutes.[50] Sextus Pompeius Festus referred to these columns in the market place as "lactaria," or "nursing columns," because people would bring their nursing infants there to be deposited.[51] Boswell believed that most children left at these locations were promptly taken and reared by others.[52] In *The Lady of Andros*, by Terence, Glycerium easily pretended to be pregnant and then, when she was ready to "deliver", sent a maid "straight away to fetch the midwife and bring a baby as well."[53] It was to the lactaria where the servant likely went.

This ready acceptance of exposure was due, in part, to the belief that a newborn was not equivalent in worthiness to a mature adult. While children would become more rational, and thereby acceptable, with education and growth, the newborn was not yet filled with the type of human strength which gave it a right to live. Seneca related how when he was first begot: "I was a creature without reason and a burden to others. You should have exposed me to death as a child."[54] The parent who abandoned a child was not identified with monstrous, or inhumane, motives but rather was seen as acting in permissible terms.

In fact, the earliest concerns of the state over the practice of exposure was not with the death of the infant, but rather that it was possible that a child could be born free, exposed for reasons of economy, and then rescued and raised as a slave. At a time when pride in being a free Roman was more important than any other aspect of life, this potential degradement was disturbing.

When Pliny the Younger was governor in the provinces of Bithynia, at the end of the first century A.D., the status of abandoned children was very unsettled. He wrote to the emperor Trajan asking about how the foundlings were to be legally handled, and what was to be the status of their maintenance.[55] Trajan replied that this issue had been frequently discussed in Rome, but that there had not yet been a general regulation extended to the provinces. He was of the opinion, however, that allowing free-born Romans to be raised in a state of servitude was wrong, and that their right of freedom should be allowed without repayment for their maintenance.[56] This meant that if one decided to raise a newborn foundling as a slave, they would have to risk losing the child later if it was shown that the infant had been a free-born Roman. Under such circumstances, the adoptive family would not be compensated for the monetary expenditures they had made.

While this attitude might seem incongruous to modern social thought, one must remember that children had no rights of any kind outside of the family unit. By not allowing the severing of the right of birth to a free parent, simply because the father chose not to raise the infant, also meant that the child would not lose the designation of being a free-born citizen of Rome. This assured that they could never be legally raised into slavery unless the action was taken under a sale by his father.

But even with this limited advantage, many voices disapproved of the extensive autocratic Roman parental authority and slowly the social and legal acceptance of exposure began to weaken. It was not until 331 A.D., however, that Emperor Constantine took away the right of a parent who exposed a child to later reclaim it by simple payment of the costs incurred. He decreed that: "If any person should take up a boy or girl child that has been cast out of its home with the knowledge and consent of its father or owner, and if he should rear this child to strength with his own sustenance, he shall have the right to keep the said child under the same status."[57] This meant that suits to recover such children by their rightful parents were finally abolished. The effect was further intensified in 336 A.D. when Constantine declared the making of eunuchs a capital offense.[58] This was an important pronouncement for it reduced the major outlet for the sale of abandoned boys which had helped to support its persistence. The first steps to prevent exposure were therefore those which declared the bonds of parenthood to be broken by the act of abandonment.

In 374 A.D., Valentinian declared, for the first time, that all parents who abandoned their children would actually be penalized.[59] He condemned the exposure of children and also made infanticide a capital offence, the first Christian emperor to hold this extreme penalty.[60]

The continuing diminution in the authority of the paterfamilias, and the moral abhorrence of abandonment, was further intensified by the Emperors Honorius and Theodosius Augustuses in 412 A.D. They held that "we leave no avenue of recovery to those who expose for measure to death" for no one can call his own a child "when he scorned when it was perishing."[61] This required, however, the testimony of a bishop or cleric that the child was in fact exposed. Nevertheless, the Roman legal system had finally changed a tradition that had been present since the very founding of Rome.

But while the illegality of exposure was now clear, the practice did not cease. Not only were children still abandoned at birth, but parents continued to try and recover their children later in life, making life miserable for the adoptive parents. In 442 A.D. a council in Vaison, in southern Gaul, complained that abandoned children were "nowadays exposed more to dogs than to kindness" because people were fearful of legal action if they picked up such a child.[62] The council clarified the position of the church that anyone who reared an exposed child was legally assured of their claim, and that any parent who later tried to bring a charge against the finder was "to be punished with the ecclesiastical sanctions for murder."[63]

While times were changing in Rome, however, the effect that Roman tradition had on conquered countries was still present. In Egypt, for example, abandonment of infants was not very common during centuries of self-rule.[64] Certain passages in the Gnomon of the Idiologus indicated that there had been some exposure of children in Egypt in ancient times, but the practice was quite rare.[65] After the customs of the Greeks and Romans were superimposed on Egyptian life, however, exposure became more prevalent. Unwanted children were often abandoned on rubbish heaps and poor people, who required an inexpensive slave, would take the baby and raise it for this purpose. This practice was inferred in the naming of such infants "coprus," or "coprise," which meant "picked off a dunghill."[66] Once the populace saw that leaving an unwanted child unprotected at birth was not a criminal act, it became more commonplace and accepted.

B. Judaism and Christianity

1. Judaism

The imagery of exposure was well known to the ancient Hebrew people. When YHWH, the Lord of the Israelites, came to Ezekiel in a vision and complained of the abominations of the people in Jerusalem, He directed the prophet to remind the Hebrews that: "No one cared enough about you to do any of these things for you out of pity for you, but you were left to die in the field, spurned, on the day you were born."[67] It was only the Lord that passed by and saved the Jews from destruction.[68]

Moses himself, the bearer of the word of God from Mt. Sinai, had been exposed as an infant to save him from the command of the Pharaoh to kill all Hebrew boys as soon as they were born "in order that they might not live."[69] When the mother of Moses gave birth, she hid him for three months rather than follow the order to throw the child into the surging waters.[70] But as the infant grew in size over the next few months, it became obvious that she could no longer continue the ruse. She therefore put Moses on a small raft along the river's edge where he floated downstream and was eventually found by the Pharaoh's daughter.[71]

Ishmael, the son of Abraham and Hagar, was also exposed, although for only a brief period of time, and at a much older age. According to the Old Testament, when Sarai and Abram were old and childless, Sarai gave Abraham her maid, an Egyptian girl named Hagar, to have as a second wife in order to provide a natural heir.[72] The union succeeded, and Ishmael became Abraham's first-born child and future progenitor of the Arabs. At first all was well. But then, when Isaac was born, Sarah, as she now was called, decided that Ishmael must not share the inheritance with her own son and demanded that Abraham cast him out of their house.[73] Abraham did not argue with his wife, and gave Hagar some bread and water and sent her into the wilderness of Beer-sheba. For a time the mother and child wandered aimlessly looking for respite but gradually, as the water was used up, Hagar weakened and despondently "left the child under one of the shrubs," in order to not watch him die of thirst.[74] The angel of God appeared and told her to pick the young boy up for "I will make of him a great nation."[75] The mother and child were saved and, like the founding of Rome by Romulus, and the liberation of the Jews by Moses, an abandoned son became a sign of future fecundity for the Arab race.

That some degree of exposure persisted during the history of the early Jews is certain, but the extent is unclear. The *Talmud* took it for granted that some children would be abandoned, and discussed appropriate ways to deal with the problem. There were enough children in this category to be included as one of the ten genealogical classes of Jews that went up from Babylon after the exile: priests, levites, Israelites, Halalim, proselytes, freedmen, mamzerim, nethinim, shetuki, and foundlings.[76] The foundlings, or "Asufi," were: "Any that was picked up from the street and knows neither the father nor his mother."[77]

Just as the issue of free-birth was important to the Romans, the correct classification of the abandoned child was critical to the Jews. There was extensive discussion in the *Talmud* on how to differentiate between an infant that was abandoned out of necessity, and one that was left out of shame. The latter was equated with an illegitimate birth, and referred to as a foundling. The child was not considered a foundling, for example, if "he has been massaged with oil, fully powdered, has beads on him, wears a tablet with an inscription or an amulet."[78] This effort on the part of the parent implied a caring concern for the infant's future. If the child was suspended from a tree, however, where a wild beast could reach him, then the child would be considered as a foundling for the parents would have taken better care of a legitimate child.[79] If the child was exposed on a sorb bush, which was considered haunted by demons, he would be considered as a foundling, but not if found near a synagogue, close to town, where many people would congregate.[80] If found in a pit of date stones, shallow water, or a public thoroughfare he was a foundling; if found in the side passages off public ways, or in swift water, he was not.[81]

In addition to the realization that foundlings were abandoned because they were illegitimate, there was also a recognition that, at times, children were "thrown away on account of poverty."[82] As we have seen in other societies, while the moral teachings of the leaders were clearly against this age-old tradition, the people trying to live desperate lives would not always reflect those commandments.

Accepting that the practice was a reality, despite the pronouncements of the Torah, the rabbis were concerned that if a father abandoned a child, and then later married her unknowingly, he could possibly be committing incest. This was a sin equal to that of murder. The rabbis therefore only allowed a foundling to marry another Jew if the person abandoned "offered evidence of parental concern."[83] It is obvious from these detailed precautions that more than theoretical issues were at stake.

But while Jews may have occasionally practiced exposure, there was never any legal acceptance or social approval like was seen among the Greeks and Romans. The practice was severely condemned by Philo, the eminent Jewish philosopher of the first century A.D. He noted with disdain that it was "a sacrilegious practice which among many other nations, through their ingrained inhumanity, has come to be regarded with complacence."[84] He passionately explained that although children were often left exposed with the excuse that they may be saved, the reality was that the parents were leaving them to suffer the most distressing fate:

> For all the beasts that feed on human flesh visit the spot and feast unhindered on the infants. Carnivorous birds, too, come flying down and gobble up the fragments.[85]

There was little doubt of how gruesome would be the fate of these innocent foundlings.

Philo described the practice of exposure among the barbarians with disgust and condemned it as being against the laws of nature. He called the murder of one's own child the worst abomination that could be committed.[86] While some parents claimed that they exposed babies in a desert place with the hope of their being saved, in reality they were only providing prey for beasts who visited the spot and "feast unhindered on the infants, a fine banquet provided by their sole guardians."[87] Because the Torah teachings were not concerned with the victim's age, Philo concluded that the act of exposure was forbidden by the writings of Moses, and equal to murder.[88]

Jewish folk-tales, nevertheless, occasionally referenced instances of infant abandonments among otherwise faithful congregants. In "The Story of a Woman Whose Upper Body was Beastlike in Form," the daughter of a rabbi was extremely learned in the ways of the Torah, but very homely in outward appearance. After her marriage, when her husband saw her for the first time without a veil, he promptly left in the morning, never to return. The young woman, now pregnant and alone, did not know what to do. When a baby was born nine months later, she swathed him in a garment, packed her own belongings, and left him at the entry of her parent's house, knowing they would raise the boy as their own child.[89]

2. Christianity

The early Christian writers, like their Jewish predecessors, abhorred the practice of exposure which they found prevalent among many contemporary societies. Yet they found themselves in the rather odd position of being accused by the Romans of the very custom they so vehemently condemned. Their response to these vile inferences was intense. Tertullian called the charge ridiculous since "we are not permitted to destroy even the fetus in the womb."[90] Athenagoras, in *Embassy for the Christians*, summarized the Christian position rationally: "The same man cannot forbid the exposure of children, equating such exposure with child murder, and then slay a child that has found one to bring it up."[91] The Apologists argued that to think Christians would accept the practice of exposure was ludicrous to anyone who understood the teachings of Jesus Christ: Christians were a peaceful people, and would never tolerate murder of anyone in general, and of their own children in particular.

But although the philosophical basis for their position was secure, we still find within the early Christian writings acceptance of the fact that abandonment of children was practiced by some of the new converts. Justin Martyr admonished the practice and noted that "almost all so exposed are brought up to prostitution."[92] He included both boys and girls in this assessment, and was mindful of the fact that those infants who did not die of the exposure were generally sold into slavery. But he warned that Christians feared to expose children "lest some of them be not picked up, but die, and we become murderers."[93]

Clement of Alexandria, in the third century A.D., also cautioned that fathers: "Unmindful of children of theirs that have been exposed, often without their knowledge, have intercourse with a son that has debauched himself, and daughters that are prostitutes."[94] Sexual contacts were not limited only to the heterosexual variety and Clement called those who abandoned their children "child killers" and added:

> What cause has a man for the exposing of a child? If disinclined to have children, he ought not to have married in the first place.[95]

Minucius Felix continued these concerns as he castigated the pagan practice of exposure. He was also critical of the loose sexual morals of the day and how this would increase the sin involved: "Since you pursue Venus promiscuously, since you engender children passim, since you often expose even those born at home to the kindness of strangers, you necessarily end up having relations with your relatives and children."[96]

Tertullian did not hesitate to compare exposure directly to infanticide, but admitted that many of the children did not die.[97] His remonstration noted that: "You expose your children, in the first place, to be rescued by the kindness of passing strangers, or abandon them to be adopted by better parents."[98] The hope of a better life for your child, however, did not obviate the iniquity of the act. Similarly, Lactantius found abandonment of children as wicked as infanticide, but acknowledged that the exposure was often made by a parent who did not necessarily wish to kill the child.[99]

St. Basil of Caesarea distinguished infant exposure into categories dependent upon the family structure. The first included those women who "despise the child they have born and abandon it in the road when it could have been saved."[100] These mothers were punished for the crime of murder, and could not plead a lesser crime. Their actions were based purely in self-serving motives and there were no extenuating circumstances to explain away their violent response. He found some compassion, however, for others who exposed their children because of extreme poverty.[101] While not directly approving of such an action, he did not mention any appropriate punishment for these mothers, and appeared to argue that it was not comparable to murder.

St. Ambrose, the Bishop of Milan in the fourth century A.D., also noted how the poor "abandon their children and expose them, and if they are recovered deny that they are theirs."[102] This realization by the Church hierarchy that poverty could force otherwise good people to do wicked deeds helped to encourage the formation of foundling homes.

Christianity was able to bolster its moral regulatory pronouncements with threats that exceeded those available to the secular world. Where criminal acts, as defined by local governments, could only be punished here on earth, Christianity emphasized eternal damnation. You might be able to escape detection by the local sheriff by exposing your infant in the middle of the night, but in the Final Judgment your guilt would be revealed. In the Apocalypse tradition according to James, there were two groups who helped expedite the punishment of parents during the Judgment of Christ. One of the groups called to testify to the angel Temlakos were children who had been exposed to death at birth. The fate of their parents depended upon the circumstances of that event.[103] This also was found in the Apocalypse of Paul, Esra, and in the vision reported by Boniface.[104] Any parent who decided to leave a child unprotected in the wild would have to face judgment by that soul before their eternal fate was determined.

C. Middle Ages and Renaissance

1. Middle Ages

Medieval life was filled with many lethal problems: disease was rampant, food often scarce, and war an ever-present hazard. Under the pressure of such serious disruptions to their day-to-day existence, parents were not always able to worry about having to care for newborn infants, and abandonment was widespread. William Lecky described exposure during the Middle Ages as "practiced on a gigantic scale with absolute impunity, noticed by writers with most frigid indifference."[105] John Boswell, as well, found that it "appears in nearly every type of historical document, from law to literature."[106] While the end of the Roman Empire suggested that exposure would become less tolerated, the harsh realities of medieval peasant life vaporized such pronouncements into thin air.

Boswell summarized the reasons for this exaggerated problem of exposure during the Medieval era as follows:

> Parents abandoned their offspring in desperation when they were unable to support them, due to poverty or disaster; in shame, when they were unwilling to keep them because of their physical condition or ancestry (e.g., illegitimate or incestuous); in self-interest or the interest of another child, when inheritance or domestic resources would be compromised by another mouth; in hope, when they believed that someone of greater means or higher standing might find them and bring them up in better circumstances; in resignation, when a child was of unwelcome gender or ominous auspices; or in callousness, if they simply could not be bothered with parenthood.[107]

This brief list of the more common causes of exposure would fit nicely into almost any historical era, but the Middle Ages seems to have particularly amplified the effect which stress placed on troubled families. Burdened with famine and fear, oppressed by local and foreign lords, and suppressed by the moral rulings of the church, the peasantry could not properly care for the large number of children born.

Two of the more accepted reasons underlying this rise in the prevalence of exposure was the relative overpopulation of a very poor populace in Europe, and the large number of illegitimate births.[108] Poverty and shame became devastating obstructions to the caring of a child after birth, and the result was the widespread use of exposure.

The poor would often abandon children in the hope that they would be rescued and become servants in more prosperous households. Such a view had already been alluded to by Juvenal who felt that the exposed child often wound up better off after abandonment than if he would have remained with the natural parent: "Fortune, in waggish Sport and silent night, smiles on these naked babes; she keeps them warm and hugs them in her Bosom, then conveys them into the houses of the Great."[109]

The outright sale of a child into slavery was no longer allowed, but it was still legal for those with means to pick up a foundling and raise it as a slave. Destitute parents would rather chance a future hope of freedom and success for their children, then commit them to a certain miserable existence by remaining where they were. There was a widespread belief that exposed children would not only likely survive, but many would even flourish and become popes, kings and heroes.[110] While such success stories were found in numerous biographies of that era, encouraging the act of exposure when times were tough, the majority of abandoned infants were likely dead before the age of ten.

In addition to the commonplace trials of poverty, the birth of bastards was probably more common during the Middle Ages than at any other time in Western history. Clerics were forbidden to marry under Church law, but they nevertheless carried on sexual liaisons and then abandoned their children to hide any signs of illegitimacy.[111] Armies spreading over Europe during the centuries of the Holy Crusade left a path of pregnant women, rejected and alone, with no ability to pay for the newborn child's care, and no support structure to ease their re-acceptance into society. The institution of marriage was not yet formalized, and women were frequently left to deal with their pregnancy in the only way they could. They had little choice but expose the newborn to the elements if they were to be able to survive themselves.

The incidence of exposure among the peasant class was so great, that early Christian theologians warned men, in the strongest possible terms, not to visit the many brothels which were around. It was not only because they were committing the sin of sexual promiscuity, but because "they might unwittingly commit incest with a child they had abandoned."[112] Priestly concerns were realistic during those Dark Ages and their alarms over this especially venial sin was appropriate.

There were many additional reasons why abandoned children were picked up and raised by foster families. Between 10-25% of married couples at the time were infertile from medical disorders and their only hope of having children was to find an exposed infant.[113] While some of these couples desired children out of love and a desire to share their home with family members, others simply desired cheap help to aide with the duties of everyday life and to provide assistance in case of infirmity or old age. Infants supplied a ready source of servants and inexpensive labor to those so in need. Where a caring parent might spend inordinate time and money over the welfare of their child, an uninterested owner would not likely squander their savings on the rearing of a slave.

Another source of succor for the exposed was the Catholic Church itself. While condemning the practice of exposure on theologic grounds, the Church actually took in many foundlings and kept them permanently under their control. This practice, known as oblation, has been extensively documented by John Boswell in *The Kindness of Strangers*, and is discussed more completely later in this chapter.

Boswell argued that Christianity may have actually increased the incidence of abandonment by its extreme ethical stand on procreation. The Catholic church prohibited attempts at birth control, a stand which remains rigidly enforced today. This assured that adherents would continually produce children as long as they remained sexually active despite their inability to afford another mouth to feed. Since the killing of a child would result in the severe punishment of burning for all eternity in Hell, these poor peasants found themselves in a moral dilemma. The church eventually eased its unyielding stance and agreed to take in abandoned children for care. But by providing a means to accept unwanted infants in its churches and monasteries through the process of oblation, and also through the care of foundlings by the development of respite hospitals, the church in essence encouraged the practice of abandonment and found itself furnishing an acceptable outlet for the very condition it was trying to prevent.[114]

But despite the widespread popular acceptance of exposure in Europe during the Middle Ages, legal rulings against the practice continued to expand. Pope Gregory, in the thirteenth century A.D., extended the denial of recovery to parents who abandoned their children and later desired to recover them by payment of their upkeep. He ruled that if children were abandoned with the knowledge or consent of their fathers, then they were automatically freed from his legal control.[115] If the Church had raised these children, however, it retained parental control without interference from the natal family.

The laws of Teruel, a province of Spain during the thirteenth century, forbade the selling of daughters and "any woman who is proven to have abandoned her child shall be punished and constrained to care for the child, according to the law."[116] The Castilian *Fuero Real* also punished abandonment. If the child was abandoned knowingly, then the parent lost all authority. But if it occurred without his knowledge, then the parent could reclaim the child by paying all expenses.[117] Punishment for infanticide, if the child should die, was severe: "Anyone who exposes an infant who then dies because there is no one to take care of him will himself be liable to death for this causing a death to take place is the same as killing someone."[118]

2. Renaissance

As the tribulations and ignorance of the Dark Ages began to vaporize into the fresh new approaches of the Renaissance, much of the civilized world finally witnessed the cultural advances which would initiate the heritage of Humanism. Arts and sciences flourished in an atmosphere of open exploration, religious debates shook the rigidity of the emerging Church, and nations once again generated strong central governments that stabilized the lives of its citizens. Adults everywhere were able to reap the advantages of this more comfortable life, but newborns were nevertheless abandoned by the hundreds of thousands.

Statistics from births in Italy during the Renaissance era document the extent of this problem. In Florence the percentage of children who were abandoned after baptism ranged from a low of 14%, at the opening of the eighteenth century, to a high of 43% in the nineteenth. In Milan, the opening of the eighteenth century witnessed a rate of 16%, and by the end it was 25%.[119] While these numbers seem astounding at first glance, they take on even greater impact when one realizes that the true figures are likely higher since the very nature of the process is so secretive that many cases will not appear in the public record for statistical analysis. Many infants were abandoned or destroyed during concealed pregnancies, and the eventual disposition by the mother was never known. This means that during some years in Italy, the abandonment rate was greater than 50% of all children born.

The situation in France was similar. According to Boswell: "In every city in France in the eighteenth century where it is known, the rate of abandonment was 10 percent or better."[120] In Toulouse in the eighteenth century, the rate of known abandonment of recorded births varied from a mean of 10%, in the first half of the century, to 17-25% on the second half.[121] In poor quarters of the city, the rate approached 40%.[122] In Lyons, almost one-third of the children born were abandoned.[123] In Paris, 9% of births were foundlings in 1721, and from 1730-1820, it ranged from 13-35%.[124] Estimates on how many children that were abandoned were taken, and raised by others, varies but it does appear that many were saved.[125] In the year 1833, 127,507 children were abandoned, somewhere between 20-30 percent of all births.[126]

Emile Zola, in *L'Assommoir*, described how the situation was even a subject of conversation among the working class. A popular folk-song comforted:

> The poor little babe that the mother abandons
> Can always find refuge, make up for her loss,
> For God in high heaven looks out for his children,
> And God's child finds shelter and love by the cross.[127]

The supposed success of the foundling homes in Paris and Stockholm were discussed over much of the world as countries debated how best to prevent the exposure of unwanted children. Many asserted that infanticide was not heard of where successful institutions were available.[128]

Spain followed the trend of other European countries. In Madrid, the admissions to the Inclusa foundling hospital in 1765 was 14.1% of all recorded baptisms in the city while from 1801-1807 it was 26.2%.[129] Spain was under the strict moral control of the Catholic Church, and births among unwedded women were likely associated with even higher abandonment rates.

Foundling hospitals were developed late in Germany, primarily because of the distractions of war throughout the Holy Roman Empire. The first one was opened in 1761 by Landgrave Frederick II of Hesse-Cassel.[130] Despite evidence that illegitimacy ratios in the eighteenth century were at five percent, there were many arguments against support of such homes because of cost, high infant mortality, lack of maternal love, and the encouragement of sexual intercourse out of wedlock.[131]

In China there was extensive exposure of children well into the nineteenth century.[132] Foundling homes were first set up in the twelfth century but then were little used until the Qing dynasty (1644-1911 A.D.) when they were reestablished.[133] Jesuit missionaries to China in the seventeenth century found thousands of babies, mostly females, thrown on the streets like refuse to be collected each morning and then dumped into a huge pit outside the city.[134] John Weyland explained that among the Chinese who lived near rivers, exposure generally involved tying a gourd around the body with the hopes that as it floated down the river, someone would decide to keep the baby and rescue it from death.[135] In a country where there were greater excesses in population than almost anywhere else on earth, it was unlikely that many were saved. Weyland added that exposure was primarily confined to the cities, and in areas near water, where crowding was common.[136]

Another form of exposure occurred in England where women who bore illegitimate children put their babies out to nurse and then abandoned them.[137] Upwards of 50,000 illegitimate children were born annually, and fully two-thirds were put out to nurse.[138] The mother would usually leave the child two to four weeks after its birth and agree to pay a set fee each week. The mortality of the children under the care of these nurses – baby farmers as they were called – was 75-90%.[139] If the baby was not left with a nurse, it was commonly left at a doorstep of a house wrapped in an old blanket, a practice which came to be known as "dropping."[140]

But it was not only by sending their illegitimate children to baby farmers that the English populace practiced child abandonment. A general carelessness about the welfare of the young developed in England during this era, and many children were left to wander the streets in pitiful disparity, begging for food from passersby with little interest in their health or well-being. Erasmus, as early as 1543, had decried the exposure of children asking how parents could be so heartless in their actions: "What is more cruel than those who are said to expose their children because bringing them up is a nuisance?"[141] He was so upset with the circumstances that he found the use of a wet-nurse equivalent to abandoning the child:

> Isn't it a kind of exposure to hand over the tender infant, still red from its mother, drawing breath from its mother, crying for its mother's care – a sound said to move even wild beasts – to a woman who perhaps has neither good health nor good morals and who, finally, may be much more concerned about a bit of money than about a whole baby?[142]

He argued that "simply to take on some hired nurse for a baby still warm from its mother is a kind of exposure."[143]

But the Renaissance, and the Age of Enlightenment which followed, did not change parental attitudes towards their offspring. The public may have been better educated in the Arts and Sciences than their earlier counterparts, but when faced with hardship, the response of many adults was self-survival. If exposure was not to be the preferred way of dealing with an unwanted birth, society would have to find the means to secure the welfare of individual families, and offer them alternative methods of care. As a realistic option, this did not occur until the 20th century.

D. Modern Society

1. Tribes

Among primitive cultures, where food was limited and birth control ineffectual, abandonment of newborns remained a common occurrence. As aptly described by Lloyd DeMause, hunter-gatherer tribes are "in the infanticidal mode."[144] And when the decision to not rear a newborn is made, it is often exposure, rather than outright slaughter, that is the procedure of choice. The practices of these tribal societies is discussed in more detail in the Chapter on Tribes.

2. Modern Times

While the social leniency towards exposure has changed in modern times, it is a reflection more of reformation within the legal definitions of child abuse and neglect, then in the attitudes of parents toward what is morally right or wrong. If there is anything we have learned from the utilization of exposure throughout the ages, it is that parents have often acted out of necessity, and that they have believed that natural law has allowed them to function in the manner they have. Church edicts and legal stipulations aside, the emotional decision that is made at the moment of birth cannot be reproduced in a courtroom of law.

The legality of exposure has been an enigma since the crime, though usually recognized as a wrongful act, has not been uniformly punished. In England, common-law required that before the exposure of a child could be considered an actual crime, there had to be an injury sustained.[145] If the child died, for example, then one could proceed with a charge of murder. If there was illness or a non-fatal injury, then abuse could be claimed. But if there was simply abandonment, and no residual damage, there was no common-law basis for criminal charges.

In America, the exposure of a child did not have to result in injury in order to be a criminal act under most state statutory law.[146] Abandonment of an infant was punishable as an illegal act by itself. While most people would agree that this approach is more sensitive to the needs of helpless children, it actually does little to prevent exposure when a parent decides that a newborn is unwanted. Punishment for the crime, by necessity, is limited and generally the infant is simply given to a foster family which is the very result the parent wanted in the first place.

Some countries, on the other hand, have extended the severity of punishment for infant exposure beyond a slap on the wrist. The Roman-Dutch common law of British Guiana, Ceylon and South Africa differentiate exposure from infanticide. The killing of a child is included under the term parricide, and is generally punished by being broken to death on a wheel, or strangulation.[147] But while not considered a capital crime, abandoning a child for understandable reasons is still not dealt with lightly:

> They, who expose their children, are mostly punished with whipping, branding and banishment, or other less punishment at discretion. Which is to be understood of those who out of poverty abandon and expose their children in public places, where they may immediately be found.[148]

The law was less lenient, however, for those who seemed to be uninterested in the fate of their child. The criminal code read: "Who, without any necessity, put away their children in some lonely place, where they may perish of cold and hunger, are punished with death."[149] If the infant was treated so inhumanely as to likely die, then the criminality of the act was seen as equivalent to murder.

With health care availability becoming a greater means to assure the survival of newborns who heretofore would have had little chance of living through the postpartum period, a new form of abandonment exists today where babies are left at hospitals by parents who simply cannot afford to care for them at home – the so-called "boarder babies."[150] These parents began with a desire to raise their child properly, but soon found their patience, and their pocketbook, exhausted. They had the child admitted to a hospital and then never returned to take them home. A study by the Child Welfare League of America, in 1992, found that 607 babies were being boarded at 72 institutions each month because of this problem, and that 85% had been exposed to either drugs or alcohol in the womb.[151]

E. Signs

When children were abandoned in ancient times, it was common for the infant to be left with some memorabilia as a means of recognition at a later date. Such a means of identity was also intended to help promote rescue of the child since it showed concern on the part of the parent which indicated that the infant was otherwise worth saving. If the discoverer wished to assure future anonymity, the signs could easily be discarded.

Some historians believe that these preparations were not devised for the purpose of prolonging the infant's life, but rather were little more than a readiness for the death process. Much as objects were placed in the tombs of adults in Egypt to help with the transfer to "life" in the hereafter, the child was left with some type of payment to be offered at "heaven's door."[152]

But while certain societies, like the Egyptians, might have intended this meaning, others, like the Jews, clearly did not have such beliefs. In the rabbinical interpretations of Talmudic law, the child was not considered as a foundling if "he has been massaged with oil, fully powdered, has beads on him, wears a tablet with an inscription or an amulet."[153] These elaborate measures indicated that the baby was legitimate, and should be cared for and raised as a Jew.

Stories of exposure utilizing similar signs abounded in classical literature. In *Ion*, by Euripides, Creusa followed an ancient custom begun by Athene, and placed with the infant son she had borne to Apollo an embroidery from her robe depicting two snakes as protectors of his safety.[154] She had woven the sign in her childhood, and had a Gorgon in the center with serpents fringed like an aegis. Included as well were a gold ornament and an olive wreath which continued to flourish, even when Ion was grown, "because the tree is holy."[155]

In *Daphnis and Chloe*, by Longus, the earliest known Greek novel, Daphnis was found by a goatherd suckled by a she-goat, dressed with a purple cloak, gold brooch and ivory dagger.[156] The baby was raised and later fell in love with Chloe, who also was found abandoned by a shepherd in a cave with a gold thread girdle, gilded sandals and gold anklets. Daphnis' heritage was eventually found to be a royal one, and the eventual marriage of the two had a happy ending because of the proper ancestry which was proven by the signs of their birth.

Heliodorus, in *An Ethiopian Romance*, told the story of Charicleia who had been exposed as an infant with a necklace of gems and a ribbon woven of silken thread on which was embroidered in native characters the story of the child in order that she might be recognized.[157]

In *The Marriage of Figaro*, by Beaumarchais, Figaro was a foundling who eventually was realized to be the abandoned son of the countess.[158] When asked for proof by the count, Figaro answered:

> My Lord! If the lace shawls, embroidered wrappings, and jewels the brigands found on me did not indicate high birth, the precautions someone had taken to give me marks of distinction would be sufficient testimony that I was a child someone valued.[159]

That such signs were also intended as partial payment to the rescuer was evident in Menander's *The Arbitration* where a child was exposed and then found by one man but given to another to raise. A dispute arose between them over who was the rightful owner of the valuable trinkets that had been left with the infant. Smicrines decided that the objects belong to the exposed child, rather than to the man who originally saved him.[160]

And it was not only in fictional tales that the use of signs was apparent. A council in Bordeaux in 1234 A.D. instructed priests that wicked women were accustomed to abandoning their children. While the practice was to be prevented, if possible, they should also tell their parishioners if: "God forbid, they are going to do this, they should use salt as a sign that the child has already been baptized."[161]

F. Famous Exposures

We have already discussed how Moses, Ishmael, Ion, and the Roman twins, Romulus and Remus, were all exposed at birth but survived to become heroic figures. Many other famous royalty were fabled to be similarly treated, either because the story of their abandonment was true, or because it lent an air of divine intervention which expanded their aura of identity with the gods.

Sargon of Akkad, the first Akkadian King in about 2400 B.C., was said to have been exposed in a fashion very similar to Moses:

> My mother was a changeling, my father I knew not,
> The brothers of my father loved the hills.
> My city is Azupiranu, with is situation on the banks of the Euphrates.
> My changeling mother conceived me, in secret she bore me.
> She cast me into the river which rose not over me.

> The river bore me up and carried me to Akki, the drawer of water.
> Akki, the drawer of water, took me as his son and reared me.[162]

In other versions of the legend, it was written that:

> My mother, the high priestess, conceived me, in secret she bore me.
> She set me in a basket of rushes, with bitumen she sealed my lid.
> She cast me into the river which rose not over me.[163]

Semiramis, who succeeded to the throne of the Assyrian Empire of Nineveh on the death of her husband Ninus and built the fabled city of Babylon, was the daughter of Derceto (Dercetis), a Syrian goddess who had offended Aphrodite and was punished by falling in love with a youth who then lay with her. From that moment of unbridled passion she became pregnant with Semiramis and because of her shame, she killed the young man, exposed her daughter in the desert, and then threw herself into a lake and was changed into a fish.[164] Semiramis was found alive by shepherds and brought up by Simmas, the chief shepherd of the royal herd.

Cyrus, the founder of the Persian empire, was the son of Mandane, the daughter of king Astyages. Before Cyrus was born, Astyages dreamed of a vine that grew from Mandane and covered all of Asia after her marriage to Cambyses. This dream was interpreted by the seers to mean that the child of Mandane would rule in his place and so when Cyrus was born, Astyages ordered Harpagus to kill him by exposure. Harpagus instead gave the infant to Mitradates with clear instructions: "It is Astyages' command to you that you take this child and expose it on the loneliest part of the hills, that it may the soonest perish."[165] The slave felt pity for the child, however, and raised him instead in his own house.[166] As an adult, Cyrus defeated Astyages and, true to the dream, became king of all Persia.

Zal, another traditional early ruler of Persia, was born to the paladin Sam during the reign of Shah Minuchihr. Because he had white hair at birth, a shameful disfigurement, his father ordered him exposed on Mt. Alburz, a remote place where the Simorgh bird placed its nest.[167] The infant lay there without shelter, and "sucked his own finger-tips and cried" until the Simorgh heard it weep and fed it with the tenderest portions of her own prey.[168] When the infant was grown, the Simorgh brought him to his father who saw how worthy the young man was of the crown and had no other blemish save his hair. He then asked for forgiveness and gave his son the name of Zal and proclaimed him as his heir.[169]

Hou Chi, a human ancestor of the Chou dynasty in China, established in 1123 B.C., was said to have been abandoned by his mother in a country lane but was protected by cows and sheep. He was then abandoned in the woods, and then again on the ice, but was eventually saved each time.[170] Another Chinese personage, Tseu Ouen, an important prime minister of Tch'ou in 604 B.C., was said to have been exposed by his mother, the daughter of the Prince of Iun, who had been seduced by Teou Pe Pi. He was supposedly nourished by a tigress before his rescue.[171]

Telephus, a traditional king of Mysia in Greece, was exposed on Mt. Parthenius by his mother Auge, the daughter of king Aleos. Auge had herself been ordered drowned by her father when found to be pregnant by Heracles. She survived and after giving birth to Telephus, exposed him knowing he would be killed if discovered. He was suckled by a hind and later found by the herdsmen of king Corythus.[172]

The Greek gods were frequently said to have fathered children from mortal women, but their offspring were often not accepted as legitimate. Hippothous, the son of Alope, king Cercyon's daughter, was ordered exposed because of his illegitimate origin as were Aeolus and his twin brother Boeotus, the sons of Arne, the daughter of king Aeolus.[173] All three lived to become heroes of the Greek Golden Era.

In the Indian epic poem, *Mahabharata*, we read the story of Shakuntala, the mother of Bharata, the eponymous ancestor of the princes who played the leading part in the tale. She told how she was the child "of a sage and a nymph, deserted at birth, cared for by birds, found and reared by Kanva," who gave her the name of Shakuntala.[174]

Other countries also have had kings who had been saved after abandonment at birth. Scyld, the founder of the Danish royal line, was claimed to have been exposed in a boat as a child.[175] Lamissio was reared by King Agelmund after being found abandoned, and later became his heir and succeeded to the throne of the Lombards.[176] Additional famous persons said to have been exposed include Ptolemy Soter, Asclepius, Coronis, Gilgamesh, Aegysthus, and the brothers Amphion and Zethus.[177]

G. Oblation

The tradition of offering children for service to the Lord dates back to the Old Testament. Its foundation is contained in the book of *Exodus* where the Lord directed Moses: "Dedicate to me all of the firstborn sons of Israel, and every firstborn male animal; they are mine!"[178] In the book of *Numbers*, Moses was further instructed:

> For every firstborn within the Israelite people belongs to me, both man and beast. At the time I slew every firstborn in the land of Egypt, I declared them dedicated to me.[179]

The practice of redeeming the first-born son endures today in the Jewish *"pidyon haben"* where a *kohen* holds the money over the boy's head and recites: "this instead of that, this in commutation of that."[180]

The *Mekilita*, which is the Midrash that deals with the interpretation of *Exodus*, agreed that this dedication meant that the first-born must be given to the priests in order to fulfill their holy tasks.[181] One example was described in the book of *Samuel* where Hannah, who was barren, prayed for a son to be born. She vowed to the Lord: "If you will grant your maidservant offspring, Then I shall set him before you all the days of his life."[182] When Hannah gave birth to Samuel, true to her oath she left him at the Tabernacle where the youth was raised by the rabbis and eventually became assistant to Eli the priest.[183]

Replenishing the priesthood from abandoned infants was also a feature of the pagan Roman faith. Juvenal, in his *Satires*, tells how the Salii, or priests of Rome, came from children who had been "picked up at a filthy pond's side."[184] They were raised in the service of the gods and remained to carry on their sacred rites.

It is therefore not surprising that the early Christian Church carried on a similar practice. What is quite astounding, however, is the frequency with which the process developed during the Middle Ages, and the large numbers of children which were abandoned to the service of the Lord Jesus Christ. Church structure, arising as it did from both Hebrew and Roman origins, was well-organized and required many men and women to carry on the priestly burden of an ever enlarging number of worshipers. While many youngsters voluntarily joined the priestly caste out of true devotion to God, children who were unwanted by their parents became a necessary supply of future novates as well. By the end of the fifth century A.D., most of the monasteries throughout the Western world began to accept young children within their walls to be raised and managed by the Church fathers.[185]

Some children were admitted after spending years in a foundling home, but the religious institutions in early medieval Europe received most of their novates in a process known as "oblation." This donation of a child as a permanent gift to the monastery was concluded with a formal acceptance and written contract, consistent with common-law principles of commercial transactions.[186] The children who were donated had little choice in the matter, even once they reached the age of majority, as the most part, this process was seen as a permanent gift, and once the child was taken up and reared, it remained the property of the church. The contract was not revocable.[187] There was a monetary payment made by wealthy parents to help in the costs of training the child, but the poor could donate their offspring for free.

In 633 A.D., the Fourth Council of Toledo clarified the basis of permanence by this process. It canonized that:

> Either parental desire or personal devotion can make a monk; both are binding. We deny henceforth any possibility of returning to the world for either category, and we forbid any resumption of secular life.[188]

This philosophy of ultimate control by a "parental desire" was accepted in the great canonical collections of the High Middle Ages.[189] Isidore of Seville said: "Anyone who has been relegated to a monastery by his parents should know that he will remain there forever."[190]

The Rule of St. Benedict, compiled in the first half of the sixth century A.D., detailed how the child was to be offered.[191] The benefits were primarily spiritual. But it is interesting to see how in one of the instruments the relationship to child sacrifice was formally made:

> Since both the Old and the New Testaments authorize the offering of children to God, as Abraham did . . . I herewith offer this my son to Almighty God and Holy Mary his mother, according to the Rule of Benedict, for the good of my soul and those of my parents . . .[192]

To many parents, it was a way of returning fruits of homage to the Lord. Most were donated before the age of twelve years old, with the majority given up shortly after being weaned.[193] It was a very humane type of abandonment, and carried no social disgrace.[194] The practice accounted for a high percentage of monks, and only began to decrease in the twelfth century A.D.[195] The Register of New Minster, at Winchester, revealed that between 1030 and 1070 A.D. there were 41 new monks initiated and of these 35, or 85%, were oblates.[196]

While the motive for many of these oblations appeared to be a genuinely religious desire to profess the Christian faith, others were little more than veiled exposures. John Boswell was generally supportive of the process, but noted that at times infants were "cast into the cloister by parents and relatives just as if they were kittens or piglets whom their mother could not nourish."[197]

One class of oblates who received complaints in the monastic literature were the numbers of defective children who were left to the care of the church. The abbot of Andres was horrified that at his monastery "were the lame, the malformed, the one-eyed, the squinting, the blind, the crippled."[198] Others complained of "the blind, lame, one-eyed, one-armed, leprous, or deaf children whom parents could not bear to keep."[199] At times, it appeared that oblation was used to donate especially those children who were born with some type of deformity. Ulrich of Cluny, in the eleventh century A.D., wrote that:

> If they have any who are lame or crippled, deaf and dumb or blind, hump-backed or leprous, or who have any defect which would make them less desirable in the secular world, offer them as monks with the most pious of vows . . . so that they themselves are spared having to educate and support them.[200]

But there were many other reasons given by parents to show that children given as oblates were, in fact, expendable. To the nobility, it offered a way to control the number of children raised within the family for dynastic purposes. There was just so many ways that property could be divided and still assure that the survivors would remain powerful. If too many children were born, it was advantageous to donate some to the Church. In addition to reducing the number of hereditary claims, the wealthy gained potential political and ecclesiastical benefits if their oblate rose to a position of power.[201] There was no forced separation of Church and State in the Middle Ages.

Another common source of oblates were daughters. Many families preferred to raise sons and searched for an acceptable dispersion of female births. The nunneries provided easy relief. One reason the raising of daughters was avoided was to prevent costly marriages.[202] Even if payments to the church at the time of donation was necessary, the cost would still be less than secular expenses. In his autobiography, Sir Simonds D'Ewes in seventeenth century England, wrote how he shipped off two of his daughters in the 1670s to nunneries and the cost was between ten and fifteen pounds a year for maintenance. This was understood to be an excellent investment: "We hope they will be pleased with this, for we have too much business and too much charge in the world to comply with all our dear relations according to the measure of our love."[203]

Another reason for oblation, especially in the High Middle Ages, was bastardy. Illegitimacy gradually became an increasing problem throughout this era so that "by the fourteenth century the influx of illegitimates, primarily the children of the priests, was staggering."[204] Oblation offered as much anonymity as with foundling homes, and for those who retained a concern for their offspring, there was a greater likelihood of the child surviving the internment. It was a problem for the church, however, for there was no way of knowing who the parentage was for requests of financial assistance.

Oblates were also offered during periods of famine when the parents could no longer afford to rear the child.[205] Such dire distress was quite common during the Middle Ages and put a burden on some monasteries who often relied on donations of food from local farms.

At times, the oblation could even be a voluntary effort on the part of the child. William Shakespeare, in *A Midsummer Night's Dream*, dramatized how this could be carried out in order to avoid punishment. Egeus was discontent over his daughter's unwillingness to marry the man he had picked out for her and brought the matter to king Theseus for judgment. Egeus argued: "I beg the ancient privilege of Athens, as she is mine, I may dispose of her, which shall be either to this gentleman or to her death, according to our law."[206] Theseus offered the young girl an option which could settle the problem. Instead of following her father's plan, she could "endure the livery of a nun, for aye to be in shady cloister mewed, to live a barren sister all your life, chanting faint hymns to the cold fruitless moon."[207]

While many of the children were comfortable with their religious lives, others were quite displeased and longed for a temporal existence. In the story of *The Prince's Vow* from Cleves, we read of Otto, the youngest son of the noble family from Hesse, who was destined to spend his life in a monastery from the moment of his birth: "His ardent young spirit recoiled in horror" from this calling, as he could not resign himself "to meet his fate."[208]

The requirement that oblates were permanently under the control of the church, even once they became an adult, led to frictional dissension among church leaders. Many felt that once the child grew to the age of majority, they should be allowed to choose whether they wanted to continue within the structure of the church, or return to secular life. Others felt that the authority of the church was supreme.

A particular noteworthy case was argued in the ninth century A.D. when Gottschalk of Orbais requested to leave the church rather than remain a monk. Initially, the Council of Mainz in 829 A.D. agreed with his request, but an appeal was made directly with the Carolinian emperor. Rabanus defended the orthodox view of the church in his treatise *On the Oblation of Children*. He noted biblical examples of extreme obedience to the Lord including the sacrifice of Isaac by Abraham; God's claim of the first-born children as his due, consigning the tribe of Levites to priestly service; Jephthah's slaying of his own daughter in fulfillment of a vow; Hannah's dedication of Samuel, again in fulfillment of a vow; and the offering of Jesus to the temple as a boy.[209] He concluded: "The same Lord who then through his oracle ordered the patriarch to offer his son as a sacrifice, now in his gospel commands the people of his church to offer their offspring to holy service."[210] This argument prevailed with the Carolinian emperor who ruled that Gottschalk of Orbais had to remain a monk despite the Council of Mainz order in 829 A.D. to free him from his vows.[211]

But times would soon change, and Pope Celestine, at the end of the twelfth century, ruled that an oblate could not be kept against his will after attaining the age of reason. His successor, Innocent III, asked oblates to reconfirm their vows at age fifteen years, and be allowed to leave if they did not wish to remain.[212] In the thirteenth century, under Pope Gregory IX, the excesses were further modified so that children were not professed until age twelve years for girls and age fourteen years for boys.[213] Pope Innocent IV added that reconfirmation of vows had to occur at age fifteen years.[214] St. Thomas Aquinas, himself an oblate at age six years and a respected scholar of the time, agreed with these principles.[215] Under the weight of all these changes, oblation waned markedly between the twelfth and fourteenth centuries and then disappeared.[216]

But before it died out, oblation was responsible for the career of many respected church leaders. The list included Paphnutius, St. Gregory, Nazianzen, Daniel the Stylite, Symeon the Stylite, Euthymios the Great, Sabas the Great, Cyril of Skythopolis, Nicolas of Sion, Theodore of Sykeon, St. Willibald, Bede, St. Boniface, Notker Balbulus, and Pope Innocent V.[217]

Endnotes

1 . Hume, "On the Populousness of Ancient Nations," Essays Moral, Political & Literary, 400.
2 . Shakespeare, The Winter's Tale, 2.3.186-189.
3 . Boswell, The Kindness of Strangers, 429.
4 . Locke, Two Treatises of Government, First Treatise, VI.56.4-5, 181.
5 . Ibid., VI.56.11-12, 181.
6 . Boswell, The Kindness of Strangers, 45.
7 . Ibid., 429.
8 . Boswell, "Exposition and Oblatio: The Abandonment of Children and the Ancient and Medieval Family," 13.
9 . Ibid.
10 . Boswell, The Kindness of Strangers, 118.
11 . Encyclopedia Britannica (1879), Volume IX, 481.
12 . Bennett, "The Exposure of Infants in Ancient Rome," 351.
13 . Malthus, "An Essay on the Principle of Population, or, A View of Its Past and Present Effects on Human Happiness; with an Inquiry into Our Prospects Respecting the Future Removal or Mitigation of the Evils Which it Occasions, (1872)" I.XIII, On Population, 222.
14 . Harrison, The Law of Athens, 71.
15 . Patterson, "Not Worth The Rearing: The Causes of Infant Exposure in Ancient Greece," 105.
16 . MacDowell, The Law in Classical Athens, 91.
17 . Bolkestein, "The Exposure of Children at Athens," 223.
18 . Plato, The Republic, 460c, 139.
19 . Aristotle, Politics, VII.XIV.10, 623.
20 . Boswell, The Kindness of Strangers, 85.
21 . Discourses 1.23. Ibid., 85-86.
22 . Seneca, Oedipus, IV.II, The Complete Roman Drama, Volume II, 700.
23 . Sophocles, Oedipus the King.
24 . Edmunds, Oedipus, The Ancient Legend and Its Later Analogues, 10.
25 25. Ibid., 18-19.
26 . Euripides, Ion, 20-24, 185.
27 . Ibid., 28-34, 186.
28 . Ibid., 1501, 250.
29 . Menander, The Arbitration, The Complete Greek Drama, 1150.
30 . Aristophanes, Thesmophoriazusae, 502-506, 173-175.
31 . Cameron, "The Exposure of Children And Greek Ethics, 105-106.
32 . Boswell, The Kindness of Strangers, 134.
33 . Ibid., 135.
34 . Bennett, "The Exposure of Infants in Ancient Rome," 347-349.
35 . Hume, "On the Populousness of Ancient Nations," 398, 399.
36 . Gibbon, The Decline and Fall of the Roman Empire, Volume I, 375.
37 . Boswell, The Kindness of Strangers, 136.
38 . Juvenal, "A Gallery of Women," 605-608, The Satires of Juvenal, 117.
39 . Lucian, "Voyage to the Lower World," 5, Volume I, 232.
40 . Dante, The Purgatorio, VII.31-33, 84.
41 . Dionysius of Halicarnassus, Roman Antiquities, II.XV.2, Volume I, 355.

42 . Malthus, "An Essay on the Principle of Population, or, A View of Its Past and Present Effects on Human Happiness; with an Inquiry into Our Prospects Respecting the Future Removal or Mitigation of the Evils Which It Occasions (1872)," On Population, I.XIV, 229.
43 . Flaceliere, Daily Life in Greece at the Time of Pericles,78.
44 . Radin, "The Exposure of Infants in Roman Law and Practice," 338.
45 . Beryl Rawson, "Children in the Roman Familia," The Family in Ancient Rome, 172. The Justininian Code, in the sixth century, deemed that all exposed children were to be considered freeborn. Ibid.
46 . Quintilian, Institutio 7.2.14. Boswell, The Kindness of Strangers, footnote 24, 62.
47 . Theodosian Code, 5.10.1, 110.
48 . Boswell, The Kindness of Strangers, 65.
49 . Ibid., 88.
50 . Ford, "The Emergence of the Child as a Legal Entity," 395.
51 . Boswell, The Kindness of Strangers, 110.
52 . Boswell, "Exposition and Oblatio: The Abandonment of Children and the Ancient and Medieval Family," 15.
53 . Terence, The Lady of Andros, III.515, 57.
54 . Seneca, "On Benefits," III.xxxi.2-3, Moral Essays, Volume III, 187.
55 . Pliny, "To the Emperor Trajan," LXXI, Letters of Gaius Plinius Caecilius Secundus, Volume IX, 392-93.
56 . Ibid., "Trajan to Pliny," LXXII, Volume IX, 393.
57 . Theodosian Code, 5.9.1, 109.
58 . Boswell, The Kindness of Strangers, 72.
59 . Ibid., 162.
60 . Ford, "The Emergence of the Child as a Legal Entity," 397.
61 . Theodosian Code, 5.9.2, 109.
62 . Boswell, The Kindness of Strangers, 172.
63 . Ibid., 173.
64 . References to exposure are sparse and generally reported only during times of severe strife or famine. In the Admonitions of Ipuwer, from the Twelfth Dynasty (1990-1785 B.C.), it was recorded that "Lo, children of nobles are dashed against walls, Infants are put out on high ground." Lichtheim, Ancient Egyptian Literature, Volume I, 153.
65 . Referencing sections 41, 92, and 107. Cameron, "The Exposure of Children And Greek Ethics," 105.
66 . Fildes, Breasts, Bottles & Babies, 8.
67 . Ezekiel 16:5. The Anchor Bible, 270.
68 . Ezekiel 16:6,7. Ibid.
69 . Acts of the Apostles, 7:19. The Anchor Bible, 61.
70 . Hebrews 11:23.
71 . Exodus 2:3-5.
72 . Genesis 16:1-3.
73 . Genesis 21:10.
74 . Genesis 21:15. The Anchor Bible, 154.
75 . Genesis 21:18. Ibid.
76 . Kiddushin, Mishnah, IV.69a.
77 . Ibid.

78 . Kiddushin, Gemara, IV.73b.
79 . Ibid.
80 . Ibid.
81 . Ibid.
82 . Ibid., IV.73a.
83 . Boswell, The Kindness of Strangers, 151.
84 . Philo, The Special Laws, III.XX.110, Volume VII, 545.
85 . Ibid., III.XX.115, 547-49.
86 . Ibid., III.XX.112, 547.
87 . Ibid., III.XX.115, 549.
88 . Ibid., III.XX.117-118, 549-551.
89 . Gorion, Mimekor Yisrael Classical Jewish Folk Tales, Volume III, 1059.
90 . Tertullian, Apology, 9.8, 31.
91 . Athenagoras, Embassy for the Christians, 35, 76.
92 . Martyr, "The First Apology," XXVII, The Writings of Justin Martyr & Athenagoras, Volume II, 30.
93 . Ibid., XXIX, 31.
94 . Clement of Alexandria, Paedogogus, III.III, Writings, 288.
95 . Boswell, The Kindness of Strangers, 158.
96 . Ibid., 159.
97 . Ibid.
98 . Ibid.
99 . Ibid., 161.
100. Ibid., 164.
101. Ibid., 165.
102. Ibid., 168.
103. Ethiopic version. Cameron, "The Exposure of Children And Greek Ethics," 111.
104. Ibid.
105. Langer, "Infanticide: A Historical Survey," 355-56.
106. Boswell, "Exposition and Oblatio: The Abandonment of Children and the Ancient and Medieval Family," 16.
107. Boswell, The Kindness of Strangers, 428-29.
108. Ibid., 341.
109. Juvenal, Satires, 6.604-606, 187.
110. Boswell, The Kindness of Strangers, 394.
111. Ibid., 403.
112. Ibid., 3.
113. Ibid., 14.
114. Ibid., 430.
115. Ibid., 325.
116. Ibid., 327.
117. Ibid.
118. Ibid., 328.
119. Ibid., 16.
120. Ibid.
121. Ibid., 2.
122. Ibid., 15.
123. Ibid.
124. Meyer, "Illegitimates and Foundlings in Pre-Industrial France," 252.

125. Boswell, The Kindness of Strangers, 44.
126. Langer, "Europe's Initial Population Explosion," 1.
127. Zola, L'Assommoir, 253.
128. Ulbricht, "The Debate About Foundling Hospitals in Enlightenment Germany: Infanticide, Illegitimacy, and Infant Mortality Rates," 222.
129. Boswell, The Kindness of Strangers, footnote 32, 16.
130. Ulbricht, "The Debate About Foundling Hospitals in Enlightenment Germany: Infanticide, Illegitimacy, and Infant Mortality Rates," 213.
131. Ibid., 227.
132. Hume, "On the Populousness of Ancient Nations," 399.
133. Jimmerson, "Female Infanticide in China: An Examination of Cultural and Legal Norms," 50.
134. Langer, "Infanticide: A Historical Survey," 354.
135. Weyland, The Principles of Population and Production, as They are Affected by the Progress of Society; With a View to Moral & Political Consequences, 133.
136. Ibid., 135-136.
137. "Report of the Committee Appointed by the Council of the Obstetrical Society," 9.
138. Curgenven, "On Baby-Farming and the Registration of Nurses," 6.
139. Ibid., 3.
140. Malcolmson, R. W., "Infanticide in the Eighteenth Century," 188.
141. Erasmus, "The New Mother," Colloquies, 273.
142. Ibid.
143. Ibid., 283.
144. DeMause, "The Fetal Origins of History," 30.
145. Quoting Rex v. Hogan, 5 Eng. Law & Eq. 553. Lynam v. People, 65 IllApp 687, 689 (1895).
146. Ibid.
147. Leeuwen, Commentaries on Roman-Dutch Law, XXXIV.2, Volume II, 267.
148. Ibid.
149. Ibid.
150. Chicago Tribune (June 24, 1992): section 1, 8.
151. Ibid.
152. Cameron, "The Exposure of Children And Greek Ethics," 107.
153. Kiddushin, Gemara, IV.73b.
154. Euripides, Ion, 20-24.
155. Ibid., 1417-1436.
156. Longus, Daphnis and Chloe, I, 20.
157. Heliodorus, An Ethiopian Romance, II, 61.
158. Beaumarchais, The Marriage of Figaro, III, 19.
159. Ibid., III, 174.
160. Menander, The Arbitration, 1152.
161. Boswell, The Kindness of Strangers, 324.
162. Roux, Ancient Iraq, 140-141.
163. The Legend of Sargon, 5-7. Pritchard, Ancient Near Eastern Texts, 119.
164. Harpers Dictionary of Classical Literature & Antiquities, 497.
165. Herodotus, The History, I.110, 85.
166. Ibid., I.108-110.
167. Dunn, The Foundling and the Werewolf, 97.

168. Ferdowsi, The Epic of the Kings, V, 36.
169. Ibid., V, 38-39.
170. Dunn, The Foundling and the Werewolf, 94.
171. Ibid.
172. Ibid., 99.
173. New Century Classical Handbook, 35, 572.
174. Kalidasa, Shakuntala and Other Writings, 98.
175. Boswell, The Kindness of Strangers, 214.
176. Ibid., 223.
177. Redford, "The Literary Motif of the Exposed Child," 213, 215-216.
178. Exodus 13:1,2. The Living Bible, 59.
179. Numbers 8:17. The Anchor Bible, 270.
180. Levenson, The Death and Resurrection of the Beloved Son, 47.
181. Mekilita de-Rabbi Ishmael, Tractate Pisha, XVI, Volume I, 130.
182. 1 Samuel 1:11. The Anchor Bible, 49.
183. 1 Samuel 2:11. Ibid., 77.
184. Juvenal, Satires, 6.602, 187.
185. Boswell, The Kindness of Strangers, 230.
186. Ibid., 228.
187. Boswell, "Exposition and Oblatio: The Abandonment of Children and the Ancient and Medieval Family," 18.
188. Mansi 10.631.49. Boswell, The Kindness of Strangers, 233.
189. Ibid.
190. Regula monachorum 4. Ibid., footnote 22, 233.
191. Ibid., 231.
192. PL 66.842. Ibid., 237.
193. Ibid., 304.
194. Ibid., 241.
195. Ibid., 297.
196. Ibid.
197. Boswell, "Exposition and Oblatio: The Abandonment of Children and the Ancient and Medieval Family," 20.
198. Boswell, The Kindness of Strangers, 299.
199. Boswell, "Exposition and Oblatio: The Abandonment of Children and the Ancient and Medieval Family," 21.
200. Boswell, The Kindness of Strangers, 298.
201. Ibid., 240.
202. Stone, The Family, Sex and Marriage, in England 1500-1800, 38.
203. Ibid., 87.
204. Boswell, The Kindness of Strangers, 302.
205. Ibid., 304.
206. Shakespeare, A Midsummer Night's Dream, I.I.42-45, 2.
207. Ibid., I.I.72-75, 3.
208. Guerber, Legends of the Rhine, 22.
209. Boswell, The Kindness of Strangers, 246.
210. Ibid., 440.
211. Ibid., 245-47.
212. Ibid., 313.
213. Ibid., 314.

214. Ibid.
215. Ibid., 314-315.
216. Ibid., 317.
217. Ibid., 242; Boswell, "Exposition and Oblatio: The Abandonment of Children and the Ancient and Medieval Family," 30.

CHAPTER VIII

FEMALE INFANTICIDE

> "At least 60 million females in Asia are missing and feared dead, victims of nothing more than their sex. Worldwide, research suggests, the number of missing females may top 100 million."[1]

As headlined in the above quotation, in many areas of the world a female infant's chance of survival to adulthood is much less than that of her male counterpart. In some cases, this is due to her being summarily disposed of at birth simply because of her sex; in others, she is so neglected that malnutrition leads to an early death. At times, parents do not even wait until their daughter is born to determine her premature fate. Prenatal testing, such as amniocentesis and ultrasound, is being used worldwide to recognize female fetuses so that an abortion can be performed as soon as possible.[2] In South Korea, the country with the highest boys-to-girls birth ratio in the world, it is estimated that 30,000 female fetuses were aborted in 1994 because parents did not want a daughter.[3] Statistics show that 114 boys in South Korea, 110 boys in Taiwan, 119 boys in China, and 112 boys in India are born for every 100 girls.[4]

Modern technology even allows couples to essentially choose the sex of their child through artificial insemination.[5] According to a recent poll, nearly twenty percent of geneticists approve of the use of abortion if a fetus is not the desired gender.[6] In 1971, India passed the liberal Medical Termination of Pregnancy Act which allowed any woman to terminate her pregnancy before 20 weeks had passed.[7] Many couples then rushed to get sex-determination tests in order to abort a female fetus. One clinic in Meerut, India performed ultrasounds on pregnant women for $35 to determine the sex of the fetus. If the finding is a girl, "they can step next door to the Child Welfare Clinic and have her aborted."[8] In 1993, the Indian Parliament attempted to stop this practice by making it illegal to divulge the sex of a fetus, but it has not had much effect.[9] A similar response has occurred in China and South Korea.[10] One reason for this move is governmental concern that there will be millions of men in the next twenty years who will not be able to find a wife.

This attitude is not restricted to developing countries where the cost-benefit ratio of raising a female infant through the rite of marriage can be quite high. In a 1985 survey of 295 U.S. geneticists, 62% say they would aid a couple who desired to know the sex of their young fetus in order to determine whether to keep it, having decided they would have an abortion if the fetus was female.[11] Most of these scientists regarded the parents right to choose the sex of their child a "logical extension" of their right to control the spacing of their childbirth.

The figures of female infanticide in the modern age are truly astounding. Estimates indicate that 30.5 million females are missing in China, 22.8 million in India, 3.1 million in Pakistan, 1.6 million in Bangladesh, 1.7 million in West Asia, 600,000 in Egypt and 200,000 in Nepal.[12] While these numbers are theoretical, and based on the difference between actual and expected sex-ratios, they are felt by experts to be reliably close to the truth.

The problem of female infanticide is deeply ingrained within the prejudice of cultural sexism. Even when a daughter is not killed at birth, female infants often have a higher mortality rate simply because they are given less food than males. In some cases it is "because family members view a daughter with diarrhea as a nuisance but a son with diarrhea as a medical crisis."[13] Dr. Amartya Sen estimated that over one hundred million females around the world are missing because they are not allowed to benefit from nutrition and health care in the developing countries.[14] Johns Hopkins researcher Margaret Bentley found that the male:female ratio in India increased as the children got older because "mothers facing limited food supply and money make sure sons get adequate nutrition and health care, while daughters frequently go hungry or sick."[15] The problem is present on such a large scale that the term "gynecide" has been suggested to denote the world-wide destruction of female infants and fetuses.[16]

This preference for sons is not of modern origin. For most of recorded history, male children have been favored over females. Anthropologists explain this priority as arising from the needs of primitive tribes to provide adequate protection and sustenance for the family unit. Finding food in a dangerous forest setting was something which only the physically stronger male was able to do, and if successive female infants were born, families had to eliminate some girls in order to maintain a majority of men to hunt and provide for defense. In addition, the rate of population increase was mostly determined by the numbers of females in a tribe, and since girls were more likely to survive the high risk period of early childhood, over-population could result if females were not selectively removed.[17]

While this primal necessity might indeed explain some male preferential treatment during the prehistoric era, a patriarchal attitude against women persisted even when conditions improved. Agricultural advancements, which did not favor one sex over another, failed to significantly alter societal partiality for males. Even the supposed democracy of religion, which preached the sanctity and equality of all human life, only allowed males to participate in important, or powerful, church positions. This sexist approach to the worship of God was prominent in Judaism, Christianity, and Islam, as well as many other religious beliefs.

Along with this cultural proclivity against women came an undercurrent of distrust. The female was generally depicted as an instigator of evil – in the image of a seductive Eve – with wiles that would drag men into a troublesome death unless the danger was anticipated. The *Celestina*, written in 1499, adhered to this view and chastised the majority of women for:

> Their deceits, their gossiping, their ingratitude, their inconstancy, their presumption, their boastfulness, their false humility, their folly, their scorn, their servility, their gluttony, their lust, their filth, their cowardice, their insolence, their sorcery, their gibes, their scolding, their want of shame, their whoring. Consider the giddy little brains concealed behind those long and delicate veils! Or within those fine and sumptuous gowns! What corruption, what cesspools, beneath those gaudy temples! They are called limbs of Satan, the fountainhead of sin, and the destroyers of Paradise.[18]

As women were increasingly burdened with this unfavorable image, their chance for survival progressively worsened.

How far back does evidence of the problem go? Comparative anthropologists have estimated that as many as 50% of newborn females were eliminated by Paleolithic parents at birth.[19] Population sex-ratios have consistently shown that the expected birth rate is 105 males to 100 females, with normal ratios hardly ever ranging beyond 102-108.[20] The slightly higher male majority at birth is later canceled by a somewhat greater mortality during early adulthood.[21] Although sex-ratios of fossil remains are subject to interpretive error,[22] H. V. Vallois determined that among 309 skeletons of human adults, a sex-ratio of 125.6 was present.[23] He believed this was secondary to female infanticide. Because of the unreliability of sex verification unless the entire skeleton is available for comparison, others have questioned this conclusion.[24]

But if there was widespread female infanticide during the early evolution of our species, many have argued that there was a rational explanation for the favoritism of males. Charles Darwin believed that infanticide, "especially of female infants," was the most important check on excessive proliferation of early man.[25] Limited food supplies not only necessitated that the numbers of tribal members be kept within a restricted number, but there was evidence that Stone Age men were aware of this problem and utilized infanticide to check their family growth.[26] If the number of individuals outgrew the available food supply, it was easier to kill a newborn female at birth than to try and prevent further procreation.

John M'Lennan also pointed out that rearing all the females would be less beneficial to the tribal culture "as they would be less capable of self-support, and of contributing, by their exertions, to the common good."[27] The rearing of girls "weakened their mothers when young, and, when grown-up were a temptation to surrounding tribes."[28] It was perceived characteristics such as these which fostered a strong male bias against members of the "weaker sex."

A. Greco-Roman Times

Most researchers have accepted that the majority of children exposed by Greek fathers were either sickly or females.[29] Donald Engels doubted that the extent of female infanticide was as extensive as claimed by others,[30] but studies, such as those reported on by Cynthia Patterson, have clearly indicated that unequal sex-ratios during that era support the prevalence of female infanticide.[31]

W. W. Tarn reported that a list of Greeks who came to Miletus in the third century B.C. showed 118 sons and 28 daughters brought as part of the colonization.[32] No family reported having more than two daughters. Tarn believed that the unequal sex-ratio was due to female infanticide although others have refuted this claim. Critics point out that females may have been brought as slaves and therefore not appeared as participants on the list. Also, that the tabulation was not meant to accurately reflect the exact number of colonizers, but were only used to validate specialized claims. Nevertheless, what indirect data does remain supports the likely presence of elective female infanticide.[33]

When a decision was made to expose a daughter during this era, it was usually because of economic reasons. The Bronze and Copper Ages were associated with improvements in agricultural methodology, but work in the field, for the most part, was still a man's job. Male family members and friends were not expendable options, but were necessary elements to assure a successful harvest. Frequent wars took a great toll on young, healthy males, and parents needed to replace this drainage by raising sons to assure a constant, productive future. Although women did face the danger of death during childbirth, the risks did not reach the male loss of life through military excursions.

Even in the cities, where manual labor was less demanding, the Greek parent faced significant economic problems with raising a daughter to the age of majority. The Athenian father was generally required to supply a large dowry at the time of his daughter's marriage, and this arrangement was a significant hardship to a struggling provider. Some fathers decided that the burden associated with the birth of a daughter was not a blessed event, and sought to either expose her before she was accepted into the family or give little sustenance in her formative years, even if this put her at risk because of malnutrition.[34]

While these matters were likely the primary reasons individual parents decided to preferentially abandon a female birth, Mark Golden has hypothesized that another reason why Greek society may have permitted the practice to proceed with little social interference was to avoid the problem of excess widows later in life.[35] Except for rare instances, such as with Amazon female warriors, women were not part of the armed forces in the ancient world since hand-to-hand combat required greater physical strength than does modern warfare. Armed conflicts were quite common, and the campaigns took a great toll on healthy young males who either gave their lives for the sake of their country or were away from home for extended periods of time. As Herodotus so succinctly describes in his *History*, skirmishes between neighboring lands were a constant arena for conflict, and peace treaties, finally signed after years of tragic loss of life, although intended to last for decades, usually held together for only a few years. This meant that many cities had a surplus of adult women, most of whom had lost their own spouse but were still capable of procreation. Such competition among surviving women could create serious domestic strife, and the elimination of some of the newborn daughters would help prevent a persistent imbalance in the sex-ratio of marriageable adults.

A similar situation developed during the rise and fall of the Roman Empire. From the earliest founding of Rome by Romulus, female infanticide was tolerated as an occasional necessity of life. Although there are no textual records from that time, Romulus was said to have "obliged the inhabitants to bring up all their male children and the first born of the females."[36] The raising of more than one daughter was very rare.[37] Among the general Roman public, the ancient axiom was: "Everyone raises a son, including a poor man, but even a rich man will abandon a daughter."[38]

Mentioned by Stobaeus in the fifth century A.D., this principle of male preference dated from as early as 300 B.C.[39] When Hilarion had to leave on a business trip in 1 B.C., he was purported to instruct his wife Alis: "If, as may well happen, you give birth to a child, if it is a boy let it live; if it is a girl, expose it."[40] A similar story was told in *The Golden Ass*, by Apuleius, where a man who left his pregnant wife for a business trip instructed that "if she were delivered of a daughter, it should be killed."[41]

When Romans abandoned infants, they were often left in a conspicuous locale, and anyone who wanted to raise the foundling could then claim it at as his own. Such children, nurtured by foster parents, were referred to as "alumni."[42] The sex-ratio of alumni were 2:1 male:female, indicating that boys were obviously favored over girls when a decision was made to rescue an exposed offspring.[43]

Sexual bias of this type continued for centuries. In the *Metamorphosis*, by Ovid, the story was told of Ligdus who informed his wife that he wanted only a boy child for daughters were known to be trouble. When his wife became pregnant, he commanded that "if it should be a girl, let her be killed."[44] The mother panicked when a girl was born and told her husband it was a boy which created problems later in life when the father found a girl for "him" to marry. The plot was comedic, but the reality was not. Iphis may have survived in literary fiction because of a unique storyline, but other young girls in real life never lived long enough to dream of a future marriage.

B. Persia

Female infanticide was a common practice throughout Arabia before the time of Mohammed.[45] The Persian world was a male-dominated society; females were generally seen as a burden, and it was not unusual for unwanted daughters to be buried alive.[46] A common proverb held that it was a "generous deed to bury a female child."[47] For the most part, it was only the infant who was killed by this method, but girls even after the age of six years, were occasionally sacrificed in a similar fashion.[48]

Certain Arab tribes were especially noted for their acceptance of female infanticide. The Tamim often disposed of girls chiefly because of the scarcity of food.[49] As with other tribal societies, it was the men who gathered sustenance for the family, and females were seen as a liability, especially during times of economic stress. While the men generally followed this custom with little restraint, it was said that the only occasion at which Othman ever shed a tear was when his little daughter, who he had ordered buried alive, wiped the dust of the grave earth from his beard as she was laid in her grave.[50]

The practice of female infanticide, according to legend, began with Cais b. Asim, the Sa'dite who was a contemporary of Mohammed. The myth contended that his niece was carried off by a robber horde and when he offered to ransom her, she refused and decided to stay with her captors. He was so indignant at this disgrace that he killed all of his daughters by burying them alive, and never again allowed a daughter to live.[51]

Such fictional accounts may have a loyal following in folklore, but social scientists find evidence of the custom in much earlier times. Balfour believed that the pagan Arabs had long practiced female infanticide, as did the Muslims of Sind. Some evidence even suggests that the conquest of India by these Mohammedan's is what first led to the development of female infanticide in that country.[52] While certain sultans tried to stem the practice, such as Sa'sa'a who saved one hundred eighty girls from being buried alive by their parents, the majority of early Persians did not consider female infanticide an evil act.[53]

Mohammed clearly recorded the presence of these killings during the sixth century A.D. When he first went to Mecca, for example, he demanded that the people not commit child-murder.[54] Later, in 652 A.D., his collected writings were compiled into the *Koran*, the holy book which comprises the moral tenets of Islam.[55] He asked with censure, for example, how would a father answer "when the female child that had been buried alive shall be asked for what crime she was put to death."[56] He further reproached the people for their negative reactions to a daughter's birth:

> And they ascribe daughters unto God! Glory be to Him! But they desire them not for themselves. For when the birth of a daughter is announced to any one of them, dark shadows settle on his face and he is sad. He hideth him from the people because of the ill tidings: shall he keep it with disgrace or bury it in the dust? Are not their judgments wrong?[57]

But the religious precepts of Islam, while finding that the killing of female infants was generally wrong, did not alter the inferior status of the female population. As the *Koran* stated: "Men are superior to women on account of the qualities with which God hath gifted the one above the other."[58]

Mixed signals such as these obviously led to some confusion among the converts and Mohammed had to admonish fathers for wanting sons rather than daughters: "What! hath your Lord prepared sons for you, and taken for himself daughters from among the angels?"[59] He argued that while daughters may indeed be less favored under the eyes of Allah, it was not permissible to take away their lives. One does not question God, one follows the law and gives thanks for any blessed receipts. So that while one may pray for the birth of a son, one may not bury the birth of a daughter:

> God's the kingdom of the Heavens and of the Earth! He createth what He will! and he giveth daughters to whom He will, and sons to whom He will.[60]

C. Judaism & Christianity

We find a similar discrepancy in the treatment of women within the Western religions of Judaism and Christianity. The murder of anyone, including a female child, was clearly prohibited as a primary sin by both religions, but that did not mean there was equality of the sexes in other aspects of secular life. According to the Holy Scripture, from the very beginning of the human race, when Adam alone was created from "clods in the soil," there had been more than an anatomic difference between men and women.[61] It was not until man was placed in the garden of Eden, for example, that God thought it time to make woman as a companion – "an aid fit for him."[62] God therefore took one of Adam's ribs and made it into a woman, so-called because she was "taken from Man."[63] What has developed since then is nothing short of orthodox sexism.

In the legends of the Jewish Haggadah, this difference between male and female was emphasized in no uncertain terms:

> When God was on the point of making Eve, he said: "I will not make her from the head of man, lest she carry her head high in arrogant pride; not from the eye, lest she be wanton-eyed; not from the ear, lest she be an eavesdropper; not from the neck, lest she be insolent; not from the mouth, lest she be a tattler; not from the heart, lest she be inclined to envy; not from the hand, lest she be a meddler; not from the foot, lest she be a gadabout. I will form her from a chaste portion of the body," and to every limb and organ as he formed it, God said, "Be chaste! Be chaste!" Nevertheless, in spite of the great caution used, woman has all the faults God tried to obviate.[64]

In the *Talmud* it was recorded that the Rabbis said: "Happy is he whose children are males, and woe to him whose children are females."[65] When a daughter was young, you worried she was to be seduced; when she was an adult, you worried she would not marry or have no children; and when she was old, you worried she would engage in witchcraft. Ben Sira noted that: "A daughter is a vain treasure to her father: through anxiety on her account, he cannot sleep at night."[66]

The *Talmud* also expressed that if one injured a minor son, "he must make for him a safe investment (out of the compensation money)," while if it was a daughter that was harmed, the father was exempt from payment.[67] In addition, the period of purification for a woman after the birth of a daughter was twice as long when compared to a son.[68]

Most of these religious practices related to sexual preference only, and there is little evidence that actual female infanticide was practiced by the Jews. But it is reasonable to assume that when the necessity for exposure was felt to be present, because of economics or shame, girls were more likely to have been left than boys.

A similar situation existed for Christianity. The outline for the role of the Christian woman was clarified in the New Testament:

> Christian women should be noticed for being kind and good, not for the way they fix their hair or because of their jewels or fancy clothes. Women should listen and learn quietly and humbly. I never let women teach men or lord it over them. Let them by silent in your church meetings. Why? Because God made Adam first, and afterwards he made Eve. And it was not Adam who was fooled by Satan, but Eve, and sin was the result.[69]

The writings of Paul confirmed this obedient role. He explained to the Corinthians that: "A wife is responsible to her husband, her husband is responsible to Christ, and Christ is responsible to God.[70] In addition: "Adam, the first man, was not made for Eve's benefit, but Eve was made for Adam."[71] He continued this thought with the Ephesians:

> For a husband is in charge of his wife in the same way Christ is in charge of his body the church. So you wives must willingly obey your husbands in everything, just as the church obeys Christ.[72]

The Church hierarchy had little room for women, and until modern times, pious females could do little else than donate their service by joining a nunnery. The initial attitude of the Church was to force celibacy on priests so that they could not be ensnared by the wily female. As Heloise sheepishly pointed out in her letters to Abelard, it was a woman who first lured man from Paradise, a woman who plunged Solomon into folly and idolatry, and a woman with whom Job fought his hardest battles.[73] No wonder, then, that women should not be given positions of authority within the Church structure.

That some Christian parents did indeed expose their female infants was evident in the writings of the early Christian theologians who were concerned over future acts of incest. Saint Justin Martyr cautioned that it was wicked to expose children for "almost all those who are exposed are raised to prostitution."[74] He then added a warning against consorting with prostitutes because it was thereby possible that one would be guilty of having intercourse with his own child.[75] Clement of Alexandria similarly advised of this danger.[76] Boswell noted that other theologians warned men not to visit brothels for they "might unwittingly commit incest with a child they had abandoned."[77] It is doubtful that such concern would have been manifest if the danger was not real.

D. Middle Ages & Renaissance

In the poem "Praise of Women," by Palladas around 400 A.D., the early medieval attitude towards women was aptly summarized: "Only twice is womankind anything but an affliction: in bride bed and in the grave.[78]

It is evident that the plight of females was to find no new advantages during the Dark Ages.

John Boswell, in his comprehensive study of exposure of children during the Middle Ages, commented on the difference in the sex-ratio of first- and second-born children recorded among the peasants at Farfa and St. Germain. The first-born infants were overwhelming likely to be male, while the second child showed little statistical sexual disparity. Boswell believed that this was due to the common practice of abandoning females until a son was born. The logic was that: "Peasants wanted at least one son and made sure that their first child was male by abandoning daughters to the service of the wealthy or to nearby monastic communities."[79]

Emily Coleman studied the polyptych, or tax census forms, of some 1700 families in the abbey of Saint Germain-des-Pres from the period 810 to 829 A.D., and found that the sex-ratios of adults ranged from 110.3 to 252.9, rather than the expected 105.[80] She also discovered that as the arable land increased, the sex-ratio became lower, suggesting that food shortages played a role in the decision to eliminate females.[81] When food was abundant, all children were able to be fed and there was little need for infanticide. When sustenance was sparse, and an infant had to be exposed or killed to protect the supply for other family members, it was more practical to choose a daughter to destroy.

These conditions persisted for centuries. Josiah Russell examined the male sex-ratio among heirs in medieval England from 1250 to 1348 and from 1430 to 1545 and found the male:female ratios to be 4:3, suggesting that female infants had been the victims of infanticide.[82] In addition, he also found that among serfs there was a similar male predominance which indicated that they may have liquidated females more than the favored classes.[83] Barbara Kellum also uncovered similar results in her research. Increased ratios of male to female children in England during the fourteenth and fifteenth centuries suggested to her that female infanticide was likely practiced among the serf population.[84]

Female infanticide was also common in Iceland during the era of Viking control.[85] In the *Icelandic Sagas*, the power of the father to "ut bera," or expose the child, was implied in several passages. In *gunnlaugs Saga*, Thorstein ordered the child which his wife was to bear in his absence to be exposed if a girl.[86]

In Irish lore, tales of female infanticide occurred among many of the ancient kings. Cormac mac Airt abandoned his daughter, Mes Buachalla, after her birth, and Ragallach, king of Connacht ordered his daughter killed as well.[87]

These findings of uneven sex-ratios were not eliminated by the social advances of the Renaissance. According to David Lynn: "Infanticide of female newborns persisted during the Renaissance along with other cruel practices towards daughters."[88] Among the lowest social level in seventeenth century Russia, female infanticide seems to have been widespread.[89] Documents showed that among slaves, there was almost a 2:1 male:female ratio.[90]

E. Tribes

Women have often fared little better in the wild than among the smoke stacks of male-dominated, modern societies. In their ethnographic analysis of 393 populations, Divale and Harris found that 208 of them practiced infanticide more than occasionally. The male:female sex-ratio of those over age fourteen in these societies was 117:100, while in those where infanticide was uncommon it was 104-108:100. The data collected in this paper provides some of the best documentation of widespread infanticide among tribal groups.

The authors interpreted their results to indicate that female infanticide was used as a major means of population control in an otherwise male-dominated world. They further explained that: "Since the reproductive potential of most sexually reproducing species is determined largely by the rate of female survivorship, the most effective mode of population control is to reduce the percentage of the population which consists of sexually active fertile females."[91] In other words, tribes destroyed their daughters at birth in order to control their population growth.

While some might determine that this practice was cruel and excessive, Divale and Harris pointed out that the method was actually more advantageous than using abortion to control the number of births. First, abortion was potentially life threatening to the mother should a complication arise, and the loss of a mothers life was more costly, from both practical and emotional reasons, than the loss of a newborn's life. Secondly, destroying a female at birth allowed a male baby to be spared, assuring the tribe a strong warrior and worker base.[92] Abortion did not allow one to predetermine the sex of the child and thereby could not select out a desired, and much needed, male birth.

Such a pragmatic view of female infanticide appears to be quite common among tribal societies. Besides the reasons given by Divale and Harris, other justifications included the danger that excess numbers of young women could be a temptation to surrounding tribes which then might lead to war and bloodshed. If there was a danger to the entire tribe because of females available for marriage, it would be safer to keep their numbers down. In the words of Fison and Hewitt: "Savages are perfectly logical people in their own way."[93]

It was also common to find female infanticide in tribes where a costly dower had to be given with a girl in marriage.[94] This reached incredible proportions of deaths among female births in India during the nineteenth century, and is discussed in detail later in this chapter.

Various authors have commented on other reasons given by families for accepting the need for female infanticide. Among the Fiji in the Pacific Islands, the justification for females being selectively killed was that they were useless in war and gave the parents so much trouble.[95] Daughters also were frequently victims in the aboriginal New Guinea tribes where some families complained that:

> Girls don't stay with us when they grow up. They marry and go to other places. They don't become warriors, and they don't stay to look after us in our old age.[96]

In the Torres Straits, parents at times said that female children were killed because of the extra trouble in attempting to keep them chaste as the boys would continually seek them out.[97]

The Loucheux, or Kutchins, in Northwest America, practiced female infanticide and the women said they did this in "a desire to spare them the miseries of life." Women of that tribe were treated as inferiors by the men and were "literally beasts of burden to their lords and masters. All the heavy work is done by them."[98]

Among the Eskimos, female infanticide was quite common with some statistics suggesting a rate as high as 66% of female births.[99] Smith & Smith reviewed the data from ten Inuit populations and found an average of 21%.[100] Joseph Birdsell estimated the numbers of females destroyed at birth to have ranged from 15-50%, while Knud Rasmussen, in his history of the Netsilik from 1922-23, calculated the numbers at an astounding 80%.[101] It should be noted that when Schrire and Steiger reviewed the multiple data collections which recorded such impressive numbers, they concluded that the results were more indicative of what transpired during short periods of stress, rather than what was representative of long term conditions.[102]

Whatever the true incidence, it is nevertheless valid that most of this information comes from studies during 1880-1930, and that the killings are much rarer in modern times.[103] The generally agreed upon reason for the selective frequency was the difficulty in obtaining enough food in such a severely frozen environment, and the necessity for male members to predominate in order to hunt and fish. E. Hoebel blamed the incidence on "approved homicide" believing that it was due to the hard life they had to endure. Weyer felt that it was an artificial check on population increase beyond the supply of food.[104] Asen Balikci determined that it was often due to the belief that the female child was a burden: "A hunter has to feed his daughter for many years and then leaves just as she is getting useful."[105] Also parents thought they "cannot afford to waste several years nursing a girl."[106] It then became an adaptive measure which increased the survival chances of the family.[107] Since males were more likely to be killed from accidents during the hunting for food, selective female infanticide would act as a balance to keep the adult population more uniform.[108]

An alternate view, expounded by Freeman, was that the killing of female infants by the Eskimos was not an issue of necessity, but rather a manifestation of male dominance.[109] This view has not been widely accepted, however, and whatever the basis for the actual societal acceptance, most of the infanticide was discontinued after the general conversion of many Eskimo tribes to Christianity in the late 1930s and 1940s.[110] It should also be noted that ethnographers generally postulated female infanticide among Eskimos on sex-ratio studies, and, according to Chapman, only once was the female infanticide observed directly.[111] These issues are discussed in more detail in the chapter on Tribes.

F. Japan

In Japan, female infanticide was used to perpetuate the patrilineal lineage in a method known as "mabiki," or "thinning." This terminology came about because of the similarity to procedures used to assure the proper growth of rice seedlings.[112] Smaller, or slower growing, rice plants were discarded by farmers so that only the heartier variety remained. This concept carried into Japanese culture so that the ideal family was seen as two sons and one daughter, with male:female ratios elevated throughout the country, especially in the rural areas.[113]

Estimates of the extent of female infanticide in certain areas of Japan indicated that an average of two out of every five live-births were destroyed.[114] According to Mildred Dickeman, ninety percent of the population of peasants would use infanticide as a method of population limitation when necessary. It allowed for removal of defectives and twins, and, "most importantly, it permitted manipulation of the sex ratio to guarantee patrilineal perpetuation of the localized peasant family."[115]

Dickeman estimated that up to 10-25% of children were killed at birth in the Tokugawa era, and that up to 50% of all females were killed.[116] Up to the Edo period, in 1867, the usual method was to obstruct the infant's nose and mouth with wet paper causing immediate suffocation, while in modern day Japan one usually finds the infant drowned in the toilet.[117]

While women in Tokyo account for only a small percentage of assault crimes, over 88% of the homicide victims under the age of one year are killed by females, usually the mother. Japanese women are traditionally relegated to a lower social status, and "they are most likely to strike out at the innocent when the limit of their control is reached."[118] Sakuta and Saito divided the infanticide cases in modern Japan into two types: the "Mabiki" type, where the motive is population control due to poverty and the inability to raise another child, and the "Anomie" type, where the victims are illegitimate and the motive is to avoid ill-repute and loss of psychological support by their lovers.[119] Funayama, et.al., suggested that cases of repeated neonaticide may be due to the light sentences generally given to women in Japan convicted of the crime.[120]

In 1966, the year of the Fire-horse (Hinoe-Uma) occurred and according to Japanese tradition this meant that girl babies born that year would be ill-fated. While the early neonatal mortality rate of accidents and violence for baby boys was not significantly different from previous years, that for girls was much higher.[121]

G. China

In China, infanticide had long been used to eliminate either deformed, or unhealthy, infants but, according to Orleans, "it was primarily aimed at the female child who, as a consumer, would be a serious burden to the poor family."[122] As poverty and overcrowding continued relentlessly into the twentieth century, female infanticide persisted as well.[123]

An old Chinese folk song points out how the status of women has always been that of a second-class citizen:

> The past in China was a pit,
>   Grim, bottomless, accursed,
> Where common folk were trodden down,
>   And women fared the worst.[124]

The very fabric of Chinese belief in the order of the universe supported the concept of male dominance. The principle of Yin and Yang in China set a superior value on everything that was masculine and females were seen as inferior when compared to the attributes of a man. The earliest records of such activity appear to date from *The Book of Songs* which originated around 800-600 B.C.[125]

In addition, under the Confucian patriarchal order which dated from the sixth century B.C., daughters were generally fated to leave the natal household and their presence was therefore seen as an expendable luxury. Many families found themselves simply unable to afford such excesses, and this led to the frequent occurrence of female infanticide.[126] As the famous poet Po Chu-i told, after his daughter was born when he was almost forty years old: "If I am spared the grief of her dying young, Then I shall have the trouble of getting her married."[127] Han Fei Tzu, who died in 233 B.C., told how: "As to children, a father and mother when they produce a boy congratulate one another, but when they produce a girl they put it to death."[128]

In *The Family Instructions* for the Yan Clan, during the Northern and Southern Dynasties (420-589 A.D.), Chen Fan said that girls created such inconvenience that:

> When the birth is near, he sends servants to keep watch, and when the labour begins they peep into the room from outside the window or the door. If a girl is born she is immediately taken and killed.[129]

Women were not able to offer ancestral sacrifice, glorify the family name through official appointments, or even perpetuate the family name since they took on the aura of their husband's family. They "traditionally obeyed their fathers in youth, their husbands in middle life, and their sons in old age."[130] Known as the "Three Obediences," this principle caused a Chinese woman to enter her husbands' family as a "humble newcomer," and while the husband could remarry if he was widowed, a woman had to remain single with no primary property rights.[131] Such female passivity was evident to Westerners from their earliest contacts with the East. Marco Polo noted how, in Cathay, the women do not gad about to parties, or listen to improper stories, but walk in the company of their mothers and "on the way they always walk with their eyes cast down in front of their feet."[132]

Social preference for boys began to enlarge during the Han Dynasty but during the Sung Dynasty (960-1280 A.D.), female infanticide became a widely practiced, and socially acceptable, response to the birth of a daughter.[133] In the *Collections* of Su Tung Po it was stated that the common method for disposal at that time was to put the newborn girl into a bucket of cold water, the designation then being referred to as a "water baby."[134] This was especially prevalent in Fukien, Kiangsi, Szechwan, Anhwei, and Yunnan and among the Hakka.[135] Similar drownings were reported frequently in Jiangxi.[136] Male illegitimates were usually saved and adopted by relatives.

During the Han dynasty (202-220 B.C.), infanticide was socially labeled as an homicide and the death penalty was possible. By the Southern Sung (1133 A.D.) it carried a three year penalty and in the Yuan Dynasty (1279-1368 A.D.) a monetary fine. By the Qin (1644-1911 A.D.) there was no specific punishment mentioned in the Criminal Code.[137]

Jesuit missionaries to China in the seventeenth century found thousands of babies, mostly females, thrown on the streets like refuse to be collected each morning and dumped into a huge pit outside the city.[138] The poor, unable to supply their children with common necessities, would often expose them in the streets of the great cities like Pekin and Canton.[139] Sir George Staunton estimated the number of children annually exposed at Pekin at about two thousand.[140] The incidence of infanticide during the Ch'ing Dynasty (1644-1911 A.D.) was so great that it reached epidemic proportions.[141] In 1697, the Kangxi emperor decreed that "the custom of drowning infant girls is to be abolished completely and anyone who disobeys this is to be punished according to the law."[142] But despite the threat of legal intervention, little change occurred.

The killing of girl babies did not abate as China moved slowly into the modern era. Like many ancient societies, the Chinese felt that the expense of raising a daughter was too great.[143] Much of this was blamed on the dowry system and the high cost of raising a daughter in a male based society.[144] For others, the female child was simply considered a burden since they could not carry on the family heritage. The dictates of Chinese familism demanded that the son perpetuate the family line and a daughter was worthless in this regard. In the Yangtze Valley of China, a girl was seen as being of less value to the parents because as soon as she matured, she would leave her parents to go live with her husband's family. As a consequence, female infanticide led to sex-ratios of only 100 girls to 135 boys.[145]

From 1851-1948 statistics indicated that almost five percent of all female births in China ended in infanticide.[146] The mother generally either "placed her head down in a bucket of water, suffocated her, or simply abandoned her to die."[147] With the population of China so large, and the people so poor, the loss of individual female infants did not create a social upheaval for reform. While the classical Han marriage systems considered the bearing of a girl as bad luck, local customs had an effect. In Szechwan, girl babies were killed because they were a burden on the family, but in Shensi, girls were considered precious.[148]

As the Communists came into control in September 1949, there was some attempt to alleviate this practice by making social acceptance of the sexes more equal and putting women to work in factories and in the fields. Despite this commendable action, however, female infanticide continued unabated.[149] In 1943, an official publication of the Nationalist government exhorted the people that "the drowning of girl infants is to be prohibited."[150] It had little effect.

In 1971, the political leaders of China realized they had to do something to lessen the rate of growth of the population, and endorsed the idea of fertility restraint in the Fourth Five-Year Economic Development Plan that year. The set of guidelines which were developed was that the ideal family should have only two children.[151] By 1978 it was apparent that the program was not working and they then embarked upon the "one child per couple" policy.[152] Under this plan, a contract would be signed which granted couples economic and educational advantages in return for their promising to not have more than one child.[153] The proposal was planned to lower the natural population increase rate (births minus deaths) from the then 1.4% to 0.5% by 1985, and to zero population growth by the end of the century.[154] In February, 1980, Chen Muhua, the vice-premier in charge of population control, explicitly outlined the goal: "We will try to attain the goal that 95 percent of married couples in the cities and 90 percent in the countryside will have only one child in due course."[155] By 1981, a nationwide quota system was in place.

If a family defiantly chose to have a second or third child, they would be taxed heavily, up to a year's income for some.[156] This resulted in a shocking increase of female infanticide as 80% of the families attempted to have their only allotted child be a son. Male:female ratios in Hupei province in 1982 reached an incredible 503:100![157] It was estimated that almost 300,000 cases of female infanticide occurred during 1982 and 345,000 in 1983.[158] Steven Mosher found that the government strongly coerced many women into having abortions, and even used infanticide to control population growth.[159] His articles not only angered the Chinese officials, but led to his dismissal from Stanford University because he would not join their "conspiracy of silence" about the problem.[160] But the people followed the directive so well, and so many newborn daughters were killed, that the policy had to be modified in 1988 because of public pressure both in China and abroad.[161] Peking originally argued that the killings were not due to the governmental policies but rather because of the feudal village attitudes that "boys are precious, girls are worthless."[162] Nevertheless, Peng Peiyn, the new Minister in charge of state family planning, said that China will now "allow couples in rural areas with one daughter to have a second child with planned spacing."[163] The city restrictions on procreation were to remain the same. In the interim, it is estimated that over a million babies, mostly female, lost their lives. Even by 1990, the recorded ratio of males to females was 1.066; without excess female destruction this ratio would have been no higher than 1.02.[164] This was due to both female infanticide, and sex-selective abortion. According to one Chinese estimate, 98 percent of fetuses aborted are female.[165]

H. India

But in no country, or historical age, was the practice of female infanticide so extensively and systematically carried out as among certain classes of feudatory Rajputs in Northern and Western India in the nineteenth century. The slaughter of newborn girls was so ingrained into the fabric of local

Indian society at that time that the British government had to impose sex-ratio quotas in some towns in order to make sure that the proportion of boys and girls remained relatively equal. If police did not actually count the number of children in the village to assure acquiescence, the killings would not have ended.

The problem was not new but had gone undetected for many centuries because "infanticide was carried out in the privacy of the women's apartment."[166] While many religious or superstitious observances were openly practiced, such as widows throwing themselves on a burning funeral pyre of their husbands in the deadly ritual known as "sati," the birth of a child was generally unwitnessed. A newborn daughter's death was a secret duty which the Indian mother felt bound to perform in order to protect the rest of their family from financial ruin.[167]

Legend had placed the blame for female infanticide on ancient times. It was said that a powerful Raja among the Jharejas could not find a suitable husband for his daughter and refused to marry her to one of lower rank. The Rajgor, or family brahmin, advised him to put the daughter to death or her unmarried state would lead to disgrace. The Raja could not agree to do this himself, and so the Rajgor consented to bear the responsibility and ordered the girl destroyed. From that time forward, female infanticide began to be practiced in increasing frequency.[168]

While such stories have few serious adherents, there were several practical reasons why the frequency of female infanticide became so enmeshed in Indian culture. First, the prestige of an Indian family often depended on the amount of wealth and manpower available to the clan, and the costs of raising a girl, and then offering a satisfactory dowry for her marriage, were very great. While many Indian cultures practiced some degree of elaborate wedding ceremonies, these particular sects engaged in lavish and expensive preparations so that it was not unusual for a family on the edge of solvency to become bankrupt from the matrimonial expense. R. K. Narayan described in *The Financial Expert* how costly was this process. Magaya complained:

> How much more blessed is he that gives away three daughters? He is blessed no doubt, but he also becomes a bankrupt.[169]

In addition, he retorted that all the money his father had went to the three daughters: "By the time my father found husbands for them there was nothing left for us to eat at home."[170]

These extravagant dowers have been postulated as the primary cause of the extensive acceptance of female infanticide. Tribes adjacent to the Rajputs, where marriages were comparatively inexpensive, showed few signs of female infanticide.[171] But the Rajputs, where the cost of marrying a daughter was great, had a common rule that if there was no reasonable prospect of a suitable marriage, the female infant's life must be forfeited.[172] There were many methods developed to accomplish this task: giving a pill of tobacco and bhang to swallow, drowning in milk, smearing the mother's breast with opium or the juice of the poisonous Datura, or covering the child's mouth with a plaster of cow-dung before it drew breath.[173] Ferishta noted how there was a custom among the Gakkars of the Punjab that:

> As soon as a female child was born to carry her to the door of the house, and there proclaim aloud, holding the child in one hand, and a knife in the other, that any person who wanted a wife might take her now, otherwise she was immediately put to death.[174]

The second reason for accepting female infanticide came from the inferior position women had in the Indian social system. Men were seen as farm hands and fighters for the family name, while women primarily performed only housework. Among the Kallars of the Madurai district, a woman who gave birth only to daughters was looked down upon by members of the community and in order to avoid the wrath of her in-laws she often would do away with the baby and report it as a natural death.[175] While this was not an uncommon world tribal view, it was maintained in India even as modern advancements changed the country from a purely agricultural culture to one more industrial and mechanized. As Bharati Mukherjee noted in her novel, *Jasmine*: "God with infinite memories visited girl children on women who needed to be punished for sins committed in other incarnations."[176]

In addition to the social deprecation associated with the birth of a daughter, there were also practical problems with having only female offspring. Under standard tradition, a son was necessary for the performance of certain funeral rites at the pyre of his father.[177] Women were not allowed to perform this task, and proper burial, as well as an assured passage into the hereafter, was at risk if there were no sons to survive.

The Rajputs were also a warrior race and the status of women was very low.[178] Daughters could not marry below their rank and had to be married before a certain age or there was social disgrace and a blot on the family honor.[179] The payment was so sacred, and inviolable, that even a partial deviation was disgraceful. The higher the rank, the more difficult it was for a daughter to find a proper match. Infanticide seemed to be the only tolerable solution.[180]

Finally, favoritism of the male was legitimized even within the Indian legal system. The *Commentaries* on Hindu laws, or *Mitakshara*, were passed down through the ages as divinely inspired. The family within this framework consisted only of male descendants. As to females: "The wives and daughters are looked upon as appendages of their husbands and fathers; the relatives through females do not belong to the family at all."[181]

This sexist concept existed for centuries. In a poem on the importance of having a son from about 600 B.C., the author explained:

> Food is man's life and clothes afford protection,
> Gold gives him beauty, marriages bring cattle;
> His wife's a friend, his daughter causes pity:
> A son is like a light in highest heaven.[182]

The birth of a daughter was seen as a liability which caused the father to never again be able to prosper throughout the rest of his life.[183]

For many parents, there was only one solution – dispose of the daughter at birth. The story of the discovery of this problem in the eighteenth century was detailed in a book by Edward Moor aptly titled: *Hindu Infanticide, An Account of the Measures Adopted for Suppressing the Practice of the Systematic Murder by Their Parents of Female Infants; With Incidental Remarks on Other Customs Peculiar to the Natives of India.*

The details of this saga seem almost fictional, but the facts are real. In 1789, Mr. Jonathan Duncan wrote to the Governor General of India on the not "unfrequent practice among the tribe of Rajkumar to destroy their daughters, by causing the mothers to refuse them nurture."[184] Duncan was the Governor of Bombay and presented his evidence officially from the Junapore area of the Benaras district.[185] His observations at that time were restricted to the Rajkumars, a clan of Rajputs.[186]

With very little delay, the British government confirmed his findings and an agreement was signed with the local authorities on December 17, 1789 "not to commit any longer such detestable acts."[187] At that time the practice appeared to be common among the Kutch, Kehtri, Nagar, Guzerat, Miazed, Kalowries and Sind inhabitants.[188] It was not until 1795 that a regulation of the law formally declared that the crime would be considered equal to murder.[189]

As the details became public, other instances of female infanticide throughout India became apparent. Captain Seton had written to Mr. Duncan in 1804 that: "Every female infant born in the Raja's family of a Ranni, or lawful wife, is immediately dropped into a hole dug in the earth and filled with milk, where it is drowned."[190] This method of elimination was so common that it even became a saying whereby people, when asked how they put their female children to death, would answer "by making them drink milk."[191]

In the late eighteenth and nineteenth centuries, female infanticide was also a well established social custom among the Jarejas of Kutch and Kathiawar and a number of clans and castes in the North-Western provinces of India such as Punjab and Oudh and in some of the Rajput states of Rajasthan.[192] It was documented among the Khonds, Rajputs, Cutch, Todahs, Hill tribes around Munniepore, and the Biluchi.[193] In the Northwest provinces, about one-half million people were suspected of the practice.[194]

Statistical evidence confirmed the worst fears of the authorities. In 1841 the Jahreja male population of Kathiawar was 5760, while females numbered only 1370.[195] It was estimated that the number of female infants destroyed yearly was 20,000 out of 125,000 families.[196] The British under Lord Lawrence arranged the Umritsur durbar in 1853 where an agreement was reached to expel from a caste every one who committed infanticide, and to adopt moderate rates of marriage expenses to discourage the killing of newborn girls.[197] Eventually it was decided to place under police supervision any tribe in northern India where the percentage of female children fell below a defined level.[198] The effectiveness of the 1880 Act could be seen by the rise in the percentage of girls from 30% in 1877, to 46.8% in 1882.[199]

Social scientists have tried to find other explanations than basic economics for this cultural outrage. Murdock believed that the practice of polyandry was a primary cause.[200] The Todas were a pastoral tribe of buffalo herders who did not view infanticide, or adultery, as a criminal act.[201] Their culture was polyandrous, meaning every woman was allowed to marry several men, and so there were fewer requirements to the progenitation of females.[202] The system of polyandry among the Todas was very well organized. When a woman married a man, it was understood that she became the wife of his brothers at the same time.[203] The terms father and mother included kinship members and not just the biological parent.[204] Unwanted children, especially girls, were suffocated at birth and buried like stillborns. If twins were born, any girls were killed.[205]

James George Frazer found that rather than causing the infanticide among the Todas, polyandry was the result. He concluded that the custom of polyandry among the Todas "was facilitated, if not caused, by a considerable excess of men over women," which was in turn caused by the practice of female infanticide.[206] The motives for this, however, were unclear.

Risley also believed that female infanticide among the Naga tribes in Assan was a consequence of exogamy, where tribes searched for wives outside their own clan, rather than a cause. He noted, however, that the Kandh's believed in female infanticide because: "It was better to destroy girls in their infancy than to allow them to grow up and become causes of strife afterwards."[207] This was because stronger neighbors would raid the tribes in quest of wives. If the females were destroyed at birth, the likelihood of such danger was avoided.[208]

In modern times, the slaughter of female newborns continues. In some parts of India, infanticide of newborn females is so common that it has a special name: "kuzhippa," or "baby intended for the burial pit."[209] According to Andal Damodaran, secretary of the Indian Council for Social Science Research: "A family keeps its first girl child, occasionally a second; all others are killed within 24 hours of birth."[210] Barbara Miller investigated female infanticide in rural India during the twentieth century and noted that daughters were seen as much more of a liability to parents in the Northern parts of the country when compared to the South.[211] Unlike other rural cultures, such as China, this bias affected girls mostly in the higher social strata.[212] Miller argued that the geographic division was primarily due to male favoritism in the Northern territories, while the South was characterized more by "feminism" which resembled the status that women had won in the Western world.[213]

Unlike the progress made in many countries across the globe, the sex-ratio in India has been declining. In 1901, there were 971 women for every 1000 men, while in 1981 this figure was only 933.[214] As late as 1955, boys comprised 63% of the Rajput children in Uttar Pradesh, although by 1975 this had fallen to 55%.[215] Over half of 1250 women surveyed in Madras admitted having killed a baby girl. Estimates indicate that four in ten girls are killed at birth nationwide.[216] Each year, twelve million girls are born in India but 1.5 million die before they reach their first birthday; only 9 million are still alive by age fifteen years.[217] While there is a law prohibiting infanticide, no one in India has yet been convicted.[218]

As if the criminal statistics are not disturbing enough, the figures do not take into account selective abortion which is likely to result in further problems in the future. The use of amniocentesis to discover the sex of the fetus in order to then abort a female is widely prevalent throughout India.[219] In one clinic in Bombay, of 8000 abortions performed, 7999 were female fetuses.[220] The impact of this practice is not small since India has the highest illegal abortion rate in the world: nearly four million women annually terminate their pregnancies.[221] Since this type of favoritism is legal, no amount of criminal sanctions will correct the problem. Unless societal pressure is made to bear upon the status of women so as to encourage parents to desire to raise a daughter equally to a son, we can expect unequal sex-ratios for many years to come. According to many observers, this will not occur until women are allowed to play a more prominent role in the production of goods and in the ability to have the legal right to own property and land.

Endnotes

1 . Kristof, "Stark Data On Women: 100 Million Are Missing," C1.
2 . Ibid., C12. In the Western Indian state of Maharashta, a law was passed prohibiting amniocentesis to determine the sex of the unborn child because it was being used to abort female fetuses. Gorman-Stapleton, "Prohibiting Amniocentesis in India: A Solution to the Problem of Female Infanticide or a Problem to the Solution of Prenatal Diagnosis," 23.
3 . American Medical News (July 29, 1996): 55.
4 . Tefft, "A Rush to Rob the Cradle – of Girls," 1.
5 . Ronald Ericsson has licensed sperm centers around the world which utilize his patented procedure to predetermine the sex of an artificial pregnancy with success rates of 75-85%. Underwood, "Choosing Baby's Gender," 66.
6 . Leo, "Baby Boys, To Order," 59.
7 . Dahlburg, "Faith & Practice: A Changing World Puts Abortion in the Spotlight," H1.
8 . Hale, "the Brutality of Growth Control," 1A.
9 . Dahlburg, "Faith & Practice: A Changing World Puts Abortion in the Spotlight," H1.
10 . Tefft, "A Rush to Rob the Cradle – of Girls," 1.
11 . Wertz & Fletcher, "Fatal Knowledge? Prenatal Diagnosis and Sex Selection," 21.
12 . Kristof, "Stark Data On Women: 100 Million Are Missing," C1.
13 . Ibid.
14 . Ibid.
15 . Hale, "The Brutality of Growth Control," 1A.
16 . Female Infanticide. <http://www.uia.org/uidademo/pro/ f3382.htm> (4/25/99).
17 . McKee, "Sex Differentials in Survivorship and the Customary Treatment of Infants and Children," 108.
18 . The Celestina, I, 8.
19 . Hoffer & Hull, Murdering Mothers: Infanticide in England and New England 1558-1803, 3.
20 . Barclay, Techniques of Population Analysis, 83.
21 . Coale & Banister, "Five Decades of Missing Females in China," 459.
22 . Nordborg has shown that female infanticide may at times not bias the sex ration, lead to a male-biased ratio or even a female-biased ration depending on the manner in which the parental preferences are implemented. Nordborg, "Female Infanticide and Human Sex Ratio Evolution," 195.
23 . Neel, "Lessons From a `Primitive' People," 816.
24 . Engels, "The Problem of Female Infanticide in the Greco-Roman World," 113.
25 . Darwin, The Descent of Man, I.IV, 134.
26 . Harris, Cannibals & Kings, 10.
27 . M'Lennan, Primitive Marriage, 165.
28 . Avebury, The Origin of Civilization & the Primitive Condition of Man, 114.
29 . Langer, "Infanticide: A Historical Survey," 354.
30 . Engels, "The Problem of Female Infanticide in the Greco-Roman World," 112.
31 . Patterson, "Not Worth The Rearing: The Causes of Infant Exposure in Ancient Greece," 120.
32 . Engels, "The Problem of Female Infanticide in the Greco-Roman World," 115.
33 . Pomeroy, "Infanticide in Hellenistic Greece," 209-213.

34 . Van Hook, "The Exposure of Infants At Athens," 135. See e.g., Golden, Children and Childhood in Classical Athens, 94.
35 . Golden, "Demography and the Exposure of Girls at Athens," 330.
36 . Dionysius of Halicarnassus, Roman Antiquities, II.XV.2, Volume 1, 355.
37 . Lindsay, The Ancient World, 168. See e.g. Langer, "Infanticide: A Historical Survey," 354.
38 . Boswell, The Kindness of Strangers, 102.
39 . Ibid.
40 . deMause, The History of Childhood, 25.
41 . Apuleius, The Golden Ass, X.23, 513.
42 . Rawson, "Children in the Roman Familia," 173.
43 . Ibid., 179.
44 . Ovid, Metamorphoses, IX.683, 229.
45 . Pakrasi, Female Infanticide in India, 16.
46 . Hastings, Encyclopedia of Religion & Ethics, Volume I, 4.
47 . Westermarck, The Origin and Development of the Moral Ideas, Volume I, 406.
48 . Smith, Kinship & Marriage in Early Arabia, 293.
49 . Ibid., 153, 155.
50 . Koran, footnote 2, 204. Referred to as 'Umar elsewhere. O'Leary, Arabia Before Muhammad, 202.
51 . Smith, Kinship & Marriage in Early Arabia, 291.
52 . Pakrasi, Female Infanticide in India, 16-17.
53 . O'Leary, Arabia Before Muhammad, 202.
54 . Ibid., 202-03; Smith, Kinship & Marriage in Early Arabia, 292-293.
55 . Mayer, Islam & Human Rights, 110.
56 . Koran, LXXI:8-9, 45.
57 . Ibid., XVI:60-62, 204.
58 . Ibid., IV:38, 415.
59 . Ibid., XVII:42, 168.
60 . Ibid., XLII.48, 274.
61 . Genesis 2:7. The Anchor Bible, 14.
62 . Genesis 2:18. Ibid., 15.
63 . Genesis 2:21-23. Ibid.
64 . Haggadah, "Woman." The Other Bible, 31.
65 . Sanhedrin, Gemara, XI.100b.
66 . Ibid.
67 . Baba Kamma, VIII, Gemara 87b.
68 . Sanhedrin, I.4a.
69 . 1 Timothy 2:10-14. The Living Bible, 965.
70 . I Corinthians 11:3. Ibid., 922.
71 . I Corinthians 11:9. Ibid.
72 . Ephesians 5:23-24. Ibid., 945.
73 . The Letters of Abelard and Heloise, 3, 131.
74 . Martyr, "The First Apology," 27, Writings, 63.
75 . Ibid., 27, 64.
76 . Clement of Alexandria, "Paedogogus", III.III, 288.
77 . Boswell, The Kindness of Strangers, 3.
78 . Creekmore, Lyrics of the Middle Ages, 4.
79 . Boswell, The Kindness of Strangers, 264.

80 . Coleman, "Infanticide in the Early Middle Ages," 49.
81 . Ibid., 53-54.
82 . Kellum, "Infanticide in England in the Later Middle Ages," 368.
83 . Damme, "Infanticide: The Worth of an Infant Under Law," 2.
84 . Kellum, "Infanticide in England in the Later Middle Ages," 368.
85 . Martinson, Growing up in Norway, 800 to 1990, 27.
86 . Westrup, Introduction to Early Roman Law, 249.
87 . Rees & Rees, Celtic Heritage: Ancient Tradition in Ireland and Wales, 220-222.
88 . Lynn, Daughters and Parents, 42.
89 . Atkinson, "Society and the Sexes in the Russian Past," 17.
90 . Ibid., footnote 50, 17.
91 . Divale & Harris, "Population, Warfare, & the Male Supremacist Complex," 530.
92 . Ibid., 530-31.
93 . Fison & Howitt, Kamilaroi & Kurnai, 135.
94 . Ibid., 137.
95 . M'Lennan, Studies in Ancient History, 91.
96 . Langness, "Child Abuse and Cultural Values: The Case of New Guinea," 14-15.
97 . Aptekar, Anjea: Infanticide, Abortion & Contraception in Savage Society, 67.
98 . Frazer, Totemism & Exogamy, Volume 3, 358.
99 . Lomis, "Maternal Filicide: A Preliminary Examination of Culture and Victim Sex," 503.
100. Smith & Smith, "Inuit Sex-ratio Variation: Population Control, Ethnographic Error, or Parental Manipulation?," 595.
101. Ibid.
102. Schrire & Steiger, "A Matter of Life and Death: An Investigation into the Practice of Female Infanticide in the Arctic," 179.
103. Ibid., 596.
104. Balikci, "Female Infanticide on the Arctic Coast," 615.
105. Ibid., 621.
106. Balikci, "The Netsilik Eskimos," 1.
107. Balikci, "Female Infanticide on the Arctic Coast," 624. In ethnographic language, it was best explained as a consequence of "parental efforts to match the number of sons with locally prevailing, but regionally variable, rates of sex-specific mortality and economic productivity." Smith & Smith, "Inuit Sex-ratio Variation: Population Control, Ethnographic Error, or Parental Manipulation?," 595.
108. Schrire & Steiger, "A Matter of Life and Death: An Investigation into the Practice of Female Infanticide in the Arctic," 162.
109. Balikci, "Netsilik," 424.
110. Ibid., 427.
111. Chapman, "Infanticide and Fertility Among Eskimos: A Computer Simulation," 317.
112. Dickeman, "Demographic Consequences of Infanticide in Man," 126.
113. Ibid., 128.
114. Ibid.
115. Ibid., 126.
116. Ibid., 128.
117. Shiono, Maya, Tabata, Fujiwara, Azumi & Morita, "Medicolegal Aspects of Infanticide in Hokkaido District, Japan," 104, 106.

118. Kumasaka, Smith & Aiba, "Crimes in New York and Tokyo: Sociocultural Perspectives," 24.
119. Sakuta & Saito, "A Socio-medical Study on 71 Cases of Infanticide in Japan," *Keio Journal of Medicine* 30 (1981): 159. Cited by Funayama, Ikeda, Tabata, Azumi & Morita, "Case Report: Repeated Neonaticides in Hokkaido," 149.
120. Ibid., 150.
121. Kaku, "Were Girl Babies Sacrificed to a Folk Superstition in 1966 in Japan?," 391.
122. Orleans, *Every Fifth Child: The Population of China*, 36.
123. Poffenberger, "Child Rearing and Social Structure in Rural India," *Child Abuse and Neglect: Cross-Cultural Perspectives*, 79.
124. Croll, *Feminism & Socialism in China*, 12.
125. Lee, "Female Infanticide in China," 164.
126. Stacey, *Patriarchy and Socialist Revolution in China*, 43.
127. Po Chu-i, "Golden Bells," in Waley, *Translations From the Chinese*, 152.
128. Yu-Lan, *A History of Chinese Philosophy*, 327.
129. Yanshi jiaxun, XBCZJC, 2:6. Lee, "Female Infanticide in China," 165.
130. Fairbank & Reischauer, *China, Tradition & Transformation*, 16.
131. Ibid.
132. Polo, *The Travels*, 167.
133. Yao, *Chinese Women: Past & Present*, 75.
134. Ibid. 91.
135. Ibid. 92.
136. Lee, "Female Infanticide in China," 166.
137. Hom, "Female Infanticide in China: The Human Rights Specter and Thoughts Towards Another Vision," footnote 22, 255.
138. Langer, "Infanticide: A Historical Survey," 354.
139. Malthus, "An Essay on the Principle of Population, or, A View of Its Past and Present Effects on Human Happiness; With an Inquiry into Our Prospects Respecting the Future Removal or Mitigation of the Evils Which it Occasions (1872)," *On Population*, I.XII, 215-216.
140. Ibid., 216.
141. Yao, *Chinese Women: Past & Present*, 93.
142. Ibid. 167.
143. Connery, *Abortion: The Development of the Roman Catholic Perspective*, 26.
144. Poffenberger, "Child Rearing and Social Structure in Rural India," 80.
145. Fei, *Peasant Life in China: A Field Study of Country Life in the Yangtze Valley*, 34.
146. Eastman, *Family Fields & Ancestors*, 21.
147. Ibid.
148. Kiel, "Forensic Science in China: Traditional and Contemporary Aspects," 213.
149. *Time Magazine*, Fall 1990, 36.
150. Orleans, *Every Fifth Child: The Population of China*, 36.
151. Tien, *China's Strategic Demographic Initiative*, 29.
152. Ibid., 87-88.
153. Yuan, Tianlu, Yu, Jingneng & Zhongtang, "China's Demographic Dilemmas," 11.
154. Mosher, "Human Rights in the New China," 31.
155. Ibid.
156. Mosher, "Forced Abortions and Infanticide in Communist China," 13.

157. Nation 246 (June 18, 1988): 848. At times, some of these incredible sex-ratio alterations could be due to the registering of only a part of the population. Lee, "Female Infanticide in China," 35.
158. Weisskopy, "China's Birth Control Policy Drives Some to Kill Baby Girls," A1.
159. Mosher, "Forced Abortions and Infanticide in Communist China," 10.
160. Ibid., 11.
161. This pressure was not swiftly applied, however. Steven Westlely Mosher, a doctoral candidate in anthropology at Stanford University, was fired after revealing the cruelties of Chinese birth control practices in a popular Taiwan weekly in 1980. The Chinese authorities complained that "the photographs taken by Mr. Mosher during his story exceeded the scope of his research topic (and) had nothing to do with any conceivable social science research topic." Shapley, "Anthropologist Fired: Stanford Plays Its China Card," 280.
162. Mosher, "Forced Abortions and Infanticide in Communist China," 22.
163. Bullough & Ruan, "China's Children," 848.
164. Coale & Banister, "Five Decades of Missing Females in China," 460.
165. Aird, "China's War on Children," 60.
166. Panigrahi, British Social Policy and Female Infanticide in India, 15.
167. Pakrasi, Female Infanticide in India, 33.
168. Ibid., 30.
169. Narayan, The Financial Expert, 8.
170. Ibid.
171. Westermarck, The History of Human Marriage, Volume III, 168.
172. Ibid., 162.
173. Encyclopedia Britannica, 1881, Volume XIII, 3.
174. Westermarck, The History of Human Marriage, Volume III, 162.
175. Krishnaswamy, "A Note on Female Infanticide: An Anthropological Inquiry," 299-300.
176. Mukherjee, Jasmine, 34.
177. Minturn & Hitchcock, The Rajputs of Khalapur, India, 96.
178. Panigrahi, British Social Policy and Female Infanticide in India, 4.
179. Pakrasi, Female Infanticide in India, 6.
180. Ibid., 13.
181. Markby, An Introduction to Hindu & Mahommedan Law, 54.
182. "Aitareya Brahmana," Poetry of the Orient, 256.
183. Arya, "The Family Structure of the Folk People of Western Uttar Pradesh," 246.
184. Letter dated October 2, 1789. Moor, Hindu Infanticide, An Account of the Measures Adopted for Suppressing the Practice of the Systematic Murder by Their Parents of Female Infants, 4.
185. Pakrasi, Female Infanticide in India, 2.
186. Panigrahi, British Social Policy and Female Infanticide in India, 16.
187. Moor, Hindu Infanticide, An Account of the Measures Adopted for Suppressing the Practice of the Systematic Murder by Their Parents of Female Infants, 8.
188. Ibid., 27.
189. Regulation XXI. Panigrahi, British Social Policy and Female Infanticide in India, 18.
190. Moor, Hindu Infanticide, An Account of the Measures Adopted for Suppressing the Practice of the Systematic Murder by Their Parents of Female Infants, 19.
191. Ibid., 27.

192. Panigrahi, British Social Policy and Female Infanticide in India, xi. It was widely prevalent in the North-Western provinces and Oudh, among the various clans of Rajputs; the Jats, Gujars, Ahirs, Tagas and Koris of certain clans, in the Punjab the Sikhs, especially the Bedis and Sodhis, the Rajputs, the Khatris, the Moyal Brahmans, the pure Pathans, and spurious Muhummadans; in Kutch and Kathiawar it was exclusively confined to the Jarejas and Jaitwas and in Ahmedabad and Kaira, the Lewa Khombees; in Rajputana and Central India the Rajputs of high rank. Ibid, 5-6.
193. M'Lennan, Studies in Ancient History, 85-87.
194. Panigrahi, British Social Policy and Female Infanticide in India, xii.
195. Ibid., 41.
196. Pakrasi, Female Infanticide in India, 33.
197. Encyclopedia Britannica, 1881, Volume XIII, 3.
198. Ibid.
199. Panigrahi, British Social Policy and Female Infanticide in India, 188.
200. Murdock, Our Primitive Contemporaries, 121.
201. Ibid., 116.
202. Aptekar, Anjea: Infanticide, Abortion & Contraception in Savage Society, 59-60.
203. Rivers, The Todas, 515.
204. Murdock, Our Primitive Contemporaries, 116.
205. Ibid., 119.
206. Frazer, Totemism & Exogamy, Volume 2, 263.
207. Hodson, "Female Infanticide in India," 91.
208. Ibid.
209. Murphy, "Killing Baby Girls Routine in India," C12.
210. Ibid.
211. Miller, The Endangered Sex, Neglect of Female Children in Rural North India, 14.
212. Ibid., 15.
213. Ibid., 24.
214. Bajpai, "India's Lost Women," 49.
215. Minturn, "Changes in the Differential Treatment of Rajput Girls in Khalapur: 1955-1975," 127.
216. Thomson, "Editorial, Why are Potential Women Being Killed?," 181.
217. Bajpai, "India's Lost Women," 49.
218. Thomson, "Editorial, Why are Potential Women Being Killed?," 182.
219. Jeffery, Jeffery & Lyon, "Female Infanticide and Amniocentesis," 1207.
220. Thomson, "Editorial, Why are Potential Women Being Killed?," 181.
221. Four Million Babies Aborted Each Year. April 28, 1998. <http://www.lioncity.com/wwwboard/messages/13.html> April 25, 1999.

CHAPTER IX

PUNISHMENT

> "More children under 5 years of age die from mistreatment by parents than from tuberculosis, whooping cough, polio, measles, rheumatic fever and appendicitis combined."[1]

A. BACKGROUND

The above quotation, from Jerome Leavitt's book on *The Battered Child*, graphically points out the dangers children face from punishment inflicted by their parents. Modern society has frequently overlooked this problem as concern for the general welfare of children has often overshadowed the plight of individual families: the forest has been seen, but the trees have been missed.

In the Declaration of the Rights of the Child adopted by the United Nations in 1959, the preamble states that: "Mankind owes the child the best it has to give."[2] To that end they voted that: "The child shall be protected from all form of neglect, cruelty and exploitation."[3] This valorous sentiment, while unanimously acclaimed by ambassadors from every major country in the world, does not reflect the all too frequent harmful conduct of parents which leaves many children in harm's way, even within the confines of their own home.

One need only scan the daily newspapers to see evidence of this wretched behavior. In the 1991 Indiana criminal trial of Dr. Gary and Gloria Shipley for the killing of their five-year-old daughter, the state prosecutor claimed that they embarked on a pattern of abuse and deprivation that ultimately Amy's body could not survive: "That, ladies and gentlemen, is murder." The defense attorney countered this claim by maintaining that the Shipleys were simply trying to discipline their child in ways they felt were in her best interests. They were "at their wits end" in trying to keep Amy in line, and that's why they locked her in the bathroom, and "that's why they fed her milk laced with ground pepper."[4] It should be noted that Gary Shipley was a practicing physician, and his wife was a registered nurse. This case manifested the "best" they could give.

In 1992, in Highland Park, Illinois, the parents of four-year-old Eduardo Mendoza Jr. were so upset over his repeated soiling of his pants that they continuously whipped him with an extension cord and kicked and bit him. The newspaper account of the boy's death stated that: "The bruises over the child's body were so extensive it took the pathologist for the Cook County

Medical Examiner's Office more than two hours to count them."[5] Mr. and Mrs. Mendoza were relatively uneducated immigrants from Mexico. This case manifested the "best" they could give.

These two brief case reports are not unique and reflect how much harm a parent can inflict upon a child in an attempt to discipline their misbehavior. The problem is not restricted to any one time or place, and the fine line between stern punishment and fatal abuse is often crossed by individuals of all cultures, education, and wealth without the realization of how grotesque the chastisement has become. Kaplun and Reich, after analyzing children murdered by their parents in New York City, concluded that "the murder of a child is the final chapter in his history of maltreatment."[6] Along the way, most of the abuse has been hidden from view.

Even though society has always developed legal restrictions to designate appropriate conduct, parents have consistently been given wide authority over the discipline and raising of their offspring.[7] Sovereignties did not generally interfere with what was seen as the natural right of a parent to raise a child in a manner they individually saw fit. This basic privilege included the prerogative to use physical punishment when necessary to maintain family order and to prevent the development of unruly habits. Even today, forty-six states in America permit corporal punishment of children, and a similar allowance exists in Australia, Barbados, Canada, Ireland, New Zealand, South Africa, Swaziland, Trinidad, Tobago, and the United Kingdom.[8]

In Egypt, as early as 3000 B.C., the maxim of training young boys was that "a boy's ears are on his back," which meant that whippings were frequently used for discipline.[9] In fact, the word for "teaching" in Egyptian is etymologically the same as that for "punishment".[10] Similarly, in Sumeria, the schools had "a man in charge of the whip" in order to punish boys who misbehaved.[11]

Adults were seen as rulers of their own child. Under the Babylonian Code of King Hammurabi, from about 2250 B.C., if a son hit his father, the boy's fingers were cut off.[12] Aristotle noted that Persians fathers ruled their children in a tyrannical manner and usually used their sons as slaves.[13] Seven centuries before the birth of Christ, Ahiqar, the adviser to the king of Assyria, found that severe discipline of children was so important that he initiated the famous aphorism "spare the rod, spoil the child."[14]

The rise of Judaism and Christianity may have lessened the incidence of child exposure, but it did little to modify the severe punishment of children when they did not follow the lessons commanded by the Lord. In the Old Testament, parents of rebellious children were even given the option of asking for the death penalty as punishment for defiant behavior. If a son did not respond to reprimands, he could be brought before the Sanhedrin and charged with a capital crime. The Biblical text demanded that guilty verdicts be handed down in specific situations:

> Anyone who reviles or curses his mother or father shall surely be put to death.[15]
>
> Anyone who curses his father, or mother shall surely be put to death – for he has cursed his own flesh and blood.[16]
>
> Anyone who strikes his father or mother shall surely be put to death.[17]

Such corrections were not left to the privacy of a parent's home, however. If anyone thought that they had a stubborn or rebellious child, they first had to strongly warn and punish the boy as best they could. If there was no improvement:

> Then his father and mother shall take him before the elders of the city and declare, "this son of ours is stubborn and rebellious and won't obey; he is a worthless drunkard." Then the men of the city shall stone him to death.[18]

Note how this retribution was directed only at sons and did not include daughters, or full grown men.[19] The *Talmud* explained that a boy could only be charged during the time "that he produces two hairs until he grows a beard right around," meaning the hairs of the genitals and not of the face.[20] Maimonides explained that this was until the "hair surrounds the entire membrum."[21] Both the mother and father had to be willing to have the child killed, and they had to show that there had first been a warning and scourging of the child before three judges.[22] If the defiant behavior continued, then the trial to determine the death penalty would be before twenty-three judges.[23]

The *Talmud* even went on to explain how these children would be punished if they ran away after being charged with being stubborn and rebellious: "If he fled before his trial was completed, and then his nether hair grew round, he is free, but if he fled after his trial was completed, and then his nether hair grew round, he remains liable."[24] The reason for the rabbis' concern was that the ultimate destiny of a rebellious son was dangerous to the entire community. Despite the biblical concern for life, and prohibition of murder, the action was necessary for "the death of the ungodly is a benefit to them and a benefit to the world."[25] His evil habits would ultimately lead to sin and this could prove to be a calamity to all Jewry.

Other sections of the biblical text provided warnings to children which supported such extreme measures: "One who curses his father and his mother – His lamp will go out in the darkness of night."[26] The Old Testament, besides authorizing fatal punishment for rebellious behavior, also encouraged lesser means to maintain the discipline of their child. In *Proverbs* the following cautionary notes were expressed:

> He who will not punish his son shows no love for him,
> For if he loves him he should be concerned to discipline him.[27]
> A senseless soul is a vexation to his father
> And bitterness to her who bore him.[28]
> A wise son values correction,
> But the insolent will not listen to rebuke.[29]
> A youngster's heart is filled with rebellion,
> But punishment will drive it out of him.[30]
> Punishment and rebuke produce wisdom,
> But the boy who gets his own way will shame his mother.[31]
> Discipline your son and he will give you happiness and peace of mind.[32]
> Discipline your son while there is still hope for him,
> And do not indulge him to his own destruction.[33]

The *Talmud* also contained similar warnings:

> Do not threaten a child. Either punish or forgive him.[34]
> He who rebukes not his son leads him into delinquency.[35]

Philo, the first century A.D. Jewish philosopher, agreed that fathers had the rights to admonish their children severely if they did not submit to threats. This included beating them, degrading them and even putting them in bonds.[36] According to Josephus, a Jewish historian from the same era, if children were talked to about their insolence, and did not listen, then they were to be stoned.[37] If the child continued to rebel, the punishment could be extended to death, "though here it requires more than the father alone or the mother alone."[38] The early Jewish philosophers found no problem with assuring that children would follow the tenets of the Lord with threats, and actions, of death.

Maimonides, the famous twelfth century Jewish philosopher and physician, did not dispute the reasonableness of this punishment but said that stoning to death for cursing a mother or father would not be proscribed unless a warning was first given about the prohibited activity. In addition, the only curses which would lead to this extreme penalty were the special names of God.[39] He agreed that if you would strike your parent and leave a mark, you would be killed by strangulation.[40]

Jewish folktales also told of how to treat "The Rebellious son." In one version, a man complained to the king that his son "raised his hand and slapped my face." The king demanded witnesses to confirm the story and when they authenticated the father's complaint, he had the son's head cut off. He added that: "Were it not that I do not pass sentence of death without witnesses, I would slay his mother, for she was faithless to you and conceived from some other man, for her son who hit you could not have come forth from your loins."[41]

In another fictional version, an old man complained that his rich son left him live in poverty and the king ordered the son's head cut off but the father relented when the man was about to be killed and asked for his life to be saved.[42] The lesson, however, was clear – parents retained the power to sternly punish their impudent offspring, even to the point of death.

The arrival of Christianity did little to change these disciplinary actions, although one does not read of stonings as appropriate punishment in the New Testament. The famous Christian Latin poet Prudentius, writing of his upbringing in the fourth century A.D., noted how "my first years wept beneath the rod with its merciless blows."[43] Such discipline was never frowned upon by stern theologians.

This rigorous upbringing continued for centuries and the intensity of the discipline was even increased during the Middle Ages. Much of this came about from the child being allied with the interests of the devil, according to many medieval sources.[44] To control the child's behavior it was necessary at times to literally beat the devil out of him. It was firmly believed that "much folly and lewdness was couched in a child's heart," and if it was "not purged, will burst forth" into enormities.[45] The rod was the means for forming the child in the religious image desired: "The more she loveth him, the sharper she beateth him."[46] Even into the sixteenth century, parents were instructed that they must bring up their children "in the fear and nurture of the Lord."[47]

In modern day society, such extreme discipline has been approved by many regional sects in order to help prepare the children for the study of biblical teachings. If the desire to follow the parent's directions did not naturally arise, it was emphasized into existence with pain. In *Light in August*, by William Faulkner, McEachern repeatedly whipped the orphan boy he found because the lad did not wish to learn his assignments. Each whipping was began with prayers to God:

> He asked that he be forgiven for trespass against the Sabbath and for lifting his hand against a child, an orphan, who was dear to God. He asked that the child's stubborn heart be softened and that

> the sin of disobedience be forgiven him also, through the advocacy of the man he had flouted and disobeyed, requesting that Almighty be as magnanimous as himself, and by and through and because of conscious grace.[48]

The Greco-Roman world also supported strict control over the raising of children. In Sparta, discipline of children became a legendary show of fortitude and strength. Boys were lashed with whips during the entire day at the altar of Artemis, frequently to the point of mental and physical exhaustion. They were required to bravely endure this castigation cheerfully, often vying with one another for the supremacy of who could suffer being beaten for the longer time.[49]

Lucian related how mothers would urge the children to hold on and endure pain with threats, even to the point of dying, to which Anacharsis remarked that any state which submits to such ridiculous treatment "wants a dose of hellebore," the popular medication prescribed by physicians for madness.[50] Seneca provided the Stoic interpretation that the parents did not dislike their children in Sparta, but rather "their own fathers call upon them to endure bravely the blows of the whip, though mangled and half dead" to build strength since "the fragile trees are those that have grown in a sunny valley."[51] Life was tough, and children had to learn early to prepare for the dangers ahead. The beatings were not meant to dishearten, or harm, the children, but rather to build endurance and the ability to survive.

But to some observers, the abuse was not based in such noble motives. In *The Clouds*, by Aristophanes, Strepsiades explained to his son that: "I've got the right to beat you now; but one day you may have a son, and you'll have the right to beat him."[52] Parental discipline seems to have taken on the adolescent mentality ascribed to present day college fraternity hazing techniques.

As the development of ancient legal systems codified the standard precepts of family function into law, the authority of the parent remained intact. The ancient Roman Twelve Tables gave the father absolute power over his children, even if this meant exposure or fatal discipline.[53] This *patriae potestas* was based in the natural order of things, and would characterize Roman law for centuries. The mother, however, did not participate in this power, and if she killed her child she could be found guilty of parricide in both the Twelve Tables and in later Roman legal development.[54]

The Romans were intent on not allowing children the right of independence until they were mature adults. They felt that the Greek constitution was lacking in this regard for it only allowed the father to rule the sons for a short period of time, and the punishment for disobedience was not very great.[55]

Dionysius of Halicarnassus explained why this was deficient:

> But mild punishments are not sufficient to restrain the folly of youth and its stubborn ways or to give self-control to those who have been heedless of all that is honorable; and accordingly among the Greeks many unseemly deeds are committed by children against their parents. But the lawgiver of the Romans gave virtually full power to the father over his son, even during his whole life, whether he thought proper to imprison him, to scourge him, to put him in chains and keep him at work in the fields, or to put him to death.[56]

The Romans, like the Jews, accepted that death could be a just punishment for familial disobedience in certain select situations. When Horatius fought victoriously for Roman victory against the Curiatii and lost his two brothers, he returned to Rome with his spoils and found his sister grieving for the loss of her betrothed, one of the enemy Curiatii. He killed her with a sword and his father Publius Horatius said at his trial that his "daughter had been justly slain."[57]

They also felt that the inability of a child to reason made it appropriate to use physical pain to force him to do right.[58] The Latin word for teaching is *disciplina*, which has taken on the standard meaning for punishment. Plutarch decried this treatment and said that "children should be led to honorable practices by means of encouragement and reasoning and not by blows and ill-treatment which are more fitting for slaves."[59] He added, however, that excessive affection could lead to an unaffectionate child.[60]

The *Institutes* of Justinian, in 533 A.D., while making certain other advances in the treatment of exposure of infants, nevertheless continued the strict *patriae potestas* of Roman family law. Children begotten in lawful marriage remained under the total control of the father and strict discipline was recommended until at least age seven years: "For children below the age of seven years, or who have just passed that age, resemble lunatics in want of intelligence."[61]

The Chinese culture saw children as a great boon to a family, for they would give their parents due honors of burial and pay respects to their memory after death. But they nevertheless placed strict disciplinary control on the child's upbringing as well, and would allow punishment to extend even to the death of the child. Their early legal system held that:

> If a son complains of injustice done to him by this father, or a younger brother by an elder, he receives a hundred blows with a bamboo, and is banished for three years, if he is in the right; if not, he is strangled. If a son should raise his hand against his father,

> he is condemned to have his flesh torn from his body with red-hot pincers.[62]

Even the modern Chinese culture values the traditional absolute rights of parents to inflict harsh physical punishment upon children and the filial piety of the child obliges them to endure or even show enjoyment over this punishment.[63]

During the Middle Ages, whippings continued to be the favored means of disciplining children. Physical violence was not frowned upon in those days, and the punitive discipline of children was "almost universal."[64] Whippings were common for children who cried, refused to eat or show affection, and especially for stubbornness or obstinate behavior.[65] The pain and suffering was seen as good for their souls. One thirteenth century adage held that: "If one beats a child until it bleeds, then it will remember, but if one beats it to death, the law applies."[66] A late sixteenth century Dutchman, Batty, even concluded that the providence and wisdom of God had especially formed the human buttocks so they could be beaten severely without injuring the body seriously.[67]

The primary motive of most medieval parents was to maintain parental control and also protect the reverence of the child's soul. There was also an awareness, however, of the tribulations of life which the child needed to face as an adult. The Middle Ages offered little protection of law, no social agencies to watch out for one's welfare, and few conveniences at home or at work. In 1580, Montaigne told how: "A boy must be broken in to the discomfort and hardship of exercise, in preparation for the discomfort and hardship of a dislocation, the colic, cauteries, gaol, and torture."[68]

Thomas Hobbes, in his seventeenth century English *Elements of Law*, agreed with these ancient paternalistic principles. He believed that the covenants of cohabitation would allow all men to have "for the most part also the sole right and dominion over the children."[69] He expanded this authority by saying that parents may alienate their children, sell or give them into servitude, and even "kill them for rebellion, or sacrifice them for peace."[70] The laws of nature demanded that parents be given extensive authority when they felt it was necessary for the protection of the expanded family.

This power was not always directed toward beneficial ends, however, and Martin Andersen-Nexo told of parents in Denmark who "rated dead things above the living child." They punished the children with a stick that hung over the child like a constant threat. And the discipline could even prove fatal:

> It certainly was owing only to the parents' infinite goodness that

> a small boy got permission to stay alive after breaking a tooth off the rake, or tearing a few knots in the old fishing net. By rights he should have been beaten to a pulp long ago.[71]

These extensive rights of parents to punish their children, even to the point of death, persisted up to the time of Colonial America. In 1646, the General Court of Massachusetts Bay enacted a law whereby "a stubborn or rebellious son, of sufficient years and understanding," which meant at least sixteen years of age, who would not obey even after being chastened, would be brought before the Magistrates in court and "such a son shall be put to death."[72] These "Stubborn Child Laws" were enacted in Connecticut in 1650, Rhode Island in 1668, and New Hampshire in 1679.[73]

Although the Stubborn Child Laws were enacted with popular consent, an actual death penalty was never imposed. Public whipping of rebellious children, however, was another legislative act that met with immediate favor and was frequently carried out.[74] Its intent to promote obedience by the infliction of both pain and shame fit in well with the social structure of Colonial America. The Puritans, like much of medieval society, did not recognize childhood as a separate human age per se, but rather treated the child as an adult as soon as they could do without their mother or nurse.[75] Tolerance of teenage impudence did not become an accepted social premise until the advent of modern times.

The Renaissance brought much advancement to the Arts and Sciences, but in the harsh discipline of children there was little change. In the eighteenth century, John Wesley typified these teachings when he advised bringing up children in a manner designed to break their wills. "Let a child from a year old be taught to fear the rod and to cry softly," he warned, justifying the Biblical proverb: "He that spareth the rod hateth his son."[76] The prevailing view was that every parent "had the sacred right to punish his offspring," even if it presumably meant the child would be worked into an early grave.[77] Children were often starved, beaten, and forced to work for material gain of the parents.[78] This was accepted as payment for the services which the adult rendered in rearing the child. By today's standard, this type of treatment would mean that a very large percentage of the offspring would be labeled as "battered children."[79]

How could such oblivion to the rights of children be tolerated by an otherwise moral society? John Locke, in his *Second Treatise on Government*, wrote that although all men were in essence equal under natural law, children were not born into a full state of equality and the parents retained a duty and jurisdiction over them. This included "the power of commanding and chastising them."[80] He was not concerned about abuse for: "God hath woven into the Principles of Humane nature such a tenderness for their offspring, that there is little fear that parents should use their power with too much rigour."[81] Nevertheless, he reasoned that even though "fathers have a power over the lives of their children, because they gave them life and being," it is not proper to act without the principle of divine justice.[82] Just because you give something to another does not give you the right to take it away as well. This latter right is reserved only for God, the Author and Giver of life.[83]

In England, the power of the father over his child adopted the Roman maxim of *patriae potestas*, but lawful correction of an underage child had to be carried out in a reasonable manner.[84] If a child died from punishment inflicted for disciplinary purposes, the parent was charged with murder. The spirit of the law, however, was sometimes overshadowed by the insignificant legal status of the child. In 1761, when the penalty for petty larceny was death, a woman who was convicted of gouging out the eyes of her children so that they would be more suitable for securing her income as beggars, was committed to prison for only a two-year term.[85]

Blackstone summarized the legal position of the English courts at that time: if a parent killed his child during moderate punishment, it was a "misadventure, since there was no intention of hurt." But if he exceeded the "bounds of moderation," and death ensued, then the appropriate felony charge was either manslaughter or murder.[86]

One particular social problem in eighteenth century England which accentuated the abuse of children was the almost epidemic presence of alcoholism. Drunken parents inflicted much abuse and suffering on their children, and inebriation was so common that it was hard to pin a manslaughter charge because juries would accept the claim that the defendant was drunk, and therefore lacked the necessary intent to do harm.[87] Even if a guilty verdict was returned, the sentence was usually minimal, and the family would soon be united with the remaining children under the care of an even more destitute parent.

Harsh punishment of children was also quite characteristic of the German peasant family. In the fictional tale *Hannele*, by Gerhart Hauptmann, a young girl of fourteen tries to drown herself because of the repeated beatings she was given by her father: "She saw no other way out of her troubles, poor child."[88] Her father countered with the excuse that was commonly given at that time:

> She's lazy. That's wot's the matter with her. I'll cure her, and mighty quick, too, if she don't stop skulkin.[89]

In Germany, hostility towards children was so great that the term "kinderfeindlichkeit", or "rage toward children", was often used to describe the strict parental attitude.[90] The common educational method to deal with misbehavior was severe corporal punishment, and in the nineteenth century Bavarian infant mortality rates were as high as 57%, partly because of the resultant injuries.[91] A common motto among the German townsmen was "to love your child means to chastise it."[92]

In the famous child abuse cases in Vienna at the turn of the nineteenth century, the Hummel trial revealed that the defendant parents would often hold the mouth of their daughter rightly shut so that her cries could not be heard. As a defense to this action, they claimed that they were simply exercising their right of parental discipline.[93] Children of that era were often thought to deserve punishment because of their naughty behavior.[94]

Even lullabies showed how mischievous children were treated with the threat of death. An ancient German lullaby read:

Sleep, baby, sleep,
See the grazing sheep?
One is black and one is white
And if my baby won't go to sleep,
He'll feel the black sheep's bite.[95]

Another from England went:

Baby, baby, naughty baby,
Hush, you squalling thing, I say.
Peace this moment, peace, or maybe
Bonaparte will pass this way.

Baby, baby, he's a giant
Tall and black as Rouen steeple,
And he breakfasts, dines, rely on't,
Every day on naughty people.

Baby, baby, if he hears you,
As he gallops past the house,
Limb from limb at once he'll tear you,
Just as pussy tears a mouse.

And he'll beat you, beat you, beat you,
And he'll beat you all to pap,
And he'll eat you, eat you, eat you,
Every morsel snap, snap, snap.[96]

Fairy tales often carried the same lessons. In the British folk tale of "Orange and Lemon," a mother warned her daughter to be very careful and not break the milk pitcher or "I'll kill you." a few days later, the girl accidently broke the pitcher and begged her mother not to kill her. But the woman chopped off her daughter's head and cooked it for dinner. The girl was then heard to say:

> My mother chopped my head off,
> My father picked my bones,
> My little sister buried me,
> Beneath the cold marble stones.[97]

A similar story was presented in "The Satin Frock," where a mother cautioned her daughter not to get a dirty mark on her new satin frock, and when the girl accidently did, the woman cut off her head and hung it on the wall.[98] In the novella, *The Cruel Mother*, a London woman had two sons:

> But she took out a little pen-knife,
> And she parted them and their sweet life.[99]

Bedtime stories and songs often held frightful lessons for the children to learn.

Tribal communities often practiced infanticide for reasons of necessity, as seen in the chapter on Tribes, but there are very few cases which have documented fatal child abuse. Treatment of children varied greatly among these diverse cultures; many were quite lenient, and tolerant, of all erratic behavior, others were very strict. The ancient Aztecs, for example, after the age of seven years utilized disciplinary measures such as sticking the child with thorns, having their hands tied and then being stuck with pointed agave leaves, whippings and even being held over a fire of dried axi peppers and being made to inhale the acrid smoke.[100] But most tribal punishment of youngsters utilized only scolding, and corporal measures were almost never required. Geza Roheim noted that natives saw the deliberate infliction of pain in the discipline of a child as "the sadistic pedagogy of the white man."[101]

Our modern age has been characterized by an expansion of governmental control over adults who are shown to be abusive to their children, yet American courts have generally recognized that the custody and care of children "resides first in the parents."[102] They have given parents almost complete immunity from civil liability for injuries to their children, unless the damage is repetitive or fatal.[103] The United States Supreme Court has recognized that "natural bonds of affection lead parents to act in the best interests of their children."[104] If a parent is going to be guilty of harming their child during discipline, it will have to be a clear showing of excess.

In the late nineteenth century, there was concern in the courts that if questions of punishment excess was left to the jury it would tend to subvert family government and greatly impair its efficacy. This led to a standard that required the administered punishment to have "proceeded from malice, and was not in the exercise of a corrective authority" if a finding of assault and battery was to be made.[105]

Today, the standard requires that parental authority be exercised "within the bounds of reason and humanity."[106] One nineteenth century Illinois case, that helped to promulgate this more humane approach, found parents who punished their blind son by imprisoning him in a cellar for long periods of time, guilty of neglect and fined them as having acted in a manner that was not appropriate to the facts.[107] At the time, this holding was considered quite liberal, but most states soon followed with similar judgments.

If parents are found to have not acted in this reasonable manner, legal concepts have developed whereby the state, acting as *parens patriae*, may restrict the parents control when it is judged to be in the best interests of the child.[108] The courts will not allow parents to subject their children to harm for activities which they may voluntarily choose for themselves. In the words of the United States Supreme Court, although parents may be free to become martyrs, "it does not follow that they are free, in identical circumstances, to make martyrs of their children."[109] The courts may use this power when there is neglect, abandonment, or failure to provide adequate food, clothing, shelter or supervision.[110]

B. CHILD ABUSE

Child abuse and neglect (CAN) includes four distinct conditions: physical abuse, neglect, emotional abuse and sexual abuse.[111] Judicial ability to take children from abusive parents and place them in foster homes became a necessity as the extent of the problem of child abuse across the civilized world became conclusive. This predicament of abuse is truly world-wide. In England, studies have shown that by age four years, some type of "smacking" is almost universal.[112] In the United States over 90% of parents have stated that they use physical punishment at some time in their child's life.[113] In Sweden, about 4% of all children are abused at least one time each year by a parent "so severely that they risked being physically injured."[114]

While there is a fine line between discipline and abuse, and statistics can often be misleading, there is still no question that the numbers of children injured each year by their parents is outrageously high. Estimates indicate that between 600,000 to nearly two million children, between the ages of three and seventeen years, will be physically abused each year in the United

States alone.[115] In 1992, the National Committee for Prevention of Child Abuse estimated the number of cases at almost three million.[116] Some estimates even range as high as 6.5 million cases yearly.[117] And while many of the injuries are minor, between 2,000 and 5,000 of these children will be abused so greatly that they will die from the cumulative damage.[118] In 1990, 0.5% of injuries recorded by the National Society for the Prevention of Cruelty to Children in England and Wales were fatal.[119] In 1996, American statistics indicated that one third of infant deaths from injury are due to homicide, and 80% of these are due to fatal child abuse.[120] One-half of the children who die from the abuse are under one year of age.[121]

Analysis of the details is staggering. In 1975, Gelles found that 1,000,000 American children were kicked, bitten, or punched by their parents; 750,000 were beaten up, and 50,000 had a gun or knife "used" on them.[122] The figures for 1992, as given by the National Committee for Prevention of Child Abuse, indicated that 25% of the parents involved in fatal cases had substance abuse as a contributing factor and that 36% neglected to provide enough basic care or sustenance to maintain the child's life. 84% of the children who died were under the age of five years, and 38% of the children were at one time in government children services systems.[123]

Parents frequently offer the excuse that the children were only being disciplined by the beatings, and that their treatment was not abusive.[124] While infants up to the age of a few weeks are usually killed because they are unwanted, after that age parents usually commit infanticide in an attempt to control the child's behavior.[125] They maintain that it was their right to physically discipline children in the manner in which they saw fit.[126] Analysis showed that they typically expected "simple, obedient, correct, appreciative responses from their infants and small children" even during ordinary activities.[127] The child's failure to perform in this manner was met with either physical attack, verbal criticism or subsequent neglect.

While some of the cases were certainly due to accidental injury during routine reprimands, there were many cases which obviously extended beyond any reasonable attempt to discipline. The degree of damage that some of these children underwent was incredible. It was often hidden from view, or explained away as accidental in origin. In 1946, Caffey drew attention to a number of injuries in infants that he thought could have been secondary to parental neglect or abuse.[128] S. H. Fisher, in 1958, suggested that willful mistreatment by parents should be considered when there is evidence of skeletal trauma.[129] While creating some stir among social welfare agencies, these discoveries did not become well known until C. Henry Kempe and his colleagues first used the term "battered child syndrome" in 1962 to describe the spectrum of abnormalities which could be seen.[130] Battered Child Syndrome was defined as a: "Term used by us to characterize a clinical condition in young children who have received serious physical abuse, generally from a parent or foster parent."[131] In 302 cases which Kempe presented in his initial report, 33 of the children died and 85 suffered permanent brain injury.

Since then, the syndrome of "battered child" has become all too well-known among social welfare workers. For the most part, the diagnosis can be made by finding "a child who has suffered serious physical injuries in circumstances which indicate it was caused wilfully rather than by accident."[132] Most children who are abused in this manner are under the age of three years.[133] A major diagnostic feature is the marked discrepancy between the clinical injuries manifested by the patient, and the story supplied by the parents.[134]

The physical abuse is usually not a constant or daily occurrence.[135] While many children visually reveal the marks of repetitive beatings or injuries, others are abused in subtler ways. It may show up, for example, in medical syndromes known as "failure to thrive due to maternal deprivation," where the infant simply presents as malnourished or chronically ill.[136] This is also referred to as a "nutritionally battered child," and the abuse is one of omission rather than commission.[137] At times, there may be actual unrelated injuries which mask, or delay, the underlying diagnosis.

There are a number of infants who are at highest risk of abuse and neglect because of problems in the family structure, or in the timing of the pregnancy itself. These include children who were products of a difficult pregnancy or delivery which left the mother either in pain or disability; children born at an inconvenient time from an unplanned pregnancy, or those who were illegitimate or of an unwanted gender; or children who were unfortunate enough to be born during a period of severe family stress and crisis, such as economic privity or a breakdown in the marriage relationship.[138] Many researchers have pointed out that the age of the mother is also a dominant risk factor, with mother's age below fifteen years putting the baby in the greatest danger.[139] The unfortunate part of child abuse, however, is that they may also simply be normal children of parents who have a tendency to anger quickly. In Chicago, ten children under age fifteen years were murdered in 1993 because of parental frustration over the inability to stop their crying.[140]

The parents who are guilty of abuse generally have the lowest possible tolerance for a number of natural activities such as crying, soiling and periodic rejection of food.[141] Sleep deprivation may promote irrational action in a parent, and the result can be devastating to the child. Maria Piers noted that some people stick their fingers in their ears and others get even with the baby by hitting back. "Finally," Piers added, "some adults manage to shut him up for good."[142]

Marybeth Tinning admitted killing three of her children by suffocation in order to stop them from crying.[143] Waneta Hoyt said that she smothered five of her children because their screaming made her feel useless. When her two-year-old son would not stop crying, "I used a bath towel to smother him."[144] Other cases have been documented to develop from frustration, or even a misplaced desire to help the child break an unwanted habit, such as bed-wetting or thumb-sucking. After the age of one year, soiling is usually the predisposing event for abuse.[145]

They also often have a low sense of self-esteem and a lack of trust in other adults.[146] They are usually vulnerable to crises in their own lives, and have difficulty in coping with their everyday problems.[147] In taking their anger out on their children, they vent discontentment from themselves, even if only for a short period of time. In most cases, the parents do not have any initial intent to kill the child and the resultant death is accidental, albeit negligent and foreseeable.[148] Much of the literature indicates that abusive parents were themselves abused by their own parents.[149]

The majority of child abusers are women. As a parallel statistic, it is also true that women, throughout history, have been the prime perpetrators of infanticide.[150] But this type of data does not correlate with any genetic deficiency in a woman's ability to raise, or discipline, her child. In almost every society, it is the woman who generally is in charge of the children for the greater part of the day and night, responsible for the feeding, cleaning, chastisement and control. From a purely mathematical perspective, the woman is then statistically more likely, in sheer numbers, to be involved in an abusive reaction.

The men who kill their children by physical abuse have certain common characteristics. They often abuse their wives as well, get into fights with both friends and strangers, have frequent brushes with the law and can best be described as "sociopaths".[151] The abuser does not generally intend to kill the child at the moment of the punishment, and the death is often an unexpected and incidental result of abuse.[152]

Lester Adelson, writing of the details of forty-six children killed over a seventeen year period in Cuyahoga County, Ohio, noted that nine children were killed by their fathers during an emotional outburst triggered by frustration and aggravation. He noted that:

> Prolonged and repeated crying episodes, defecation in their clothing, persistent harassment and other temper-abrading and eroding activities goaded the fathers to the point where they resorted to excessive violence either as a disciplinary measure or as an outlet for their explosive anger and sense of futility. No mother killed with such provocation.[153]

Repetition of abuse may also be another characteristic feature. Wiltshire was the first part of Britain to start child-maltreatment registers, and over a twenty-one year period, 147 families were followed after having neglected or maltreated one or more children at home. Of the 560 children that were born to these families, 513 suffered maltreatment and 41 died.[154] In only three cases was the parent convicted of manslaughter or infanticide, yet in thirteen other deaths, the official cause of death was listed as asphyxia or inhalation of gastric contents: a typical finding in cases where the child is smothered.[155]

A new category of fatal child abuse is the "shaking baby syndrome" in which a young child is shaken so hard and violently that the brain stem, spinal cord and/or brain are heavily damaged by ruptured blood vessels.[156] This is a common method of abuse of very young infants and the damage is often permanent in both the brain and eyes.[157] Even death may result from intra-cranial bleeding, and the younger the infant, the more vulnerable he is to this complication because of the weakness of the neck muscles and heaviness of the head.[158] In the six-county Chicago area in 1992, shaking was found to be a cause, or contributing factor, in over ten percent of the children under age fifteen years who were murdered.[159]

The usual reason given for the shaking is to try and get the baby to stop crying. Lorenzo Ellison, charged with killing a four month old infant in this way, said that he had tried to amuse the infant to stop him from crying, but there was no response. After shaking the baby the infant died and at autopsy showed brain hemorrhage.[160] This is the most common cause of death because the brain, after ricocheting about the skull, will tear blood vessels and brain tissue and then swell, constrict blood vessels, and eventually lead to fatal neurologic damage. Because there is no external bruising, or signs of abuse, the condition may be mistaken for Sudden Infant Death Syndrome.[161] It is estimated that for every fatal case, there are three who survive with permanent brain damage.[162]

There have also been a number of cases recently described where the infanticide appears to be a form of epileptic reaction triggered by crying which revived childhood memories of punishment. The hitting of the child during this seizure reaction has proven fatal in a reported ten cases.[163] There have also been cases termed "Munchausen's Syndrome by Proxy" where the parents create a physical illness in their child, rather than in themselves, to gain attention and medical treatment.[164] A particularly novel method of attempted infanticide can be seen in Moslem countries where sewing needles are occasionally inserted into the baby's soft fontanelle in an effort to cause death.[165] Many of these children survive the implantment and develop medical problems later in life.

Burning the child is a common method of abuse and between 4-9%

of all children hospitalized for burns are victims of abuse.[166] As noted by Feldman: "Abused children are often held under flowing hot water or immersed in tubs of drawn hot water."[167]

Today, most states have statutes that provide criminal penalties for the physical abuse of children.[168] Under such laws, for corporeal punishment to be used by parents the method must be limited to that necessary to discipline alone, and also must be reasonable and appropriate to the child's misbehavior.[169] If the state feels that the parents are not providing a safe environment for the child, they may step in under the role of *parens patriae* to protect the child's welfare.[170] This means that the child is taken from the family and placed in a foster home setting. Discussing the problem of children in potentially dangerous family situations, William Grinker, the New York commissioner of the Human Resources Administration, had a policy: "When in doubt, pull them out."[171]

To show how extensive the damage by parents to their own children can be, the Illinois Department of Children and Family Services published a guide which alerted physicians to signs of the syndrome. Included were the following physical findings to suggest abuse:

1. Dead on arrival to a medical facility.
2. Victim of unexpected death.
3. Severe or multiple injuries unexplained by known unintentional (accidental) trauma.
4. Multiple or moderately severe injuries that are unexplained or incompatible with the history given.
5. Multiple or moderately severe injuries that are explained by a variety of conflicting histories.
6. One or more injuries (of any degree of severity) which the child or another party states are inflicted.
7. A condition known to be characteristic of abuse without other plausible explanation. Such conditions include but are not limited to:

a. *Central Nervous System*
- eggshell fractures
- subdural hematomas
- retinal hemorrhages
- unexplained coma

b. *Skin*
- whip or loop marks (from beatings)
- immersion burns, particularly if symmetrical
- cigarette burns

- symmetrical abrasions or lacerations (as from bondage)
- tattoos
- slap marks (bruises with shape of fingers)
- bruises in different stages of healing and/or outside normal distribution (e.g. bruises on back, buttocks, perineum, inner thighs, face, neck and earlobe)

c. *GI/Abdomen*

- ruptured viscus
- duodenal hematoma
- intra-abdominal hematoma
- lacerated or contused organ (liver, kidney, spleen)

d. *Skeleton*

- torus fractures of humerus or femur
- metaphyseal chip fractures
- any fracture in a child too young to walk
- multiple fractures in various stages of healing

e. *Sexual Abuse*

- sexually transmitted disease in prepubertal child (gonorrhea, syphilis, condyloma acuminata, genital herpes, chlamydia, trichomonas)
- unexplained vaginal laceration
- unexplained rectal laceration
- unexplained penile or perineal trauma
- sperm/semen in vagina, throat or anus (or any other part) of child
- labia minora greater than 4 mm apart in position of rest
- lacerated hymen in prepuberal child

8. Malnutrition or slow growth unexplained by medical illness
9. Severe illness due to delay in medical care.[172]

The final answer to this problem does not appear close at hand, but one possible solution may come from legal channels which provide some chance of discovery before the abuse is fatal. In 1979, Sweden became the first country to ban physical punishment of children.[173] Their aim was not to prosecute and incarcerate parents, but to educate the public in order to change the attitudes and practice of those who find such discipline acceptable. In sixteen years, only one parent was actually punished by a small fine for spanking his eleven-year-old son.

C. SEXUAL ABUSE

The occurrence of sexual intercourse between a parent and child, though generally seen as a taboo, has been present in almost every civilization known to man. According to many psychiatrists, incestuous craving is the most "constant and universal sexual force in the life of the individual."[174]

In the Old Testament, after Lot fled Sodom and Gomorrah with his two daughters, they lived in a cave for fear of retribution from the surviving citizens. One day the older girl confided to her sister that there were no men which their father would let them marry, and that they soon would become too old to ever have children, or a family of their own. She therefore suggested: "Come, let's fill him with wine and then we will sleep with him, so that our clan will not come to an end."[175] The older girl was soon impregnated with Moab, the ancestor of the Moabites, and the younger girl with Benammi, the ancestor of the nation of the Ammonites.[176] The biblical text never mentions any punishment for this sin, and in other sections does not explicitly call the act of incest a crime.

Other ancient legal codes also showed leniency towards incest. The Code of Hammurabi, from about 1700 B.C., punished marital infidelity or intercourse with a betrothed maiden by death. But the penalty for incest was not so severe: "If a seignior has had intercourse with his daughter, they shall make that seignior leave the city."[177] This penalty is quite benign for a code that otherwise calls for an "eye for eye" retribution.

In modern times, certain tribal societies have allowed marriage between adults and infant children under the age of five. Claude Levi-Strauss described how one woman, with a child from a previous marriage, married a two-year-old boy among the Chukchee: "When she was nursing her own child, she also nursed her infant husband."[178] According to the Talmud, a child of three years and one day could marry with her fathers permission.[179] This age was agreed to by Maimonides as well.[180]

The question of sexual abuse is what led Freud to his designation of the Oedipal complex to explain infant sexuality. His initial studies suggested that seduction by others is what caused neuroses, primarily in women, because so many of his patients complained of episodes of this type while undergoing psychoanalysis. Freud had studied with Charcot in Paris, and at that time Dr. Ambroise Auguste Tardieu, professor legal medicine at the University of Paris and dean of the Faculty of Medicine, had published a book outlining the brutal abuses that children suffered at the hands of their caretakers, often parents.[181] This led to an entire literature on the sexual assault of children which indicated that sexual attacks were very common.[182] For reasons that are still debated, Freud was later to recant this theory, and blame the remembrances on fantasies rather than facts. He would not believe that the numbers of sexual attacks were as great as his patients claimed.

Most of the time, however, society has identified the intimate union of an adult and a child as sexual abuse. The problem arises in determining who is a child, and how intimate the union must be to satisfy this designation.

According to Steele, sexual abuse is "the exploitation of the child for the purpose of satisfying the adult."[183] Richard Krugman defines it as the "involvement of dependent, developmentally immature children in sexual activities that they do not fully comprehend and therefore to which they are unable to give informed consent and/or which violate the taboos of society."[184] The 1974 federal Child Abuse Prevention & Treatment Act defines it as the "obscene or pornographic photographing, filming, or depiction of children for commercial purposes, or the rape, molestation, incest, prostitution or other such forms of sexual exploitation of children under circumstances which indicate that the child's health or welfare is harmed or threatened."[185] The age determination of "children" is then dependent on local statutory law.

The problem today has reached dangerous levels. The American Humane Society estimated that in 1969, 200-300,000 female children were molested in the United States, and that 5,000 of these girls were ravaged by their father.[186] As adults, about one-third of American women and one-sixth of American men state that, at some time in their life, they have been victims of sexual exploitation.[187] About 2-5% of these will have been from members within the immediate family circle. Surveys of adults in several industrialized countries suggest that 10-15% of children are victims of sexual abuse.[188] Publicity over the problem has led to increased public awareness, and recent figures indicate that over 75% of the reported incest cases involve a father or stepfather.[189] In Canada, 98% of the sexual assaults are by the father.[190] As with child abuse in general, those that sexually abuse their children often were mistreated themselves in their youth. Studies show that about 25-30% of proven incest offenders were molested themselves as children.[191]

It is very unusual for a father who has used a daughter as a sexual object to actually kill the child afterwards.[192] More frequently, the initial event is not intended, but once the relationship between father and daughter becomes sexualized, "he relates to her more as if she were his wife."[193] But instances certainly occur and cannot be discounted. Delay described a man who tied an apron on his fourteen-year-old daughter's face and: "After beating her with an electric cord, he planned to masturbate, but instead found his daughter dead."[194] Another recent case involved a man who impregnated his two young daughters and "then beat one to death with a baseball bat because she planned to reveal him as the baby's father."[195] The man pled guilty to the killing of his fourteen-year-old daughter and admitted to attacks on his twelve-year-old as well.

Endnotes

1 . Leavitt, The Battered Child, 3.
2 . Kempe, "Recent Developments in the Field of Child Abuse," xxi.
3 . Declaration of the Right of the Child by the United Nations General Assembly, November 20, 1959. Taylor & Newberger, "Child Abuse in the International Year of the Child," 1205.
4 . Chicago Tribune (August 8, 1991): section 2, 1. A similar case of death due to pepper laced milk being given to discourage the taking of a bottle was reported by Adelson. Adelson, "Homicide by Pepper," 391.
5 . Chicago Tribune (August 21, 1992): section 2, 1.
6 . Kaplun & Reich, "The Murdered Child and His Killers," 812.
7 . Philo, "The Special Laws," II.XL.231, The Works of Philo, 590.
8 . Taylor & Newberger, "Child Abuse in the International Year of the Child," 1208.
9 . The Age of God-Kings, 69.
10 . Ancient Egypt, 91
11 . Radbill, "A History of Child Abuse and Infanticide," 173.
12 . Code 195. The Code of Hammurabi, 73.
13 . Aristotle, Nicomachean Ethics, VIII.1160b.26-27, The Works of Aristotle, Volume I, 413.
14 . Matthews & Benjamin, Old Testament Parallels, 179.
15 . Exodus 21:17. The Living Bible, 66.
16 . Leviticus 20:9. Ibid., 104.
17 . Exodus 21:17. Ibid., 66.
18 . Deuteronomy 21:18-21. Ibid., 167.
19 . "`A son', but not a daughter; `A son', but not a full-grown man." Sanhedrin, Mishnah, VIII.68b.
20 . Ibid.
21 . Maimonides, The Book of Judges, Treatise III, VII.5, 159.
22 . Ibid., VIII.71a.
23 . Ibid.
24 . Ibid., VIII.71b.
25 . Ibid.
26 . Proverbs 20:20. The Anchor Bible, 120.
27 . Proverbs 13:24. Ibid., 94.
28 . Proverbs 17:25. Ibid., 109.
29 . Proverbs 13:1. Ibid., 93.
30 . Proverbs 22:15. The Living Bible, 516.
31 . Proverbs 29:15. The Anchor Bible, 169.
32 . Proverbs 29:17. The Living Bible, 520.
33 . Proverbs 19:18. The Anchor Bible, 116.
34 . Talmudic Anthology, 70.
35 . Ibid., 124.
36 . Philo, "The Special Laws," II.XLI.232, The Works of Philo, 590.
37 . Josephus, Antiquities, IV,.VIII.24, The Works of Flavius Josephus, 275.
38 . Philo, "The Special Laws," II.XLI.232, The Works of Philo, 590.
39 . Maimonides, The Book of Judges, Treatise III, V.2, 150-151.
40 . Ibid., V.5, 151.
41 . Gorion, Mimekor Yisrael Classical Jewish Folk Tales, Volume III, 1395.

42 . Ibid.
43 . Prudentius, "Hymns," Preface, 7, The Poems of Prudentius, Volume I, xxix.
44 . Ford, "The Emergence of the Child as a Legal Entity," 401.
45 . Byman, "Child Raising and Melancholia in Tudor England," 75.
46 . Ibid., 76.
47 . Ibid., 70.
48 . Faulkner, Light in August, 133.
49 . Plutarch, "Ancient Customs of the Spartans," Moralia, Volume III, 443-45.
50 . Lucian, "Anacharsis, A Discussion of Physical Training," 39, The Works of Lucian of Samosata, Volume III, 211.
51 . Seneca, "On Providence," I, Moral Essays, Volume I, 31.
52 . Aristophanes, The Clouds, 1457-1458, 171.
53 . Justinian, The Institutes, I.IX.1, 12.
54 . Ibid., IV.XVIII.6, 206.
55 . Dionysius of Halicarnassus, Roman Antiquities, II.26.3, 387.
56 . Ibid., II.26.3-4.
57 . Livy, History of Rome, I.XXVI.9, 93.
58 . Wiedemann, Adults & Children in the Roman Empire, 27.
59 . Plutarch, "The Education of Children," Moralia, Volume I, 41.
60 . Ibid., 43.
61 . Justinian, The Institutes, III.XIX.10, 138.
62 . Hegel, The Philosophy of History, 128-129.
63 . Wu, "Child Abuse in Taiwan," 148.
64 . Hunt, Parents & Children in History, 134.
65 . Ibid., 135.
66 . deMause, The History of Childhood, 40.
67 . Stone, The Family, Sex and Marriage, in England 1500-1800, 122.
68 . Montaigne, Essays, I.27, 59.
69 . Hobbes, The Elements of Law, II.IV.7, 104.
70 . Ibid., II.IV.8, 105.
71 . Andersen-Nexo, "Life Sentence," 287.
72 . Sutton, "Stubborn Children: Law & the Socialization of Deviance in the Puritan Colonies," 31.
73 . Ibid.
74 . Bremner, Children & Youth in America, A Documentary History, Volume I 1600-1865, 38-39.
75 . Pollock, Forgotten Children, 3.
76 . Ford, "The Emergence of the Child as a Legal Entity," 403.
77 . Inglis, Sins of the Fathers, 23.
78 . Ibid., 18.
79 . deMause, The History of Childhood, 40.
80 . Locke, Two Treatises of Government, Second Treatise, 67.16, 312.
81 . Ibid., 67.17-19.
82 . Ibid., First Treatise, VI.52.3-4, 178.
83 . Ibid., VI.52.8-13.
84 . Eversley, Law of the Domestic Relations, 487.
85 . Lorence, "Parents and Children in Eighteenth Century Europe," 8.
86 . Blackstone, Commentaries on the Laws of England, Book the Fourth, 14.II.1, Volume IV, 182.

87 . Rose, *The Massacre of the Innocents: Infanticide in Britain 1800-1939*, 13.
88 . Hauptmann, "The Assumption of Hannele," I, *Dramatic Works*, Volume 4, 23.
89 . Ibid., Act II, 63.
90 . Ende, "Battering and Neglect: Children in Germany, 1860-1978," 250.
91 . Ibid., footnote 13, 275.
92 . Ibid., 253.
93 . Wolff, *Postcards From the End of the World*, 73-74.
94 . Marie Kutschera claimed one of her children was a slut, one plotted to poison her, one was stealing the brandy and one involved in precocious sexual practices. Ibid., 126.
95 . Piers, *Infanticide*, 28.
96 . Ibid., 29-30.
97 . Briggs, *A Dictionary of British Folk-Tales*, Volume I, 442.
98 . Ibid., 476.
99 . Ibid., Volume II, 397.
100. Ruhrah, "Aztec Methods in Child Training," 22.
101. Roheim, "The Western Tribes of Central Australia: Childhood," 202.
102. Prince v. Commonwealth of Massachusetts, 321 US 158, 166, 64 SCt 438, 442 (1944).
103. Thomas, "Child Abuse & Neglect, Part I: Historical Overview, Legal Matrix, & Social Perspectives," 293-294.
104. Parham v. J.R., 442 US 584, 603, 99 SCt 2493, 2504 (1979).
105. State v. Jones, 95 NC 588, (1886).
106. Fletcher et al v. The People, 52 Ill 395, 397 (1869).
107. Fletcher et al v. The People, 52 Ill 395 (1869).
108. Prince v. Commonwealth of Massachusetts, 321 US 158, 164, 64 SCt 438, 442 (1944).
109. Prince v. Commonwealth of Massachusetts, 321 US 158, 170, 64 SCt 438, 444 (1944).
110. Davidson & Horowitz, "Protection of Children From Family Maltreatment," 269.
111. Belsey, "Child Abuse: Measuring a Global Problem," 69.
112. Scott, "The Psychiatrist's Viewpoint," 191.
113. Steinmetz & Strauss, "The Family as Cradle of Violence," 50.
114. Somander & Rammer, "Intra- and Extrafamilial Child Homicide in Sweden 1971-1980," 53.
115. Krugman, "Advances and Retreats in the Protection of Children," 531.
116. *Chicago Tribune* (April 7, 1993): section 1, 1.
117. Straus & Kantor, "Stress and Child Abuse," 49.
118. Kleinman, Blackbourne, Marks, Karellas & Belanger, "Radiologic Contributions to the Investigation and Prosecution of Cases of Fatal Infant Abuse," 507.
119. Belsey, "Child Abuse: Measuring a Global Problem," 70.
120. Overpeck, Brenner, Trumble, Trifiletti, & Berendes, "Risk Factors For Infant Homicide in the United States," 1211.
121. Durfee, Gellert, & Tilton-Durfee, "Origins and Clinical Relevance of Child Death Review Teams," 3173.
122. Citing R. J. Gelles. Williams, "Introduction," 11.
123. *Chicago Tribune* (April 7, 1993): section 1, 1.
124. This was the excuse at the trial of Marie Kutschera. Wolff, *Postcards From the End of the World*, 125.

125. Kunz & Bahr, "A Profile of Parental Homicide Against Children," 360.
126. Costa & Nelson, Child Abuse & Neglect: Legislation, Reporting & Prevention, 4.
127. Steele, "Psychodynamic Factors in Child Abuse," 86.
128. Cameron, Johnson & Camps, "The Battered Child Syndrome," 4.
129. Fisher, "Skeletal Manifestations of Parent Induced Trauma in Infants and Children," 956.
130. Kempe, Silverman, Steele, Droegemueller & Silver, "The Battered-Child Syndrome," 17.
131. Ibid.
132. Cameron, Johnson & Camps, "The Battered Child Syndrome," 2.
133. Ibid., 5.
134. Ibid., 7.
135. Steele, "Psychodynamic Factors in Child Abuse," 58.
136. Ibid., 64.
137. Adelson, "Homicide by Starvation," 460.
138. Steele, "Psychodynamic Factors in Child Abuse," 67.
139. Overpeck, Brenner, Trumble, Trifiletti, & Berendes, "Risk Factors For Infant Homicide in the United States," 1213.
140. Chicago Tribune (September 10, 1993): section 1, 16.
141. Inglis, Sins of the Fathers, 68-69.
142. Piers, Infanticide, 31.
143. Eggenton, From Cradle to Grave, 227.
144. Chicago Tribune (April 1, 1994): section 1, 15.
145. Krugman, "Fatal Child Abuse: Analysis of 24 Cases," 69.
146. Steele, "Psychology of Infanticide Resulting From Maltreatment," 78.
147. Ibid., 79.
148. Ibid., 77.
149. Costa & Nelson, Child Abuse & Neglect: Legislation, Reporting & Prevention, 6.
150. Steinmetz, The Cycle of Violence, 89.
151. Steele, "Psychodynamic Factors in Child Abuse," 71.
152. Ibid., 72.
153. Adelson, "Slaughter of the Innocents," 1346.
154. Oliver, "Dead Children From Problem Families in NE Wiltshire," 115-116.
155. Ibid., 116.
156. Chicago Tribune (November 22, 1990): section 2, 20.
157. Collins, "On the Dangers of Shaking Young Children," 143.
158. Ibid., 146.
159. Chicago Tribune (June 22, 1993): section 1, 6.
160. Chicago Tribune (November 24, 1992): section 1, 1.
161. Chicago Tribune (June 22, 1993): section 1, 6.
162. Ibid.
163. Pontius, "Infanticide in Limbic (?) Psychotic Trigger Reaction in a Man With Jacksonian and Petit Mal (?) Seizures: `Kindling' by Traumatic Experiences," 935.
164. Taylor & Newberger, "Child Abuse in the International Year of the Child," 1207. In one case a four-year-old child was subjected to repeated subcutaneous and intravenous injections of fecal material and the resultant infectious disease was thought to be of immune deficiency origin. Kohl, Pickering & Dupree, "Child Abuse Presenting as Immunodeficiency Disease," 466.
165. Abbassioun, Ameli, & Morshed, "Intracranial Sewing Needles: Review of 13 Cases," 1046.

166. Feldman, "Child Abuse by Burning," 197.
167. Ibid., 200.
168. Horwitz & Davidson, Legal Rights of Children, 267.
169. Ibid., 269.
170. Ibid., 264.
171. Voice (October 22, 1991): Metro, 12.
172. Protocol for Determining if an Injury is a Result of Child Abuse or Neglect, 4-5.
173. Children and Violence, Innocenti Digest, Intrafamilial-Physcial, <http://www.unicef-icdc.org/information/digests/ violence/intra02.htm> (4/25/99).
174. Rascovsky & Rascovsky, "The Prohibition of Incest, Filicide and the Sociocultural Process," 271.
175. Genesis 19:32. The Living Bible, 15.
176. Genesis 19:37,38.
177. Code of Hammurabi, 154. Pritchard, Ancient Near Eastern Texts, 172.
178. Levi-Strauss, The Elementary Structures of Kinship, 487.
179. Seder Nezikin, 376.
180. Maimonides, The Book of Women, Book Four, 18.
181. Masson, The Assault on Truth, Freud's Suppression of the Seduction Theory, 15.
182. Ibid., 27.
183. Steele, "Psychodynamic Factors in Child Abuse," 106.
184. Krugman & Jones, "Incest and Other Forms of Sexual Abuse," 286.
185. Child Abuse Prevention and Treatment Act, Public Law 93-247, Jan 31, 1974.
186. Radbill, "Children in a World of Violence: A History of Child Abuse," 11-12.
187. Krugman & Jones, "Incest and Other Forms of Sexual Abuse," 287.
188. Belsey, "Child Abuse: Measuring a Global Problem," 75.
189. Cole, "Incest Perpetrators, Their Assessment and Treatment," 689.
190. Canadian Legal FAQs, National Child Abuse FAQs. <http://www.extension.ualberta.ca/legalfaqs/nat/chi-07.htm> (April 25, 1999).
191. Ibid., 692.
192. Scott, "Parents Who Kill Their Children," 123.
193. Summit & Kryso, "Sexual Abuse of Children: A Clinical Spectrum," 118.
194. Ibid.
195. Chicago Tribune (January 30, 1992): section 2, 4.

CHAPTER X

SHAME

"The bastard, like the prostitute, thief and beggar, belongs to that motley crowd of disreputable social types which society has generally resented, always endured."[1]

A. Historical Survey

Kingsley Davis, in the above quotation, summarized the general attitude that society has always placed upon the birth of a child outside the accepted husband-wife relationship. Throughout history, cultural mores in almost every known civilization has disapproved of offspring when there was no formal marriage bond. If an unmarried woman became pregnant, she was usually ostracized by the community-at-large and her children were treated as outcasts.[2] For the most part, this exclusion was limited to the female. As Will Durant pointed out: "The men never thought of applying the same restrictions to themselves; no society in history has ever insisted on the premarital chastity of the male."[3]

Such a sexist policy was relatively easy for the authorities to carry out since the pregnant woman was readily identifiable but only her words could specify the man. Ann Higginbottham described the situation in Victorian England where, for the woman, "The infant at her breast was her stigma, her burden, her curse."[4] To hide the mark of shame which resulted from a bastard birth, women often turned to drastic means. The "Scarlet Letter" of illegitimacy, and its resultant life of isolation and suffering, became one of the commonest reasons for newborn infant exposure or abandonment in almost every country of the world.[5]

The likelihood that a bastard child would be killed at birth bore an inverse relationship with the frequency of illegitimacy within the particular societal structure. In a community where the numbers of such births were rare, the shame of the act was considered to be the most severe, and the probability of infanticide increased. The mother dreaded the consequences of severe castigation, which were certain to occur after the birth became known, and acted to conceal the pregnancy and dispose of the infant before its arrival was manifest. In the words of Lombroso, the result was that "fear of shame impels to crime," a maxim that has proven true for centuries.[6]

The basis for this disgrace seems as ancient as the written word itself. While it might appear that natural instincts to procreate would overcome such restrictive taboos, the historical data suggests that various moralistic prohibitions were in place in the earliest societies of mankind. The result of these prohibitions was to ostracize a woman from the society of traditional married partners, either out of competitive fear from other wives, or the concern that legitimate children could be adversely affected by the inclusion of illegitimate offspring. To provide stability within a group structure, pairing off of one male and one female, in a permanent and restricted union, was the agreed-upon format.

Yet many anthropologists believe that such unions of marriage were not the initial alliance among primitive parents. It is postulated that the family in prehistoric times rather consisted of a mother and child core unit, with the father merely an instinctive progenitor.[7] As is commonly seen in many animal groupings, the male left the family once a child was born, and it was then up to the mother to provide sustenance for both her offspring and herself. While this process might have been successful in other mammalian species, where food gathering capability was more equal between the two sexes, such a system was not an evolutionary effective mechanism in the human species. Women were generally not physically able to perform the task of raising the young alone in the wild, and the lives of her children were therefore endangered if there was not the support of a protective male.

Marriage then became necessary in order to assure that there was adequate protection for the offspring in order to guarantee perpetration of the race.[8] Men were necessary for food gathering and defense; women primarily cared for the children and the home. Each had their function clearly demarcated, and the marriage bond assured that the roles would continue in a mutually conducive, and lasting, fashion. Although occasional instances in civilization could be found where such bonding did not occur, "societies without marriage are rare."[9]

Once the safety of the union was secure, the next issue which arose to strengthen the need for a marital bond was the question of inheritance. As goods were accumulated, the question of ownership after death of the father led to potential danger of confrontations among the surviving children. This could seriously harm all the participants if some means of determining priority was not available through accepted legal principles. Marriage became the method by which settlement of property rights could be restricted to the lineage of the legal wife. A fixed ceremony was developed which clearly separated wives and concubines. The eldest legal child, usually of male lineage, could then be identified, and a succession of the estate became assured.[10] This paternalistic system required "complete fidelity from the woman, (and) generated in the male a proprietary attitude towards her."[11]

As soon as marriage became the normal social structure for family life, control over sexual intercourse outside the marriage bond, for either moralistic or competitive purposes, quickly followed. Infidelity and promiscuity were banned and most societies, as well as religious creeds, developed severe penalties for those who disobeyed the moral code. Obviously, catching someone in the midst of a licentious act was conclusive evidence of guilt, but most intimate relationships were hidden from view. The only obvious sign of culpability was clinical evidence of pregnancy, and any unmarried woman who was found in such a state was usually shunned. To try and escape this ostracism, women frequently attempted to conceal the pregnancy by both seclusion and loose fitting outer wear. They then destroyed the illegitimate birth by infanticide or exposure.[12] Detection of such activity could be very difficult.

Legal reaction to sexual relations among the unmarried adult was varied, but often extreme. In order to try and prevent the illicit activity by evoking intense fear of discovery, severe punishment of promiscuity was a common trend among early societies. The Laws of Eshnunna, the Diyala region east of Baghdad which flourished around 2000 B.C., held that seizing a betrothed girl and taking her virginity "is a capital offence and he shall die."[13] In the Code of Hammurabi, from around 1700 B.C., if a wife was caught with another man, they were both bound together and thrown into the sea to drown.[14] If a man took a virgin betrothed maiden and lay with her, he was put to death.[15] The lesson was simple: if you were caught defiling a woman outside the marriage bond, you risked the penalty of death.

While capital punishment was resorted to by many civilizations, other less severe penalties were also developed. Most required that marriage be forced upon the couple, or that a large monetary payment be made which could financially ruin the wrong-doer. Under the Middle Assyrian Laws of around 1300 B.C., if a virgin was dishonored by a married man, the father "shall give his daughter who has been ravished as a spouse to her ravisher," while if the man already had a wife, he would pay one-third in silver the price of a virgin.[16]

The ancient Egyptians were somewhat unique and did not hold any child a bastard, even though he was born of a slave or unmarried mother. Diodorus of Sicily, in 56 B.C., noted that "they have taken the general position that the father is the sole author of procreation and that the mother only supplies the fetus with nourishment and a place to live."[17] Egyptian folktales, however, generally held that legitimacy of birth produced a good character while illegitimacy produced a bad one.[18]

Similarly, the Lawcode of king Lipit-Ishtar, the fifth ruler of the Dynasty of Isin in Sumer and Akkad during the early second millennium B.C., did not set up rigid punishment for those found guilty of unfaithfulness. It rather mildly stated that:

> If a man's wife has not borne him children but a harlot from the public square has borne him children, he shall provide grain, oil, and clothing for that harlot; the children which the harlot has borne him shall be his heirs, and as along as his wife lives the harlot shall not live in the house with his wife.[19]

In the Old Testament, however, such behavior among Jews was not tolerated. If a man married a woman, and found out she was not a virgin, he could accuse her before a religious court and she would then be tested by spreading her garment before the judges.[20] If his accusations were true:

> The judges shall take the girl to the door of her father's home where the men of the city shall stone her to death. She has defiled Israel by flagrant crime, being a prostitute while living at home with her parents; and such evil must be cleansed from among you.[21]

It was not only the woman who was at risk under Jewish law. If a man was discovered committing adultery, both he and the other man's wife were to be killed and "in this way evil will be cleansed from Israel."[22] If the girl was engaged to marry, and did not scream for help when she was seduced, she would be stoned to death.[23]

The old Hebrews looked on an illegitimate pregnancy as a serious crime and punished it severely. When Judah found out that Tamar, his daughter-in-law, was pregnant as a result of prostitution, he ordered her to be brought out in the square and burned.[24] But she revealed to him that the child was his, as he had unwittingly slept with her on an earlier visit, and her life was spared.[25] When she later gave birth to twin sons, the midwife tied a scarlet thread around the wrist of the child who appeared first as a sign of shame.[26]

Even though the child might be an innocent by-product of the immoral union, according to Hebraic teaching it would not escape the wrath of God. According to the *Wisdom of Solomon*:

> But the children of adulterers will not reach maturity,
> and the seed of unlawful union will be destroyed.
> For even if they attain length of life, they will be of no account,
> and in the end their old age will be without honor.
> And if their end come swiftly, they will be without hope
> or consolation on the day of decision.
> For hard is the end of an unjust generation.[27]

The punishments for adultery were likewise great. If a priest's daughter was adulterous, she was felt to have profaned her father and was slain by burning.[28] If she was an "arusah," or a betrothal still living in her father's house, the death was by stoning, and for other cases it was death by strangulation. The seducer under Biblical rule was seen as being even more culpable than the seduced, and in most cases this suspicion fell upon the woman.[29] For a betrothed damsel who played the harlot, death would be demanded and, depending on the circumstances, she would either be killed by strangulation, stoning at the entrance of the city gate, or stoning at the door of her father's house.[30]

According to the Jewish historian Josephus, if a man was to have sex with an unespoused virgin, he would have to marry her. If the girl was espoused, however, then both were to be put to death.[31] Cohabitation was seen as a means of procreation and not pleasure.[32]

Philo, the first century A.D. Jewish philosopher, accepted this stern approach and demanded that men and women must come to marriage together as virgins. He added that while many nations would permit men after the age of fourteen to copulate with harlots, a courtesan was not even permitted to live in Israel.[33] If any woman was found guilty of plying this trade, she would be put to death.

It is of interest that while Philo did not have approve of illicit sex in his own era, the Bible was replete with procreation outside the marriage bond, even among the venerable Patriarchs. Abraham, the very progenitor of the Hebrew race, was given a concubine by Sarai when they were unable to have children, and much of the Old Testament is peppered with instances of similar family relationships. But Judaism, after entry into the Promised Land, continued to deplore the sexual union of unmarried couples. Moses Maimonides, in the twelfth century, told how children born of adultery are "always despised to every way of life and in every nation."[34] If a bastard child did survive, there was a mark of shame that followed him even after his death. Under Jewish law, a bastard was not allowed to enter the sanctuary of the temple, "nor any of his descendants for ten generations."[35] In addition, a bastard could not marry a daughter of Israel. The *Talmud* stated that one of those who were to be subjected to the punishment of scourging was "an Israelite that married a bastard."[36]

That illegitimate children were nevertheless still produced among the Hebrews could be seen by the laws which developed to deal with them. The Babylonian *Talmud* extensively discussed how foundlings were to be considered either as legitimate children or bastards by the manner in which the infant was abandoned. By the detail of these rabbinical holdings, it is apparent that there were a number of exposures which primarily were due to the shame produced by the birth of an illegitimate child.

Yiddish folklore also contained parables of illicit behavior. In "A Tragic Tale," a brother and sister live together, after the death of their parents, in order to not divide their fortune. The girl became pregnant and was forced to run away because the town people were angered by this incestual condition. In order to hide her sin when the infant was born, "she wrapped it up and put it into a basket with two thousand rubles," along with a note saying the boy was Jewish and left it at the synagogue.[37]

Christianity continued the teaching of a very strict and dogmatic prohibition of sex outside the marriage bond. The very birth of Jesus was a problem which was dealt with through the imagery of divine conception. Mary and Joseph were engaged to be married when Mary, despite still being a virgin, discovered she was pregnant. Joseph, "being a man of stern principle," decided to break the engagement, but he wanted to do it quietly so as to not publicly disgrace her.[38] An angel, however, told Joseph in a dream not to hesitate marrying Mary for "the child within her has been conceived by the Holy Spirit," and will bear him a Son who will save his people from their sins.[39] It is later related in Luke, that the angel Gabriel had appeared to Mary in Nazareth, and explained to her that she will become impregnated by the Holy Spirit, "and the power of God shall overshadow you; so the baby born to you will be utterly holy – the Son of God."[40]

Early canon law, which was based on the teaching of Paul, promoted a life of celibacy which held that it would be better if one "could get along without marrying."[41] But the theologians were nevertheless pragmatic and agreed that if one could not control themselves in sexual matters than "it is better to marry than to burn with lust."[42]

When promiscuity did occur, it was generally the woman who was punished. As the church tried ever harder to force women to conform to the marital requirement, women who gave into their emotions were driven even more to conceal their pregnancies and then kill their illegitimate offspring upon delivery.[43] As is often the case with any harsh discipline or law – secular or religious – the greater the punishment, the more likely wrong-doers will commit further crimes to keep from being caught. So it was with the shame of a bastard birth.

But to the early Church Fathers, vitally important principles were at stake, and there was no ethical way to accept the concept of sexual intercourse outside the marital bond. St. John Chrysostom warned that a child who was born illegitimate was disgraced and caused a severe injustice to be done. He was well aware of the deadly consequences of such actions and how debauchery was commonly a precipitating cause of the sin of infanticide after birth: "You see how drunkenness leads to whoredom, whoredom to adultery, adultery to murder."[44] Tertullian, as well, remonstrated that adulterous conceptions were often slaughtered in a manner that doubly worsened the sinful activity. Not only was it evil in the eyes of God to engage in sex with someone other than a spouse, there was now the added crime of murder.[45]

But despite this strident theologic tone, the penalties that were proscribed by the Church could do little more than warn of punishment in the afterlife to come. The Church was limited to the prescription of penance, and the length of the sentence varied as to the degree of the sin. In the penitence ascribed as punishment for murdering a child by Bede in the eighth century, a mother who killed her child before the fortieth day of life was to do penance for one year; a child who "has become alive" will account as a murder but: "It makes a great difference whether a poor woman does it on account of the difficulty of supporting the child or a harlot for the sake of concealing her wickedness."[46] It was almost as if the church would forgive the killing of a child from reason of poverty in order to control infanticide from shame.

In ancient Greek society, illegitimate children fared little better. There were no religious leaders exhorting the venial sin of intercourse outside the marital bond, but there was still a problem which encouraged its avoidance. The social identity of a person in ancient Greece was designated by family affiliation. Without a recognized father, who was responsible for approving acceptance of all children into the family structure, the bastard had no legal guardian. The mother was not authorized to fulfill that role under Greek law, and illegitimate offspring were generally not sanctioned by the biologic father.[47]

But because an unwanted Greek child did not have any sanctioned legal rights, it did not necessarily mean that he or she was slaughtered at birth. While there was no fervent moral condemnation for the act, there was still a demand for healthy infants by other families who were unable to bear children. According to Cynthia Patterson, women would often find an alternative route than destruction of the newborn:

> Given that women communicated with other women in carrying out household duties or during religious festivals, and that childbirth and child care were female responsibilities, it is possible that there may have been something of a "feminine network" which could place an unwanted infant in the hands of a woman wanting to be a mother.[48]

Since nobody really wanted to care for a disabled infant, an "unwanted" baby usually meant a bastard birth.

The Greeks, as well as the Romans which followed, also found a convenient explanation for supposed virgin births within their religious format. Rather than facing the stigma of an illegitimate child from an illicit relationship, there developed the explanation of mating a mortal woman with a god so that the mother could remain virginal in the strict sense of the word. The list of such offspring was very extensive, and some of the most famous Greek heroes were said to have been products of such divine conception. Livy, in his *History of Rome*, told how the famed city was founded by twins supposedly born to a Vestal Virgin, and he noted that the mother accepted the boys birth: "Whether actually so believing, or because it seemed less wrong if a god were the author of her fault."[49] Ovid was somewhat more direct: "Many have gotten into decent bedrooms pretending to be gods."[50]

But while many a daughter in the ancient world tried to explain away her pregnancy with hopes of assuaging her parent's anger, fathers were often not satisfied with the explanations put forth, and infanticide was a not uncommon result. When king Orchamus found out that his daughter Leucothoe had an illicit affair with the Sun, he buried her alive under the sand.[51] Aleos ordered his daughter Auge drowned when he discovered that she was pregnant from Heracles.[52] And King Aeolus ordered his grandchild abandoned and sent his daughter, Canace, a sword with a note saying "you know from your desert what it may mean" when he found out about her illegitimate tryst with her brother.[53] Etearchus ordered his daughter Phronime thrown into the sea by Themison,[54] and Aeschines related how a father killed his unchaste daughter by walling her up in an empty house.[55]

The attitude of strict Greek fathers was perhaps best summarized by Agenor, the father of Europa. His daughter had been taken by Zeus in the form of a bull, and was later found to be pregnant. The sire's advice to his unchaste progeny was simple and direct:

> Sinful Europa, why delay your dying? Here is an ashtree: you luckily still have your sash: hang until your neck has been broken.[56]

Such were the fables that Greeks used to teach their children the fundamentals of appropriate moral behavior. But it was not only mortal fathers who were ashamed of their sullied children. Even the gods could at times be so upset by the actions of their offspring that they would have them killed. Rhesus, according to Euripides, was thrown into the Strymon river by his mother, one of the Muses, for she was shamed before her sisters by her pregnancy.[57]

The Romans had similar stories to tell. Appius Claudius charged the virgin Verginia with being a lustful slave to a man, and her father Verginius, driven mad with grief over her disgrace and shame, then slew her as a "righteous parricide."[58] This story was repeated by many Roman authors with favor, and Cicero stated that the slaying occurred in the Forum on account of the mad lust of one of the decemvirs.[59] No matter what the true facts may have been, there were no outcries for the father to be taken away in chains to pay for the life of his child.

Shakespeare, in *The Winter's Tale*, portrayed the anger which infidelity can arouse in a husband made aware of his wife's bastard birth:

> This brat is none of mine; It is the issue of Polixenes. Hence with it, and together with the dam Commit them to the fire![60] If thou refuse And wilt encounter with my wrath, say so; The bastard brains with these my proper hands Shall I dash out.[61]

In the Middle Ages, the dilemma of persecution continued to harass the unmarried mother, and the lives of her offspring remained endangered. During the sixth and seventh centuries, this was somewhat less conspicuous in Ireland because of the Brehon laws which required that the tribe raise and foster any unwanted child, including those that were born out of wedlock. Nevertheless, even in the Emerald Isle, reports of infanticide did occasionally persist among children of "irregular origin."[62]

In the eighth century A.D., Boniface noted that "harlots" in the Germanic lands generally killed the children they bore rather than leave them in churches.[63] Gregory the Great found a fishpond with over six thousand infant heads that were thought to be the remains of similarly unwanted babies.[64] One of the reasons for this slaughter was the punishment that awaited the discovery of an illegitimate birth in Germany. Teutonic law required that the man be killed if the crime was proven, and that the fallen girl be either sold into slavery, or killed as well.[65] Concealment and infanticide were the only means to escape this harsh fate.

The Church in Europe was well aware of this circumstance and responded by developing foundling homes to help care for the large number of abandoned children. Regino of Prum, around 906 A.D., suggested that women put their children up for adoption, rather than kill them. He agreed with the canonical decrees that exhorted women to leave these babies at the church door, rather than expose them to the elements and to death. One such decree stated that:

> We advise all priests to announce publicly to their congregations that if any woman should conceive and give birth as the result of a clandestine affair, she must not kill her son or daughter . . . but should have the baby carried to the doors of the church and left there, so that it can be brought to the priest in the morning and taken in and brought up by some one of the faithful. She will thus avoid being guilty of murder and, even worse, of parricide.[66]

This may have done some good since the punishment of parricide was to be sewn up in a sack with various animals and then thrown into the river or sea to drown.

The Celt tradition found another way to test the status of a newborn. When a question of legitimacy of offspring was raised, the judgment would be left to the Rhine river: "Bastards were drowned, but the river bore the true born on its surface to land."[67] Since women often exposed their unwanted children at the rivers edge, rather than kill them directly, the veracity of the tradition was frequently challenged.

Throughout Renaissance Europe, the problem of illegitimacy seemed to intensify. In the sixteenth-century Essex court records of England, for example, only three of the thirty mothers who killed their babies were married.[68] Prostitution was common, and ineffective means of birth control left unmarried women in a trap from which there was no other escape. Once the "woman's curse" failed to appear, all the prospective party could do was patiently wait for nine months to pass, and then drown the newborn infant and secretly bury it before a discovery was made. So common was this scenario that in 1556, King Henry II of France obliged women to declare premarital pregnancies to a judicial official in order to prevent the expectant concealment and eventual infanticide.[69] If a woman was found to be pregnant, and had not given proper notification, she could be given the death sentence. It was hoped that fear of this severe punishment would dissuade young women from risking premarital sex.

The idea of punishing concealment of the pregnancy as a crime equal to murder itself caught on in many other European countries. In England, the burden of proof placed upon the prosecution was eased so that a woman who concealed a birth was automatically assumed to be guilty of murder unless she could prove that the infant was still-born. If she had been charged with homicide, the common-law assumption of "innocent until proven guilty" would have remained intact. The 1623 Act of James I provided that if a woman gave birth to a bastard child and concealed the birth, then she could be found guilty and punished by death, even without there having to be proof that the child was born alive.[70]

This English law proved so discriminatory that juries were reluctant to bring in a guilty verdict and resorted to judicial evasion. Women were found innocent at times simply by showing that they provided clothes for the expected child, or knocked on the wall during the birth process, disproving the charge of concealment.[71] While society was ready for drastic action to combat the rise of infanticide, this particular inequitable treatment of heretofore law-abiding young women was too much to bear.

William Hunter, the great English surgeon, addressed the London Medical Society in 1783 on the callous and unfair attitude of this new law.

He noted that in most of these cases "the mother has an unconquerable sense of shame, and pants for the preservation of her character."[72] He admitted that many of the mothers-to-be may have thought of ways to conceal the birth from family and friends so that disposal of the infant could be accomplished. But once they were taken into labour, Hunter argued that they forgot their criminal intent and did not desire to kill the baby. Instead:

> Their schemes are frustrated; their distress of body and mind deprives them of all judgment and rational conduct; they are delivered by themselves just where they happen to be; they faint away, and on recovering consciousness find the child apparently lifeless.[73]

How could it be justice to pronounce a death penalty on such a miserable wretch as this? Juries agreed with this compassionate approach, and despite the healthy number of prosecutions brought by the authorities for concealment, few convictions were forthcoming.

Nevertheless, the problem of ever increasing numbers of children born out of wedlock continued to plague the European Continent. By the eighteenth century, a marked increase in sexual immorality, seduction, and illegitimacy began to make the social problem critical. In England it reached its peak between 1800 and 1845.[74] In Iceland between 1827-1830, the illegitimacy ratio reached sixteen percent, the highest known for any European area at that time.[75] Some countries, like Switzerland and the Netherlands, were able to maintain low levels of bastardy, but most others, like Scandinavia and Austria, achieved very high levels.[76]

One of the reasons for this sudden rise in unmarried pregnancies was the sexual abuse of women who labored as domestic servants. According to William Langer: "The evidence suggests that in all European countries, from Britain to Russia, the upper classes felt perfectly free to exploit sexually girls who were at their mercy."[77] It was taken for granted that masters of a household and their sons could sleep with their servants at will, and that traveling men were entitled to the favors of pretty girls from the lower classes, almost as a matter of right and social distinction. The women were to not only submit to these favors, but were to consider themselves fortunate to be chosen. If the girl became pregnant, however, "she was left to shift for herself."[78] The gentleman's honor code did not include financial payments for any residual favors.

If a pregnancy showed itself overtly, the woman was summarily fired. One reason that many prostitutes during that era were former domestic servants was that they were dismissed without a reference when they became pregnant, or even if they made allegations of sexual advancements against their master.[79] In *Joseph Andrews*, by Henry Fielding, written in

1742, Lady Booby immediately dismissed her maid who she suspected was pregnant. Her reasoning was to the point: "Pray pay her wages instantly. I will keep no such sluts in my family."[80]

No wonder then that the first impulse to arise when a young domestic found herself with the clinical signs of pregnancy was to seek out an abortion, or conceal the pregnancy until birth and then abandon the infant to a foundling home or the fates. If the infant was abandoned and later found dead, the attitude of most men was typified by that of Axel in Hamsun's *Growth of the Soil*: "Infanticide meant nothing to her, there was nothing extraordinary in the killing of a child; she thought of it only with the looseness and moral nastiness that was to be expected of a servant-girl."[81]

This attitude was also reflected in the perception toward legal prosecution for infanticide. Despite the large number of suspected newborn murders in England at the time, as when a child was found buried in a garden or abandoned in the field, from 1730-1774 only sixty-one infanticide cases were actually tried at the Old Bailey in London.[82] This small number was reflective of the general laxity within the administration toward prosecuting women for the crime. When charges were brought, however, over one-half of those cases taken to trial involved unmarried servant women.[83]

For those who did not kill their offspring, the difficulty of raising them amidst poverty and filth was intense. With good intentions, some women tried to both retain employment, and rear a child as best they could. But too often the money ran out and the children were then abandoned to their own wiles on the streets. This created a disturbance among the well-to-do which attracted much social and literary attention. In 1729, Jonathan Swift decried satirically:

> That horrid Practice of Women murdering their Bastard children; alas! too frequent among us; sacrificing the poor innocent Babes, I doubt, more to avoid the expense than the shame.[84]

He estimated that there were 120,000 children a year in Ireland that were begging on the streets in need of support, many of them illegitimate and abandoned. His plan proposed that they be taken at one year of age and then fattened and raised for consumption and sold to "Persons of Quality and Fortune."[85] This would supply a quantity of fresh flesh that would be in season throughout the year and help solve the complaints of the upper class in London that the waifs were constantly in the way.

There is no historical evidence that Swift's wry proposal was ever put into practice, but a more practical solution to the problem was eventually forthcoming in the formation of foundling homes as discussed in the chapter on Exposure. Thomas Coram realized that the primary cause of such large numbers of abandoned children was simply that: "Foundling equals bastard . . . and bastard equals disgrace."[86] After many years of fund raising and political maneuvering, he finally obtained a charter to open a home in London on March 22, 1739.[87]

Coram's awareness of the role of illegitimacy was not restricted to the English shores. Meyer estimated that of the foundlings abandoned in Paris in the nineteenth century, over 80% were bastards, although others have estimated a lower number.[88] The actual illegitimacy ratio during this period of time ranged from 4.75% to 8.84%.[89] Of interest, in 1793 France actually abolished the term bastardy, and substituted the term "extra-marital children", which lasted only a short period of time, and was succeeded by the term "natural children."[90] It was not to be a name change alone that would settle the disgrace of children born out-of-wedlock.[91]

Foundling hospitals, despite their admirable expectations, were not to be the hoped-for answer as many of the children they received soon died from neglect, malnutrition, and disease. At San Gallo, 20% of the infants died within one month of admission and another 30% in one year. Only 32% lived to age five years. In Dublin, the mortality rate between 1750-1759 was 89% and the hospital was finally closed in 1830. In Paris infant mortality rates of 80-90% were common.[92] The mortality rates were often so high in the winter that one commentator called it "a veritable hecatomb."[93]

Following the failure of the use of abandonment to handle the numbers of unwanted births, outright killings of the newborn surged again. Some claimed that "infanticide had taken the place of desertion as the mother sought to avoid the shame and disapproval of the community in which she lived".[94] In nineteenth century Australia, the majority of newborn deaths listed as stillbirth were illegitimate and likely homicidal in nature.[95]

In nineteenth century England, illegitimacy and poverty were shown to be the commonest reasons for infanticide. According to R. Sauer: "The sense of shame and fear of humiliation arising from having to face illegitimacy alone was so acute in some of these women, that even murder became a feasible means to avoid opprobrium."[96]

It was particularly the servant women, in the wealthier sections of London, that killed their newborn infants in great numbers.[97] William Acton found in 1857, that 57% of the bastard births in London were from mothers who worked as domestic servants.[98] Of course, many single women found that being a servant was one of the only jobs they could find during that time. From 1857-1881, 11.6% of the female population worked in this capacity.[99] The full skirt fashion of the time allowed a pregnancy to be hidden until delivery. After that, once the newborn was disposed of, no sign of shame remained.

In the English countryside it was also common for men to leave a woman to fend for herself: "When a country man gets a girl into trouble in nine cases out of ten he comes to London to escape responsibility."[100] Pollak noted how most of the women who attempted to kill their newborns were "live-in maids who are afraid of losing their jobs."[101]

Not that men were immune from the law, however, if they were charged with killing such an illegitimate child. In a short story by Victor Hugo about a Guernsey bachelor whose servant was noticed to have looked pregnant, and then suddenly lost weight without the appearance of a child, when the body of an infant was found buried in his yard, he was quickly convicted and hung.[102]

In addition to strict rules of virtuous conduct placed upon women, Victorian England was also noted for its preference by men of late marriage or permanent bachelorhood. In 1851, 30% of all men over the age of twenty years were unmarried in England, and 35% in Scotland.[103] Women were expected to remain virginal while waiting for a marriage proposal. Jane Austen, in *Pride and Prejudice*, described how even the image of wrong-doing could ruin a girl's reputation:

> Loss of virtue in a female is irretrievable – that one false step involves her in endless ruin – that her reputation is no less brittle than it is beautiful – and that she cannot be too much guarded in her behavior towards the undeserving of the other sex.[104]

All of this did not actually stop sexual intercourse before marriage, much like prohibition in America did not eliminate the ingestion of alcoholic beverages. But it did lead to a large number of bastard births. From 1861 to 1870, the number of children born in wedlock in the United Kingdom was 7,043,090 while those out of wedlock was 457,006 (6.5%).[105] The real number of those born out of wedlock was actually greater since many of the births were never registered.

With little attempt to understand, or help, the unwed mother, discrimination against her "ran like a red thread through the history of western civilization."[106] Men were generally seen as the source of money to pay for the child's care, but moral guilt was fastened exclusively on the mother and the penalty was usually a cruel life followed by a vindictive death.[107] Kurt Hamsun, in his famous novel *Growth of the Soil*, portrayed this attitude in the trial of Barbro who had killed her newborn illegitimate son:

> Society despises the unmarried woman who bears a child. Not only does society offer her no protection, but it persecutes her, pursues her with contempt and disgrace. Atrocious! No human

> creature with any heart at all could help feeling indignant at such a state of things. Not only is the girl to bring a child into the world, a thing in itself surely hard enough, but she is to be treated as a criminal for that very fact.[108]

It is of interest that while the unwed mother was shown little compassion by society in general, when she was finally charged with the killing and concealment of her child, her image was surprisingly changed. Juries would often show more sympathy to her portrayal on the stand at trial then they would have in the street. This resulted in a very low conviction rate for the charge of infanticide, as opposed to other types of homicide. Political commentators were indignant at this result. "Let no murderess be made a heroine of, and the practice may be lessened," said Dr. William Ryan.[109] But since the majority of infanticides were among the unmarried women, he added that society should look with a more forgiving eye, and pity at the "unhappy victims of seduction."[110]

An article in Lancet in 1861, which decried the killing of children to make money on burial insurance, also explained that "seduction, misery and shame . . . are powerful incentives operating upon many a mother to destroy her offspring."[111] Social awareness of the problem an unwed mother faced began to rise. Writing of the problem in 1869, Curgenven noted that the mortality rate of illegitimate children in England was 54-90%, while that of legitimate children of the lower classes was 10-30%.[112] Solutions began to be crystallized in the late nineteenth century.

A study by a select committee on Infant Mortality in Britain in 1871, summarized the causes of the excessive infant mortality among illegitimate children as follows:

1. The ignorance and poverty of the parents, or in the case of an illegitimate child – the mother.

2. Early seductions.

3. The difficulty experienced by the mothers of illegitimate children in maintaining them.

4. The insufficient legal protection afforded to young girls against their own weakness and ignorance and the arts of the seducer.

5. The grossly unjust favour which the law of bastardy shows to the fathers of illegitimate children.

6. The overwork of mothers during pregnancy.

7. The custom by which married women return to work immediately after the birth of their infants, leaving those infants to the care of nurses.

8. The total want of a simple legal method by which a married woman can compel her husband to support her and her children.

9. The relation of personal slavery in which the law of England places every woman towards her husband.[113]

In America the situation was similar to that of Europe. During the Puritanical Era of the eighteenth century, young girls were publicly hung on the gallows for destroying their children in an attempt to avoid the shame and scandal from premarital pregnancies. The rigid moral codes strictly forbade sex before marriage and the death penalty was promoted in Sunday sermons as a lesson to be learned and applauded by the parishioners.[114] Not only were the Puritans extremely intolerant of sexual relations outside the marriage bond, but they felt that murder of an unbaptized infant kept the infant from entering heaven which thereby mocked the intent, and authority, of God.[115] Their trials, and subsequent executions, were widely attended and supported by the populace. Ministers would frequently admonish the women just before they were killed. Cotton Mather in 1646 related how when one woman tried to conceal her illegitimate infant by killing it and stuffing it into a chest, she was nevertheless found and punished for "the blood of the child cried, when the cry of the child itself was thus cruelly stifled."[116] In order to prevent concealment, public registration of births, marriages and deaths was maintained in many of the colonies with great care.[117] This chronicle helped to uncover any act of deception.

But in America, as in Europe, despite the harshness of these disciplinary methods, the problem of illegitimate births and deaths continued. Before 1680 only about 3.3% of brides had children within 6 months of their wedding. Between 1761-1800, this proportion had risen to 16.7%.[118] If one measured it at nine months from the wedding, it was 33%.

In Canada, most of the women charged with the crime of concealment were single and employed as domestic servants. As in England, these young girls could not usually find other means of support, and once hired they were commonly exploited sexually by their employer's entire family.[119] While having to accept sexual advances in order to keep her job, she was nevertheless expected to practice birth control by some methodology: "If she bore an illegitimate child, she would lose her job and be ostracized from society at large."[120] As Blackhouse noted: "The concealment of the pregnancy followed by infanticide must have seemed preferable to disgrace, loss of employment and shelter, and even starvation."[121] With such an enormous burden, the actions they took to extricate themselves did not seem so extreme. Looking back on the lives they led, "the courage and resourcefulness that these women exhibited in total secrecy and isolation, and often in complete ignorance of the natural processes of pregnancy and childbirth, is striking."[122]

In Russia, the dread of a shameful birth similarly drove women to kill their infants shortly after delivery. In *The Power of Darkness*, Tolstoy told of how the mother of a sixteen-year-old, unmarried pregnant girl demanded that the father of the newborn infant help her bury the bastard in the cellar. When the young man asked if there was some other way than killing the poor infant, she answered "you should have thought about it a year ago."[123] It was better to bury it in the earth, she explained, then risk the disgrace which would follow: "Mother earth will not blab to any one: she'll keep it close."[124] Tolstoy obviously felt great disgust over this common attitude, and when the father tried to bury the child beneath a floor board he cried about "how the little bones crunched and how it whimpered."[125] At the end of the story he confessed his guilt and was taken away by the police.

Even in 1970, one of every ten births in Russia was out of wedlock – a total of over 400,000 illegitimate babies a year.[126] According to L. Kuznetsova "one cannot conceal the fact that the unmarried mother often becomes the target of humiliating abuse – and stones of malice are tossed at her child as well."[127]

In Corsica, the Penal Code of 1810 required three elements for the crime of infanticide: newborn victim, born alive, with death deliberately caused.[128] Guilty parties were given the death sentence, even though ordinary homicide was only punished by hard labor for life. The reasoning for this differential was the intent to use punishment as a specific deterrent to the crime. In Stephen Wilson's review of infanticide during the nineteenth century, the primary motive was to avoid dishonor and shame associated with a bastard birth.[129]

In Argentina, the nineteenth century humanistic approach to the crime of infanticide led to an entirely different tactic. The offense was uniquely defined as: the killing, through either neglect or violence, of a child by its mother "in order to hide her dishonor."[130] If convicted of this felony, a woman only faced imprisonment for three to six years. In contrast to the centuries earlier approach in Europe, the accused here had to establish she was an honorable person by demonstrating that she attempted to conceal the pregnancy and birth.[131] One's reputation was an expediency worth killing for.

And it was not only the civilized countries that abhorred illegitimate children. In most uncultured societies, offspring of prenuptial children were killed. Robert Briffault noted that: "Infanticide is not regarded in the lower stages of culture as a criminal act, but is viewed from the point of view of expediency as a Malthusian measure, and no child is reared when it is inconvenient to do so."[132]

Among the Bedouins near Massua, if a young girl bore a child, it was killed by the grandmother.[133] Phyllis reported on how a young unmarried Yemenite woman gave birth to a child and the woman's mother handed her a knife and said "you brought this on, you will get rid of it", and then left the room.[134]

Native American Indians practiced similar beliefs. As the Euro-American exploration spread across California, many Indian women were forced into concubinage with white men and the resultant births created numerous infants of mixed blood. For a long period, these newborns were killed as a means of nonviolent resistance. Every white child born "was secretly strangled and buried."[135] The Sinkyone and Lassik tribes were particularly noted for this practice.[136] Among the Wappo, any unwanted child could be killed by the mother, and no social stigma was applied by other members of the tribe.[137]

The Iroquois Indians of Northeastern America told with reverence the legend of Degandawida where a redeemer was born of the virgin Djigosasee. The grandmother, however, did not believe her child's story of a virgin birth and tried to destroy the newborn child by cutting a hole through the ice and thrusting him into the lake. The child would not sink, and survived both this, and all other attempts at harm.[138] As a grown man, along with his disciple Hiawatha, he became a prophet, saint, mystic and poet of the American Indian culture.[139]

Shame might come even from legitimate marriages, if the marriage occurred between members of different social castes. While most of the illegitimate births have occurred through fornication between unmarried couples, there have also been classes from adultery, incest, forbidden caste unions, and procreation by avowed celibates.[140] In colonial America, marriage between a white and a black was prohibited, and their children were considered "spurious and mixt issue," or "abominable mixtures."[141] Among the Ka-'U in Hawaii, if a low caste woman bore a child fathered by a member of the higher caste, the child was killed in order to prevent adulteration of the purity of the bloodlines.[142] The Tswana condoned killing a child who was felt to bear an evil omen. While illegitimate children were not placed in this category, their killing was treated more leniently than that of other offspring. If the corpse of an infant was found, the Chief would call the unmarried women of the village together in order to test their breasts for milk. The culprit would then be smeared with a mixture of medicines to cause intense pain as expiation for the crime.[143] The Narrinyeri in Victoria generally murdered any infant born before the mother was married.[144]

Even today, the illegitimate birth rate as a percentage total of the live-birth rate in many areas is quite high. In countries such as Japan and the Mideast, where there is intense social pressure against illegitimate births, the rate is often less than 1%.[145] In Jamaica, however, during the 1960's it was recorded as high as 74%, in Panama 70%, and in Guatemala and El Salvador the rate was 67%.[146] In the United States, the rates were 9.7% for the total population, with the rate for nonwhites some 7-10 times that for whites.[147] In 1990, 28% of births in the U.S. were to unmarried women, a total of 1,165,384 infants.[148]

A number of modern authors have noted that a prominent feature in many of these young, unmarried girls is a denial of the pregnancy. The denial can actually at times induce physical changes whereby the biological manifestation of the pregnancy, such as enlarged abdominal girth, may not be seen.[149] Gerchow recorded that some of these patients may even continue to have some degree of menstrual blood flow, something which would never occur in a normal pregnancy.[150]

These women have an unusually high likelihood of committing infanticide after the child is born. Edward Saunders hypothesized that: "When they were no longer able to deny the reality with the birth of the child, they became acutely disorganized and murdered their infants."[151] In some studies, fear of being abandoned by their own mother, if the child was discovered, was the precipitating event.[152] Gummersbach found that the single personality factor that clearly separated those who killed their infant, from those who sought abortion, was extreme passivity.[153] Concealment of their pregnancy, even from themselves, was their only way of coping with the emotional stress. Helplessness, lack of experience, immaturity and panic were all factors leading the woman to kill her unwanted child as soon as it was born.[154]

B. Literature

The plight of the unwed mother to withstand the pressures of an unsympathetic society, and the tragic effects this caused upon her innocent child, has been a favorite literary topic of authors throughout the ages. The plot combines all the emotional elements of human nature which captivates both the interest, and the horror, of diverse nations and cultures.

In many of the stories, the bastard child became the main character of interest. Heliodorus, in *An Ethiopian Romance*, narrated the tale of queen Persinna who exposed her newborn infant because the child was white rather than the blackened tint of native Ethiopians. To not be shamed by a charge of adultery, she abandoned the infant in the wilds for:

"I preferred to deliver to the hazards of chance rather than to certain death or, at any rate, the infamy of bastardy."[155] The ploy worked, and the child was saved and grew up to become the beautiful Chariclea, a major participant in the storyline.

Famous for the portrayal of intense personal drama, Greek theater provided frequent instances of exposure of an illegitimate child by a mother who was acting out of shame or fear. Many of these offspring were supposedly the progeny of a mortal mother and a god. These were often tales of woe for, as the epode in *Ion*, by Euripides, warns: "Our legends, our tales at the loom, never tell of good fortune to children born of a god and a mortal."[156]

In many, the infant was rescued and grew to become a hero or king. Amphion and Zethus, twin sons, were born to Zeus and Antiope, the daughter of Nycteus of Thebes. She exposed them on Mount Cithaeron but they were saved by a herdsman.[157] When grown they helped to build Thebes and became masters of the city.[158] Asclepius, the famous Greek physician and co-founder of modern medicine along with Hippocrates, was by some accounts said to have been exposed by his mother who had gotten pregnant by Apollo.[159] Another version said he was exposed in Thelpusa and was reared by Autolaus.[160]

Not all of the children of gods who were exposed at birth survived to become famous later in life. Psamathe, the daughter of Crotopus at Argos, was impregnanted by Apollo and, in fear of her father, exposed the child at birth. The baby was destroyed by sheepdogs of Crotopus and Apollo, in anger, sent Vengeance to punish the Argive city.[161]

Another popular theme through the ages was to dramatize the frailty, or evil nature, of the spurned mother through the infant's appearance or plight. In *Titus Andronicus*, by William Shakespeare, Queen Tamora bore a black child by the Moor Aaron and then sent the infant to him with instructions that "bids thee christen it with thy dagger's point."[162] Her son, Demetrius, said that "By this our mother is for ever shamed."[163] Whether the reference is to the affair with the Moor, or to the infanticidal act, is unclear.

In the same play, Titus was unsure of how to deal with the refusal of his daughter to marry the man he chose and asked the emperor, Saturninus, if it was right of rash Virginius to slay his own daughter because "she was enforced, stained and deflowered."[164] Saturninus answered that the act was correct because "the girl should not survive her shame, and by her presence still renew his sorrows."[165] Titus then killed his daughter Lavinia for his woes was equal to that of Virginius.

The dramatic affect of how the birth of a bastard infant can change a young girl's life was vividly portrayed in Menander's touching play, *The Girl From Samos*. Chrysis was berated by her lover Demeas for even thinking of keeping a baby born out of wedlock.[166] The usual practice was obviously to destroy the illegitimate child, but Chrysis desired to keep her infant and raise it by herself once it was born. Her neighbors told her she had gone crazy to let the baby live.[167] When she refused to give the baby up, Demeas threatened to murder her in anger.[168]

The ancient Roman playwright, Terence, in *The Mother-In-Law*, told of how Pamphilus returned home from abroad and found his wife Philumena about to deliver a child. Her mother tried to assuage his outrage by explaining that she was raped while he was away, but that he should not be angered for the "child shall immediately be exposed, and you shall be none the worse; and by this means you will not only suffer no inconvenience but protect your unlucky wife's reputation besides."[169] While Phidippus was expected to agree with this obviously rational solution to the illegitimate pregnancy, he instead scolded the woman for her attitude. "Could ye be so damnable malicious as to wish death for the poor child?" he asked incredulously.[170] His wife responded that the one evil that could crown all her other disasters would be to be "forced to bring up a child whom we don't know the father of."[171]

Sir Walter Scott, in *The Heart of Midlothian*, included the tale of the trial of Effie Deans, a young girl charged "for concealing her pregnancy, and giving no account of the child which she has borne," a felony that was created by a 1690 Scottish statute.[172] Under that intolerant Act which duplicated the English Stuart Act, her crime was a capital offense which demanded that a woman who concealed her pregnancy be found guilty for murder. Effie's reasons were clear to the court: "The dread of this public shame was so great, that, rather than face it, the unwed pregnant woman disguised her condition as best she could, and did away with the infant at birth."[173] There was little sympathy from her father who felt that "I wadna gie one o' my grey hairs for her life, if her gude name be gone."[174] Effie was found guilty and ordered by the judge to be hanged, but was saved by a reprieve by Queen Caroline.

In 1858, George Eliot, in *Adam Bede*, told the story of Hette Sorrel, a young unmarried woman who was brought to trial for murdering her illegitimate child shortly after its birth. The father of the child, Arthur Donnithorne, escaped any punishment for most people felt that there was no reason to think that "the guilt of the crime lies with him . . . It is not for us men to apportion the shares of moral guilt and retribution."[175] At the trial, Hette even tried to deny her pregnancy, but there were eye witnesses to the event and she was found guilty and sentenced to death by hanging.[176] Her life was eventually saved by her father's ability to obtain a pardon. Happy endings were often not so apparent in real life.

The writers of the last three decades of the eighteenth century Age of Enlightenment turned their attention to the discovery and elimination of the causes of unmarried motherhood rather than concentrating on the punishment.[177] They generally were very sympathetic to the woman's plight and claimed that the excessive severity of the laws led to the crime, rather than preventing it.[178] Pestaluzzi characterized this belief when he wrote in frustration and anger: "O you judges! the girl loved her babe, but because of your penal laws she killed it."[179]

In eighteenth century Germany, the theme of the seduction of young innocent girls who fell victims to the intolerance of the middle class and performed infanticide was quite popular among the "Sturm und Drang" authors, which included Goethe.[180] The women, typically innocent and sharing childlike naivete, were usually executed by a ruthless judge, while the seducer emerged without penalty. The topic even surpassed the frequently used theme of the hostile brothers who proceed, out of jealousy and pride, to turn family ties to hatred.[181]

The authors generally felt that punishment in Germany was out of proportion to the circumstances and looked only at the facts of the killing rather than realizing the reasons leading up to the crime. One editorial in the magazine *Briefwechsel* asked: "How long shall we lead to the block these unfortunate girls as sacrificial victims, whose love and the natural weakness of their sex, whose adornment of innocence and modesty has made them to be mothers and murderesses?"[182]

Goethe battled with these dilemmas in *Faust* when Gretchen (Margarete) became pregnant by Faust and related:

> How firmly I could once inveigh
> When any young girl went astray!
> For others' sins I could not find
> Words enough to speak my mind!
> Black as it was, blacker it had to be,
> And still it wasn't black enough for me.
> I thanked my stars and was so game,
> And now I stand exposed to shame![183]

Her dying brother Valentine told her that she was a whore and that: "All the decent citizenry will from you, harlot, turn away as from a plague corpse in their way."[184] She would no longer be able to step up to the altar rail or dancing floor, but would have to slouch to a dismal corner:

> Where the beggars and cripples crouch.
> And even though God may forgive,
> Accursed here on earth you still will live.[185]

Gretchen eventually drowned her child in the lake and later, while awaiting her execution in prison, dreamed of the event.[186] Her punishment was more from within the tempest of her soul, than the horror of her sentence of death.

Goethe was said to have based his theme on the trial of Susanna

Margaretha Brandt in Frankfurt in 1772. The "Gretchen Tragedy", as the storyline became known, was quite popular and was copied in operas by Berlioz, Boito, and Gounod and also by other "Sturm und Drang" German writers. Charles Gounod, in his version of *Faust*, had Marguerite in prison at the end of the opera, patiently waiting to be executed for the murder of her child.[187] In *Mephistopheles*, by Arrigo Boito, Marguerite had become obviously insane after poisoning her mother in addition to drowning her illegitimate child.[188] The audience was to find some degree of sympathy in the dissolution of Marguerite's soul, rather than in the vicious retribution of the state.

In Schiller's moving poem, "The Infanticide," an unmarried young woman awaits her death on the scaffold advising: "Sisters, trust your youthful roses ne'er, Trust them ne'er to false man's treach'rous vow!"[189] She tells her newborn son that he will seek in vain for his father who "wilt curse the moment of our bliss, When the Bastard's name inflicts its stain."[190]

Many other famous tales also contained the saga of an illegitimate birth. In *the History of Tom Jones*, by Henry Fielding, when the infant Tom was found in the bed of Mr. Allworthy, the servant claimed that the unknown mother must be a hussy: "I should be glad to see her committed to Bridewell, and whipt at the cart's tail."[191] When her master says that he is glad she "hath not done worse," the woman advises how it would have been better for the baby to have been left at the churchwarden's door for "it is two to one but it lives till it is found in the morning."[192]

In *The Master and Margarite*, by the Russian author Milkhail Bulgakov, the unfair burden placed upon the mother in these cases was portrayed. Friede visited Hell in a dream and met a young woman who had been raped by the owner of a cafe. Nine months later she gave birth to a boy and immediately carried him into the woods, stuffed a handkerchief in his mouth, and buried him alive. At her trial, she weepfully defended her conduct with claims that she could not afford to raise the child. Friede listened to her story intently and then angrily asked where was the cafe owner? Why was he not in Hell along with the guilty mother? The reply was what had he to do with the sordid details, it "wasn't he who stifled the child."[193]

Jean-Paul Sartre, in *No Exit*, tells of Estelle Rigault who had an extramarital affair with Roger and when she found herself pregnant she went to Switzerland where the baby was born. Although Roger wanted her to keep the baby, and pleaded for her to follow his advice, she attached the newborn to a rock and threw it from her balcony into the water. In anguish, Roger then shot himself.[194]

Similarly, W. Somerset Maugham, in *The Unconquered*, relates the rape of a French country maiden by a German soldier who was part of the conquering army during the wartime invasion of France. He later found the girl pregnant in Soissons, and desired to marry her. The mother of the young girl hoped for the marriage to take place, but when the baby was born the girl took the infant to a brook and held it under the water till it was dead. She performed the task immediately after the birth for "I was afraid if I waited I shouldn't have the courage."[195]

The severe puritanical attitude of the clergy in eighteenth century America was caustically portrayed by Maxwell Anderson. In *The Wingless Victory*, Reverend Phineas McQueston, of Salem, Massachusetts, berated an unmarried mother and cast her out with her bastard infant:

> We can make no distinction between the sin and the fruits of the sin. It would be as well if her were to die – and better for your soul.[196]

As occurred with witches as well, the cleansing of the soul often meant that the young girl's life would have to be taken.

Probably the most sympathetic outpouring of empathy over the treatment of bastard births can be seen in the *Growth of the Soil*, by Kurt Hamsun. In this famous novel, the servant-girl Barbro disposes of an illegitimate birth and then is tried for murder. In a moving defense, Fru Heyerdahl points out that it is society which is to blame, and not the frightened, persecuted and shamed woman, now distraught and weakened with an attempt to hide her pregnant state:

> The child is at least killed in kindness. The mother tries to save herself and the child she loves from the misery of its life. The shame is more than she can bear, and so the plan gradually forms itself in her mind, to put the child out of the way . . . But it is the fault of society that it is so; the fault of a hopeless, merciless, scandalmongering, mischievous, and evil-minded society, ever on the watch to crush an unmarried mother by every means in its power![197]

She also castigates the men who seem to always judge but never are called to judgment themselves:

> Why is the man to go free? The mother found guilty of infanticide is thrust into prison and torture, but the father, the seducer, he is never touched. Yet being as he is the cause of the child's existence, he is a party to the crime; his share in it, indeed, is greater than the mother's; had it not been for him, there would have been no crime. Then why should he be acquitted? Because the laws are made by men.[198]

Men who commit infanticide have been mostly overlooked on the fictional front, although not totally ignored. Sam Shepard, in his Pulitzer prize-winning play *Buried Child*, tells how Dodge drowned his wife's infant son who was born after they had not slept together for over six years. Shame, along with anger, forced him into the move, and he later explained away his actions with a comment on the nature of man: "You think just because people propagate they have to love their offspring?"[199] Infanticide was not something that should seem out of place, even within the confines of a family home.

Endnotes

1 . Macfarlane, "Illegitimacy and Illegitimates in English History," 71.
2 . Williamson, "Infanticide: An Anthropological Analysis," 65-66.
3 . Durant, Our Oriental Heritage, 46.
4 . Higginbotham, "Sin of the Age: Infanticide and Illegitimacy in Victorian London," 321-22.
5 . Hastings, Encyclopedia of Religion & Ethics, Volume I, 3.
6 . Lombroso & Ferrero, Female Offenders, 251.
7 . Werner, The Unmarried Mother in German Literature, 12.
8 . Ibid., 13.
9 . Durant, Our Oriental Heritage, 37.
10 . Werner, The Unmarried Mother in German Literature, 13-14.
11 . Durant, Our Oriental Heritage, 48.
12 . Encyclopedia Britannica, 1881, Volume XIII, pg 3.
13 . The Laws of Eshnunna, 26. Pritchard, Ancient Near Eastern Texts, 162.
14 . Code of Hammurabi, 129. Ibid., 171.
15 . Code of Hammurabi, 130. Ibid.
16 . Middle Assyrian Laws, Tablet A.55. Assyrian Laws, transl. G. R. Driver & John C. Miles (Oxford: Clarendon Press, 1935), 423.
17 . Diodorus of Sicily, The Library of History, I.80.3-4, Volume I, 275.
18 . El-Shamy, Folktales of Egypt, 108.
19 . Lipit-Ishtar Lawcode, 27. Pritchard, Ancient Near Eastern Texts, 160.
20 . Deuteronomy 22:18.
21 . Deuteronomy 22:21. The Living Bible, 167.
22 . Deuteronomy 22:22. Ibid.
23 . Deuteronomy 22:23.
24 . Genesis 38:24.
25 . The young lady was a childless widow and had disguised herself as a prostitute in order to copulate with Judah. Genesis 38:14.
26 . Genesis 38:28. The Living Bible, 36.
27 . The Wisdom of Solomon, 3:16-19, 130.
28 . Sanhedrin, Gemara, VII.50a.
29 . Ibid., VII.50b.
30 . Kethuboth, Gemara, IV.44b-45a.
31 . Josephus, Antiquities, IV.VIII.23, 273.
32 . Ibid., IV.VIII.24, 275.
33 . Philo, On Josepth, IX.43, 163-165. See e.g. Deuteronomy 23:17.
34 . Maimonides, The Guide of the Perplexed, III.49, 611.
35 . Deuteronomy 23:2. The Living Bible, 168.
36 . The Mishnah, Makkoth, 3.1, 405.
37 . Weinreich, Yiddish Folktales, 186.
38 . Matthew 1:18-19. The Living Bible, 745.
39 . Matthew 1:20-21. Ibid.
40 . Luke 1:35. Ibid., 800.
41 . I Corinthians 7:6. Ibid., 918.
42 . Ibid.
43 . Werner, The Unmarried Mother in German Literature, 25.
44 . S. John Chrysostom, "The Epistle of St. Paul the Apostle to the Romans, The Homilies of S. John Chrysostom, Archbishop of Constantinople, 413.

45 . Tertullian, "On Modesty," V, 66.
46 . McNeill & Gamer, "Penitentials Tentatively Ascribed by Abers to Bede," II.11, Medieval Handbooks of Penance, 225.
47 . Patterson, "Not Worth The Rearing: The Causes of Infant Exposure in Ancient Greece," 115.
48 . Ibid., 116.
49 . Livy, History of Rome, I.IV.2, 17.
50 . Ovid, Metamorphoses, III.282-83, 66.
51 . Ibid., IV.213-250, 88-89.
52 . Classical Mythology, 368.
53 . Ovid, Heroides, 83-84, 95-96, 139.
54 . Herodotus, The History, IV.154, Volume II, 357.
55 . Viljoen, "Plato and Aristotle on the Exposure of Infants at Athens," 62.
56 . Horace, Odes and Epodes, 149.
57 . Euripides, Rhesus, 926-928.
58 . Orosius, The Seven Books of History Against the Pagans, 63.
59 . Cicero, The Republic, II.XXXVII.63, 175.
60 . Shakespeare, The Winter's Tale, 2.3.93-96.
61 . Ibid., 2.3.138-141.
62 . Robins, The Lost Children, 3.
63 . Boswell, The Kindness of Strangers, 210.
64 . Ibid., footnote 107, 211.
65 . Werner, The Unmarried Mother in German Literature, 23.
66 . Boswell, The Kindness of Strangers, 223.
67 . Rees & Rees, Celtic Heritage, 238.
68 . Emmison, Elizabethan Life: Disorder, 156-157.
69 . Shorter, The Making of the Modern Family, 51.
70 . Hoffer & Hull, "Murdering Mothers: Infanticide in England and New England 1558-1803," 20.
71 . Parry, "A Dissertation by William Hunter on the Uncertainty of the Signs of Murder in the Case of Bastard Children," 1143.
72 . Ibid.
73 . Ibid.
74 . Laslett, "Introduction: Comparing Illegitimacy Over Time and Between Cultures," 26.
75 . Ibid.
76 . Ibid., 28.
77 . Langer, "Infanticide: A Historical Survey," 357.
78 . Ibid.
79 . Smout, "Aspects of Sexual Behaviour in Nineteenth-Century Scotland," 196.
80 . Fielding, Joseph Andrews, 19.
81 . Hamsun, Growth of the Soil, 266.
82 . Malcolmson, "Infanticide in the Eighteenth Century," 191.
83 . Ibid., 202.
84 . Swift, "A Modest Proposal for Preventing the Children of poor People in Ireland From Being a Burden to their Parents or Country; and for making them Beneficial to the Publick," Gulliver's Travels & Other Writings, 489.
85 . Ibid., 490.
86 . McClure, Coram's Children, 9.

87 . Ibid., 28, 33.
88 . Boswell, The Kindness of Strangers, footnote 34, 17.
89 . van de Walle, "Illegitimacy in France During The Nineteenth Century," 270.
90 . Ibid., 264.
91 . Even in modern France, the impulse to abandon a child at birth led to the law of secret childbirth, generally called "Childbirth Under X," where the identity of any mother who so desires will be protected and the resultant child is then given to an adoptive family. This law was passed in 1941 when many couples were separated by war. Bonnet, "Adoption at Birth: Prevention Against Abandonment or Neonaticide," 503.
92 . Rose, The Massacre of the Innocents: Infanticide in Britain 1800-1939, 2.
93 . Langer, "Checks on Population Growth: 1750-1850," 98.
94 . Robins, The Lost Children, 155.
95 . Thearle & Gregory, "Child Abuse in Nineteenth Century Queensland," 93.
96 . Sauer, "Infanticide and Abortion in Nineteenth-Century Britain," 85.
97 . Behlmer, "Deadly Motherhood: Infanticide and Medical Opinion in Mid-Victorian England," 419.
98 . Ibid., 420.
99 . Ibid.
100. Bishop, Women and Crime, 96.
101. Pollak, The Criminality of Women, 21.
102. Hugo, "Monster & Infanticide," The Works of Victor Hugo, 449.
103. Rose, "The Massacre of the Innocents: Infanticide in Britain 1800-1939," 17.
104. Austen, Pride and Prejudice, 316.
105. Philanthropus, The Institution of Marriage in the United Kingdom, Appendix B, 387.
106. Piers, Infanticide, 65.
107. Ibid.
108. Hamsun, Growth of the Soil, 342.
109. Ryan, "Child Murder In Its Sanitary and Social Bearings," 15.
110. Ibid.
111. "Infanticide," Lancet, 314.
112. Curgenven, "On Baby-Farming and the Registration of Nurses," 8.
113. Infant Mortality: Its Causes and Remedies, 30.
114. Jones, Women Who Kill, 49.
115. Ibid., 50.
116. Mather, "A Whoredom Unmaked," America Begins, 119.
117. Winthrop, "A Heretic Bears a Monster," America Begins, 121.
118. Wells, "Illegitimacy and Bridal Pregnancy in Colonial America," 353.
119. Blackhouse, "Desperate Women and Compassionate Courts: Infanticide in Nineteenth-Century Canada," 457.
120. Quoted from Lori Rotenberg. Ibid., 458.
121. Ibid.
122. Ibid.
123. Tolstoy, "The Power of Darkness," IV, The Portable Tolstoy, 800.
124. Ibid., 801.
125. Ibid., 805.
126. Madison, "Social Services for Women: Problems and Priorities," 319.
127. Ibid.

128. Wilson, "Infanticide, Child Abandonment, and Female Honour in Nineteenth-Century Corsica," 765. The average number of cases prosecuted yearly was two. Ibid., 764.
129. Ibid., 773.
130. Codigo penal de la Republia Argentina (Buenos Aires: Sud America, 1887), sec. 1, title 1, chap. 2, arts 100, 101. Ruggiero, "Honor, Maternity, and the Disciplining of Women: Infanticide in Late Nineteenth-Century Buenos Aires," 354.
131. Ibid., 357.
132. Briffault, The Mothers, Volume I, 27.
133. M'Lennan, Studies in Ancient History, 98.
134. Piers, Infanticide, 19.
135. Castillo, "The Impact of Euro-American Exploration & Settlement," 104.
136. Elsasser, "Mattole, Nongatl, Sinkyone, Lassik, and Waiaki," 196.
137. Sawyer, "Wappo," 259.
138. Henry, Wilderness Messiah, 30-31.
139. Ibid., 29.
140. Laslett, "Introduction: Comparing Illegitimacy Over Time and Between Cultures," 7.
141. Wells, "Illegitimacy and Bridal Pregnancy in Colonial America," 351.
142. Handy, Craighill & Pukui, The Polynesian Family System in Ka-'U, Hawaii, 79.
143. Schapera, A Handbook of Tswana Law and Custom, 261-62.
144. Smyth, The Aborigines of Victoria, 52.
145. Hartley, Illegitimacy, 25.
146. Ibid.
147. Ibid., 25, 49.
148. Chicago Tribune (February 26, 1993): section 1, 3.
149. Brozovsky & Falit, "Neonaticide, Clinical and Psychodynamic Considerations," 679.
150. Ibid., 680.
151. Saunders, "Neonaticides Following `Secret' Pregnancies: Seven Case Reports," 370.
152. Brozovsky & Falit, "Neonaticide, Clinical & Psychodynamic Considerations," 681.
153. Saunders, "Neonaticides Following `Secret' Pregnancies: Seven Case Reports," 370.
154. Milcinski, "Abortion and Infanticide in Yugoslavia," 164.
155. Heliodorus, An Ethiopian Romance, IV, 95.
156. Euripides, Ion, 502-508, 205.
157. New Century Classical Handbook, 114.
158. Ibid., 91.
159. Pausanias, Description of Greece, II.XXVI.4, Volume I, 387.
160. Ibid., VIII.XXV.11, Volume IV, 27-29.
161. Ibid., I.XLIII.7, Volume I, 235.
162. Shakespeare, The Tragedy of Titus Andronicus, IV.ii.71, 61.
163. Ibid., IV.ii.113, 62.
164. Ibid., V.iii.38, 88.
165. Ibid., V.iii.41-42.
166. Menander, The Girl From Samos, The Complete Greek Drama, Volume II, 1131.
167. Ibid., 1133.

168. Ibid., 1135.
169. Terence, The Mother in Law, III, The Comedies of Terence, 77.
170. Ibid., IV, 85.
171. Ibid., IV, 86.
172. Scott, The Heart of Mid-Lothian, I.V, 52.
173. Editorial note by John Henry Raleigh. Ibid., xxvi.
174. Ibid., II.VI, 196.
175. Eliot, Adam Bede, XLI, 406.
176. Ibid., XLIII, 419.
177. Werner, The Unmarried Mother in German Literature, 40.
178. Infanticide as a theme was treated only by male authors. Kord studied almost 1600 plays by women of the eighteenth and nineteenth century, and not one dealt with the subject of infanticide. Kord, "Women As Children, Women As Childkillers: Poetic Images of Infanticide in Eighteenth-Century Germany," 459.
179. Werner, The Unmarried Mother in German Literature, 56.
180. Ibid., 1. "Treatises by Beccaria, Kant, Pestalozzi, and Voltaire called for the abolition of the death penalty for infanticide, while poetic treatments of the theme by the writers of the Storm and Stress movement depicted the plight of the guilty mothers." Kord, "Women As Children, Women As Childkillers: Poetic Images of Infanticide in Eighteenth-Century Germany," 452.
181. Werner, The Unmarried Mother in German Literature, 2.
182. Ibid., 4.
183. Goethe, Faust, I.3577-3584, 126.
184. Ibid., I.3751-3753, 132.
185. Ibid., I.3761-3763.
186. Ibid., I.4550-4562, 161.
187. IV.2. Simon, 100 Great Operas and Their Stories, 167.
188. III. Ibid., 327.
189. Schiller, The Poems of Schiller, 28.
190. Ibid., 27.
191. Fielding, The History of Tom Jones, A Foundling, I.III, 6.
192. Ibid.
193. Bulgakov, The Master and Margarite, 23, 283.
194. Sartre, No Exit, 37.
195. Maugham, "The Unconquered," The Complete Short Stories, 486.
196. Anderson, The Wingless Victory, I, 5.
197. Hamsun, Growth of the Soil, 343.
198. Ibid., 343-344.
199. Shepard, Buried Child, III, 126.

CHAPTER XI

SACRIFICE

"For a murder does not become a sacrifice by being committed in a particular spot."[1]

A. Historical Survey

Clement of Alexandria, the second century A.D. Greek theologian, commented above on the deplorable practice of human sacrifice among pagan heathens, and gave little credence to the excuse that it was homage to some angry or demanding deity. The sacrificial act was nothing less than outright homicide, and its performance within the tenets of a religious belief did not change the criminal nature of the deed. Today, such a conclusion would evoke little academic or philosophical argument; throughout much of our history, however, such sentiment was very controversial.

For centuries before the birth of Christ, infants had frequently been sacrificed by many civilizations to various idols or divinities. Otherwise rational and successful societies practiced the rite in elaborate ceremonies that were intended to pacify the pertinacious nature of their gods. In their own way, they believed totally in the value of the deadly process, and the children were given up readily by parents with little sign of remorse. If so many diverse cultures thereby found the offering of their offspring beneficial, can we merely pass them off as chaotic, or pathologic, customs? I think not. We cannot simply exchange our present moral values with those of our ancestors and throw off their determinations with a shrug of ethical disapproval. Somehow we must find a more rational explanation for their behavior.

But Clement of Alexandria was correct, and we also cannot fail to question each and every occurrence simply because it was called, at the time, a religious observation. The dilemma we face in trying to analyze the reasoning of our ancestors in sacrificing the lives of their children comes in deciding when the offering was an act of veneration, and when it was simply blind carnage.

As human beings, we all share certain innate genetic traits which guide the expression of our social behavior. These mannerisms are instinctive, and, while we may develop some voluntary control over their outward presence, we cannot totally eliminate its underlying force. The motivation behind these activities is referred to as "natural law." And, like the sled dogs in Jack London's *Call of the Wild*, we are inextricably drawn to a particular life pattern by genetic material that has been inherited from very ancient ancestors.[2]

The way in which diverse human societies have all developed a similar belief in some type of supernatural deity to which they have ascribed power over every critical aspect of their lives, is one sign of this genetic bondage. Be it within the sanctuaries of ancient Sumeria or the temples of modern America, humans beings worship omnipotent gods who require adherence to a set of instructions known as the divine law. If the precepts of the gods are not followed, dire consequences surely will follow.

Since the anger of the gods has been a constant threat in all of these religious beliefs, appeasements have had to be arranged which generally include some type of sacrificial activity. By relinquishing an item of value to the gods, it is hoped that gratuitous repayment will be generated in the form of promoting fertility, warding off disease, preventing calamity or easing the passage of the dead out of this world.[3] If an individual fails to acquiesce to the god's demands, not only will the life of that one person be affected, but the entire population could possibly be put at risk.

This power of the Almighty is remarkably ubiquitous. According to religious tenets, the gods created earthquakes and storms, controlled the movements of men, and were responsible for the growing of crops and the supply of food. The more dependent the people were on day-to-day regeneration of basic life needs, the more important was the support of the gods. In the thirteenth century A.D., the Arab scholar Ibn Khaldun remarked on the clear economic base of this relationship:

> The frugal inhabitants of the desert and those of settled areas who have accustomed themselves to hunger and to abstinence from pleasures are found to be more religious and more ready for divine worship than people who live in luxury and abundance.[4]

If one cannot buy the basic necessities of comfort during life here on earth, then you can still hope for equality in the justice of the eternal hereafter.[5]

The ancient Sumerian, Egyptian, and Assyrian civilizations all worshiped gods in this regard. In the Sumerian pantheon, for example, the country was dependent on Enlil:

> Without Enlil, the Great mountain,
> No city would be built, no settlement founded,
> No stalls would be built, no sheepfolds established,
> No king would be raised, no high priest born.

The rivers – their floodwaters would not bring over flow,
The fish in the sea would not lay eggs in the canebrake,
The birds of heaven would not build nests on the wild earth,
In heaven the drifting clouds would not yield their moisture,
Plants and herbs, the glory of the plain, would fail to grow,
In fields and meadows the rich grain would fail to flower,
The trees planted in the mountain-forest would not yield their fruit.[6]

With such omnipotence, the gods could not be overlooked. If they were dissatisfied, disaster was certain. One of the sacrifices appropriate in especially trying times, was that of a fellow human being; often, that person was a child. This action was not meant to belittle the importance of human life, it was rather an attempt to elevate it to the highest degree of placation. In order to save other mortal lives from calamity, one or more individuals would have to be given up in the supreme act of piety and faith. As Nigel Davies noted: "Their object was, therefore, more to preserve than to destroy life."[7]

Philo of Byblos told how ancient peoples in dangerous situations would often sacrifice their own children for the sake of the whole population: "It was customary for the rulers of a city or nation, rather than lose everyone, to provide the dearest of their children as a propitiatory sacrifice to the avenging deities."[8] He described how King Kronos, who the Phoenicians called El, sacrificed his only son, Anobret, on an altar in royal attire "when war's gravest dangers gripped the land."[9] Kronos did not love his son less than other concerned parents, but the forfeiture of his son was the only way to save the welfare of the entire country.

This unimpassioned attitude was not restricted to just one religion or one period of time. Eli Sagan contended that: "Sacrifice is a form of religious action that has persisted throughout all the changes religion has undergone from primitive to historical times."[10] We see evidence of it in the Judaeo-Christian teachings, as well as in the aboriginal tribes of New Guinea. Under Eastern philosophy: "A sensible man `feared the gods' and scrupulously followed their prescriptions."[11]

Even into modern times, human sacrifice can be found in isolated instances, although it is generally accepted as pathologic behavior under present day ethical values. When John Baker examined women at Broadmoor State Asylum in England who had been convicted of infanticide and found to be insane, he recounted a number of cases where a child was offered up as a sacrifice to appease an angry deity: "In one case the sacrificial altar was the child's bassinet, under which the mother proceeded to kindle a fire."[12] In days past the killer may have been diagnosed as a sibyl, or a witch; now she is remembered only as a schizophrenic murderer.

The question remains, however, that if the Gods, who are the ultimate authority over our actions and beliefs, personally demand that a particular person be killed, and one is certain that God is speaking directly to them in a clear, unquestionable manner, is not that act of sacrifice then acceptable and forgiven under the doctrine of divine justice? After all, who can claim that a commandment of the All-Powerful Lord is wrong?

That is a difficult question to answer. Most cultures have appointed high priests or judges to assess the will of God, and not left the interpretation up to untrained individuals. The priesthood is somehow qualified to "understand" such complex issues, and God is more likely to speak through them than through the common man. But the opinions of priests are nevertheless still subject to mortal mistakes, and their conclusions are often disagreed with, even by followers of the same religious sect. Nevertheless, while it is relatively easy to know who is a prophet and who a fake through retrospective analysis, it is not so easy to make the differentiation at the moment in time when the query is raised. Not until a disbelieved prophecy rings glaringly true do the rest of us realize the false nature of a forecaster's knowledge.

Nonetheless, we have been often guided by those with supposed knowledge of the divine will. Rabanus Maurus, in his defense of oblation in 819 A.D,, pointed to the willingness of Abraham to sacrifice Isaac as proper adherence to a divine law that supersedes that of mortal man. It would be a greater evil for someone to pass secular judgment on such an action, and "maintain that a worldly and temporal law should be given precedence over the divine and eternal law," than to obey the commandment of God.[13] When God calls, all must answer; it is not something that mortal legislators can redefine.

If Maurus is correct, and Abraham is to be congratulated for his devotion to God when he was willingly to sacrifice his only son Isaac, then how can we call some misguided servant of another deity an abhorrent murderer? After all, only a privileged few can hear the words of God. Others simply see the external act and judge the result within the limitations of their fallible human knowledge. How do we tell when the person has heard the true commandment from the Lord above, and when there has only been an hallucinatory imagination?

Tertullian accepted the word of God as statements ascribed to the teaching of Jesus Christ. He scorned those who believed that Diana of the Scythians, or Mercury of the Gauls, or Saturn of the Africans, or Jupiter in Latium would demand that a human be sacrificed in order to appease their insatiable appetite for blood.[14] But is that not what the Scythians, or the Gauls, or the Africans said about Christianity as well? We judge morality by what we believe within our own set of ethical tenets, and then insist that those who do not agree are wrong.

Many great sages throughout the ages have followed the conclusion that God cannot condone killing, and have not been willing to accept that murder was allowable under any divine authority. Plutarch, in his moral essay "Superstition", concluded that:

> Would it not then have been better for those Gauls and Scythians to have had absolutely no conception, no vision, no tradition, regarding the gods, than to believe in the existence of gods who take delight in the blood of human sacrifice and hold this to be the most perfect offering and holy rite?[15]

The debate between religious fanatics and moral humanists may rage forever, but it is not likely that a simple, mutually agreeable answer will emerge. Nonetheless, our historical record shows that many parents have felt that spilling the blood of their own children on a sacrificial altar was something which was required by God, and, in all piety, they acquiesced.

1. Antiquity

Signs of infant sacrifice date back to the very beginnings of human presence on earth. Neanderthal man, living about 200,000 to 70,000 B.C., is thought to have practiced ceremonial sacrifice as reflected in archaeologic remains. In Uzbekistan, Southern Russia, a child's skull surrounded by six pairs of Siberian mountain goat horns strongly suggested that some type of ritual sacrifice was performed.[16] And, in the great bas-relief from Laussel, France, where drawings dating back to the Paleolithic era can be found, the figure of a menstruating goddess holding her menstrual blood horn can be clearly seen with indications that she was to be placated by the sacrifice of human infants.[17]

As early man evolved, the worship of the gods appears to have changed little. At Ofnethohlen, in Germany, a mass burial from about 20,000 B.C. showed thirty-three skulls, of which twenty were children showing signs which suggested some type of sacrifice.[18] In Northern Africa, thousands of bones of sacrificed children have been dug up by archaeologists with inscriptions designating these as first-born sons of noble families as far back as 7000 B.C.[19] Inscriptions on burial urns in Sardinia indicate that three thousand first-born sons of noble families, between the ages of one month and four years, were sacrificed by first being strangled, and then burned as offerings to Tanit.[20] The matriarchal Babylonian goddess Ishtar was placated by the sacrifice of human infants,[21] while the Pelasgians offered every tenth child as a sacrifice of propitiation in times of scarcity.[22] In addition, the ancient kings of Tyre offered their sons in sacrifice, and the ancient Syrians sacrificed to Jupiter and Juno.[23] Archaeologists in the Gezer excavations have found the skeletons of numerous children under the age of eight days in earthenware jars.[24] Infants bodies were also discovered in foundations in Egypt laid as late as the 22nd Dynasty from around 950-720 B.C.[25]

In Carthage, the specter of human sacrifice in the ancient world reached its infamous zenith. There was such an overflow of blood in this Punic power that the rest of the world finally rebelled against the slaughter. Despite accepting the morality of exposing infants, the Greeks condemned the Carthaginians for their offering infants in sacrifice to their gods.[26] Philo, writing of barbarian nations, but likely referring particularly to Carthage, noted that they have "long admitted child sacrifice as a holy deed and acceptable to God."[27] The extent of child sacrifice in Carthage is discussed later in this chapter.

Ancient Greece, while abhorrent of the practice in Carthage, was not totally impervious to the breadth of sacrifice within their own society. The Greeks were very superstitious people, and believed in the power of their gods to bring on personal disaster if they were not appeased. The very origin of the word "superstition" dates back to this era when people would often spend whole days in prayer and sacrifice to ensure that their children would outlive them. The term applied to these people were "superstitious," from *superstes*, meaning a survivor, and the word later acquired the wider application we know today.[28]

Greek fables regularly told of the extremes to which men would go to obtain the good grace of the gods. At times, human sacrifice would be made to assure benevolent climatic activity. As seen later in this chapter, King Agamemnon sacrificed his daughter Iphigenia to the goddess Diana in order to obtain favorable winds necessary for the fleet to sail to the Trojan War. When King Athamas asked the oracle at Delphi how to end the drought in his land, he was told that it would not end until one of his children had been sacrificed. He then sent for his son, Phrixus, and daughter, Helle.[29] A golden ram forewarned the children of their danger and during their escape Helle fell off the ram's back and drowned in the sea.[30]

Other children were killed in order to assure the security of the state. In Attica, one of the heroes from whom the Athenian tribes received their name – the Eponymoi – was a man named Leos who was said to have given up his daughters, at the command of the oracle, for the safety of the commonwealth.[31] He was revered for this generous act, as was Erechtheus of Attica who sacrificed his daughter to Pherephatta for a similar reason.[32]

But it was not always rational concern for the welfare of others that led to infanticide, at times it was anger that stimulated a fatal reaction. The rage of Medea against her husband Jason had sacrificial elements. Seneca, the Roman tragedian, professed that she offered the loss of her sons to the ghost of her brother, who she and Jason had killed during their escape from Colchis, the country of the Golden Fleece. As she slew her elder son with a knife she swore: "Let this hand that slew thee with the sword now offer sacrifice unto they shade."[33]

To a plebeian Greek, it was easy to accept the fact that particular circumstances might require a child to be sacrificed for the general good. Intellectuals, however, did not always see the piety or necessity of such a brutal act. Empedocles attacked the practice and was not swayed with the arguments of "greater good." He attacked it as a murderous act and charged that:

> Changed in form is the son beloved of his father so pious, who on the altar lays him and slays him. What folly![34]

Aeschylus argued that "you cannot burn flesh or pour unguents, not innocent cool tears, that will soften the gods' stiff anger."[35] To kill another human being was therefore a futile, and worthless, deed, with no chance of changing what the Fates had deemed to happen. But while the wise men might caution against the futility of superstition and magic, the commoner held tightly to his age old beliefs.

The ancient Romans also told of children sacrificed to appease the gods. In one story, the daughters of king Orchomenus were seized with a longing to cannibalize one of their own infants. They cast lots to see which child should be sacrificed, and the lot fell on the son of Leucippe, Hippasus. As the women performed their bloody rite, Hippasus was torn limb from limb.[36] Marius, the Roman, also was said to have sacrificed his daughter to mollify an evil-averting deity.[37]

Lactantius, the third century A.D. Christian author and appointee of Diocletian, castigated the Roman who he claimed immolated children to Saturn. They were depraved, he wrote, to call the "foul and horrible crime against the human race" a sacrifice.[38]

Shakespeare portrayed some of these sentiments in *Titus Andronicus*, where the son of Queen Tamora was sacrificed to placate the shadows of the Roman soldiers who were killed in the war. The victorious king passionately explained how enemy human blood must be shed in order for the ghosts of those who have passed before to be allowed to rest in peace: "To this your son is mark'd and die he must, t'appease their groaning shadows that are gone."[39]

In the New World, evidence of human sacrifice has been found in many diverse civilizations. In southern Mexico, the Olmecs, who prospered around 1200 B.C., sacrificed human beings to their gods and practiced ritual cannibalism.[40] The ancient Aztecs, who thrived in the thirteenth century, were estimated to have sacrificed up to 20,000 victims in religious rituals to assure pacification of the sun god, Huitzilopochtli.[41] Ortiz gave larger estimates and concluded that up to 250,000 victims were sacrificed yearly in Central Mexico, and 15,000 yearly in the capital city of Tenochtitlan alone.[42]

When children were sacrificed by the Aztecs, it was usually to the rain god, Tlaloc.[43] The children were taken to the tops of mountains and killed in an effort to secure the growth of their crops.[44] Whereas adults were frequently eaten after the sacrifice, children were less often consumed.[45] Girls were generally beheaded, and then some were skinned and the pelts worn by the priests during sacred ceremonies.[46] The children came from all social classes, including the nobles.[47] Infants were often bought from their parents as compensation both for property loss and also for some obligation that the family may have incurred to the state.[48] According to the Codex Maliabecchi, drowning was the standard method for disposing of the victims. At the feast of Tocoztli, "they sacrificed young children and young girls, and also newborn babies."[49] Children were also sacrificed at the feast of Zazitocoztli, Ecaloaliztli and Michayehuitl. The annual loss during all of these feasts was estimated at two thousand per year, although some people placed the estimates in the many thousands.[50] While Tenochtitlan was the largest center for sacrifice in the Aztec empire, there was evidence of a similar practice in towns throughout the country.[51] The Inca Empire also practiced human sacrifice at the time of the Aztecs, however the annual sacrifice there could only be measured in the hundreds.[52] This has been explained by some as due to their more secure food supply. But as seen in the chapter on Tribes, vestiges of infanticide still can be found in current Peruvian cultures.

2. Judaism

James Frazer interpreted much of the Old Testament writings as indicating that the ancient Hebrews frequently sacrificed their first-born children.[53] To reach this conclusion, he had to make many controversial assumptions, and very literal translations, which are at variance with those of most biblical scholars. In the book of *Exodus*, for example, the Lord instructed Moses: "The first-born of thy sons shalt thou give unto Me."[54]

Frazer knew of passages which later called for redemption of human children, but believed that the Semitic people in the Old Testament were well aware of the common custom of first-born sacrifice among the Carthaginians, Phoenicians, Canaanites, Moabites, and Sepharvites, and that "the Hebrew custom of redeeming the firstborn is a modification of an older custom of sacrificing them."[55]

Most interpreters of the Bible do not take the directive to literally mean actual sacrifice, however.[56] In other sections of that chapter, the Lord instructed the Jewish people that they may purchase the first-born of the animals back from the Lord, but they "must buy back your firstborn sons."[57] The Mekilta, which contains the rabbi's interpretations of the meanings of the book of *Exodus*, clarified that while the word "firstborn" referred both to men and beasts in the actual text, it was only the beasts who were slaughtered on the altar.[58] The sacrifice of humankind was meant to be taken in the devotional, and not the literal, sense. The Lord took for Himself all of the first-born in Israel after the Passover killing of the oldest Egyptian sons during the Exodus, but then accepted the priestly obedience of the Levites in substitution for them.[59] Although the first issue of the womb would continue to be sacred to the gods, "for practical purposes," the celestial authorities would be satisfied with a lamb instead of a human being.[60] The primitive demand for sacrifice, however, was never actually abolished.

In the opening paragraph of *Leviticus*, for example, Moses was instructed by the Lord: "When you sacrifice to the Lord, use animals from your herds and flocks."[61] And in *Numbers* it is recorded that:

> You may never accept the firstborn sons, nor the firstborn of any animals that I do not permit for food. Instead, there must be a payment of two and a half dollars made for each firstborn child. It is to be brought when he is one month old.[62]

This practice survives today in the "pidyon haben," or redemption of the first-born ceremony.[63]

But the Israelites were nevertheless a stubborn and unruly people throughout their history in the Promised Land, and they frequently reverted to episodes of conduct which more closely resembled their neighbors than their Patriarchs.[64] As Peter Riga pointed out, the Jews, along with the neighboring pagans, used sacrifices to please God in a form of external penitence.[65] The records of the eighth and seventh centuries B.C., according to Nigel Davies, clearly "demonstrate beyond all doubt that the Israelites of the period made burnt offerings of their sons in the Tophet fires lighted in the valley of Gehinnon outside Jerusalem."[66] The tophet was a drum that produced a great din in order to prevent parents from hearing the cries of their children as they were burned in the sacrificial flame.

Moses mentioned the practice but spoke of other nations being guilty of the crime and forbade the Jews to do the same:

> Don't follow their example in worshiping their gods. Do not ask, "How do these nations worship their Gods?" and then go and

> worship as they do! You must not insult the Lord your God like that! These nations have done horrible things that he hates, all in the name of their religion. They have even roasted their sons and daughters before their gods.[67]

This diatribe left no room for doubt that the instructions of the Jewish leader to his brethren were clearly to refrain from any form of human sacrifice. If any question did remain, Moses added what was to be the punishment for anyone who did not follow this command. If an Israeli "presents his child to be burned to death as a sacrifice to heathen gods, (he) must be killed."[68] One wonders if there was the necessity of giving such a warning unless some of the Hebrews were indeed guilty of transgression.

But despite these clear pronouncements against child sacrifice, we do see many instances in the Bible where offerings by the Jews occurred. And the numbers are not small if one believes the statistics of Elijah who was told by the Lord that there are "7,000 men in Israel who have never bowed to Baal nor kissed him!"[69]

Ahaz, the son of Jotham and king Judah, who ruled for sixteen years in Jerusalem from about 743-727 B.C., was said to be evil and not follow the precepts of his ancestor David.[70] In the Valley of Hinnom: "He even passed his son through fire, imitating the abominations of the nations whom YHWH dispossessed before the Israelites."[71] Such were the ways of the Israelites at that time, and Ahaz "followed the ways of the kings of Israel and even made molten images for Baal."[72] As punishment for these actions, the Lord sent the king of Syria to defeat Ahaz, and deported large numbers of Jews to Damascus.[73] The sages taught that at his death, no eulogizes were made and that he would have "no portion in the world to come," as retribution for his wicked ways.[74]

The Bible also told of how the people of Israel, under King Hoshea, were defeated by King Shalmaneser of Assyria, and were then exiled to Assyria.[75] There, they began to follow the evil customs of that nation including the worshiping of false idols: "They abandoned all the commands of YHWH, their God; they made themselves molten images – two calves; they made a pole of Asherah; they bowed down to all the heavenly host; they worshiped Baal."[76] They even "passed their sons and their daughters through fire."[77] The Lord, in anger at these atrocities, swept away the Israelites and left only the Jewish tribe of Judah as a remainder of the Chosen People. But the Hebrews still did not repent and walked in the same evil path which Israel had done before them. The Lord then destroyed them as well, and finally all of Israel was carried off to Assyria where they were replaced by colonists from various countries. These peoples worshiped their own gods:

> The people of Babylon made Succoth-benoth; the people of Cutha made Nergal; the people of Hamath made Ashima; the Avvites made Nibhaz and Tartak; and the Sepharvites were burning their sons in fire to Adrammelech and Anammelech, gods of Sepharvaim.[78]

And though an exiled Hebrew priest was sent to teach them to worship only the Lord who had made a covenant with Israel:

> Israel didn't listen, and the people continued to worship other gods. These colonists from Babylon worshiped the Lord, yes – but they also worshiped their idols. And to this day their descendants do the same thing.[79]

King Manasseh of Judah, who reigned from about 697-642 B.C., restored the cult of Baal and Asherah. He "passed his son through fire," which is generally taken to be indicative of a Canaanite divinatory act, although there have been some attempts to distinguish it from an actual sacrifice.[80] He rebuilt the altars to Baal that his father Hezekiah had destroyed, and "he made his sons to pass through the fire in the valley of Ben-Hinnom."[81] The sages disparaged him, and also accused him of murdering Isaiah, the son of Amoz, who had prophesied against him. He was responsible for much bloodshed in Jerusalem and was punished by God, according to the sages, by being delivered into the hands of the king of Assyria. Unlike Ahaz, Manasseh later returned to the throne and gave up the worship of all idols.[82]

King Josiah, who ruled Judah from around 640-609 B.C., later destroyed all the equipment used in the worship of Baal, Ashera, and the Sun, Moon, and Stars, and also the altar of Topheth in the Valley of the Sons of Hinom "so that no one could pass his son or daughter through fire to Molech."[83] He was the grandson of Manasseh, and ascended his father's throne at age eight.[84]

In the book of *Jeremiah*, stories of sacrificial activity during the reign of king Josiah, of Judah, and his sons Jehoiakim and Zedekiah, were described.[85] The Lord, angered at the blasphemous activity, told Jeremiah that the people of Judah had sinned and built an altar called Topheth in the Valley of Ben-Hinnom: "In order to burn their sons and daughters in the fire – a thing that I never commanded, nor did it even enter My mind."[86] This is repeated later in the chapter when the Lord complained that they built high altars to Baal, "in order to burn their sons in the fire as burnt offerings to Baal – a thing that I never commanded, never ordered, and that never even entered my mind."[87] God threatened to bring terrible evil on Israel for having forsaken Him and turning the valley into a place of shame and wickedness by: "Sending up sacrifices in it to other gods of whom neither they nor their fathers have known."[88] He proposed to wipe Jerusalem off the earth and lay siege to the city until food was gone. And then: "I will make them eat the flesh of their own sons and daughters."[89]

In the book of *Ezekiel*, the Lord reminded Jerusalem how He had nurtured and protected the Jews, but that now, instead of showing gratitude and respect, they made images of gold and silver and:

> You took your sons and your daughters that you bore me and sacrificed them to them for food. As if your harlotry was not enough, you slaughtered my sons as an offering and delivered them over to them![90]

The Lord explained how He had scattered the Jews in the wilderness for not obeying His laws and let them adopt the customs and laws of the land.[91] He had hoped they would draw back in horror as they "burnt their firstborn children as offerings to their gods."[92] But now the children were still going to the Place of Sacrifice and, like their fathers before them: "You defile yourselves by the offer of your gifts and by delivering up your sons to the fire."[93] He angrily declaimed: "They have worshiped idols and murdered my children whom they bore to me, burning them as sacrifices on their altars."[94] And to add further insult: "When they had murdered their children in front of their idols, then even that same day they actually came into my Temple to worship!"[95] Because of all these sins and worship of abominable idols, "and in accordance with the blood of your children which you gave them," the Lord decried that I am going to condemn you to be punished as an adulterer and a murderer.[96]

The prophet Isaiah confirmed many of these stories. He lived during the reigns of King Uzziah, King Jotham, King Ahaz, and King Hezekiah of Judah, and told of how the people worshipped idols and "slay your children as human sacrifices down in the valleys, under overhanging rocks."[97] The *Talmud* was to later reflect the Jewish response to these sacrifices, and may have even indicated that some Jews continued to sacrifice their children by burning them to Molech.[98]

One particular sacrifice which created great controversy among later commentators was that by Jephthah, a warrior from Gilead appointed by the Israelites to command their army against the Ammonites. Jephthah vowed to the Lord that if He would help him to victory, then: "Anything coming out the doors of my house to meet me, when I return with victory from the Ammonites, shall belong to Yahweh; I will offer it up as a burnt offering."[99] After his victory he returned home and his only child, a daughter, ran out to greet him. When he recognized who it was, he tore his clothes and exclaimed: "Ahh! My child! You have brought me low!" for he had made a vow to the Lord that he could not take back.[100] The child would have to die by his own hands in fulfillment of a vow he could not break.

Although many readers of the bible would be outraged at the willingness of Jephthah to kill his own daughter because of a vow, others commended his obvious devotion to the sanctity of the Lord. St. John Chrysostom, the patriarch of Constantinople from 398-404 A.D., defended these seemingly brutal actions of Jephthah. He lamented that many heathens impugned believers of the bible, and called them cruel and inhumane on account of this sacrifice.[101] But the girl had to die, Chrysostom argued, for if the Lord had disallowed this sacrifice, and not required Jephthah to fulfill his oath, than many others would have sworn similar vows in the future, without understanding the importance of their commitment. In the course of time, their impiety would have led to many more cases of child-murder.[102] It therefore became, like the story of Abraham and Isaac, an example of the need to put loyalty to God above even the love of your own child.

Josephus, the first century A.D. Jewish historian, went even further in supporting the moral of this story and said that the sacrifice "was not ungrateful to her, since she should die upon the occasion of her fathers victory, and the liberty of her fellow-citizens."[103] Abhorrent of murder in general, Josephus could still find acceptance in a particular instance, when the welfare of the entire country was at stake.

While most rabbis decried sacrificial practices, and warned their congregations of its dire consequences, there was still an awareness that fear and ignorance somehow excused the actions of guilty participants. Netanyahu related how a Tannaitic dictum of the second century A.D. stated that:

> The sacrifice of one's offspring to idolatry – the most hideous crime on all counts – does not entail the prescribed punishment when the act was committed under duress, in error, or through deliberate misguidance.[104]

Rabbi Ishmael explained that when one faced the alternative of either death or the performance of idolatrous worship, one should choose to live. This was because the Law was given "to live by it and not die by it," unless the act had to be performed in public.[105] Rabbi Akiba, however, said that one should not violate the law, and perform either idolatry or murder, in order to stay alive.[106] If God determined that your time on earth was complete, you should go in a willing, and obedient, manner.

Of even greater importance to the future unity of Judaism was the sacrifice which never occurred, but which was heralded as the supreme devotion to god – the story of Abraham and Isaac which is covered later in this chapter. Once again, the attempted sacrifice of a child was seen as an act of honor rather than horror.

Although there is documentation of King Solomon having committed child-sacrifice, he did build idols to false gods. Within the sight of Jerusalem, he "built a temple on the Mount of Olives, across the valley from Jerusalem, for Chemosh, the depraved god of Moab, and another for Molech, the unutterably vile god of the Ammonites."[107] While little was made of these transgressions during his lifetime, he was punished by the Lord for these indiscretions by having the kingdom taken away from his son.[108]

The Bible contained many warnings to not sacrifice children or suffer the consequence of severe retribution. Twice in *Leviticus* there were warnings not to sacrifice children to Molech:

> You shall not give any of your children to Molech, burning them upon his altar.[109]
>
> Who sacrifices his child as a burnt offering to Molech shall without fail be stoned by his peers.[110]

The Mishnah called for anyone who "offers any of his seed to Molech," to be stoned to death.[111] There was a condition, however, that:

> He that offers any of his seed to Molech is not culpable unless he gives up (the child) to Molech and passes him through the fire: if he gave him up to Molech but did not pass him through the fire, or if he passed him through the fire but did not give him up to Molech, he is not culpable.[112]

This somewhat confusing passage appeared to require, like modern criminal law, that there be both intent to sacrifice, and the act of sacrifice, before punishment was to be given for offering a child to Molech. This would then mean that if the child was "passed through the fire" for some other reason than an offering to Molech, there would be no unlawful conduct. It seems that the willingness to consider homage to a false idol, rather than the actual sacrificial offering of a child, was the more heinous act.

In the Jewish folktale of "Sacrificers of Children," the story was told of a poor man who lived in the days of Rabbi Abraham ibn Ezra. He sat bemoaning his tribulations and poverty when suddenly an old man appeared and told him that if he sacrificed his only son to him he would bless him with vast amounts of gold, silver, cattle and sheep. The man was overwhelmed with joy at this prospect, but knew that he must keep the fate of the son from his wife. He told her that he was going to take their son to school where he could learn Bible, Mishnah and Torah. Instead he took the boy to a spot on top of the shill and: "Prepared wood and fire and bound his son and took the knife and slaughtered him and sacrificed him to the satyrs who leaped and danced there."[113] He became wealthy, as promised, and other men soon found out and said that they would sacrifice their sons as well in order to obtain equal riches. They then offered their sons up "to the aforementioned demon like the first man who had chosen that abomination."[114] They similarly became wealthy and the practice was continued each and every year. The killings continued until Rabbi Abraham ibn Ezra came and showed them their wicked and profane ways and doomed them to the depths of destruction if they did not change. When they agreed to modify their conduct, their wealth disappeared and they were left as before, except for one thing – "while their children whom they had slaughtered were lost entirely."[115] The story was told "to awaken the hearts of the Children of Israel so that they should not be in too great a hurry to grow wealthy."[116]

The Middle Ages were a time of deep danger and distress for many Jews as anger was vented against them for being the killers of Christ. Many Jews committed suicide, rather than being forced to become baptized into the Christian faith. Those who survived often became anxious and despondent over their despoiled state. The story was told of Isaac the Righteous who was said to have brought a sin-offering to God for having allowed himself to be baptized:

> He took his two children, his son and daughter, at midnight and led them through the courtyard; he brought them before the Holy Ark, and slew them there for the sanctification of the Name of God . . . With their blood he sprinkled the pillars of the Holy Ark [saying]: This blood is my reconciliation for all my evil-doing.[117]

3. Christianity

While Judaism was often identified with the devotion manifested by Abraham's willingness to sacrifice his son, Isaac, as a mark of his obedience to the bidding of the Lord, the very essence of Christianity was built upon the sacrifice of an only son, Jesus Christ, although the deed was one of divine nature. This redemptive act of God was promulgated as an act of love throughout the gospel teachings. We read, for example, in the book of *John*: "For God loved the world so much that he gave his only Son so that anyone who believes in him shall not perish but have eternal life."[118]

The crucifixion of Jesus on the cross fulfilled traditional sacrificial concepts, and was likened to the Jewish atonement for sin.[119] But where Moses required the sprinkling of blood in order to cleanse every offering to God, for "without the shedding of blood there is no forgiveness of sins," Christ did not have to die over and over again but "came once for all, at the end of the age, to put away the power of sin forever by dying or us."[120] Jesus took away the sins of all men, as told in the Gospel of St. John, "and the blood of Jesus his Son cleanses us from every sin."[121] This was something which the animal sacrifices could never do, for "it is not possible for the blood of bulls and goats really to take away sins."[122] But the New Testament provided more than just a reminder of the people's disobedience, for:

> Christ gave himself to God for our sins as one sacrifice for all time, and then sat down in the place of highest honor at God's right hand, waiting for his enemies to be laid under his feet. For by that one offering he made forever perfect in the sight of God all those whom he is making holy.[123]

In the book of *Romans*, the people were told to believe in God for: "Since he did not spare even his own Son for us but gave him up for us all, won't he also surely give us everything else?"[124] God paid a ransom with "the precious lifeblood of Christ," in order to save the people He loved.[125]

This personal, demonstrative caring for each individual person was quite unique among religions at the time, and left a deep impression on those who converted to Christianity. No matter how evil their prior life had been, there was a chance to be forgiven. As John Calvin noted, the benefit of the death of Christ was that: "We see it to be a sacrifice by which he expiates our sins in the sight of God, and so appeases the wrath of God and restores us to grace with him."[126]

The Christians also continued to pay homage to Abraham for his willingness to sacrifice Isaac when commanded to do so by God. Origen, in the third century A.D., advised the fathers of the Church to be constant in purpose as Abraham was: "Offer your son to God joyful, immovable in faith."[127] And for those who believed in the justice of the Lord, take heart and:

> Behold God contending with men in magnificent liberality: Abraham offered God a mortal son who was not put to death; God delivered to death an immortal son for men[128]

But where the sacrifices offered by the Lord and by Abraham were to be revered, early Church Fathers clearly distinguished the practices of barbarians who committed murder in their attempts at sacrificial offerings. Tertullian warned that killing another human being, even in a sacrificial way, was murder, and that it made no difference "whether it is committed for a religious purpose or according to one's own choosing."[129] St. Augustine nevertheless worried that parishioners might not fully understand the differences. Seeing the danger of lauding the actions of Abraham to a populace which had been aware of child sacrifice in other religions, he cautioned not to see Abraham's devotion as a role model for killing, or as an excuse for their hasty actions: "But every one that shall resolve to sacrifice his son unto God shall not be cleared of guilt in such a resolution, because Abraham was praised for it."[130]

Despite these apprehensive statements, later Christian writers extolled the actions of martyrs who gave their lives, or the lives of their children, in steadfast devotion to the teachings of the Church. St. Valerian, in the fifth century A.D., told of one mother who sacrificed her seven sons rather than submit to the demands of a blasphemous ruler. He did not severely castigate her for this crime, but instead praised her as an example for the entire congregation:

> If, therefore, our father Abraham offered one son in sacrifice and pleased God, how much more has this mother pleased Him? At one time she immolated 7 sons to God, with prayers of approving desire.[131]

It was once again apparent that general principles were to be set aside when certain factual conditions warranted support.

4. Middle Ages and Renaissance

The offering of children in homage to the gods continued well into the Middle Ages. Child sacrifice was commonly practiced by the Irish Celts and the Gauls.[132] The ancient Irish were said to have sacrificed to the idol Cromm Cruach "the firstling of every issue and the chief scions of every clan," in order to assure a good harvest on Mag Slacht in the County Cavan.[133] Most of this appeared to be economically based:

> To him without glory they would kill their piteous wretched offspring, with much wailing and peril, to pour their blood around Cromm Cruaich. Milk and corn they would ask from him in return for one-third of their healthy issue.[134]

It is thought that this cult was first introduced into Ireland by Heremon, the nineteenth King of All Ireland, around 1015 B.C.[135] St. Patrick was also said to have preached against the burning of first-born children at the fair of Taillte.[136]

In Norway, humans were sacrificed to Odin and to Mars, and the Swedes sacrificed their king, Olaf Woodcutter, to appease Odin during a famine.[137]

Human sacrifices were also made to Thos, Wodan and Fricco. The bodies of the victims were often hung in the open after the sacrifice, and Adam of Bremen chronicled one occasion when seventy-two bodies were seen hanging together.[138] The heathens of Gotland were said to sacrifice their sons and daughters for similar reasons.[139]

In ancient Russia, the villagers sacrificed their first-born children to the god Perun.[140] Prince Sviatoslav reigned in Russia from 962 to 971 A.D., and after his death his younger son, Vladimir, succeeded after a bloody war in 978 A.D. Vladimir encouraged a resurgence of paganism and crowded his castle with idols. One chronicler said that: "The people sacrificed to them, calling them gods, and brought their sons and daughters to sacrifice them to these devils."[141]

There was also evidence of ancient offerings among Eastern cultures as well. The Shang Dynasty in China, around 1800 B.C., "sacrificed humans and animals in order to seek help and guidance from their ancestral spirits and gods of nature."[142] In the Indian legend of king Somaka, it was told that he had a hundred wives but no sons. Finally a son was born but he wanted a hundred, and not just one. The family priest told him to sacrifice the son, Jantu, and his other wives would smell the smoke and bring forth sons. The boy was sacrificed and, true to the prophecy, ten months later one hundred sons were born.[143] Other versions told this story of the merchant Dhanadatta who was also willing to sacrifice one son in order to obtain one hundred more.[144]

One reason that some cultures accepted sacrifices of this type, was that they did not fear death itself. They believed that while the body might die, the soul would live eternally. In the Katha Upanishad *Conquest of Death* it was explained that:

> The Knowing Self is not born, it dies not; it sprang from nothing, nothing sprang from it. The Ancient is unborn, eternal, everlasting; he is not killed, though the body is killed.[145]

A human being therefore need not fear death for "a mortal ripens like corn, like corn he springs up again."[146] If an infant's sacrifice brought benefit in the present, the future life reborn would benefit even more.

This allowed an adult to willingly sacrifice all he possessed in order to achieve heavenly reward. Vajasravasa was agreeable to surrendering even his son Nachiketas to this end, for he knew that earthly existence was meager when compared to heavenly abode. His piety was rewarded with the naming of the fire-sacrifice rite after the boy.[147]

But the gods were many, and their appetites seemingly insatiable. Where the Ganges river met its destination into the sea, infants were often thrown to the sharks as an offering to the Water Goddess. The British were not able to outlaw this practice until 1802.[148] The first-born son of the Mairs, a Hindu tribe, used to be sacrificed to Mata, the smallpox goddess.[149]

In modern India, the aboriginal Khonds of Gumsur and Ganjam practiced sacrifice to avert evil occurrences, and in Bengal children were thrown into the Ganges river to fulfill a vow by the parents.[150] James Frazer noted that: "Khonds in distress often sold their children for victims, considering the beatification of their souls certain, and their death, for the benefit of mankind, the most honourable possible."[151]

Sacrifice was also a common event among many tribal peoples in ancient times. According to S. F. Cook: "As an institution, human sacrifice has been known to all primitive peoples at all times in the world's history."[152] In Peru, a son was occasionally sacrificed if the father was sick and the priest said he would die without the homage paid. The sacrifice was meant to satisfy an idol so as to save the father's life.[153] A. de Herrera also noted that the Indians of the Peruvian valleys, between San-Miguel and Caxamalca, sacrificed their children to the idols which they held in great veneration.[154] Among the Amazon tribes, one of the sacred superstitions related to the use of musical instruments at certain festivals which were forbidden to be seen by women. If some girl was said to have seen them, either by accident or design, her father was required to sacrifice her.[155]

In eastern Africa, the Senjero used to sacrifice their first-born sons in order to assure a good harvest.[156] Among the Baganda of Central Africa, some chiefs had to sacrifice their own child at a water well to the water-spirit as a means of securing prosperity.[157] The first-born son was sacrificed at times to Ruwa, the chief god, among the Chagga on Mt. Kilimanjaro in East Africa.[158] Reports of sacrifices of this type have occurred even into the modern era. In Zimbabwe, as late as 1929, a king's daughter was sacrificed to bring rain in a ceremony that was centuries old.[159]

The Kutonaqa Indians of British Columbia would sacrifice their first-born children to the Sun in order to assure health and prosperity for the family.[160] The Coast Salish Indians of the same region would sacrifice their first child to the Sun as well for similar reasons.[161] The Indians of Florida were said to have sacrificed their first-born male children.[162]

B. Carthage

Carthage was founded by Phoenicians who left Tyre and originally called the city Qart Hadasht, the "New City."[163] Tradition held that Elissa of Tyre, also known as Dido by the North Africans, fled her murderous brother, King Pygmalion, and founded the city on a hilltop called the Byrsa.[164] The traditional date given for the establishment was around 814 B.C. The city population grew rapidly and, by the third century B.C., the Carthaginian inhabitants numbered three times that of Rome.[165] It was hailed as the center of Punic power in the Mediterranean region.

The Carthaginians, probably more than any other society in the history of man, put child sacrifice on a level that was felt necessary to maintain stability of the state. This continued with only brief interruptions for a period of almost six hundred years.[166] It was to become a source of condemnation from authors and statesmen all around the globe, and synonymous with the designation of "barbaric" or "pagan" activity.

Diodorus of Sicily, around 20 B.C., wrote detailed accounts of how the Carthaginians sacrificed infants to their chief god, Baal Hammon, and later to the goddess Tanit. He described how they sacrificed the noblest of their sons to Cronus in ancient times, but then had stopped for many years. In 310 B.C., however, they were defeated at the hands of the Greek general Agathocles, and the elders decided that this was due to the displeasure of their gods over the absence of satisfactory homage.[167] They then selected two hundred of the noblest children, as they had done in the past, and sacrificed them to the gods in a public ceremony. The children were placed on the outstretched hands of a statute of Cronus and then fell into a gaping pit filled with fire.[168]

Kleitarchos, a Greek author in the third century B.C., retraced these horrible rites and recounted how when the flames engulfed the child, the limbs of the statute contracted "and the open mouth seems almost to be laughing" as the body slipped into the brazier: "Thus it is that the `grin' is known as `sardonic laughter,' since they die laughing."[169] As the infants bodies rolled into the flaming pit, the cries of the parents was drowned out by flutes, tambourines, and lyres. The ashes and bones were then gathered and collected in a small urn and placed with others in the sacrificial precinct of the goddess Tanit.[170]

Plutarch reported how Gelon, the ruler of Gela from 491-483 B.C. and of Syracuse from 485-478 B.C., vanquished the Carthaginians off Himera and as part of the peace treaty made them stop sacrificing their children to Cronus.[171] He wrote how the Carthaginian mothers "stood by without a tear or moan," and that the "whole area before the statute was filled with a loud noise of flutes and drums so that the cries of the wailing should not reach the ears of the people."[172] He related how with full knowledge and understanding, they would offer up their own children and those who had none would buy little ones from poor people and then cut their throats "as if they were so many lambs or young birds."[173]

According to Tertullian, who was born in Roman Carthage around 160 A.D., babies used to be sacrificed publicly to Saturn even down to the proconsulate of Tiberius, and then secretly beyond that.[174] The parents would fondle their babies so that they would not be crying when they were sacrificed.[175] He claimed that the holy crime was still being committed and that Tiberius, a contemporary of Christ, had tried to stop the practice by "lashing the Punic priests to trees and leaving them to die of exposure."[176] In his *Apology* he also moralized that it makes no difference whether infanticide was carried out for a religious purpose or according to one's own choosing.[177]

Archaeologic excavations of the area in 1921 lent support to the historical claims of extensive infant sacrifice.[178] Thousands of earthen vases were discovered stacked twenty to thirty feet below the surface near the old commercial port of Carthage, now called Salammbo. They all contained the ashes of burned babies.[179] Under the funeral pyre, where Queen Dido supposedly immolated herself after founding the city, were found urns containing the charred bones of thousands of very young children. Similar remains were later found in Sardinia, an area of Punic conquest. Inscriptions on the urns indicated that the victims were first-born sons of noble families. They were "first strangled and then burned as offerings to Tanit."[180] After the sacrifice, the parents would bring the bones to be buried in an area known as the Tophet, which was called the Precinct of Tanit. Excavations in Carthage have found one such area that held as many as 20,000 burial urns.[181]

This scene of music drowning out the cries of infants as they were prepared for the sacrifice to the gods has passed through the years to many authors. Moloch appeared in *Paradise Lost* by Milton as one of the followers of Satan:

> Horrid king besmeared with blood of human sacrifice, and parents tears, though for the noise of drums and timbrels loud their children's cries unheard, that passed through fire to his grim idol.[182]

In his novel, *Salambo*, Gustave Flaubert told how the Carthaginians were losing the battle for their town due to a prolonged drought that was felt to be caused by the anger of the god Moloch, the Devourer. Sacrifices usually involved children who "were burned on the forehead, or on the nape of the neck with woolen wicks," but this time nothing had worked.[183] Since the survival of the very Republic was at stake, only an immolation by fire would purify Carthage and the ancients decided that the son of King Hamilcar, along with thirteen other children, had to be sacrificed. As the children were flung into the flames, the priests would cry out: "They are not men but oxen. Lord, eat!"[184] That night, rain fell and the sacrifice had prevailed on the mercy of the gods.

The Carthaginians apparently accepted the necessity of sacrificing children on the belief that human blood was required to maintain the supernatural powers of the gods.[185] Weyl hypothesized that this practice may actually have been dysgenic to the Carthaginians by removing the children most likely to succeed and become eminent, i.e. the first-born of the upper class:

> If the observed differences in psychometric intelligence between first-born and subsequent births are partially due to genetic factors then the birth order of sacrificial victims must have been relevant to the impoverishment of the Punic gene pool.[186]

Perhaps because of this weakened superstructure, or perhaps because their time had simply come, the Romans destroyed and leveled much of the city in 146 B.C. This put a stop to child sacrifice at Carthage, although it continued to linger in other parts of North Africa for some time.[187]

C. Abraham and Isaac

Certainly the most widely discussed sacrifice of all time, and the one which still remains a timeless mixture of mystery and awe, was the biblical tale of the attempt, rather than the completion, of the sacrifice of Isaac by his father Abraham. This story – known as the "Akeda" – is part of the high holy holiday of Rosh Hashanah in synagogues across the world. It is presented as a model of unlimited faith and reveals the deep intensity of Abraham's obedience to the commandments of his one and only God. As a prime example of how trust in the Lord should be maintained, even to the point of sacrificing a beloved child, it is proudly, and reverently, put forth as depicting the very essence of what it means to be a devout Jew. In the words of Elie Wiesel: "This strange tale is about fear and faith, fear and defiance, fear and laughter . . . Here is a story that contains Jewish destiny it its totality."[188]

To a truly pious believer, the story of Abraham is an affirmation that devotion to God rises above all else. That despite the pressures for personal gain or comfort, or even love of another human being, one must always remember: "You shall love YHWH your God with all your heart and with all your soul and with all your might."[189] But to a Jew who is torn between the natural love of a child and the love of God, the command to kill is a chilling test of blind submission that shakes the foundation of belief. Nowhere else in the biblical text is another human being directly condemned to be murdered in the name of the Lord. While God permits those who commit blasphemy to be executed, there are no other instances where personal direction to do so is ordered by the Almighty.[190] And when the event does happen, when God finally does test the endurance to kill, it is not because of anything that Isaac had done to anger the Lord, but rather as a simple test of his father's faith.

This story of unlimited obedience to an unseen Deity requires much fortitude and faith. The paradigm is not restricted to Judaism alone, but is also an important part of the Christian liturgy. In the Catholic Church, the story of the sacrifice is told during the Holy Saturday Easter Vigil and is part of the second cycle of Lent during the service of Mark.[191]

In the Lutheran Church, the story is told at the Easter Vigil as "a foreshadowing of the sacrifice of the Son of God and suggests the death that Baptism effects."[192] It is also part of the liturgical first Sunday of Lent.[193] The lesson demonstrates how God asked Abraham to sacrifice Isaac as a test of faith, the same faith which leads to the renewal and growth during the Lent service.[194] The Evangelical Covenant Church describes the story as part of the first Sunday in Lent, part B, but does not include it in the Easter service.[195]

Through all of these services, almost 1,783,660,000 Christians, and 17,615,000 Jews, sit in church or synagogue every year, during one of the holiest times of that year, and are reminded by their rabbis or priests of how the willingness to sacrifice your only child to the commandment of God is not only an accepted act of homage, it is the very essence of what is required of a faithful believer.[196] In addition, even larger numbers of Moslems accept the actions of Abraham in equally reverent terms. The *Koran* describes this deed as a decisive test of man's obedience to Allah and exclaims that the choice was well made: "Peace Be on Abraham! Thus do we reward the well-doers."[197]

Such incredible adherence, by so many disparate cultures, to the command for an infanticidal act has no parallel in all of human history. The story reflects the inherent discrepancy between the evolutionary nature of man, which demands propagation of the species, and the divine pronouncements of religion, which denigrates man before his God. Where self-survival, or love of one's own kind, is supreme among the animal species, humankind has always been willing to bow in obedience to some mystical higher form.

To try and understand the nature of this saga, we must analyze more thoroughly the events which preceded the biblical incident. Abraham was one hundred years old, and already had a son Ishmael with the Egyptian handmaid Hagar, when God called Sarai, who was ninety years old and childless, and announced that she was to become pregnant despite the advanced nature of her years.[198] When a son was indeed born, their joy was limitless and they named the infant Isaac, which meant "laughter."[199]

Sarah, as she was now known after the birth of Isaac, became jealous of Abraham's illegitimate son and concubine. Although it was she who first suggested that Abraham lie with Hagar in order to have an heir when it appeared that his bloodline could never be continued through herself, she now demanded that he get rid of Hagar and her illegitimate child. Abraham was initially unsure of what to do, but God reassured him that Sarah's insistence was proper "for it is through Isaac that your line shall be continued."[200] Sarah directed him to abandon Ishmael in the wild, like an unwanted child, and Abraham agreed.

Years later, when Isaac was twenty-five years old, the divine promise to foster the future of the Jewish race through Isaacs' seed was put to the ultimate test. For reasons which have been contested for ages, God decided to verify Abraham's faith and obedience. He called Abraham personally, and not through the intermediary of an angel, and told him to make an "*ola*," or offering:

> Take your son, your beloved one, Isaac whom you hold so dear, and go to the land of Moriah, where you shall offer him up as a burnt offering on one of the heights that I will point out to you.[201]

Rabbi Yoshe-Ber, in interpreting this part of the biblical text, pointed out that the Lord had to tell Abraham of this task because "no angel would have accepted the assignment."[202]

Without any argument, without even any attempt to question the reason for such a violent request, Abraham left the very next morning to carry out his appointed task. He did not tell Sarah or Isaac of the nature of his trip and after three days, when they reached the final destination, Abraham told the servants to stay in the camp and began to climb the mountain with his beloved only son. He placed the wood for the burnt offering on Isaac's shoulders, as one would do with a sacrificial animal, and carried the knife and flint himself.[203]

As they slowly ascended the mountain, each with their own heavy load, Isaac asked innocently: "Father, there is the wood, and the firestone, but where is the sheep for the burnt offering?"[204] Abraham answered: "God will see to the sheep for his burnt offering, my son."[205] By this time, Isaac had begun to sense his gruesome destiny. His path was yet straight and unaltered, for he knew he had the blessing of the Lord.

When they arrived at the site designated by God, Abraham bound Isaac's arms and legs and then laid him on the altar. He lifted the knife to plunge into the body of his son, and as the moment of truth approached, the Angel of God suddenly shouted to him from heaven above:

> Abraham! Abraham! Lay not your hand upon the boy, nor do the least thing to him! Now I know how dedicated you are to God, since you did not withhold from me your own beloved son.[206]

The need for the sacrifice to be completed was gone, and Isaac was allowed to fulfill God's promise to populate the earth with a multitude of his descendants. Abraham, who had so intently concentrated on his task that the angel had to call out his name twice, had proven beyond all doubt that he was totally devoted to adoration of the Lord.

Some issue has been made of the manner in which the story ends in the biblical text. After Abraham is assured that the blessing of the Lord is now bestowed upon both him and his offspring: "Abraham then returned to his servants, and they left together for Beer-sheba."[207] As Shalom Spiegel remarks: "One would think it was only the father who returned, and his son was not with him."[208] While Isaac did not die according to the Akedah, "Scripture regards him as though he had died and his ashes lay piled on the altar."[209] Mention is seldom made of Isaac in later biblical accounts. Even when Sarah dies, for example, it is only Abraham who mourns for her; Isaac is never mentioned.[210] This three year absence, until he marries Rebeccah, is claimed by the Midrash to be due to his spending time in Paradise as a reward for the trial he had been put through.[211]

This performance of Abraham, this willingness to sacrifice even his only son, has been viewed as the mark to which all truly pious Jews must aim. For the sincere adherent, there must be such intense faith in divine communication that no one must question God, no matter how painful the request might appear. As noted by Joshua ben Sira, Abraham when tested "was found loyal."[212] For, in the words of Kierkegaard, "no sacrifice was too hard when God required it."[213]

Philo, the noted first century A.D. Jewish philosopher, wrote extensively on this story, and his comments are very revealing about the attitude of religious leaders towards child sacrifice in that era. In general, like all loyal Jews, Philo found the decision of Abraham inspiring: it was supremely indicative of man's ability to obey the commandments of the Lord. He was proud of how Abraham received this divine message to sacrifice his son, and "showed not change of color nor weakening of the soul," – his faith was unshaken.[214] And when Abraham raised the knife over Isaac's body, in order to complete the ritual sacrifice, his determination was so strong that the angel of the Lord had to call Abraham twice by name "to turn him and draw him back from his purpose and thus prevent his carrying out the slaughter."[215] Philo was not dismayed at this intensity; God Almighty reigned above all mortal life, even one's own children.

But where Philo was characteristic of those who exalted the action of Abraham because of the faith shown to the glory of God, he also attempted to excuse the sacrifice with motives that were less than spiritual. With an almost deft flip of his hand, Philo explained that Abraham had been reared among the Chaldeans, and lived the greater part of his life with the common custom of child sacrifice: "His realization of its horrors was rendered less powerful by the regularity of such a practice."[216]

While it was true that many Semitic tribes in the region did indeed accept the practice of infanticide, Philo's acceptance of it being "rendered less powerful" for this reason is unsettling. The most eminent Jewish philosopher of the time has provided a social defense for Abraham which implies that Jews could be made more tolerant of child sacrifice simply by the nature of its frequent occurrence. It is almost as if custom, no matter how cruel or contrary to Jewish law, can provide a defense for impious action. Such an attitude borders on heresy.

Philo also sought to justify the event by noting that Abraham showed no base, or self-serving, motive for the attempted sacrifice, and that there was no effort to search for fame. Abraham went alone "lest he should appear to be making a boastful parade by bringing witnesses to his pious conduct."[217] This meant that Abraham was not seeking to teach others by his conduct, but rather was only following the directions of his God. In so doing, he could not be faulted for the sin of vain-glory which would have put a different light on the undertaking.

It is of interest that St. Augustine, writing centuries later, felt that Abraham was tempted by the offering "to prove his pious obedience, and so make it known to the world, not to God."[218] Without condemning Abraham for this motive, St. Augustine nevertheless provided a reasoning which might have affected the lesson taught by Abraham's faith. A true Christian, according to Augustine, does not act for self-serving reasons, but rather in love and devotion to the teachings of Jesus Christ and His disciples. Abraham may have been enticed by the prospect of worldly fame, but Augustine did not feel that the eventual outcome depended on this motivation.

The writings of Philo also show that he struggled, on a purely emotionally and human level, with Abraham's apparent equanimity after being ordered to kill his only legitimate child. Philo concluded that, despite Abraham's position as patriarchal father of the Jews, he was still a man susceptible to human traits and could not be expected to go against the custom of the times. To react differently would have made him the first "to initiate a totally new and extraordinary procedure," which is something that would have been against nature and impossible to do.[219] Sounding more like a modern psychoanalyst than a philosopher, Philo sifted through the legendary tale and embraced the facts which bothered him in trusting confidence. The Jewish Patriarchs had never taken on the image of saints, and had all been guilty of some actual, or potential, sin which indicated the mortal nature of their existence. And so it was with Abraham as well. But his description of Abraham as a man not capable of questioning the judgment of God to sacrifice his own son simply because it was the general custom of the times, may have astounded even the readership to which his remarks were directed.

Philo's writings continued this process of excusing Abraham's actions with justifications that eventually became strangely inconsistent with many of his other views. He emphasized that the sacrifice of Isaac was "truly meaningful" since it involved the loss of an only son:

> For a father to surrender one of a numerous family as a tithe to God is nothing extraordinary, since each of the survivors continues to give him pleasure, but when there is only one son, it shows his acceptability of God.[220]

"Nothing extraordinary" would certainly fit the attitude of the pagan world, but the loss of any life would be anathema to a Jew.

Philo finally added another possible explanation which even negated the actual sacrifice of Isaac and replaced it with an allegoric reconstruction. He discerned that the name of the boy in the Chaldaean language was "Isaac," but when it was translated into the Jewish tongue, it was "Laughter." He therefore opined that what Abraham was thereby sacrificing was the emotion and not the body of his son.[221] Rather than killing Isaac in order to show his devotion to God, he was giving up "Laughter" which was something belonging to God alone.

I will leave Philo's meandering here, not because we completely understand his inner conviction of whether Abraham's actions were morally right or wrong, but rather because his conflict establishes the basis for our own questioning. It reveals how even a devout theologian struggled for an explanation that will translate divinely guided obedience into behavior that is acceptable for the common man.

Josephus, the first century A.D. Jewish historian, also searched for ways to buffer the impact of Abraham's homicidal intent. He first rationalized that the motive of God to even request the sacrifice was because He was "desirous to make an experiment of Abraham's religious disposition toward Himself."[222] After all, the Lord had blessed Abraham in many ways and made both him, and his son Isaac, superior to his enemies. Surely He could expect that Abraham would not question anything asked of him, just as Jews everywhere should not shirk their own gratitude for being the Chosen People.

And Josephus believed that God's premonition was correct; Abraham rightly concluded that "it was not right to disobey God."[223] But while Abraham had little doubts of his own, he did not tell Sarah, or any of the servants, "otherwise he should have been hindered from his obedience to

God."[224] Sarah would not likely have accepted the explanation that her son must die because God requested a sacrifice of homage. Abraham therefore purposely decided to not test his own conviction by discussing the matter with his wife before beginning on his journey. The Lord had made a request, Abraham had decided to respond. That would be enough.

Josephus contended that Abraham did provide an explanation to Isaac to assuage the boy's fears. He believed that Abraham said to his son:

> I suppose He thinks thee worthy to get clear of this world neither by disease, neither by war, nor by any other severe way, by which death usually comes upon men, but so that he will receive thy soul with prayers and holy offices of religion, and will place thee near to Himself.[225]

Isaac was appointed a position of martyrdom, and was promised beatification and nearness to God for eternity in life after death.

The Akedah provides another traditional interpretation of why God decided to test Abraham. It tells that when Isaac was thirty-seven years old, Satan questioned God on why He praised Abraham so much.[226] Satan, in his infinite desire to harm mortal man, recounted to God how all the people prayed to You when they wanted something, but after their request was granted, they forgot about You. Look at Abraham, Satan said slyly, he plays with his child and does not honor You. God dismissed the accusation and answered that Abraham was an upright man and if asked, would even sacrifice Isaac. "Agreed," Satan cried out, clapping his twelve wings in glee and excited about his successful attempt to cause the death of Isaac. The obedience of Abraham would thereby show not only the piety of man in reverence to the Lord, but also the failure of Satan to succeed in harming the devout Jew.

In the *Zohar*, the magnus opus of the Spanish Jewish Kabbalah from the late thirteenth century, the story of Isaac's sacrifice was reflective of the final element in the saga of the Jews as the Chosen People. Isaac, according to this tradition, was thirty-seven years old, the age of majority, when Abraham was ordered to sacrifice him. If Isaac had refused to go, Abraham would not have been punished for his failure since he was no longer responsible for Isaac's actions.[227] But Abraham did not discuss the matter with his son: "For until he executed judgment by binding Isaac he could not attain perfection."[228] Abraham thereby brought his son to the altar in order to fulfill the final phase of preparing God's chosen people by achieving the sanctity necessary to be worthy of the task.

Christianity could easily have bypassed this venerable, though troublesome, aspect of the Old Testament but instead, the Church accepted the actions of Abraham as pious, and extended its meaning in new directions. In the New Testament, we find a resurrection explanation which allowed Abraham to sacrifice Isaac in much the same way as the Lord allowed his own son, Jesus, to be killed. In the book of *Hebrews*, it was written that Abraham "believed that if Isaac died God would bring him back to life again."[229] He trusted God and, in fact, this was what actually happened – "Isaac was doomed to death, but he came back again alive!"[230] This extension of the nature of Abraham's action towards the Resurrection of Christ was also evident in the Book of Mormon. The offering of Isaac by Abraham was seen as "a similitude of God and His only begotten Son."[231] Much like Isaiah was given the prophetic vision of the true Jewish savior as Jesus Christ, Abraham's deed was also tied in with the beliefs that were to culminate in Christianity.

This resurrection theme was accepted by other important early Church Fathers. Origen argued that the equanimity of Abraham during the ordeal was because he "had received the promises, thinking that God is able to raise him up even from the dead . . . He knew the Christ was to be born from his seed."[232] He also pointed to the importance of the journey taking Abraham three days to reach the site of the sacrifice. When the Jews had departed from Egypt, they offered sacrifices to God on the third day, and it was on the third day after the crucifixion of Jesus Christ that the Son of God was resurrected.[233] As even more proof of the relationship, Origen pointed out that Isaac himself had to carry the wood up the mountain, just as Christ had to carry the wood of the cross.[234] The parable of Abraham and Isaac could therefore be nothing else but a reflection of the very death of the Son of God Himself.

St. Augustine lent support to the resurrection views expressed by Origen. He felt that Abraham could never have believed that God actually wanted a human sacrifice, but rather that:

> When the divine commandment thundered, it was to be obeyed, not disputed. Yet Abraham is worthy of praise, because he all along believed that his son, on being offered up, would rise again.[235]

This faith of Abraham was warranted because God had told him directly that it was through Isaac that a nation of descendants would populate the earth.[236] God had assured Abraham that: "In Isaac shall thy seed be called."[237] It was therefore reasonable for Abraham to have complete faith that in following the command to sacrifice, Isaac would not die, even if this required a rising of the dead after the sacrifice was completed.

Later Jewish commentators also accepted a resurrection theory to the Akedah. R. Judah taught that when the Abraham's knife touched Isaac's throat, "his soul flew clean out of him, but the soul returned when the voice of the Lord was heard.[238] They then said a prayer: "Blessed art Thou, O Lord, who quickens the dead."[239] Some Talmudic Sages related this resurrection to the passage in *Isaiah* which tells how "God's light of life" will fall upon the people like dewdrops.[240] In the Midrash Lekah Tob the Lord restores the soul of Isaac "by means of the dewdrops for the Resurrection of the dead."[241]

Abraham's all-encompassing trust in the directive of the Lord was something to be extolled throughout the New Testament. In the book of *Romans*, the actions of Abraham were praised: "Abraham is the father of us all when it comes to these matters of faith."[242] And in the book of *James*, the faith of Abraham was made complete "by what he did, by his actions, by his good deeds."[243] The true believer did not question what was asked of him in observance of the Lord's command.

St. Clement of Rome, the first century A.D. successor to St. Peter, similarly discussed how Abraham went through with the sacrifice since he knew that Isaac could not die. Abraham was granted a son in old age because of his faith in the Lord and it was through this very nature of obedience that "he offered him as a sacrifice to God."[244] But he knew that the Lord had promised to make a great people from the seed of Isaac, and that this could not be possible if Isaac would die at the time of the sacrifice. Clement eased the burden on Abraham even more by revealing that Isaac was also aware of this security and how "with confidence because he knew the future, Isaac cheerfully let himself be led to the altar."[245]

Prudentius, the fourth century A.D. Christian Latin poet, told how Abraham was the:

> Forerunner of all men of faith, Who willed to give his only son, In sacrifice, that sire foresaw, Descendants numerous as the stars.[246]
>
> Thus teaching us, with lively faith in God, to place upon the altar as a pious gift, The dearest and the only treasure of our heart.[247]

The model for all men's actions was to be faith in the Almighty, even if this required the willingness to commit murder in the name of the Lord. It was the hereafter in which we were to be judged, and the standards to be met were not of secular invention.

Later reformationists offered similar theologic explanations to the Akeda. According to Calvin, all of Abraham's undertakings were again founded on the promise: "In Isaac shall thy seed be called". He found the strength of Abraham admirable:

> We can imagine what anguish took hold of the holy man when he realized that in the person of his son the very hope of eternal life was

> to be extinguished. And yet by faith he escaped such dark thoughts, and did as he was commanded. What a wonderful power it was that enabled him to overcome so many and so arduous obstacles.[248]

The by-words to be remembered by all these learned men were Faith, Faith, Faith.

But all was not necessarily well with the tale, and some concerns were evident in the writings of various Church leaders. The Old Testament clearly had said that murder was wrong, and this meant that one could not even commit suicide: "For he that kills himself, kills not other but a man."[249] How then was it allowable to sacrifice a child, even in devotion to God? St. Augustine found a rational answer within the biblical concept that it was lawful to kill only when commanded by God: "Abraham was not only freed from being blamed as a murderer, but he was also commended as a godly man in that he would have killed his son Isaac, not in wickedness, but in obedience."[250] The greatest sin of all was failing to follow the personal commandments of the Lord. If your conduct was acceptable to God, it was mandatory that it be acceptable to the rest of mankind.

Augustine, however, saw the danger in lauding the actions of Abraham too much. He cautioned others to not see Abraham's devotion as a role model for killing, or as an excuse for their hasty actions: "But every one that shall resolve to sacrifice his son unto God shall not be cleared of guilt in such a resolution, because Abraham was praised for it."[251] After all, "What can the human mind conceive more dreadful than for the father to be the murderer of his son?"[252] Within this dreadful act, nevertheless, came the lesson for all Christians to learn of having faith in the judgment of God.

During the Middle Ages, biblical stories were often told in pageants at various times of the year, and the saga of Abraham was a popular theme. In the Brome story of *Abraham and Isaac*, Isaac's concerns over the singular decision made by his father were empathically depicted. As Isaac was led towards the mountain top, his awareness of the uneasy situation was evident. Father, he said, "my heart beginneth to quake to see that sharp sword in your hand."[253] When Abraham admitted that he must kill him, Isaac pleaded poignantly:

> Kill me father? Alas, what have I done? If I have trespassed against you aught, With a yard ye make me full mild; And with your sharp sword kill me nought, For iwis, father, I am but a child.[254]

But as Isaac realized that he could not change his father's mind, he told Abraham to do God's bidding: "For, be I once dead and from you go, I shall be soon out of your mind."[255] In the epilogue at the end of the play, the Doctor explained how the moral of the story was: "How we should keep, to our power, God's commandments without grudging."[256] In the difficult times of the Dark Ages, faith that life in the hereafter would be more comforting than the present was all that many peasants had available to maintain a stoic existence.

More modern commentators often agree that the myth of the Akeda simply symbolizes the historical transition among the ancient Hebrews "from child sacrifice to animal sacrifice."[257] This explanation, however, still accepts the existence of child sacrifice, and relegates the importance of the story to hyperbole based on fact rather than faith. While elements of the rationale may be true, and the frequency of child sacrifice abated by the substitution of animal victims, the resilient belief in Abraham's actions as a mark of faith in Almighty God demands that a more comprehensive understanding of the meaning of the tale be supplied.

Through all the centuries of commendation over the actions taken by Abraham, little has been written about his lack of any attempt to question the Lord's command. Such silence in the face of an order to kill his only son is disturbing, and not explained by reluctance to debate the Divine will. The Bible relates an earlier event where the Lord had told Abraham at Mamre that He had heard that the people of Sodom and Gomorrah were utterly evil.[258] Abraham knew what this meant – the city would be wiped off the face of the earth by God's wrath. In sympathy with the lives of innocent citizens, Abraham queried the Lord further. "Will you stamp out the innocent along with the guilty?" he asked with audacious concern.[259] "What if there were fifty goodly people in the city", he persisted. Wouldn't it be unfair for the "Judge of all the world" to destroy them along with the rest of the populace?[260] "Shall he who is Judge of all the world not act with justice?" Abraham demanded?[261] The Lord agreed to save the city if fifty such citizens could be found. Abraham then continued to ask for forgiveness if forty-five people were found, then forty, then thirty, then twenty, and finally even if only ten such worthy men were found. In the words of Erich Fromm, Abraham's attitude was not that "of a meek supplicant but that of the proud man who has a right to demand that God uphold the principle of justice."[262]

If Abraham realized he had the authority to question the Lord's command about Sodom and Gomorrah, why did he not then challenge Him the same way when the life of Isaac, his only legitimate son, was at stake? I have never encountered a satisfactory answer to this query, but if Abraham had sought to change the mind of the Almighty, it is possible that the entire future history of the world would have been changed.

It is of interest that although Abraham did not seek to question the motives of the Lord, the Egyptian Pharaoh, who had refused to let the

Hebrews leave the country even after the land was devastated by nine plagues forecast by Moses, immediately let the Exodus begin when the life of his firstborn male child was taken.[263] The celebration of this fatal night of Passover was made a solemn part of the Jewish calendar by the Lord so that the people would always be reminded of how His power was greater than that of any mortal king, and how the Jews were to always obey His commandments or face His terrible wrath.

D. Agamemnon and Iphigenia

In Greek legendary history, a similar sacrificial dilemma that faced Abraham was said to have been thrust upon the great general of the Greek force that prepared to sail for Troy, King Agamemnon. The tale began with the seduction of Helen, the most beautiful woman in the world, by Paris, son of Hector and prince of Troy. They exchanged vows of love and escaped back to his native land while Menelaus, the husband of Helen and brother of king Agamemnon, vowed revenge when he returned home and found the pair gone. The two men then gathered the Greek forces in a large armada of ships in the Bay of Aulis.[264] Agamemnon had been chosen general, and the troops were ready to sail but the winds suddenly died down and the ships became stalled in the water. Calchas, the famous seer brought along to help in the planning of battle, advised Agamemnon that the reason for the atmospheric delay was that Diana, the virgin goddess, had been angered because Agamemnon had promised to sacrifice to her the loveliest thing each year, and, in the confusion of preparing for war, he had neglected the offering that season. In order to now appease her ire, and assure a change in the weather, Calchas warned that virgin blood must be shed.[265]

After further counsel, Agamemnon realized that the virgin blood which must flow was that of his own lovely daughter, Iphigenia. Like Abraham, Agamemnon was faced with the difficult decision of having to sacrifice a child to appease a God. But where Abraham had received his orders directly from the Almighty Lord, Agamemnon was hearing the word of God through a human interpreter.

In many versions of the story, Agamemnon's decision was labored and intense. It was not an easy choice, and the king's love for his daughter was pitifully and tragically intense. But despite his horrified reluctance to place Iphigenia on the sacrificial altar, the fate of the army depended on the pacification of the gods, and eventually "the king subdued the father," and Agamemnon proceeded with the bloody offering.[266] Kierkegaard labeled this action that of the tragic hero where "the father will turn his face away, but the hero will raise the knife."[267]

The Greek playwrights spared no tears in portraying the final event:

"Her supplications and her cries of father were nothing, nor the child's lamentation to kings passioned for battle."[268] As he lifted her to the altar, "she struck the sacrificers with the eyes' arrows of pity."[269]

Unlike the offering of Isaac, there was no divine intervention in this Greek tragedy, and when the sacrifice was completed, the winds arose and the armada sailed away to defeat the Trojans in a grisly ten year war as chronicled in the famous heroic poem, *The Iliad*, by Homer.

Ovid could not believe that Iphigenia was actually killed, and claimed that Diana, the virgin goddess, yielded and placed a deer in the stead of Iphigenia as a replacement victim, in much the same way that a lamb was accepted with Isaac.[270] Pausanias said that Hesiod, in his *A Catalogue of Women*, also believed that Iphigenia did not die.[271] But what has survived to modern times is the legend that Agamemnon carried out the deed, and let his daughter be killed for the good of the country and the pride of his men.

While Agamemnon eventually won the war, and returned home triumphantly, he quickly paid the ultimate price for his unsympathetic temerity. It was this sacrifice of their daughter which turned Clymenestra's love into hatred against her husband, and she plotted his death at the hands of her lover. Clymenestra would not be swayed by arguments that her daughter's life was rightfully exchanged for the preparation of war. In *Agamemnon*, by the Roman tragedist Seneca, her nurse had argued that the loss of Iphigenia "freed our Grecian fleet from long delay, and waked from their dull calm the sluggish seas."[272] Clymenestra answered scornfully: "Oh, shameful thought, that I, the heaven born child of Tyndarus, should give my daughter up to save the Grecian fleet.[273] There was no way that words of praise would assuage her anger and she killed her husband and then was left to bear the fatal brunt of her son's anger as well. In *Electra*, by Sophocles, she had further justified her actions by telling her surviving daughter that: "This father of yours, whom you never stop weeping for, did a thing no other Greek had dared to do, when he so ruthlessly sacrificed your sister to the gods."[274] But she has survived the ages as a woman willing to commit parricide for the love of another man, and her act of revenge has not found much commiseration or appeal.

Endnotes

1 . Clement of Alexandria, "Exhortation to the Heathen," III, Writings, Volume I, 49.
2 . London, Call of the Wild.
3 . Sagan, Cannibalism: Human Aggression and Cultural Form, 52.
4 . Khaldun, The Muqaddimah, 67.
5 . "To everyone who is victorious, I will give fruit from the Tree of Life in the Paradise of God." The Revelation 2:7. The Living Bible, 1005.
6 . Roux, Ancient Iraq, 91.
7 . Davies, Human Sacrifice, 13.
8 . Philo of Byblos, The Phoenician History, 3.44, 63.
9 . Ibid.
10 . Sagan, Cannibalism: Human Aggression and Cultural Form, 50.
11 . Roux, Ancient Iraq, 97.
12 . Baker, "Female Criminal Lunatics: A Sketch," 22.
13 . Boswell, The Kindness of Strangers, 440.
14 . Tertullian, "Scorpiace," 7, Apologetical Works, Volume XI, 395.
15 . Plutarch, "Superstition," 171.BC, 13, Moralia, Volume II, 493.
16 . Davies, Human Sacrifice, 32.
17 . DeMause, "The Fetal Origins of History," 34.
18 . Davies, Human Sacrifice, 32.
19 . deMause, The History of Childhood, 27.
20 . Weyl, "Some Possible Genetic Implications of Carthaginian Child Sacrifice," 69-70.
21 . McCully, "Archetypal Psychology As A Key For Understanding Prehistoric Art Forms," 529.
22 . Ryan, "Child Murder In Its Sanitary and Social Bearings," 2.
23 . Ibid.
24 . Ibid., 161.
25 . Davies, Human Sacrifice, 37.
26 . Weyl, "Some Possible Genetic Implications of Carthaginian Child Sacrifice," 71.
27 . Philo, On Abraham, XXXIII.181, 91.
28 . Cicero, De Natura Deorum, II.XXVIII.72, 193.
29 . Frazer, The Dying God, VI, 162.
30 . Hamilton, Mythology, 118.
31 . Pausanias, Description of Greece, I.V.2, Volume I, 25.
32 . Clement of Alexandria, "Exhortation to the Heathen," III, Writings, Volume I, 48-49.
33 . Seneca, Medea, V.i, 616.
34 . Plutarch, "On Superstition," 13.171C, Moralia, 493.
35 . Aeschylus, Agamemnon, 69-71, 37.
36 . Frazer, The Dying God, 164.
37 . Clement of Alexandria, "Exhortation to the Heathen," III, Writings, Volume I, 48-49.
38 . Lactantius, The Divine Institutes, I.14, 82.
39 . Shakespeare, The Tragedy of Titus Andronicus, I.i.125-6, 6.
40 . Barbarian Tides, 160.
41 . Voyages of Discovery, 149.
42 . Ortiz de Montellano, "Aztec Cannibalism: An Ecological Necessity?," 611.

43 . Voyages of Discovery, 158.
44 . Davies, Human Sacrifice, 62.
45 . Harner, "The Ecological Basis for Aztec Sacrifice," 119-120.
46 . Beane & Doty, Myths, Rites, Symbols: A Mircea Eliade Reader, Volume I, 246.
47 . Cook, "Human Sacrifice and Warfare as Factors in the Demography of Pre-Colonial Mexico," 85.
48 . Ibid.
49 . Ibid.
50 . Ibid., 86.
51 . Ibid., 87.
52 . Harner, "The Ecological Basis for Aztec Sacrifice," 119.
53 . Frazer, The Dying God, 173.
54 . Exodus 22:28b. The Holy Scriptures, 60. See e.g., Numbers 18:14-15.
55 . Frazer, The Dying God, 179.
56 . There are some scholars who do believe that child sacrifice was at one time a part of the official cults of YHWH. Levenson, The Death and Resurrection of the Beloved Son, 11.
57 . Exodus 13:13. The Living Bible, 59. You must also be prompt in "the redemption payment for your oldest son." Exodus 22:29. Ibid., 68. And: "Your sons must all be redeemed." Exodus 34:20. Ibid., 80.
58 . Mekilita de-Rabbi Ishmael, Tractate Pisha, XVI, Volume I, 129.
59 . Numbers 3:11-13. This practice has its tradition today as the *pidyon ha-ben.* Numbers, The Torah, A Modern Commentary IV, 40.
60 . Spiegel, The Last Trial, 63.
61 . Leviticus 1:2-3. The Living Bible, 86.
62 . Numbers 18:16. Ibid., 130.
63 . Lustig, "On the Origin of Judaism: A Psychoanalytic Approach," 363.
64 . Exodus 32:9, 33:5, 34:9.
65 . Riga, Sin & Penance: Insights Into the Mystery of Salvation, 67-68.
66 . Davies, Human Sacrifice, 64.
67 . Deuteronomy 12:30-31. The Living Bible, 160-61.
68 . Deuteronomy 18:10. Ibid., 164.
69 . I Kings 19:18. Ibid., 302. When Paul was explaining to the Romans that God had not rejected the Jews, he reminded them that he himself was a Jew and a member of Benjamin's family. He noted that Elijah had claimed to God that he was the only one left in all the land who still loved God and was told: "No, you are not the only one left. I have seven thousand others besides you who still love me and have not bowed down to idols." Romans 11:4. Ibid., 907.
70 . 2 Chronicles 28:1.
71 . 2 Kings 16:3. The Anchor Bible, 184.
72 . 2 Chronicles 28:2. The Anchor Bible, 158.
73 . 2 Chronicles 28:5.
74 . Wollman-Tsamir, The Graphic History of the Jewish Heritage, 113.
75 . 2 Kings 17:3,6.
76 . 2 Kings 17:16. The Anchor Bible, 203.
77 . 2 Kings 17:17. Ibid.
78 . 2 Kings 17:30-31. Ibid., 208.
79 . 2 Kings 17:40-41. The Living Bible, 325.
80 . 2 Kings 21:6. He also practiced black magic and used fortune telling.

81 . 2 Chronicles 33:6. The Anchor Bible, 195.
82 . Wollman-Tsamir, The Graphic History of the Jewish Heritage, 114.
83 . 2 Kings 23:4,10. The Anchor Bible, 279.
84 . Wollman-Tsamir, The Graphic History of the Jewish Heritage, 114.
85 . Jeremiah 1:1-3.
86 . Jeremiah 7:31. The Anchor Bible, 54.
87 . Jeremiah 19:5. Ibid., 127.
88 . Jeremiah 19:4. Ibid.
89 . Jeremiah 19:9. Ibid., 128.
90 . Ezekiel 16:20,21. The Anchor Bible, 271.
91 . Ezekiel 20:23,24.
92 . Ezekiel 20:26. The Living Bible, 647.
93 . Ezekiel 20:31. The Anchor Bible, 362.
94 . Ezekiel 23:37. The Living Bible, 651.
95 . Ezekiel 23:39. Ibid.
96 . Ezekiel 16:36-38. The Anchor Bible, 272.
97 . Isaiah 57:5. The Living Bible, 572.
98 . Sanhedrin, 7.7, The Mishnah, 392.
99 . Judges 11:31. The Anchor Bible, 206.
100. Judges 11:35. Ibid.
101. St. John Chrysostom, The Homilies, "To the People of Antioch," 237.
102. Ibid., 238.
103. Josephus, "Antiquities," V.VII.10, The Works of Flavius Josephus, Volume I, 329.
104. Sifra, Quedoshim, X.5.3.13. Netanyahu, The Marranos of Spain, 6.
105. Sanhedrin, Gemara, VIII.74a. Ibid., 7.
106. Ibid., 8.
107. I Kings 11:7. The Living Bible, 292.
108. 1 Kings 11:11-13.
109. Leviticus 18:21. Ibid., 103.
110. Leviticus 20:2. Ibid., 104.
111. Mishnah, Fourth Division Nezikin, Sanhedrin, 7.4, 391.
112. Ibid., 7.7, 392.
113. Gorion, Mimekor Yisrael Classical Jewish Folk Tales, Volume II, 756.
114. Ibid., 757.
115. Ibid., 759.
116. Ibid.
117. Finucane, Soldiers of the Faith, 187.
118. John 3:16. The Living Bible, 839.
119. Davies, Human Sacrifice, 66.
120. Hebrews 9:22,26. The Living Bible, 981.
121. 1 John 1:7. Ibid., 997.
122. Hebrews 10:4. Ibid., 981.
123. Hebrews 10:12-14. Ibid.
124. Romans 8:32. Ibid., 904.
125. 1 Peter 1:18,19. Ibid., 991.
126. Calvin, "The Catechism of the Church of Geneva," Theological Treatises, Volume XXII, 100.
127. Origen, "Homilies On Genesis," VIII.7, The Fathers of the Church, 142.

128. Ibid., VIII.8, 144.
129. Tertullian, "Apology," 9.6, Apologetical Works, 31.
130. St. Augustine, The City of God, I.XXV, Volume I, 30.
131. Saint Valerian, "The Martyrdom of the Mother and Her Seven Sons," Homilies, 417.
132. deMause, The History of Childhood, 27.
133. Frazer, The Dying God, 183.
134. Dorson, Peasant Customs & Savage Myths, Volume I, 351.
135. Graves, The White Goddess, 131.
136. Davies, Human Sacrifice, 46.
137. Turville-Petre, Myth & Religion of the North, The Religion of Ancient Scandinavia, 46.
138. Ibid., 244.
139. Ibid., 253.
140. Frazer, The Dying God, 182.
141. Light in the East, 123-124.
142. Barbarian Tides, 146.
143. Davies, Human Sacrifice, 77.
144. Van Buitenen, Tales of Ancient India, 103.
145. Yutang, The Wisdom of China and India, 46.
146. Ibid., 42.
147. Ibid., 43.
148. Davies, Human Sacrifice, 78.
149. Rose, "Unlucky Children," 63.
150. Panigrahi, British Social Policy and Female Infanticide in India, 1.
151. Frazer, The Golden Bough, Spirits of the Corn, Volume I, 245.
152. Cook, "Human Sacrifice and Warfare as Factors in the Demography of Pre-Colonial Mexico," 82.
153. Frazer, The Dying God, 185.
154. Ibid.
155. Wallace, A Narrative on the Travels of the Amazon and Rio Negro, 349.
156. Frazer, The Dying God, 182.
157. Frazer, The Golden Bough, Aftermath, 163.
158. Ibid., 331.
159. Davies, Human Sacrifice, 143.
160. Frazer, The Dying God, 184.
161. Ibid.
162. Ibid.
163. Barbarian Tides, 108.
164. Matthews, "The Phoenicians," 174.
165. Empires Besieged, 55.
166. Stager & Wolff, "Child Sacrifice at Carthage – Religious Rite or Population Control?," 32.
167. Diodorus of Sicily, The Library of History, 20.14.3-4, 179.
168. Ibid., 20.14.6, 181.
169. Stager & Wolff, "Child Sacrifice at Carthage – Religious Rite or Population Control?," 33.
170. Matthews, "The Phoenicians," 166.
171. Plutarch, "Gelon," 175.1, Moralia, 27.

172. Ibid., "On Superstition," 13.171CD, 493.
173. Plutarch, "Superstition," 13, Moralia, Volume II, 493.
174. Tertullian, Apology, 9.2-3, 30.
175. Ibid., 9.4, 31.
176. Weyl, "Some Possible Genetic Implications of Carthaginian Child Sacrifice," 72.
177. Tertullian, Apology, 30-31.
178. Weyl, "Some Possible Genetic Implications of Carthaginian Child Sacrifice," 69.
179. Picard, Carthage, 36.
180. Weyl, "Some Possible Genetic Implications of Carthaginian Child Sacrifice," 70.
181. Stager & Wolff, "Child Sacrifice at Carthage – Religious Rite or Population Control?," 32.
182. Milton, Paradise Lost, I.392-396, 67.
183. Flaubert, Salammbo, 222.
184. Ibid., 233-234.
185. Weyl, "Some Possible Genetic Implications of Carthaginian Child Sacrifice," 70.
186. Ibid., 75.
187. Stager & Wolff, "Child Sacrifice at Carthage – Religious Rite or Population Control?," 35.
188. Wiesel, Messengers of God, 69.
189. Deuteronomy 6:5. The Anchor Bible, 330.
190. "The prophet who tries to lead you astray must be executed." Deuteronomy 13:5. The Living Bible, 161. This is even if it is a "brother, son, daughter, or beloved wife . . ." Deuteronomy 13:6,7. Ibid.
191. Lectionary for Mass, 50, 95.
192. "Manual on the Liturgy," Lutheran Book of Worship, 332.
193. Ibid., 17-18.
194. "First Sunday in Lent," 1.
195. Covenant Book of Worship, 319.
196. World Almanac & Book of Facts, 718.
197. Koran, XXXVII:109-110, 83.
198. Romans 4:19. The Living Bible, 900.
199. Genesis 21:3,6. The Anchor Bible, 153.
200. Genesis 21:12. Ibid., 154.
201. Genesis 22:2. Ibid., 161.
202. Weinreich, Yiddish Folktales, 22.
203. Genesis 22:6.
204. Genesis 22:7. The Anchor Bible, 161.
205. Genesis 22:8. Ibid.
206. Genesis 22:11-12. Ibid., 162.
207. Genesis 22:19. Ibid.
208. Spiegel, The Last Trial, 3.
209. Ibid., 3-4.
210. Genesis 23:2.
211. Spiegel, The Last Trial, 7.
212. Sir 44:20. Levenson, The Death and Resurrection of the Beloved Son, 175.
213. Kierkegaard, Fear and Trembling, 36.
214. Philo, On Abraham, XXXII.170, 87.
215. Ibid., XXXII.176, 89.
216. Ibid., XXXIV.188, 93.

217. Ibid., XXXIV.190, 95.
218. St. Augustine, "The City of God," XVI.XXXII, Basic Writings of Saint Augustine, Volume 2, 352.
219. Philo, On Abraham, XXXV.193, 95.
220. Ibid., XXXV.196, 97.
221. Ibid., XXXVI.201-202, 99.
222. Josephus, "Antiquities," I.XIII.1, The Works of Flavius Josephus, 97.
223. Ibid., I.XIII.2, 98.
224. Ibid.
225. Ibid., I.XIII.3, 99.
226. Frankel, The Classic Tales, 68-75.
227. Zohar, 72-73.
228. Ibid., 73.
229. Hebrews 11:19. The Living Bible, 983.
230. Hebrews 11:19. Ibid.
231. Book of Mormon, Jacob 4:5, 113.
232. Origen, "Homilies On Genesis," 1, The Fathers of the Church, 137.
233. Ibid., 4, 140.
234. Ibid., 6, 140-141.
235. St. Augustine, "The City of God," XVI.32, The Works of Aurelius Augustine, Volume II, 147.
236. Genesis 21:12,13.
237. St. Augustine, "The City of God," XVI.XXXII, Basic Writings of Saint Augustine, Volume 2, 352.
238. Spiegel, The Last Trial, 30.
239. Ibid., 30-31.
240. Isaiah 26:19. The Living Bible, 550.
241. Spiegel, The Last Trial, 32.
242. Romans 4:16. The Living Bible, 900.
243. James 2:22. Ibid., 988.
244. Clement of Rome, Epistles, "To The Corinthians," 10, 15.
245. Ibid., 31, 28.
246. Prudentius, The Poems of Prudentius, "A Hymn For Epiphony," 45-48, Volume I, 85.
247. Ibid., "The Origin of Sin," 5-8, Volume II, 79.
248. Calvin, Commentaries, V, Volume XXIII, 246.
249. St. Augustine, "The City of God," The Works of Aurelius Augustine, I.XIX, Volume I, 25.
250. Ibid., I.XX, 26.
251. Ibid., I.XXV, 30.
252. Calvin, Institutes of the Christian Religion, II.X.11, Volume I, 376.
253. Brome, Abraham and Isaac, 148-150, 57.
254. Ibid., 168-172, 58.
255. Ibid., 201-202, 59.
256. Ibid., 441-42, 67.
257. Falk, A Psychoanalytic History of the Jews, 71.
258. Genesis 18:20.
259. Genesis 18:23. The Anchor Bible, 132.
260. Genesis 18:24-25. Ibid.

261. Genesis 18:25. Ibid.
262. Fromm, You Shall be as Gods, 28.
263. Exodus 12:31.
264. Euripides, Iphigenia in Taurus, 8, 123.
265. "Virgin blood must satisfy the virgin goddess' anger." Ovid, Metamorphoses, XII.29-30, 286.
266. Ibid., XXII.
267. Kierkegaard, Fear and Trembling, 68.
268. Aeschylus, Agamemnon, 228-230, 41.
269. Ibid., 240-241, 41.
270. Ovid, Metamorphoses, XII.32-33, 286.
271. Pausanias, Description of Greece, I.XLIII.1, Volume I, 229.
272. Seneca, Agamemnon, II.I.160-161, 720.
273. Ibid., II.I.162-164, 720.
274. Sophocles, Electra, 84.

CHAPTER XII

POVERTY & FAMINE

> "I have been assured by a very knowing American of my acquaintance in London, that a young healthy child well nursed is at a year old a most delicious nourishing and wholesome food, whether stewed, roasted, baked or boiled."[1]

In the above quotation from *A Modest Proposal*, Jonathan Swift satirically described above how a tender young infant, like that of a choice baby lamb, can make a tasty dish that was both a source of nutrition, and profit. He wryly suggested that this source of sustenance deserved further consideration by society-at-large to improve upon the problems of hunger, as well as a number of other social ills that were rampant in eighteenth century London at that time. Unwanted excess children could be sold to the highest bidder for food, thereby reducing the welfare rolls in an otherwise productive and effective manner. While the readers of Swift may not have taken his recommendations seriously at the time – rightfully so – there have been many times throughout recorded history where such monstrous episodes did indeed occur.

Most people in the civilized world, and I fortunately include myself on this extensive list, can afford to live a reasonably secure and comfortable life. Not that problems do not threaten the future of our existence, – we live in troubled and insecure times – and not that a significant proportion of our population do not need more in the way of the basic necessities of life, but at least there is usually enough food for most of us to eat, and our children can often go to bed with fulfillment of the minimum nutritional requirements. But many millions of people all over the world continue to suffer the pangs of poverty and starvation and the World Bank has recently estimated that one-third of the world, or over one billion people, are hungry and malnourished, while another two billion are in need of vitamin supplementation.[2] Such widespread privation can cause devastating reactive behavior, and infanticide has been one of the unfortunate manifestations in a mind crazed with extreme destitution.

This should come as no surprise to students of human psychology. Certainly the most intense natural drive seen throughout the animal kingdom is that of self-preservation, and man is no exception to the general rule. When one's life is in immediate danger, all organisms immediately seek a way to survive, and in the process even loving parents can turn deadly to their nearby offspring. While lack of water will cause weakness, dehydration and finally death within days, lack of food leaves one in a ravenous, progressively unstable state for days to weeks. Here-to-fore moral taboos, such as homicidal battles over food or cannibalism, can become accepted life-saving measures. As Malthus aptly noted: "Famine seems to be the last, the most dreadful resource of nature."[3] Swift's sardonic recommendations aside, lack of food has caused many children to perish at the hands of a previously loving parent: whether fed to prevent the death of an older sibling, or sold in order to save another family member, infants have been sacrificed like cattle in times of stress.

A. POVERTY

One does not have to be extremely "poor" to have difficulty meeting the burden of raising a child to adulthood. It has been estimated that it costs between $145,000 to $221,000 to raise a child to age eighteen years in middle class America today.[4] In times past, the hardship has been just as great. Adam Smith, in his famous treatise on *The Wealth of Nations*, aptly summarized the dilemma: "Poverty, though it does not prevent the generation, is extremely unfavourable to the rearing of children."[5]

The commonest reason parents disposed of newborn infants in ancient Rome and Greece was that they could not afford to raise them to maturity.[6] Rather than rejoice in the birth of their children, the less opulent deemed it an act of paternal tenderness to relieve their newborns from the impending miseries of life by exposing them to death shortly after birth.[7] Since exposure was not considered a crime, it was easy to dispose of a newborn and not worry about the negative economic impact on the rest of the family.

But such callous disregard for life could not last for long, and the Roman Emperor, Constantine, finally issued an edict to give relief to parents who declared that they could not afford to raise their children. In 315 A.D., he decreed a law which he hoped would restrain parents from committing parricide for economic reasons. Under his direction, if any "parent should report that he has offspring which on account of poverty he is not able to rear, there shall be no delay in issuing food and clothing, since the rearing of a newborn infant will not allow any delay."[8] Through this law, Constantine thereby assured that public funds would be made available to those who were unable to provide for their own children in order to prevent the murder, or exposure, of impoverished infants. This admirable concern would later become the prototype model for foundling hospitals, and was comprised into the Theodosian Code, although it was rejected in Justinian's collection.[9]

These legal pronouncements appeared to have some immediate effect on the populace of the Roman Empire, although it provided only a partial, and temporary, relief. While some children were spared from infanticide because of the liberal provisions, there still remained a large population with limited funds. In addition, ancient prejudices, such as preference for sons rather than daughters, remained intact. At Veleia, for example, statistics showed that economic aide was asked for 246 male children but only 35 girls.[10] It was easier to dispose of a daughter surreptitiously, than to ask for life-saving support.

Most of the poor during this era simply abandoned their children because they could not feed them. Others were so despondent that they committed infanticide out of what they perceived as merciful goals. Plutarch wrote that when poor men did not rear their children it was because they considered poverty "the worst of evils," and could not endure their children sharing it.[11]

Among the Jews, who generally showed very low rates of exposure or infanticide, the impact of destitution nevertheless took a great toll. While very little factual information exists on the numbers of children actually exposed, evidence indicates that most cases were due to economic distress and poverty. The Babylonian *Talmud* related that, at times, one could find "children thrown away on account of poverty."[12]

Early Christian Fathers also documented the problem among their brethren. St. Basil of Caesarea noted that poverty was often given as an excuse for those who exposed their children at birth.[13] St. Ambrose, the Bishop of Milan in the fourth century A.D., described how the poor "abandon their children and expose them, and if they are recovered deny that they are theirs."[14] Lactantius was not tolerant of this activity and advised that "if someone really cannot support children because of poverty, better he should abstain from relations with his wife than undo the work of God with guilty hands."[15] Once you undertook the responsibility of having a child, you could not summarily dismiss it in this way and still remain faithful to the teachings of Jesus Christ.

Mohammed, as well, was aware of the relationship between infanticide and poverty. In the *Koran*, his directives were clear: "And do not kill your children for fear of poverty; We give them sustenance and yourselves (too); surely to kill them is a great wrong."[16] The concern was due to the especially high prevalence of female infanticide among the Arab tribes, and Mohammed made the elimination of this crime a high priority item.

During the Middle Ages, poverty was often associated with infanticide. Marco Polo explained that in the province of Manzi, the custom was that poor women exposed their babies at birth because they had no means of rearing them.[17] Mary McLaughlin noted that the poor were: "at the mercy of the chronic cycles of famine, malnutrition, disease and death, and their children were by far the most common victims of the parental negligence and despair, of the abandonment, exposure, and even infanticide, which must be counted among major threats to young life."[18]

The Christian Church took note of this unfortunate reality and modified its punishment for infanticide when the killing was secondary to an impoverished condition. In the *Penitential* of Theodore, the Archbishop of Canterbury from 668-690 A.D., a woman who was found guilty of infanticide would have to do penance for fifteen years; if she was poor, however, the penance was only seven years.[19] The penalty for abortion under this system was only one year. While abortion was not countenanced by the Church, the message was clearly that it was less of a sin than infanticide. In the penance supposedly given by Bede in the eighth century, a mother who killed her child before the fortieth day was to do penance for one year; a child who "has become alive" will account as a murder but: "It makes a great difference whether a poor woman does it on account of the difficulty of supporting the child or a harlot for the sake of concealing her wickedness."[20] Another eighth century penitential noted that a "woman who exposes her unwanted child because she has been raped by an enemy or is unable to nourish and sustain (him), is not to be blamed, but she should nevertheless do penance for three weeks."[21]

Roman-Dutch law, which formed the common law of British Guiana, Ceylon and South Africa, punished the exposure and resultant death of children as a capital offence when there was no apparent necessity for the actions of the parent.[22] When there were reasons of poverty, however, and when the exposure was in a public place, the punishment was only whipping, branding or banishment.[23]

The modern era continued to show an increasing frequency of infanticide among the poor. In nineteenth-century England, illegitimacy and poverty were the primary reasons that parents killed their children. There was a decline in baptisms in England between the sixteenth and nineteenth centuries, and one major reason was that many infants were destroyed immediately at birth because the parents could not afford to raise them.[24] While baptism was necessary to save an infant from eternal perdition, the rite notified the entire community of the birth. The only way out, at least in the mind of many frightened couples, was to abandon the child secretly and exchange short-term relief for possible eternal damnation.

The poor suffered a similar fate in America. The lower east side of Manhattan during the nineteenth century was the most congested area in the world. With a population density of 250,000 per square mile, it was twice as crowded as the most heavily populated area of London. In 1865, a ward by ward survey found tenement house infants "lying unattended in filth, with sores and illnesses, or already dead."[25] Neglect and moral lassitude were commonly associated with the depravity of extreme poverty.

In 1996, children continued to be disposed of by the poor. In Hungary, a hospital installed an incubator at its entrance to encourage distressed parents to give up their babies instead of killing them. Economic troubles had recently prompted a large increase in the killing of infants, and one police official noted that: "The state of the country's economy is closely linked with infanticide."[26]

Even fairy tales portrayed the trials of the poor with murmured understanding. In the Grimm's tale of "Hansel and Gretel," a woodcutter and his wife took their two children into the woods and left them there alone. The wife said it was necessary so that all four of them did not die of hunger.[27] Of course, as in most "fairy tales," the children did not succumb to the trial and a happy ending was delivered to readers whose reality was often less fortunate.

From Terra d'Otranto, in Italy, there was the tale of "Chick" where a husband and wife have seven children but were so poor that they had no food. They decided to leave the children in the forest alone, for "it's better to lose them all at once than watch them waste away like candles."[28] In the French tale of "The Lost Children," a married couple living in Gargeac left their son and daughter, Jean and Jeannette, in the woods where the wolves would eat them because they cost too much to raise.[29]

Another form of poverty, even harder to endure because of the associated loss of dignity, is the pitiable institution of slavery. Throughout most of our history, people have been forced to work for others under despicable, inhumane conditions. Like animals of burden, they have been treated with little concern for their families or welfare, and their loss of life becomes merely an economic event rather than a cause for sorrow. Religious advancements, like Judaism and Christianity, did little to change this status. St. Paul, for example, told the slaves that they were to obey their masters and be eager to serve them:

> Serve them as you would Christ. Don't work hard only when your master is watching and then shirk when he isn't looking; work hard and with gladness all the time, as though working for Christ.[30]

Although many were born into servitude, others were freeborn citizens who became innocent victims of war. To the victors went the spoils, and the most valuable prizes were frequently the subjects of defeated nations. Men were often killed, while women and children were brought back in chains to perform the labor of the land. People of all color, race and sex were subject to this life of deportation and a weary, angry, blood-ravaged soldier was not a compassionate owner. In *The Life of Henry the Fifth*, William Shakespeare narrated how king Henry encouraged the Governor of Harfleur to permit his town to be taken without a fight:

Take pity of your town and of your people
Whiles yet my soldiers are in my command,
Whiles yet the cool and temperate wind of grace
O'erblows the filthy and contagious clouds
Of heady murder, spoil, and villainy.
If not – why, in a moment look to see
The blind and bloody soldier with foul hand
Defile the locks of your shrill-shrieking daughters;
Your fathers taken by the silver beards,
And their most reverend heads dashed to the walls;
Your naked infants spidded upon pikes,
Whiles the mad mothers with their howls confused
Do break the clouds . . .[31]

With such a graphic representation of would happen if they resisted, it is easy to understand why the Governor capitulated to Henry's demands, forcing the entire town into a state of hated slavery.

Philo recounted how the Dardanian women, taken prisoner by the Macedonians, held slavery to be the worst possible disgrace and threw their children into the deepest part of the river exclaiming: "You at least shall not be slaves but ere you have begun your life of misery shall cut short your destined span and pass still free along the final road which all must tread."[32] He also detailed how the Xanthians, when attacked by Brutus, fought as long as they could and when their strength was finally spent they slaughtered their women, parents and children to complete their allotted term as free men.[33] To be slaves of the Romans was deemed a fate worse than death.

But such was the fortune of most citizens who were captured during the Greek and Roman conquests. The very word "slave" was derived from the practice of military leaders to order the preservation, and sale, of captives rather than killing them.[34] The income generated from this practice made many a general wealthy, and was often the impetus for their entering into such a dangerous means of employment. Slaves were noted at times to destroy their own children at birth "that they may not be involved in trouble by being compelled to raise children in addition to their enduring slavery."[35]

Xenophon, in his narrative of the war between Cyrus and his brother Artaxeres, described how the Greek army, hired by Cyrus and led by Cheirisophus, viciously and unrelentingly attacked the Taochians. When their stronghold ran out of defenses: "The women threw their little children down from the rocks and then threw themselves down after them, and the men did likewise."[36]

Livy, in the *History of Rome*, noted a number of similar events during the wars of Philip of Macedonia. He related how Theoxena tried to flee from Philip but to no avail. When she was about to be captured, she killed her two children and then threw herself, along with the dead children, into the sea.[37]

Livy goes on to tell how Taurea Vibellius reported that when his native city of Capua was taken in 211 B.C., he killed his wife and children "that they might suffer no indignity," and then killed himself.[38] In 200 B.C., when Philip attacked Abydus, the men "ran to kill their wives and children and then they themselves sought death by every path."[39]

St. Augustine reported the story of the city of Saguntum which was under siege by Hannibal. As it became evident that they would be captured, the men of the city "made a huge fire in the market-place, and therein entombed all their parents, wives, children and friends, after they had slain them first, and lastly themselves."[40]

Fictional accounts of mercy killings were no less vivid. In *Doctor Zhivago*, by Boris Pasternack, Pamphil was afraid that he would be killed, and his family taken prisoner, by the rebellious Bassalygo:

> His constant fear for his family in the event of his own death rose to a new climax. In his imagination he saw them handed over to slow torture, watched their faces distorted by pain, and heard their groans and cries for help. In his desperate anguish – to forestall their future sufferings and to end his own – he killed them himself, felling his wife and three children with that same, razor-sharp ax that he had used to carve toys for the two small girls and the boy, who had been his favorite. The astonishing thing was that he did not kill himself immediately afterward.[41]

The killing of newborns by slaves continued into the American slave society of the eighteenth century. In Massachusetts, a black servant Susanna killed her child "because she thought it would be happier out of the world than in it, where its mother had a hard lot."[42] All across the South, many slave women felt the same anguish for the children they bore and followed this infanticidal practice, especially when the babies were fathered by their white masters.

In Mawell Anderson's play, *The Wingless Victory*, the wife of Nathaniel McQeuston was a black princess of the Celebes, but when she found their life together impossible in eighteenth century Salem, Massachusetts, she decided to commit suicide by ingesting a poison she had brought from home. So that her daughters would not be left to a life of whoredom or slavery, she gave them the poison to take as well.[43]

Toni Morrison, in *Beloved*, told how Sethe lived through the horrors of slavery but could never let it happen to her own offspring. When her last baby was born, a daughter whose father was a slave-holder, she killed the girl it in a way which the baby could not understand:

> What it took to drag the teeth of that saw under the little chin; to feel the baby blood pump like oil in her hands; to hold her face so her head would stay on; to squeeze her so she could absorb, still, the death spasms that shot through that adored body.[44]

Love alone was not enough to support a family torn apart by the horrors of slave labor.

B. FAMINE AND CANNIBALISM

But if the loss of dignity was a catalyst to kill, the most potent stimulus to incite the event was hunger. The impact of hunger on the actions of a human being are overwhelming and generally beyond voluntary control. Joseph Conrad noted that: "No fear can stand up to hunger, no patience can wear it out, disgust simply does not exist where hunger is, and as to superstition, beliefs, and what you may call principles, they are less than chaff in a breeze."[45]

Under such trying circumstances, a parent's willingness to die in an attempt to save their child's life is truly tested. Many choose to put their children before themselves. Victor Hugo, in *Ninety Three*, described how Michelle Flechard was found by the Red Bonnets, a Parisian battalion, huddling in the woods with her three hungry children. The family had been without food for three days and when the sergeant gave Michelle a piece of bread, she broke it into three pieces and gave each child something to eat:

> "She didn't keep any for herself," grumbled the sergeant. "Because she's not hungry," said a soldier. "Because she's a mother," said the sergeant.[46]

Similarly, in the Penobscot Indian legend of the "Corn Mother," when the populace became so congested that the food supply was used up and the tribe was overcome with starvation, the Great Mother decided that the only way to stop the tears was to have herself be killed and then buried in an adjacent land. Her family resisted, but her persistence finally allowed them to agree to her demands. In the field where she was buried, great crops of corn soon began to sprout and the surviving members of the tribe were assured a continuing supply of sustenance.[47]

But in real life, not all mothers or fathers are the same. When food was scarce, the person – or child – adjacent to you became a potential source of nourishment for self-survival. Not only could there be flesh to eat if the individual was killed, but there would also be one less person to drain the available food supply. According to Hobbes, such action was excusable under the Natural Law:

> When a man is destitute of food, or other thing necessary for his life, and cannot preserve himself any other way, but by some fact against the Law; as if in a great famine he take the food by force, or stealth, which he cannot obtain for money, nor charity; or in defence of his life, snatch away another man's Sword, he is totally Excused.[48]

There is archeological evidence that Neanderthal man, living some 220,000 years ago in Central Europe, practiced cannibalism as well as the first Homo Sapiens, Cro-Magnon Man, 75,000 years ago.[49] These postulates are based on human bone fragments with teeth marks that appear to be of human, rather than animal, causes.

Evidence is also found in ancient mythology. In the Atrahasis story of the ancient Sumerian civilization, humans were created by the gods in order to take care of the world. They procreated rapidly, however, and the earth soon became over-populated. The noise created by all of the people disturbed the gods who then attempted to lessen their numbers by sending a famine upon the land. Stories of its devastation included episodes of cannibalism: "In the sixth year, a daughter is cooked for dinner, a son's eaten for food."[50]

The Old Testament was filled with prophecies foretelling of severe famines as punishment for the actions of the Hebrews not following the precepts of the Lord's commandments. Moses told the people of Israel, before they crossed the Jordan River into the Promised land, that if they did not obey all the commandments of the Lord, curses would fall upon them: "You will even eat the flesh of your own sons and daughters in the terrible days of siege that lie ahead."[51] And to emphasize this even more Moses continued:

> The most tender and delicate woman among you – the one who would not so much as touch her feet to the ground – will refuse to share with her beloved husband, son and daughter. She will hide from them the afterbirth and the new baby she has borne, so that she herself can eat them.[52]

This warning by Moses was repeated elsewhere, that if the Israelites did not obey, "you shall eat your own sons and daughters."[53]

A similar portent was given by Ezekiel, who prophesied in Babylonia around 593 B.C. Because the people had rebelled against the judgments of the Lord, and became more wicked than other nations, His anger would be vented and: "Surely parents will eat children in your midst, and children shall eat their parents."[54] Jeremiah, as well, told of how the valley would no longer be called Topheth, or Ben-Hinnom Valley, but "The Valley of Slaughter," for: "I will see to it that your enemies lay siege to the city until all food is gone, and those trapped inside begin to eat their own children and friends."[55]

Such forebodings appeared to come true during a siege in Samaria by King Ben-hadad of Syria, when the king of Israel was asked by a woman to help with the deadly famine that was killing the people of the town. She proposed that they eat his son one day and her's the next. The king agreed and then boiled his son which they proceeded to eat.[56] A similar story was told of the famine in Jerusalem which was so great that:

> With their own hands the kindly women cooked their children.
> This was the food they had, when my people was ruined.[57]

In the Babylonian *Talmud*, Rabbi Nehemiah explained the reasoning for such debauchery : "For the crime of robbery locusts make invasion, famine is prevalent, and people eat the flesh of their sons and daughters."[58]

One particular cause of such hunger was wartime sieges where towns were cut off from needed supplies and the entire population slowly starved until they surrendered. When Numantia was stormed by Scipio in 133 B.C., Petronius related that "some women were found with half-eaten bodies of their children hidden in their bosoms" after a fifteen month blockade.[59]

Josephus also described the siege of Jerusalem by the Romans which led to intense starvation. The story of Maria of Azov, who killed and ate her son during this trial, was told in the painting "Hunger, Madness and Crime," by the nineteenth century Belgian, Antoine Joseph Wierty.[60] Depicted was a woman with bared breast and disordered hair sitting by a cauldron with a blood stained knife and an emaciated corpse of her infant. In *Purgatory*, when Dante viewed the wasted forms of the penitents, he reflected on this one woman: "See the people who lost Jerusalem when Mary preyed on her child!"[61] Josephus had referred to her as Mary, or Miriam, the daughter of Eleazar who was starving during the Roman war on Jerusalem and took her own son and said "be thou my food."[62] She then slew and roasted him for desperate sustenance.

The New Testament does not contain similar traditional stories of cannibalism, but the connection between divine strength and human flesh was made very clear through the use of the sacrament of bread and wine. After crossing the Sea of Galilee into Jerusalem, Jesus was faced with multitudes of people who were starving and desirous of bread. They said to him:

> You must show us more miracles if you want us to believe you are the Messiah. Give us free bread every day, like our fathers had while they journeyed through the wilderness![63]

Jesus then explained that the true bread is a person and that He alone – Jesus Himself – was the Bread of Life.[64] The people murmured in protest to this apparent sacrilegious statement, but Jesus explained that the eating of his flesh had been ordained in order to redeem humanity:

> Unless you eat the flesh of the Messiah and drink his blood, you cannot have eternal life within you. But anyone who does eat my flesh and drink my blood has eternal life, and I will raise him at the Last Day. For my flesh is the true food, and my blood is the true drink.[65]

Some of these same concepts were seen in the New World Indian tribes. While the ancient Aztecs did not generally eat the children they sacrificed to the rain god Tlaloc, the majority of their adult sacrifices were consumed after they were killed.[66] This has led some historians to speculate that the victims may have actually been part of the basic food supply. The maize-bean diet of the Aztecs was unpredictable, secondary to crop failures, and was also deficient in essential amino acids and fats unless eaten in great quantity.[67] Since consuming only this primary food substance would cause widespread nutritional deficiency, it was possible that human flesh, as a supplement of excellent protein and vitamin value, became more acceptable. This theory has been rebuffed by others who argued that the eating of sacrificial victims was only a necessary completion to the sacred act of sacrifice with the energy of their victim transferred to their own store of strength in the process.[68] But it is nevertheless true that the Inca Empire, which existed in Peru around the same time as the Aztecs, had a much more secure food supply and the sacrifices there were many fold fewer than the Aztecs.[69]

Cannibalism of children during times of severe food shortage continued to be described into the Middle Ages. Ralph Glaber, writing in the eleventh century, told how a mighty famine raged in the Roman world for five years and many people starved to death:

> The horrible famine compelled men to make their food not only

> of unclean beasts and creeping things, but even of men's, women's and children's flesh, without regard even of kindred; for so fierce waxed this hunger that grown-up sons devoured their mothers, and mothers, forgetting their maternal love, ate their babies.[70]

The *Siete Partidas* law of the Castilians allowed cannibalism in defense of the state. It stated that: "A father who is besieged in a castle he holds from his lord, may, if so beset with hunger that he has nothing to eat, eat his child with impunity rather than surrender the castle without permission of the lord."[71]

An Italian chronicler declared that in 1212 A.D., in Sicily, there was a famine so severe that mothers ate their children while a Hebrew chronicler related the same story during a terrible siege in Toledo, Spain during the fourteenth century.[72] In the *Inferno*, Dante recounted the story of Count Ugolino who was jailed without food in the Mew with his four children. Hungry and alone, one child came crying and said to him: "Father, it will be far less painful to us if you eat of us; you did clothe us with this wretched flesh, and do you strip us of it?"[73]

During the severe crop failures in England in 1315-1317 A.D., Johannes de Trokelow, a well-known chronicler, claimed that parents killed their children and ate them.[74] Jasper Danckaerts related how during the Dutch War with the English, the Lord punished the people with an infestation of weevils which caused a great loss of the grain crop. One mother killed her own child and ate it and was then arrested and condemned to be hung. On the scaffold she said that "what she had done she did in the mere delirium of hunger, for which the governor alone should bear the guilt," since it was his actions which caused the visitation from God.[75] Her last minute defense appears to have been unheeded.

Tribal practices not uncommonly included the eating of children during periods of food shortage. Among the Eskimos, infanticide was often a necessity when traveling in inclement weather. A child who could not walk was an additional burden which the mother could not bear on long journeys for food and shelter. During times of plenty, very few cases of infanticide could be found among the Eskimos.[76] But in times of famine, children have been reported to have been killed, and then eaten, among the central Eskimos.[77] It was understood by the Eskimos of Greenland that a child must be sacrificed before their parents when food was scarce.[78] The Inuit Eskimos of Quebec were noted to practice infanticide, and even cannibalism, during times of famine in the nineteenth century.[79]

The Indians of Northeastern America occasionally practiced cannibalism and during times of severe crop failure, the Mohawks would eat the flesh of women and children.[80] The Mohave Indians also believed in the legend of the discovery of growing watermelons from seeds so that the people "no longer had to kill their children in order to survive."[81]

The Australian aboriginals were very fond of their offspring, and very indulgent to those that were kept. But if tribal numbers increased too rapidly, infanticide became a necessity.[82] Cannibalism among the Aranda ranged from mothers eating their children during periods of drought, to every second child being killed and fed to the preceding child in order to assure it's growth.[83] Geza Roheim explained that:

> When the Yumu, Pindupi, Ngali, or Nambutji were hungry, they ate small children with neither ceremonial nor animistic motives. Among the southern tribes, the Matuntara, Mularatara, or Pitjentara, every second child was eaten in the belief that the strength of the first child would be doubled by such a procedure.[84]

Once the infant had gone through the ceremony of having received a name, it would rarely be eaten as nourishment for mothers or older children.[85]

Among the Maori of New Zealand, infanticide was never seen unless the food was short.[86] Elsdon Best detailed how the Maori told tales of infanticide during long drawn out sieges when:

> Desperate with hunger, the children in a besieged fortified village have been sacrificed. The practice followed was to exchange children, so that parents might not eat their own children.[87]

The Polynesians also were fond of their children and yet had laws which required infanticide when more than one or two children were born to a family because of the scarcity of food.[88] Among the Marquesians, in south-east Hawaii, children were sometimes eaten during seasons of extreme scarcity.[89] The Tikopia practiced infanticide to allow the older children to grow healthy since the scarcity of food often severely weakened many of the youngsters.[90]

In the *Good Earth*, Pearl Buck wrote of the tribulations of famine in China and how an old man told Wang Lung that "there have been worse days. Once I saw men and women eating children."[91] Wang Lung answered that there will never be such a thing in his house, but later his wife gave birth to a fourth child during hard times and soon after the baby cried he found it dead: "Upon the neck he saw two dark, bruised spots."[92]

Theodore White, in his early travels as a correspondent, reported how the severe famine in China in 1942, during their war with Japan, caused such destruction that some of the people resorted to cannibalism. In one village:

> A mother was discovered boiling her two-year old to eat its meat. In another case a father was charged with strangling his two boys to eat them.[93]

In Chengchow, which was the epicenter of the famine, the population had been reduced from 120,000 to 30,000.[94] Unlike the severe drought which killed many during the reign of Emperor Kuang-hsu in 1893, "this death was man-made."[95]

Folk-tales from many countries of the world have told of behavior that related to killing and hunger. In the British tale of "The Milk-White Doo," a man caught a hare and had his wife bake it for dinner. During the cooking, the woman tasted the hare until it was all gone and then had nothing left to serve her husband. She therefore killed her son Johnnie, and cooked him for dinner, in order to not be punished by her hungry husband.[96]

In the gruesome Italian folk tale from Abruzzo, "The Three Blind Queens," three queens were ordered killed by the minister and in order to save their lives they gouged out their eyes for the proof of their death. They then lived in a cave and each gave birth to a baby. When they ran out of food, they drew lots to see whose baby they would eat in order to remain alive. They ate the child of the eldest first, and then the one of the middle sister. When the youngest sister turn came, she ran away with her baby in order to save his life.[97]

Endnotes

1 . Swift, "A Modest Proposal for Preventing the Children of Ireland from Being a Burden to Their Parents or Country," Satires and Personal Writings, 23.
2 . Chicago Tribune (November 30, 1993): section 1, 4.
3 . Malthus, "An Essay on the Principle of Population, as It Affects the Future Improvement of Society. With remarks on the speculations of Mr. Godwin, M. Condorcet, and other writers (1798)," On Population, VII, 51
4 . U.S. News & World Report (March 10, 1986): 63. Six years ago the estimated cost was $75,500. Ibid.
5 . Adam Smith, The Wealth of Nations, Books I-III, I.VIII, 182.
6 . Balsdon, Roman Women, 196.
7 . Gibbon, The Decline and Fall of the Roman Empire, Volume I, 375.
8 . Theodosian Code, 11.27.1, 318.
9 . Blackstone, Commentaries on the Laws of England, Book the First, Section Four, I.2.
10 . Balsdon, Roman Women, 197.
11 . Plutarch, "On Affection For Children," VI.5, Moralia, 355.
12 . Kiddushin, Gemara, IV.73a.
13 . Hexaemeron 6, Homilia VIII. Boswell, The Kindness of Strangers, 165.
14 . Hexaemeron 18.58. Ibid., 168.
15 . Institutes 6.20. Ibid., 161.
16 . Surah XVII:31. Qur'an, 181.
17 . Polo, The Travels, 174. He also explained that "the poor and needy sell some of their sons and daughters to the rich and noble, so that they may support themselves on the price paid for them and the children may be better fed in their new homes." Ibid., 199.
18 . McLauglin, "Survivors and Surrogates," 120.
19 . McNeill & Gamer, "The Penitential of Theodore," XIV.25-26, Medieval Handbooks of Penance, 197.
20 . Ibid., "Penitentials Tentatively Ascribed by Abers to Bede," II.11, 225.
21 . Penitentiale Valicellanum 1.40. Boswell, The Kindness of Strangers, 220.
22 . Leeuwen, Commentaries on Roman-Dutch Law, XXXIV.3, Volume II, 267.
23 . Ibid.
24 . Sauer, "Infanticide and Abortion in Nineteenth-Century Britain," 85.
25 . English, "Pediatrics and the Unwanted Child in History: Foundling Homes, Disease, and the Origins of Foster Care in New York City," 700.
26 . Chicago Tribune (May 20, 1996): section 1, 10.
27 . Grimm's Fairy Tales, 320.
28 . Calvino, Italian Folk Tales, 449.
29 . Delarue, The Borzoi Book of French Folk Tales, 97.
30 . Ephesians 6:5-7. The Living Bible, 951.
31 . Shakespeare, The Life of Henry V, III.iii.28-40, 90.
32 . Philo, "Every Good Man Is Free," XVII.115, Loeb Classical Library, Volume IX, 77.
33 . Ibid., XVIII.119, 79.
34 . Justinian, Institutes, I.III, 6.
35 . Dio Chrysostom, Discourses, "On Slavery and Freedom," II.8, 151.
36 . Xenophon, Anabasis, IV.VII.13, 73.

37 . Livy, History of Rome, XL.IV.14-15, Volume XII, 13.
38 . Ibid., XXVI.XV.14, Volume VII, 59-61.
39 . Ibid., XXXI.XVIII.6, Volume IX, 55.
40 . St. Augustine, The City of God, III.XX, Volume I, 100.
41 . Pasternack, Doctor Zhivago, II.12.8, 372.
42 . Jones, Women Who Kill, 48.
43 . Anderson, The Wingless Victory, III.II, 131.
44 . Morrison, Beloved, 251.
45 . Conrad, Heart of Darkness, 113.
46 . Hugo, Ninety Three, 12.
47 . Erdoes & Ortiz, American Indian Myths & Legends, 13.
48 . Hobbes, Leviathan, II.XXVII, 346.
49 . Hogg, Cannibalism & Human Sacrifice, 14.
50 . Matthews & Benjamin, Old Testament Parallels, 23.
51 . Deuteronomy 28:53. The Living Bible, 172.
52 . Deuteronomy 28:56-57. Ibid., 173.
53 . Leviticus 26:29. Ibid., 111.
54 . Ezekiel 5:10. The Anchor Bible, 100.
55 . Jeremiah 19:6,9. The Living Bible, 596.
56 . 2 Kings 6:28.
57 . Lamentation 4:10. The Anchor Bible, 76.
58 . Shabbath, Gemara, II.32b.
59 . Petronius, Satyricon of Titus Petronius Arbiter, 141.
60 . Shahar, Childhood in the Middle Ages, 138.
61 . Dante, "Purgatory," XXIII.29-30, The Divine Comedy, 297.
62 . Josephus, "The Jewish War," VI.III.4, The Works of Flavius Josephus, Volume II, 425.
63 . John 6:30-31. The Living Bible, 843.
64 . John 6:35.
65 . John 6:53-55. Ibid., 844.
66 . Harner, "The Ecological Basis for Aztec Sacrifice," 119-20.
67 . Ibid., 127.
68 . Ortiz de Montellano, "Aztec Cannibalism: An Ecological Necessity?," 611, 615.
69 . Harner, "The Ecological Basis for Aztec Sacrifice," 119.
70 . Coulton, Life in the Middle Ages, 3.
71 . Boswell, The Kindness of Strangers, 329.
72 . Ibid., 330.
73 . Dante, "Inferno," XXXIII.61-62, The Divine Comedy, 353.
74 . Hanawalt, "The Female Felon in Fourteenth-Century England," 260.
75 . Danckaerts, "A Plague of Weevils," America Begins, 117.
76 . Garber, "Eskimo Infanticide," 98.
77 . Aptekar, Anjea: Infanticide, Abortion & Contraception in Savage Society, 160.
78 . Mirsky, "The Eskimo of Greenland," 75.
79 . D'Anglure, "Inuit of Quebec," 480.
80 . Henry, Wilderness Messiah, 29.
81 . Devereux, "Mohave Indian Infanticide," 133.
82 . Howitt, The Native Tribes of South-East Australia, 748.
83 . Roheim, "The Western Tribes of Central Australia: Childhood," 199.
84 . Ibid., 200.

85 . Ibid.
86 . Mead, Cooperation & Competition Among Primitive Peoples, 454.
87 . Best, The Maori, Volume I, 413.
88 . Andersen, Myths & Legends of the Polynesians, 444.
89 . Ellis, Polynesian Researches, 328-329.
90 . Dickeman, "Demographic Consequences of Infanticide in Man," 123.
91 . Buck, The Good Earth, 67.
92 . Ibid., 71.
93 . White, In Search of History, 148.
94 . Ibid., 149.
95 . Ibid., 150.
96 . Briggs, A Dictionary of British Folk-Tales, Volume I, 414.
97 . Calvino, Italian Folk Tales, 407-408.

CHAPTER XIII

REVENGE

> "Both these women had bitter cause to destroy their own dear flesh – revenge on a husband."[1]

Ovid, the first century A.D. Roman poet, above described above how two wronged women – Medea and Procne – killed their children instead of their husbands in order to bring about a punishment worse than death. They so desired to wreak havoc on the men, they were willing to destroy their own sons in the process.

Revenge is such a powerful motive that it can cast aside all other feelings which might otherwise temper rational behavior. When hatred festers and gathers strength until there is only one single overwhelming desire to reap revenge on the offending person, nothing will prevent its completion short of death. In the words of Madame Defarge, who desired to "exterminate" the entire family of Charles Darnay during the class rebellion of the French Revolution, it was futile for someone to mention compassion and try and change her mind: "Tell the Wind and Fire where to stop, not me!"[2] While adults generally bear the brunt of such malignant retaliation, children are occasionally caught in the web of vengeance, and killed without regret, even by their own parent.

Plutarch was not outraged at this reason for infanticide, but did raise the question on whether blood-revenge, in response to the killing of a family member, was an accepted rationale. He discussed the story of Merope, who had concealed the birth of her infant son, Aeptys, and then sent him away to be raised, after Polyphontes had murdered her father and brother and then forced her to marry him.[3] Aeptys later returns under an alias name to revenge his father's death and, in order to gain access to Polyphontes, says he is the one who murdered the infant son. Merope does not recognize her true son, and attempts to revenge the murder by killing Aeptys with an ax. At the last minute her act is turned aside. But Plutarch nevertheless questions whether the murder would have been wrong under the circumstances known:

> Which would be the greater misdeed, to omit the punishment of an enemy because of the son, or to slay a child under the impulse of anger against an enemy?[4]

We will see that many instances of actual murder will raise the question in a more than theoretical sense.

A. Revenge Against Spouse

Seneca, the first century A.D. Roman tragedian, noted how potent was the strength of female revenge: "No force of flame or raging gale, or whizzing bolt so fearful is, as when a wife, by her lord betrayed, burns hot with hate."[5] A woman, caught in a web of retaliation, is capable of the most dastardly deed, according to Seneca, and to satisfy her anger, she would resort even to something as drastic as infanticide. The murder of a child, in revenge against a spouse, is not an uncommon occurrence throughout recorded history, and has been dubbed by some authorities as the "Medea syndrome" or "Medea complex."[6] It is a woman who bears the designation of this tragedy, but while women may in fact represent a majority of the cases, there is also a significant number of men who kill their children in order to punish their wife. In the world's literature on infanticide reported by Resnick, revenge-killing occurred in up to 24% of murders by mothers, and 16% by fathers.[7]

Browne noted that the actual murder often took place at the exact moment when the wife was extremely angry with her husband.[8] It was an impulse-killing with the fatal blow often delivered before reconsideration of the response. Many of these women also had profound thoughts of suicide, and often equated the child's murder with their own desire to die.[9] They were diagnosed as having an acute psychotic reaction brought about by an affective impulse translated directly to a violent reaction.

In England, d'Orban similarly determined that retaliating women who killed their children "were a highly unstable and disturbed group who had the highest combined score on measures of stress."[10] Bourget referred to them as "unstable individuals who deliberately kill their children to manipulate and cause suffering to their spouses."[11] Over and over again, the women showed that it was the desire for revenge that precipitated the killing of their child.

And the model which all researchers turn to for comparison, the most famous of all revenge killings, is the Greek legend of Medea. This tale has gathered interest for centuries, and in the words of Grillparzer: "Since then all other horrors seem mere jest."[12]

The standard storyline of the tragedy was presented by Euripides in 431 B.C. Medea was a barbarian princess and sorceress, who had an infamous knowledge of potions and drugs. Her father, King Aeetes of Colchis, kept a Golden Fleece which Jason and the Argonauts, came to steal. Medea fell in love with Jason, and gave him magic potions to help slay the fire-breathing dragons which protected the Golden Fleece. Without her help, Jason never would have succeeded in his heroic quest, and the Argonauts would have returned home empty-handed and unworthy of lasting fame. She even assured their escape with the stolen prize by killing her own brother who tried to overtake them once the daring deed was discovered.

Initially, all seemed blissful and well as Medea and Jason married and had two children, Aeson and Absyrtus. Then, during a trip to Corinth, Jason fell in love with the daughter of King Creon. He told Medea he planned to marry the princess and retain custody of his two sons, and suggested she leave the country for her own welfare. Just like that, after all Medea had done to make her husband famous, she was forgotten in a moment of passion for another woman. At first, Medea was anguished and severely depressed. She even lamented her disheartened mood with thoughts of suicide. But then her anger began to rise, and she pondered how she could make Jason pay for his torturous infidelity. Her conclusion was consistent with the most egregious of all Greek tragedies; she first sent a robe laced with poison as a feigned present to the young princess, and then murdered her own children to complete her revenge.[13] As Jean Anouilh was to have her say centuries later: "I followed you in blood and crime, and I need blood and crime to leave you."[14]

The saga of Medea's grief offers a wide array of human emotions which test the very essence of mortal adoration and enmity. It reveals how outrage over lost love can override even the innately strong, maternal attachment of a woman for her own children. According to Ovid, Medea had been able to subdue dragons and maddened bulls, as well as "fierce fire with wise drugs," but she did not have "the power to escape the flames of her own passion."[15]

In most early fictional depictions, Medea was portrayed as callous and evil, traits which have identified her to the present day. But one must remember that she was deeply in love with Jason, and the intensity of her grievous loss was overwhelming. She did not use her children as mere pawns, and loved them as dearly as life itself. She contemplated other actions than the one she eventually took, as reflected in the words of Euripides: "Ah, wretch! Ah, lost in my sufferings, I wish, I wish I might die."[16] But as time passed, and the hurt festered, she realized that it was only through the loss of his sons that Jason could be made to suffer as much as she had done.

At first Medea requested that she be allowed to leave the country with her children, but when Jason refused, saying they are "my very spring of life, my sore heart's comfort, and my joy," Medea saw clearly where to vent her anger.[17] She realized "in his armored strength this flaw reveals the place to strike."[18] Although the thought of losing her sons was great, they: "Must pay the penalty of these your father's crimes – my heart with horror melts, a numbing chill pervades my limbs, and all my soul is filled with sinking fear."[19] Propertius aptly summarized her choice: "The mother, clearly though she loved her children, appeased her anger by their slaughter."[20]

Once her decision was made, the method chosen was brutal. Seneca told how her vengeance was "as some wild Bacchanal . . . her face revealing every mark of stricken woe, with flushing cheek and sighs deep drawn, wild cries, and tears, and laughter worse than tears."[21]

Many modern authors have interpreted her actions with varying degrees of compassion. If you search long enough through the hundreds of stories, plays, poems and other literary commentaries on this intriguing fable, you can find almost every possible explanation for Medea's actions. But the fact remains that the "Medea Syndrome" is one which commonly occurs either in the literal, or the psychologically sublimated, sense. Children bear the brunt of their parents emotions, and when they do, the effects may be powerfully beneficial or devastatingly deadly.

In the ancient Greek legend of Procne, revenge against a husband took on an even more grotesque turn. Procne had married Tereus of Thrace, a son of Ares, and when their son Itys was still a young boy, she asked to see her sister, Philomela, who they had left many years before. Tereus journeyed to Athens to accompany the young woman back to Thrace and on the return trip he raped Philomela and then cut out her tongue to prevent her telling the tale of what happened. The girl wove the story into a wondrous tapestry, however, and when Procne found out the truth, the two sisters plotted their revenge. Procne cut her young son's throat and then boiled him in a pot and served it to Tereus for supper.[22] When the father realized what he was eating, he ran after the two women to kill them but the gods turned Procne into a nightingale and Philomela into a swallow before he could reach them.[23]

Many ancient authors, while accepting the revenge of Medea, found the action of Procne abhorrent. Achilles Tatius noted how:

> So far greater were the agonies of jealousy than those of the womb; women care nothing but to avenge themselves on him who has wronged their bed, even if they suffer in their revenge a woe equal to that which they inflict.[24]

Ovid reprimanded her revenge but noted that:

> Child-blood on Medea's hands excites our horror, dismembered Itys brings tears to the eye: Parental savagery rampant. Yet both these women had bitter cause to destroy their own dear flesh – revenge on a husband.[25]

It is intriguing to postulate why Medea would evoke such dramatic understanding, when her actions were provoked only by infidelity, while

Procne reaped only disdain after responding to a violent, disfiguring rape of her sister.

In modern day literature, a husband's anger was portrayed by Gerhart Hauptmann in *Flagman Thiel.* Thiel's son was killed by a train and in his grief and madness he imagined that it was the fault of his wife, the boy's stepmother. "Beast of a mother!" he cried, and then realized that her own baby, his step-son, still lived:

> A red mist enveloped his senses. Two baby eyes penetrated through it. He felt something soft, fleshy between his fingers.[26]

He choked the throat of the child and then realized the result of his actions and let the baby go. In a desire to harm his detested wife, he was willing to kill the only child he had left.

B. Revenge Against Others

In his treatise on anger, *De Ira*, Seneca noted the potential fatal outcome of that intense emotion. He warned that: "Men in anger invoke death upon their children, and are hostile to their closest friends and must be avoided by those dearest to him."[27] His cautionary advice to refrain from close relationships with those who are prone to sudden anger has borne true through the centuries. The kinship of family or friends has not assured a safe environment during periods of irrational outburst, and many children have been killed when they were perceived by their parents as being "in the way."

According to legend, Theseus, the Greek hero and friend of Heracles, was granted three wishes from Neptune in reward for the valiant services he rendered the god. Theseus asked for no favor, however, until an angry outburst against his son, Hippolytus, after his second wife, Phaedra, falsely stated that the boy had made unwelcome advances upon her. In truth, Phaedra had desired the love of Hippolytus, and when she was spurned by his refusal, she sought to punish him at the hands of his father. Theseus angrily wished for the death of his son, and prayed to the gods to not let him "live to behold another sun's bright rays."[28] Since his request could not be refused, the gods acquiesced and Hippolytus was immediately killed when the horses of the chariot he was in bolted and dragged him to a bloody end.[29] Once his outburst was over, and the truth became known, Theseus was overwhelmed with grief.[30] Seneca portrayed him as breaking down in tears. Asked why he would cry if he hated his son so much, he answered: "Because I slew, not lost my son."[31] The realization of personal responsibility in causing the boy's death, which was so fervently desired during the outburst of hatred, was regretted when the circumstances calmed.

A similar saga appeared in early Irish literature where Ronan was told that his son, Mael Fothartaig, entreated his wife in his absence. He violently ordered the boy killed despite the lad's exclaiming that it was "a sad deception that has been put upon you, to kill your only son unjustly . . . I no more thought of lying with her than I would lie with my mother."[32] But Mael was executed and when the truth was finally revealed, Ronan sat at his son's grave for three days and nights and wailed: "Woe is me that Mael Fothartaig was slain for the guilt of a lustful woman."[33]

Many other folk-tales contained similar aspersions against a woman's credibility. In the Serbian tale of "The Stepsisters," Paul's wife hated his sister, Yelitza, because she thought her husband preferred the love of Yelitza to her own. She tried desperately to turn him against her by first killing his favorite horse and saying it was the sister who performed the deed. Paul asked Yelitza if indeed it was her fault and when she denied any involvement, he believed her. The wife next killed his favorite falcon, and once again Paul believed his sisters version. Finally, in desperation, she killed her own infant in the cradle with a knife, and then left the bloody weapon in the sister's bed. Paul finally believed his wife's accusation and ordered his sister to be killed by the grotesque method of quartering.[34]

In the Mexican folktale of "The Flower of Lily-Lo," the parents of three sons preferred the youngest one most of all. The other two were very jealous and one day they killed the boy while looking for the flower of Lily-Lo to help cure their mother's illness. The flower later revealed the story of what happened, and for revenge the parents shut the boys in a room and "lighted a fire inside and threw a lot of chili peppers on the flames so they would choke to death."[35]

Occasionally, anger or jealously has taken some very strange turns in attempts at retaliation. In Orlando, Florida, in 1992, a woman tried to infect her two-year-old daughter with the AIDS virus by repeatedly biting the child because of jealousy against the child's grandmother. The mother had become infected with the virus and felt that the daughter was beginning to love the grandmother more. She decided to then give her daughter AIDS so that the grandmother would not be able to care for the girl.[36]

C. CURSES

One way in which revenge could be satisfied, without having to take direct participation in the bloody loss, was to put a curse on the victim and let the gods apply the injury. While scientific validation is lacking to prove that such a method actually works, it has been a belief that has crossed time and space for ages. Voodoo practice exists in many parts of the world even today, and every practicing Christian and Jew still believes that impious actions will be punished when the Day of Judgment arrives. Superstition covers every aspect of our lives, but in this section I will only discuss the curses that have been fabled to lead to a child's death.

Biblical curses were common, and their effects dramatic. Joshua declared a terrible curse on anyone who might try and rebuild Jericho after he caused the walls to come "tumbling down," and warned that any builder who disobeyed would find his eldest son die when the foundation was laid, and the youngest son die when the gates were set up.[37] Discrediting the force of this threat, a man from Bethel named Hiel began to rebuild Jericho:

> When he laid the foundations, his oldest son, Abiram, died; and when he finally completed it by setting up the gates, his youngest son, Segub, died. For this was the Lord's curse upon Jericho as declared by Joshua, the son of Nun.[38]

Curses on children also occurred because of the sins of their parents. King Ahab had desired to buy the vineyard of Naboth, but was turned down when the man did not want to leave his home. The king's wife, Jezebel, then had two scoundrels falsely accuse Naboth of cursing God and the king, and he was stoned to death for the blasphemy. The property was thereby freed up, and the king took possession. But when Ahab moved into the house, God sent Elijah with a message that for this wrongful deed, none of his male descendants would survive.[39] Ahab tore his clothing, put on rags and slept in humble sackcloth in an attempt to atone for his sin and assuage God's anger. But the curse remained, although God did take some measure of empathy and allowed Ahab to die before having to witness the death of his sons. Soon after the kings demise, the sons died.[40] The son of David and Bath-sheba also died, according to Nathan, because David had sinned and given great opportunity to the enemies of the Lord to despise and blaspheme Him.[41]

This particular aspect of hereditary curses was not favored in other sections of the Bible. The true law of Moses was "that the fathers shall not die for the children's sins, nor the children for the father's sins."[42] This was echoed by Job who cried out that God should punish the man who sins and not his children.[43] But the Lord was a vengeful Ruler, and the threat of generational punishment was often presented as a means to control mortal misbehavior.

A variant of this type of curse is portrayed in *The Jew of Malta*, by Christopher Marlowe. In this tale of avarice and greed, the wealthy Jewish merchant, Barabas, seeks to take revenge on the governor of Malta by feigning an engagement of his own daughter to the governor's son. When the young woman's preferred love is killed in a duel with the son, she decides to enter a nunnery and Barabas swears that "ne'er shall she grieve me more with her disgrace."[44] He poisons her, and the entire nunnery, in his rage.

D. Step-Parents

The hatred of step-parents for their step-children has always been a common theme in literature and folklore. Many cultures have accepted as fact that animosity would naturally develop between step-parents and their newly acquired children. Juvenal claimed that in Rome: "At last it's defined as proper to kill a stepson."[45] He warned orphan boys to keep a close watch on the food they were served: "The meat pies are hot, but also hot with a mother's poison."[46]

Often, the killing involved intertwining themes of incestual love. King Athamas of Orchomenus in Boeotia was led down a misguided path similar to that of Theseus. He was told by an oracle that the famine in his land would not cease until he sacrificed one of his children. This advice was prearranged by his second wife, Ino, who was jealous of the children by his earlier marriage with Nephele. The king obeyed the suggestion and sent for his son Phrixus, and daughter Helle, in order to sacrifice them on the altar. The children were forewarned, however, by the ram with a fleece of gold and during their escape on the ram's back, Helle fell into the sea and was drowned.[47]

Many other tales had frightening storylines, but happier endings. In the famous Grimm fairy tale, "Snow White & the Seven Dwarfs, the wicked step-mother queen decided to kill Snow White when the mirror on her wall said that the girl, rather than the queen, was the "fairest of all." She first directed the huntsman to take Snow White into the woods and kill her and bring back her heart as a token. When that failed she brought the girl a poison comb, and then a poison apple but through all the attempts at murder, Snow White survived. As most modern children know from the ending in the Walt Disney movie version, Snow White not only outlived the wicked queen, but married the handsome prince and lived happily ever after.[48]

In Celtic lore, the step-mother of Niall of the Nine Hostages, exposed him beneath the green of Tara because of jealousy. After he was there for three days he was found by Torna and saved.[49]

Ancient Irish folklore told of Cormac Conn Longes, of Ulster, who married Etain, the daughter of king Etar. When Cormac revealed a daughter he had by his first wife, she ordered the child to be killed. Two slaves were sent to bury the child in a pit, but they took pity on her and she was saved.[50] A similar order to kill step-children was given by Aoife, after her marriage to Bodb. She was jealous of the love he had for the four children, and after failing to kill them by means of a sword she took them to the lake and changed them into swans with a magic wand.[51]

In Russian folklore, the story of "Jack Frost" involved a step-mother who ordered her husband to take his daughter and leave her in the open field in the bitter frost. The old man grieved, but followed the wishes of his domineering wife. The girl was left to die in the open and Jack Frost came to freeze her but instead took pity on her and gave her a fur coat to remain warm.[52] Similarly, in "The Grumbling Old Woman," a stepmother had her husband abandon his daughter in the forest to "get her out of my way." The girl was saved by a wood-goblin who turned into a brave youth.[53]

In the Mexican folktale of "The Little Guana," a step-mother forced her husband to choose between her and his own children. He was afraid of the woman and took his kids to a mountain where he abandoned them. They found their way out and the father returned them to the site once more, but again they were saved.[54]

Happy endings, however, were not always a part of folktale legends. The British tale of "The Cruel Stepmother" told of a rich nobleman in Scotland, Malcolm, who was brother to Fingal, king of Morveni. His wife died after giving birth to a daughter, Beatrix, and he later remarried. The step-mother hated Beatrix because of her beauty and she later gave birth to a son who became the darling of his father. She killed the boy with a knife, and then "laid it, with the knife reeling in gore, into the arms of the innocent Beatrix." The father, in anger, then cut off the right arm of Beatrix, then her right leg and finally her tongue and left her in the forest.[55]

Other British tales included "The Friar and the Boy" where a step-mother looked upon her step-son with an evil eye and told the father "put away this boy, who is a cursed plague to me."[56] In "The Little Bird," a step-mother killed her step-daughter for breaking a milk jug and then baked her in a pie.[57] Similarly, "The Rose Tree" told how a step-mother cut off her daughter's head and then stewed the heart and liver for her husband's supper. A bird was then heard to sing:

> My wicked mother slew me,
> My dear father ate me,
> My littler brother whom I love,
> Sits below, and I sing above,
> Stick, stick, stone dead.[58]

From Marche, Italy, came the tale of the "Water in the Basket" where a step-mother beat her step-daughter every day and then poured boiling water on her in order to kill her. She mistook her own daughter for the girl, however, and killed her instead.[59]

In Yiddish folklore, a cruel step-mother told her step-son, Moyshele, that if he broke the pot she needed for cooking, she would chop off his head. Not satisfied with only this threat, she told Sheyndele, her step-daughter, that if she broke the plate she would cut off her leg. The family rooster broke the pot and the step-mother then cut off Myshele's head and cooked it for supper. He was later heard to sing:

> Murdered by my mother, eaten by my father, and Sheyndele, when they were done, sucked the marrow from my bones, and threw them out the window.[60]

An Iraqui tale, "The Little Red Fish and the Clog of Gold," told of a fisherman whose wife died and left him the object of marriage by many other women. He told one widow who desired to marry him that he would never marry for: "Stepmothers hate their husband's children even though their rivals are dead and buried."[61] He relented eventually, however, and the step-mother, true to his fears, later killed his daughter with a mixture of arsenic and lime so that her own daughter could marry the prince.[62]

Endnotes

1 . Ovid, Amores, II.14.31-33, 129.
2 . Dickens, A Tale of Two Cities, III.12, 427.
3 . Arnold, "Preface to Merope," On the Classical Tradition, 42.
4 . Plutarch, Moralia, 998.E
5 . Seneca, Medea, III.iii, Volume II, 604.
6 . Stern, "The Medea Complex: The Mother's Homicidal Wishes To Her Child," 330.
7 . Resnick, "Child Murder by Parents: A Psychiatric Review of Filicide," 329.
8 . Browne & Palmer, "A Preliminary Study of Schizophrenic Women Who Murdered Their Children," 71.
9 . Ibid., 71, 75.
10 . d'Orban, "Women Who Kill Their Children," 569.
11 . Bourget & Labelle, "Homicide, Infanticide, and Filicide," 668.
12 . Grillparzer, Medea, V, 111.
13 . Euripides, The Medea.
14 . Anouilh, Medea, 64.
15 . Ovid, Heroides, XII.163-168. See e.g., Ovid, Tristia, II.387-388, 83; Ovid, Metamorphoses, VII.398, 165.
16 . Euripides, Medea, 96-97, 62.
17 . Seneca, Medea, III.ii, 602.
18 . Ibid., III.ii.
19 . Ibid., V.i, 614.
20 . Propertius, The Elegies, 243.
21 . Seneca, Medea, III.i, 596.
22 . Ovid, Metamorphoses, VI.630-640, 150.
23 . Hamilton, Mythology, 271.
24 . Tatius, Clitophon and Leucippe, V.5.7-8, 247.
25 . Ovid, Amores, II.XIV.29-33, 129.
26 . Hauptmann, "Flagman Thiel," Teutonic Literature in English Translation, 124.
27 . Bacon, "Moral Philosophy," Third Part, VI, Opus Majus, 688-689.
28 . Seneca, Phaedra, III.ii, 655.
29 . In the version of the story by Racine, it is Phaedra's nurse, Oenone, who invokes Theseus' wrath with the false accusation of Hippolytus. Racine, Phaedra, V, 293.
30 . Cicero, De Officiis, III.XXV.94, 371.
31 . Seneca, Phaedra, IV.I, 661.
32 . Dillon, Early Irish Literature, 90.
33 . Ibid., 91.
34 . Petrovitch, Hero Tales & Legends of the Serbians, 206-208.
35 . Paredes, Folktales of Mexico, 127.
36 . Chicago Tribune (December 12, 1992): section 1, 10.
37 . Joshua 16:26.
38 . I Kings 16:34. The Living Bible, 299.
39 . I Kings 21:21.
40 . I Kings 21:29.
41 . II Samuel 12:14.
42 . 2 Chronicles 25:4. Ibid., 381.
43 . Job 21:19.

44 . Marlowe, The Jew of Malta, III.IV, 235.
45 . Juvenal, "A Gallery of Women," 630-631, The Satires of Juvenal, 118.
46 . Ibid., 636-637, 118.
47 . Frazer, The Dying God, 161-62.
48 . Grimm's Fairy Tales, 163-169.
49 . Rees & Rees, Celtic Heritage: Ancient Tradition in Ireland and Wales, 238.
50 . Dillon, Early Irish Literature, 26.
51 . Ibid., 64.
52 . Russian Fairy Tales (New York: Pantheon Books, 1965), 366.
53 . Ibid., 341.
54 . Paredes, Folktales of Mexico, 89-90.
55 . Briggs, A Dictionary of British Folk-Tales, Volume I, 199.
56 . Ibid., 250.
57 . Ibid., 378.
58 . Ibid., 472.
59 . Calvino, Italian Folk Tales, 353-55.
60 . Weinreich, Yiddish Folktales, 54-56.
61 . Bushnaq, Arab Folktales, 181.
62 . Ibid., 187.

CHAPTER XIV

MONEY

> The wet nurse system was "objectively a disguised form of infanticide."[1] "Another's Child is no more natural to a Nurse than a Plant to a strange and different Ground."[2]

These curt appraisals of the motives behind the common practice of new mothers hiring themselves out to breast feed the infants of other women was a view that was held by many European social critics during the Renaissance Era. While such expansive condemnations were clearly exaggerations, designed to make social change by ascribing the heinous actions of a few to all who breast fed for profit, it nevertheless indicates how many observers believed that widespread abuse permeated the operation so pervasively that the system itself should be dismantled. It is difficult to tell precisely how skewed were their concerns for while many wet-nurses throughout history were loving and genuinely interested in the welfare of the babies they cared for, many others did indeed view their profession only as a means to make a comfortable living. Driven by monetary greed, with little care for the welfare of their infant charges, the wages they received was often spent without any regard to providing proper service, and many infants assigned to their care died from malnutrition or disease.

Wet-nursing was not the only way in which infants have been used as a commodity in order to accrue income. Historically, the value of an infant's life was frequently determined by the forces of supply and demand, as well as the inevitability of death.[3] Many parents in ancient times sold their children for profit. The Thracians used to sell their children for export,[4] and even the early Christian Church realized that the sale of children was a reality of the time and did not pass judgment on its legality or morality.[5]

While both boys and girls were sold to the highest bidder as slaves, daughters were often commonly sold as part of a marriage pact. It was the welfare of the father, or of the family, that was determinative of who the prospective buyer would be, and the wishes of the child were seldom taken into consideration. In fact, the infant's chance of surviving after birth in various tribal communities was directly correlated with the economic incentive of future marriage. In Torres Straits, where families used to be kept small through the practice of abortion and infanticide, there was little female infanticide because daughters could be later sold to the highest bidder in marriage.[6] On Bank Island, and among the matrilineal Zuni, there was also a large bride price which kept the level of infanticide low.[7]

Without such economic value, some families, both ancient and modern, saw a newborn infant simply as a debit that could not fit into their tight budgetary plans. This concern was not only for the welfare of a biologic family unit, it also held true for an entire state. In 1954, Kingsley Davis wrote:

> A birth rate of 30 or more per 1000 inhabitants is a drag on any nation. It is certainly a drag from a short-run military point of view, because it loads the age structure with children who increase non-military costs; it withdraws women from the industrial labor force; it increases ill-health and mortality; and it places a great burden on educational and other facilities.[8]

To relieve this economic pressure, newborn infants were often killed. And if they were allowed to live, they were usually neglected. The misuse of children for economic advantage became legendary in England during the Renaissance era. According to Ruth Inglis, they were "starved, beaten, neglected and worked beyond their capacities by the poor for material gain."[9] They were maimed in order to beg, abandoned in order to allow the mother to maintain employment, and forced to work in dirty, dusty places like chimneys and coal mine tunnels where their small size allowed them to perform services adults could not render. If there was any way to make money off a child, history showed examples of that advantage being taken.

A. BURIAL SOCIETIES

One particularly grisly way in which the death of a child led to economic gain for the parents in nineteenth century England was a perverse use of expenses under an insurance plan to pay for funerals called "burial societies."[10] These programs paid a parent for the death of an insured child, and the amount received was often considerably more than the cost of the actual burial itself.[11] Where a funeral might cost between one to two pounds, a club generally paid three to five pounds (five to eight dollars) in the event of a child's death.[12]

And if this advantage was not enough, some parents joined several burial clubs for each child, and then collected the payments of all when the baby died. The supposed reasoning for this practice was insecurity in the financial stability of any particular club, but cases were documented where up to ten clubs were contracted to provide payment for the funeral expense.

By joining a number of burial clubs at the same time, a large amount of money could be made by withdrawing feeding from a young infant and allowing death to occur from what could be masked as medical disease.[13] The children were often removed from the breast after only a few weeks, or given unwholesome food and clothing and unduly exposed to the weather.[14] In one case, a woman was said to have refused medical care saying "no, thank you, he is in two burial clubs."[15]

Because the infant was often extremely wasted before medical assistance was sought, a physician could not state with certainty whether the causation was natural or deliberate.[16] The infant lived only a short period of time, and the physician signed the death certificate as best he could. Even if the scenario suggested infanticide, few medical practitioners looked more deeply into the case.[17] Police seldom reported the deaths to the coroner, relying on an 1808 statute which ensured that bodies were usually buried with all speed, leaving little time for investigation.[18] And there was no requirement for a medical practitioner to state a cause of death on a death certificate until the Births & Deaths Registration Act of 1874.[19] According to J. D. J. Havard: "The moral depravity and apathy to the fate of their children shown by the poor during this period was appalling."[20]

In addition to hastening death by withholding feedings from young infants, parents had ready access to a number of potent tonics which were legally available over the drugstore counter to treat ailing children. These medicines contained large amounts of cocaine or laudanum and could be given in amounts that would result in a painless, quiet demise.[21] The most common of these, "Godfrey's cordial," was usually started at age three to four weeks in order to quiet the child during restless nights. While some children obviously benefitted from the therapeutic effect, many physicians felt that over-usage of these drugs was the primary cause of death in children under the age of one year.[22]

The history of these clubs lasted over a century. They were initially formed under the Friendly Societies Act of 1793, and the numbers of applicants quickly reached incredible levels. By 1858 there were over 20,000 registered societies in England and Wales with over 2,000,000 members.[23] By 1891, Prudential had life insurance on over 2,400,000 children on its books.[24]

Social activists finally began to pressure the government to help correct this situation in the middle of the nineteenth century. The extent of the problem began to be discussed in 1843 with the report by Edwin Chadwick to the Home Secretary. In that expose he referred to the practice of burial insurance for children as a "bounty on neglect and infanticide."[25] The Friendly Society Act of 1846 provided that no insurance would be effected for children under the age of six years, but this only applied to burial clubs that came into existence after the Act was passed.[26]

Joseph Kay in 1850 admonished that:

> There can be no doubt, that a great part of the poorer classes of this country are sunk in such a frightful depth of hopelessness, misery and utter degradation, that even mothers forget their affection for their helpless little offspring and kill them, as a butcher does his lambs, in order to make money by the murder, and therewith lessen their pauperism and misery.[27]

Yet, despite these claims, a Select Committee in 1854, did not find the problem extensive since they could only find four persons having been convicted of murdering their children for this reason from 1841 to 1853.[28] In 1861, the respected medical journal Lancet ran a series of articles which berated the continued usage of these burial clubs. They pointed out that a father could be held financially responsible for the maintenance of his child, as long as the child was alive, but was not punishable for its death should it perish through his neglect.[29] Even if a father was found to be guilty of negligent care, he still could actually gain a financial savings from the death of his infant! Statistics were pointed to which showed that while infants of laboring men outside the clubs died at the rate of 36% before reaching age five, children of the same age who were insured in the burial clubs died at the rate of 62 to 64%.[30] Statistics from a relatively healthy town like Preston, remarkable for the health and longevity of its inhabitants, showed that the child death rate in the burial clubs was four times that of the poor hovels of Dorsetshire laborers.[31] One common expression of the time was: "Aye, aye, that child will not live, it is in the burial club!"[32] Little wonder, one editor wrote, that infants should be found dead through the avarice of fathers.[33] This situation was "a grave question of State."[34]

That most of the problem was due to poverty was revealed by closer analysis of its prevalence. As the evidence of abuse continued to mount, others kept up the cry for reform. In 1872, Charles Cameron, editor of the North British Daily Mail, called the practice productive of an immense amount of crime, and is a direct encouragement to parties to put children out of the way for the sake of the benefit."[35] In 1874, the Fourth Report of the Commissioners Appointed to Inquire into Friendly and Benefit Building Societies heard from witness after witness how parents would criminally neglect their children to the point of death in order to gain the financial payments.[36] But still no action was taken by the governmental authorities.

Finally, in 1888, the London Society for the Prevention of Cruelty to Children was formed by the Reverend Benjamin Waugh and one of its first roles was to spearhead an attack against child life insurance.[37] Progressively, the legislature began to pass more stringent acts to prevent cruelty to children in 1889, 1894 and 1904,[38] and the abuse finally began to end with the passage of the Comprehensive Children's Bill in 1908.[39]

B. WET-NURSES

As pointed out earlier, another way for a mother to make money was to be hired out as a wet-nurse either to private patrons, or foundling homes.[40] This practice dated back to the very beginnings of modern civilization. One of the earliest references to the use of other women as a source of breast feeding was in a Sumerian lullaby, from the third millennium BC, where the wife of Shulgi, ruler of Ur, sang to her son of a "nursemaid, joyous of heart" who would suckle him after birth.[41]

Ancient societies widely utilized wet-nurses, and prominent physicians highly recommended the practice. With our modern emphasis on breast feeding by the child's own mother, this attitude on the part of the medical profession may seem to be a strange recommendation. But we must remember that baby food was otherwise very difficult to prepare, and the basic sustenance for the first few years of life came from mother's milk. Animals, such as goats and cows, were often providers of milk as well, but there was no capability of storage, and infections from this source were common. Because of the long period of time the mother would have to breast feed her child, there was a need to have some type of supplement to reduce the resultant strain. If a family was not wealthy enough to hire a wet-nurse, they were forced to make do with "other animals' milk, honey, butter, mashed bread, farinha, chopped meat, or other substitutes."[42]

Soranus, the Greek physician who practiced in Rome during the second century A.D., wrote in his treatise *Gynecology*, about how to select the proper wet-nurse:

> One should choose a wet nurse not younger than twenty nor older than forty years, who has already given birth twice or thrice, who is healthy, of good habitus, of large frame, and of a good color. Her breasts should be of medium size, lax, soft and unwrinkled, the nipples neither big nor too small and neither too compact nor too porous and discharging milk overabundantly. She should be self-controlled, sympathetic and not ill-tempered, a Greek and tidy.[43]

From the very start, concern over transference of undesired traits from the wet-nurse to the infant was apparent.

Religious teachings generally recommended that the mother provide breast feeding for her own child. The rabbinic teachings of the Talmud held that a child should be breast fed for twenty-four months, but there is no reference that utilizing a wet-nurse was considered a sin.[44] Philo even described how the sister of Moses told the king's daughter, after the infant was found adrift in the river, that she knew of a woman, in reality her mother, who had lately been with child, and could be hired "ostensibly for wages."[45] It was obvious that this was primarily to function as a wet-nurse.

The wages a woman could expect for this service was quite appealing. In 13 B.C., a contract for wet-nursing in Egypt called for sixteen payments of ten silver drachmas and two cotyls of oil every month.[46] This was a very stable income for women whose job opportunities were otherwise limited.

But as with any lucrative business, avarice often became an early ancillary motive. Plutarch admonished that most nursemaids were insincere and "love for pay."[47] He said that women should nurse their infants themselves for they will do it with greater care and affection.[48] Even if there were twins, he continued, there was no need for assistance since nature fashioned women's breasts double to provide an adequate source of nutrition.[49]

What caused alarm to many critics, was the frequent association of a child's death with feeding by a wet-nurse. In the *Code of Hammurabi*, from the second millennium B.C., there was even reference to how such a charge should be punished:

> When a seignior gave his son to a nurse and that son has died in the care of the nurse, if the nurse has then made a contract for another son without the knowledge of his father and mother, they shall prove it against her and they shall cut off her breast because she made a contract for another son without the knowledge of his father and mother.[50]

It is obvious that Hammurabi correlated the death of the child with the opportunity to receive higher wages.

Thomas of Chobham, in the thirteenth century, found such a likely correlation between the hiring of a wet-nurse and the resultant death of the child, that he equated a refusal of a mother to nurse her child as a sin equal to that of overlaying.[51] He also warned that a wet-nurse, in order to provide adequate milk for her charges, would have to deny some to her own child.[52] This easily could explain the high mortality rate among the children of such mothers and if the woman was careful to adequately feed her own offspring first, then there would be a deficient supply for the other infants.

Erasmus, in 1543, vilified mothers who did not nurse their own children and compared them with those who exposed the child in the wilds. "There's no class of living creatures that does not nurse its own young", he chided.[53] It was wrong, and also fatal, to not breast feed your own:

> Isn't it a kind of exposure to hand over the tender infant, still red from its mother, drawing breath from its mother, crying for

> its mother's care – a sound said to move even wild beasts – to a woman who perhaps has neither good health nor good morals and who, finally, may be much more concerned about a bit of money than about a whole baby?[54]

In Tudor England, if a mother refused to nurse her child, it indicated that the woman had neglected her duties. Genetic inheritance had not yet become accepted, and many scientists believed that traits like virtue and vice were transmitted through the mother's milk. By using a wet-nurse, there was the possibility of degradation of the child's behavior through the menial tendencies of the nurse.[55] Joseph Addison warned that:

> Many instances may be produced from good Authorities and daily Experience, that Children actually suck in the several Passions and depraved Inclinations of their Nurses, as Anger, Malice, Fear, Melancholy, Sadness, Desire, and Aversion.[56]

While short-term feedings were not likely to be dangerous, the mother was warned not to obviate her natural responsibilities beyond those brief interruptions.[57]

Despite all of these antagonistic professional opinions, the practice of putting to children to wet-nurse was very widespread. While women found it difficult, impractical, and at times impossible, to nurse their own children, men continued to find their decisions abhorrent. In 1600, the French physician Guillemeau said that: "There is no difference between a woman who refuses to nurse her own children and one that kills her child as soon as she has conceived."[58] Similarly, in 1748, Dr. William Cadogan, the esteemed British physician, noted that: "The ancient custom of exposing them to wild beasts or drowning them would certainly be much quicker and more humane way of despatching them."[59]

Even the great French humanist, Rousseau, who calmly admitted that he gave his own children to foundling homes, lamented how mothers had despised their first duty and refused to nurse their own children. They would contrive all sorts of reasons for neglecting this task, and the nurses they found were of no benefit to a child. His rationale was simple: "The woman who nurses another's child in place of her own is a bad mother; how can she be a good nurse?"[60]

Joseph Addison, the English essayist and poet, was even more vitriolic in his attack on the system of wet-nursing. In an essay published in The Spectator in 1711, he criticized mothers who hired such nurses:

> It is unmerciful to see, that a Woman endowed with all the

> Perfections and Blessings of Nature, can, as soon as she is delivered, turn off her innocent, tender, and helpless Infant, and give it up to a Woman that is (ten thousand to one) neither in Health nor good Condition, neither sound in Mind nor Body, that has neither Honour nor Reputation, neither Love nor Pity for the poor Babe, but more Regard for the Money than for the Whole Child, and never will take further Care of it than what by all the encouragement of Money and Presents she is forced to.[61]

But throughout much of eighteenth century Europe, "wet nursing, like prostitution, was one of the two ever-available sources of income for poor young women."[62] In France, up to 90% of the infants born to urban mothers were put out to wet-nurse.[63] In general, wet-nurses were paid twice that of regular household help or dry-nurses.[64] They could not afford to lose this financial base, even if it meant that they had to dispose of their own children. In essence, they were income producing property to be rented out as either whores or wet-nurses.[65]

In England, the practice reached incredible proportions and the nurses, ofttimes referred to as "baby-farmers," would care for more infants than they would be capable of feeding. One reason that they became so popular was the widespread belief among the medical profession that breast feeding could produce a serious illness in certain women. One of these, the insanity of lactation, was felt to be due to a state of exhaustion which developed from the rigors of breast feeding:

> Many mothers, who for various reasons are totally unfitted to do so, undertake the nursing of their children, and their systems are unable to withstand the severe strain which lactation entails, with the result that the attack of insanity develops.[66]

As late as 1927, J. Stanley Hopkins wrote:

> Childbirth and lactation entail a severe stress on the female sex, and, under certain circumstances, are liable to cause insanity, during the course of which attempts at infanticide and suicide are common.[67]

The mortality rate among these baby-farmers was from 75-90%.[68] Most of the children were illegitimate, and up to 35,000 a year were cared for in this fashion.[69] The nurse would frequently be paid from three to five shillings per week per child, and when responsible wet-nurses would reach their limit of three to six infants, they would usually place the rest with the baby-farmers.[70] Hospitals would advertise the availability of mothers whose infants died at birth as wet-nurses.[71]

In the novel *Esther Waters*, George Moore related how the young destitute Waters was forced to hire out as a wet-nurse after the birth of her baby at fifteen shillings per week, and then paid six shillings per week to have her own child cared for by such a woman. This, despite the fact that "I've always heard that children die that are put out to nurse."[72] The sequence was bluntly described:

> The children of two poor girls had been sacrificed so that this rich woman's child might be saved . . . Fine folks like you pays the money, and Mrs. Spires and her like gets rid of the poor little things. Change the milk a few times, a little neglect, and the poor servant girl is spared the trouble of bringing up her baby and can make a handsome child of the rich woman's little starveling.[73]

Disraeli wrote of this practice in *Sibyl*, published in 1845, and noted how their expenses were quite low:

> Laudanum and treacle, administered in the shape of some popular elixir, affords these innocents a brief taste of the sweets of existence, and keeping them quiet, prepares them for the silence of their impending grave.[74]

In 1865, the trial of Charlotte Winsor, a Devonshire entrepreneur who "smothered illegitimate infants for a fee," created a sensation in England and began the long process towards reform.[75] Drs. Ernest Hart and Alfred Wiltshire placed an advertisement in the newspaper for a nurse to assume responsibility for an unwanted bastard child and established beyond doubt "that many of these women carried on the business (of adoption) with a deliberate knowledge that the children would die very quickly."[76] Along with other laymen and physicians, the Infant Life Protection Society was formed and, eventually, the 1872 Infant Life Protection Act was passed to correct some of the grotesque criminal excesses. It was greatly aided by the appearance of common, and affordable, milk substitutes in the 1860s.[77]

One unique twist on this practice was said to have occurred in Tasmania where dogs were so valuable that women deserted their infants at times for the sake of suckling puppies.[78] In addition, the modern epidemic of drug dependence has taken its toll on children of addicts who are either damaged by the drug which is transported transplacental or through breast milk, or by the violent actions of the parent while under the influence of the drug.[79]

C. SLAVERY

The selling of children for slavery was a common practice in ancient society. In the Old Testament, such sales were not considered a sin, but rather a necessity that was tolerated as long as there were regulations governing the transaction. Under normal rules, women had fewer liberties than men: "If a man sells his daughter as a slave, she shall not be freed at the end of six years as the men are."[80]

The primary reason for the biblical sales were economic, as described by Nehemiah: "What was happening was that families who ran out of money for food had to sell their children or mortgage their fields, vineyards, and homes to these rich men."[81] The Mikilita interpreted the Biblical passages as allowing for the sale of a daughter by the father up to the time of her maidenhood. The mother, however, was not allowed to sell her daughter, or a father to sell his son.[82] The Babylonian *Talmud* agreed that a daughter could be sold for money.[83] After marriage, however, the daughter was not able to be sent into servitude by the parent.[84]

The Greek historian Herodotus related how in ancient Babylon the custom held that once a year the girls of the village who were ripe for marriage were brought together and sold in a great auction.[85] After the conquest of Babylon, and the general ruin which followed, there was even greater pressure to sell children in order to obtain money for food. A common saying was that a parent "who is destitute of a livelihood prostitutes his female children."[86]

In Greece, the sale of children was widespread until forbidden by law during the direction of Solon.[87] The Roman *patriae potestas*, in addition to recognizing the right of a father to determine whether his legitimate infant was to live or die, also permitted a sale for profit. Emperor Constantine, in 313 A.D., legitimized this authority by edict in order to reduce the numbers of infants being abandoned. He felt that selling a child was preferable to destroying it. If a father sold his offspring, he did not permanently lose his *potestas* but could reclaim the child by payment of the cost of upbringing at a later date.[88] This satisfied the concerns of the biologic parents, but created dissension among the families who purchased the children. They felt that their expenditures should have given them a greater right of retention. Constantine amended the rules in 323 A.D., and added regulations which did not hinder the legality of the sale, but made reclamation less available.[89]

In *The Comedy of Errors,* by William Shakespeare, Egeon, a merchant of Syracuse, buys twin sons born at the same time as his own children to grow up with them as slaves. The parents were "exceeding poor," and simply unable to bear the burden of the children.[90]

Christianity did not accept the sale of children as an ethical transaction.

The early Church Fathers took a strong moral stand against the mistreatment of children who were seen as belonging to God, and not to the parent. There could be no *patriae potestas* for the true father was the Divine Father, the Almighty Himself. Nevertheless, the church recognized that the reality of life was a constant struggle for survival, and occasionally there would be the need to sell a child rather than watch it die of starvation. St. Basil of Caesarea described this situation with compassion:

> He turns his glance at length on his children: by selling them he might put off death. Imagine the struggle between the desperation of hunger and the bonds of parenthood. The former threatens him with a horrible death; nature pulls him back, persuading him to die with his children. Often he starts to do it; each time he stops himself; finally he is overcome, conquered by necessity and inexorable need.[91]

While finding pity in the actions of the parent, Basil was outraged by the conduct of the auctioneer:

> After a thousand tears (the father) comes to sell a beloved child, but no pity moves you; you do not defer to nature. Hunger has made him desperate; you delay and dissemble, prolonging his agony. He asks for the price of food in return for his own heart.[92]

St. Ambrose, the bishop of Milan in the fourth century A.D., came to a similar conclusion. He found that parents did have some justification for their need to sell a child, but the creditors position was very inhumane.[93]

Valentinian III, in 451 A.D., began to change the complacency of the church towards these immoral actions. He issued an edict against the sale of children, noting that a very terrible famine had recently devastated all of Italy, and: "People have been reduced to selling their children and relatives to escape the danger of imminent death."[94] While mortal life was not to be deprecated, concerns over remaining obedient to the teachings of Jesus Christ were even more important. It would do no good to assuage the misery facing us here on earth and now with conduct that would lead to an eternity of suffering in Hell. The selling of children was a sin that damned the parent forever.

His remonstrance, however, was not quickly heeded. During the sixth century in Italy, a number of laws allowed for the sale of children in time of need.[95] Cassiodorus described a great fair in southern Italy where the peasants sold their children at a market.[96] Dante commented on this practice when he witnessed in *Purgatory*, as an example of the sin of Avarice, the soul of a man who was willing to part with his own child for an appropriate fee: "I see (him) selling his daughter and bargaining over her as pirates do with other slave-women."[97]

Of course the economic value of a child was not only in the potential sale, but also in income generated by his labor. Visigothic law, during the sixth century A.D., allowed a parent to put their infants in the care of another, as long as there was payment given until the child was ten years: "After that, nothing further is to be paid, since the child himself can work off his support through his own labor."[98] Medieval children were expected to begin to be able to fend for themselves at a very early age.

The *Annals of Ulster*, during the early Middle Ages in Ireland, recorded sales of children in order to save their parents from destitution.[99] In the seventh century A.D., the *Penitential* of Theodore noted that a father, "driven by necessity," may sell his son into slavery without sin.[100] The ninth century chronicles of Languedoc related that both Spanish Christians and Jews sold some of their offspring into slavery after the economic disruptions of the Muslim invasion.[101]

In Ireland, at the start of the twelfth century, desperate parents sold their children during a famine according to contemporary chroniclers.[102] Similar sales also occurred in England according to some sources.[103] David Hume explained that:

> To rear a child in London, till he could be serviceable, would cost much dearer, than to buy one of the same age from Scotland or Ireland; where he had been bred in a cottage, covered with rags, and fed on oatmeal or potatoes.[104]

Like young saplings, these children were reared only to be sold on the world market. He further concluded that:

> To kill ones own child is shocking to nature, and must therefore be somewhat unusual; but to turn over the care of him upon others, is very tempting to the natural indolence of mankind.[105]

In Germany, the *Schwabenspiegel* civil code, authorized:

> If a man sells his child for a reason that is legally binding, he acts properly. But he should not sell him to someone who might kill him, or sell him into prostitution.[106]

Another section allowed the recovery of an abandoned child if the parent first repaid any cost incurred.[107] The Germanic states allowed this sale of children far down into the Middle Ages.[108]

The *Siete Partidas*, which supplanted the Castilian *Fuero Real* in Spain during the thirteenth century, upheld the right of parents to sell children under trying circumstances: "A father who is oppressed with great hunger or such utter poverty that he has no other recourse can sell or pawn his children in order to obtain food."[109] This authority did not extend to the mother.

In more modern times, Theodore White, during his travels to China as a wartime correspondent during the Sino-Japan conflict, reported on the miserable conditions among the poor peasantry. Severe food shortages had led to extreme hardship, and in some areas there was famine of great proportions. In Chungking: "Families sold their children; nine-year-old boys brought four hundred Chinese dollars, four-year-old boys two hundred dollars."[110] When one had to survive, even a child became expendable.

In Japan, the sale of children during times of food shortage dates back to the seventh century.[111] During the Edo period (1600-1868 A.D.) such transactions were behind many courtesans and prostitutes but finally became illegal in 1872.[112]

In nineteenth century American literature, the killing of children by slave mothers, in order to prevent their having to grow up in such a painful and unjust environment, was presented as an altruistic act that induced compassion, rather than revulsion, in the reader's mind.[113] Probably the most well-known description was by Harriet Beecher Stowe in *Uncle Tom's Cabin*, the book which helped to divide the country between North and South over the economic issue of slave labor. In that fictional tale, Cassy tells Tom how her first two children were sold into slavery by a white man who she had been forced to live with because he had threatened to harm her children if she did not agree. After he reneged on his promise, she tried to buy her children back with the help of another man who befriended her but failed and never saw her children again. When she had a son by her new owner, she made up her mind that she "would never again let a child live to grow up!"[114] She gave the infant some laudanum and then suffocated it at her bosom as he slept. This empathetic action contrasted sharply with the attitude of the white slave-holders at the time who primarily saw such killings as criminal acts which were secondary to the vices inherent in the Black slave race.[115]

Endnotes

1 . Badinter, Mother Love, Myth and Reality, 112.
2 . Addison, The Spectator, 246 (December 12, 1711), Volume II, 455.
3 . Rose, The Massacre of the Innocents: Infanticide in Britain 1800-1939, 5.
4 . Herodotus, The History, V.6, 358.
5 . Boswell, "Exposition and Oblatio: The Abandonment of Children and the Ancient and Medieval Family," 16-17.
6 . Aptekar, Anjea: Infanticide, Abortion & Contraception in Savage Society, 41.
7 . Ibid., 42.
8 . Davis, "The Demographic Foundations of National Power," 74.
9 . Inglis, Sins of the Fathers, 18.
10 . Forbes, "Deadly Parents: Child Homicide in Eighteenth- and Nineteenth-Century England," 188-199.
11 . Ibid., 189.
12 . Havard, The Detection of Secret Homicide, 52.
13 . "Infanticide," 314-315.
14 . Ibid., 314.
15 . Havard, The Detection of Secret Homicide, 53.
16 . Forbes, "Deadly Parents: Child Homicide in Eighteenth- and Nineteenth-Century England," 196.
17 . "Infanticide," 314.
18 . Havard, The Detection of Secret Homicide, 58.
19 . 37 & 38 Vict. c. 88, S. 20. Ibid., 69.
20 . Ibid., 52.
21 . Forbes, "Deadly Parents: Child Homicide in Eighteenth- and Nineteenth-Century England," 191.
22 . Havard, The Detection of Secret Homicide, 53.
23 . Rose, The Massacre of the Innocents: Infanticide in Britain 1800-1939, 136-37.
24 . Ibid., 139.
25 25. Forbes, "Deadly Parents: Child Homicide in Eighteenth- and Nineteenth-Century England," 190.
26 . 9 & 10 Vict. c. 27. Havard, The Detection of Secret Homicide, 59.
27 . Langer, "Infanticide: A Historical Survey," footnote 24, 365.
28 . Forbes, "Deadly Parents: Child Homicide in Eighteenth- and Nineteenth-Century England," 190.
29 . "Infanticide," 315.
30 . "Premiums for Infanticide," Lancet 2 (1861): 299.
31 . Ibid.
32 . Sauer, "Infanticide and Abortion in Nineteenth-Century Britain," 88.
33 . One could actually make 104 pounds sterling by the infants death. "Infanticide," 315.
34 . "Premiums For Infanticide," 299.
35 . Forbes, "Deadly Parents: Child Homicide in Eighteenth- and Nineteenth-Century England," 192.
36 . Ibid., 194.
37 . Rose, The Massacre of the Innocentes: Infanticide in Britain 1800-1939, 151.
38 . Forbes, "Deadly Parents: Child Homicide in Eighteenth- and Nineteenth-Century England," 198.

39 . Rose, The Massacre of the Innocents: Infanticide in Britain 1800-1939), 158.
40 . Moseley, "The History of Infanticide in Western Society," 346.
41 . Fildes, Breasts, Bottles & Babies, 6.
42 . Levenstein, "`Best For Babies' Or `Preventable Infanticide?' The Controversy Over Artificial Feeding of Infants in America, 1880-1920," 76.
43 . Soranus, Gynecology, II.XII.19, 90-91.
44 . Kethuboth, Gemara, V.60a.
45 . Philo, "On The Life Of Moses," I.III.17, Loeb Classical Library, 285.
46 . Fildes, Breasts, Bottles & Babies, 9.
47 . Plutarch, "The Education of Children," 5, Moralia, Volume I, 15.
48 . Ibid., 13-15.
49 . Ibid., 15.
50 . "The Code of Hammurabi," 194, Ancient Near East Texts, 175.
51 . Kellum, "Infanticide in England in the Later Middle Ages," 370.
52 . Ibid., footnote 19, 384.
53 . Erasmus, "The New Mother," Colloquies, 273.
54 . Ibid.
55 . Byman, "Child Raising and Melancholia in Tudor England," 71.
56 . Addison, The Spectator, December 12, 1711, Volume II, 455.
57 . Ruhrah, Pediatrics of the Past, 79.
58 . Lorence, "Parents and Children in Eighteenth Century Europe," 3.
59 . Ibid., 3-4.
60 . Rousseau, Emile, I, 17.
61 . Addison, The Spectator, December 12, 1711, Volume II, 454-55.
62 . Piers, Infanticide, 47.
63 . Hrdy, "Fitness Tradeoffs in the History and Evolution of Delegated Mothering with Special Reference to Wet-Nursing, Abandonment and Infanticide," 416.
64 . Fildes, Breasts, Bottles & Babies, 162.
65 . Piers, Infanticide, 47-48.
66 . Hopwood, "Child Murder and Insanity," 96.
67 . Ibid., 95.
68 . Curgenven, "On Baby-Farming and the Registration of Nurses," 3.
69 . Ibid., 6.
70 . Ibid., 4.
71 . Thearle & Gregory, "Child Abuse in Nineteenth Century Queensland," 95.
72 . Moore, Esther Waters, XVIII, 120.
73 . Ibid., XVIII, 123, 126-7.
74 . Disraeli, Sybil, 131.
75 . Behlmer, "Ernest Hart and the Social Thrust of Victorian Medicine," 712.
76 . Ibid., 713.
77 . Levenstein, "`Best For Babies' Or `Preventable Infanticide?' The Controversy Over Artificial Feeding of Infants in America," 77.
78 . Aptekar, Anjea: Infanticide, Abortion & Contraception in Savage Society, 65.
79 . One woman was convicted of endangerment after she disregarded warnings from her social worker not to breast feed if she took drugs and then caused the death of her two month old son. New York Times (September 11, 1994): section L, 36.
80 . Exodus 21:7. The Living Bible, 66.
81 . Nehemiah 5:2-3. Ibid., 406.
82 . Mekilita de-Rabbi Ishmael, Volume III, 19-20.

83 . Kiddushin, Gemara, I.3b.
84 . Ibid., II.45a.
85 . Herodotus, The History, I.196, 122.
86 . Ibid., I.196, 123.
87 . Todd, The Primitive Family as an Educational Agency, 116.
88 . Boswell, The Kindness of Strangers, 69-70.
89 . Code of Justinian, 8.46.10. Ibid., 70.
90 . Shakespeare, The Comedy of Errors, I.i.56.
91 . Hexaemeron 6, Homilia VIII. Boswell, The Kindness of Strangers, 165.
92 . Destruam 4, Homilia in Illud Lucae. Ibid., 166.
93 . De Tobia 1.8.29. Ibid., 168-69.
94 . TC, Novels of Valentinian 33. Ibid., 170.
95 . Ibid., 201.
96 . Cassiodorus Senator, Variarum liber 8.33. Ibid., 201-202.
97 . Dante, "Purgatory," XX.80-81, The Divine Comedy, 261.
98 . LV 4.4.3. Boswell, The Kindness of Strangers, 206.
99 . Ibid., 214.
100. 2.13.1. Ibid., 220.
101. Annales Anianenses. Ibid., 217.
102. Ibid., 281.
103. Ibid.
104. Hume, "On the Populousness of Ancient Nations," Essays Moral, Political & Literary, 387.
105. Ibid., 400.
106. Boswell, The Kindness of Strangers, 326.
107. Ibid.
108. Sumner, Folkways, 257.
109. 4.17.8. Boswell, The Kindness of Strangers, 328.
110. White, In Search of History, 152.
111. The request was first made by peasants in 676 A.D. but not granted until 691 A.D. Kitahara, "Childhood in Japanese Culture," 46.
112. Ibid., 47.
113. Liggins, "Death is Better Than Slavery: Representations of Infanticide in Nineteenth Century American Literature," 295
114. Stowe, Uncle Tom's Cabin, Chapter XXXIV, "The Quadroon's Story," 427.
115. Ibid., 297.

CHAPTER XV

DEPRESSION & INSANITY

"Thy sorrow I will greatly multiply by thy conception; children thou shalt bring in sorrow forth."[1]

A. POSTPARTUM DEPRESSION

If one accepts the surviving manuscripts of the Old Testament as the true account of the history of mankind, then the story of Adam and Eve, and God's choice of punishment for their forewarned disobedience, aptly explains the reasons why women have had to endure the painful agonies of childbirth. If the Bible is simply good literature, we are faced with an unsatisfactory evolutionary dilemma.

In the process of giving birth to a new human being, we have an event – the generation of life, the reproduction of the species – which by all rights should be confronted with expectant joy and composure. Childbirth should logically, at least from a scientific perspective, be a naturally pleasant process, or at least a painless one, since the very survival of the human race depends on continual voluntary fecundity. How can one expect women to have more than one child if the mechanism is so distressing and dangerous?

The Bible provides a satisfactory answer to its faithful followers. The reason for the travail was that Eve did not listen to the Lord's command, and took the apple from the Tree of Knowledge after being assured by the snake that the command was meant to be broken. Once she encouraged Adam to eat the forbidden fruit, she was destined to then "bear children in intense pain and suffering."[2] John Milton, in the quotation at the start of this chapter, interpreted the Lord's design to be more than just physical pain from the act of childbirth, and intended to include sorrow and despair.

Milton's prophecy has proven uncannily true. Childbirth has indeed frequently caused sorrow and despair, along with numerous other problems, for many mothers throughout the history of human civilization. Not only can a young mother expect severe emotional stress for many months both during and after her pregnancy and delivery, but at times the process may even lead to permanent insanity.[3] Modern data from studies of normal pregnancy indicate that from 20-40 percent of women report emotional disturbance, or some type of cognitive dysfunction, in the early postpartum period.[4] Maternity blues, which is not considered a psychiatric disorder but can lead to crying and irritability, may be seen in from 50-80 percent of women during the first postpartum week.[5]

New mothers frequently complain of irritability, dysphoria, anxiety, emotional lability, tearfulness, and fatigue, especially if they are delivering for the first time. For many, these complaints are only a minor inconvenience which pass after a short period of time. But while the majority of women suffer only a transient emotional letdown, about 8-12% will develop a more serious depression which can lead to thoughts of suicide and desires to harm their baby.[6] Although infanticide itself may be a clinical rarity, "intrusive infanticidal ideation is clinically common."[7] If the mother has a previous history of clinical depression, there is an even greater likelihood of exacerbation during the postpartum period.[8] This can exist for up to one year following delivery, although the highest risk for severe problems requiring hospitalization lasts about one month. Where the frequency of postpartum psychosis is about 1 in 500 in primiparous women, it is about 1 in 3 for those who have been previously affected.[9]

As part of this adaptive reaction, it is common for a new mother to blame her baby not only for the discomfort she had to go through during the delivery process, but also for the pregnancy and the postpartum depression itself.[10] These women are torn between a natural, inbred love for their child, and instincts of anger and distress over their feelings of melancholy and pain. Robert Briffault believed that the first instinctive reaction of the mother to a newborn infant was one of revulsion, and not of love:

> If the mother has not followed Froebel's exhortations and come to love her child before birth, there is a brief interval occasionally dangerous to the child before the maternal instinct is full aroused.[11]

It is during this early period of resentment that the danger of infanticide is most evident. Of all children that are killed by their mothers during the first year of life, almost 50% perish on the first day following birth.[12]

In addition to the severe emotional stress produced by these series of events, physiologic changes may also be a causative factor in postpartum depression. Lactation has long been linked to the development of depressive symptoms, and investigators believe that it is the major reason for extension of these complaints beyond the immediate postpartum period.[13] Breast feeding produces hormonal changes which delay the onset of cyclical ovulation as a means to prolong the period of time that the breast tissue can continue to produce milk. In many human societies, this supplementary provision continues for up to two to four years because of the limited food supply and slow development of infant growth.

Some evidence has also accumulated that the use of ergot alkaloids during the purpureum may increase the risk of infanticide by affecting the mother's psychological state.[14] But most investigators believe that hormonal alterations from the pregnancy termination itself are what increases the infanticidal tendency. Recent studies have centered on the role of alterations in steroid metabolism, biogenic amines and the adenosine phosphate system.[15] Some authors have argued that the change in endocrinal activity could explain infanticide in humans as it appears to do in laboratory animals.[16] In the immediate postpartum period there is a rapid drop in estrogen and progesterone levels, and a large increase in the hormone prolactin. This correlates with the peak presentation of postpartum psychosis, but clinical trials have not substantiated the causative role for these hormonal variations.[17] Other possible causations include high levels of cyclic adenosine monophosphate, rapid drop in the level of cortisol, persistent increase of alpha-2-adrenoceptor, low levels of tryptophan, decreased endorphins, or alterations in thyroid hormone.[18]

Psychiatric classifications of postpartum depression have evolved over the years; in the nineteenth century, physicians categorized the mental disorders connected with gestation as: insanity of pregnancy, which was related to the stress of the pregnancy itself; puerperal insanity, which was due to the delivery; and insanity of lactation, which developed during breast feeding.[19]

The insanity of lactation was felt to be due to a state of exhaustion which developed from the rigors of breast feeding. It was during this period that child-murder occurred most frequently.[20] As late as 1927, J. Stanley Hopwood wrote:

> Childbirth and lactation entail a severe stress on the female sex, and, under certain circumstances, are liable to cause insanity, during the course of which attempts at infanticide and suicide are common.[21]

He determined that over 25% of all murders committed in London by people considered not responsible for their actions were perpetrated by insane nursing mothers.[22]

John Baker reported in 1902, from the State Asylum at Broadmoor in England, that 5% of infanticides occurred from insanity of pregnancy, 35% from puerperal insanity and 60% from the insanity of lactation.[23] The puerperal cases were generally single mothers who had the highest recovery rate of their insanity, and were generally discharged after a comparatively short detention.[24]

Because of the widespread acceptance within the medical community that the effects of pregnancy and delivery could temporarily alter the reasoning of a new mother's mind, the claim of insanity as a legal defense to infanticide was often assured. Where many seventeenth century juries would pardon the murderess by a finding of "temporary phrenzy,"[25] the word for the defense in the nineteenth century was "puerperal mania."[26] The result of this mental disorder classification in England, as well as other countries which followed their legal standard, was that the killing of a newborn infant in the postnatal state became strictly defined under the term "infanticide," and a charge of murder was not an appropriate consideration. The English approach was summarized by one legislator as necessary because these were cases where:

> Disturbed women who, when they have recovered from the effects of childbirth or lactation, return to reality to discover that the blessings of motherhood have evaded them, that for them it has been a curse. A mother returns from her confused or withdrawn condition to discover that she has killed her own child.[27]

Today, the psychiatric syndromes associated with pregnancy are categorized as postpartum blues, puerperal psychosis and depression. Postpartum blues (baby-blues, maternity blues) is the emotional lability and tearfulness which characteristically occurs in the first week or two after delivery. It is found in up to 80% of all mothers, but is generally short-lived, and is not associated with any significant danger of infant harm.[28]

Postpartum, or puerperal, psychosis is most likely to appear in the first few weeks after delivery. It is similar to cases described by Baker in 1902 where women in the postpartum period developed a form of mania associated with the termination of the flow of breast milk, disappearance of the lochia, and elevated temperatures from non-infectious causes. Manifestations of injury in the English series included cases where: "The child's head is dashed against the bed-post, or a pair of scissors is driven into the brain, or the throat is cut, or the head battered in with a poker."[29]

This category of psychosis is the most serious type of postpartum depression, and is the one most likely to be associated with infanticide. It has its peak incidence between day three and day fourteen, and occurs in about 1-2 mothers per 1000 births. The risk of danger to the mother or infant in this condition is so great that as soon as the diagnosis is suspected the mother should be hospitalized immediately.[30] The illness is characterized by agitation, restlessness, insomnia, mood lability, tearfulness, elation, progression to a state of confusion and then a fulminate psychotic episode with signs of mania and delirium.[31]

The final category, depression associated with pregnancy, is classified as an atypical psychotic syndrome, DSM-III-R, and does not have any unique feature of depression except the timing associated with the delivery of a child.[32] Its prevalence is higher in women with a previous history of affective illness and while most cases will last for an average of six to eight weeks, many others will continue for up to one year after delivery.[33] Moderate depression, seen for as long as two years, can still be classified as secondary to the postpartum state.

The intensity of the depression in these patients is quite varied. Some mothers enter such a severe state of estrangement that they turn entirely away from other people and are unable to experience them as fellow human beings. When this syndrome of severe withdrawal occurs, the lives of her young children are particularly endangered.[34]

Another more common reaction is one of hopelessness and insecurity. According to the family members of one young woman who tried to poison her children:

> What she really wants is a decent husband. She's overwhelmed by the fact she has three kids to take care of alone.[35]

Homicides during this melancholic period are generally from drownings or poisonings rather than violent deaths.[36]

In America, infanticide is not restricted to a particular age of victim, or sex of offender, although an attempt to raise this issue was introduced in the United States Senate by Senator Presley in 1989.[37] When a child is killed by its mother, the case is handled as a homicide and in states where the death penalty is available, it is possible that a capital punishment will be applied. Claiming Postpartum Depression as a defense is somewhat hampered since the classification under American Psychiatric Association is as an atypical psychotic syndrome, DSM-III-R, and does not have any unique feature of depression except the timing associated with the delivery of a child.[38] It has, however, been successful in a small number of cases.[39] From 1986-1991, twenty women have introduced evidence of postpartum depression or postpartum psychosis into their defense against a charge of infanticide, and juries have acquitted one-half, and given one-quarter heavy sentences and one-quarter light sentences.[40]

B. PREMENSTRUAL SYNDROME

Modern medical advances have led to the discovery of many diseases which kill large numbers of human beings but are newly arisen through some type of evolutionary aberration. The AIDS epidemic is an example of this condition as it appears that the causative virus is some type of variant infection which has not caused similar problems in the distant past. Other problems, however, though new to modern medical terminology, have affected mankind for many years. One important breakthrough of such research has been in the area of hormonal affects on human behavior. It is now clearly apparent that a series of complaints may develop in women due to hormonal changes during the luteal phase of the menstrual cycle that can lead to a variety of cyclical mood swings. This syndrome has variously been described under the terms Premenstrual Syndrome (PMS), Premenstrual Aggravation (PMA), Late Luteal Phase Dysphoric Disorder (LLPDD), Premenstrual Tension Syndrome (PMTS), and Premenstrual Tension (PMT). The American Psychiatric Association designates the disorder under the DSM-III-R category.[41]

The reactions of women to PMS have been remarkably similar worldwide, and differ only with minor variation in every country which has been studied. While typical symptoms may commonly include breast pain, fatigue, stomach cramps and back pain, there are also frequent occurrences of severe depression and panic attacks which can lead to unpredictable, and even fatal, behavior. All in all, over 150 different symptoms have been attributed to PMS in one publication or another.[42]

It is now believed that the pathophysiology of PMS is due to the interactions of cyclic changes in estrogen and progesterone, the primary female hormones associated with menstrual flow, and certain neurotransmitters like serotonin.[43] The exact mechanism of action of these substances, however, is still uncertain but its similarity to the postpartum disorders is striking.

In addition to biochemical causation, there may be psychological components which either intensify, or determine, the clinical presentation. Women with PMS generally have greater amounts of conflict within their nuclear family.[44] This may be a secondary finding due to the disruptive nature of the PMS disorder on interpersonal relationships, or it may be a primary factor in the etiology of the illness itself.

Similar to the transient psychiatric syndromes of the postpartum state, PMS has been accepted as a legal defense to criminal activity by causing temporary "insanity." This concept dates back to the early nineteenth century when acquittals for shoplifting because of suppression of menstrual periods was first allowed in the courtrooms of Europe.[45] Various studies in France indicated that from 44-84% of female violent crimes were committed during the premenstrual or early menstrual phases.[46] PMS in France was thereby accepted as a complete defense to criminal action and recognized as a form of insanity.[47] In England, PMS has been upheld as a mitigating factor in order to reduce the severity of a sentence because of diminished responsibility.[48]

In America, the legal status of the illness is still in the developmental stage, but evidence so far supports acceptance of the English approach. In 1982 a New York woman was charged with child abuse and argued that she had no criminal intent because she blacked out as a result of PMS. The court accepted the evidence and dropped her charges from a felony to a misdemeanor.[49]

While many attorneys applaud the use of PMS as a defense in criminal cases, other commentators have worried that the claim reinforces stereotypic views of women as unable to control themselves due to "raging hormones":

> The fear is than even though this defense is clearly beneficial to women who legitimately suffer from this syndrome, the raging hormone theory acts as a double-edged sword ultimately working to the detriment of women in general.[50]

It is too soon to determine the full extent of this problem in modern day society, but some historians have already begun to postulate how the disorder may have affected past behavior. The famous case of Lizzie Borden, the New England murderess, has been ascribed by some to be a classic case of a woman who has suffered the ultimate effects of PMS.[51] Whether other infamous women will survive such scrutiny awaits to be seen.

C. INSANITY

To many, the mere fact that a parent could purposely kill their own child is enough evidence to diagnose mental instability, if not outright insanity. Such an act would be considered so vile and unnatural as to not be consistent with normal human behavior. While this type of deductive reasoning is clearly appealing to those who believe in the natural "goodness" of man, such a broad generalization is plainly incongruous and cannot explain away, simply on the basis of insanity, the large numbers of infanticides which have occurred in human history. That is not to say, however, that individual cases do not exist where the action is clearly aberrant.

Insanity has been defined as "any mental disorder characterized by temporary or permanent irrational or violent deviations from normal thinking, feeling, and behavior."[52] While the legal definition of the term could include more moderate lapses in judgment, and fit a wide array of infanticides already discussed in previous chapters, in this section I am going to refer only to those cases of insanity which demonstrate the extreme type of madness that leaves one in a totally unreasoned frame of mind.

Throughout most of our history, this type of madness has generally been ascribed to the workings of some god or devil. A typical example of this conduct was recorded in the Greek legend of Pentheus, the child of Agave and Echion, who inherited the royal crown of Cadmus. When Pentheus was informed that Dionysus (Bacchus), the child of Zeus and Semele who was the deity that bestowed wine on men, had begun to appear throughout the land, he refused to honor the god and outlawed the nightly Bacchic revels. This rejection angered Dionysus, and Pentheus was warned by the seer Tiresias that his insolence was dangerous and even endangered his life. Tiresias counseled Pentheus that Dionysus should be accepted, but the king steadfastly resisted.

One day, Pentheus was told by a herdsman that members of a Bacchant tribe – roaming bands of women who honored Dionysus during nighttime rites – were terrorizing the farm towns and fields. Pentheus went to see for himself, and hid in a pine tree to observe their actions. His subterfuge was necessary for men were forbidden to witness such affairs. When the leader of the ceremony, his own mother Agave, noticed the figure of a man in the tree, she ordered the other women to attack. Pentheus realized the mortal danger he was in and cried out: "Murder not thou thy son – thy very son!"[53] But his pleas were unheeded and Agave, with foaming lips and eyes that rolled wildly, tore out his left arm while the others, including her two sisters, then literally ripped him apart. When the women were done with their maniacal deed, Agave impaled his head on her thyrsus and carried it proudly home.[54] In the story as told by Euripides, Agave bragged to the chorus that she had slain a monster. But when she realized it was her own son who was killed, she shrieked out in anguish "hard my heart beats, waiting for its doom."[55]

A similar story was told of Leucippe, the daughter of king Minyas of Orchomenus, who killed her son Hippasus in an overwhelming fit of madness.[56] Leucippe, along with her sisters Alcithoe and Arsinoe, had refused to join Dionysus in his nighttime revels, as had Pentheus, and in anger the god drove them mad with an insatiable desire for human flesh. The women drew a victim by lot, and chose Hipassus who they quickly tore apart and devoured.[57] They were then turned into the Oleae and the Psoleis who stood in Greek mythology for mourning and grief.[58]

It was not only women who were vulnerable to such paroxysms of horror, men showed similar tendencies. Heracles (Hercules), the son of Zeus and Alcmene, was honored in many of the Greek fables as the most admired of mortal men. In the *Homeric Hymns* he was referred to as the greatest man who ever lived on earth.[59] But in the story of his madness by Euripides, Hercules returned from his twelve labors to find his wife and children about to be slain by Lycus. He initially planned to save them, but was then seized in a fit of madness sent by Hera, the wife of Zeus who had hated him since his birth. She directed Madness, the child of murky Night, to "stain him with the blood of kin, that he shall slay his sons."[60] Hercules then proceeded to murder his three sons and wife, thinking they were his enemy Eurystheus and his sons. In rage he killed one son with an arrow and then as the other, "coaxing hands stretched out to clasp the knees of his mad father, begs with piteous tones," he hurled him to his death as well.[61] When the deed was done, he fell asleep and when he awoke, he cried: "Woe's me for the river of blood he hath spilt!"[62] He thought of killing himself in grief, but his friend Theseus comforted him and advised that "the curse of childrens blood shall meet a friends eyes."[63] He counseled Hercules to suffer for the agony of his loss, but to recover and be strong. Theseus then took him to Pallas for purification to cleanse his hands of the taint of blood.

In a similar fable, Hera, the wife of Zeus, was incensed at Athamas for helping to raise the illegitimate child of Zeus and Semele.[64] She drove Athamas insane, and when he next saw his wife Ino carrying his two young sons, he mistook them for a lioness and her two cubs. Dante described how he took one son, Learchus, and "whirled him round and dashed him on a rock."[65] Ino fled in terror and threw the other son, Melicertes, into a boiling cauldron and then leapt into the sea along with the dead child.[66]

Christianity also accepted that madness could result from divine causation. When Jesus Christ was first preaching the new law to his Jewish brethren, he demonstrated his powers by healing the sick and infirm. Frequently it was the mentally deranged that were brought to him for care. One man took his son directly to Jesus when the disciples could not help him, and: "Jesus rebuked the demon in the boy and it left him, and from that moment the boy was well."[67]

But as time passed, and the teachings of Judaism and the Church overshadowed the pagan mythologic beliefs, such fictional explanations of insane crimes did not find sympathetic ears. When the gods were invoked in cases of infanticide or murder, it was the devil at play, and the fate of such killers was often a sentence of death.

There are many instances where parents have been convicted of viciously killing their children under such unstable mental states. This was especially true of the witch hunts in America during Colonial times. In 1638, Dorothy Talbie, of Salem, Massachusetts, was convicted in the murder of her daughter and was said to be "so possessed with Satan that he persuaded her to break the neck of her own child, that she might free it from future misery."[68] The gallows were to free her from the trials of life here on earth as well.

Modern medical thought has replaced the older spiritual interpretations with specific psychiatric diagnoses. In 1975, Browne studied nine schizophrenic women who had murdered at least one of their children and described scenarios which mimicked the fictional myths. All of the mothers felt that they "were saving their child from some pain or unhappiness by murdering them."[69] Afterwards, all of the women were profoundly depressed, and most also attempted suicide, indicating that they were able to feel intense guilt after the attack, even though there appeared to be little compunction during the murder itself. Society did not demand their death, as had some earlier cultures, but "purification" in a life of institutional care was generally deemed appropriate. After two thousand years, the ghost of Theseus seems to have returned in the guise of modern medical justice.

One recent variant on the issue of insanity and infanticide has been the reported correlation between limbic psychotic seizures and the stimulus to murder in a small number of patients. In some cases, the crying of a baby has been determined to be the trigger event which set off a form of epileptic seizure resulting in the killing of the child.[70]

D. SUICIDE

In one of the most moving fictional moments in all Western literary history, Charles Dickens ended his story of the French Revolution with the suicidal death of Stryver, the hard-nosed lawyer who took the place of Darnay on the guillotine and gave up his life in order to save that of a man he found more worthy. His last words, spoken just before his head was sliced off in front of a cheering, revengeful crowd were: "It is a far, far better thing that I do, than I have ever done; it is a far, far better rest that I go to, than I have ever known."[71]

Such honorable sentiments echo one of the reasons that suicide accounts for almost 1.2% of the annual deaths in the United States, and ranks tenth on the list of common causes of death.[72] In fact, three times as many people commit suicide as commit murder.[73] Worldwide, an estimated fifteen million threaten to kill themselves each year, and 365,000 actually die.[74] It is oddly considered by most criminal statutes as illegal conduct, equivalent to attempted murder, and although many people today feel that it should be legalized for those who suffer from terminal disease, assisting the suicide of another individual may still be considered as an aide to a homicidal act. This anomaly is not restricted to the legal arena. Suicide has been condemned by most western religious institutions, and yet many spiritual leaders have praised the deed as valorous in select situations. In the Old Testament, the word "suicide" never actually appears.[75] But there are a number of suicides which are described and not followed by negative commentary.

Of the five actual reports of suicide, four involve the death of only one individual. When the Philistines were closing in on King Saul after routing the Israelites in battle, the famous leader requested his armor-bearer to kill him so that he would not be captured and tortured. The young man resisted, so Saul took his own sword and fell upon the point of the blade.[76] Another Israeli king, Abimelech, who has been remembered mostly for the wickedness of his reign, requested a similar fate after being hit by a millstone which was thrown at him by a woman from a rooftop as he attacked the city of Thebez. He did not want it said that he was killed by a woman, and so he convinced his armor-bearer to pierce him with his sword and died.[77] Ahithophel, one of King David's counselors who sided in a conspiracy against the king with Absalom, later felt publicly disgraced when Absalom did not follow his advice and went home and hanged himself.[78] General Zimri, who assassinated King Elah of Israel and then declared himself king, lived only seven more days because the Israeli army did not support him and backed General Omri instead. When Zimri saw that the city he ruled was taken by the general's men, he went into the palace and burned it and died in the flames.[79]

In one suicide, the act was performed primarily to kill others in the process. This valiant deed, known to every child who attended Sunday school or saw the movie version with Victor Mature, involved the story of mighty Samson, the biblical equivalent of Hercules. Samson killed himself by bringing down the temple columns in order to destroy the hated Philistines. In one great selfless act, he gave up his life and "those he killed at the moment of his death were more than those he had killed during his entire lifetime."[80] This type of suicide, based on revenge against an enemy, has come to be referred to by some as "Samsonic."[81]

In the New Testament, there is a report of only one suicide – that of Judas Iscariot, the disciple who betrayed Jesus for thirty silver coins. After Jesus was sentenced to death, Judas deeply regretted what he had done and returned the money to the Jewish leaders saying: "I have sinned, for I have betrayed an innocent man."[82] He then went out and hanged himself.[83]

While there were elements in certain of these suicides to imply a disgraceful ending brought about by wrongful activity, there still remained no direct biblical commandment to prohibit its future use. Josephus, the first century A.D. Jewish historian, called the act of suicide and "impious act" against God, but still agreed that the brave citizens of Masada, who killed themselves instead of surrendering to the Romans, were to be honored with great respect.[84]

St. Augustine initially formulated the theologic ban of suicide in *The City of God*.[85] He stated that God's command, "Thou Shalt Not Kill," was to be taken as forbidding self-destruction.[86] In addition, he warned that "a person taking his own life is, of course, a homicide."[87] Augustine allowed only one valid excuse for taking your own life and that was where the act was commanded, or abetted, by God. For this reason, he pardoned Samson "on the grounds that the Spirit of the Lord, who wrought miracles through him, had bidden him to do so."[88]

The writings of Augustine formed the basis for the Church to finally legislate against suicide in the sixth century A.D.[89] By taking their own life, those who committed suicide were guilty of murder, and would be punished in Hell for all eternity to come. Dante portrayed the souls of those who committed suicide in the Seventh Circle of Hell, continually badgered by Harpies shrieking among the withering trees.[90]

In societies like Egypt and India, however, suicide was not seen as against any religious tenets. In fact, many Eastern religions favored the event as a means to denigrate the temporary attachment of the divine soul to its earthly physical form. Among Indian women, the commission of suicide by throwing themselves on the flaming pyres of their husbands – a ritual known as "sati" – was an act of honor and love. Even today, suicide by immolation is not an infrequent means that radical elements resort to in their graphic dissension against political regimes. Such acts, akin to those of military personnel from as far back as ancient Greece to modern Japan, represent a valiant form of heroic action which is performed for the common good. The French sociologist, Emile Durkheim, referred to this type of suicide as "altruistic."[91]

In modern times, infanticide as a result of suicide is rare when compared to other etiologies. But, as pointed out by Peter Marzuk:

> Although these incidents are infrequent, they probably account for 1000 to 1500 combined suicide and homicide deaths annually in the United States alone, placing their mortality on par with other diseases such as pulmonary tuberculosis (1467 deaths), viral hepatitis (1290 deaths), influenza (1943 deaths), and meningitis (1156 deaths).[92]

In his review of case reports from the world's literature, Marzuk found between 16-29% of mothers, and from 40-60% of fathers will commit suicide immediately after murdering their children.[93] While the infanticide rate of children under the age of one correlates in many nations with the suicide rate, in America there is no clear statistical association.[94]

John Baker, studying women convicted of infanticide at the State Asylum at Broadmoor in England, found that suicide was particularly prevalent in association with infanticides due to insanity of lactation.[95] These women were profoundly disturbed and often stated that they no longer desired to live. But they also believed that "to die alone and leave their children is impossible for them," and so they would first take the life of their child, and then attempt suicide.[96] After the murder was completed, many experienced a feeling of relief, "as if some tension were removed from their over-wrought brain."[97] The suicide may then have been prevented or postponed so that a planned double-suicide inadvertently turned into a single infanticide. J. Stanley Hopwood found that of 166 cases of women admitted to the Criminal Lunatic Asylum at Broadmoor in England, 98 cases had suicide ideations and 59 actually attempted suicide.[98]

In studies of infanticide from the early twentieth century in America, researchers frequently found an association with suicide in the majority of cases.[99] Lauretta Bender, who studied cases at Bellevue Hospital in New York, even concluded that "child murder by parents is a suicidal act as a result of identification processes."[100] She found that in schizophrenics and manic-depressive psychoses, the mother often first developed a suicidal drive that was then converted into a tendency to kill both the child and herself. Only after further development did the impulse become one to kill the child alone. Under these circumstances "the child becomes an integral part of the escaping personality."[101] In a study of nine schizophrenic women who murdered one or more of their children, Browne & Palmer found that all of them had either contemplated or attempted suicide at some time.[102]

The temporal relationship between suicide and infanticide is worldwide. In Sweden, 35% of children killed by their parents from 1971-1975 were part of a homicide-suicide, and from 1976-1980 it was 27%.[103] The numbers of male and female perpetrators in this study were about equal, and most of the killings during a suicide were from shooting while from the non-suicide it was strangulation.[104]

In England, Gibson and Klein noted that of 113 women who killed their children between 1955-60, 62% of them committed suicide before trial.[105] In a study from Ireland, 30% of mothers who attempted infanticide, also attempted suicide.[106]

Results from Canada between 1961-1983 indicate that while 19% of killings of children over the age of one year was associated with a suicide, none of the infanticide cases were followed by a suicide.[107] Another study revealed that suicide was attempted or successful in 41% of mothers who killed at least one of their children and 66% of fathers.[108] In Quebec, between 1988-1990, there were 39 cases of homicide-suicide, and 35% of the victims were children.[109]

In a study of 296 infanticides in Copenhagen from 1946-1960, 94 of the children were poisoned and in 92 of these cases, there was an attempted suicide on the part of the killer.[110] Seventy-two of the children were killed by their mothers, eight by their fathers, and seven by loco parentis.

In Japan, "joint suicide," or the killing of one's child followed by oneself, is not an uncommon crime. In 1977, 17% of all homicide victims were children who were slain by a parent who then committed or attempted suicide.[111] When the suicide involves the whole family it is called "ikka shinju," while a father-child suicide is "fushi shinju," and a mother-child one "boshi shinju".[112] "Oya-ko Shinju," or parent-child suicide, is not seen as infanticide but rather as a single death, or "death at the center of the heart."[113] This blurred sense of self-boundary comes from the Buddhist philosophy. It accounts for about two percent of all suicides in the present era.[114] The mother more commonly commits the suicide, and the reasons given are usually increased fatigue associated with the raising of young children without assistance, and anxiety over the child's future.[115]

Not all studies have confirmed this large percentage of suicide attempts coinciding with a child homicide. Lester Adelson, for example, reported that of forty-six children killed in Cuyahoga county, Ohio, in a seventeen year period, only three children died when parents wanted to "take the children with them."[116] It is obvious that statistics will vary both because of regional differences and also the amount of investigation that is made into the underlying reasons for the murder.

When suicide is considered by the parent, it generally is thought of before the actual act of infanticide.[117] But in some cases, depression intensifies after the parent fully comprehends the fatal result of their actions, and then, even if there was a failed suicide gesture before, the realization of the infant's murder leads to another suicide attempt that is more intensive and successful.[118] In Adelson's study of forty-one assailants, eight committed suicide after they were convicted of murder, while only three had attempted it before.[119] In the series of cases reported by Bartholomew, mothers who committed neonaticide were usually young and unmarried and generally did not have any suicidal intent at the time of the murder. After the crime was completed, however, a significant number then developed suicide ideation.[120]

The most common diagnosis in mothers who commit infanticide, and then survive a suicide attempt, is psychotic depression. The child is typically seen as solely dependent on her for care and she "sees a need to escape and `save' herself and her children from a painful, ruinous world."[121] By viewing the child as an extension of herself, the mother will try and prevent her child from suffering the same fate that she has had to endure.[122] Afraid to abandon her child to the evils of the world after her own suicide, she takes the child's life as well.[123]

With men, the infanticide-suicide combination often involves anger over the infidelity, or loss, of a wife. In Anderson, Indiana, Terry Jones had called a 911 dispatcher with the grim tale of his response to his believing his wife was having an affair on the Internet: "I just killed my wife. I just killed both my kids."[124] Shortly after he killed himself as well.

Endnotes

1 . Milton, Paradise Lost, X.193-195, 517.
2 . Genesis 3:16. The Living Bible, 3.
3 . Hopwood, "Child Murder and Insanity," 95.
4 . Kane, "Postpartum Disorders," Comprehensive Textbook of Psychiatry IV, Volume II, 1238.
5 . Parry, "Postpartum Psychiatric Syndromes," Volume I, 1063.
6 . Time 131 (June 20, 1988): 81.
7 . Button & Reivich, "Obsessions of Infanticide. A Review of 42 Cases," 235. In a review of 42 cases at the University of Kansas Medical Center where infanticidal ideation was the principal symptom, one-half of the women developed the problem in association with pregnancy. Ibid., 239.
8 . Kane, "Postpartum Disorders," 1239.
9 . Parry, "Postpartum Psychiatric Syndromes," 1060.
10 . Piers, Infanticide, 33.
11 . Briffault, The Mothers, Volume I, 112.
12 . Iffy & Jakobovits, "Infanticide: New Medical Considerations," 272.
13 . Hopwood, "Child Murder and Insanity," 95.
14 . Iffy & Jakobovits, "Infanticide: New Medical Considerations," 272.
15 . Kane, "Postpartum Disorders," 1239.
16 . Cowlishaw, "Infanticide in Aboriginal Australia," 268.
17 . Parry, "Postpartum Psychiatric Syndromes," 1060.
18 . Ibid., 1060-62.
19 . Hopwood, "Child Murder and Insanity," 96.
20 . Ibid., 97.
21 . Ibid., 95.
22 . Ibid., 96.
23 . Baker, "Female Criminal Lunatics: a Sketch," 16.
24 . Ibid., 19.
25 . Behlmer, "Deadly Motherhood: Infanticide and Medical Opinion in Mid-Victorian England," 413.
26 . Ibid.
27 . In a Bill submitted to Parliament on June 23, 1965. Abse, "Infanticide and British Law," 316.
28 . Romito, "Postpartum Depression or the Medicalization of Maternal Unhappiness. A Critical Review," 7.
29 . Baker, "Female Criminal Lunatics: a Sketch," 20.
30 . Parry, "Postpartum Psychiatric Syndromes," 1064.
31 . Ibid., 1062.
32 . Gitlin & Pasnau, "Psychiatric Syndromes Linked to Reproductive Function in Women: A Review of Current Knowledge," 1413.
33 . Romito, "Postpartum Depression or the Medicalization of Maternal Unhappiness. A Critical Review," 8-10.
34 . Piers, Infanticide, 37-38.
35 . Chicago Tribune (March 8, 1991): section 2, 7.
36 . Baker, "Female Criminal Lunatics: a Sketch," 20.
37 . Senate Concurrent Resolution No. 23 introduced by Senator Presley, February 9, 1989. Iffy & Jakobovits, "Infanticide: New Medical Considerations," 269.

38 . Gitlin & Pasnau, "Psychiatric Syndromes Linked to Reproductive Function in Women: A Review of Current Knowledge," 1413.

39 . In the first case to use this defense, a qualified psychiatrist testified that the defendant was suffering from "post partum psychosis with infanticide, a mental disorder which frequently occurs with the delivery of a child." People v. Skeoch, 408 Ill 276, 280, 96 NE2d 473, 375 (1951).

40 . Reece, "Mothers Who Kill: Postpartum Disorders and Criminal Infanticide," 702.

41 . Hurt, Schnurr, Severino, Freeman, Gise, Rivera-Tovar, & Steege, "Late Luteal Phase Dysphoric Disorder in 670 Women Evaluated for Premenstrual Complaints," 525.

42 . Keye, The Premenstrual Syndrome, 114.

43 . Mortola, "Assessment and Management of Premenstrual Syndrome," 877.

44 . Kuczmierczyk, Labrum, & Johnson, "Perception of Family and Work Environments in Women With Premenstrual Syndrome," 787.

45 . Vanezis, "Women, Violent Crime and the Menstrual Cycle: A Review," 11.

46 . Ibid.

47 . Lewis, "Premenstrual Syndrome as a Criminal Defense," 427.

48 . Keye, The Premenstrual Syndrome, 17.

49 . People v. Santos, unreported, No. 1K046229 New York Criminal Court, November 3, 1982. Ibid., 17, 26.

50 . Lewis, "Premenstrual Syndrome as a Criminal Defense," 438.

51 . Vanezis, "Women, Violent Crime and the Menstrual Cycle: A Review," 12.

52 . Funk & Wagnalls, New Comprehensive International Dictionary of the English Language, 655.

53 . Euripides, Bacchanals, 1121, 95.

54 . Ibid., 1122-1141, 95-97.

55 . Ibid., 1288, 111.

56 . Morford & Lenardon, Classical Mythology, 209.

57 . The New Century Classical Handbook, 566, 720.

58 . Frazer, The Dying God, 164.

59 . "Hymn to Herakles," Homeric Hymns, 65.

60 . Euripides, The Madness of Hercules, 831-832, 195.

61 . Seneca, Mad Hercules, IV.i, Volume II, 492.

62 . Euripides, The Madness of Hercules, 1050, 213.

63 . Ibid., 1155-56, 223.

64 . Apollodorus, The Library, 3.4.3, Volume I, 319.

65 . Dante, Inferno, XXX.10-11, 371.

66 . Apollodorus, The Library, 3.4.3, Volume I, 319.

67 . Matthew 17:18. The Living Bible, 762.

68 . Hoffer & Hull, Murdering Mothers: Infanticide in England and New England 1558-1803, 40.

69 . Browne & Palmer, "A Preliminary Study of Schizophrenic Women Who Murdered Their Children," 75.

70 . Pontius, "Infanticide in Limbic (?) Psychotic Trigger Reaction in a Man With Jacksonian and Petit Mal (?) Seizures: 'Kindling' by Traumatic Experiences," 940.

71 . Dickens, A Tale of Two Cities, III.15, 470.

72 . Hankoff & Einsidler, Suicide, Theory & Clinical Aspects, xiii.

73 . Meerloo, Suicide and Mass Suicide, 80.

74 . Ibid., 82.
75 . The Oxford English Dictionary first uses the term in 1651 AD, and Alvarez could find no earlier usage of the word before the Religio Medici of Sir Thomas Browne in 1635 AD. Alvarez, "The Background," Suicide: The Philosophical Issues, 12.
76 . I Samuel 31:4.
77 . Judges 9:53-54.
78 . II Samuel 17:23.
79 . I Kings 16:18.
80 . Judges 16:30-31. The Living Bible, 219.
81 . Bardis, History of Thanatology, 4.
82 . Matthew 27:4. The Living Bible, 775.
83 . Matthew 27:5.
84 . Josephus, "Wars", III.VIII.5, The Works of Flavius Josephus, Volume II, 315.
85 . Cassidy & Russo, "Religion: A Catholic View," 76.
86 . Augustine, St., The City of God, I.XX, Volume I, 26.
87 . Ibid., I.XVII, 21.
88 . Ibid., I.XXI, 26.
89 . Alvarez, "The Background," 12.
90 . Dante, Inferno, XII, 167.
91 . Bardis, History of Thanatology, 72.
92 . Marzuk, Tardiff & Hirsch, "The Epidemiology of Murder-Suicide," 3179.
93 . Ibid., 3181.
94 . Lester, "The Murder of Babies in American States: Association With Suicide Rates," 1202.
95 . Baker, "Female Criminal Lunatics: a Sketch," 21.
96 . Ibid.
97 . Ibid., 22.
98 . Hopwood, "Child Murder and Insanity, 103.
99 . Bender, "Psychiatric Mechanisms in Child Murderers," 32.
100. Ibid., 46.
101. Ibid.
102. Browne & Palmer, "A Preliminary Study of Schizophrenic Women Who Murdered Their Children," 71.
103. Somander & Rammer, "Intra- and Extrafamilial Child Homicide in Sweden 1971-1980," 48.
104. Ibid., 50.
105. d'Orban, "Women Who Kill Their Children," 568.
106. Lukianowicz, "Attempted Infanticide," 15.
107. Silverman & Kennedy, "Women Who Kill Their Children," 124.
108. Rodenburg, "Child Murder by Depressed Parents," 43.
109. Buteau, Lesage, & Kiely, "Homicide Followed by Suicide: A Quebec Case Series, 1988-1990," 554.
110. Harder, "The Psychopathology of Infanticide," 197.
111. Kawanishi, "Japanese Mother-Child Suicide: The Psychological and Sociological Implications of the Kimura Case," 33-34.
112. Wagatsuma, "Child Abandonment and Infanticide: A Japanese Case," 129-130.
113. Bryant, "Oya-Ko Shinju: Death at the Center of the Heart," 5.
114. Ibid., 7.
115. Ibid., 10.

116. Adelson, "Slaughter of the Innocents," 1346.
117. Hopwood, "Child Murder and Insanity," 104.
118. Resnick, "Child Murder by Parents: A Psychiatric Review of Filicide," 331.
119. Adelson, "Slaughter of the Innocents," 1346-47.
120. Bartholomew, "Repeated Infanticide," 441.
121. Marzuk, Tardiff & Hirsch, "The Epidemiology of Murder-Suicide," 3181.
122. Resnick, "Child Murder by Parents: A Psychiatric Review of Filicide," 331.
123. Ibid., 329.
124. Chicago Tribune, January 16, 1999, section 1, pg 9.

CHAPTER XVI

EUTHANASIA

> "What is novel, over the few million-or-so years of human existence, is the idea that succor of all viable babies is a desirable social goal."[1]

William Silverman, commenting on the modern debate raging over the ethics of abortion and neonatal death, noted that the accepted premise that all babies have a natural right-to-life is flawed and extremely impractical from a societal standpoint. The history of human civilization has been in general agreement. When a newborn infant was born into ancient society with such serious deformities that independent life was limited, the problem was solved by either killing the infant, or not providing sustenance in a process known as "culling." Modern ethicists have euphemized the term and referred to it as "euthanasia."

Hippocrates, the father of modern medicine, clearly recommended that "no cure is to be applied in desperate sicknesses," and this aphorism was applied in a wide context, including the treatment of newborns.[2] Asclepius, the son of Apollo and co-founder of the medical profession, believed that medication was for the benefit of people of sound constitution with treatable ailments. He did not find it necessary, let alone ethically required, that all diseases undergo restorative therapy.

Over the last decade, a trend towards the more ancient approach of non-heroic treatments has resurfaced across a broad front of professional and social support. Quality of life, rather than quantity, has become an important key-word in this movement, and many physicians now accept that allowing a patient to die is not a defeat or ethical wrong.[3] In the words of Robert Cooke, "medicine is the science of care, not the science of cure."[4] When a physician decides that the medical condition of a patient is so disordered that there is no reasonable chance of survival beyond a few months, the patient is deemed "terminal." Simple comfort care, without any attempts to aggressively maintain life, may then be appropriate and this treatment generally is known as "hospice" care. If there is a more active decision to actually hasten death, rather than simply keep the patient comfortable, then the term "euthanasia" applies.

There are various ways of defining this concept, but in general it is the action of inducing a "painless, peaceful death."[5] As Arval Morris, Professor of Law at the University of Washington in Seattle, nicely stated: "Euthanasia is a matter of deciding in favor of death on the ground that death is in the better interests and is preferable to life for the one who is to die."[6]

This preference of death over life is not shared by all concerned parties however, and a heated argument over both the morality of euthanasia in general, and the methods by which it should be allowed in particular, has gathered strength. To better understand why otherwise caring, intelligent health care providers, ethicists and religious leaders should disagree so vehemently over something so basic as how to face the inevitability of death, it is necessary to further define certain aspects of the problem.

When action is taken to actually kill a patient, in the medical rather than criminal sense, such activity is called "active," or "positive," euthanasia. Except for a small group of activists, most proponents of the right-to-die movement do not recommend this procedure. According to the Council on Ethical and Judicial Affairs of the American Medical Association in 1988: "What is termed "active euthanasia" is a euphemism for the intentional killing of a person; this is not part of the practice of medicine with or without the consent of the patient."[7] The American College of Physicians, in 1989, confirmed their belief that even if such euthanasia was legalized, it "would violate the ethical standards of medical practice."[8]

Many proponents nevertheless believe that this rigid stance is archaic, and there have been a number of attempts to legalize active euthanasia via what has been termed "physician assisted suicide." Oregon was the first state in the nation to pass such a law in 1994, although it was not until 1997 that the Oregon Supreme Court held that the law was constitutional.[9] Similar measures have so far failed in California and Washington.

If a means to save a life is available, but for any purposeful reason is withheld, the term "passive" or "negative" euthanasia is used.[10] Although the person responsible for behaving in this manner does not directly terminate the life of a patient, they still cause death from an ethical perspective. The reasoning is that: "Deliberately withholding action while being aware that action is possible constitutes a conscious attempt to determine what happens."[11] This means that you cannot claim non-culpability simply because you did not "pull the trigger." In the words of Leonard Weber: "There is no significant moral difference between giving a baby a lethal injection and with-holding permission for surgical correction of duodenal atresia, with the result that the baby starves to death."[12]

The utilization of these concepts has primarily centered around the treatment of patients with terminal disease. According to most Hospice criteria, these patients are not expected to live more than six months, even with the best medical care, and therefore the person's comfort becomes of primary concern. With respect to the care of a disabled newborn, the standard designation of "terminal disease" is generally not appropriate. When individuals desire to not treat an infant because of euthanasia concerns, it is not the time limit of life that is determinative, but rather whether the outlay of such aggressive treatment for a prolonged period of time, both from an economic and comfort standpoint, is appropriate. If the infant, for example, has severe neurologic or gastrointestinal malformations which interfere with independent life support function, and these defects are not curable with modern technology, deciding whether to continue artificial feedings in order to maintain life indefinitely would be a passive euthanasia issue.

The problem of caring for these offspring is not of minor proportions. About seven percent of normal term pregnancies will have some type of birth defect.[13] In addition, another seven percent result in low birth weight babies which is associated with an increased infant mortality and morbidity.[14] This means that almost fourteen percent of live-births have significant health hazards which may threaten life either quantitatively or qualitatively.

In 1982, the standard infant mortality in this country was 11.2 per 100 live births.[15] Among infants who were born under 2.2 lb, almost 25% had physical or mental disorders.[16] About 30,000 babies will be born in America each year into a life that will be "harshly limited and impaired."[17] The cost of carrying for these infants in 1981 was estimated to be about $40,000 to $100,000 per child.[18]

It is obvious from these statistics that attempting to aggressively care for, and maintain the life of, the entire category of defective infants will involve enormous effort simply to assure survival beyond the first few months of life. After that, continuing medical care and attempts at rehabilitation will be so expensive that present day sources of funding will be quickly depleted. All of this sophisticated treatment costs money – lots of it – and in an age of limited means to further increase taxes and insurance premiums, it is legitimate to ask whether society has an ethical obligation to treat all of these newborns, or whether some infants can be left to expire from the insufficient anatomic systems with which they were born. As Dr. Marcia Angell rightfully asked: "Do we have the right to inflict a life of suffering on a helpless newborn just because we have the technology to do so and despite the fact that we ourselves would have the legal right to reject such a life?"[19]

The role parents play in this decision-making process is hotly debated. There is no agreement on whether a parent can simply decide that the expenditure of money and time to treat such a child is simply not worth the effort, and requests that the infant, lawfully born to them, not be treated with any artificial life-sustaining methods.

The United States Constitution protects the right of a parent to raise their children in a manner consistent with their own beliefs as part of the fundamental component of the right to personal privacy.[20] In addition, the

Anglo-American legal tradition has generally upheld a parent's authority to make decisions for their infants on the recognition that they "are the best determiners of their infants best interest."[21] In Britain, parental consent is given a great deal of standing as "there is no justification for usurping parents' rights" when deciding on options such as the non-treatment of severely deformed newborns.[22]

Like most other constitutional rights, however, this authority is not absolute and if the child's health appears to be in jeopardy, the courts may step in and take whatever steps are necessary to save the child's life.[23] This action is legitimized because the state maintains an interest to preserve the lives of all its citizens, even those who do not desire to have their lives preserved.[24]

Competent adults may refuse medical treatment, even if their actions are likely to be lethal. With respect to children, this autonomy is less concrete. There is a great deal of leeway in allowing parents to make such judgments for their children, as long as the actions appear reasonable, and in the best interests of the child.[25] But because a minor is not able to make an independent choice, the parents do not have complete freedom in this regard. In deciding whether the parent's decision is appropriate, the courts often use a "substituted judgment" test which analyzes whether the child, if competent, would have agreed with the choice.[26] If there is child abuse or neglect, it is determined that the child would not have willingly agreed to such treatment. Similarly, any parent who refuses to provide care to a deformed newborn can be viewed as acting abusive or neglectful. If a child's health is seriously affected by a parent's decision, there can be withdrawal of the child into the care of local authority.[27]

This necessity of basic medical services does not only depend upon state statutory legislation, which can expand the legal requirement even further, but is also guaranteed by the United States Constitution. On its face, this hallowed document guarantees a persons "right to life" which has been interpreted to include newborn infants.[28] The Declaration of Independence quite succinctly states:

> That all men are created equal, that they are endowed by their Creator with certain unalienable Rights, that are among these Life, Liberty and the pursuit of Happiness.[29]

It is therefore possible that if a parent does not actively pursue an attempt to maintain their disabled newborn's life, they could be found guilty of violating the child's rights. According to most legal scholars: "It is now well settled that parents are under a duty to prevent avoidable and premature termination of life."[30]

Accepted medical ethics support many of these legal concepts. In 1977, the AMA House of Delegates at the Clinical Convention adopted the following guidelines: "The intentional termination of the life of one human being by another – mercy killing – is contrary to that for which the medical profession stands and is contrary to the policy of the American Medical Association."

But professorial statements do not always correlate with the actual workings of those on the frontline of medical care. Polls of physicians in 1961 and 1971 indicated that from 60-80% of practitioners had participated in some form of passive euthanasia.[31] Since there was complete anonymity in these questionnaires, the extent of the practice was not really known.

Then, in 1973, the medical world was "stunned" by the admission of two pediatric specialists in the intensive-care nursery of a large academic hospital, that many infants were allowed to die from the intentional withdrawal of treatment.[32] In that study, 299 deaths in a special-care nursery were reported and 43 (14%) were related to the withholding of treatment to severely impaired children.[33] There was no mandatory family conference, no orders to DNR (Do Not Resuscitate), no living wills or legal counsel; the health care professionals simply felt enough was enough and allowed the children to die.

While many health care workers had long known that many of these children were not receiving "aggressive" medical care, the magnitude was never solidified by statistical data. This 1973 study clearly showed that many disabled infants were allowed to die and that the health care profession was a willing, and at times even a supportive, participant. The authors were sympathetic to this beneficent approach and concluded that "the burden of decision making must be borne by families and their professional advisers because they are most familiar with the respective situations."[34]

This led to an extensive debate over the ethical issues surrounding the treatment of infants who have severe congenital disabilities. Questions surfaced over whether such actions were illegal or unethical. Was this simply a matter for the parents to decide, or did the state have an interest in protecting the lives of all of these infants? Since handicapped newborns had constitutional rights, they had to be protected from harm.[35] Yet in cases of extreme disability, even the law could understand the vagaries of human dilemma, as evidenced by the federal circuit court conclusion:

> Frequently, however, correction of a life-threatening physical defect or use of heroic life-sustaining measures preserves the life of an infant who continues nevertheless to suffer from mental or physical defects so great as seriously to impair the infant's expected quality of life and chances for an independent existence.[36]

In 1982, a series of events began which was to catapult this entire process into the public eye, and advance the concept of euthanasia to its present-day status. The very essence of culling, and right-to-life, was brought into the legal arena and thereby, via ethicists, physicians, attorneys, politicians, and concerned parents, into the reality of our everyday life.

In order to better understand the issues raised in this heated debate, it is necessary to outline some factual information concerning the birth of two very special, and very disabled, infants. On April 9, 1982, the parents of a newborn infant with Down's syndrome and esophageal obstruction, dubbed "Baby Doe" by the courts, refused to allow doctors at a Bloomington, Indiana hospital to operate and bypass the blockage to ingestion of food which was leading to a rapidly worsening nutritional depletion. Without surgery the child would starve to death since it could not eat food on its own. On April 10, based on the advice of the treating physicians who felt that the infant could survive the necessary surgery, the hospital initiated judicial proceedings to override the parent's decision.

That very night, an Indiana trial court reviewed the hospital's plea and denied the request. A few days later, on April 12, the presiding judge in the case asked the local Child Protection Committee to review his decision.[37] The Committee held an emergency hearing and found no reason to disagree with the court. The infant died six days after birth, and an autopsy showed Down's syndrome with an esophageal atresia and tracheo-esophageal fistula that could have been surgically repaired.[38]

After being informed of the publicity surrounding this case, President Ronald Reagan on April 30, 1982 sent a memorandum instruction to the Secretary of the Department of Health & Human Services (HHS) directing him to notify health care providers of the mandatory treatment of handicapped infants as stated under Section 504 of the Rehabilitation Act of 1973.[39] This statute was a civil rights provision written into a vocational rehabilitation law that provided handicapped individuals with civil rights protection similar to that extended to ethnic and racial minorities by the Civil Rights Act of 1964, and to women by Title IX of the Education Amendments of 1972.[40] The statute was originally intended to protect employees against job discrimination, and by attempting to extend the law to the medical issues represented in the Baby Doe case, the Reagan Administration was acting under what they viewed was a moral necessity.[41]

On May 18, 1982, the director of the HHS office of Civil Rights, issued a notice reminding all health care providers that it was unlawful "to withhold from a handicapped infant nutritional sustenance or medical or surgical treatment required to correct a life threatening condition."[42] The Reagan administration had thereby committed itself to a principle of "nondiscrimination on the basis of handicap" that rejected "any and all quality-of-life judgments."[43] If a normal infant could be kept alive by proven methods of medical care, then a disabled infant required the same treatment to be given, irrespective of the parent's wishes.

After months of preparation, on March 7, 1983, an "Interim Final Rule" was promulgated by the Secretary of the HHS which provided for expedited hospital compliance with the Secretary's ruling and unrestricted access to hospital records.[44] This rule clarified that it would be unlawful for hospitals receiving federal financial assistance to withhold treatment from handicapped infants if required to correct a life-threatening condition.[45] The government declared it had the right to be able to review the treatment given to such patients without the consent of the family, or the hospital staff. Because the hospitals accepted at least part of their operating income from federal funds, HHS demanded that all hospital records be made available for utilization review.

On April 6, 1983, the American Medical Association filed a complaint seeking that these Interim Final Rules be deemed invalid. The American Academy of Pediatrics filed a similar suit eight days later and the Honorable Gerhard Gesell, U.S. District Judge for the District of Columbia, ruled that the Secretary had acted improperly and that the rules were arbitrary and capricious.[46] Gesell determined that the primary purpose of the rules was to require physicians to take into account only the medical considerations of the case, and did not allow the parents to have an influence on their decision.[47] This was not something which was within the purview of the government to require by a simple rule-making process.

On July 5, 1983, the Department of HHS issued new "Proposed Rules" which supported their stand requiring care of the disabled newborn, but modified certain restrictions.[48] It received 16,739 comments, of which 97% were in support.[49] Of interest, 141 pediatricians sent in comments, and 72% were opposed to the government's position.

After evaluating the responses, HHS promulgated its new final rules on January 12, 1984 which were to take effect on February 13, 1984.[50] These rules established procedures "relating to health care for handicapped infants" which purported to govern the actions of hospitals in dealing with this problem.[51] The final rule, issued on January 9, 1984 was somewhat less intense than the initial proposal.[52] On March 12, 1984 the AMA amended their complaint and filed suit to declare these Proposed Rules invalid and their relief was initially granted.[53]

On October 11, 1983, after the Interim Final Rules of HHS had been declared invalid, but before the Final Rules were promulgated, a child with multiple congenital defects known as "Baby Jane Doe" was born at St. Charles Hospital in Port Jefferson, New York. She had spina bifida, microcephaly, hydrocephalus, a malformed brainstem, and such an extremely high risk of severe retardation that she would likely never interact with her environment or with other people.[54] Despite these extensive problems, her pediatric neurosurgeon had recommended transfer to the University Hospital where he planned surgical correction of some of the defects. The parents, after consulting a number of health care professionals and family members, elected not to consent to the surgery. At the time they felt that survival, with the deficiencies that would remain, was not in the baby's best interest.[55]

On October 16, 1983, an unrelated attorney named A. Lawrence Washburn, Jr., hearing of the details of the case and the parents decision, filed suit in the New York Supreme Court seeking the appointment of a guardian ad litem to direct the hospital to perform the required surgery. The trial court, acting in what it felt was the infant's possible interest in life, granted his request and appointed William E. Weber as guardian ad litem.[56] The next day, however, the Appellate Division of the New York Supreme Court reversed this decision.[57] One week later, on October 28, 1983 the New York Court of Appeals, the state's highest court, affirmed the action of the Appellate Division.[58] In their decision, they chastised those who sought "to displace parental responsibility for and management of" the infant's care.[59] This holding was based in the belief that such matters were best left to the parents and their medical advisors.

While the state of New York proceedings were in progress, on October 19, 1983 the HHS received a complaint from a private citizen that Baby Jane Doe from New York was being discriminated against because of the failure to perform the surgery. The department then made requests for the hospital to make their records available for inspection. This was part of the initial promulgated rules which were denied in federal court. The hospital refused, and the government then filed suit to invoke its general authority. The district court allowed the parents to intervene as defendants and ruled against the government.[60] Judge Leonard Wexler reasoned that there was no authority for the government to step in and review hospital records. He felt that the hospital could not perform surgery without parental consent and therefore could not be guilty of discrimination, the reason given by the government for its action.

The Court of Appeals affirmed this decision, as did the United States Supreme Court. These appeals basically found that parenteral consent was required for any medical care irrespective of statutory wording of infant status.[61] The consent was felt to be an indelible principle of medical care and could not be changed by legislative action.

This decision, to leave the responsibility of withholding treatments in severely handicapped neonates during the first few days following birth to the parents, had the backing of a number of proponents in the medical, legal, and ethical literature.[62] According to Earl Shelp, Assistant Professor of Medical Ethics at Baylor College of Medicine, the bond of love that united parents to their children disposed them to act in the best interest of the neonates welfare.[63] It was necessary to judge conduct "in light of the circumstances," and not label it as "illegitimate in view of the end attained."[64] While proponents of euthanasia beamed with success, the victory soon proved pyrrhic.

The United States Congress, under pressure from the Reagan administration, eventually took enforcement of this problem out of the hands of the Courts with passage of amendments to the Child Abuse Prevention and Treatment Act (CAPTA) of 1984.[65] This law followed the initial wishes of President Reagan and the HHS and required that all deformed infants be given aggressive treatment in situations where other infants would likely receive similar care. It eliminated much of the parental decision-making process.[66] Treatment under this standard was required unless it was obviously inhumane and had virtually no chance of saving the life of the infant.[67] In addition, if treatment was withheld for any reason, it had to be reported for investigation and verification by governmental sources.[68] States were only obligated to adopt these rules within the governance of private hospital settings if they accepted funds available to their child abuse and neglect agencies from the CAPTA program.[69]

These scenarios, except for the extent of the legal battles, are not isolated instances. There are a number of Baby Doe proceedings presently in progress in other parts of the country.[70] Infants born with a congenital defect have been deemed to be "handicapped individuals" protected under Section 504 of the Rehabilitation Act of 1973.[71] If a hospital desired to withhold ventilator treatment from such a baby, even if that infant had anencephaly – a condition that is universally fatal shortly after birth – this would violate the Act.[72]

Most parents tend to decide on what appears best by either intuition or common sense; few act without feelings of love and genuine concern. When a decision is made to allow a newborn to die, it is generally well thought out, and agreed upon by many other family members and health care personnel.

But the debate among ethicists over the dilemma posed by the consideration of euthanasia has spawned extensive philosophical arguments. Most ethicists agree that there is little moral difference between "direct" euthanasia, where death is induced by doing something actively to end life, and "indirect," where something is done that foreseeably will result in death, such as withholding feedings.[73] This type of treatment generally involves only feeding the infant "on demand," but when the child is either too ill to feed, or is anatomically unable to accept food, there is no "demand" ever present. The end result, in the words of Dr. John M. Freeman, is that: "With the gentle help of sedation and feeding on demand . . . children starve to death without making too much noise."[74]

Is this action truly criminal infanticide, or is it an acceptable way to let "nature take its course?" On one end of the spectrum is the argument that all human life is sacred, and therefore one human being can never take the life of another human being under any circumstance. Since human life is a gift from God, it is outside of our responsibility to judge whether another person should live or die.[75] Life is "unconditionally good", in the sense of the Deity, and there can be no allowance of euthanasia on quality-of-life grounds.[76] This is the classical view expressed by most theologians.[77]

Orthodox Judaism accepts this sanctity of life argument and strictly prohibits active euthanasia. In the *Talmud* it is written that even if you kill a child that is falling off a roof, it is still considered murder for the sanctity of life is the same whether that life has just seconds, or years, to exist.[78] The Babylonian *Talmud*, from the fifth century A.D., declares that: "He who closes the eyes of a dying person while the soul is departing is a murderer."[79] Even if the mother gives birth to a creature with a double back, or a double spine, the *Talmud* held it "has the status of a person and killing it would be considered infanticide which is prohibited."[80] Oriental Jews, nevertheless, consider the disabled newborn to be the result either of a curse on the family or caused by external evil forces.[81] Much of this likely comes from Confucian ideology which views newborns with deformities as monsters, and a sign that the ancestors of the couple were without virtue.[82]

Maimonides, the twelfth century A.D. Jewish philosopher and physician, agreed with these principles and stated that: "Whether one kills a healthy person or a patient who approaches death, or even a dying person, one is liable to capital punishment."[83] And the principle also holds true for both normal, or deformed, children.

Rabbi Immanuel Jakobovits, president of the Institute of Judaism and Medicine in Jerusalem, has become a modern spokesman for the orthodox Jewish view on this issue. In opposing euthanasia, he stated that human life has "infinite value," meaning that every moment, every fraction of life, must be spared.[84] In other words: "The title to life is absolute from the moment of birth."[85]

Even if the child would take part in the decision, euthanasia would be considered wrong under this holding. If it is performed without the consent of the person, it is murder, while if done consensual it is equivalent to suicide.[86] In the words of Paul Ramsey, Professor of Religion at Princeton University: "We have no moral right to choose that some live and others die, when the medical indications for treatments are the same."[87] One cannot morally be allowed to decide that the value of one life is greater than another.[88]

This view is also argued by "Vitalists" who maintain that all life is valuable and that treatment may never be withheld, regardless of prognosis.[89] Since life is so sacred, one should not use handicap to determine when treatment should be given.[90] When viewed in an ethical perspective, handicapped individuals are still "perfect specimens".[91] Such a strict "right-to-life" holding requires newborns to receive whatever services are needed to maintain biological function.[92]

It is of interest that Pope Pius XII, in 1957, held that only ordinary means are necessary to preserve life since: "Life, death, all temporal activities are in fact subordinate to spiritual ends."[93] Ordinary means in this context were generally understood to mean "those which held out a prospect of benefit, alleviation or cure, and did not entail an undue burden in terms of pain, anxiety, expense, etc."[94] Some observers read into this statement that euthanasia might be considered by the Church to be appropriate at times when heroic, rather than ordinary, treatments would be necessary to keep the infant alive. Vatican II, however, which was convened in 1962, clearly dismissed this interpretation and negated the concept of euthanasia. They held that life is reverent and "whatever is opposed to life itself, such as any type of murder, genocide, abortion, euthanasia, or willful self-destruction," is infamous.[95] The Church was not to tolerate murder of any kind, and included would be even mercy killing.

But the argument within the Church on how aggressively to treat a dying patient was not quieted by these holdings. Pope John Paul II, in 1980, confirmed that "no one and nothing can, in any way, authorize the killing of an innocent human being," but distinguished this from withholding treatments "that can only yield a precarious and painful prolongation of life."[96] While active euthanasia was prohibited, passive killings, by only supplying ordinary methods of therapy, appeared to be acceptable.

An opposing view to this inviolate right-to-life, is one which holds that it is "better to be dead than to suffer too much or to endure too many deficits of human function."[97] It is an approach that favors the quality of a persons life rather than the quantity of years one lives. Proponents of this view do not accept that there is a "right" to life that is inherent and inviolate simply because the physical attributes of physiologic life are present and functioning. Rather, there is an expectation that one will live within the bounds that are determined by "consensus in the society to which the man belongs."[98] This means that the family of man may ethically, and legally, decide the limits which members of that culture must meet if continued existence is to be expected. Since rights are dependent on a social commitment within society, there can be no intrinsic natural, or absolute, right-to-life.[99]

The extent to which a newborn's life can be taken under this type of approach depends upon the society, or on the instance in question. As Eike-Henner Kluge explained: "Mere membership in the species homo sapiens, or mere possession of a living human body no longer guarantees personhood."[100] By personhood is meant the qualities which entitle someone to claim the right-to-life.

For some, the decision of whether to allow a newborn this designation of personhood depends on whether the infant is likely to become a functioning adult. Henry Aiken argues that: "The right to biological survival are entirely contingent upon the ability of the individual in question to make, with the help of others, a human life for himself."[101] If human life, as we define it, is not possible, it is then acceptable to allow for merciful termination of life, or even perhaps "obligatory" termination under certain circumstances.[102] This premise not only allows one to not aggressively treat a newborn with significant disabilities from a moral perspective, it permits the commission of infanticide if conditions such as extreme pain are present.

Within these two extremes lie many varied definitions of when euthanasia is appropriate, and when it infringes on basic human rights. While it is difficult to categorize all of them in one simplistic outline, certain determinative principles are commonly raised.

The first important factor which often is considered is the right of self-determination. Ethicist Earl Shelp argues that this axiom of autonomy allows any human being to have a say in how he will live his life, and when that life will be brought to an end. While the state may have an interest in preserving life in general, it does not have the right to interfere with a particular adult who voluntarily chooses to terminate his life. But the right of self-determination cannot be raised by an infant, and therefore some other person must be designated to make the decision on behalf of the newborn's welfare. In general, it is the parent who is given this responsibility, but in the case of disabled newborns we have already seen how the executive and legislative branches of government have severely restricted their authority.[103]

Whoever is designated to judge what should be done to care for a severely disabled infant must be guided by the principle of beneficence, which provides a duty to help further the important and legitimate interests of the infant.[104] In addition, there are principles of justice which assure that the fate of child is not intermingled with those of the guardian, and that the child receives his or her due.[105] According to Jonathan Glover, a philosopher at Oxford University, this means we must make a resolution by substituting ourselves for the defective infant.[106]

This transference of the decision-making chore to another human being is not acceptable to those who follow strict right-to-life proposals for a number of reasons. One basis is that even if conditions favored a plausibly justifiable homicide under the stringent conditions of extreme necessity, there is no stable way of blocking its extension to cases that would be unacceptable.[107] Once you allow a killing under a complex set of facts, it would be very difficult to equally judge a similar, although slightly varied, set of facts and find euthanasia unacceptable. The holding on one would taint the reasoning of the other.

There is also the ethical question of having a single person decide the life of another without qualifications which would include medical, legal, ethical and social training. Schaeffer and Koop demand that "no one should be making decisions to kill self-sustaining infants."[108] They point out, however, that if anyone is to decide the disabled infants fate it should be deformed adults, rather than medical ethicists, who are queried on whether a life with disability is better than no life at all. In their interviews of disabled patients on whether the quality of their existence was acceptable, the answer was usually "I'm very glad to be alive."[109]

Once a determination is made that a particular individual does have the right to decide the fate of the infant, ascertaining which infants should be allowed to live, and which should be considered beyond capability of satisfactory existence, is the next issue to be faced. Most ethicists believe that this decision should not be based on a specific diagnosis or deficiency, but rather on whether there are attributes which suggest that the infant will eventually be able to develop attributes of becoming a "person." Raymond Duff, one of the co-authors of the initial newborn nursery article in 1977 that led to this difficult debate, has become a strong advocate of selective non-treatment of newborns and follows this "person-oriented" rather than "disease-oriented" approach.[110] It demands that judgment not be made simply by the medical diagnosis on the face of the hospital chart.

There are few people who would disagree with this sensible conclusion. But how do you decide if the infant in question is equivalent to a potential adult – or, in the jargon of the ethicist, a person? I will not attempt to review all of the writings on this incredibly complex question, but it is interesting to highlight some of the methods recommended in order to better appreciate its relationship to questions of infanticide.

Eike-Henner Kluge, Associate Professor of Philosophy at the University of Victoria, characterizes an entity as a person "if and only if, either it now is perceptually aware, reasons and makes judgments, and is self-aware, or it is in a state of constitutive potential with respect to these."[111] Infants are possibly "persons" under this definition, because of their constitutive potential.[112] But only the infants who meet the defining criteria for personhood would be included in the list that Kluge believes should survive after birth with heroic measures.[113] Infants who cannot have potential for personhood, such as those with anencephaly, should therefore be "euthanized," for "the absence of the right to life creates a duty to kill."[114]

A similar approach is taken by Mary Anne Warren, a professor of philosophy at San Francisco State University, who counts infants as persons, as opposed to genetically determined human beings, when there is consciousness, reasoning ability, self motivated activity, the capacity to communicate and the presence of self-awareness.[115] If these are not available, and no one wants to pay for its care, "then its destruction is permissible."[116]

Peter Singer, a professor of philosophy at Monash University in Australia, argues that newborns are non-persons for they are not rational and self-conscious. This makes their destruction morally acceptable and different than considerations to adult human beings.[117]

Joseph Fletcher, a retired professor of biomedical ethics, argues that the value of human life depends on more than "merely being alive" and that "it is better to be dead than to suffer too much."[118] He contends that if abortion is considered ethically acceptable for genetically damaged fetuses, then euthanasia of defective newborns is justified.

One can quickly see that this process of determining whether a particular infant is a "person" is critical to the judgment of whether its euthanasia is an infanticide. You cannot be guilty of murder under this assessment if there is no capability of "normal" life. Such a Utilitarian view only asks whether the infant can live a meaningful life; if it cannot, it is quite acceptable to then terminate its existence.

Richard McCormick, a moral theologian at the Kennedy Institute of Ethics, agrees with this stratagem. He concludes that the relational potential of the neonate should be used as the guideline to determine non-treatment.[119] While it may be difficult to ascertain with accuracy how valuable a life the newborn might live, it is a more valid principle to follow than simply examining the infant at birth:

> Life is a value to be preserved only insofar as it contains some potentiality for human relationships. When in human judgment this potentiality is totally absent, or would be because of the condition of the individual, totally subordinated to the mere effort for survival, that life can be said to have achieved its potential.[120]

In addition to taking into account the life of the infant, there are also those who raise concerns over the lives of those who must undertake the responsibility of taking care of such a disabled child. John Fletcher, assistant to the director of the National Institutes of Health, finds that the "plight of parents" is a necessary, yet often neglected, part of the decision and that it is allowable to withdraw care in such cases from "terribly damaged newborns."[121]

Kuhse and Singer have emphasized that: "When the parents will be the ones who must care for a severely handicapped infant it is the parent who should have the right to decide whether the infant lives or dies."[122] There are limited resources available in the world and, since the newborn does not have an inherent right to life, the "community might properly decide that its resources are more urgently spent on other tasks than caring for handicapped new-born infants whose parents are not prepared to care for them."[123] This so-called social utilitarianism balances the potential productivity of life with the social and economic costs of the treatment.[124] In 1981, the cost of neonatal care in the U.S. was estimated at almost three billion dollars per year.[125] How to continue paying for such enormous expenditures is something which cannot be ignored.

Finally, it should be noted that euthanasia is not restricted to the newborn nursery alone. Similar killings have often occurred after parents have been forced to watch their children suffer for many years. Our modern era has generally required that such mercy-killings be considered criminal homicide. In 1925, Dr. Harold E. Blazer was tried in Colorado for killing his daughter, an incurable invalid whom he had nursed for thirty-two years. The jury was unable to reach a verdict and his case was dismissed.[126] Louis Greenfield, in 1932, killed his seventeen-year-old son who had been paralyzed and mentally retarded.[127] Bryan Helfenbein shot his ten-year-old son in the head as "an act of love" as he "had led a terrible life and saw his boy was going to lead a terrible life."[128]

In 1947, the United States Supreme Court took a dim view of such mercy killings. On October 12, 1939 a man by the name of Repouille had put to death his twelve-year-old son because the child had "suffered from birth from a brain injury which destined him to be an idiot and a physical monstrosity malformed in all four limbs. The child was blind, mute, and deformed. He had to be fed; the movements of his bladder and bowels were involuntary, and his entire life was spent in a small crib."[129] The man had four other children to care for and found this compromised by the burden of caring for the disabled son. He was indicted for manslaughter but only convicted in the second degree with a jury verdict recommending "utmost clemency." Except for this one act he had a clear record and felt he had enough of a "good moral character" to apply for nationality as a United States citizen. The Supreme Court held that these actions showed he was not of good moral character and that the prevalent moral feelings in this country would "be outraged by the conduct in question."[130]

At times, a parent may act to kill their child out of mercy even when there is no obvious physical or mental abnormality. In one review of the reported cases of infanticide in the world's literature, mercy was given as the most common motive for killing in 56% of mothers and 35% of fathers who attempted to prevent a real, or supposed, harm to their child which they concluded was more devastating than death.[131] Harder, on the other hand, in his review of infanticide in Denmark, found no certain cases where the killing occurred out of pity.[132] The true percentage lies somewhere between these two extremes.

Endnotes

1 . Silverman, "Mismatched Attitudes About Neonatal Death," 12.
2 . Marcus, The Jew in the Medieval World, 5.
3 . On November 8, 1994, Oregon became the first place anywhere to legalize physician-assisted death by a 52%-48% vote. American Medical News (November 28, 1994): 1.
4 . Kluge, The Ethics of Deliberate Death, 24.
5 . Funk & Wagnalls New Comprehensive International Dictionary of the English Language, 439.
6 . Morris, "Law, Morality, and Euthanasia for the Severely Defective Child," 144.
7 . "American College of Physicians Ethics Manual. Part 2: The Physician and Society; Research; Life-Sustaining Treatment; Other Issues," 333.
8 . Ibid., 334.
9 . ACP Observer, 17 (December, 1997): 3.
10 . Kluge, The Ethics of Deliberate Death, 11.
11 . Ibid., 13.
12 . Weber, "In Defense of the Legal Prohibition of Infanticide," 131.
13 . Shelp, Born to Die? Deciding the Fate of Critically Ill Newborns, 55.
14 . Ibid., 56.
15 . Ibid., 55.
16 . Rosenblum & Budde, "Historical and Cultural Consideration of Infanticide," 11.
17 . Ellis, "Letting Defective Babies Die: Who Decides?," 393.
18 . Rosenblum & Budde, "Historical and Cultural Consideration of Infanticide," 11.
19 . Angell "Handicapped Children: Baby Doe & Uncle Sam," 660.
20 . Quilloin v Woolcott, 434 US 246, 255 (1978).
21 . King, "Federal & State Regulations of Neonatal Decision Making," 96.
22 . Mason & Meyers, "Parental Choice and Selective Non-Treatment of Deformed Newborns: A View From Mid-Atlantic," 68.
23 . Ibid., 69.
24 . Crossley, "Selective Nontreatment of Handicapped Newborns: An Analysis," 501.
25 . Ibid., 500.
26 . Ibid., 502.
27 . Mason & Meyers, "Parental Choice and Selective Non-Treatment of Deformed Newborns: A View From Mid-Atlantic," 68.
28 . U.S. Constitution, Amendment V.
29 . Encyclopedia Britannica (1973), Volume 7, 161.
30 . Gostin, "A Moment in Human Development: Legal Protection, Ethical Standards and Social Policy on the Selective Non-Treatment of Handicapped Neonates," 51.
31 . Ellis, "Letting Defective Babies Die: Who Decides?," 399.
32 . Long, "Infanticide for Handicapped Infants: Sometimes It's a Metaphysical Dispute," 79.
33 . Duff & Campbell, "Moral & Ethical Dilemmas in the Special-Care Nursery," 891.
34 . Ibid., 894.
35 . Gostin, "A Moment in Human Development: Legal Protection, Ethical Standards and Social Policy on the Selective Non-Treatment of Handicapped Neonates," 32.
36 . American Academy of Pediatrics v Heckler, 561 F.Supp. 395, 396 (DC 1983).

37 . In re the Treatment and Care of Infant Doe, No. GU8204-004A (Ind. Cir. Ct., Apr. 12, 1982), cert. denied sub nom., Infant Doe v. Bloomington Hospital, 464 U.S. 961 (1983).
38 . Pless, "The Story of Baby Doe," 664.
39 . Public Law 93-112, 29 U.S.C. 794 (1982 & Supp. III 1985). Gostin, "A Moment in Human Development: Legal Protection, Ethical Standards and Social Policy on the Selective Non-Treatment of Handicapped Neonates," 59.
40 . Huefner, "Severely Handicapped Infants With Life-Threatening Conditions: Federal Intrusions Into The Decision Not To Treat," 175.
41 . Ibid., 176.
42 . 47 Fed. Reg. 26,027 (1982).
43 . Arras, "Toward an Ethic of Ambiguity," 25.
44 . Non-Discrimination on the Basis of Handicaps, 48 Fed Reg 9630 (1983)(interim final rule modifying 45 C.F.R. 84.61).
45 . Published March 7, 1983. 48 Fed. Reg. 9630.
46 . American Academy of Pediatrics v Heckler, 561 F.Supp 395 (D.D.C. 1983).
47 . American Academy of Pediatrics v Heckler, 561 F.Supp. 395, 400 (DC 1983).
48 . Non-discrimination on the Basis of Handicap Relation to Health Care for Handicapped Infants, Proposed Rule, 48 Fed. Reg. 30,846 (July 5, 1983)(proposed rules modifying 45 C.F.R. 84.61).
49 . Kuhse & Singer, Should the Baby Live?, 43.
50 . 49 Fed. Reg. 1622 (1984). Huefner, "Severely Handicapped Infants With Life-Threatening Conditions: Federal Intrusions Into The Decision Not To Treat," 179.
51 . 45 CFR 84.55 (1985). Bowen v American Hosp. Assn. 476 US 610, 613, 106 SCT 2101, 2105 (plurality opinion, 1986).
52 . Non-Discrimination on the Basis of Handicap in Programs and Activities Receiving or Benefitting from Federal Financial Assistance: Procedures and Guidelines Relating to Health Care for Handicapped Infants, Final Rule, 49 Fed. Reg. 1622, 45 C.F.R. 84.55 (1984). See Kuhse & Singer, Should the Baby Live?, 43-44.
53 . United States v University Hospital 729 F.2d 144 (1984).
54 . U.S. v. University Hosp., State U. of New York, 729 F2d 144, 146 (2nd Cir 1984).
55 . King, "Federal & State Regulations of Neonatal Decision Making," 89.
56 . U.S. v. University Hosp., State U. of New York, 729 F2d 144, 146 (2nd Cir 1984).
57 . Weber v StonyBrook Hospital, 95 AD2d 587, 467 N.Y.S.2d 685 (per curiam) (1983).
58 . Weber v Stony Brook Hospital, 60 NY2d 208, 456 NE2d 1186, 469 N.Y.S.2d 63 (1983)(per curiam), cert denied, 464 U.S. 1026 (1983).
59 . Murray & Caplan, "Beyond Babies Doe," 9.
60 . United States v University Hospital, State Univ of N.Y. at Stony Brook 575 F.Supp. 607 (E.D.N.Y. 1983).
61 . Bowen v American Hosp. Ass'n, 476 US 610, 623, 106 SCt 2101, 2114 (1986). The supreme court had earlier heard the case as Heckler v. American Hosp. Ass'n and renamed it reflecting the change in command at HHS.
62 . Gostin, "A Moment in Human Development: Legal Protection, Ethical Standards and Social Policy on the Selective Non-Treatment of Handicapped Neonates," 32.
63 . Shelp, Born to Die?, 13.

64 . Ibid., 14-15.
65 . 42 U.S.C. 5101-05 (1984).
66 . Newman, "Baby Doe, Congress and the States: Challenging the Federal Treatment Standard for Impaired Infants," 2.
67 . Ibid., 4.
68 . Gostin, "A Moment in Human Development: Legal Protection, Ethical Standards and Social Policy on the Selective Non-Treatment of Handicapped Neonates," 63.
69 . The Department of Health and Human Services reported that after investigating 49 cases of alleged discriminatory withholding of medical care under enforcement of the Baby Doe Regulations, they could find no evidence of discrimination in any of the cases. 49 Fed. Reg. 1646-1649 (1984). Turnbull, "Incidence of Infanticide in America: Public and Professional Attitudes," 382.
70 . Baby Doe born in Bloomington, Indiana with Downs syndrome and a surgically correctable blockage of the digestive tract. American Academy of Pediatrics v. Heckler, 561 F.Supp. 395 (DC 1983).
71 . Bowen v. American Hospital Ass'n, 476 U.S. 610, 624, 106 S.Ct. 2101, 2110, 90 L.Ed.2d 584 (1986).
72 . In re Baby K, 832 F.Supp. 1022, 1028 (E.D.Va. 1993), affm'd 16 F3d 590 (4th Cir 1994). The appeal court stated that "It is beyond the limits of our judicial function to address the moral or ethical propriety of providing emergency stabilizing medical treatment to anencephalic infants. We are bound to interpret federal statutes with their plain language and any expressed congressional intent." In the Matter of Baby K., 16 F3d 590, 598 (4th Cir 1994).
73 . Fletcher, "Infanticide & the Ethics of Loving Concern," 15-16.
74 . Varga, "The Ethics of Infant Euthanasia," 442.
75 . Smith, Concerning Human Life, 3.
76 . Fletcher, "Infanticide & the Ethics of Loving Concern," 19.
77 . Ibid., 17.
78 . Jacobovits, Jewish Medical Ethics, 46.
79 . Rosner, Studies in Torah Judaism: Modern Medicine and Jewish Law, 118.
80 . Ibid., 75.
81 . Strauss, "Culture, Rehabilitation, and Facial Birth Defects: International Case Studies," 57.
82 . Qiu, "Morality in Flux: Medical Ethics Dilemmas in the People's Republic of China," 22.
83 . Code of Maimonides, Hil. Rotze'ach, 2:7. Jakobovits, "Jewish Views on Infanticide," 26.
84 . Kuhse & Singer, Should the Baby Live?, 19.
85 . Weir, Selective Nontreatment of Handicapped Newborns: Moral Dilemmas in Neonatal Medicine, 150.
86 . Smith, Concerning Human Life, 20.
87 . Ramsey, Ethics at the Edges of Life, 192.
88 . Kary, "A Moral Distinction Between Killing and Letting Die," 332.
89 . Steinbock, "Infanticide," 103.
90 . Gostin, "A Moment in Human Development: Legal Protection, Ethical Standards and Social Policy on the Selective Non-Treatment of Handicapped Neonates," 37.
91 . According to Moshe Tendler, a Professor of Talmudic Law. Ibid., footnote 16, 37.
92 . Blustein, "Morality and Parenting: An Ethical Framework for Decisions About

The Treatment of Imperiled Newborns," 26.

93 . Pope Pius XII: Acta Apostolicae Sedis. McCormick, "To Save or Let Die," 174.
94 . Johnstone, "The Sanctity of Life, the Quality of Life and the New `Baby Doe' Law," 263.
95 . "Pastoral Constitution on the Church in the Modern World," 27, The Documents of Vatican II, 226.
96 . Lammers & Verhey, On Moral Medicine, 442, 444.
97 . Fletcher, "Infanticide & the Ethics of Loving Concern," 20.
98 . Himsworth, "The Human Right to Life: Its Nature & Origin," 169.
99 . Kluge, The Ethics of Deliberate Death, 120.
100. Ibid., 6.
101. Aiken, "Life & the Right to Life," 180.
102. Ibid.
103. Shelp, Born to Die?, 12.
104. Ibid., 19.
105. Ibid., 23.
106. Weir, Selective Nontreatment of Handicapped Newborns; Moral Dilemmas in Neonatal Medicine, 170.
107. Devine, The Ethics of Homicide, 150.
108. Schaeffer & Koop, Whatever Happened to the Human Race, 62.
109. Ibid., 65.
110. Weir, Selective Nontreatment of Handicapped Newborns; Moral Dilemmas in Neonatal Medicine, 62.
111. Kluge, "Infanticide as the Murder of Persons," 35.
112. Ibid., 40.
113. Kluge, The Ethics of Deliberate Death, 138. Kluge considers the characteristics of personhood to be self-awareness, rationality, symbolic awareness of reality and the capability of language, awareness of itself as a free causal agent and volition. Ibid., 126.
114. Ibid., 139.
115. Weir, Selective Nontreatment of Handicapped Newborns; Moral Dilemmas in Neonatal Medicine, 156.
116. Ibid., 157.
117. Ibid., 158.
118. Fletcher, "Infanticide & the Ethics of Loving Concern, 20.
119. Weir, Selective Nontreatment of Handicapped Newborns; Moral Dilemmas in Neonatal Medicine, 166.
120. McCormick, "To Save or Let Die," 175.
121
. Weir, Selective Nontreatment of Handicapped Newborns; Moral Dilemmas in Neonatal Medicine, 161.
122. Kuhse & Singer, Should the Baby Live?, 189.
123. Ibid., 192.
124. Gostin, "A Moment in Human Development: Legal Protection, Ethical Standards and Social Policy on the Selective Non-Treatment of Handicapped Neonates," 38.
125. Fleischman, "Caring for Babies in Danger," 17.
126. Wilson, Death by Decision, 29.
127. Ibid., 30.
128. Chicago Tribune (April 23, 1991): section 2, 1.

129. Repouille v. United States, 165 F2d 152 (CA2 1947).
130. Repouille v. United States, 165 F2d 152, 153 (CA2 1947).
131. Resnick, "Child Murder by Parents: A Psychiatric Review of Filicide," 329.
132. Harder, "The Psychopathology of Infanticide," 200.

CHAPTER XVII

POWER

"Three things seek my death,
  Hard at my heels they run -
Hang them, sweet Christ, all three -
  Devil, maggot and son."[1]

In the above quotation from an ancient Irish poem, aptly titled "Devil, Maggot & Son," a father angrily told how his own son evoked mortal fear in him, equal to that of the Devil himself. It was a chilling revelation to realize such danger from within the bonds of family ties, but one which has menaced many a man in times past. Like proverbial cute little kittens which grow into rough alley-cats, instances of children overthrowing their parents to achieve their own power base has not been rare in literature or in life.

For the most part, such fatal familial revolts have only affected people of wealth or power. Certainly, jealousy has caused many children from the middle and lower class to break away from the constraints of their family life, but few disputes have led to homicidal acts. The climb to success is seldom easy, however, and eminent men have only had to search their own checkered past to see what avenues their children might take to attain a similar goal. There is plenty of space at the bottom of life's triangle, but only room for one at the top.

Even in the liturgy of ancient religions, the gods had reason to fear the children they bore. In Greek mythology, Cronos was warned that his children would eventually usurp his power and he attempted to bypass this destiny by swallowing each newborn immediately after his wife Rhea gave birth.[2] This was done with the intention that no other of the proud children of the line of Ouranos should ever hold the king's position among the immortals.[3] When he was finally fooled by Rhea, after the birth of Zeus, into swallowing a stone wrapped in swaddling clothes instead of the actual infant god, his fate was sealed. Zeus, when grown, returned to dethrone his father and throw him into chains, fulfilling the very prophecy which Cronos vainly tried to prevent.[4] The Roman orator Cicero, later tried to dismiss the impact of this infanticidal story with the explanation that Cronos meant "satiated with years," and that the devouring of his sons meant rather that "time devours the ages," and not that the father devoured the son.[5] But such interpretive freedom was much too academic for the average Greek child who listened to these stories with literal amazement and did not search for hidden meanings.

The lesson in Fate was also not lost on Zeus, for when he later married his first wife Metis, Earth told him that she would bear a daughter and then a son who "would be the lord of heaven."[6] Finding his own role of lord much to his liking, Zeus then swallowed Metis to prevent her from having any further children.[7]

Other societies maintained similar fables for their gods. The Phoenicians borrowed the Greek text and told a story of Kronos, the son of Ouranos, who destroyed his son Sadidos because he was suspicious of the young man's ambition.[8] The Romans, as well, accepted the Greek mythology as consistent with appropriate responses on the part of their gods.

We need not look only to fables for occasions where parricide hastened the succession of royalty, however. Under most imperial inheritance procedures, the throne passed to the king's eldest child, usually a son, immediately upon the death of the monarch. Not infrequently, children found the appeal of ultimate power too attractive to wait until nature took its course, and many a son was led to the throne prematurely by subterfuge and murder of a slowly aging parent.

In response to these well-accepted threats, some rulers resorted to infanticide in order to eliminate the real danger from overly ambitious offspring. Oedipus, for example, was exposed by his father Laius because an oracle had told him he would be slain by his own child. Three days after his son was born, King Laius pierced the boy's ankles, "and by the hands of others cast him forth upon a pathless hillside."[9]

King Acrisius was similarly told in a prophecy that his grandson would kill him, and so he locked his daughter Danae up in an underground chamber of bronze to prevent her having access to suitors. When Zeus entered her guarded cell in a golden shower through the ceiling, she became pregnant and Acrisius had her put adrift in a basket, along with her infant Perseus.[10] The chest was carried to Seriphus where Dictys recovered it and reared Perseus to adulthood. While competing one day in a pentathlon, Perseus hurled a discus and accidently struck Acrisius on the foot and killed him, once again fulfilling the dire prophecy.[11]

In an analogous story, Astyages, the Persian ruler, dreamed that a vine grew from his daughter, Mandane, and covered all of Asia after her marriage to Cambyses. He was told by the oracles that this meant her offspring would rule in his place one day. When she then gave birth to a son, Cyrus, Astyages ordered the infant exposed.[12] The steward charged with this task found the command too severe and gave it to Harpagus who raised the boy as his own.[13] True to the prophecy, as in the case of Zeus, the boy eventually grew to manhood and defeated Astyages to become king himself.

The very founders of Rome, Romulus and Remus, were said to have been exposed on the banks of the Tiber because Aulius, the Alban king, feared the overthrow of his own royal power.[14] There was very little that a royal authority would not do to maintain their regal position. Zal, another traditional early ruler of Persia, was born to the paladin Sam during the reign of Shah Minuchihr. Because he had white hair at birth, a shameful disfigurement, his father ordered him exposed on Mt. Alburz.[15] This was because: "Sam felt his worldly ambitions frustrated and, in great fear that he might become the butt of ridicule, he strayed from the path of wisdom and chose a strange course."[16]

Chinese history, which generally greatly respected elders and parents, revealed similar instances where power overcame filial bonds. The Ch'in dynasty lasted from 221-207 B.C. and was characterized by the rule of a particularly brutal king. A short time before his death, he uncovered a fatal intrigue involving his son. To protect himself from harm, despite the advancement of his own years, he had the young man instantly executed.[17] Similarly, in 515 A.D., the widow of the newly deceased Chinese emperor, Empress Dowager Ling, seized power in the name of her son who was still a child. She was a devout Buddhist, but in 528 A.D., fearing that her son was becoming too independent, she killed him and enthroned a younger son in his stead.[18] Wu Zhao, or Empress Wu, also smothered her own infant daughter to implicate the Empress of Gaozong, and then when she was in power she disposed of one of her sons, who was the successor to the Prince, and replaced him with a more compliant younger son.

King Herod, the man who was made king of the Jews by the Romans, went to Caesar and accused his own sons of trying to take over his reign. He had tortured his eunuch servants until they told him that his son, Alexander, had wanted to take over the kingdom and that Herod was dying his hair black to cover up his age.[19] Alexander admitted that "the father may have a suspicion upon all his sons, as intending some treachery to him."[20] Herod presented his case against an assembly, as was the custom of the Jews at that time. Saturninus, one of the jurors, found the sons guilty but said they should not be killed for: "To put one's son to death is a greater misfortune than any other that could befall him by their means."[21] The others on the jury, however, inflicted the death penalty which Herod requested. Alexander and Aristobulus were then strangled by Herod's command.[22] At a later trial before Quintilius Varus, Herod accused his other son, Antipater, of taking power from him and had him killed with poison.[23]

It was not only a desire to maintain solitary control that led to infanticide, but statesmanship and honor have also been so closely guarded that the killing of a child has been deemed to be necessary. Brutus ruled Rome in the 244th year after its founding. He charged his two young sons, and also the two brothers of his wife, the Vitelli, with a plot to recall the Tarquin kings. Rome was now an independent city, and in order to assure this continued freedom, he had his family members beheaded.[24] Virgil found compassion in this act and defended the payment of such an extreme penalty "for fair freedom's sake."[25]

St. Augustine noted how Torquatus, another Roman, "slew his own son, not for fighting against his country, but only for going against his command, being general (he being a valorous youth and provoked by his enemy, year and getting the victory); because there was more hurt in his contempt of authority than good in his conquest."[26] This action was detested by Augustine, who reminded his readers that earthly goods and possessions are "never so dear as children."[27]

Such honorable ideals, however, was not usually the view of royalty. King Philip of Macedonia hated the Romans intensely, and set up his throne as defiantly standing for opposition to everything Roman. When his son Demetrius cultivated friendship within the outlawed city, Philip was forced to have him killed or lose credibility among those he ruled.[28] He sent Demetrius to Astraeum in Paeonia, and had Didas poison him there.[29]

In 1388 A.D., the Earl of Foix had a falling out with the king of Navarre, the brother of his wife. He then found poison in his son's purse which he interpreted as being for him. He threw his son in prison and then threatened to kill him with a knife and when a small amount of blood was drawn, the boy was so afraid he fell down and died on the spot.[30]

To help reduce the threats from children for dynastic considerations, while at the same time helping bridge relationships with the Church in medieval Europe, noblemen often would donate children to the service of the Church in the process known as "oblation." The general adage was: "The fewer full grown male relatives a king had around him, the easier he slept at night."[31] To keep the number of offspring under control, oblation was "certainly more humane than murdering them."[32]

There were also tales of fathers killing sons in mortal combat, without knowing the identity of their victim. One of the most well-known of these stories is contained within the Persian epic *Shah-nama*, or *The Epic of the Kings*, by Ferdowski, one of Iran's greatest poets who lived from 932-1020 A.D. One section related how Rustum, the Persian heroic warrior and son of Zal, had a son, Sohrab, by the princess Tahmina whom he had loved in his early youth. They were then separated for years, and Tahmina told Sohrab that he must conceal the identity of his father. One day, Rustum led the Persian army against the Tartars who had recruited Sohrab to be their champion. The two men met in single combat, unaware of their father-son relationship. Sohrab saw in Rustum a resemblance to himself, and also noted similarities to stories about his father that were told by his mother. He worried for a moment whether it could be true, and opined that: "I must not venture to give battle to my father and shamelessly confront him."[33] But the battle was fated to occur and Rustum mortally wounded the lad before realizing that it was his own son that he destroyed. Sohrab, in turn, when realizing that his slayer was his father, rued just before he died:

> If thou art Rustem, cruel is thy part,
> No warmth paternal seems to fill thy heart;
> Else hadst thou known me when, with strong desire,
> I fondly claimed thee for my valiant sire.[34]

In his modern version of the tale, Matthew Arnold also had Sohrab ask his father with his dying breath for a tomb where visitors may witness the place of his death and cry: "Sohrab, the mighty Rustum's son, lies there, Whom his great father did in ignorance kill!"[35]

A similar tale was found in the Irish legend of Cu Chullain, a warrior similar in reputation to Rustum. In *The Wooing of Emer*, it was told that he had a son with Aife, the Amazonian warrior, who raised the lad and told him never to reveal his real name.[36] The boy grew to become a mighty warrior and one day had to fight Cu Chullain in combat. Emer, the daughter of Forgall, warned Chullain not to fight the boy for he was his son. "Do not murder your only son!" she cried, but to no avail for Chullain did not believe her.[37] In the battle, the lad received a mortal blow and as he lay dying revealed his real identity to his victorious father. When Chullain claimed to have not recognized his son, the boy wryly added, "it is not a wonder you did not know me when I cast my spear crooked and feebly against your bush of blades."[38]

Tribal customs have also often sought to protect the chief from perceived dangers when children were born. In Baganda, Africa, the first child born to a chief was awaited with considerable anxiety, for it was thought that if the child was a boy then the father would die. As the midwife carefully delivered the first baby born, she checked to see if it was a male, and if so would then strangle the infant and tell everyone that the child was born dead.[39] In Shoshong, South Africa, in 1866, it was reported that king Sekhomo was so jealous of the popularity of his son Khame, that he determined to kill him. He engaged the evil magicians, "moloi", to go at night and kill the young man but Khame surprised them and smashed their magic apparatus.[40]

Among North American Indian legends, the story was told of Toscas wo-hah, Chief of the Cascades. He had two hundred wives and was powerful and strong. When any of the wives brought him a new baby, the Chief would kill it if it was a boy: "He was afraid the boy would grow up and become stronger than himself."[41] Only his daughters were allowed to live. One day, his wife Ni-ti-it had a son and lied, in order to save his life, by telling the Chief it was a girl. The boy grew to become even more powerful than the Chief and one day defeated him in battle. A similar story was also told where the mother was named Nom-i-neet.[42]

But even modern thought has not overlooked the jealousy which can develop between parent and child. Samuel Johnson, in *Rasselas*, noted that:

> In families where there is not poverty, there is commonly discord. If a kingdom be, as Imlac tells us, a great family, a family likewise is a little kingdom, torn with factions and exposed to revolutions. An unpracticed observer expects the love of parents and children to be constant and equal, but this kindness seldom continues beyond the years of infancy. In a short time the children become rivals to their parents; benefits are allayed by reproaches, and gratitude debased by envy.[43]

It appears, therefore, that the human species can revert to more primitive, animalistic attitudes of survival in the wild where progeny become dangerous rivals, rather than supportive friends, when one's authority and control are at stake.

Is it simply secondary to the ancient adage that "Power corrupts," or is a more natural, genetic reason at play? As Lady Macbeth chillingly admitted, even the death of a child should not stand in the way of her desire for dynastic power:

> I have given suck, and know how tender 'tis to love the babe that milks me; I would, while it was smiling in my face, have plucked my nipple from his boneless gums and dashed the brains out, had I so sworn as you have done to this.[44]

Endnotes

1 . O'Connor, The Fountain of Magic, 32.
2 . Hesiod, Theogony, 460-467, 24.
3 . Ibid., 460-462.
4 . Aeschylus, Eumenides, 641-42, 169.
5 . Cicero, De Natura Deorum, II.XXV.64, 185.
6 . Apollodorus, The Library, I.iii.6, Volume I, 2.
7 . Hesiod, Theogony, 890-891, 35.
8 . Philo of Byblos, The Phoenician History, 2.21, 51.
9 . Sophocles, Oedipus the King, 716-720, 41-42.
10 . Apollodorus, The Library, 2.4.1, 72.
11 . Ibid., 2.4.4, 73.
12 . Herodotus, The History, I.108, 84.
13 . Ibid., I.111, 85.
14 . Cicero, The Republic, II.II.4, 113.
15 . Dunn, The Foundling and the Werewolf, 97.
16 . Ferdowsi, Shah-nama, V., 35-36.
17 . Fitzgerald, A Concise History of East Asia.
18 . Empires Besieged, 126.
19 . Josephus, Antiquities, XVI.VIII.1, The Works of Flavius Josephus, Volume I, 569.
20 . Ibid., XVI.I.3, 334.
21 . Ibid., XVI.IX.3, 370.
22 . Ibid., XVI.IX.7.
23 . Ibid., XVII.V.
24 . Orosius, The Seven Books of History Against the Pagans, 50.
25 . Virgil, Aenead, VI.820, Virgil's Works, 125.
26 . St. Augustine, The City of God, V.XVIII, Volume I, 166.
27 . Ibid.
28 . Livy, History of Rome, XLI.XXIII.11, Volume XII, 263.
29 . Ibid., XL.XXIV.3-8, 77.
30 . Froissart, The Chronicles, 26, 180-187.
31 . Boswell, The Kindness of Strangers, 257.
32 . Ibid., 258.
33 . Ferdowski, Shah-nama, 75.
34 . "The Death of Sohrab," Poetry of the Orient, 78.
35 . Arnold, "Sohrab & Rustum," 792-793, Poetical Works, 85.
36 . Dillon, Early Irish Literature, 16.
37 . Ibid., 17.
38 . Colum, A Treasury of Irish Folklore, 57.
39 . Roscoe, The Baganda: An Account of Their Native Customs and Beliefs, 54.
40 . Holub, Seven Years in South Africa: Travels, Researches, and Hunting Adventures, Between the Diamond-Fields and the Zambesi, Volume I, 335-336.
41 . Hines, The Forgotten Tribes, Oral Tales of the Teninos and Adjacent Mid-Columbia River Indian Nations, 95-96.
42 . Ibid., 99.
43 . Johnson, Rasselas, 26, 100.
44 . Shakespeare, Macbeth, 1.7.55-60. Lady Macbeth was supposedly childless but

her boast, while an expression of fantasy, clearly shows how far she was willing to go in order to become queen. Calef, "Lady Macbeth and Infanticide or `How Many Children Had Lady Macbeth' Murdered?," 536-537.

CHAPTER XVIII

TWINS

"Twins have such great shadow that if they come near a sick person he will die: hence twins must be killed."[1]

The above superstition characterized the attitude of the Lovedu, a Bantu tribe in South Africa, where dire consequences were prophesied about the birth of twins. Such children were considered evil and had to be killed immediately after birth or it was thought that great damage would result to the mother's family or tribe. Such practices are likely to shock the modern Western reader, for today we not only consider most infant births a blessed event, but perceive multiple ones as cause for even greater celebration. After all, how often is a person fortunate enough to be rewarded with two offspring at the same time?

Actually, statistics show that the event is not that uncommon. In the United States twins are born once every eighty-six births. The occurrence will vary with rates of 1.79 being seen in Belgians and only 0.01 among the Cochin Chinese.[2] Caucasians, in general, have a higher rate of twin birth than the Mongoloid race.

There were also many ancient societies who found this type of birth a joyous occasion to be celebrated rather than feared. Tacitus wrote how Livia, the sister of Germanicus, gave birth to twin sons and was elated: "This, as a rare event, causing joy even in humble homes."[3] In the *Aenead*, by Virgil, Sergestus was given the Cretan slave girl Pholoe with twin sons on her breast as a prize which was to be honored over other equally attractive women hostages.[4]

And it is not a uniformly negative reaction among all tribal cultures as well. The Lepchas of Sikkim considered twins of the same sex lucky, although if the sexes were disparate, it was lucky only if the girl was born first.[5] In the Baganda liturgy, the birth of twins was seen as the direct intervention of the god Mukasa, and an important event to be celebrated.[6] Twins were also seen as fortunate among the Xosa of Africa, who planted euphorbia alongside the hut in order to protect against evil influences.[7] The Yoruba of Nigeria have the highest twinning rate in the world and consider the children to be imbued with magical powers.[8] Although they were considered evil and generally killed in ancient times, twins now are revered and their birth proclaims joy, happiness, and good luck. Among the Great Benin tribes twins were a good omen except in the Arebo area.[9] The Tembu and Fingo tribes of South Africa saw twins as lucky and planted two trees, or "Naaboom," when they were born.[10] The Mohave Indians, Yman tribes of southwest America, West African Ashanti, East African Shilluk, Balinese of Indonesia and Papago of southwestern United States also saw twins as a fortunate occurrence.[11]

But there were many instances when twins were considered to be a sign of malevolence and evoked fear and prophecies of destruction. In such instances, infanticide was promoted by custom and accepted as necessary to protect the rest of the family members. In addition, in some tribal societies when twins were of the opposite sex it was assumed that they had committed incest within the womb and forfeited their right to live on the basis of this sin.[12] The most common method in ancient times was to combine a ritual killing and banishment of both the mother and the twin.[13]

Gary Granzberg studied seventy tribal societies and found that eighteen did not permit one or both of the twins to live, a rate of over twenty-five percent.[14] The reasons for such drastic action varied, but seemed to revolve around economic, technological, and ecological issues. The most common reason twins were killed in Granzberg's research was that the society had insufficient facilities to properly rear two children at once and still allow the mother the ability to fulfill her other responsibilities.[15] As Dickeman pointed out, the maternal workload was so great that raising two infants at the same time was not feasible.[16] Lester confirmed the findings of Granzberg with relation to the inferior status of women and difficulty in raising twins, but did not uncover any statistical correlation with societal aggression.[17] He found that it was generally the man who made the decision to kill a twin.[18]

While the elimination of a least one of a pair of twins under these circumstances was a practical application of a limited means of sustenance, there were other interwoven feelings of trepidation which shadowed the unusual phenomenon. A review of tribal practices will further clarify the extent of this problem. As the general topic of infanticide in tribal populations general was already covered extensively in the chapter on Tribes, only the references to twin infanticide will be covered in this section.

Among Eskimos, twins were generally either separated, or, if one was a female, destroyed.[19] Many observers reasoned that an Eskimo woman could not possibly rear both children, and the custom was therefore prudent.[20] Because boys could support their parents when they were grown, if both twins were boys, one was often given to another family to be raised rather than be killed.[21] There was little evidence that Eskimos destroyed twins because of any magical concerns.

The Australian aborigines would usually kill one or both twins. The Yolngu, in Australia, commonly destroyed one of the twins.[22] The Narrinyeri, as well, would usually kill at least one infant, but often would destroy both.[23] The Aranda believed that the first-born of a twin, or "aldoparinja," was the child of an evil wind which entered the already pregnant women and was therefore a demon which had to be killed.[24] The Arunta of Central Australia felt that twins were unnatural and killed them immediately.[25] The grandmother would either stuff the infants mouth with coal or sand or beat its head with a stick. The Warramunga tribes saw the twin as uncanny and killed it so that after destruction of the body, the soul would return to the Alcheringa and then be reincarnated.[26]

Among the Siuai of Bougainville, the weaker of the two twins was usually killed.[27] In the Benin territory, twins were regarded as visitations of a devil and both the twins, and the mother, were generally sacrificed to appease the evil spirit whose ill-will brought them into being.[28]

Junod studied the Thonga tribes of South Africa and found that no child was ever killed at birth unless it was a twin.[29] They looked on the birth of twins as a great misfortune and in former times one of the pair, usually the feebler one, was put to death.[30] This was accomplished either by starvation or strangulation with a rope, and the child was then buried in a broken pot.[31]

The A-ki-ku-yu of British East Africa considered twins unlucky. They believed that twins could prevent a woman from ever bearing again if they were the first-born, and therefore killed at least one. If they came later, the prejudice did not exist.[32] Triplets were always unlucky, and were killed no matter when they were born.

The Ibo of Nigeria considered the birth of twins an evil and unnatural event. Among the south-eastern tribes it was believed that one twin was the child of a devil which had secretly mated the mother, and since it was impossible to tell which was the devil's baby, both must die.[33] The infants were crammed into old water pots and then put away and covered with leaves.[34] Twins were treated similarly in the southeast corner of Lake Victoria Nyanza and among the natives of Bukara Island. Modern legislation has condemned this practice, but it appears to still be present in some of the tribal cultures.[35] In 1991, a questionnaire circulated among the Efik, Ibibio and Annang tribes of south-eastern Nigeria indicated that 9% considered twins taboo.[36]

The Amhara of Ethiopia considered twins a great calamity and referred to them as "menta." Because it would be too difficult for the mother to suckle two babies for two years, the weaker twin was usually neglected. In Portuguese East Africa the birth of twins was seen as an appalling misfortune and one was usually put to death.[37] One of the twins were also put to death among the !Kung bushmen of the Kalahari Desert that borders Namibia and Botswana.[38] In the island in Lake Victoria Nyanza in Africa twins were exposed,[39] while the Arebo killed twins directly.[40]

Among the Buka Passage islands that formed part of New Guinea, twins were disliked and although they were not outright killed, they were often not given proper attention. This generally resulted in the death of one or both.[41]

The Akha in India did not see twins as children, but rather as evil spirits who had to be disposed of as quickly as possible.[42] The infants would usually have either charcoal, or rice husks, stuffed in their mouth and they were then left in the jungle to die. It was believed that if the children were not destroyed in this fashion, epidemics or crop failure would result. One of a pair were also killed among the Todas of Southern India who commonly practiced female infanticide as well.[43]

Twins were seen as an evil spirit among the Piaroa of Venezuela and the Indians of the Guianas.[44] Among the Tehetehara of Northeast Brazil, infanticide was rare but did occur with twins who were thought to be the result of sexual relations between the mother and a dangerous supernatural being.[45] The Tapinape, in a similar belief, would bury the twins at birth. The Aztecs of Mexico,[46] and the Witotos of Northwestern Amazonia also killed one of a pair of twins.[47]. The Aztecs had a strict taboo on infanticide and abortion in order to increase the need for man power. They did, however, allow for the killing of a twin where the last born was killed at birth.[48]

The Central Pomo of Northern California practiced infanticide against twins, although they seldom killed other children.[49] This was also the case with the Kawaiisu of the Sierra Nevada region of California,[50] the Death Valley and Big Smoky groups of the Western Shoshone,[51] the Southwest Indians north of the Meso-American border,[52] the Wailaki of California,[53] and the Cahto of California.[54] The Konkow Indians of California considered it so unlucky to give birth to twins that in addition to killing the children, the mother was often killed as well.[55] Among the Maidu of California, twins were seen as an ill-omen and both were killed. Other tribes would only kill one twin in the belief that they would fight when they grew up.[56] The Cree of Northwestern Canada immediately killed one of a pair of twins, usually the girl.[57] Twins were often killed by the Tikopians of Melanesia and the Bontoc Igorot of the Phillipines.[58] One of a pair were killed among the Ainus of Northern Japan.[59]

While practical and economic reasons for the killing of twins was the underlying basis in most primitive cultures, fear and ignorance have been the primary reason in more "advanced" societies. In the Middle Ages, there was a belief that women could not conceive twice consecutively which meant that twins could not be born from the same father. Earlier Greek mythology also felt this to be likely as with the legend of Heracles (Hercules) who was born a twin and felt to be the offspring of Zeus, rather than his mortal father, Amphitryon.[60] While earlier Greek civilizations accepted that one of the children could be the issue of a god, the Medieval mind did not see the same benefit and one of the twins was usually abandoned.[61]

Endnotes

1 . Krige & Krige, The Realm of a Rain-Queen, 218.
2 . Newman, Multiple Human Births, 38.
3 . Tacitus, Annals, III.84.
4 . Virgil, Aenead, V.284-5, 89.
5 . Gorer, Himalayan Village: An Account of the Lepchas of Sikkim, 288.
6 . Roscoe, The Baganda: An Account of Their Native Customs and Beliefs, 64.
7 . Soga, The Ama-Xosa: Life and Customs, 295-296.
8 . Oruene, "Cultic Powers of Yoruba Twins: Manifestation of Traditional and Religious Beliefs of the Yoruba," 221.
9 . Roth, Great Benin: Its Customs, Art and Horrors, 35-36.
10 . Laubscher, Sex, Custom & Psychopathology, 90.
11 . Williamson, "Infanticide: An Anthropological Analysis," 65.
12 . Ford, "Control of Conception in Cross-Cultural Perspective," 765.
13 . Oruene, "Cultic Powers of Yoruba Twins: Manifestation of Traditional and Religious Beliefs of the Yoruba," 222.
14 . Granzberg, "Twin Infanticide: A Cross-Cultural Test Of a Materialistic Explanation," 405.
15 . Ibid., 406.
16 . Dickeman, "Demographic Consequences of Infanticide in Man," 116.
17 . Lester, "The Relation of Twin Infanticide to Status of Women, Societal Aggression, and Material Well-Being," 58.
18 . Ibid., 59.
19 . Hoebel, The Law of Primitive Man, 75.
20 . Garber, "Eskimo Infanticide," 100.
21 . Ibid.
22 . Hippler, "Culture and Personality Perspective of the Yolngu of Northeastern Arnhem Land: Part I – Early Socialization," 227.
23 . Smyth, The Aborigines of Victoria, 52.
24 . Roheim, "The Western Tribes of Central Australia: Childhood," 195.
25 . Spencer & Gillen, The Arunta, Volume I, 39.
26 . James, Primitive Ritual and Belief: An Anthropological Essay, 10.
27 . Oliver, A Solomon Island Society: Kinship and Leadership Among the Siuai of Bougainville, 501.
28 . Newman, Multiple Human Births, 6.
29 . Junod, The Life of a South African Tribe, Volume I, 41.
30 . Ibid., Volume II, 433.
31 . Ibid., Volume II, 434.
32 . Routledge & Routledge, With a Prehistoric People, 149.
33 . Asindi, Moira, Etuk, & Udo, "Brutality to Twins in South-eastern Nigeria: the Existing Situation," 378.
34 . Basden, Niger Ibos, 182.
35 . Ibid., 183.
36 . Asindi, Young, Etuk, & Udo, "Brutality to Twins in South-eastern Nigeria: the Existing Situation," 379.
37 . Maugham, Portuguese East Africa: The History, Scenery & Great Game of Manica and Sofala, 271.
38 . Kuhse & Singer, Should the Baby Live?, 101.
39 . Levy-Bruhl, Primitive Mentality, 150.

40 . M'Lennan, Studies in Ancient History, 98.
41 . Blackwood, Both Sides of Buka Passage, 164.
42 . Bernatzik, Akha and Miao: Problems of Applied Ethnography in Farther India, 78.
43 . Murdock, Our Primitive Contemporaries, 118.
44 . Williamson, "Infanticide: An Anthropological Analysis," 65.
45 . Wagley, "Cultural Influences on Population: A Comparison of Two Tupi Tribes," 273.
46 . Murdock, Our Primitive Contemporaries, 383.
47 . Ibid., 463.
48 . Carsch, "The Family, Child Rearing and Social Controls Among the Aztecs," 9.
49 . Dickeman, "Demographic Consequences of Infanticide in Man," 123.
50 . Zigmond, "Kawaiisu," 403.
51 . Thomas, Pendleton & Cappannari, "Western Shoshone," 270.
52 . Griffin, "Southern Peiphery: East," 335.
53 . Elsasser, "Mattole, Nongatl, Sinkyone, Lassik, and Waiaki," 196.
54 . Myers, "Cahto," 245.
55 . Riddell, "Maidu & Konkow," 381.
56 . Heizer, "Natural Forces and Native World View," 652.
57 . Smith, "Western Woods Cree," 260.
58 . Aptekar, Anjea: Infanticide, Abortion & Contraception in Savage Society, 71.
59 . Murdock, Our Primitive Contemporaries, 178.
60 . Morford & Lenardon, Classical Mythology, 354.
61 . Shahar, Childhood in the Middle Ages, 122.

CHAPTER XIX

LOVE OF ANOTHER

> "A son, a little child of unknown promise is dead; a fragment of time has been lost."[1]

There are occasions where a person suddenly finds himself having to choose between equally beloved people or creeds that have clashed to such a degree that the simultaneous existence of both is not possible. Such a choice is always difficult, but it is particularly onerous and tragic when the one having to choose is a parent, and the life in danger is his or her own child. Under such dire straits, how does one judge the actions of such an embattled executioner?

In the above quotation, the Greek philosopher Seneca summarized the Stoic position on the prospective value of a child's life. Putting all of the youngster's potential into perspective, there were many other things which had greater practical importance: honor, friends, and nationalism, just to name a few. When a Greek parent was abruptly faced with the possible loss of one dearly beloved object in order to spare the survival of another, they sometimes chose the rational, rather than emotional, option. It may have been a cold or calculated assessment, but the fact remains that children have a clearly unpredictable future and a minimally productive present. In addition, there was always the opportunity of replacing one child with another by future generation, or there may have already been other children alive who were not in any present danger. The same was not necessarily true of the alternate choice.

Such a callous appraisal of the positive attributes of children may be uncomfortable to those who are loving parents, devoted to nothing more intensely than the welfare of their offspring. Over the centuries, however, many respected, educated and reverent parents put extreme importance in things such as honor, or friends, or the survival of the country in which they lived. If faced with having to choose between such objects and their own children, some of these otherwise rational adults would have steadfastly protected their beliefs, even if it resulted in their child's death. These parents did not have a deficient paternal or maternal instinct, but rather had a greater overriding love which made the infant's life expendable by comparison. In this chapter, I will discuss some of the past and present "loves" which have been seen to supersede that of a child.

A. GOD

The biblical story of Abraham and Isaac, discussed earlier in the chapter on Sacrifice, typified the terrible predicament a parent may find himself in when one's devotion to God conflicts with the life of one's own child. In most religions, love and reverence to the Almighty God overrides all other mortal bonds. The truly pious believer must be willing to sacrifice any life, even their own, if the Lord so directs. In Judaism, this belief was voiced by the martyrs of Mainz who cried out, in defense against the rampaging townspeople who were preparing to destroy their synagogue:

> Oh, our good fortune if we do His will! Oh, the good fortune of everyone slain and butchered and killed for the Unification of His name. There is none better to sacrifice our lives to than our God.[2]

They went on to take their own lives, including cutting the throats of their children. They were slain and sacrificed "for the Unification of the Glorious and Awesome Name."[3]

Such a devotion brought Abraham to the brink of killing his only son, Isaac, when the voice of the Lord commanded him to sacrifice the boy in a burnt offering. For over five thousand years, the Jewish faithful, and devotees of other religions as well, have found this willingness of Abraham to follow God's directive inspirational and commendable.

If you accept the Old Testament as a holy text that accurately reflects the recollection of the facts as related by the Lord to Moses, you trust that Abraham responded to the true word of the true God. Such an act of faith could only be doubted by a confirmed atheist. The problem we face in other such cases is determining when the voice directing infanticide is that of the real Saviour, and when it is a false prophet.

Philo, the first century A.D. Jewish philosopher, noted with disdain how barbarian nations "have for long admitted child sacrifice as a holy deed and acceptable to God."[4] These nations have done horrible things, he severely reprimanded, referring to the biblical text where it was revealed that "they have even roasted their sons and daughters before their gods."[5] This condemnation, of course, came from an extremely pious Jew who believed that Abraham's willingness to offer his only son was laudatory, and that the commands of Yahweh were to be strictly obeyed without any questions asked. The obvious difference to Philo was that his God was the true God, and the barbarians were performing murder before a false idol.

The Almighty God of the Jews, and subsequently of the Christians and Muslims as well, was a very angry and demanding Deity. He expected that His commandments were to be followed without failure. While He might show compassion to the welfare of His chosen people in general, He was not adverse to utilizing death as a means to candidly reprimand those who disobeyed His commands. When Moses came down from Mt. Sinai and found the people worshiping a golden calf-idol, he told the Levites to kill those who disobeyed and then extolled them with:

> Today you have ordained yourselves for the service of the Lord, for you obeyed him even though it meant killing your own sons and brothers; now he will give you a great blessing.[6]

Josephus pointed out this trait in the biblical tale of Nadab and Abihu, two of Aaron's sons who were instructed to follow the proper order of temple worship. When they did not bring the sacrifices which Moses had ordered, the Lord punished them by causing a fire to flash up at the altar and burn them to death.[7] Josephus noted that their loss was not to be mourned for: "Moses entreated their brethren and their father not to be troubled for them, and to prefer the honor of God before their grief about them."[8]

And during the terrible days in Jerusalem, when Antiochus IV, Epiphanes, tried to force the conversion of the Jews by ordering them to eat of swine's flesh, seven brothers elected to be tortured and killed rather than profane themselves in this way.[9] And their elderly mother, agreed with their choice to die rather than disobey the commandments of God for "when two alternatives lay before her, religion, or the immediate salvation of her sons according to the tyrant's promise, she loved religion better, which preserves to eternal life according to God's promise."[10] This belief that the precepts of God were more important than life itself was woven into the very fabric of Jewish, Islamic and Christian history.

The Christians were told, in even clearer terms as documented in the New Testament, how necessary it was to follow the teachings of Jesus Christ, the Son of God who was sent to expiate the world of sin. When Jesus was questioned by the Pharisees in Judea over his new teachings which differed from the instructions of Moses, He answered that dedication to God was the only way to assure a peaceful life in the hereafter.[11] He then instructed Peter that:

> Anyone who gives up his home, brothers, sisters, father, mother, wife, children, or property, to follow me, shall receive a hundred times as much in return, and shall have eternal life.[12]

It was clear that a family member was not to interfere with devotion offered to Jesus Christ. In Galilee, Jesus told a crowd of followers:

> Anyone who wants to be my follower must love me far more than

> he does his own father, mother, wife, children, brothers, or sisters – yes, more than his own life – otherwise he cannot be my disciple.[13]

He reminded his twelve disciples: "If you love your son or daughter more than me, you are not worthy of being mine."[14]

This allegiance was not based in theory alone, but was expected to withstand even instances where the life of a loved one had to be lost. When the "true" word of God, the Gospel of Jesus Christ, was to be spread among the people of Israel, Jesus warned that: "Brother shall betray brother to death, and fathers shall betray their own children."[15] The disciples were destined to be hated by those they tried to convert. They were to be arrested and whipped, scorned and even killed, but all who would endure their sufferings would be saved. The message of salvation, was to take a deadly toll:

> Don't imagine that I came to bring peace to the earth! No, rather, a sword. I have come to set a man against his father, and a daughter against her mother, and a daughter-in-law against her mother-in-law, a man's worst enemies will be right in his home![16]

This message of supreme devotion and faith was continued by the Church Fathers. Origen advised the people to be as constant in purpose as was Abraham: "Offer your son to God joyful, immovable in faith."[17] For it was God that determined the eternal life of man. And it was He who offered even his own son for the grace of all mankind. If you followed God's commands, then even the death of your child should not be withheld:

> Behold God contending with men in magnificent liberality: Abraham offered God a mortal son who was not put to death; God delivered to death an immortal son for men[18]

St. Valerian, writing in the fifth century A.D., praised the story of the mother who sacrificed her seven sons, and then followed with martyrdom of her own life, in a blessed devotion to God:

> If, therefore, our father Abraham offered one son in sacrifice and pleased God, how much more has this mother pleased Him! At one time she immolated seven sons to God, with prayers of approving desire. Then she offered herself as the eighth victim.[19]

Her actions were to stand as encouragement to others of heavenly glory and "an example of outstanding virtue."[20]

To be a good Christian, one had to love God above anything or anyone else. The *Ethiopic Didascalia*, a supposed message to the Christian Church from the Twelve Apostles, noted that: "He that loveth his son or his daughter more than me is not worthy of me."[21] The Brotherhood of Man was never to be equated with allegiance to the Almighty God.

Moslems were no less devoted to the word of God as recorded by Mohammed in the Koran. The fervor of this obedience is graphically witnessed today by Moslem fundamentalists who are willing to sweep aside any form of resistance to the teachings of their religious leaders. No matter what action is required, their rulers are followed as the direct descendants of God. In the words of Fakhr ud-Din Gurgani, in the eleventh century A.D.:

> Three kinds of obedience are obligatory to the reasonable man, and those three are connected; they spell for the heart enjoyment of desire, and for the soul, good name; honorable life in this world, eternal paradise in the next. Do not turn your head away from the command of these three, if you would gain both worlds! One is the command of the Judge of the world, which liberates the soul forever. Second, the command of the Prophet Muhammad, which is rejected by a faithless unbeliever. Third, the command of the Sultan that rules the world, splendor of the religion of God in the realm.[22]

A Muslim would follow the directive of his king as intensely as he would the laws of the Koran.

Such allegiance was not confined to monotheism. The Greek and Roman gods were equally demanding of strict obedience, and failure to appease their edicts could result in dire consequences. Although it was seldom necessary to sacrifice a human child to assure placation, the killing of Iphigenia by Agamemnon is evidence of how devoted the Greeks were in obeying the commands of their gods.[23]

We also see the god's displeasure, however, if a child's blood is spilled unnecessarily. When Tantalus sacrificed his own son, Pelops, in order to demonstrate his satisfaction when the gods came to dine at his house, the gods were abhorred. The boy was "met by the cruel sword, even while he ran to gain his father's kiss," but was restored to life by the gods and Tantalus punished by having him stand wearily while "above his head hangs ready food, more swift to take its flight than Phineus' birds."[24]

Other pagan gods, however, were less offended and even required the offering of human flesh, often that of the infant variety. Civilizations which practiced such rites appear to have shown little reluctance to follow the fatalistic commands, believing that obedience was next to godliness. The priesthood, delegated the responsibility of interpreting the requirements of the gods, would be under particular stress during times of war or famine, and were not adverse to requesting infanticide in order to appease the anger of the deity. This is discussed more thoroughly in the chapter on Sacrifice.

B. FAMILY

Choosing between saving the life of a mortal and remaining devoted to the Lord of Heaven may be relatively easy for some faithful devotees, but deciding which member of one's own family to save brings forth an incredibly difficult assignment. How does one determine which son or daughter, husband or wife, mother or father, brother or sister is the most beloved? A family is filled with many strata of loves, and picking out one as more cherished than another can be an impossible task.

One relationship which has demonstrated very strong bonds over the years is that of brother-sister. This was graphically illustrated in the Persian story of the wife of Intaphrenes. King Darius, the Persian ruler from 521-485 B.C., had Intaphrenes and his entire family arrested for suspicion of being part of a conspiracy against the throne. Typical Persian justice was swift, and all who were detained were summarily sentenced to be executed by decapitation. The wife of Intaphrenes, however, begged Darius for mercy and her beauty moved him to offer her the opportunity to survive and save only one other family member. She had before her a husband of many years, a brother and multiple children. She finally appealed for her brother to be set free stating:

> My lord, I can get a husband again, if it is God's pleasure, and other children if I lose these; but my father and mother being dead, in no way can I have another brother.[25]

Plutarch, commenting on this choice in his treatise on *Moralia*, adjudged her decision as very meritorious.[26]

This genetic attachment between siblings also led to a troubled decision for Althaea, the mother of Meleager in Greek legend. Meleager had killed Althaea's two brothers, Plexippus and Toxeus, after they had insulted his lover, Atalanta. Althaea, after hearing of the parricide, was faced with the agonizing decision of whether to avenge the shades of her brothers by taking the life of her own son, or overlooking her filial ties in favor of Meleager. To a Greek, an unavenged murder would leave the spirits of the dead to roam through Hades for all eternity, a fate which was worse than death itself. Yet the mournful mother could only fulfill this responsibility by killing her only child. After a long tormenting night, she finally decided that she must choose her brothers first:

> At last the sister in her overcomes the mother, devoted to appease with blood the shades of her own blood-kin, she must spill the blood of her own son, a mother undevoted.[27]

As she prepared to burn the magical brand which would lead to her son's death, she cried out: "I gave you the gift of life; you owe the debt of death."[28] Althaea understood that her revenge of one evil deed was through the commission of an equally horrendous one and when the act was done, she hung herself in grief. Ovid commented that at the moment Meleager died, Althaea proved a "better sister than a mother."[29]

Similarly, Athaliah, the daughter of Ahab and Jezebel, took revenge on the children of her son for the killings of her parents and brother. She "stifled my maternal tenderness" and repaid murder for murder.[30]

In an unusual extension of this sibling preference, Attalus, the king of Pergamus, exposed all his own children so that he could leave his crown to the son of his brother Eumenes.[31] A nephew thereby became more worthy than a son because of brotherly love.

But of all the difficult choices to be made among various family members, being forced to decide among one's own children who is to live, and who is to die, may be the most agonizing decision a parent ever has to make. How can one make such a selection? Do you save the oldest child, the one first-born? Or do you pick the strongest? The most capable? The most attractive? Who becomes the most expendable in such a dismal scenario?

For many families who have been faced with this dilemma, the answer has resided within the age of the infant. When there are multiple healthy offspring alive, and all are of otherwise equal emotional and productive value, it is most often the newborn infant who is left unprotected. This is generally because the newborn has not yet formed a strong attachment to the rest of the family, and the resultant loss is not as great as with the older children. Of course, as we have earlier discussed in previous chapters on female infanticide and culling, the presence of the sex and health of the infant is always taken into consideration first.

Perhaps the most likely time in which such a choice will have to be made is during famines associated with tribal societies. Australian aboriginals, in order to assure the survival of an older child, will even feed them the flesh of a younger child in a form of cannibalism that has escaped social condemnation. Even if the child is not provided as part of the food base, there are times where its sustenance cannot be maintained as it would take too much nutriment away from the other siblings, and put their continued survival at risk. The parent must therefore choose to feed only some of the children, and practicality is the only guideline to follow. In her evaluation of infanticide in a small South American town whose inhabitants were extremely poor, Piers found that it was usually the seventh or eighth child in a family who was the one doomed to die in order that an older child could live.[32]

The infant mortality rate of many tribal societies is very high. Among the East Sepik in Papua New Guinea, 400 per 1000 children will not survive infancy. Under these conditions, closely spaced newborns are often killed in order to assure the survival of the older sibling. Under these conditions, infanticide is rather an "adaptation to" and not "a cause of" the high mortality.[33] Of all infants born in 1966, 11% were killed, twice as many females as males.[34]

And then were times where the decision was made because one particular child was a favorite, even though all of the children were generally beloved. Again, it was generally the older child who was chosen because of closer parental ties. In Communist China, only one son was generally permitted to be exempt from military service. One family was described where a second son was born unexpectedly late in life. When the older boy was drafted into the army, the mother "went home and beat her new baby to death," in order to prevent the loss of her favorite son.[35]

C. COUNTRY

Love of one's country has often superceded even that of other family members in many areas of the world. This was particularly evident during the Greek and Roman eras, when the state took on an almost super-human personna. Philo of Byblos told how ancient peoples in dangerous situations would often sacrifice their own children for the sake of the whole population: "It was customary for the rulers of a city or nation, rather than lose everyone, to provide the dearest of their children as a propitiatory sacrifice to the avenging deities."[36] He related how Kronos, who the Phoenicians called El, sacrificed his only son, Anobret, on an altar in royal attire "when war's gravest dangers gripped the land."[37]

Aristotle reasoned that such devotion was quite rational and understandable. He explained that when several families united, they became a village; and when villages then coalesced they became a state. This meant that: "The state is by nature clearly prior to the family and to the individual, since the whole of necessity is prior to the part."[38] No single person, even one's own child, retained primary importance in such a system of law.

Epictetus, the first century A.D. Greek Stoic philosopher, also accepted that the universal agreement among men was "that the whole is superior to the part, and the state to the citizen."[39] An individual could never claim to be more important than his country which would survive beyond the life of any mortal man.

Many Greeks were honored for their support of this concept and their willingness to put the survival of the state before their own children. Statesmen of the highest reputation showed no reluctance to putting their offspring to death in an attempt to promote the strength of their country.[40] It was felt by most commentators of the time that actions of this type were necessary for otherwise the "cities and countries cannot but fail."[41] Pausanias described in his travelogue the silver statue to the Eponymoi, from whom the ten tribes of Athens were established. Leos was among these famous figures and was said to "have given up his daughters, at the command of the oracle, for the safety of the commonwealth."[42] Such actions were honored rather than abhorred in the ancient world.

A similar crisis was said to have developed during the war between the Lacedaemonians and Messenians. The Messenians were losing, and Euphaes, the respected oracle, said that a maiden, whose "father gives her freely for the slaughter," had to be sacrificed to the god.[43] After the lots were cast, Lycisus is first chosen but it is determined that the maiden is not his real daughter so Aristodemus offers his own daughter in her place.[44] The young woman's lover then claims that she should not be killed because she is pregnant, and Aristodemus, "in a fury of passion," kills the girl and opens her belly to show that the statement was false.[45]

In Sparta, devotion to the state was particularly passionate. Children were trained early on to endure the hardships of life with few luxuries – a "spartan" existence – and adults lived a life of privation without the need of comfort or frivolity. Parents saw the survival of their sons as totally subservient to the welfare of the state. Argileonis, the mother of Brasidas, typified this attitude when she responded to compliments about the heroic behavior of her son who died a valiant death in battle: "Sirs, my son was a good and honorable man, but Sparta has many a man better than him."[46] When Damatria heard that her son survived the fighting, but proved a coward under stress, she determined that he was unworthy of her love and killed him upon his return from the war.[47] Another Spartan mother heard her son ran away from the enemy and wrote: "Either clear yourself of this (report) or stop your living."[48] Spartan soldiers were expected to die a heroic death rather than live a pusillanimous life.

The biologic Spartan family was imperceptibly entwined with citizenry throughout the entire state. When one mother, who had sent five of her sons to the war, met a worn and injured returning survivor, she reservedly asked of how the battle went. The man recognized who she was, and compassionately responded that all five of her sons had unfortunately been killed. "I did not inquire about that, you vile harlet," she replied, "but how fares our country?"[49]

For many Spartan men, death on the battlefield was more noble than winning at the Olympic games, and more worthwhile than living a long, but otherwise dishonorable, life.[50] In the words of one mother of a son who gave his life in battle, "I bore him that he might die for Sparta."[51] Another said: "Lay him away, and let his brother take his place."[52]

But where the individual death of commoners, even those whose actions were valiantly heroic, was soon forgotten, the fate of an elite few became legendary. The story of the flight of Helen to Troy, and the resultant Trojan War which followed for ten long years, has retained incredible literary magnetism since Homer initially began to sing the verses over two thousand years ago. But if it was not for the willingness of a father to kill his own child for the sake of his country, the tale may never have been told. As Racine had him reason" "How could I dare to put the State below my daughter, and grow old at home unsung?"[53] The tale of Agamemnon and Iphigenia is detailed in the chapter on Sacrifice.

The Romans placed an equal emphasis on the critical role of the state. Cicero argued that one's moral obligation was to their country first, then parents, and then the children.[54] Polybius, in his *History of Rome*, noted that:

> There have also been instances of men in office putting their own sons to death, in defiance of every custom and law, because they rated the interests of their country higher than those of natural ties even with their nearest and dearest.[55]

Even political office was felt to supersede family ties. Seneca comforted one grieving father by reminding him that "there are countless cases of men who have buried sons and returned to their duties."[56] The loss of a son would be only a "mere sting," and by prolonging one's grief would be a show of weakness.[57]

Lucius Junius Brutus was considered a great patriot by Virgil for having killed his own sons in the cause of Roman freedom: "Though a father, for the sake of splendid freedom he will yet condemn his very sons who stirred new wars."[58] He was later called unnatural for this act by Servius in the late fourth century A.D.[59]

Germanicus stated with honor and pride that "neither wife nor son are dearer to me than my father and the state."[60] The reasoning was clear: "Princes were mortal; the State was everlasting."[61] It was said that when Germanicus died, the Romans were so grieved that "new-born babies of wedded parents were thrown forth to be destroyed."[62]

Soldiers showed similar devotion to their military leaders. In *Pharsalia*,

Lucan told of Laelius, a centurion who boastfully declared to Caesar: "Tell me to plunge a sword into my brothers breast, my father's throat, or the belly of my wife, now great with child, and I will not fail you."[63]

One reason the people were so intently devoted to their state leaders was the confluence between the rulers of the land and the mythological gods. Kings from many countries claimed divine heritage in the era before Christ including Rome, Greece, and Egypt.[64] The Scandinavians, Celts, Germans, and English also saw their kings as divine, and their heraldry formed a bridge between the worlds of gods and of men.[65]

This led to an unbridled allegiance to the king who stood in the stead of the state. The "Siete Partidas" law of the Castilians, for example, allowed:

> A father who is besieged in a castle he holds from his lord, may, if so beset with hunger that he has nothing to eat, eat his child with impunity rather than surrender the castle without permission of the lord.[66]

Among the Persians, Herodotus related how Boges was praised by Xeres for his actions when Eion was under siege by Cimon. When there was no food left, he piled up a great pyre and slew and cast into the fire his children, wife, concubines and servants, and then threw himself on the fire as well after scattering the gold and silver.[67] There was nothing which loyal followers would not do for their military and political leaders.

And leaders would demand equal obedience, and valor, from their own children. In *Tamburlaine*, by Christopher Marlowe, the mighty king killed his own son Calyphas because of his cowardly manners: "Folly, sloth, and damned idleness . . . Thou hast produced a greater enemy" than the curse of Asia.[68] He refused to let his men bury "this effeminate brat, for not a common soldier shall defile his manly fingers with so faint a boy."[69]

While some of these motives were ethically defensible, if not even laudable, there were certainly times where interest in the state was linked with personal gain rather than the corporate good. Philo, the first century A.D. Jewish philosopher, noted that many parents had patriotically accepted that their children had to be "sacrificed for their country to serve as a price to redeem it from wars or drought or excessive rainfall or pestilence."[70] But he cautioned that in many cases there were less laudatory motives for choosing the state's welfare over the life of their own children. Some, for example, seemed rather to be acting "partly through desire for glory and honor, to win fame at the time and a good name in the future."[71] Such an endeavor would be detestable:

> If anyone throws away a son or a daughter through desire for

glory he will be justly blamed rather than praised, for with the life of his dearest he is purchasing an honour which he ought to cast aside.[72]

D. FRIENDS

In more ancient civilizations, the ability to survive the rigors of life often depended more on the availability of a network of friends than on genetically inherited advantages. There was no guarantee of protection from marauding neighbors through local militia, and harvesting of crops could not be completed without the cooperative efforts of many individuals. Archytas of Tarentum voiced the sentiment, shared by many others, that: "Nature abhors solitude."[73] It was very difficult for one man to live alone, and as friendships were formed to solidify a more secure way of life, the bonds attained a level of allegiance that rivaled even those of the biologic family.

In Roman times, friends often were given more love and affection than one's own children. Seneca chided one man for being womanish as he grieved after recently losing a young son: "Had you lost a friend – which is the greatest blow of all – you would have not grieved, but rather rejoiced for knowing him."[74] Lucian admired the story of Abauchas who let his wife and children almost die in a fire to save his friend Gyndanes and then explained: "I can beget other children easily enough . . . but it would be long before I get another friend as Gyndanes."[75]

In the Middle Ages, there was a popular tale of a knight who sacrificed his children to get blood as a cure for a friends leprosy.[76] And in the Portuguese tale of "Pedro and the Prince," a prince killed his only son in order to obtain blood that would bring back to life his dear friend, Pedro, who had risked his own life to save that of the princess.[77] An African tale, "The Quality of Friendship," told of a similar killing to obtain blood to restore the sight of a friend.[78]

E. LOVERS

From conjugal love to illicit sexual passion, the literary accounts of the depths to which intense carnal desire can reach ranges from dime store trash to the Nobel Prize. There is no dearth of material dedicated to this theme, but in real life, as well as in the printed word, many unions have been fatally parted in the eternal saga of unrequited love. "All is fair in love and war" may have been intended as an aphorism for behavior of the chase, but its message can just as easily describe a legacy of slaughter.

The lessons of this devotion are not restricted to select cases alone. Among certain Indian cultures, it was customary for a widow to throw herself on the burning funeral pyre of her husband in a suicidal offering of love. The intensity of this sacrifice – known as "sati" – was memorialized in a Persian poem from the seventeenth century:

> Then like a ruby, she entered the flames, and gazed on the fire with so ravished a look that the fire was afraid of touching her;
> So impatient she was because of her heart's desire, that the heart of the fire became as cold as icy water!
> When the blood-spilling fire-flood surged on again and arose in resurrection,
> She entered its midst like a strong wind that swept the dust from her face and the smoke from her flames...
> With her lashes she swept the flames from his hair, and with her blood she washed the smoke of the fire from his face.
> She embraced him more nearly than her soul, and when she had found her well-beloved, she gave up her life to him.[79]

Multiple references to similar feelings can be found throughout recorded history. The Roman poet, Juvenal, told the story of a married woman, Hippia, who fell rapturously in love with the gladiator Sergius. When her paramour was forced to leave the country, she brazenly abandoned her family and followed him with an attachment that was overwhelming. She preferred this character "to her children, to her country, to her sister, and to her husband."[80]

In *Desire Under the Elms*, Eugene O'Neill dramatically portrayed this raging affection in association with an infanticidal theme. In the play, Abbie fell in love with, and then became pregnant by, Eben, her elderly husband's son. After she gave birth to a son, Eben began to believe that Abbie had wanted his child only to assure inheritance of the farm for herself. In anger, he planned to break their incestual affair and told her of his intentions. Abbie passionately clung to him and begged him to stay, forswearing the intensity of her love:

> If I could make it -'s if he'd never come up between us – if I could prove t' ye I wa'n't schemin' t' steal from ye – so's everythin' could be jest the same with us, lovin' each other jest the same, kissin' an' happy the same's we've been happy afore he come?[81]

She then went to the cradle, where the tiny infant lay, and put a pillow over the baby's face until he stopped breathing in the hope her beloved Eben would stay.[82]

The modern criminal stage has also seen well-publicized stories of women who killed their children in response to abandonment by a lover.

Elizabeth Diane Frederickson Downs shot her three children, fatally wounding one, and then drove to a hospital emergency room, claiming that they had all been assaulted by an unknown male assailant. One clue to her guilt lay in the finding of a large rose tattoo on her back with the word "Lew" etched just beneath – a reference to the lover who had just jilted her, Lew Lewiston.[83]

It was not only illicit love, but marital bliss as well, that could be associated with such ardor. D. H. Lawrence, in *The Rainbow*, described how the Brangwen's became totally encompassed in passionate love, even after their children were born: "Their children became mere offspring to them, they lived in the darkness and death of their own sensual activities."[84] Their love was not one of tenderness, but rather of lust and "the maddening intoxication of the senses, a passion of death."[85]

Thomas Hardy added another category of women who would react to the loss of one man by reinforcing their desire for another. He explained how "some widows can guard against the wounds their children give them by turning their hearts to another husband and beginning life again."[86] In the process of this affirmation of rebirth and love, the safety and care of their children were cast aside.

F. SELF-SURVIVAL

In *Andromache*, by Euripides, Menelaus vented his anger against Paris, the man who had abducted his wife and started the Trojan war. He ordered Andromache, the widow of Hector and mother of Paris, to atone for her dead son's crime by either choosing to die herself, or forfeit the life of her last living child:

> If you decide to die, the boy survives. If you put your own skin first, he dies instead. It's one of the two."[87]

We never actually see a resolution within the context of the play, as the scene shifted to another storyline, but as Andromache pondered her horrifying alternatives, obvious shivers quaked through her spine. She dearly loved her living son, but could that love be so extant as to be willing to die?

Perhaps at times, some parents have felt that it would be better to die than see their child be killed, but not often. There are a number of instances where a parent has chosen to live, and thereby directed the death of their child. Legend tells of Aun (On), the ancient king of Sweden, who sacrificed nine of his sons at Upsala, to the god Odin, in order that his own life might be spared.[88] The poet Thiodolf told the story in verse:

In Upsal's town the cruel king
Slaughtered his sons at Odin's shrine -
Slaughtered his sons with cruel knife,
To get from Odin length of life.
He lived until he had to turn
His toothless mouth to the deer's horn;
And he who shed his children's blood
Sucked through the ox's horn his food.
At length fell Death has tracked him down,
Slowly but sure, in Upsal's town.[89]

In more modern times, tribal custom occasionally has held that the life of a chieftain was endangered by the birth of a son. In Uganda, a first-born infant son of a chief is strangled after delivery: "This is done to ensure the life of the father; if he has a son born first he will soon die, and the child inherit all he has."[90]

Even if there was not endangerment to life, some parents killed their newborns in order to not be faced with future disruptions and stress. Slaves in ancient days frequently were stated to practice infanticide on children born to them. Dio Chrysostom noted that some slave women:

> Destroy the child before birth and others afterwards, if they can do so without being caught and yet sometimes even with the connivance of their husbands, that they may not be involved in trouble by being compelled to raise children in addition to their enduring slavery.[91]

G. OATHS

The sanctity of forswearing an oath, as representing that a promise would be secured by the guarantee of a man's honor, has been widely accepted for ages. Rather than disavow such a pledge, many parents have purposely acted in ways which have harmed their children, and some have even committed infanticide. These actions were taken not only because of the shame associated with renouncing an oath, but also because of the belief that non-performance would nonetheless result in death or destruction. Part of this deduction was purely superstitious, but there were also numerous pronouncements by religious leaders that failure to execute a sworn deed would result in disfavor with the gods. In the words of Rabbi Judah the Nasi: "Children die as a punishment for unfulfilled vows."[92] And in the New Testament: "When a man takes an oath, he is calling upon someone greater than himself to force him to do what he has promised, or to punish him if he later refuses to do it; the oath ends all argument about it."[93]

A prime example of this intense commitment was depicted in the Biblical story of Jephthah, a warrior from Gilead appointed by the Israelites to command their army against the Ammonites. Jephthah vowed to the Lord that if He would help him to victory then: "Anything coming out the doors of my house to meet me, when I return with victory from the Ammonites, shall belong to Yahweh; I will offer it up as a burnt offering."[94] Whether because of divine assistance, or superior military strength, the Israelites were indeed victorious. Jephthah returned home triumphantly, and as he neared his home he expected some animal to run up to him in order to guarantee the promised sacrifice to the Lord. Instead, his only child, a beloved daughter, ran out to greet him. "When he saw her he tore his clothes in anguish," for he had made a vow to the Lord that he could not take back.[95] The young girl was prepared for her death, and accepted her fate with equanimity: "Father, you must do whatever you promised the Lord, for he has given you a great victory over your enemies the Ammonites."[96]

Josephus, the first century A.D. Jewish historian, rationalized the brutality of this event by noting that the sacrifice "was not ungrateful to her, since she should die upon the occasion of her father's victory, and the liberty of her fellow-citizens."[97] As we have earlier seen with the superiority of the state to any single individual, the loss of a child was secondary to the gain of the entire Jewish community.

St. John Chrysostom, the fourth century Greek Church theologian, argued that the young girl had to be slain in order to retain the future sanctity of sworn oaths. He realized that some unbelievers impugned the actions of God for allowing the killing to occur, and repelled their claims that the decision was cruel and inhumane.[98] He maintained that this was rather an example of providence and clemency, for if the Lord had forbidden this sacrifice to occur, through some last minute divine forgiveness, then many other faithful followers would have not learned the lesson of respect for swearing in the name of the Lord. People would have then increased the number of such vows, knowing that they could disregard them if they so desired, and this would have resulted in many more cases of inadvertent child-murder over time.[99] Jephthah's daughter had to die so that the world would know that a vow pledged to the Lord could be completely relied upon as a sacred and valid promise.

St. Augustine, however, was not as disposed to accept the rationality of Jephthath's actions. He had pardoned Abraham's willingness to kill Isaac as an act of attempted murder because Abraham was acting in direct obedience to the orders of God. Under this set of facts, the action was not outlawed by the Biblical commandment "thou shalt not kill," which otherwise would have demanded that Abraham be seen as a blasphemous criminal. But the killing by Jephthah was not comparable because: "It is a doubtful question, whether it ought to hold as a command from God that Jephthah killed his daughter that met him on his return."[100] According to Augustine, one cannot choose to murder another human being, and thereby disobey one of the most holy Biblical directives, simply on the need to not disavow an oath. Sworn behavior is not equivalent to the commandment of God.

Dante, as well, did not agree with Jephthah's action. While vows were not to be taken lightly, oaths were not to be kept "with stubborn wall-eyed foolishness," as was witnessed in this biblical tale.[101] But even to modern scholars, it is the "rashness and imprecision with which he pronounces his vow, not his willingness to carry it out by sacrificing his daughter" that is flawed.[102]

The Old Testament contained other stories connecting infanticide with strict obedience to an oath. King Saul, in an attempt to discipline the soldiers in his army during the battle with the Philistines, swore to his men that whoever ate any food before the enemy was slain would be cursed.[103] This was done to maintain the defensive lines and prevent any break in attention. His son, Jonathan, however, had not heard the command and ate some honeycomb during a pause in the action. Afterwards, he was told of the curse and said: "That's ridiculous! A command like that only hurts us."[104] As the fighting continued once again, the Israelites found their advantages eroding away. Saul went to the altar and asked the Lord whether they should continue the battle, but unexpectedly got no reply and realized that something was wrong. He questioned the men whether anyone had insulted the Lord through disobedience of his command: "I vow by the name of the God who saved Israel that though the sinner be my own son Jonathan, he shall surely die!"[105] At the time Saul made this oath it was only intended as a bold statement, for he did not know that it was actually Jonathan who had eaten that day. But when he later found out the truth, he grievously told the lad that "you must die, may God strike me dead if you are not executed for this."[106] According to Josephus, Jonathan was willing to submit to the penalty for "death will be to me very acceptable when it proceeds from thy piety."[107] But the troops arose and defied Saul's edict for the valiant actions of Jonathan had saved Israel in many previous campaigns.[108] A compromise was eventually made and Jonathan did not have to die.

Another biblical oath was fulfilled with the figurative loss of Samuel, who was given in an act of oblation to the Lord. Hannah, who had not been able to conceive a child and was in danger of being barren because of her advanced age, prayed at the Tabernacle to be given a son. She promised that if the Lord made her pregnant: "I will give him back to you, and he'll be yours for his entire lifetime."[109] When she later gave birth to a healthy infant son, her joy was intense. But when the baby was weaned, in obedience to her promise, she brought him back to the Tabernacle and gave him to Eli the priest to give "to the Lord for as long as he lives."[110]

The Greek legend of the sacrifice of Iphigenia by her father, Agamemnon, was similarly based on a solemn oath. Agamemnon had vowed to the goddess Diana that he would sacrifice the most beautiful creature born that year within his realm, if she would allow him to prosper in all his obligations. The wealth and fame of Agamemnon was magnificent, and he now was general of the Greek armada that was harbored at the Bay of Aulis. But because he had forgotten to make an offering that year, the winds had died down and the seer, Calchas, said it was because of Diana's anger. Agamemnon was then forced to sacrifice Iphigenia – for in that year nothing was born more beautiful than she. When he at first resisted the command, Ulysses told him: "You owe your daughter's life to Greece. You promised it to us."[111] Cicero, the Roman orator who normally was very tolerant of actions taken to promote the welfare of the state, believed Agamemnon ought to have broken his vow rather than commit so horrible a crime.[112]

In the Indian *Upanishads*, Vagasravasa, desirous of attaining heavenly rewards through abstention from worldly treasures, promised to surrender all that he possessed. When his only son, Nakiketas, asked him "to whom wilt thou give me," his father realized that his son was a possession as well. Since he had forsworn to rid himself of even his son, he answered, "I shall give thee unto death." Because of an oath, a young boy was killed.[113]

In the *Ramayana*, the story was told of an ancient Indian king who accidently killed a fourteen-year-old boy and in payment for his misdeed he swore to the parents that they could have any reparation they desired, short of his kingdom and his life. The grieving father angrily asked that the king's son should also be taken from him at the same age, and the king agreed, since he did not have a child, and had no plans for one in the future. But a son, Rama, was born two years later, and when the boy was fourteen years old the man returned to remind the king of his oath. The king vacillated but Rama told his father: "The word of a king may not be broken. The duty of a son is to obey."[114] He then went into exile, but did not die and was raised in a foreign land.

Another happy ending was seen in the Grimm fairy tale, "The King of the Golden Mountain." This fable told of a rich merchant who lost all of his holdings in a shipwreck and faced a future life of poverty. One day he met a little black mannikin who offered him all the gold he desired if he promised to bring him in twelve years time the first thing which rubbed against his legs when he returned home. The man agreed, believing it would only be his dog. But as occurred in the biblical tale of Jephthah, when he arrived home, his son ran up and grabbed his leg to steady himself and the merchant was horror-stricken. At the end of the twelve years, the son was given up but lived and became king of the golden mountain.[115]

Oaths were sacred not only to human beings, but also to the Gods. In Greek mythology, Phaeton was born to the Sun God and the nymph Clymene. As a youth he questioned his divine origin, so his mother sent him to India to find his father and realize the truth of his heritage. The boy traveled far, and finally met Phoebus in the palace of the Sun and was reassured that he was truly His son. As further proof of his filial attachment, Phoebus swore to grant any of his wishes and solemnized it: "I call witness that dreadful lake, which I never saw, but which we gods swear by in our most solemn engagements."[116] Phaethon then asked for only one wish – to ride in his father's chariot. The Sun tried to dissuade the boy, knowing that it would lead to his demise, but failed: "The oath is sworn and must be kept – but I beg you to choose more wisely."[117] Phaethon, however, was not to be dissuaded and took the chariot out by himself. The mighty horses could immediately feel the difference in their reins and began to head off track. As they neared the earth, Zeus destroyed the chariot with a bolt in order to save humanity from total destruction, and Phaethon was killed. Cicero, as he had done earlier with the decision of Agamemnon, advised that it would have been much better if the fathers promise had not been kept.[118]

H. HONOR

While refusing to break an oath, even if it jeopardized the life of your child, was primarily due to a code of honor, there were other aspects of this principle which evoked similar dedication. Montaigne, in one of his sixteenth century essays, aptly explained how pride could cause inanimate concepts to equate with the life of a mortal being in certain individuals:

> There are few lovers of poetry who would not be prouder to be the father of the Aenead than of the handsomest youth in Rome, and who would not more gladly endure the loss of the son than of the poem.[119]

That such events did occur has been referenced in many literary works. In the Biblical story of Lot, two angels, disguised as travelers, came to the city of Sodom to meet with Lot and were invited in as guests for the night. When they were preparing to retire to bed, the Sodomites surrounded the house and shouted for Lot to send out the men so "we can rape them."[120] Lot pleaded with them not to destroy the honor of his protective hospitality and said:

> Look – I have two virgin daughters, and I'll surrender them to you to do with as you wish. But leave these men alone, for they are under my protection.[121]

Offering sanctuary in one's home implied a promise of safety which came even before the welfare of family members.

Jewish folk tales related similar stories. In "The Brother's Wife," a mother with a young infant son was attacked by a man who threatened to strangle her infant if she repelled his advances. "Do what you will," she said stoically, "for your sake I shall not go to hell and lose my share of the world to come."[122] The man proceeded to strangle the infant and then ran away; but the woman's chastity was not broken.

Such feelings typified the chivalry of the Middle Ages which characteristically put one's honor above all else. In the *Song of Roland*, Blancandrin directed king Marsilion to send their own sons as hostages to king Charlemagne:

> I'll send mine own, though he should die therefore. Better by far the heads of them should fall than we should lose honour, estate and all.[123]

It was this same attitude which caused dueling to become the emblem of integrity whereby one was willing to sacrifice their own life, or take the life of another, in response to simple acts of shame. Such pride could be found world-wide.

In *Titus Andronicus*, by William Shakespeare, Titus returned from war with the Goths where twenty-one of his sons had died in battle. When he proceeded to try and force his daughter Lavinia to follow his demands, his son Mutius arose to protect his sister and barred his father's way. Titus immediately killed the lad and admonished his other sons that they were not his own if they tried to dishonor him. A son was unworthy "that hath dishonour'd all our family."[124]

Shakespeare continued this subplot of honor in *Much Ado About Nothing,* when Hero was left at the altar by Claudio who claimed that she was no longer a virgin. Leonato, the shocked father, then vents his anger on his daughter and says:

> Do not live, Hero do not ope thine eyes;
> For, did I think thou wouldst not quickly die,
> Thought I thy spirits were stronger than thy shames,
> Myself would, on the rearward of reproaches,
> Strike at thy life.[125]

Another example of this Athenian authority was nicely portrayed by Shakespeare in *A Midsummer Night's Dream*. King Theseus was asked to rule on the right of Egeus to decide who his daughter will marry. Egeus has given his consent to Demetrius, but claims that Lysander has bewitched the young girl with verses of feigning love. He therefore came to the king with a rightful fathers plea: "I beg the ancient privilege of Athens, as she is mine, I may dispose of her, which shall be either to this gentleman or to her death, according to our law."[126] Theseus agrees that this power is intact but offers the maiden an option to "endure the livery of a nun, for aye to be in shady cloister mewed, to live a barren sister all your life, chanting faint hymns to the cold fruitless moon."[127] If she does not otherwise accept this option, or marry who her father wishes, she must die.

The Irish legend of Cu Chulainn told how the champion of Conchobar of Ulster was forced to battle his own son, Conlai, because he had come to challenge the honour of Chulainn's city.[128] Even when warned that Conlai was his only son, Chulainn said: "I would kill him for the honor of Ulster."[129] It could not matter to a soldier who was sworn to uphold the honor of his city, who had made the challenge.

A somewhat stranger tale appeared in Irish lore about the Danes who lived in Ireland for a time and were known as Na Lochlannaigh. They were renowned for their secret recipe of how to brew beer from heather. The ingredients were closely guarded from the Irish, and as the number of Danes dwindled by attrition, there was the distinct likelihood that the Irish would never learn the highly desired formula. Finally, only a father and son were left alive with knowledge of the secret. The Irish planned to kill them both, but first questioned the father on how to make the beer. The older man was afraid that if he did not answer, he would be killed and his son would divulge the formula, in violation of their honor code. He therefore agreed to tell but demanded that they first had to kill his son since he "could not bear the shame of having his son hear him divulge this information."[130] The young man was murdered and then the father told the Irish that they might as well kill him too, for he would never divulge the confidential method.

In the Italian folk tale, "The Wildwood King," there was a king with three daughters, the youngest of which was so beautiful that no one would marry the older two. Fearing a life of spinsterhood if the youngest was not eliminated, they jealously told their father that the younger sister ran away with a common soldier in one of their dreams. The king then ordered the girl killed, "Lest the dream come true and his younger daughter disgrace the royal house."[131]

Many other tales existed of daughter's being slain by their parent because of shameful actions, as discussed in the chapter on Shame. A family reputation could be irreversibly stained if the disreputable actions were not severely disciplined. In the Japanese tale of "Gappo and His Daughter Tsuji," by Suga Sensuke, the daughter of Gappo had scandalized the family by making love to her stepson. When she returned to his house,

Gappo told his wife: "I'll not let her cross our threshold nor let her touch the gate. She must be dead!"[132] Out of paternal love and obligation to her husband, he vowed: "I cannot permit so vile a creature to live."[133]

Galdos told of a similar attitude in his moralistic novel of *Dona Perfecta.* When the grande lady's daughter desired the love of a man they considered an atheist, the parents agreed that: "It would be better to see her dead, to see her buried and food for the worms, than to see her in his power."[134]

Endnotes

1 . Seneca, "On Consolation to the Bereaved," XCIX, Ad Lucilium Epistulae Morales, Volume III, 131.
2 . Spiegel, The Last Trial, 18.
3 . Ibid., 19.
4 . Philo, "On Abraham," XXXIII.181, Loeb Classical Library, 91.
5 . Deuteronomy 12:31. The Living Bible, 161.
6 . Exodus 32:29. Ibid., 78.
7 . Numbers 3:4.
8 . Josephus, "Antiquities," II.VIII.7, The Works of Flavius Josephus, 211.
9 . The Fourth Book of Maccabees, 5.1, 8.3, 9.1, 169, 189, 193.
10 . Ibid., 15.3, 221.
11 . Matthew 19:17. The Living Bible, 764.
12 . Matthew 19:29. Ibid., 765.
13 . Luke 14:26. Ibid., 822.
14 . Matthew 10:37. Ibid., 754.
15 . Matthew 10:21. Ibid.
16 . Matthew 10:34-36. Ibid.
17 . Origen, "Homilies On Genesis," VIII, The Fathers of the Church, 142.
18 . Ibid., VIII, 144.
19 . St. Valerian, "The Martyrdom of the Mother and Her Seven Sons," Homilies, 417.
20 . Ibid.
21 . Ethiopic Didascalia, XXV.4, 111.
22 . Gurgani, Vis and Ramin, 3, 6.
23 . See discussion later in this chapter.
24 . Seneca, Thyestes, I.II, 757.
25 . Herodotus, The History, III.119, 261-262.
26 . Plutarch, "On Brotherly Love," 7.481, Moralia, Volume VI, 267.
27 . Ovid, Metamorphoses, VIII.474-477, 196.
28 . Ibid., VIII.502, 196-197.
29 . Ovid, Tristia, I.VII.17-19, 39.
30 . Racine, Athaliah, II.vii.724, 270.
31 . Hume, "On the Populousness of Ancient Nations," Essays Moral, Political & Literary, 399.
32 . Piers, Infanticide, 16.
33 . Townsend, "Infant Mortality in the Saniyo-Hiyowe Population, Ambunti District, East Sepik Province," 179.
34 . Ibid., 180.
35 . Stacey, Patriarchy and Socialist Revolution in China, 199.
36 . Philo of Byblos, The Phoenician History, 3.44, 63.
37 . Ibid.
38 . Aristotle, Politics, I.3.1253a, 55.
39 . Epictetus, The Discourses, 18.
40 . Philo, "On Abraham," XXXIII.180, Loeb Classical Library, 89, 91.
41 . Ibid., XXXIV.184, 91.
42 . Pausanias, Description of Greece, I.V.2, Volume I, 25.
43 . Ibid., IV.IX.4, 221.
44 . Ibid., IV.IX.6, 223.

45 . Ibid., IV.IX.6, 223.
46 . Plutarch, "Ancient Customs of the Spartans," Moralia, Volume III, 445.
47 . Ibid., 459.
48 . Ibid., 461.
49 . Ibid., III.7, 463.
50 . Ibid., III.21, 467.
51 . Ibid., III.8, 463.
52 . Ibid., III.12, 467.
53 . Racine, Iphigenia, I.i.77-78, 57.
54 . Cicero, De Officiis, I.XVII.58, 61.
55 . Polybius, The Histories, VI.54.
56 . Seneca, "On Consolation to the Bereaved," XCIX, Ad Lucilium Epistulae Morales, Volume III, 133.
57 . Ibid., XCIX, 137.
58 . Virgil, Aenead, 6.1087-1089(823-824), 165.
59 . Boswell, The Kindness of Strangers, footnote 11, 59.
60 . Tacitus, Annals, I.42, 29.
61 . Ibid., III.6.
62 . Suetonius, "Caligula," 5, The Lives of the Twelve Caesars, 215.
63 . Lucan, Pharsalia, I.78, 36.
64 . Frazer, "The Magic Art," The Golden Bough, Volume II, 173, 177, 195.
65 . Turville-Petre, Myth & Religion of the North, The Religion of Ancient Scandinavia, 190.
66 . Boswell, The Kindness of Strangers, 329.
67 . Herodotus, The History, VII.107, 504-505.
68 . Marlowe, Tamburlaine, Part Two, IV.124-125, 146.
69 . Ibid., IV. 160-162, 147.
70 . Philo, "On Abraham," XXXIII.179, Loeb Classical Library, 89.
71 . Ibid., XXXIV.184, 91, 93.
72 . Ibid., XXXIV.187, 93.
73 . Cicero, On Friendship, XXIII.88, 83.
74 . Seneca, "On Consolation to the Bereaved," XCIX, . Ad Lucilium Epistulae Morales, Volume III, 67.
75 . Lucian, "A Dialogue of Friendship," The Works of Lucian of Samosata, Volume III, 70.
76 . Boswell, The Kindness of Strangers, 331.
77 . Pedroso, Portugese Folktales, 25-29.
78 . Abrahams, African Folktales, 115.
79 . Nau'i, "Indian Summer," 121.
80 . Juvenal, Satires, 6.111, 137.
81 . O'Neill, Desire Under the Elms, III.ii, 49.
82 . Ibid., III.iii, 50.
83 . Rule, Small Sacrifices, 46, 66. The killing was postulated "as a kind of sacrifice upon the altar of Lew's love." Ibid., 179.
84 . Lawrence, The Rainbow, VIII, 237.
85 . Ibid.
86 . Hardy, The Return of the Native, 217.
87 . Euripides, Andromache, 380-382, 88.
88 . Frazer, The Dying God, 160.

89 . Ibid., 161.
90 . Roscoe, "Further Notes on the Manners and Customs of the Baganda," 30.
91 . Dio Chrysostom, "On Slavery and Freedom," II.8, Discourses, Volume II, 151.
92 . Shabbath, Gemara II.32b.
93 . Hebrews 6:16. The Living Bible, 978.
94 . Judges 11:31. The Anchor Bible, 206.
95 . Judges 11:35.
96 . Judges 11:36. The Living Bible, 214.
97 . Josephus, "Antiquities," V.VII.10, The Works of Flavius Josephus, Volume I, 329.
98 . Chrysostom, "The Homilies on the Statutes, or To the People of Antioch," The Homilies of S. John Chrysostom, 237.
99 . Ibid., 238.
100. Augustine, The City of God, I.XX, Volume I, 26.
101. Dante, "Paradise," V.65, The Divine Comedy, 77.
102. Levenson, The Death and Resurrection of the Beloved Son, 19.
103. I Samuel 14:24.
104. I Samuel 14:29. The Living Bible, 238.
105. I Samuel 14:39. Ibid., 239.
106. I Samuel 14:44. Ibid.
107. Josephus, "Antiquities," VI.VI.5, The Works of Flavius Josephus, Volume I, 368.
108. "We vow by the life of God that not one hair on his head will be touched." I Samuel 14:45. The Living Bible, 239.
109. 1 Samuel 1:11. Ibid., 227.
110. 1 Samuel 1:28. Ibid.
111. Racine, Iphigenia, I.iii.285-86, 65.
112. Cicero, De Officiis, III.XXV.94, 371.
113. Upanishads, "Katha-Upanishad," First Valli, Volume II, 1-2.
114. Ramayana, 65.
115. Grimm's Fairy Tales, 241-243.
116. Bulfinch, Mythology, 41.
117. Ibid.
118. Cicero, De Officiis, III.XXV.94, 371.
119. Montaigne, Essays, II.8, 158.
120. Genesis 19:5. The Living Bible, 14.
121. Genesis 19:8. Ibid.
122. Gorion, Mimekor Yisrael Classical Jewish Folk Tales, Volume III, 1104.
123. Song of Roland, 3.43-45, 52.
124. Shakespeare, The Tragedy of Titus Andronicus, I.i.345, 14.
125. William Shakespeare, Much Ado About Nothing, 4.1.123-127.
126. Shakespeare, A Midsummer Night's Dream, I.i.42-45, 2.
127. Ibid., I.i.72-75, 3.
128. Cavendish, Legends of the World, 184.
129. Dillon, Early Irish Literature, 17.
130. Cavendish, Legends of the World, 187.
131. Calvino, Italian Folk Tales, 403.
132. Sensuke, "Gappo and his Daughter Tsuji," 249.
133. Ibid.
134. Galdos, Dona Perfecta, 185.

CHAPTER XX

POPULATION CONTROL

"The most widely used method of population control during much of human history was probably some form of female infanticide."[1]

As Marvin Harris noted above in his discussion of the origins of modern culture, the concept of controlling family size is not new, although the methodology practiced to accomplish this goal has undergone major modification in recent times. Before the availability of safe birth control technology, the easiest, safest, and most efficacious way to prevent the accumulation of future offspring, putting aside moral implications, was to eliminate newborn daughters soon after birth. Such a homicidal response to the delivery of a child may be hard for many modern social commentators to understand, but we should not be quick to condemn an action that was often necessitated by conditions beyond the parent's control. It was not that our ancestors lacked concern for their newborn children, but rather that they realized that allowing another child in the family to live, especially one that would begin procreation soon after puberty, unfavorably affected the survivability of the entire group.[2] The reality was that population growth beyond the available arable food supply put the lives of all residents at stake. Without any other effective means of birth control, the incidence of infanticide would have to remain high.

Our modern age has spent much effort in attempting to control the extent of this problem. We now live in an era of birth control pills, condoms, vaginal gels, spermicidal foam, diaphragms, relatively safe means of abortion, and access to information and medical care to determine voluntarily when our children are to be born. And yet, despite all of these safe and accessible birth control modalities, the population growth of the world is at the highest rate in humankind's experience.[3] Despite all the technology developed by scientific advancements, most of the world's population continues to procreate without artificial interference.

In earlier times, voluntary population control was basically implemented by celibacy, delayed marriages, unsafe abortion, infanticide and abandonment.[4] Certain societies also resorted to sending excess numbers of citizens to other countries in a process known as colonization. This was particularly popular among the ancient Greeks, who took advantage of their superior strength and knowledge to expand geographically at will. Plato, in *Laws*, discussed the utilization of this method to maintain the optimum strength of the ideal state. He recommended that the number of households in the country should be kept at 5040 and, if the number increased beyond that amount, one of the means to reduce the citizenry would be to send out colonies of people that seemed suitable to outside lands.[5]

While we know of many instances in which this actually occurred, there is some question as to when it was relied on for aggrandizement, and when it was for population control. If too many sons were born to a powerful family, for example, one or more of them might have been forced to emigrate, not because the number of siblings was too great to feed, but because there were no means to assure an adequate inheritance. Along with the lost legacy went a contingent of slaves, friends, and other family members to assist in the development of a new community. W. W. Tarn, who researched the Greeks arriving in Miletus in the third century B.C., noted that one particular colonization brought one hundred eighteen sons and twenty-eight daughters, and no family listed more than two daughters. He believed this likely indicated the presence of female infanticide in the Greek population at large, but others have pointed out that colonization did not necessarily catalog the number of participants as a reflection of the population, but rather for other purposes.[6] It was obvious, however, that the process was primarily a male-oriented endeavor.

Plato's conceptual government was reproduced centuries later in *Utopia*, the ideal state imagined by Sir Thomas More. Colonization was used by the Utopians whenever "the numbers swell beyond the limit for the whole island."[7] Nearby lands would be taken over and new cities, built on the exact model of the mother country, were constructed. Neither Plato, nor More, discussed the danger of conflict between those who did the colonizing and those whose land was being taken away. Matters such as exist today on the West Bank of Jerusalem were apparently of no concern to theoretic philosophers. But the likelihood that colonization would create serious conflicts was real, and as the nations of the world closed upon each other's territory, the efficacy of colonization as a method for population control was destroyed. If growth was to be curtailed, other means of regulation had to be found. Infanticide became the preferred method since it functioned as a means of fertility control at both the population and family levels.[8]

Putting aside moral considerations, careful analysis of the situation shows that this decision was rationally based. Infanticide had the advantage of allowing parents to select the healthiest, and most desirable, children if an unlimited number of offspring was not possible.[9] From a societal standpoint such eugenic goals were very important. If membership in the family had to be limited, it was obviously propitious to assure that the healthiest, and fittest, would survive. This was best accomplished by evaluating the child after birth to determine if proper conditions for future societal needs were present. Such forecasting was obviously not possible with the use of abortion. Natality studies reveal how necessary was this control. While the mean number of children born to procreating families ranges from seven to ten, not all of these offspring will survive to become generating adults.[10] Thomas Malthus estimated that, under typical circumstances, the doubling time of most human populations was from 10-25 years. This rapid expansion of consumers could not be maintained by the available food supply, and he postulated that "such growth must soon initiate either internal or external limitation."[11] Malthus outlined this dilemma of reproduction in his *First Essay on the Principle of Population* in 1798. The unequal distribution of the bounties of nature was caused by "the constant tendency in all animate life to increase beyond the nourishment prepared for it."[12] Since population increased in a geometrical ratio, and the subsistence to feed that growth increased in only an arithmetical ratio, the difficulty of providing proper subsistence would constantly operate to check further population growth by limiting the food supply.[13]

Malthus explained that part of the natural response to this condition was a lowered fertility ratio. He pointed out that tribal societies which hunt and travel for food cannot allow women enough time to give the necessary attention for raising of infants. According to his studies, this resulted in a diminution of the birth rate by endogenous control. Mother Nature had a wonderful way of attempting to modulate the number of children born. But the effort was not satisfactory, for the scarcity of food also led to a general increase in "vicious habits," such as the increased frequency of child abandonment.[14] The strongest proof of this distress was infanticide, for it "violates the most natural principle of the human heart."[15] As a scientist, Malthus was able to identify the clarity of cause and effect; as a human being he could not accept that it was consistent with the spirit of man.

Charles Darwin, in 1859, incorporated this phenomenon into his famous theory of evolution. He theorized that as more individuals are produced than can possibly survive:

> There must in every case be a struggle for existence, either one individual with another of the same species, or with the individuals of distinct species, or with the physical conditions of life.[16]

The outcome of this conflict would generally be in favor of those who were the "fittest," which put the newborn infant at a distinct disadvantage.

But it is not only in the procurement of food that population growth negatively impacted the lives of procreating adults. Parents also encountered other economic disadvantages during the early years of child rearing, before the children were able to work and help perform objective functions of family life. Many families simply could not afford to care for a new child every year, and without means to control this birth they rapidly slid into deep poverty. This appeared to be the prime reason that most ancient families, in civilized areas at least, attempted to reduce the numbers of children they reared.[17] Hesiod, writing around 700 B.C., noted how:

> One single-born son would be right to support his father's house, for that is the way substance piles up in the household; if you have more than one, you had better live to an old age.[18]

But preventing the birth of a child was not an easy matter. Abortion was quite dangerous, and there was also a high degree of failure. Complications included the death of the mother, or permanent sterility resulting from the secondary infections. Even in the 1800s, over one-third of Americans who underwent abortion died as a result of complications.[19] This was therefore something which only had value in select situations, but could not be relied on for effective, and safe, population control.

Voluntary abstinence was unreliable and did not even prevent the birth of children to Christian priests who took a vow of celibacy throughout the Middle Ages. Delayed marriage did nothing to control the birth of illegitimate children, the numbers of which have been earlier discussed in the chapter on Shame. And while natural spermicidal preparations have been part of the folk pharmacopeia of almost every culture and tribe, their ready availability and efficacy has always been substandard.

With infanticide the economic cost to the parents was low, and the methodology was effective and safe. This made it especially attractive to the impoverished peasants of under-developed countries.[20] In addition, the weak, premature or deformed infants could be removed from further care.[21] The adult female population was not at risk, and the process could be easily manipulated. From the standpoint of natural selection, it was "an effective means of controlling population" and was preferred by many societies.[22]

Darwin believed that infanticide, and especially female infanticide, was the most important check on the proliferation of early man.[23] Many other authors agreed that it may have been the most widely used method of population control.[24] The eminent historian William Langer concluded that its use as a method of population control extended through to the end of the nineteenth century.[25]

Throughout history we see attestation to this practical application of infanticide. The main mechanism in stabilizing human growth during the earliest history of man, that of the Pleistocene period, was most likely infanticide.[26] How the first case came about we will never know, but according to John M'Lennan:

> The moment infanticide was thought of as an expedient for keeping down numbers, a step was taken, perhaps, the most important that was ever taken in the history of mankind.[27]

James Neel has studied the Yanomama tribe in southern Venezuela and northern Brazil as a model on how primitive populations likely practiced spacing of children. Infanticide, along with intercourse taboos and abortion, reduced the average effective live-birth rate among these Indians to approximately one child every four to five years among the childbearing period.[28] The infanticide was primarily directed at infants whose older siblings were thought to be not yet ready for weaning, usually at three years of age. This growth rate created a steady population density that equated well with the available food supply.

During Greco-Roman times, abandonment was often used to control the family size and was, according to John Boswell, "a gentler check on overall population than infanticide."[29] While Boswell compassionately differentiated the actions of exposure and infanticide, primarily because of the opportunity for rescue after exposure due to the "kindness of strangers," most children who were abandoned to the elements likely died.

Many authors have emphasized that the Greek philosophers accepted the use of infanticide to limit the size of the state, but this supportive evidence must be cautiously interpreted.[30] Certainly, Plato and Aristotle did not object to the use of infanticide for control of certain elements of children born to the state. Plato, however, in *Laws*, noted that there were many contrivances to help lower the fertility rate of the citizens, and if these did not work, the ancient device of colonization was a proper means of reducing their numbers.[31] It is not clear in his writings, when he would have recommended exposure for pure population control. Aristotle, similarly accepted the need of infanticide in the case of deformed children, but actually argued for abortion, rather than exposure, as limiting the numbers of unwanted children.[32] Whether his advice was followed by the women who were forced to go through the abortion cannot be ascertained.

But whatever the method chosen, the Greeks certainly did practice population control out of necessity. Even under the most favorable circumstances, Averil Cameron argued that "it would be impossible for any family to maintain all the children which it could bring into the world even if the mother were capable of nursing more than one at a time."[33] This simple practicality may have been one of the reasons that most governments of that era did not consider infanticide a crime.[34]

In the Middle Ages, voluntary methods of birth control continued to be quite limited and a "type second" family unit, where demography was "close to instinctual nature," remained the social mean. Many medieval parents often did not actually know how many children they had.[35] When families felt that the number and sex of their children needed to be regulated, abandonment was the primary choice.[36]

This carried on into the Renaissance and Jean-Louis Flandrin claimed that infanticide was the principal method of birth control in France as late as the seventeenth century:

> Women pregnant out of wedlock would regularly murder their new-born bastards, and married couples had no compunction about smothering or abandoning unwanted children in hard times.[37]

In nineteenth century England, proposals of infanticide as a method to control population appeared in print, albeit of the satirical type. Jonathan Swift, in *A Modest Propsal*, in 1729, advocated controlling population size by destruction of children, but rather than have the youngsters simply disposed of, he suggested that they be grown for food, like pigs prepared for a slaughter. In this way not only could the numbers of inhabitants be checked at an appropriate level, but the scarcity of food could be improved at the same time. While the proposal was obviously tongue-in-cheek, the numbers of abandoned children on the streets of London at the time was a problem that was not. Social action obviously needed to be taken, but the authorities were having little success.

It seemed that satire was the only way to promote change. In 1838, Marcus, in "On the Possibility of Limiting Populousness," similarly proposed that surplus children could be submersed in hot water, or asphyxiated with gas, in order to reduce over-population.[38] In a more serious tone, the London Dialectical Society, in 1869, incurred the wrath of many welfare activists by appealing to physicians to use means to help in "keeping back" families.[39] This overt suggestion to allow newborns to die at birth, rather than aide in their recovery as they has sworn to do with their Hippocratic Oath, was likely made out of frustration, but it nevertheless showed the need for some type of assistance in checking the growth of the poor and hungry in the English cities and country towns.

Change would indeed eventually come, but the problem was never completely eliminated. In Charles Dickens' *Great Expectations*, Mr. Jaggers coldly admitted that "all he saw of children, was, their being generated in great numbers for certain destruction."[40] And even as late as 1948, Julian Huxley argued that hospital treatment, or other means of encouraging the survival of infants from members of the lowest strata, should not be encouraged "lest the removal of the last check on natural selection should make it too easy for children to be produced or to survive."[41]

The less civilized areas of the world, although subject to a slower population growth, still required control of their numbers to remain within the confines of an adequate food supply. Primitive tribes often used infanticide as a eugenic measure to attain this goal.[42] It was born of necessity, and not of superstition, despite the fact that some of the children who were killed may have had the additional factors of shame or deformity promoting their disposal. As R. Brough Smyth pointed out, the killing was a practicality: "It is not a rite – it is not a sacrifice."[43] Tribesmen generally did not have the wherewithal to cultivate food through agricultural techniques, and so had little choice but to control their profusion by this means: "The soil of their territory can maintain but a certain number of human beings."[44]

In their ethnographic analysis of 393 populations, Divale and Harris found that 208 of the tribes practiced infanticide more than occasionally. The male:female sex ratio of those over age fourteen in these societies was 117:100, while in those where infanticide was uncommon it was 104-108:100. The authors concluded that female infanticide was used as a major means of population control in an otherwise male dominated world and that:

> Since the reproductive potential of most sexually reproducing species is determined largely by the rate of female survivorship, the most effective mode of population control is to reduce the percentage of the population which consists of sexually active fertile females.[45]

While this method seemed cruel and excessive, they nevertheless pointed out that it was more advantageous than using abortion to control births. First, the loss of a mother's life was more costly, from both practical and emotional reasons, than the life of a newborn; and secondly, male fetuses could be spared to provide a warrior and worker base.[46] All considered, they believed that the use of infanticide to control the number of tribal members was rationally based.

Will Durant put the blame for this policy directly on the shoulders of primitive women. To Durant, the woman desired to escape the burden of rearing offspring:

> Primitive men do not usually care to restrict population; under normal conditions children are profitable, and the male regrets only that they cannot all be sons. It is the woman who invents abortion, infanticide and contraception.[47]

This view is clearly sexist, and is not shared by many other historians.

In China, up to the time of the Communist Revolution, the main mechanism of excess population control was infanticide.[48] The pressure of population on the land was a strong limiting factor on the number of children born and if a birth could not be prevented, the newborn was eliminated in order to reduce the risk of famine. Chinese culture did not attempt to justify the practice, but it was tolerated because the only alternatives were poverty and crime.[49] John Weyland noted that infanticide was chiefly confined to the crowded cities and river-ways, but that the numbers were not enough to provide a check on population growth.[50]

The primary cause of this problem was the poorly productive nature of Chinese farmland tillage. Crop production, per acre of land, had always been very small, and rudimentary equipment, along with little ability to store and move food to outlying areas quickly, created a constant threat of hunger. In *Satan Never Sleeps*, Pearl Buck recorded how poverty and famine caused starving parents to act with callous disregard: "They left their children on purpose and called them 'lost,' so that there was one hungry mouth the less when they reaped the few grains left in a harvested field."[51] In Cochin-China, all children born in the first three years of marriage were killed in an attempt to limit the population growth.[52]

While many of the infanticides were purposeful, a similar effect was also achieved by neglectful parental care. According to Francis Place:

> Great numbers of the children who are born in this country, are half destroyed by neglect and improper food, and that, after pining away a few weeks or a year or two of existence, they perish miserably, without any chance of approaching maturity.[53]

This particular type of mortality increased as the annual earnings of the family decreased.[54]

But the world has never seen the use of infanticide to control the population growth as occurred in China only a few decades ago. According to the third national census in China, 1,008,175,288 people inhabited the People's Republic of China on July 1, 1982. This was equal to the estimated population of the entire earth in 1850.[55] In 1971, the political leaders of China realized they had to do something to lessen the rate of growth of the population, and endorsed the idea of fertility restraint in the Fourth Five-Year Economic Development Plan that year. The set of guidelines which were developed was that the ideal family should have only two children.[56] By 1978 it was apparent that the program was not working and they then embarked upon the "one child per couple" policy.[57] This resulted in a vast increase in female infanticide as families attempted to have their only allotted child be a son. So many newborn daughters were killed in response to governmental controls, that the policy had to be modified in 1988.[58] In the interim, it was estimated that over a million babies lost their lives.

Such dire results, following well-meaning intentions, points out how difficult it is to achieve a proper population balance. In America, we have not yet had to face the problems of over-population that are seen in most Third World countries. We continue to grow enough food to not only feed ourselves, but also provide assistance to others in need. But the accumulation of people, ever worsening by advances in medical and hygienic care, will some day arrive at our own cities and towns, and on that day our well-publicized social moral fiber will finally be tested. Garrett Hardin warned of this problem when he pointed out how nature had always taken care of population control for us in the past with epidemics which would stabilize the population numbers. But he warned that abortion and even euthanasia may become necessary: "Because widespread disease and famine no longer exist, we have to find other means to stop population increases."[59] When famine spreads over our land, and we are forced to watch our own infants turn into shriveled bags of leathery flesh, will we continue to condemn abortion and infanticide as antithetical to the welfare of God-fearing, law-abiding minds? And in the aftermath of poverty and hunger, with self-survival looming large over a weakly tethered existence, will we, as a race, be able to survive the trials of Nature without sacrificing the lives of other human beings? I do not know the answer to these repugnant questions, but it seems clear to me that history has not suggested that the answer will be a resounding yes.

Endnotes

1 . Harris, Cannibals and Kings: The Origins of Cultures, 5.
2 . Ibid.
3 . Small, "Contraception: Use and Failure," 89.
4 . Lorence, "Parents and Children in Eighteenth Century Europe," 9.
5 . Plato, Laws, V.740E, Volume I, 367.
6 . Engels, "The Problem of Female Infanticide in the Greco-Roman World," 112-120.
7 . More, Utopia, II.V, 58.
8 . Scrimshaw, "Infanticide in Human Populations: Societal & Individual Concerns," 460.
9 . Ibid., 461.
10 . Dickeman, "Demographic Consequences of Infanticide in Man," 120.
11 . Ibid.
12 . Malthus, "An Essay on the Principle of Population, or, A View of Its Past and Present Effects on Human Happiness; with an Inquiry into Our Prospects Respecting the Future Removal or Mitigation of the Evils Which It Occasions (1872)," I.I, On Population, 152.
13 . Malthus, "An Essay on the Principle of Population, as It Affects the Future Improvement of Society. With remarks on the speculations of Mr. Godwin, M. Condorcet, and other writers (1798)," I. Ibid., 9.
14 . Malthus, "An Essay on the Principle of Population, or, A View of Its Past and Present Effects on Human Happiness; With an Inquiry Into Our Prospects Respecting the Future Removal or Mitigation of the Evils Which it Occasions (1872)," I.II. Ibid., 164.
15 . Malthus, "An Essay on the Principle of Population, as it Affects the Future Improvement of Society with Remarks on the Speculations of Mr. Godwin, M. Condorcet, and other Writers (1798)," IV. Ibid., 25.
16 . Darwin, The Origin of Species, 3, 78.
17 . Hume, "On the Populousness of Ancient Nations," Essays Moral, Political & Literary, 398.
18 . Hesiod, Works & Days, 376-378, 63.
19 . Sauer, "Infanticide and Abortion in Nineteenth-Century Britain," 83.
20 . Wagatsuma, "Child Abandonment and Infanticide: A Japanese Case," 131.
21 . Oates, Child Abuse and Neglect, 41.
22 . Martinson, Growing Up in Norway, 800 to 1990, 26.
23 . Darwin, The Descent of Man, I.II, 277.
24 . Johnson, "The Socioeconomic Context of Child Abuse and Neglect in Native South America," 62.
25 . Hardin, Exploring New Ethics for Survival, 181.
26 . Williamson, "Infanticide: An Anthropological Analysis," 66.
27 . M'Lennan, Studies in Ancient History, 81.
28 . Neel, "Lessons From a `Primitive' People," 816.
29 . Boswell, The Kindness of Strangers, 133.
30 . Cameron, "The Exposure of Children And Greek Ethics," 108.
31 . Plato, Laws, V.740E, Volume I, 367.
32 . Cameron, "The Exposure of Children And Greek Ethics," 109.
33 . Ibid., 107.

34 . Moseley, "The History of Infanticide in Western Society," 351.
35 . Hunt, Parents & Children in History, 42.
36 . Boswell, "Exposition and Oblatio: The Abandonment of Children and the Ancient and Medieval Family," 12.
37 . Blackhouse, "Desperate Women and Compassionate Courts: Infanticide in Nineteenth-Century Canada," 447.
38 . Behlmer, "Deadly Motherhood: Infanticide and Medical Opinion in Mid-Victorian England," 415.
39 . Ibid.
40 . Dickens, Great Expectations, III.51, 382.
41 . Huxley, Man in the Modern World, 50.
42 . Harrisson, Savage Civilization, 267.
43 . Smyth, The Aborigines of Victoria, 53.
44 . Ibid., 54.
45 . Divale & Harris, "Population, Warfare, & the Male Supremacist Complex," 530.
46 . Ibid., 530-31.
47 . Durant, Our Oriental Heritage, 49.
48 . Williamson, "Infanticide: An Anthropological Analysis," 68.
49 . Fei, Peasant Life in China: A Field Study of Country Life in the Yangtze Valley, 33.
50 . Weyland, The Principles of Population and Production, As They Are Affected By The Progress of Society; With a View To Moral & Political Consequences, 134-136. In Pekin, a city of three million people, about nine thousand exposed infants were picked up yearly by the police, and it was estimated that five thousand were still-born deliveries. Ibid., 132.
51 . Buck, Satan Never Sleeps, 110.
52 . Briffault, The Mothers, Volume II, 27.
53 . Place, Illustrations & Proofs of the Principle of Population, 14.
54 . Fairchild, People, The Quantity & Quality of Population, 170.
55 . Tien, China's Strategic Demographic Initiative, 2.
56 . Ibid., 29.
57 . Ibid., 87-88.
58 . Nation 246 (June 18, 1988): 848.
59 . Carnell, Brian, "Garrett Hardin," Overpopulation.Com. <http://www.overpopulation.com/garrett-hardin.html>, 4/25/99.

CHAPTER XXI

INFANT IMAGE

> "There is nothing so imperfect, so helpless, so naked, so shapeless, so foul, as man observed at birth, to whom alone, one might almost say, Nature has given not even a clean passage to the light; but, defiled with blood and covered with filth, and resembling more one just slain than one just born, he is an object for none to touch or lift up or kiss or embrace except for someone who loves with a natural affection."[1]

Plutarch's deprecatory description of the appearance of a newborn child causing more repugnance than joy seems oddly out of place in our modern age where great emphasis is generally placed upon the miracle of birth. Today, we usually view the sight of a young baby as the very essence of innocence and cheer. We see the struggling infant, gasping out its first audible cry, as reflecting the creation of life which has been granted us by the Almighty God. It truly imbues one with the magnificence of the human spirit. Not only parents, but all adults alike seem to automatically desire to cuddle and protect the child; to assure that the drama of birth will successfully end in the establishment of a being filled with the magical spirit of humankind.

David Hume noted how this beneficent desire was especially intense on the part of the natural parent:

> As soon as the helpless infant sees the light, though in every other eye it appears a despicable and a miserable creature, it is regarded by its fond parent with the utmost affection, and is preferred to every other object, however perfect and accomplished.[2]

After all, how could anyone see danger in such a feeble, dependent thing as a newborn human being?

But not everyone throughout history has seen the newborn child with such pious devotion. Rather than viewing the infant as an expression of pristine human traits, many have felt the much time would have to pass before the baby achieved the distinction of being endowed with human attributes. The Romans, for example, believed that until the seventh day after birth, when the umbilical cord fell off, "a child is more like a plant than an animal."[3]

If you carefully examine the roles of parent and child in a rigidly scientific manner, there is a certain amount of reason to this rather impassive assessment. While there is certainly some modicum of compensation for both sides in the love and affection which develops within most filial relationships, the interests of each are actually antagonistic. The modern poet, John Dickson, notes in his poem "Maternity Ward":

> Behold the enemy,
> dropping into life like petals on water,
> whisked from fluid to substance to blanket
> to numbered basket in the sterile room
> screaming, "Take this cup from me!"[4]

Children are clearly an economic and defensive burden to their family; according to William Sumner, they "add to the weight of the struggle for existence of their parents."[5] If the outcome of the battle is already somewhat in doubt, the life of the newborn is in serious danger. In this context, Sumner saw infanticide as a primary act of self-defense by the parents "against famine, disease, and other calamities of overpopulation."[6] It was a variant of the process of self-survival, and may have had a reasonable basis when the parents were under severe stress.

And even if there was not a sense of danger, many viewed the newborn as simply an inconvenience, a trifling worthless piece of matter whose survival was of little concern. Diogenes related how Aristippus, the student of Socrates, was accused of exposing his son and replied: "Phlegm, too, and vermin we know to be of our own begetting, but for all that, because they are useless, we cast them as far from us as possible."[7] While not agreeing with the breadth of this disdainful remark, Montaigne nevertheless admitted that:

> I cannot entertain that passion for caressing new-born infants, that have neither mental activities nor recognizable bodily shape by which to make themselves lovable; and I have never willingly suffered them to be fed in my presence.[8]

For those who cherished the ultimate potential attributes of human life, the beginnings may have held little value.

Even when the child was not excessively disliked, many scholars saw little enough potential to support the development of love. Seneca, the Greek Stoic philosopher, believed the child had no capacity to reason: "A child is as yet no more capable of comprehending the Good than is a tree or any dumb beast."[9] Edward Gibbon, known for his extensive study of the history of the Roman Empire, noted that most children in his own era died before the age of nine years old: "Before they possess the faculties of the mind or body."[10] William Howells, writing in the nineteenth century, admitted that "there is not much that a man can actually do with a small baby, either for its pleasure or his own."[11]

But if some people saw children as only inconveniences to be tolerated until grown, of more disastrous portent was the identification of infants with the hidden evil nature of man – a reflection of the Devil himself. Through this characterization, infants took on a persona which demanded a destructive response. Within the ethics of Christian theology, the concept of Original Sin held that every human birth was tainted and required that each infant be expiated by the rite of baptism in order to be rid of this stain. In the sixteenth century, Calvin propagated this view with particular intensity. He said that man displeased God by his outrageous ingratitude: "After having been thrown into such a confusion, man was fruitful in his cursed seed, to beget descendants like himself; that is, vicious, perverse, corrupt, void, and deprived of all good, rich and abundant in evil."[12] For many theologians, these despicable traits begin within that first passage out of the womb causing the innocently swaddled newborn to carry an onerous burden of malevolence.

Educated, pious, and respected individuals have often agreed with this characterization. In 1968, Anthony Storr concluded: "It is widely accepted that the infant is potentially aggressive from the moment of its birth."[13] Not only was the newborn human being evil, it was menacing as well.

These views have been closely associated with the segregation of newborns from their inherent legitimacy as human beings. The infant was seen merely as an animal, "and the fact of his birth gave him no admission, as of right, into any social relation."[14] He faced an immediate battle for existence against, at times, imposing odds which could not be overcome. If infanticide was the result, infant image was the conception.

A. CHILDBIRTH

Today we have pain relieving drugs, Lamaze training, and specialized aides to help women reduce the degree of suffering during childbirth. But despite all of these methods, the giving of birth, though often filled with love and gratitude, still remains a bloody, harrowing, and life-threatening experience.

Little wonder then that mothers have often been hostile, and even malicious, toward their newborn children after undergoing the rigorous pain and discomfort of prolonged childbirth. Exhausted from loss of blood and sleep, the spent woman might react with anger and resentment rather than love. While nurturing frequently reappears after a period of rest, the first few weeks after delivery can be unpredictably dangerous to the newborn infant.

Many societies add an additional burden to this already difficult circumstance. Viewing birth as a mark of impurity, the mother and child are often placed into immediate isolation from family and friends for a period of "purification." Josephus related how after the birth of a boy, a Jewish woman could not come into the temple for forty days, and after a girl for eighty days.[15] The *Code of Jewish Law* considered a woman unclean for seven days after the birth of a son, and fourteen days after a daughter.[16]

Most tribal practices contained similar confinements. In Tahiti, on the Alaskan island of Kadia, and among the Bribri Indians, women were kept in a special temporary hut for up to three weeks after childbirth. Also, if anyone touched the child during this period of time, they had to be isolated as well.[17] Among the Lepchas in Sikkim, during the first three days of life, the baby was referred to as a rat-child and was not considered officially born until the third day of life.[18] Among the Koraggars of West India, the mother and child were regarded as unclean for five days and then were restored to purity by a tepid bath.[19] In Baganda, the mother was guarded by midwives for nine days and then the child was brought out and washed in a purification ceremony known as "kasiki".[20] Among the Xosa tribe, the period of time was ten days.[21] The Peruvian Amahuaca did not judge a child fully human until it was three years old.[22]

Why have so many diverse cultures developed such a fearful and protective approach to the birth of a child? The answer is not clear. One possible explanation is that there is a protective nature to the delay. Throughout our history, and even into the modern era, the mortality rates of newborn infants has always been quite high. If a parent, or family group, developed an immediate, positive attachment to the newborn child, there was the likelihood that some natural means of death would result in emotional disaster. This could lead to problems in future procreation.

But it is not only the mother that may prove a danger to the newborn, there are social exigencies as well. The rigors of obtaining food and shelter, surviving disease, and fending off natural enemies is something that the entire family must face, and at times this has led to the necessity of forgoing care of the helpless newborn child. In such cases, as Tyler concluded: "Infanticide arises from hardness of life rather than from hardness of heart."[23]

Perhaps in response to this natural harm, the general principle of criminal law has restricted the protected status of life to some period of time after the birth of the child. The basis for common law in England presumed that "a child is born dead."[24] This was an application of the general principle "*presumitur pro negante*," and the fact of live-birth had to be established by valid evidence. America followed a similar axiom.

Such separation by age has been favorably commented on by many philosophers and legislators. Although John Locke advised that "all men by nature are equal,"[25] he modified the breadth of this statement by clarifying that children "are not born in this full state of equality, though they are born to it."[26] The parents retained jurisdiction over infants for a temporary time in order to take care of them during the "imperfect state of childhood."[27]

Mercier, an English physician, summed up this concept in 1911 when he rationalized that there was a minimum of harm with infanticide compared with other murders:

> The victim's mind is not sufficiently developed to enable it to suffer from the contemplation of approaching suffering or death. It is incapable of feeling fear or terror. Nor is its consciousness sufficiently developed to enable it to suffer pain in appreciable degree. Its loss leaves no gap in any family circle, deprives no children of their breadwinner or their mother, no human being of a friend, helper or companion.[28]

B. DELAYED ACCEPTANCE

By believing that a child was not fully human until it was accepted as a member of the social group, it was easier for a culture to allow infanticide to be morally legitimate.[29] Typically the child was seen as an unsolicited being and there was no moral or mystical fault in refusing to accept him into the family or tribal structure. Such acceptance included the naming of a child, the intake of food, or the development of adult characteristics. The delay could take anywhere from a few days to a few years. According to Clellan Ford, this period of time was critical since: "Infanticide is most readily condoned if it occurs before the infant is named and has been accepted as a bona fide member of its society."[30]

In ancient Athens, a child could not be exposed after the "Amphidromia," a family ceremony where the child was carried around the hearth by the nurse and given a name.[31] Similarly, in early Scandinavia once an infant was given baptism or food, it was illegal to kill it.[32]

From the time of Augustine it was held by the Romans that ensoulment took place either at conception, or, in the more popular view, about forty days thereafter.[33] The exposure of an infant was seen as a morally neutral act since "the infant had not yet begun to participate in the life of its social group."[34] The Institutes of Justinian, in 533 A.D., summarized the Roman reasons why children were not given much legal substance until age seven years: "An infant, or one still near to infancy, differs but little from a madman, because pupils of such an age have no understanding at all."[35]

Under Jewish law, a newborn was not considered viable until it reached the age of thirty days. When the Israelite census was ordered by God, only males from the age of one month up were to be counted for a child had to live a month before being considered fully viable.[36] In the book of *Leviticus*, when the Lord gave Moses directions on what to charge the Jews for maintaining the Temple, the valuations began at the age of one month.[37] Maimonides, the respected Jewish philosopher and physician of the twelfth century, related in his Code how an infant thirty days old or less had no valuation:

> For up to that time the imaginative form that compels the parents to love it is not yet consolidated. For this imaginative form increases through habitual contact and grows with the growth of the child.[38]

In *The Guide of the Perplexed*, Maimonides added that an infant was not counted among those who have contact with the air until seven days after birth had passed: "It is as if before that period it were an abortion."[39] Ben Zion Uziel, the chief rabbi of Israel in the 1950s, said that if you kill an infant under thirty days of age you cannot be executed because its life was still in doubt.[40]

Catholicism likewise held that children did not reach the age of reason until seven years of age when they became an "impubes."[41] A minor, in the exercise of his rights, was dependent on the power of his parents or guardians unless explicitly excused by canon law.[42] Canon law simply called a person before the age of seven years an infant, a child, or a little one and regarded it as an incompetent and without the use of reason.[43]

Primitive cultures followed similar practices. In New Guinea, the infant was really not regarded as truly human until it had survived for several years. Before this passage of time, it could be killed as a form of population control.[44] In Tahiti, if the newborn breathed long enough to open its eyes it was not killed as it was then regarded as having its own "iho," or personality, and thereby had a claim on life.[45] Among the Western tribes in Central Australia, as soon as the child received a name, he was protected from being eaten by other family members.[46]

Among the Eskimos, female infanticide was quite common, but if the child was named early, the chances for survival were increased among the Netsilik. This appeared to be due to the feeling that the name carried a personal, supernatural power and that killing a named child would offend the reincarnated ghost.[47] The decision to kill the child occurred shortly after birth, however, and therefore there was little time for discussion.[48]

The Peruvian Amahuaca did not consider children as fully human until they were three years old.[49] In Ecuador, Peru, and Bolivia even today, "children are not really considered `people' until they have survived the first year or so of life."[50] In Japan, it was believed that a baby was not a human being until the spirit entered its body as manifested by the first birth cry and therefore it was not homicide to kill the newborn before this time.[51] Some societies believed that mothers were more likely to kill their children shortly after delivery because their love had not yet "awakened."[52] Many attributed the development of an attachment to the newborn with institution of breast feeding. Once the nurturing process was started, infanticide was a rare phenomenon.[53]

C. SIN

Children who in some way looked "different" than others of their age were often imputed a subhuman origin by primitive peoples. Oftentimes, they were killed; if they did survive they were ostracized and either became beggars or seers. The concept that infants were filled with sin and evil, however, was a particularly Christian development.

Even though newborns were seldom given equal protection under the law throughout history, they were not generally seen as having deficiencies of morality. In fact, it was usually assumed that infants were born pure, and that human imperfections developed during the maturation process of our mortal years on earth. Christianity changed this belief and saw things quite differently. Human beings were indeed created pure – in the form of Adam and Eve – but the expulsion from the Garden of Eden, because of the eating of the forbidden fruit, had changed the essence of man for all eternity to come. As Prudentius explained:

> Through sordid union with the flesh it fell Into iniquity; stained by Adam's sin It tainted all the race from him derived, And infant souls, inherit at their birth, The first man's sin; not one is sinless born.[54]

Christian parents "beget no offspring worthy in God's sight," and must constantly strive to overcome "the evil monsters reigning in our captive heart."[55]

These views were agreed upon by nearly every Church Father. St. Augustine believed that "not even a child of one day is without sin," and emphasized that "we are conceived in the sin of our parents and are born in their inequities."[56] This became known as the concept of "Original Sin." In the words of Philalethes:

> When Adam sinned, his descendants inherited from him original, or birth sin. By original sin is meant that inbred taint of moral evil

> in which all mankind are conceived and born, and which manifests itself in actual sin.[57]

John Calvin, the French theologian who along with Luther changed the face of Christianity by breaking away from the Roman papal control, was one of the most ardent believers of this pathway of sin. Original Sin, or "that inbred taint of moral evil in which all mankind are conceived and born," was something which was inherited by all of Adam's descendants.[58] This act was "not a trivial fault but a heinous crime."[59] The effect on every person born was complete:

> All of us descending from an impure seed, come into the world tainted with the contagion of sin . . . Before we behold the light of the sun we are in God's sight defiled and polluted.[60]

Infants were: "A seed bed of sin, and therefore cannot but be odious and abominable to God."[61]

Even though Calvin agreed that man acted spontaneously, and of free will, when he was guided by the Holy Spirit: "We maintain that his whole nature is so imbued with depravity, that of himself he possess no ability whatever to act aright."[62] The hereditary corruption was extended to all his offspring as Original Sin.[63]

But while the Christian Church adamantly believed that our passage into the mortal world was stained with this indelible heritage, there was a way of relief provided to the faithful through baptism. This rite of applying Holy Water to cleanse the soul was the only salvation available to remove the stain of Original Sin.[64] The term comes from the Greek noun meaning "dipping or washing," and refers to the baptism of Christ in the waters of the river Jordan by John the Baptist.[65] This act was originally performed by John who baptized people to show that they had turned to God, and away from their sins, in order to be forgiven.[66] As Jesus had told Nicodemus: "Unless one is born of water and the Spirit, he cannot enter the Kingdom of God."[67] But where John could only baptize with unblessed water,[68] he explained to his followers that someone with higher authority would be coming soon: "And he will baptize you with fire – with the Holy Spirit."[69]

The reason for this grace was that God, the Father, remained in love with His children, despite the blasphemy of Adam and Eve. Jesus explained to his disciples that "those who believe and are baptized will be saved."[70] But timing was critical, for if the child died, for any reason, before baptism, his souls was eternally damned. Dante, in the *Divine Comedy*, placed these pitiful babes in Purgatory: "The little innocents seized by the fangs of death before they were cleared of human guilt."[71] Adults as well, according to

Dante, were banished to the Underworld but resided in Limbo, the first Circle of Hell, where the Unbaptized and the Virtuous Pagans dwelled, even though they did not sin during their lifetime. This concept of Limbo, or *Limbus Puerorum*, had been formulated by St. Thomas Aquinas in the thirteenth century as an attempt to view the concept of original sin as one of nature and not the person.[72] In this way, innocents like un-baptized newborns would not have to perish for all eternity in the damnation of Hell. Christian justice was harsh, however, and even "though they have merits it is not enough, for they had not baptism, which is the gateway of the faith thou holdest."[73] The innate corruption of the child would have to be purified by this sacred rite so that the child could be admitted into the kingdom of God.[74]

The critical importance of being given baptism meant that the un-baptized infant was identified with the most evil and sinful existence possible. In the Middle Ages, the horror with which such children were seen was intense.[75] Burchard of Worms, in the eleventh century, explained that the custom of burying an un-baptized infant with a stake through its heart was so it would not arise and injure others.[76] Like the legendary werewolf itself, the un-baptized infant was a captive in the devil's power.[77] Baptism extended beyond the pollution of original sin and was used as a form of exorcism of the Devil during these Dark Ages.[78]

The effects of this belief did not die quickly. In 1676, Richard Allestree wrote "the newborn babe is full of the stains and pollution of sin, which it inherits from our first parents through our loins . . ."[79] In 1638, Dorothy Talbie, of Salem, Massachusetts, was convicted of murdering her daughter and was said to be "so possessed with Satan that he persuaded her to break the neck of her own child, that she might free it from future misery.[80]

But gradually the intensity of fear diminished and the taint of Original Sin became more theoretic than real. In 1831, Bronson Alcott attempted to raise his infant daughter more humanely than the traditional Calvinist position that the "infant is depraved by the taint of original sin."[81] He believed that this was one of the worst and most impious doctrines and could cause parents to treat their children with cruelty: "Ye would stamp upon the infant the seal of sin that ye may find an excuse for your own sin."[82] As the twentieth century approached, the danger of damage from un-baptized infants was assuaged, and the rite of purification became more an act of love and faith than protection.

D. HATRED AND FEAR

Attempts to harm the fetus can predate any attempts at infanticide itself. Sigmund Freud, in *The Interpretation of Dreams*, discussed such a condition in one of his woman patients:

> Like so many young married women, she had been far from pleased when she became pregnant; and more than once she had allowed herself to wish that the child in her womb might die. Indeed, in a fit of rage after a violent scene with her husband, she had beaten with her fists on her body so as to hit the child inside it. Thus the dead child was in fact the fulfillment of a wish, but of a wish that had been put aside fifteen years earlier.[83]

Freud believed that most dreams were the fulfillment of hidden wishes which the patient may not realize existed.[84] Common connections included impressions which dated back to events of earliest childhood, as well as death-wishes between parents and their children.[85] As the pregnant mother-to-be found herself suddenly in a condition that subconsciously reminded her of these suppressed infant feelings, she lashed out at the cause – the fetus in her womb – with vehemence.

Other modern authors have also found the death wish of a mother towards her child to be very widespread. Joseph Rheingold hypothesized that this lethal aspiration stemmed from a desire to escape the punishment that the women imagined their own mothers wreaked upon them.[86] While unable to respond defensively in their childhood, they now vented their anger and frustration at their own offspring.

That such impulses were not simply a new phenomenon was appreciated by Lloyd deMause who pointed out that while modern psychotherapy often found impulses of mothers to stab, mutilate, abuse, decapitate and strangulate their children, the further back in history one went, the more likely those impulses were likely to be carried out.[87] Although some of these cases had been ascribed to mental illness, Hirschmann and Schmitz found that in Germany, psychotics actually comprised a small percentage of parents who killed their newborn infants, although a much larger percentage when it was an older child who was killed.[88] Seemingly normal, well adapted and successful women were capable of showing suddenly severe, and lethal, reactions to the birth of their child.

Dorothy Bloch has written extensively on how infanticidal fear dominates the fantasies of many children.[89] She believes that the assumption of a different identity is a common defense against this threat as the child often blames himself for the destructive feelings of the parent and then develops a fanciful lifestyle.[90] The most frequent instance of this occurrence is that of homosexuality.[91]

And the problem was not restricted to the mother alone. As far back as ancient Greece, Plutarch noted how Greek fathers did not necessarily see their children with the same love and attachment as the mother. He repeated the view of Evanus who said that a child was often seen as fear or pain for the father.[92] After a lifetime of struggle, there were distinct disadvantages to the birth of a child. Because of the likelihood that a man's inheritance would go to his biological offspring, he would often lose many friends when a child was born.[93] While a child could provide future security many years later, a good friend was hard to find and yet was essential to daily life. The underlying reasons may not have been ideal, but a common proverb was: "A rich man with an unknown heir's a power."[94]

This fear and concern over their own welfare often manifested itself in physical abuse and punishment. In Germany, hostility towards children was so great that the term "kinderfeindlichkeit," or rage toward children, was often used.[95] Bavarian infant mortality rates were as high as 57%,[96] and then, as now, a desire to discipline often resulted in a fatal injury. The motto, "to love your child means to chastise it," was followed with reverent care.[97]

This predicament was world-wide, and not restricted to only one country. In England, studies showed that by age four years, some type of "smacking" was almost universal.[98] In the United States over 90% of parents stated that they use physical punishment at some time in their child's life.[99] In Sweden, about 4% of all children were abused at least one time each year by a parent "so severely that they risked being physically injured."[100] Details of this problem are discussed more thoroughly in the chapter on Punishment.

E. SUPERSTITION

1. Changelings

During the Middle Ages, superstition, rather than science, dominated the view of the world. The medieval mind, even the religious or scientific one, was ready to believe in mystery and magic as readily as we accept the truthfulness of the evening news. There were goblins in the forest, witches among the town womenfolk, and the devil was certainly residing within the souls of certain newborn infants. When a baby was born with some type of physical abnormality, or when it acted in ways which were irritative or unique, it was not seen as a normal human being, but rather as a "changeling." These were infants left by supernatural creatures who had come in the middle of the night and taken the real child, exchanging in its place one that was under the direct control of Satan.[101] As Martin Luther claimed, they were children that "Satan lays in the place of the genuine child, that people may be tormented by them."[102]

This superstition predated the Christian era and was commonly seen among the Celts, Germans and Slavs.[103] Celtic tradition held that fairies would steal a child for their own purpose and then leave an ugly, old looking, changeling in its place. Methods of retrieving the lost child included abandoning the one left in its stead on a dung hill or boundary ditch, exposing it to fire, or casting it into a river or lake. This would supposedly allow the real child to be restored, although it is obvious that many such children were ultimately destroyed.[104] Other equally fatal cures included tormenting the changeling by making it scream and cry so that a fairy would take the undesired baby away,[105] placing the infant close to the fire so it would disappear up the chimney, or putting it in a basket which was then hung over a fire.[106] Bartholomew Iscanus, the Bishop of Exeter from 1161-1181 A.D., condemned this practice which caused people to set a child "on the house roof or in an oven to recover its health."[107] But the superstition remained, and if the child did indeed die, many a parent could at least find solace in their becoming free of the influence of the Devil.

Children with any type of disability or deformity were especially regarded as changelings.[108] Also, children who were unusual in appearance or who behaved inappropriately would be seen as being under the control of an evil force.[109] If a child cried interminably, or had abnormal eating habits, it was a changeling. At times, the community even blamed the mother herself for giving birth to such a child, and in order to protect themselves against future danger, she was killed as a witch.[110]

These "reasonable" explanations for unusual events enjoyed popular acceptance for they provided a reason why an infant did not turn out as desired. It also provided an excuse to withdraw care or concern. In Shakespeare's *Henry the Fourth*, king Henry lamented that his son Percy was not as valiant as the son of Lord Northumberland: "O that it could be proved that some night-tripping fairy had exchanged in cradle clothes our children where they lay."[111]

These superstitions were widespread. One tale was told by Stephen of Bourbon, the Dominican Inquisitor, who detailed how mothers would bring their infants to the spot where the greyhound of the Seigneur of Villar, Guinefort, was buried and was fabled to be the protector of children. They would abandon their infants there in hopes of having their real child returned.[112]

A variant of the story was described by Henry Fielding in *Joseph Andrews*. Throughout the book, the story of a young man's attempt to maintain his virtue was detailed and eventually Joseph fell in love with a young woman, Fanny, who he decided to wed. At the end of the story we find out that Fanny was the real daughter of Joseph's parents who was stolen by gypsies and in her stead, the cradle contained "a poor sickly boy, that did not seem to have an hour to live."[113] The mother was grief stricken, but decided to rear the young boy as her own nevertheless.

2. Tribal Customs

Superstition has always reigned supreme in tribal religion, and the fate of a newborn depended upon local customs which determined the cause of a particular trait or appearance. Many tribes considered certain manifestations unlucky or dangerous, and referred to them as "Thola," or evil signs, which could only be cleansed by putting the child to death.[114]

In Madagascar, infants born in March or April, or on a Wednesday or Friday, were exposed, drowned, or buried alive by certain tribes.[115] The Kamchadales killed infants who were born in stormy weather.[116] More commonly, however, it was some physical appearance which caused a dangerous premonition.

One commonly observed function was the cutting of teeth. This superstition was widely spread throughout much of Africa. Livingstone wrote "if a child cuts the upper front teeth before the lower, it is killed, as unlucky."[117] Some specific instances included the inland Igbirras of Northern Nigeria, where if an infant cut its first tooth on the upper jaw, it was often killed.[118] The Ibo, of Nigeria, also killed children whose upper teeth cut first as they believed these children would be dominated by a wicked disposition and prove hateful both to gods and to men.[119] Other anomalies which the Ibo saw as an abomination, or "alu," and which resulted in immediate death, was a child born with teeth or those with any developmental abnormalities.[120]

Among the A-ki-ku-yu, any child whose upper teeth were cut first were designated as ill-omened children and killed at birth. They either were suffocated by the mother or put out in the fallow land with grass placed in its mouth and nostrils.[121] In Bondei, such unfortunate infants were also considered unlucky and killed.[122]

In one of the islands in Lake Victoria Nyanza, if a child cut its upper teeth first, it portended great disaster if it was allowed to live and therefore it was immediately killed.[123] In the Belgian Congo such children were called "Kiliba Kinkula," and were thrown into the water, or exposed to wild beasts.[124] The Bakuas also put to death such infants.[125] Among the Lovedu, a Bantu tribe in South Africa, children whose upper teeth appeared first were felt to be full of "muridi," a shadow of evil power, and were killed.[126] In British East Africa, a child born feet first was smothered otherwise "their crops will all wither up from drought".[127] In Casembe's country, if a child was seen to turn from one side to the other in sleep it was killed.[128]

The Tehetehara of Northeast Brazil would kill infants at birth if they had certain abnormalities which were considered supernaturally caused.[129] This included twins, who were felt to be born from a sexual relation between the mother and a dangerous supernatural being, and other anatomic anomalies. The Machiguenga of South America believed that excessive crying without reason was an expression of anger and may lead a mother to reject the infant and lead to infanticide.[130] In Binbinga and the coastal Australian areas, a child would be killed if it caused its mother much pain before birth.[131]

3. Omens

Many an infant has been foreordained with hatred and fear because of portentous signs that occurred before the birth process. Such tales were especially common among the Greeks who endowed their mythology with omens, even among their gods. Cronos (Saturn), the first powerful God who ruled the Heavens above, was warned by Gaia and Ouranos that some day he would be defeated by one of his own sons.[132] In a fashion that was to become commonplace among gods and kings alike when such portents were given, Cronos decided to eliminate his destined fate by killing his children at birth. In this way no son would ever be allowed to live to an age to harm him. As his fertile wife Rhea then delivered a baby, year after year, he swallowed each one as if they were a pitted olive.[133] In almost endless grief, Rhea gave birth to Hestia, Demeter, Hera, Pluto and Poseidon and then watched as Cronos swallowed each one immediately after they were born.[134] Finally, Rhea developed a plan to save her next child from destruction. She decided that immediately after birth she would substitute a huge stone in swaddling clothes for the real child, and then give it to Cronos to swallow. When her next baby son, Zeus, was born, the ruse worked and Cronos swallowed the stone and was satiated. Zeus is then sent to Ida to be raised away from the sight of his father. In order to drown out his infant cries, which would have warned Cronos of the plot, the Curetes and Corybantes beat on their shields and helmets to make noise.[135] Zeus was saved.

This lesson was even not lost on Zeus, who took special precautions to bypass the fate of his father. When he later married his first wife Metis, Earth told Zeus that she would bear a daughter, and then a son who "would be the lord of heaven."[136] Finding his own role of lord much to his liking, and remembering what happened to Cronus, Zeus then swallowed Metis to prevent her having further children.[137]

The story of Oedipus typified this danger to mortals and is perhaps the most well-known tale of its kind. According to Sophocles, an oracle told Laius, the father of Oedipus, that "his doom would be death at the hands of his own son."[138] When Oedipus was born, Laius had him exposed in an attempt to bypass the Fates, but the omen was to come true as Oedipus survived and later killed his father in a quarrel.

This characteristic veracity, despite all attempts to escape, was seen in many other famous tales. Acrisius, the son of Abas, king of Argos, was told by an oracle that he would lose his life at the hand of his grandson. He therefore imprisoned his daughter, Danae, to prevent her every becoming a mother.[139] Zeus, however, poured through the roof of her brazen subterranean chamber in a golden shower and she eventually delivered a son, Perseus. She raised the boy secretly until he was four years old and then the king heard his laughter and put the two of them in a coffer and cast them into the sea. They were carried to the island of Seriphus where they were found, and saved, by Dictys.[140] As in many portentous dream tales, Persus, when grown, returned to Argos and inadvertently killed Acrisius by an errant throw of a quoit.[141]

Cyrus, the founder of the Persian empire, was the son of Mandane, the daughter of king Astyages. Before Cyrus was born, Astyages dreamed of a vine that grew from Mandane and covered all of Asia after her marriage to Cambyses. This dream was interpreted by the seers to mean that the child of Mandane would rule in his place and so when Cyrus was born, Astyages ordered Harpagus to kill him by exposure. Harpagus instead gave the infant to Mitradates with clear instructions on what to do, but the slave felt pity for the child and raised him instead in his own house.[142] As an adult, Cyrus defeated Astyages and, true to the dream, became king of all Persia.

Worldwide, there are many tales of dangerous omens. In the Thai classic story of *Ramakien*, Lakshmi, the celestial consort of Phra Narai, was born on earth as Nang Seeda in order to share the mortal adventures of her lover. She picked as her parents Nang Monto and Totsagan. At the moment of her birth she uttered a cry which terrified the demons. It was then predicted that she would cause the death of Totsagan and the downfall of Longka where they lived. She was therefore "cast adrift on the sea in a glass bowl."[143] The gods assured her safety, however, and she was saved and brought up by the king of Mitila.

A similar story was told of Zoroaster, the traditional founder of the ancient Persian religion. At the moment of his birth, the whole of Good Creation rejoiced when he laughed instead of cried. The demons, however, were terror-struck by this omen of good and inspired his father to try and kill him at once. The man first tried to burn the boy but the wood would not light. He then laid the child in front of a herd of stampeding cattle, but the lead bull swerved away and protected the boy. A similar event occurred with a group of stampeding horses. Finally the father put the child into the lair of a she-wolf who he expected would devour him. Instead, Zoroaster was suckled and survived.[144]

In the Celtic tradition, there was the story of Balor, a robber who lived on Tory Island and was told by a druid that he would be slain by his grandson. He confined his daughter, Ethne, in a high tower and had her watched by twelve women. Mackinealy was nevertheless able to gain access to her vault and nine months later she gave birth to three sons who Balor ordered drowned. One of the boys fell out of the sheet that carried them to the water and was saved.[145]

Other Irish tales included that of Ragallach, king of Connacht, who was told by a druid that he would be killed by his own child. When his wife gave birth to a daughter, he ordered it destroyed. The child was saved by a swineherd, however.[146]

F. Overlaying

In Medieval England, church documents indicated that the most common means of infanticide at the time was "overlaying" – a condition where an infant was taken into the parent's bed to either feed or sleep, and then suffocated when the mother's body covered its face.[147] Examples of such disaster date back to the Old Testament where the decision of king Solomon to decide the real mother of a living child was related as an example of his uncommonly wise justice. In that famous case, one woman had rolled over on top of her three day old baby as they slept in bed and caused the baby to smother to death. Two mothers then appeared before Solomon with one living child and each claimed it was her own. One woman said the son of the other woman was killed and then she got up in the night and took my son from beside me while I was asleep, and laid her dead child in my arms and took mine to sleep beside her.[148] The other denied the story and swore the child was her own. Neither would change her story, despite all attempts at resolution. King Solomon then decided that he would slice the baby in two with a sword, and then give half to each woman to settle the dispute.[149] When one woman gave up her claim to save the baby, she was judged to be the real mother.[150]

In this classic ancient case of "tough" justice, the response by the mother whose child died indicated that the death was likely accidental. But many cases throughout history were not so innocent. Overlaying was a simple way to eliminate an unwanted newborn and escape any claim of responsibility. The problem became so widespread during the Middle Ages that various ecclesiastical decrees stipulated that mothers were not to sleep in the same bed as their children under the age of one year.[151] Three Penitential texts specifically condemned overlaying: the Penitential of Columbanus (seventh century A.D.); the St. Hubert Penitential (ninth century); and the Penitential of Haltigar (ninth century).[152] These regulations applied to both mothers and fathers, and usually involved penance for two years, while that for infanticide lasted from seven to fifteen years.[153] In 1217, the Synod of Salisbury issued warnings to nursing mothers to not take their children in bed with them because of the dangers of overlaying, and many of these instructions were directed to the wet nurses as well.[154] In the *Statues of Winchester I*, in

1224, the church warned of excommunication and instructed that: "Women should be restrained from keeping their children close by in bed lest they smother them while in sleep.[155] "

In the *Statutes of Coventry* this was repeated for children under the age of three years.[156] Damme, in fact, found at least fifteen references in ecclesiastical statutes of councils during this era that pointed out the dangers of taking a child into bed.[157] Other canons, as well, included overlaying as a crime against a fellow man that deserved church punishment.[158] But overlaying was not actually elevated from a venial to a major sin until 1237.[159]

Of interest, all of these warnings were only directed to women.[160] While it was common to have the overlaying occur during breast-feeding, there were a number of cases that developed during the night when either the husband, or wife, could suffocate the child. Whether the problem was truly one only of feminine causation, or whether this was another example of sexism in the Ecclesiastic courts, has not been clearly determined. The Danish synod had seen overlaying as a responsibility of the mother alone, but the tribunals elsewhere would also bring various men before the court to be charged.[161]

The prosecution in a case of overlaying did not need to allege an intent to kill the infant, as careless negligence was enough guilt and was punished with an equal intensity.[162] Abelard, for example, considered overlaying an inadvertent act and not murder; nevertheless:

> He does not question the imposition of heavy penance on the mother, not because she had sinned, since she was innocent and had acted out of compassion for the infant, but as a caution to her and other women to act more carefully in the future.[163]

The problem of overlaying continued well beyond the Middle Ages. William Congreve, in *Love for Love*, depicted Valentine as putting a pox on Twitnam who was the mother of one of his children: "A thoughtless, two-handed whore, she knows my condition well enough, and might have overlaid the child a fortnight ago, if she had any forecast in her."[164]

It was a common cause of death in Norway in the sixteenth century, and the frequency was too high to be explained by accidents alone.[165] There was evidence, as late as 1745 in Pomerania, of the punishment of overlaying by public penance.[166] And in *The Gentleman's Magazine*, from January 1746, a Florentine device called an "arcutio" was highlighted which indicated active public interest in the problem. It was a small wooden cradle where a child was lain when breast feeding in bed in order to help prevent overlaying.[167]

Even up to the nineteenth century, overlaying remained a problem in England. In 1894, the London coroner noted that a thousand infants were overlain each year in London alone.[168] It was particularly frequent on Saturday nights when the cause was believed to be gross carelessness brought on by excess alcohol intake. An article in the *British Medical Journal* noted that: "Perfectly healthy children are sacrificed to the bad habit of making them sleep with their parents."[169] In 1909 in England overlaying was made a specific criminal offense and there were twenty reported deaths from it in 1920 in Birmingham, England.[170]

In ante-bellum Virginia, during the 1850's, the mortality of children under the age of one year of age was 16-20%. While many of these were due to infectious problems, overlaying was stated to be the cause in four percent of the cases.[171] Savitt believes that many of these were actually due to Sudden Infant Death Syndrome (SIDS).[172]

The modern description of crib deaths, or Sudden Infant Death Syndrome (SIDS), pointed out that past cases of suffocation or overlaying may have at times been crib deaths which otherwise affects healthy babies between two to twelve months of age.[173] It is believed that 7-10,000 young infants die in this country every year from SIDS which is the major cause of death for infants between the ages of one week and one year.[174]

Separating the homicidal death from the crib death, however, can be very difficult. SIDS became a certifiable cause of death in 1963.[175] In 1968, Asch presented the hypothesis that the majority of SIDS deaths actually represent maternal homicide secondary to postpartum depression, but his paper was not substantiated by any case reports.[176] When forensic evidence of suffocation is evident in a SIDS death, however, it is likely that the underlying causation was homicide.[177]

Some researchers have pointed out that up to ten percent of such "unexpected" deaths may not have been natural.[178] In Wauconda, Illinois, for example, Gail Savage had been the subject of intense medical investigation in an attempt to determine the mysterious malady which took three of her children, all aged under one year, and all diagnosed as having SIDS. But the Chicago newspapers shocked the public on September 10, 1993 with the story that:

> On Thursday, 10 weeks after her third child, 5-month-old Cynthia, was buried, authorities said Savage admitted to killing all three of her children, smothering them in a blanket.[179]

She said that she suffocated the children because she was frustrated by their crying. Her claim that the babies died from SIDS was initially believed because there were no tell-tale signs of abuse. According to one pediatric pathologist: "It is not just difficult to tell the difference between a child who died from SIDS and one who is suffocated, it is impossible."[180]

In Illinois, other cases originally labeled as SIDS had their death certificates amended after later review by the Cook County Chief Medical Examiner and policy was changed in 1997 so that once a family had a death of a child due to SIDS, if any other child later died from unexplained causes, the first child's death certificate would automatically be changed to undetermined death as well.[181]

Endnotes

1 . Plutarch, "On Affection For Children," 496, <u>Moralia</u>, Volume VI, 349.
2 . Hume, "The Sceptic," <u>Essays</u>, 162-163.
3 . Plutarch, "The Roman Questions," IV.102, <u>Moralia</u>, 153.
4 . Dickson, <u>Waving at Trains</u>, 1.
5 . Sumner, <u>Folkways</u>, 267.
6 . Ibid., 269.
7 . Diogenes Laertius, <u>Lives of Eminent Philosophers</u>, III.VIII.81, 209.
8 . Montaigne, <u>Essays</u>, II 8, 139.
9 . Seneca,"On the True Good as Attained by Reason," CXXIV, <u>Ad Lucilium Epistulae Morales</u>, Volume III, 441.
10 9. Lorence, Parents and Children in Eighteenth Century Europe," 5.
11 . Howells, <u>A Modern Instance</u>, 188.
12 . Calvin, <u>Commentaries</u>, II, 59.
13 . Storr, <u>Human Aggression</u>, 2.
14 . Hearn, <u>The Aryan Household</u>, 344.
15 . Josephus, "Antiquities," III.XI.5, <u>The Works of Flavius Josephus</u>, Volume I, 105.
16 . <u>Code of Jewish Law</u>, 158.1, Volume IV, 32.
17 . Frazer, <u>The Golden Bough</u>, 242.
18 . Gorer, <u>Himalayan Village: An Account of the Lepchas of Sikkim</u>, 289.
19 . James, <u>Primitive Ritual and Belief: An Anthropological Essay</u>, 12.
20 . Roscoe, <u>The Baganda: An Account of Their Native Customs and Beliefs</u>, 53.
21 . Soga, <u>The Ama-Xosa: Life and Customs</u>, 293.
22 . Williamson, "Infanticide: An Anthropological Analysis," 64.
23 . Werner, <u>The Unmarried Mother in German Literature</u>, 20.
24 . Atkinson, "Life, Birth & Live-Birth," 134.
25 . Locke, <u>Two Treatises of Government</u>, II.54.1-2, 304.
26 . Ibid., II.55.1-2, 304.
27 . Ibid., II.58.1-3, 306.
28 28. Williams, <u>The Sanctity of Life & the Criminal Law</u>, 18.
29 . Williamson, "Infanticide: An Anthropological Analysis," 64.
30 . Ford, "Control of Conception in Cross-Cultural Perspective," 765.
31 . Williams, "The Legal Evaluation of Infanticide," 116.
32 . Werner, <u>The Unmarried Mother in German Literature</u>, 21.
33 . Kellum, "Infanticide in England in the Later Middle Ages," 369.
34 . Flaceliere, <u>Daily Life in Greece at the Time of Pericles</u>, 78.
35 . Justinian, <u>The Institutes</u>, III.XIX.10, 138.
36 . Numbers 3:15. If a newborn died before the age of one month it was considered a stillborn, and no funeral or mourning practices were observed. <u>Numbers, The Torah, A Modern Commentary IV</u>,
37 . Leviticus, 27:6.
38 . Maimonides, <u>The Book of Asservations</u>, Treatise IV, I.3, volume XV, 171. Between the ages of thirty-one days and 5 years a male child was worth five shekels and a female three shekels; from age 5 years and one day to twenty years a male was worth twenty shekels, and a female ten shekels; from age twenty years and one day to sixty years a male was worth fifty shekels and a female thirty shekels; and over the age of sixty years a male was worth fifteen shekels and a female ten shekels. Ibid.

39 . Maimonides, The Guide of the Perplexed, III.49, 611.
40 . Biale, Women and Jewish Law, 222.
41 . Canon 88. Abbo & Hannan, The Sacred Canons, Volume I, 127-128.
42 . Canon 89. Ibid., Volume I, 129.
43 . Bouscaren & Ellis, Canon Law: A Text & Commentary, 88.2, 77.
44 . Langness, "Child Abuse and Cultural Values: The Case of New Guinea," 14.
45 . Oliver, Ancient Tahitian Society, Volume I, 63.
46 . Roheim, Children of the Desert: The Western Tribes of Central Australia, Volume I, 70.
47 . Balikci, "Female Infanticide on the Arctic Coast," 617.
48 . Ibid., 620.
49 . Williamson, "Infanticide: An Anthropological Analysis," 64.
50 . Scrimshaw, "Infant Mortality and Behavior in the Regulation of Family Size," 393.
51 . Wagatsuma, "Child Abandonment and Infanticide: A Japanese Case," 131.
52 . Wolff, Postcards From the End of the World, 58.
53 . Johnson, "The Socioeconomic Context of Child Abuse and Neglect in Native South America," 63.
54 . Prudentius, "The Divinity of Christ," 909-914, The Poems of Prudentius, Volume II, 34-35.
55 . Ibid., "The Origin of Sin," 11-14, Volume II, 79.
56 . St. Augustine, Against Julian, I.3.10, 11.
57 . Philalethes, Baptismon Didache or Scriptural Studies on Baptisms, Especially Christian Baptism, Volume VIII, 51.
58 . Ibid.
59 . Calvin, Institutes of the Christian Religion, II.I.4, Volume I, 212.
60 . Ibid., II.I.5, 214.
61 . Ibid., II.I.8, 217-18.
62 . Calvin, "The Necessity of Reforming the Church," Theological Treatises, Volume XXII, 198.
63 . Calvin, Institutes of the Christian Religion, II.I.5, Volume I, 214.
64 . Philalethes, Baptismon Didache or Scriptural Studies on Baptisms, Volume VIII, 51.
65 . Matthew 3:13-17. O'Connor, Child Murderess and Dead Child Traditions, A Comparative Study, 17.
66 . Luke 3:3. The Living Bible, 803. See e.g., John 1:6.
67 . John 3:5. Ibid., 838.
68 . John 1:26.
69 . Luke 3:16, Ibid., 803-804. Paul told the disciples in Ephesus that: "John's baptism was to demonstrate a desire to turn from sin to God and that those receiving his baptism must then go onto believe in Jesus." Acts 19:4. Ibid., 884. See e.g., Acts 11:16.
70 . Mark 16:16. Ibid., 799.
71 . Dante, "Purgatory," VII.31-33, The Divine Comedy, 97.
72 . O'Connor, Child Murderess and Dead Child Traditions, A Comparative Study, 18.
73 . Ibid., "Inferno," IV.34-35, 61.
74 . Calvin, Institutes of the Christian Religion, IV.17, Volume II, 541.
75 . Kellum, "Infanticide in England in the Later Middle Ages," 379.

76 . Ibid.
77 . Ibid.
78 . DeMause, "The Evolution of Childhood," 10.
79 . Ibid.
80 . Hoffer & Hull, Murdering Mothers: Infanticide in England and New England 1558-1803, 40.
81 . Strickland, "A Transcendentalist Father: The Child Rearing Practices of Bronson Alcott," 11.
82 . Ibid., 12.
83 . Freud, The Interpretation of Dreams, 154.
84 . Ibid., 158.
85 . Ibid., 189, 255.
86 . DeMause, "The Evolution of Childhood," 25.
87 . Ibid.
88 . Harder, "The Psychopathology of Infanticide," 220.
89 . Bloch, "Fantasy and the Fear of Infanticide," 30.
90 . Bloch, "The Threat of Infanticide and Homosexual Identity," 579.
91 . Ibid., 580.
92 . Plutarch, "On Affection For Children," 4, Moralia, Volume VI, 353.
93 . Ibid., 355.
94 . Ibid.
95 . Ende, "Battering and Neglect: Children in Germany, 1860-1978," 250.
96 . Ibid., footnote 13, 275.
97 . Ibid., 253.
98 . Scott, "The Psychiatrist's Viewpoint," 191.
99 . Steinmetz & Strauss, "The Family as Cradle of Violence," 50.
100. Somander & Rammer, "Intra- and Extrafamilial Child Homicide in Sweden 1971-1980," 53.
101. Haffter, "The Changeling: History and Psychodynamics of Attitudes to Handicapped Children in European Folklore," 58.
102. Darbyshire, "Infanticide: Lambs to the Slaughter," 33.
103. Shahar, Childhood in the Middle Ages, 138.
104. Rees & Rees, Celtic Heritage, 243.
105. Shahar, Childhood in the Middle Ages, 132.
106. Kellum, "Infanticide in England in the Later Middle Ages," 379.
107. Coulton, Life in the Middle Ages, 33.
108. Moseley, "The History of Infanticide in Western Society," 352.
109. Ibid., 353.
110. Haffter, "The Changeling: History and Psychodynamics of Attitudes to Handicapped Children in European Folklore," 59.
111. Shakespeare, Henry the Fourth, Part One, I.i.85-87.
112. Shahar, Childhood in the Middle Ages, 133.
113. Fielding, Joseph Andrews, 338.
114. M'Lennan, Studies in Ancient History, The Second Series, 94.
115. Westermarck, The Origin and Development of the Moral Ideas, Volume I, 395.
116. Ibid., 395.
117. Levy-Bruhl, Primitive Mentality, 152.
118. Aptekar, Anjea: Infanticide, Abortion & Contraception in Savage Society, 70.
119. Basden, Niger Ibos, 184.

120. Ibid., 262-63.
121. Routledge & Routledge, With a Preshistoric People, 150.
122. Westermarck, The Origin and Development of the Moral Ideas, Volume I, 395.
123. Levy-Bruhl, Primitive Mentality, 150.
124. Ibid., 153.
125. M'Lennan, Studies in Ancient History, The Second Series, 94.
126. Krige & Krige, The Realm of a Rain-Queen, 218.
127. Levy-Bruhl, Primitive Mentality, 150.
128. Ibid., 152.
129. Wagley, "Cultural Influences on Population: A Comparison of Two Tupi Tribes," 273.
130. Johnson, "The Socioeconomic Context of Child Abuse and Neglect in Native South America," 64.
131. Spencer & Gillen, The Northern Tribes of Central Australia, 609.
132. Hesiod, Theogony, 464-465, 24.
133. Ibid., 467, 24.
134. Apollodorus, "Library," 1.1.5-6, Volume I, 7.
135. Ovid, Fast I, IV.210, 203.
136. Apollodorus, The Library, I.iii.6, Volume I, 2.
137. Hesiod, Theogony, 890-891, 35.
138. Sophocles, Oedipus Rex, II, 36.
139. Harpers Dictionary of Classical Literature & Antiquities, 12.
140. Ibid., 467.
141. Ibid., 12.
142. Herodotus, The History, I.108-110.
143. Cadet, The Ramakien, 40.
144. Cavendish, Legends of the World, 134.
145. Rees & Rees, Celtic Heritage, 214.
146. Ibid., 222.
147. Damme, "Infanticide: The Worth of an Infant Under Law," 3.
148. I Kings 3:20. The Living Bible, 283.
149. I Kings 3:25.
150. I Kings 3:27.
151. Moseley, "The History of Infanticide in Western Society," 356.
152. O'Connor, Child Murderess and Dead Child Traditions, A Comparative Study, 27.
153. Ibid., 26-27.
154. Ford, "The Emergence of the Child as a Legal Entity," 399.
155. Damme, "Infanticide: The Worth of an Infant Under Law," 3.
156. Ibid., 4.
157. Ibid.
158. Dunstan Con. 52, AD 963; Const. 15, Edmund, AD 1236; Const. 2 Zouche, AD 1347; Const. 4 Thorsby, AD 1363. Reichel, "Church Discipline," A Complete Manual of Canon Law, Volume II, footnote 167, 64.
159. Greenwald & Greenwald, "Medicolegal Progress in Inquests of Felonious Deaths: Westminster, 1761-1866," 238.
160. Damme, "Infanticide: The Worth of an Infant Under Law," 4.
161. Shahar, Childhood in the Middle Ages, 130.
162. Helmholz, "Infanticide in the Province of Canterbury During the 15th Century," 381.

163. Shahar, Childhood in the Middle Ages, 129.
164. Congreve, Love for Love, I.iv.190-193, 20.
165. Martinson, Growing Up in Norway, 800 to 1990, 29.
166. Lea, History of Auricular Confession and Indulgences in the Latin Church, Volume II, 90.
167. Fildes, Breasts, Bottles & Babies, 196-97.
168. "A Thousand Infants Overlain," 36.
169. Ibid.
170. Radbill, "Children in a World of Violence: A History of Child Abuse," 9.
171. Savitt, "Smothering & Overlaying of Virginal Slave Children: A Suggested Explanation," 402.
172. Ibid., 400.
173. Raring, Crib Death, 19-20. In England it is referred to as "Cot Death". Knight, "Forensic Problems in Practice: Infant Deaths," 447.
174. DeFrain, Taylor & Ernst, Coping with Sudden Infant Death, 3.
175. Kukull & Peterson, "Sudden Infant Death and Infanticide," 485.
176. Asch, "Crib Deaths: Their Possible Relationship to Post-Partum Depression and Infanticide," 214. See e.g., Cashell, "Homicide as a Cause of the Sudden Infant Death Syndrome," 256.
177. Emery, Gilbert & Zugibe, "Three Crib Deaths, A Babyminder and Probable Infanticide," 205.
178. Emery, "Child Abuse, Sudden Infant Death Syndrome, and Unexpected Infant Death," 1097.
179. Chicago Tribune (September 10, 1993): Section 1, 1.
180. Ibid., 16.
181. Chicago Tribune (September 27, 1997): Section 1, 5.

CHAPTER XXII

CONCLUSION

"Historically, the value of infant life is determined by the forces of supply and demand and contemporary attitudes to the inevitability of death. Dead babies were quickly replaceable when the birth rate was high."[1]

Lionel Rose, writing of the frequency of infanticide in England during the nineteenth century, summarized the historical status of children, not only in the British Isles, but across the world in cold, hard economic facts. Where many valuable commodities were desperately needed because of their rarity or unique beneficial traits, babies were "quickly replaceable," a matter of "supply and demand." This callous, fiscal assessment, so seemingly cruel and unjust to modern humanistic beliefs, did not meet with incredulity or shock at the time: life was hard, the future uncertain, and infant mortality was something you came to expect, not question. In our present age, however, social conscience has developed to the point where people are appalled by talk of children being ill-treated, let alone of being quickly replaceable if they should happen to die. The concept that a parent may be excused for committing infanticide stirs up feelings of anger and disbelief, and what may have transpired in the past is viewed as nothing more than a vestige of barbarian behavior.

This reformation attitude may play well on the Humanistic stage of life, but it is a naive, idealized bandwagon that totally ignores incontestable facts about how human parents react to their offspring. If we can place our emotional defense aside, and examine Rose's proposition in cold, scientific terms, his characterization of the historical value of an infant's life is quite accurate. Prior to the twentieth century, the worth of children was generally a matter of little concern to most civilizations, perhaps because they were so used to the frailty of life that there was little expectation that infants would survive the dangerous passage to adulthood. Death was a constant visitor from many directions, and there was no time to brood over the loss of a young child when more babies could be easily generated in the future.

It was not that our ancestral parents were deficient in their capacity to love and nurture offspring as we do today; it was rather that there were times when the realities of life superseded all other emotional bonds, and an infant had to be evaluated as any other disposable possession. If dire financial straits, or peril to life, or famine, or drought endangered the ability of an entire family to survive, parents were forced to make decisions from a brutally practical perspective. Too much depended on their continued survival for them to become enmeshed in an emotional mistake. A realistic appraisal of the available options left them little choice, and many committed infanticide as a low-risk solution to insurmountable problems. As Hugh Gallagher pointed out, the child is "a victim, ready-made."[2] It is a fact that ten to fifteen percent of human infants ever born have been killed by their parents following case scenarios such as these; the fiction lies in its general disbelief.

There are many reasons why society has remained ignorant of the commonality of this crime.[3] Numerous killings have been hidden from public view by concealment of the delivery process, or have been camouflaged as miscarriages of pregnancy or stillbirths.[4] Others were simply not prosecuted as civil authorities did not attach much importance to something which was seen as a personal family matter, and not a concern of the state. In addition, there were even ethical arguments which condoned the necessary killing of a newborn child: "Because infants lack memory, linguistic capacities, and the like, they can be killed without serious objection."[5]

We have also been insulated from reports of child-murder today as the necessity for infanticide has been reduced by the widespread acceptance of abortion. In China, between 1970-1979, forty-seven million abortions were performed.[6] In the Western World, up to two million unwanted pregnancies are legally terminated each year. This leaves descriptions of infanticide as front page news, implying a rare and sensational act rather than a burning social issue.

And after all the excuses are said and done, there is also the matter of feigned concern, for despite all of our vocal support of child welfare, there was a Society for the Prevention of Cruelty to Animals many years before there was one to protect the well-being of our children. While all agree that kicking a cur in the street is inhumane, most parents vehemently demand the right to raise their own children in a manner they individually see fit – even if their method is abusive or deadly. Parents may picket a multinational corporation for needless pollution of the environment, but it is likely they will remain silent when questions are raised about their authority to discipline their offspring over matters of personal or religious concern.

I began this book with one purpose in mind – to understand, as stated in the Introduction: "How someone can take their own child, and strangle it to death?" When I first raised this question many years ago, I thought the issue to be suggestive of some unique pathologic alteration of Nature's way. It did not seem rational that evolution would maintain an inherited tendency to kill one's offspring when survival was already in such a delicate balance. Darwinian natural selection of genetic material meant that only the survival of the fittest was guaranteed; a tendency toward infanticide must certainly be a sign of unfit behavior that would not pass this reasonable standard. But the answer which has emerged from my research indicates that one of the most "natural" things a human being can do is to voluntarily kill its own offspring when faced with a variety of stressful situations.

The extent of this infanticide has been overlooked, likely because it was believed to represent only an occasional psychopathic act. But in the wake of material that has been presented in the first twenty-two chapters of this book, it is obvious that this explanation is wrong. The real reason for this hidden homicidal dilemma – this indelible stain of infanticide – is not of aberrant origin, it is rather contained within the vagaries of normal human behavior. Be it transcription of inherited DNA, as I believe, or the transference of Original Sin through the retribution of a wrathful God, our inherent nature is to place the very lives of our offspring at risk if they interfere with the survival of comfort or self.

This conclusion comes from a tripartite analysis: the so-called "Natural Law," or collection of innate instincts which arises from genetic transference of behavioral traits; Divine intervention, as referenced in the relationship which has historically developed between Man and his Gods; and the written record of man-made laws which documents the importance human beings have placed on what is concluded to be "illegal" activity. While abnormal psychiatric behavior is something which will always occur in select situations, it is not pertinent to the deductions of my present analysis.

Let me emphatically state that I am not desecrating the position of man by this conclusion; the pages of this book are not the ravings of an angry misanthrope. But the idyllic belief that humans act only humanely is naive. If we are to improve upon our past record of achievement, we must first understand the inherent nature of our evolutionary make-up. There are many strengths which our species should be proud of, but there are significant others which are very undesirable. The best way to deal with these latter weaknesses is to buttress them with floodlights of awareness.

That man is capable of beastly behavior is not an innovative statement. There have been many cynics throughout the centuries who have claimed that man is not the rational, ethical organism he purports to be. Anatole France, summarizing the irony of so-called freedom and democracy during the French Revolution, noted that:

> What we call morality is simply and solely a desperate enterprise, a forlorn hope on the part of our fellow men to reverse the order of the Universe, which is constant strife and murder, blind, ceaseless and implacable.[7]

There is a large contingent of historians who believe that France's view of Mother Nature is correct. One does not have to search our historical record on earth very far to find constant strife, and ever-present murder. Over and over again, the lofty ambitions of man seem to result in actions which are more bestial and self-serving than worthy of praise. Killing each other has been a constant human pastime as we are forever enmeshed in territorial disputes, and settle our differences with violence rather than arbitration.

But many of these killings have had, at least in part, some semblance of rational explanation so that our beneficent impression of Man has not been totally destroyed. By evoking excuses like punishment for moral depravity, defense of personal rights and family, and religious directives like the Holy Crusades, the homicide of billions of human beings has been absolved. Nevertheless, no matter how facetious or real these credible defenses appear, it is difficult to try and understand how a parent can willingly kill his own child. For most people, such activity is so gruesome that it is not capable of a plausible vindication. Even more troubling has been the frequent societal acceptance that such destruction is not a criminal act. Shulamith Shahar noted that the killing of older children was generally regarded as murder by many societies, but the killing of newborn infants was often accepted without protest. In fact, many societies actually considered it "an accepted norm."[8] Mildred Dickeman called it a "normative, culturally sanctioned behavior."[9]

And so we find that whether because of economic necessity, or the birth of a disabled infant; whether for shame, or population control, or to obtain power and wealth; whether for superstition, or punishment, or mercy, or love, the killing of children has been a constant companion of human development and yet the carnage has almost been forgotten by historians and sociologists in the commentaries of our time. Very few authors have researched the frequency of this slaughter, and no one has theorized that the presence of infanticide is relevant to our normal human nature.

Until now. The data is clear, the conclusion overwhelmingly supported by the pages of this book. The impulse to kill our own children is so common that it must be part of our natural genetic inheritance. Somewhere within the DNA sequence of purines and pyrimidines, the double helix which has so much control over how we think and act, lies a genetic code which promotes destruction when a particular set of facts is presented. Reflexual, automatic, without the benefit of second thought, a child is killed in order that someone else may live.

Why does such a deadly trait exist? There are only two possible explanations. Either our nature is evil, and, as Arthur Schopenhauer concluded, "man is at bottom a savage, horrible beast."[10] Or there must be some benefit derived to our species as a whole which promotes the survival of our race despite the large disposal of our offspring. Perhaps it is a mechanism whereby unstable, or dangerous, individuals lessen the likelihood that their noxious trait will be inherited by causing the death of their own children. Perhaps, like the generative potential of infanticide among certain mammals in the wild, our reproduction rate is fostered when the loss of an infant occurs. Or perhaps it is a way to assure that the culling of unsatisfactory elements will result so that resources are not wasted on unproductive progeny. Evolution has usually proven that the end justifies the means, even if the method is mayhem.

Whatever the benefit achieved, evidence of an infanticidal gene is clear and the first area of proof comes from investigation into what has been termed the "Natural Law." This inherent nature guides our behavior, and is instinctive in each individual to a varying degree of expression. While we may develop some voluntary control over its presence, we cannot totally eliminate its underlying force. Like Jack London's *Call of the Wild*, we are inextricably drawn to a particular life pattern by genetic material that has been passed down from very ancient ancestors. The mannerisms which come so natural to every human being is not a chance event but is characteristic of our species-specific genetic code. According to Erich Fromm, these instincts even determine the basis for moral behavior: "The sources of norms for ethical conduct are to be found in man's nature itself."[11] While Fromm did not believe man was inherently evil, the principle of natural law still applies.

Some have hypothesized that our inheritance is similar to that of other organisms throughout the animal kingdom. The Institutes of Justinian, in the sixth century A.D., defined natural law as: "That which she has taught all animals; a law not peculiar to the human race, but shared by all living creatures."[12] Samuel Johnson, as well, felt that living according to nature, "in obedience to that universal and unalterable law with which every heart is originally impressed," can be learned by observing the "hind of the forest and the linnet of the grove," animals who are alike regulated by instinct as man himself.[13]

While the assessment that all animals have a similar principle and guidance of life has limited appeal, most scientists and religious advocates would argue that the rational thought process of man separates him from the rest of the animal world. The ability to communicate with language, understand complex principles, and generate new concepts and ideas, would require a natural law which, at least in some ways, is distinct from other animal species. Such a view seems common-sense for, as Alexander Pope poetically concluded, "the proper study of mankind is Man."[14]

But even if we accept a separation based upon the obvious chasm between the innovative mind of man and the reflexual response of the lower animal kingdom, there is one intense force that still unites all living beings alike: the impulse to survive. First and foremost, the desire to continue living is a dominant compulsion that reigns supreme in the hidden depths of our being. Even a devout theologian like St. Thomas Aquinas had to admit that: "Whatever is a means of preserving human life and of warding off its obstacles belongs to the natural law."[15]

This correlation of natural law with the survival instinct, has been noted by many observers of human behavior.[16] It is so intense that it usually will easily overshadow almost every other instinct of Man. The Stoic philosophers accepted this fundamental instinct to such a degree that Zeno admitted that no action is inherently wrong when it refers to the physical act alone.[17] Where occasional cases are found which reveal the attenuation of this drive, such as in suicidal deaths, most human beings would choose to live rather than give up their life for some theoretical cause. When Elisabeth Badinter discovered that poor country women had to sometimes endanger the lives of their own children in order to make money as wet-nurses, she compassionately explained: "Given the circumstances of their lives, the most one can conclude is that in their cases the survival instinct dominated the maternal instinct."[18]

Charles Darwin, in 1859, took a more calculating stance and incorporated this phenomenon into his famous theory of evolution. He postulated that as more individuals are produced than can possibly survive: "There must in every case be a struggle for existence, either one individual with another of the same species, or with the individuals of distinct species, or with the physical conditions of life."[19] The outcome of this conflict would generally be in favor of those individuals who were the "fittest," a concept that assured that the progeny who survived to propagate the race were strong and possessed physical and mental advantages over their neighbors. The teachings of Darwin pointed out that there was some beneficial effect to almost every trait which an animal showed: "This preservation of favourable individual differences and variations, and the destruction of those which are injurious, I have called Natural Selection, or the Survival of the Fittest."[20] If an attribute gave one individual a survival advantage over another, it was likely to be selected out and saved during the evolutionary process.

Today, few naturalists dispute the Darwinian explanation of evolutionary selection. But the human newborn infant is at an obvious disadvantage in such a primitive scheme. Its very existence requires a longer period of parental supervision and sustenance than any other animal species, and its positive attributes, so vital later in life, are not immediately apparent at birth. If the newborn is so deficient in survivability factors, and the parent contains a natural trait to disregard the baby at the first signs of danger, how can we then explain the apparent success of Homo sapiens up to the present day. After all, despite the short period of time we have existed in geologic terms, our mastery of the earth defies comparison.

Putting aside the obvious disclaimer that our hold over the earth is tenuous and capable of self destruction in favor of many other species at any time, there are still reasonable explanations to de-emphasize this infanticidal tendency. One answer could be that the incidence of infanticide is a mere aberration, and does not play a significant role in the survivability of mankind. Gillian Cowlishaw typified this attitude when he argued that the prevalence of infanticide in the human species, when compared to animals, was quite rare and due to some "loosening of the genetic ties" which biologically provided that a mother would nurture her young.[21] Under this theory, the general nature of mankind assured that satisfactory supportive care would be provided to children, and the sporadic appearance of infant-murder was of little concern to general population growth.

While this view could certainly explain our successful evolution, it simply is not true. The incredible prevalence of infanticide in the human species, as shown in this book, is too great to be cast off as some accidental or chance occurrence. If ten to fifteen percent of infants have been killed by their parents, and many more have been given neglectful, though non-fatal, care, there must be some other protective device in place to assure that rampant destruction does not affect the likelihood that our race will endure.

A possible modulation of this impulse to kill is apparent to any observer of young infants. One of the more remarkable traits of human babies, much more than is seen with any other animal species, is the facial and vocal response – laughter and cooing – to the stimulus of its parents. A human child interacts in ways that do not relate to other survivability factors seen in the wild, such as grooming or defensive tactics against outside predators. While it is difficult to define the emotion of pleasure in words alone, the aura of a parent's visage as it observes a child's face light up and grin is expressive enough to understand how pacifying is the effect of this interaction.

Is the reason for this unique stimulus simply joy and shear happiness of life? I think not. As with all other reflexes in nature, there is a distinct beneficial advantage to this remarkable trait, and that is to retain the love of a parent who might otherwise turn deadly as the trials of child-rearing begin after birth. With the fatigue of little sleep, the anger of annoyance, and the irritation of jealousy, the human infant is at greater risk of bodily harm from its own parent than any other enemy. Nothing in nature endangers the human infant as it does the young of other species where entire litters are taken as sources of food for some hungry predator's brood. Human beings have learned to protect their lair in ways which have all but eliminated this external threat, but the infant nevertheless remains in mortal danger from within the family circle. Although medieval parents feared that devils raided their cribs and replaced infants with changelings, and gypsies have been legended to steal babies and then sell them as slaves, of even greater concern is the infanticidal tendency of the parent himself. But our species has evolved a protective device with the mollification associated with an infant's squeal of laughter and glee. Even in the first few weeks of life, when the baby does little else than sleep and eat, one can find facial expressions which, incredibly enough, resemble a smile. Before eyesight or hearing is significantly developed to promote recognition, the baby offers its parent an appearance of gratitude and joy. This play between the baby and adult is not for mere pleasure alone; it has the hidden function of reducing the parental tendency to anger or kill. By bonding a more secure relationship during the dangerous early years, survivability of the child is more assured. If such mollification of parental anger is not promoted, fatal injuries are very likely to occur.

This necessity for stimulation of affection is not only a requirement to prevent violent actions on the part of the parent, it is also vital to the emotional development of the child as well. In *Jude the Obscure*, by Thomas Hardy, Little Father Time, the son of the destitute Jude, bemoans his fate and tells his step-mother that;" I think that whenever children be born that are not wanted they should be killed directly, before their souls come to 'em, and not allowed to grow big and walk about!"[22] The step-mother is not sympathetic to his plight, and the young boy soon commits suicide in an altruistic act, believing his parents would be better off without children, by hanging himself after first disposing of his little half-brother and half-sister. Jeffrey Berman saw this storyline as an indictment of Nature:

> The brutality of a scheme in which the living are condemned to inevitable death. Nature itself appears to be a defective parent, allowing one species to survive, temporarily, at the expense of another.[23]

Darwin's survival-of-the-fittest evolutionary scheme works daily on an intra-familial level as clearly as it does on species over millions of years.

The next support for the universality of the infanticide trait among human beings comes from a survey of religious practices that have been ever-present among human-kind. From the very first time that Man stood erect and looked with amazement at the heavens above, he has worshiped some type of powerful deity in an attempt to promote a more successful existence. Much of this homage was likely instrumental in developing a code of ethics and morals that has formed a strong foundation for the growth and development of our species. But otherwise rational and successful civilizations have also, for time immemorial, practiced human sacrifice, often of their own offspring, in elaborate ceremonies that were intended to pacify the pertinacious nature of their gods. Inhabitants from all areas of the world implicitly believed in the value of this deadly process, and innocent children were frequently given up by their parents readily, and with little sign of remorse. If so many diverse cultures could find the sacrifice of their offspring both necessary and beneficial, can we merely pass the practice off as a chaotic, or pathologic, custom? I think not.

Within the framework of every religious creed, a request from the Almighty, even one demanding the forfeiture of a human life, was something that could not be disobeyed. Rabanus Maurus, in his defense of oblation in 819 A.D., pointed to the willingness of Abraham to sacrifice Isaac as adherence to a divine law that superseded that of any mortal man. It was a greater evil for someone to pass secular judgment and determine matters of morality for themselves, rather than follow the commandments of the Lord. A worldly and temporal law could never be given precedence over the divine and eternal law.[24] When God called, all must answer; it was not something that mortal legislators could redefine as unethical or illegal.

This attitude was not restricted to just one religion or one period of time. Eli Sagan contended that: "Sacrifice is a form of religious action that has persisted throughout all the changes religion has undergone from primitive to historical times."[25] We see evidence of it in the Judaeo-Christian teachings, as well as in the pagan aboriginal tribes of New Guinea. Even under Eastern philosophy: "A sensible man "feared the gods" and scrupulously followed their prescriptions."[26]

Signs of infant sacrifice date back to the very beginnings of human presence on earth. Neanderthal man, living about 200,000 to 70,000 B.C., practiced ceremonial sacrifice as reflected in many archaeologic remains. In the great bas-relief cave painting from Laussel, France, during the Paleolithic Era, the figure of a menstruating goddess holding her menstrual blood horn can be clearly seen with indications that she was to be placated by the sacrifice of human infants.[27]

As man evolved, the deadly worship of the gods changed little. In Northern Africa, thousands of bones of sacrificed children have been dug up by archaeologists with inscriptions designating these as first-born sons of noble families as far back as 7000 B.C.[28] In Sardinia, inscriptions on burial urns indicate that three thousand first-born sons of noble families, between the ages of one month and four years, were sacrificed by first being strangled and then burned as offerings to Tanit.[29] The ancient kings of Tyre offered their sons in sacrifice, and the ancient Syrians sacrificed to Jupiter and Juno.[30] The Pelasgians offered every tenth child as a sacrifice of propitiation in times of scarcity.[31] Infants bodies were discovered in foundations in Egypt laid as late as the Twenty second Dynasty from around 950-720 B.C.[32]

In the New World, the ancient Aztecs, who thrived in the thirteenth century A.D., were estimated to have sacrificed up to 20,000 victims in religious rituals to assure pacification of the sun god, Huitzilopochtli.[33] Ortiz gave larger estimates and concluded that up to 250,000 victims were sacrificed yearly in Central Mexico, and 15,000 yearly in the capital city of Tenochtitlan alone.[34] Aztec children were often bought from their parents for the purpose of these sacrifices.[35] The Inca Empire also practiced human sacrifice at the time of the Aztecs, however the annual sacrifice there could only be measured in the hundreds.[36]

Even with the development of monotheism, and the traditional Mosaic commandment to not commit murder, the acceptance of child-sacrifice did not cease. Moses clearly forbid the Jews from practicing the sacrilege of their neighbors. But the entire Jewish religion has nevertheless been based on the faith of Abraham to follow the directive of God to sacrifice his only son, Isaac, in proof of his obedience. Abraham's silent willingness to act in this manner never faltered as he led his son to his expectant death. As he raised the knife to slay Isaac on the altar at the mountain top, the angel of the Lord had to call out twice before Abraham would desist. Such devotion was the mark to which all faithful Jews would aim for the next two thousand years.

The lessons from the New Testament were even more direct. Not only was God willing to sacrifice His only Son, Jesus Christ, for the welfare of mankind, but allegiance to God was clearly put above the love of one's own child. Jesus reminded his twelve disciples: "If you love your son or daughter more than me, you are not worthy of being mine."[37]

This fidelity was not based in theory alone, and was expected to withstand impulses to save the life of a loved one rather than follow the lessons of the Lord. When the "true" word of God, the Gospel of Jesus Christ, was to be spread among the people of Israel, Jesus warned that: "Brothers will betray each other to death, fathers will betray their own children, and children will betray their parents to be killed."[38]

The message of supreme devotion and faith was continued unabated by the early Church Fathers. Origen advised the people to be as constant in purpose as was Abraham: "Offer your son to God joyful, immovable in faith."[39] For it was God that determined the eternal life of man, and it was He who offered even His own son for the grace of all mankind. If you followed God's commands, then even the death of your child should not be withheld:

> Behold God contending with men in magnificent liberality: Abraham offered God a mortal son who was not put to death; God delivered to death an immortal son for men[40]

This uneasy union of religious fervor and infanticidal request is a part of every holy text in the religious development of man. How do we explain this constant need to show devotion to God with a compliance to sacrifice the life of one's own child? Few have even broached the question with a nominal query. Would a true God really ever ask for the slaughter of a mortal life to prove obedience and love? Would the very Founder of ethical codes and moral conduct condone the killing of another human being simply to show mortal man that their eternal rest depended on some blind acquiescence to a written word? Despite the argument that it is not within the mind of man to understand or question the workings of God, I simply do not believe that such a depiction is true. If it is genuinely acceptable to God to allow infanticide to be practiced, then my task is complete and the conclusion of this book assured: infanticide becomes a trait of man that is divinely ordered. But if it is not divine will, and the killings must have some other explanation, then it appears reasonable to assume that the constant reference to sacrificial death is a reflection of our inherent "natural law." In developing, or even following, the word of God, the Free Will of Man has interposed infanticide into the process by impulse rather than design. Homage becomes homicide, and devotion death. We assure our self-survival by a willingness to kill others and thereby lessen any risk to ourselves. Love thy neighbor is a matter of law; love thyself is a matter of awe.

Finally, to complete the tripartite support for the genetic basis of an infanticidal trait, the legislative and legal writings of the multiple cultures of man reference attitudes which clearly support the right of a parent to treat his child in any manner he saw fit. I say this not in the generic, but in the truly chauvinistic use of the word "men," for women have played almost no part in the descriptive legal texts which have gauged the determination of justice into the modern era. Without implying that women would necessarily have changed the essence of the law if they had been allowed input and control, it is a fact that our history has been primarily generated by the y, rather than the *x*, chromosome.

As one searches the ancient legal texts for some pattern in the definition of infanticide as a crime, it immediately becomes apparent that the earliest legal systems did not attach much significance to the killing of a child by their fathers. Children generally were not afforded a separate legal existence but rather were regarded as possessions of their progenitors.[41] The child was little more than a chattel that could be kept, or disposed of, at the father's whim. Male parents were granted the right to kill or expose their children either by custom or by direct legislation.[42] Many societies, and especially those tribes dependent on a hunter/gatherer existence, demanded the culling or abandonment of deformed and unproductive infants, and female babies were often destroyed because of a desire to raise sons who were considered more valuable because of their superior strength.

Such acceptance of infanticide was not an isolated phenomenon and seems to have evoked only an occasional, though spirited, reaction from social critics. The majority view clearly placed infants on a subordinate level with adults, and legal opinion uniformly found that parents could dispose of their young children with impunity. The Ages spoke unhesitatingly in favor of the social endorsement of infanticide.

And with social acceptance came an epidemic spread of infanticidal acts. The history of every modern civilization is replete with evidence of intentional child-harm. While much of this falls under the purview of child abuse, and therefore homicide through negligence rather than with malice aforethought, it is infanticide nonetheless, despite the defense that a parent may do whatever they feel is right in the raising of their offspring, even if their actions ultimately lead to the untimely death of an innocent human life.

So with this strata of support, I have concluded that it is a normal – a "natural" – trait for a human being to be willing to kill his or her own child, especially during the first year of life, and that there are genetic factors which are determinative of this compulsion. Now that we are aware of our deadly destiny, there are certain things we can do to turn this weapon of destruction into a ploughshare of peaceful coexistence. Three critical areas for future social action are:

(1) The present-day argument – and I use the word argument rather than debate because there is very little substantive interaction between advocates today – over when life begins, and whether abortion is murder of the fetus or the right of a woman to choose when to complete a pregnancy, is misguided and likely to splinter our society into a condition of social chaos. While it is valid to discuss the morality of abortion in theologic or academic circles, the social arena must now realize that if abortion is ever declared illegal, we will be faced with a million-or-so infanticides each year, based upon all of the evidence which has accumulated in the past. History shows that ten to fifteen percent of unwanted births will result in the murder of the newborn infant; no amount of criminal legislation will prevent that fact. Unless governments are prepared to financially support women throughout their pregnancy and delivery process, and then provide administrative care for the undesired baby's development, it would be wrong to suddenly take away

the right of a mother to choose not to carry the pregnancy through.

I want to emphasize that this is a purely pragmatic social view and should not dissuade Pro-Life and Pro-Choice advocates from promoting their collective views. If one believes that life begins at conception, and abortion is equivalent to murder, or that it is a fundamental right for a woman to decide when to have a child, it is understandable that all attempts to prevent such actions, short of criminal activity, would be resorted to in order to assure a moral public stance. But it is naive to believe that the controversy can focus only on questions of fetal and maternal rights, and not include an awareness of the effects such actions may have on the resultant child to be born. Exchanging a "murderous" abortion for a "murderous" infanticide is of little moral benefit and we should not rattle our sabers unless we are willing to go to war. The battlefield of this particular skirmish is likely to be strewn with the bodies of newborn babies unless we all take care to carefully consider the true meaning of our legislative intent.

(2) Our present criminal justice system must be modified to take into account the natural tendency of a parent to harm their child. The killing of a child under the age of one year by its parent is not equivalent to other forms of homicide, and should not be treated as such. The English model of defining infanticide as a separate criminal act which is punished as a form of manslaughter, based on the presumption that there are pressures placed upon such individuals that are unique and out of their control, deserves consideration in America and other countries of the world. Without excusing the commission of infanticide, we have to realize that there is a natural tendency for parents to kill their newborn child, for reasons which vary from temporary insanity to acts of self-survival, and that prevention by judicial statutes is not likely to occur.

For this reason we should consider enactment of laws similar to that of the 1938 Infanticide Act in England:

> Who causes the death of her child under the age of 12 months by wilful act or omission, but at the time of the act or omission the balance of her mind was disturbed by reason of her not having fully recovered from the effect of giving birth to the child or by reasons of the effect of lactation consequent on the birth of the child.[43]

Whether this should include actions of a father, as well as a mother, needs serious consideration since we no longer accept that the birth of a child is simply an act that can be relegated to, or blamed upon, the female sex.

There is also the need to expand our understanding of Child Abuse, and take into account the incredible pressures which are placed upon parents, especially those who are poor, in trying to raise children with little assistance. Too many reformers are willing to only castigate parents who harm their child, and few understand that simple counseling and advice will do nothing to eliminate the problem at hand. The abusive use of punishment has had centuries of support, and if we are to protect our future progeny from the effects of such care, we must begin by education in the schools, and in the home, of ways to deal with the frustration of raising a child in our own image.

(3) While we may pray to a deity bathed in human imagery and form, it is obvious that our Maker has endowed us with more bestiality than sense. As we are thrust into the twenty-first century, we are going to learn more about our genetic heritage than I believe we are prepared to accept. Mapping of human chromosomes is expanding at an incredibly rapid pace, but it so far has been restricted to physically definable attributes. Somewhere in that maze of molecules lies a gene which controls the impulse to kill, and part of that process involves the impulse to kill one's own child. We will find that such psychological traits are not unique, and that much of how we act is not likely to be explained away in motives that have classically been seen as rational and humane.

Such research must be supported, however, and our beliefs must include the realization that killing may not always be wrong. Quintilian noted that "to slay a man is often a virtue and to put one's own children to death is at times the noblest of deeds."[44] The entire euthanasia movement has funneled a similar belief into the treatment of the terminally ill. While both of these views are inherently correct, they also are reflective of our innate acceptance of the purposeful elimination of our fellow man. Once it is considered proper to condone the murder of one individual, there will only be disputation on exactly what factually must be met in many other cases as well. As long as there is a genetic code which promotes the killing of children in a wide variety of situations, it will be difficult to quench its effect.

The motto placed above the oracle of Apollo at Delphi said simply: "Know thyself." It is advice which I can little improve upon for the present age.

Endnotes

1 . Rose, The Massacre of the Innocents: Infanticide in Britain 1800-1939, 5.
2 . Gallagher, By Trust Betrayed, 121.
3 . As Shirley Wheeley pointed out, infanticide "is something we know about, have always written about, yet often fearfully avoid, not daring to look it in the eye." Wheeley, "Looks that Kill the Capacity for Thought," 208.
4 . "It is manifestly impossible to gather reliable statistics on the incidence of infanticide because so many cases are undiscovered, never proved or rarely solved." Adelson, "Some Medicolegal Observations on Infanticide," 60-72.
5 . Post, "Infanticide and Geronticide," 318.
6 . Tien, Tianlu, Yu, Jingneng, & Zhongtang, "China's Demographic Dilemmas," 13.
7 . France, The Gods Will Have Blood, 80.
8 . Shahar, Childhood in the Middle Ages, 126.
9 . Dickeman, "Demographic Consequences of Infanticide in Man," 108.
10 . Schopenhauer, On Human Nature, 18.
11 . Fromm, Man For Himself, 7.
12 . Justinian, Institutes, I.II, 3.
13 . Johnson, Rasselas, 22, 90-91.
14 . Pope, "An Essay on Man," II.I.2, Selected Poetry, 133.
15 . Aquinas, Summa Theologica, Part I of Second Part, Question 94, Article II, Volume 20, 222.
16 . Thomas Hobbes placed this as the 1st Natural Law: "The Right of Nature, which Writers commonly call Jus Naturale, is the Liberty each man hath, to use his own power, as he will himselfe, for the preservation of his own Nature; that is to say, of his own Life." Hobbes, Leviathan, I.XIV, 189.
17 . Copleston, A History of Philosophy, Volume I, Part II, Greece and Rome, 140.
18 . Badinter, Mother Love, Myth and Reality, 50.
19 . Darwin, The Origin of Species, 3, 78.
20 . Ibid., 4, 91.
21 . Cowlishaw, "Infanticide in Aboriginal Australia," 268.
22 . Hardy, Jude the Obscure, "At Christminster Again," II, 328.
23 . Berman, "Infanticide and Object Loss in *Jude the Obscure*," 156.
24 . Boswell, The Kindness of Strangers, 440.
25 . Sagan, Cannibalism: Human Aggression and Cultural Form, 50.
26 . Roux, Ancient Iraq, 97.
27 . DeMause, "The Fetal Origins of History," 34.
28 . deMause, The History of Childhood, 27.
29 . Weyl, "Some Possible Genetic Implications of Carthaginian Child Sacrifice," 69-70.
30 . Ryan, "Child Murder In Its Sanitary and Social Bearings," 2.
31 . Ibid.
32 . Davies, Human Sacrifice, 37.
33 . Voyages of Discovery, 149.
34 . Ortiz de Montellano, "Aztec Cannibalism: An Ecological Necessity?," 611.
35 . Davies, Human Sacrifice, 212.
36 . Harner, "The Ecological Basis for Aztec Sacrifice," 119.
37 . Matthew 10:37. The Living Bible, 754.
38 . Mark 13:12. Ibid., 794.

39 . Origen, "Homilies On Genesis," VIII.7, The Fathers of the Church, 142.
40 . Ibid., VIII.8, 144.
41 . Ford, "The Emergence of the Child as a Legal Entity," 393.
42 . Encyclopedia Britannica, 1879, Volume IX, 482.
43 . Infanticide Act (1938). 1 & 2 Geo. 6, Ch. 36. Kellett, "Infanticide and Child Destruction – The Historical, Legal and Pathological Aspects," 9.
44 . Quintilian, Institutio Oratio, XII.I.37, Volume IV, 377.

BIBLIOGRAPHY

ARTICLES

Abbassioun, K., Ameli, N. O., & Morshed, A. A., "Intracranial Sewing Needles: Review of 13 Cases," Journal of Neurology, Neurosurgery, and Psychiatry 42 (1979): 1046-1049.

Abse, Leo, "Infanticide and British Law," Clinical Pediatrics 6 (1967): 316-317.

Adelson, Lester, "Some Medicolegal Observations on Infanticide," Journal of Forensic Sciences 4 (1959): 60-72.

Adelson, L., "Slaughter of the Innocents," New England Journal of Medicine 264 (1961): 1345-1349.

Adelson, Lester, "Homicide by Starvation," Journal of the American Medical Association 186 (1963): 458-460.

Adelson, Lester "Homicide by Pepper," Journal of Forensic Science 9 (1964): 391.

Adelson, Lester, "Pedicide Revisited," American Journal of Forensic Medicine & Pathology 12 (1991): 16-26.

Aiken, Henry David, "Life and the Right to Life," Ethical Issues in Human Genetics, edit. Bruce Hilton, Daniel Callahan, Maureen Harris, Peter Condliffe, & Burton Berkley, New York: Plenum Press, 1973, 173-183.

Aird, John S., "China's War on Children," American Enterprise (March/April 1996): 58-61.

Alvarez, A., "The Background," Suicide: The Philosophical Issues, edit. M. Pabst Battin & David J. Mayo, New York: St. Martin's Press, 1980, 7-32.

"American College of Physicians Ethics Manual. Part 2: The Physician and Society; Research; Life-Sustaining Treatment; Other Issues," Annals of Internal Medicine 111 (1989): 327-335.

Amundsen, Darrel W., "Visigothic Medical Legislation," Bulletin of the History of Medicine 45 (1971): 563-569.

Amundsen, Darrel W., "Medicine and the Birth of Defective Children," Euthanasia and the Newborn: Approaches of the Ancient World, edit. Richard C. McMillan, H. Tristram Engelhardt & Stuart F. Spicker, Dordrecht, Holland: D. Reidel Publishing Co., 1987, 3-22.

Andersen-Nexo, Martin, "Life Sentence," Teutonic Literature in English Translation, edit. James E. Miller Jr., Robert O'Neal, & Helen M. McDonnell, Glenview, Illinois: Scott, Foresman and Company, 1970, 286-295.

Angell, Marcia, "Handicapped Children: Baby Doe & Uncle Sam," New England Journal of Medicine 309 (1983): 659-661.

Arboleda-Florez, Julio, "Infanticide, Some Medicolegal Considerations," Canadian Psychiatric Association Journal 20 (1975): 55-59.

Arima, Eugene Y., "Caribou Eskimo," Handbook of North American Indians, edit. William C. Sturtevant, Arctic, edit. David Damas, Washington, D.C.: Smithsonian Institution, 1984, 447-462.

Arras, John D., "Toward An Ethic of Ambiguity," The Hastings Center Report 14 (1984): 25-33.

Arya, Satya Prakash, "The Family Structure of the Folk People of Western Uttar Pradesh," Folklore, International Monthly 13 (1972): 241-262.

Asch, Stuart S., "Crib Deaths: Their Possible Relationship to Post-Partum Depression and Infanticide," Journal of the Mount Sinai Hospital 35 (1968): 214-20.

Asindi, Young, Moira, Etuk, H. V. Imabong, & Udo, J. J., "Brutality to Twins in South-eastern Nigeria: the Existing Situation," Journal of Tropical Pediatrics 39 (1993): 378-379.

"A Thousand Infants Overlain," British Medical Journal 1 (1895): 36.

Atkinson, Dorothy, "Society and the Sexes in the Russian Past," Women in Russia, edit. Dorthy Atkinson, Alexander Dallin, & Gail Warshofsky Lapidus, Stanford: Stanford University Press, 1977, 3-38.

Atkinson, Stanley B., "Life, Birth & Live-Birth," Law Qarterly Review 20 (1904): 134-159.

Bajpai, Shailaja, "India's Lost Women," World Press Review 38 (April 1991): 49.

Baker, John, "Female Criminal Lunatics: A Sketch," Journal of Mental Science 48 (1902): 13-27.

Balikci, Asen, "Female Infanticide on the Arctic Coast," Man 2 (1967): 615-625.

Balikci, Asen, "The Netsilik Eskimos," Man The Hunter, edit. Richard B. Lee & Irven DeVore, Chicago: Aldine Publishing Co., 1968, 78-82.

Balikci, Asen, "Netsilik," Handbook of North American Indians, edit. William C. Sturtevant, Arctic, edit. David Damas, Washington, D.C.: Smithsonian Institution, 1984, 415-430.

Barstow, Anne, "Witch Hunts: The Sex Factor," Ms 16 (1987): 85.

Bartholomew, A. A., & Bonnicci, A., "Infanticide: A Statutory Offence," Medical Journal of Australia 2 (1965): 1018-1021.

Bartholomew, Allen A., "Repeated Infanticide," Australian & New Zealand Journal of Psychiatry 23 (1989): 440-442.

Bean, Lowell John, & Theodoratus, Dorothea, "Western Pomo and Northeastern Pomo," Handbook of North American Indians, edit. William C. Sturtevant, California, edit. Robert F. Heizer, Washington, D.C.: Smithsonian Institution, 1978, 289-305.

Behlmer, George K., "Deadly Motherhood: Infanticide and Medical Opinion in Mid-Victorian England," Journal of the History of Medicine and Allied Sciences 34 (1927): 403-427.

Behlmer, George K., "Ernest Hart and the Social Thrust of Victorian Medicine," British Medical Journal 301 (1990): 711-713.

Belsey, Mark A., "Child Abuse: Measuring a Global Problem," World Health Statistics Quarterly 46 (1993): 69-77.

Bender, Lauretta, "Psychiatric Mechanisms in Child Murderers," Journal of Medicine Nervous Disorder 80 (1934): 32-47.

Bennett, H., "The Exposure of Infants in Ancient Rome," The Classical Journal 18 (1923): 341-351.

Berman, Jeffrey, "Infanticide and Object Loss in *Jude the Obscure*,", Compromise Formations: Current Directions in Psychoanalytic Criticism, edit. Vera J. Camden, Kent, Ohio: Kent State University Press, 1989, 155-181.

Birdsell, Joseph B., "Some Predictions for the Pleistocene Based on Equilibrium Systems Among Recent Hunter Gatherers," ManThe Hunter, edit. Richard B. Lee & Irven DeVore, Chicago: Aldine Publishing Co., 1986, 229-240.

Blackhouse, Constance B., "Desperate Women and Compassionate Courts: Infanticide in Nineteenth-Century Canada," University of Toronto Law Journal 34 (1984): 447-478.

Bloch, Dorothy, "Fantasy and the Fear of Infanticide," Psychoanalytic Review 61 (1974): 5-31

Bloch, Dorothy, "The Threat of Infanticide and Homosexual Identity," Psychoanalytic Review 62 (1975-76): 579-99.

Blustein, Jeffrey, "Morality and Parenting: An Ethical Framework for Decisions About The Treatment of Imperiled Newborns," Theoretical Medicine 9 (1988): 23-32.

Bolkestein, H., "The Exposure of Children at Athens," Classical Philology 17 (1922): 222-235.

Bonnet, Catherine, "Adoption at Birth: Prevention Against Abandonment or Neonaticide," Child Abuse & Neglect 17 (1993): 501-513.

Bonney, Frederic, "On Some Customs of the Aborigines of the River Darling, New South Wales," Journal of the Royal Anthropological Institute of Great Britain and Ireland 13 (1884): 122-136.

Boswell, John Eastburn, "Exposition and Oblation: The Abandonment of Children and the Ancient and Medieval Family," American Historical Review 89 (1984): 10-33.

Bourget, Dominique, & Bradford, John M. W., "Homicidal Parents," Canadian Journal of Psychiatry, 35:233-238, 1990.

Bourget, Dominique & Labelle, Alain, "Homicide, Infanticide, and Filicide," Psychiatric Clinics of North America 15 (1992): 661-673.

Brodsky, Isadore, "Congenital Abnormalities, Teratology and Embryology: Some Evidence of Primitive Man's Knowledge as Expressed in Art and Lore in Oceania," Medical Journal of Australia 1 (1943): 417-420.

Browne, William & Palmer, Anthony, "A Preliminary Study of Schizophrenic Women Who Murdered Their Children," HospitalCommunity Psychiatry 26 (1975): 71-75.

Brozovsky, Morris & Falit, Harvey, "Neonaticide, Clinical and Psychodynamic Considerations," Journal of the American Academy of Child and Adolescent Psychiatry 10 (1971): 673-683.

Bryant, Taimie, L., "Oya-Ko Shinju: Death at the Center of the Heart," UCLA Pacific Basin Law Journal 8 (1990): 1-31.

Bugos, Paul E. Jr., & McCarthy, Lorraine M., "Ayoreo Infanticide: A Case Study," Infanticide, Comparative & Evolutionary Perspectives, edit. Glenn Hausfater & Sarah Blaffer Hrdy, New York: Aldine Publishing Co., New York, 1984, 503-520.

Bullough, Vern L., & Ruan, Fang-Fu, "China's Children," The Nation 246 (June 18, 1988): 848-849.

Buteau, Jacques, Lesage, Alain D., & Kiely, Margaret C., "Homicide Followed by Suicide: A Quebec Case Series, 1988-1990," Canadian Journal of Psychiatry 38 (1993): 552-556.

Button, J. H. & Reivich, R. S., "Obsessions of Infanticide. A Review of 42 Cases," Archives of General Psychiatry 27 (1972): 235-240.

Byman, Seymour, "Child Raising and Melancholia in Tudor England," Journal of Psychohistory 6 (1978): 67-92.

Calef, Victor, "Lady Macbeth and Infanticide or `How Many Children Had Lady Macbeth' Murdered?," Journal of the American Psychoanalytic Association 17 (1969): 528-48.

Callaghan, Catherine, A., "Lake Miwok," Handbook of North American Indians, edit. William C. Sturtevant, California, edit. Robert F. Heizer, Washington, D.C.: Smithsonian Institution, 1978, 264-273.

Cameron, A., "The Exposure of Children And Greek Ethics," Classical Review 46 (1932): 105-114.

Cameron, J. H., Johnson, H. R. M., & Camps, F. E., "The Battered Child Syndrome," Medicine, Science & the Law 6 (1966): 2-21.
Campbell, T. N. "Coahuiltecans and Their Neighbors," Handbook of North American Indians, edit. William C. Sturtevant, Southwest, edit. Alfonso Ortiz, Washington, D.C.: Smithsonian Institution, 1983, 343-358.
Campion, John F., Cravens, James M., & Covan, Fred, "A Study of Filicidal Men," American Journal of Psychiatry 145 (1988): 1141-1144.
Carsch, H., "The Family, Child Rearing and Social Controls Among the Aztecs," International Anthropological and Linguistic Review 3 (1958): 8-21.
Cashell, Alan W., "Homicide as a Cause of the Sudden Infant Death Syndrome," American Journal of Forensic Medicine & Pathology 8 (1987): 256-8.
Cassidy, James P., & Russo, Priscilla M., "Religion: A Catholic View," Suicide, Theory and Clinical Aspects, edit. L. D. Hankoff & Bernice Einsidler, Littleton, Massachusetts: PSG Publishing Co., Inc., 1979, 73-81.
Castillo, Edward D., "The Impact of Euro-American Exploration & Settlement," Handbook of North American Indians, edit. William C. Sturtevant, California, edit. Robert F. Heizer, Washington, D.C.: Smithsonian Institution, 1978, 99-127.
Chapman, Michael, "Infanticide and Fertility Among Eskimos: A Computer Simulation," American Journal of Physical Anthropology 53 (1980): 317-327.
Cheung, P. T. K., "Maternal Filicide in Hong Kong, 1971-1985," Medicine, Science & the Law 26 (1986): 185-192.
Coale, Ansley J., & Banister, Judith, "Five Decades of Missing Females in China," Demography 31 (1994): 459-478.
Cole, Wendy, "Incest Perpetrators, Their Assessment and Treatment," Psychiatric Clinics of North America 15 (1992): 689-701.
Coleman, Emily, "Infanticide in the Early Middle Ages," Women in Medieval Society, edit. Susan Mosher Stuard, University of Pennsylvania Press, Inc., 1976, 47-70.
Collins, Camilla, "On the Dangers of Shaking Young Children," Child Welfare 53 (1974): 143-146.
Cook, S. F., "Human Sacrifice and Warfare as Factors in the Demography of Pre-Colonial Mexico," Human Biology 18 (1946): 81-102.
Cowlishaw, Gillian, "Infanticide in Aboriginal Australia," Oceania 48 (1978): 262-283.
Crossley, Mary A., "Selective Nontreatment of Handicapped Newborns: An Analysis," Medicine & Law 6 (1987): 499-524.
Cummings, P., Theis, M. K., Mueller, B. A., & Rivara, F. P., "Infant Injury Death in Washington State, 1981 Through 1990," Archives of Pediatric & Adolescent Medicine 148 (1994): 1021-1026.
Curgenven, J. Brendon, "On Baby-Farming and the Registration of Nurses," Meeting of the Health Department of the National Association for the Promotion of Social Science, London March 15 (1869): 3-6.
Dahlburg, John-Thor, "Faith & Practice: A Changing World Puts Abortion in the Spotlight," Los Angeles Times (January 24, 1955): H1.
Daly, Martin & Wilson, Margo, "Evolutionary Social Psychology and Family Homicide," Science 242 (1988): 519-524.
Damas, David, "Central Eskimo: Introduction," Handbook of North American Indians, edit. William C. Sturtevant, Arctic, edit. David Damas, Washington, D.C.: Smithsonian Institution, 1984, 391-396.
Damme, Catherine, "Infanticide: the Worth of an Infant Under Law," Medical History 22 (1978): 1-24.

Danckaerts, Jasper, "A Plague of Weevils," America Begins, edit. Richard M. Dorson, New York: Pantheon Books Inc., 1950, 116-118.

D'Anglure, Bernard Saladin, "Inuit of Quebec," Handbook of North American Indians, edit. William C. Sturtevant, Arctic, edit. David Damas, Washington, D.C.: Smithsonian Institution, 1984, 476-507.

Darbyshire, P., "Infanticide: Lambs to the Slaughter," Nursing Times 81 (August 14, 1985): 32-35.

Darlington, H. S., "Ceremonial Behaviorism," The Psychoanalytic Review 18 (1931): 306-328.

Davidson, Howard A., & Horowitz, Robert M., "Protection of Children from Family Maltreatment," Legal Rights of Children, edit. Robert M. Horowitz & Howard A. Davidson, New York: McGraw-Hill, 1984, 262-312.

Davies, D. Seaborne, "Child-Killing in English Law," The Modern Approach to Criminal Law, edit. L. Radzinowicz & J. W. C. Turner, London: Macmillan & Co., Ltd., 1945.

Davis, Kingsley, "The Demographic Foundations of National Power," Population, Evolution, and Birth Control, edit. Garrett Hardin, San Francisco: W. H. Freeman and Co., 1969, 71-74.

D'Azevedo, Warren L., "Introduction," Handbook of North American Indians, edit. William C. Sturtevant, Great Basin, edit. Warren L. D'Azevedo, Washington, D.C.: Smithsonian Institution, 1986, 1-14.

DeMause, Lloyd, "The Evolution of Childhood," The History of Childhood, edit. Lloyd DeMause, New York: Psychohistory Press, 1974, 1-73.

DeMause, Lloyd, "The Fetal Origins of History," Journal of Psychohistory 9 (1981): 1-89.

DeMause, Lloyd, "The History of Child Assault," Journal of Psychohistory 18 (1990): 1-29.

de Meer, K., "Mortality in Children Among the Aymara Indians of Southern Peru," Social Science & Medicine 26 (1988): 253-258.

de Meer, Kees, Bergman, Roland, & Kushner, John S., "Socio-cultural Determinations of Child Mortality in Southern Peru: Including Some Methodological Considerations," Social Science & Medicine 36 (1993): 317-331.

Desmond, Annabelle, "How Many People Have Ever Lived on Earth," Population, Evolution, and Birth Control, assembl. Garrett Hardin, San Francisco: W. H. Freeman and Company, 1969, 44-46.

Devereux, George, "Mohave Indian Infanticide," Psychoanalytic Review 35 (1948): 126-139.

Dickeman, Mildred, "Demographic Consequences of Infanticide in Man," Annual Review of Ecology & Systematics 6 (1975): 107-137.

Divale, William Tulio & Harris, Marvin, "Population, Warfare, & the Male Supremacist Complex," American Anthropologist 78 (1976): 521-538.

Donovan, James M., "Infanticide and the Juries in France," Journal of Family History 16 (1991): 157-176.

d'Orban, P. T., "Women Who Kill Their Children," British Journal of Psychiatry 134 (1979): 560-571.

Douglas, Mary, "Population Control in Primitive Groups," British Journal of Sociology 17 (1966): 263-273.

Drapkin, "Social Reaction to Deviant Behaviour Among the Incas of Peru," International Symposium on Society, Medicine and Law, edit. H. Karplus, Amsterdam: Elsevier Scientific Publishing Co., 1973, 1-10.

Duff, Raymond S., & Campbell, A. G. M., "Moral & Ethical Dilemmas in the Special-Care Nursery," New England Journal of Medicine 289 (1973): 890-894.

Durfee, Michael J., Gellert, George A., & Tilton-Durfee, Deanne, "Origins and Clinical Relevance of Child Death Review Teams," Journal of the American Medical Association 267 (1992): 3172-3175.

Edwards, Susan S. M., "Neither Bad Nor Mad: The Female Violent Offender Reassessed," Women's Studies International Forum 9 (1986): 79-87.

Elsasser, Albert B., "Mattole, Nongatl, Sinkyone, Lassik, and Waiaki," Handbook of North American Indians, edit. William C. Sturtevant, California, edit. Robert F. Heizer, Washington, D.C.: Smithsonian Institution, 1978, 190-204.

Ellis, T. S., "Letting Defective Babies Die: Who Decides?," American Journal of Law & Medicine 7 (1982): 393-423.

Emery, John L., Gilbert, Enid F., & Zugibe, Frederick, "Three Crib Deaths, A Babyminder and Probable Infanticide," Medicine, Science & the Law 28 (1988): 205-11

Emery, John L., "Child Abuse, Sudden Infant Death Syndrome, and Unexpected Infant Death," American Journal of Disease of Children 147 (1993): 1097-1100.

Ende, Aurel, "Battering and Neglect: Children in Germany, 1860-1978," Journal of Psychohistory 7 (1980): 250-279.

Ende, Aurel, "The Psychohistorian's Childhood and the History of Childhood," Journal of Psychohistory 9 (1981): 173-178.

Engels, Donald, "The Problem of Female Infanticide in the Greco-Roman World," Classical Philology 75 (1980): 112-120.

English, Peter C., "Pediatrics and the Unwanted Child in History: Foundling Homes, Disease, and the Origins of Foster Care in New York City," Pediatrics 73 (1984): 699-711.

Feldman, Kenneth W., "Child Abuse by Burning," The Battered Child, edit. Ray E. Helfer & Ruth S. Kempe, Chicago: University of Chicago Press, 1987, 197-213.

Ferngren, Gary B., "The `Imagio Dei' and the Sanctity of Life: The Origins of an Idea," Euthanasia and the Newborn, edit. Richard C. McMillan, H. Tristram Engelhardt, Jr., & Stuart F. Spicker, Dordrecht, Holland: D. Reidel Publishing Co., 1987.

Ferngren, Gary B., "The Status of Defective Newborns from Late Antiquity to the Reformation," Euthanasia and the Newborn, edit. Richard C. McMillan, H. Tristram Engelhardt, Jr., & Stuart F. Spicker, Dordrecht, Holland: D. Reidel Publishing Co., 1987, 47-64.

Filshie, G. Marcus, "Termination of Pregnancy," Handbook of Family Planning, edit. Nancy Loudon, Edinburgh: Churchill Livingstone, 1985, 234-249.

"First Sunday in Lent," Celebrate 22 (1991): 1.

Fisher, S. H., "Skeletal Manifestations of Parent Induced Trauma in Infants and Children," Southern Medical Journal 51 (1958): 956-960.

Fleischman, Alan R., "Caring for Babies in Danger," Which Babies Shall Live?, edit. Thomas H. Murray & Arthur L. Caplan, Clifton, New Jersey: Humana Press, 1985, 15-22.

Fletcher, Joseph, "Infanticide & the Ethics of Loving Concern," Infanticide & the Value of Life, edit. Marvin Kohl, Buffalo: Prometheus Books, 1978), 13-22.

Forbes, Thomas, "Deadly Parents: Child Homicide in Eighteenth- and Nineteenth-Century England," Journal of the History of Medicine 41 (1986): 175-199.

Ford, Clellan S., "Control of Conception in Cross-Cultural Perspective," Annals of the New York Academy of Sciences 54 (1952): 763-768.

Ford, D., "The Emergence of the Child as a Legal Entity," TheMaltreatment of Children, edit. Selwyn M. Smith, Baltimore: University Park Press, 1978, 393-414.

Fremantle, Anne, "The Age of Belief," The Great Ages of Western Philosophy, Boston: Houghton, Mifflin Co., Volume I, 1962.

Funayama, Masato, & Sagisaka, Kaoru, "Consecutive Infanticides in Japan," American Journal of Forensic Medicine and Pathology 9 (1988): 9-11.

Funayama, Masato, Ikeda, Takuya, Tabata, Noriko, Azumi, Jun-Ichi, & Morita, Asahiko, "Case Report: Repeated Neonaticides in Hokkaido," Forensic Science International 64 (1994): 147-150.

Garber, Clark M., "Eskimo Infanticide," Scientific Monthly 64 (1947): 98-102.

Garrett, Wilbur, "Where Did We Come From?," National Geographic 174 (1988): 434-437.

Geyer-Kordesch, Johanna, "Infanticide and Medico-legal Ethics in Eighteenth Century Prussia," Clio Medica 24 (1993): 181-202.

Giladi, Avner, "Some Observations on Infanticide in Medieval Muslim Society," International Journal of Middle East Studies 22 (1990): 185-200.

Gilberg, Rolf, "Polar Eskimo," Handbook of North American Indians, edit. William C. Sturtevant, Arctic, edit. David Damas, Washington, D.C.: Smithsonian Institution, 1984, 577-594.

Gillespie, Beryl C., "Mountain Indians," Handbook of North American Indians, edit. William C. Sturtevant, Subarctic, edit. June Helm, Washington, D.C.: Smithsonian Institution, 1981, 326-337.

Gitlin, Michael J., & Pasnau, Robert O., "Psychiatric Syndromes Linked to Reproductive Function in Women: A Review of Current Knowledge," American Journal of Psychiatry 146 (1989): 1413-1422.

Gluckman, L. K., "Abortion in the Nineteenth Century Maori: A Historical and Ethnopsychiatric Review," New Zealand Medical Journal 93 (1981): 384-386.

Golden, Mark, "Demography and the Exposure of Girls at Athens," Phoenix 35 (1981): 316-331.

Gore, Rick, "The Dawn of Humans, Expanding Worlds," National Geographic 191 (May, 1997):84-109.

Gorman-Stapleton, Odesa, "Prohibiting Amniocentesis in India: A Solution to the Problem of Female Infanticide or a Problem to the Solution of Prenatal Diagnosis," ILSA Journal of International Law 14 (1990): 23-43.

Gostin, Larry, "A Moment in Human Development: Legal Protection, Ethical Standards and Social Policy on the Selective Non-Treatment of Handicapped Neonates," American Journal of Law & Medicine 11 (1986): 31-78.

Grant, Campbell, "Eastern Coastal Chumash," Handbook of North American Indians, edit. William C. Sturtevant, California, edit. Robert F. Heizer, Washington, D.C.: Smithsonian Institution, 1978, 509-519.

Granzberg, Gary, "Twin Infanticide: A Cross-Cultural Test Of a Materialistic Explanation," Ethos 1 (1973): 405-412.

Greenwald, Gary I., & Greenwald, Maria White, "Medicolegal Progress in Inquests of Felonious Deaths: Westminster, 1761-1866," Journal of Legal Medicine 2 (1981): 193-264.

Griffin, William B., "Southern Periphery: East," Handbook of North American Indians, edit. William C. Sturtevant, Washington, D.C.: Smithsonian Institution, 1983, 329-342.

Haffter, Carl, "The Changeling: History and Psychodynamics of Attitudes to

Handicapped Children in European Folklore," Journal of the History of Behavioral Sciences 4 (1968): 55-61.
Hale, Ellen, "The Brutality of Growth Control," Detroit News and Free Press, (July 10, 1994): 1A.
Hanawalt, Barbara, "The Female Felon in Fourteenth-Century England," Viator, Medieval & Renaissance Studies 5 (1974): 253-268.
Hanawalt, Barbara, "Among the Lower Classes of Late Medieval England," Journal of Interdisciplinary History 8 (1977): 1-22.
Hara, M., Inoue, T., Tsuda R., & Ito, Y., "A Brief Statistical Survey on Medico-Legal Activities During the Period of Two Decades Four Years," Igaku Kenkyu Acta Medica 59 (1989): 1-6.
Harder, Thoger, "The Psychopathology of Infanticide," Acta Psychiatrica Scandinavia 43 (1967): 196-247.
Harner, Michael, "The Ecological Basis for Aztec Sacrifice," American Ethnologist 4 (1977): 117-135.
Heiger, Arnold, A., "Filicide: An Update," Connecticut Medicine 50 (1986): 387-389.
Heizer, Robert F., "Natural Forces and Native World View," Handbook of North American Indians, edit. William C. Sturtevant, California, edit. Robert F. Heizer, Washington, D.C.: Smithsonian Institution, 1978, 649-653.
Helm, June, "Dogrib," Handbook of North American Indians, edit. William C. Sturtevant, Subarctic, edit. June Helm, Washington, D.C.: Smithsonian Institution, 1981, 291-309.
Helmholz, R. H., "Infanticide in the Province of Canterbury During the 15th Century," History of Childhood Quarterly:Journal of Psychohistory 2 (1974): 379-390.
Hewitt, J. N. B., "A Constitutional League of Peace in the Stone Age of America," An Iroquois Source Book, Political & Social Organization, edit. Elisabeth Tooker, New York: Garland Publishing, Inc., 1985, Volume I, 527-545.
Higginbotham, Ann R., "Sin of the Age: Infanticide and Illegitimacy in Victorian London," Victorian Studies 32 (1989): 319-333.
Himsworth, Sir Harold, "The Human Right to Life: Its Nature & Origin," Ethical Issues in Human Genetics, edit. Bruce Hilton, Daniel Callahan, Maureen Harris, Peter Condliffe, & Burton Berkley, New York: Plenum Press, 1973, 169-172.
Hippler, Arthur E., "Culture and Personality Perspective of the Yolngu of Northeastern Arnhem Land: Part I – Early Socialization," Journal of Psychological Anthropology 1 (1978): 221-244.
Hirschfeld, Yizhar, "Tiberias," Biblical Archeology Review 17 (1991): 48.
Hodson, T. C., "Female Infanticide in India," Man 14 (1914): 91-92.
Hom, Sharon K., "Female Infanticide in China: The Human Rights Specter and Thoughts Towards Another Vision," Columbia Human Rights Law Review 23 (1992): 249-314.
Hopwood, J. Stanley, "Child Murder and Insanity," Journal of Clinical & Experimental Psychopathology 73 (1927): 95-108.
Hrdy, Sarah Blaffer, "Fitness Tradeoffs in the History and Evolution of Delegated Mothering with Special Reference to Wet-Nursing, Abandonment and Infanticide," Ethology & Sociobiology 13 (1992): 409-442.
Huefner, Dixie Snow, "Severely Handicapped Infants With Life-Threatening Conditions: Federal Intrusions Into The Decision Not To Treat," American Journal of Law & Medicine 12 (1987): 171-205.
Hunton, R. B., "Maori Abortion Practices in Pre and Early European New Zealand," New Zealand Medical Journal 86 (1977): 567-570.

Hurt, Stephen W., Schnurr, Paula P., Severino, Sally K., Freeman, Ellen W., Gise, Leslie H., Rivera-Tovar, Ana, & Steege, John F., "Late Luteal Phase Dysphoric Disorder in 670 Women Evaluated for Premenstrual Complaints, American Journal of Psychiatry 149 (1992): 525-530.

Iffy, Leslie, & Jakobovits, Akos, "Infanticide: New Medical Considerations," Medicine & Law 11 (1992): 269-274.

"Infanticide," Lancet 2 (1861): 314-315.

"Infanticide," Saturday Review 20 (1865): 162.

Jakobovits, Immanuel, "Jewish Views on Infanticide," Infanticide & The Value Of Life, edit. Marvin Kohl, Buffalo: Prometheus Books, (1978): 23-31.

Jason, Janine, "Child Homicide Spectrum," American Journal of Disease in Children 137 (1983): 578-581.

Jason, Janine, Carpenter, Mary M., & Tyler, Carl W. Jr., "Underrecording of Infant Homicide in the United States," American Journal of Public Health 73 (1983): 195-197.

Jason, Janine, Gilliland, Jeanne C. & Tyler, Carl W. Jr., "Homicide as a Cause of Pediatric Mortality in the United States,"Pediatrics 72 (1983):191-197.

Jeffery, Roger, Jeffery, Patricia, & Lyon, Andrew, "Female Infanticide and Amniocentesis," Social Science and Medicine 19 (1984): 1207-1212.

Jenkins, C. L., "Health in the Early Contact Period: A Contemporary Example From Papua New Guinea," Social Science & Medicine 26 (1988): 997-1006.

Jimmerson, Julie, "Female Infanticide in China: An Examination of Cultural and Legal Norms," UCLA Pacific Basin Law Journal 8 (1990): 47-79.

Jochens, Jenny M., "The Church & Sexuality in Medieval Iceland," Journal of Medieval History 6 (1980): 377-392.

Johnson, Orna, "The Socioeconomic Context of Child Abuse and Neglect in Native South America," Child Abuse and Neglect, edit. Jill Korbin, Berkeley: University of California Press, 1981, 56-70.

Johnson, Patti J., "Patwin," Handbook of North American Indains, edit. William C. Sturtevant, California, edit. Robert F. Heizer, Washington, D.C.: Smithsonian Institution, 1978, 350-360.

Johnstone, Brian V., "The Sanctity of Life, the Quality of Life and the New `Baby Doe' Law," Linacre Quarterly 52 (1985): 258-270.

Juviler, Peter H., "Women & Sex in Soviet Law," Women in Russia, edit. Dorothy Atkinson, Alexander Dallin & Gail Warshofsky Lapidus, Stanford: Stanford University Press, 1977, 243-265.

Kaku, Kanae, "Were Girl Babies Sacrificed to a Folk Superstition in 1966 in Japan?," Annals of Human Biology 2 (1975): 391-393.

Kane, Francis J., "Postpartum Disorders," Comprehensive Textbook of Psychiatry IV, edit. Harold I. Kaplan & Benjamin J. Sadock, Baltimore: Williams & Wilkins, 1985.

Kaplun, David & Reich, Robert, "The Murdered Child and His Killers," American Journal of Psychiatry 133 (1976): 809-813.

Kary, Carla, "A Moral Distinction Between Killing and Letting Die," Journal of Medicine & Philosophy 5 (1980): 326-332.

Kawanishi, Yuko, "Japanese Mother-Child Suicide: The Psychological and Sociological Implications of the Kimura Case," UCLA Pacific Basin Law Journal 8 (1990): 32-46.

Kaye, Neil S., Borenstein, Neal M., and Donnelly, Susan M., "Families, Murder, and

Insanity: A Psychiatric Review of Paternal Neonaticide," Journal of Forensic Sciences 35 (1990): 133-139.

Kellett, R. J., "Infanticide and Child Destruction – The Historical, Legal and Pathological Aspects," Forensic Science International 53 (1992): 1-28.

Kellum, Barbara A., "Infanticide in England in the Later Middle Ages," History of Childhood Quarterly:Journal of Psychohistory 1 (1974): 367-388.

Kelly, Isabel, "Coast Miwok," Handbook of North American Indians, edit. William C. Sturtevant, California, edit. Robert F. Heizer, Washington, D.C.: Smithsonian Institution, 1978, 414-425.

Kempe, C. Henry, Silverman, Frederick N., Steele, Brandt F., Droegemueller, William, & Silver, Henry K., "The Battered- Child Syndrome," Journal of the American Medical Association 181 (1962): 17-24.

Kempe, C. Henry, "Recent Developments in the Field of Child Abuse," TheAbused Child in the Family and in the Community, edit. C. Henry Kempe, Alfred White Franklin & Christine Cooper, Oxford: Pergammon Press, 1980, xv-xxi.

Kiel, Frank W., "Forensic Science in China: Traditional and Contemporary Aspects," Journal of Forensic Sciences 15 (1970): 201-34.

King, Nancy M. P., "Federal & State Regulations of Neonatal Decision Making," Euthansia and the Newborn, edit. Richard C. McMillan, H. Tristram Engelhardt, Jr., & Stuart F. Spicker, Dordrecht, Holland: D. Reidel Publishing Co., 1987, 89-115.

Kitahara, Michio, "Childhood in Japanese Culture,"Journal of Psychohistory 17 (1989): 43-72.

Kleinman, Paul K., Blackbourne, Brian D., Marks, Sandy C., Karellas, Andrew, & Belanger, Patricia L., "Radiologic Contributions to the Investigation and Prosecution of Cases of Fatal Infant Abuse," New England Journal of Medicine 320 (1989): 507-511.

Kluge, Eike-Henner W., "Infanticide as the Murder of Persons," Infanticide and the Value of Life, edit. Marvin Kohl, New York: Prometheus Books, 1978, 32-45.

Knight, Bernard, "Forensic Problems in Practice: Infant Deaths," Practitioner 217 (1976): 447.

Kohl, Steve, Pickering, Larry K., & Dupree, Elton, "Child Abuse Presenting as Immunodeficiency Disease," Journal of Pediatrics 93 (1978): 466-68.

Kord, Susanne, "Women As Children, Women As Childkillers: Poetic Images of Infanticide in Eighteenth-Century Germany," Eighteenth-Century Studies 26 (1993): 449-466.

Krishnaswamy, S., "A Note on Female Infanticide: An Anthropological Inquiry," The Indian Journal of Social Work 45 (1984): 297-302.

Kristof, Nicholas D., "Stark Data On Women: 100 Million Are Missing," New York Times November 5 (1991): C1.

Krueger, Christine L., "Literary Defenses and Medical Prosecutions: Representing Infanticide in Nineteenth-Century Britain," Victorian Studies 40 (1997): 271-295.

Krugman, Richard D., "Fatal Child Abuse: Analysis of 24 Cases," Pediatrician 12 (1983-85): 68-72.

Krugman, Richard D., "Advances and Retreats in the Protection of Children," New England Journal of Medicine 320 (1989): 531-532.

Krugman, Richard, & Jones, David P. H., "Incest and Other Forms of Sexual Abuse," The Battered Child, edit. Ray E. Helfer & Ruth S. Kempe, Chicago: University of Chicago Press, 1987, 286-300.

Kuczmierczyk, A. R., Labrum, A. H., & Johnson, C. C., "Perception of Family and Work Environments in Women With Premenstrual Syndrome," Journal of Psychosomatic Research 36 (1992): 787-795.

Kukull, Walter A., & Peterson, Donald R., "Sudden Infant Death and Infanticide," American Journal of Epidemiology 106 (1977): 485-6.

Kumasaka, Yorihiko, Smith, Robert J., & Aiba, Hitoshi, "Crimes in New York and Tokyo: Sociocultural Perspectives," Community Mental Health Journal 11 (1975): 19-26.

Kunz, Jenifer, & Bahr, Stephen J., "A Profile of Parental Homicide Against Children," Journal of Family Violence 11 (1996): 347-362.

Langer, William L., "Checks on Population Growth: 1750-1850," Scientific American 226 (1972): 92-99.

Langer, William L., "Europe's Initial Population Explosion," American Historical Review 69 (1963): 1-17.

Langer, William L., "Infanticide: A Historical Survey," History of Childhood Quarterly: Journal of Psychohistory 1 (1974): 353-366.

Langness, L. L., "Child Abuse and Cultural Values: The Case of New Guinea," Child Abuse and Neglect: Cross-Cultural Perspectives, edit. Jill Korbin, Berkeley: University of California Press, 1981, 13-34.

Lansdowne, Robyn, "Infanticide: Psychiatrists in the Plea Bargaining Process," Monash University Law Review 16 (1990): 41-63.

Lapena, Frank R., "Wintu," Handbook of North America Indians, edit. William C. Sturtevant, California, edit. Robert F. Heizer, Washington, D.C.: Smithsonian Institution, 1978, 324-340.

Laslett, Peter, "Introduction: Comparing Illegitimacy Over Time and Between Cultures," Bastardy and Its Comparative History, edit. Peter Laslett, Karla Oosterveen & Richard M. Smith, Cambridge: Harvard University Press, 1980, 1-68.

Lee, Bernice J., "Female Infanticide in China," Women in China, edit. Richard W. Guisso & Stanley Johannesen, Lewiston, New York: The Edwin Mellen Press, 1981, 163-178.

Leo, John, "Baby Boys, To Order," U.S. News & World Report 106 (January 9, 1989): 59.

Lester, David, "The Relation of Twin Infanticide to Status of Women, Societal Aggression, and Maternal Well-Being," Journal of Social Psychology 126 (1986): 57-59.

Lester, David, "The Murder of Babies in American States: Association With Suicide Rates," Psychological Reports 71 (1992): 1202.

Levenstein, Harvey, "`Best For Babies' Or `Preventable Infanticide?' The Controversy Over Artificial Feeding of Infants in America, 1880-1920," Journal of American History 70 (1983): 75-94.

LeVine, Sarah & LeVine, Robert, "Child Abuse and Neglect in Sub-Saharan Africa," Child Abuse and Neglect, edit. Jill Korbin, Berkeley: University of California Press, 1981, 35-55.

Liggins, Saundra, "Death is Better Than Slavery: Representations of Infanticide in Nineteenth Century American Literature," Society for the Interdisciplinary Study of Social Imagery (March, 1995): 295-301.

Lewis, James W., "Premenstrual Syndrome as a Criminal Defense," Archives of Sexual Behavior 19 (1990): 425-441.

Lithell, Ulla-Britt, "Breast-Feeding Habits and Their Relation to Infant Mortality and Marital Fertility," Journal of Family History 6 (1981): 182-194.
Lomis, Marsha J., "Maternal Filicide: A Preliminary Examination of Culture and Victim Sex," International Journal of Law and Psychiatry 9 (1986): 503-506.
Long, Thomas A., "Infanticide for Handicapped Infants: Sometimes It's a Metaphysical Dispute," Journal of Medical Ethics 14 (1988): 79-81.
Lorence, Gogna W., "Parents and Children in Eighteenth Century Europe," History of Childhood Quarterly:Journal of Psychohistory 2 (1974): 1-30.
Lukianowicz, N., "Attempted Infanticide," Psychiatria Clinica 5 (1972): 1-16.
Lull, Richard Swan, "The Antiquity of Man," The Evolution of Man, edit. George Alfred Baitsell, New Haven: Yale University Press, 1923, 1-38.
Lustig, Eric, "On the Origin of Judaism: A Psychoanalytic Approach," The Psychoanalytic Study of Society 7 (1976): 359-367.
Lyman, Richard B. Jr., "Barbarism and Religion: Late Roman and Early Medieval Childhood," The History of Childhood, edit. Lloyd deMause, New York: The Psychohistory Press, 1974, 75-100.
Macfarlane, Alan, "Illegitimacy and Illegitimates in English History," Bastardy & Its Comparative History, edit. Peter Laslett, Karla Oosterveen & Richard M. Smith, London: Edward Arnold, 1980, 71-85.
Mackay, R. D., "The Consequences of Killing Very Young Children," Criminal Law Review January (1993): 21-30.
Madison, Bernice, "Social Services for Women: Problems and Priorities," Women in Russia, edit. Dorothy Atkinson, Alexander Dallin, & Gail Warshofsky Lapidus, Stanford: Stanford University Press, 1977, 307-332.
Malcolmson, R. W., "Infanticide in the Eighteenth Century," Crime in England, 1550-1800, edit. J. S. Cockburn, Princeton: Princeton University Press, 1977, 187-209.
Mapes, C. C., "Infanticide – The Slaughter of the Innocents," The Medical Age 15 (1892): 741-747.
Marks, M. N., & Kumar, R., "Infanticide in England and Wales," Medicine, Science & Law 33 (1993): 329-339.
Martin, P. J., "Editorial," Edinburgh Medical & Surgical Journal 26 (1826): 34-37.
Mary-Rousseliere, Guy, "Iglulik," Handbook of North American Indians, edit. William C. Sturtevant, Arctic, edit. David Damas, Washington, D.C.: Smithsonian Institution, 1984, 431-446.
Marzuk, Peter M., Tardiff, Kenneth, & Hirsch, Charles S., "The Epidemiology of Murder-Suicide," Journal of the American Medical Association 267 (1992): 3179-3183.
Mason, J. K. & Meyers, David W., "Parental Choice and Selective Non-Treatment of Deformed Newborns: A View From Mid-Atlantic," Journal of Medical Ethics 12 (1986): 67-71.
Mather, Cotton, "A Whoredom Unmaked," America Begins, edit. Richard M. Dorson, London: Indiana University Press, 1971, 119.
Matthews, Samuel W., "The Phoenicians," National Geographic 146 (1974): 149-177.
May, Margaret, "Violence in the Family: An Historical Perspective," Violence and the Family, edit. J.P. Martin, New York: John Wiley & Sons, Ltd., 1978, 135-167.
Mays, Simon, "Infanticide in Roman Britain," Antiquity 67 (1993): 883-888.
McClellan, Catharine, "Tutchone," Handbook of North American Indians, edit. William C. Sturtevant, Subarctic, edit. June Helm, Washington, D.C.: Smithsonian Institution, 1981, 493-505.

McCormick, Richard A., "To Save or Let Die," Journal of the American Medical Association 229 (1974): 172-176.

McCully, Robert S., "Archetypal Psychology As A Key For Understanding Prehistoric Art Forms," History of Childhood Quarterly:Journal of Psychohistory 3 (1976): 523-551.

McDermaid, Gladys, & Winkler, Emil Guenther, "Psychopathology of Infanticide," Journal of Clinical & Experimental Psychopathology 16 (1955): 22-41.

McKee, Lauris, "Sex Differentials in Survivorship and the Customary Treatment of Infants and Children," MedicalAnthropology 8 (1984): 91-108.

McLaughlin, Mary M., "Survivors and Surrogates," The History of Childhood, edit. L. DeMause, New York: Psychohistory Press, 1974, 101-182.

Mead, Margaret, "The Arapesh of New Guinea," Cooperation & Competition Among Primitive Peoples, edit. Margaret Mead, Boston: Beacon Press, 1937, 20-50.

Meldman, Jeffrey A., Legal Concepts of Human Life: The Infanticide Doctrines, Marquette Law Review, 52:105-115, 1968.

Meyer, Jean, "Illegitimates and Foundlings in Pre-Industrial France," Bastardy & Its Comparative History, edit. Peter Laslett, Karla Oosterveen & Richard M. Smith, London: Edward Arnold, Ltd., 1980, 249-263.

Milcinski, Janez, "Abortion and Infanticide in Yugoslavia," International Symposium on Society, Medicine, and Law, edit. H. Karplus, Amsterdam: Elsevier Scientific Publishing Company, 1973, 163-171.

Milgrom, Jacob, "Lex Talionis and the Rabbis," Bible Review 12 (April 1996): 16, 48.

Minturn, Leigh, "Changes in the Differential Treatment of Rajput Girls in Khalapur: 1955-1975," Medical Anthropology 8 (1984): 127-132.

Mirsky, Jeannette, "The Eskimo of Greenland," Cooperation & Competition Among Primitive Peoples, edit. Margaret Mead, Boston: Beacon Press, 1937, 51-86.

Montag, Beverly A., & Montag, Thomas W., "Infanticide, A Historical Perspective," Minnesota Medicine May (1979): 368.

Morris, Arval A., "Law, Morality, and Euthanasia for the Severely Defective Child," Infanticide and the Value of Life, edit. Marvin Kohl, Buffalo: Prometheus Books, 1978, 137-158.

Mortola, J. F., "Assessment and Management of Premenstrual Syndrome," Current Opinion in Obstetrics & Gynecology 4 (1992): 877-885.

Moseley, Kathryn, "The History of Infanticide in Western Society," Issues in Law & Medicine 1 (1986): 345-361.

Mosher, Steven, "Forced Abortions and Infanticide in Communist China," Human Life Review 11 (1985): 7-34.

Mosher, Steven W., "Human Rights in the New China," Society 23 (1986): 28-35.

Murphy, Paul, "Killing Baby Girls Routine in India," San Francisco Examiner (May 21, 1995): C12.

Murray, Thomas H., & Caplan, Arthur L., "Beyond Babies Doe," Which Babies Shall Live?, edit. Thomas H. Murray & Arthur L. Caplan, Clifton, New Jersey: Humana Press, 1985, 1-12.

Myers, James E., "Cahto," Handbook of North American Indians, edit. William C. Sturtevant, California, edit. Robert F. Heizer, Washington, D.C.: Smithsonian Institution, 1978, 244-248.

Myers, Steven A., "The Child Slayer," Archives of General Psychiatry 17 (1967): 211-213.

Myers, Steven A., "Maternal Filicide," American Journal of Disease of Children 120 (1970): 534-536.

Nau'i, Mohammed Riza, "Indian Summer," transl. Mirza Y. Dawud & Ananda K. Coomaraswamy, Poetry of the Orient, edit. Eunice Tietjens, New York: Alfred A. Knopf, 1934.

Neel, James V., "Lessons From a `Primitive' People," Science 1 (1970): 815-822.

Newman, Stephen A., "Baby Doe, Congress and the States: Challenging the Federal Treatment Standard for Impaired Infants," American Journal of Law & Medicine 15 (1989): 1-60.

Nordborg, Magnus, "Female Infanticide and Human Sex Ratio Evolution," Journal of Theoretical Biology 158 (1992): 195-198.

Ober, William B., "Infanticide in Eighteenth-Century England. William Hunter's Contribution to Forensic Problem," Pathology Annual 21 (Part I)(1986): 311-19.

O'Donovan, Katherine, "The Medicalisation of Infanticide," The Criminal Law Review (1984): 259-264.

Oliver, J. E., "Dead Children From Problem Families in NE Wiltshire," British Medical Journal 286 (1983): 115-117.

Ortiz de Montellano, Bernard R., "Aztec Cannibalism: An Ecological Necessity?," Science 200 (1978): 611-617.

Oruene, T. O., "Cultic Powers of Yoruba Twins: Manifestation of Traditional and Religious Beliefs of the Yoruba," Acta Geneticae Medicae et Gemellologiae 32 (1983): 221-228.

Osborne, Judith A., "The Crime of Infanticide: Throwing Out the Baby with the Bathwater," Canadian Journal of Family Law 6 (1987): 46-59.

Overpeck, Mary D., Brenner, Ruth A., Trumble, Ann C., Trifiletti, Lara B., & Berendes, Heinz W., "Risk Factors For Infant Homicide in the United States," New England Journal of Medicine 339 (1998):1211-1216.

Parry, Barbara L., "Postpartum Psychiatric Syndromes," Comprehensive Textbook of Psychiatry VI, edit. Harold I. Kaplan & Benjamin J. Sadock, Baltimore: Williams & Wilkins, 1995, Volume I, 1059-1066.

Parry, L. A., "A Dissertation by William Hunter on the Uncertainty of the Signs of Murder in the Case of Bastard Children," British Medical Journal 165 (1931): 1143-44.

Patterson, Cynthia, "Not Worth The Rearing: The Causes of Infant Exposure in Ancient Greece," Transactions of the American Philosophical Association 115 (1985): 103-123.

Paulson, Jerome A., & Rushforth, Norman B., "Violent Death in Children in a Metropolitan County: Changing Patterns of Homicide, 1958 to 1982," Pediatrics 78 (1986): 1013-1020.

Pless, John E., "The Story of Baby Doe," Correspondence, New England Journal of Medicine 309 (1983): 664.

Poffenberger, Thomas, "Child Rearing and Social Structure in Rural India," Child Abuse and Neglect: Cross-Cultural Perspectives, edit. Jill Korbin, Berkeley: University of California Press, 1981, 71-95.

Pomeroy, Sarah B, "Infanticide in Hellenistic Greece," Images of Women in Antiquity, edit. Averil Cameron & Amelie Kuhrt, Wayne State University Press, 1983, 207-222.

Pontius, Anneliese A., "Infanticide in Limbic (?) Psychotic Trigger Reaction in a Man With Jacksonian and Petit Mal (?) Seizures: `Kindling' by Traumatic Experiences," Psychological Reports 67 (1990): 935-45.

Post, Stephen G., "Infanticide and Geronticide," Aging and Society 10 (1990): 317-328.

"Premiums for Infanticide," <u>Lancet</u> 2 (1861): 999.
Protocol For Determining If An Injury Is A Result Of Child Abuse Or Neglect, Illinois Department of Children and Family Services, 1987.
Qiu, Ren-Zong, "Morality in Flux: Medical Ethics Dilemmas in the People's Republic of China," <u>Kennedy Institute of Ethics Journal</u> 1 (1991): 16-27.
Radbill, Samuel X., "A History of Child Abuse and Infanticide," <u>Violence in the Family</u>, edit. Suzanne K. Steinmetz & Murray A. Straus, New York: Dodd, Mead & Co., 1974, 173-179.
Radbill, Samuel X., "Children in a World of Violence: A History of Child Abuse," <u>The Battered Child</u>, edit. Ray E. Helfer & Ruth S. Kempe, Chicago: University of Chicago Press, 1987, 3-22.
Radin, Max, "The Exposure of Infants in Roman Law and Practice," <u>Classical Journal</u> 20 (1925): 337-342.
Ransel, David L., "Abandoned Children of Imperial Russia: Village Fosterage," <u>Bulletin of the History of Medicine</u> 50 (1976): 501-510.
Rascovsky, Arnaldo, & Rascovsky, Matilde, "The Prohibition of Incest, Filicide and the Sociocultural Process," <u>International Journal of Psycho-Analysis</u> 53 (1972): 271-76.
Rawson, Beryl, "Children in the Roman Familia," <u>The Family in Ancient Rome</u>, edit. Beryl Rawson, Ithaca: Cornell University Press, 1986, 170-200.
Redford, Donald B., "The Literary Motif of the Exposed Child," <u>Numen</u> 14 (1967): 209-228.
Reece, Laura E., "Mothers Who Kill: Postpartum Disorders and Criminal Infanticide," <u>UCLA Law Review</u> 38 (1991): 699-757.
"Report of the Committee Appointed by the Council of the Obstetrical Society, June 2, 1869," <u>Transactions of the Obstetrical Society of London</u>, London: J.E. Adlard, Bartholoomer Close, XI (1870): 9.
Resnick, Phillip J., "Child Murder by Parents: A Psychiatric Review of Filicide," <u>American Journal of Psychiatry</u> 126 (1969): 325-334.
Riddell, Francis A., "Maidu & Konkow," <u>Handbook of North American Indians</u>, edit. William C. Sturtevant, <u>California</u>, edit. Robert F. Heizer, Washington, D.C.: Smithsonian Institution, 1978, 370-386.
Rodenburg, Martin, "Child Murder by Depressed Parents," <u>Canadian Psychiatric Association Journal</u> 16 (1971): 41-48.
Roheim, Geza, "The Western Tribes of Central Australia: Childhood," <u>The Psychoanalytic Study of Society</u> 2 (1962): 195-232.
Romito, Patrizia, "Postpartum Depression or the Medicalization of Maternal Unhappiness. A Critical Review," <u>Acta Obstetrica Gynecologica Scandinavia</u> 154 (69 Suppl)(1990):7-37.
Roper, A. G., "Ancient Eugenics," <u>Mankind Quarterly</u> 32 (1992): 383-419.
Roscoe, J., "Further Notes on the Manners and Customs of the Baganda," <u>Journal of the Anthropological Institute</u> 32 (1902): 25-80.
Rose, H. A., "Unlucky Children," <u>A Quarterly Review of Myth, Tradition, Institution & Custom</u> 13 (1902): 63-68.
Rosenblum, Victor G., & Budde, Michael L., "Historical and Cultural Consideration of Infanticide," <u>Infanticide & the Handicapped Newborn</u>, edit. Dennis J. Horan & Melinda Delahoyde, Provo, Utah: Brigham Young Press, 1982, 1-16.
Ruggiero, Kristin, "Honor, Maternity, and the Disciplining of Women: Infanticide in Late Nineteenth-Century Buenos Aires," <u>Hispanic American Historical Review</u> 72 (1992): 353-373.

Ruhrah, John, "Aztec Methods in Child Training," Bulletin of the History of Medicine 1 (1933): 19-22.

Russell, J. C., "Population in Europe 500-1500," The Middle Ages, edit. Carlo M. Cipolla, The Fontana Economic History of Europe, Harvester Press, Volume I (1976): 25-70.

Ryan, William Burke, "Child Murder In Its Sanitary and Social Bearings," Sanitary Review and Journal of Public Health (London, 1858): 4.

Sakuta, Tsutomu, & Saito, Satoru, "A Socio-medical Study on 71 Cases of Infanticide in Japan," Keio Journal of Medicine 30 (1981): 155-168.

Sargent, Carolyn F., "Born to Die: Witchcraft and Infanticide in Bariba Culture," Ethnology 27 (1988): 79-95.

Sauer, R. "Infanticide and Abortion in Nineteenth-Century Britain," Population Studies 32 (1978): 81-93.

Saunders, Edward, "Neonaticides Following `Secret' Pregnancies: Seven Case Reports," Public Health Reports 104 (1989): 368-372.

Savishinsky, Joel S., & Hara, Hiroko Sue, "Hare," Handbook of North American Indians, edit. William C. Sturtevant, Subarctic, edit. June Helm, Washington, D.C.: Smithsonian Institution, 1981, 314-325.

Savitt, Todd L., "Smothering & Overlaying of Virginia Slave Children: A Suggested Explanation," Bulletin of the History of Medicine 49 (1975): 400-404.

Sawyer, Jesse O., "Wappo," Handbook of North American Indians, edit. William C. Sturtevant, California, edit. Robert F. Heizer, Washington, D.C.: Smithsonian Institution, 1978, 256-263.

Sayre, James W., & Sayre, Robert F., "American Children and the `Children of Nature'", American Journal of Diseases of Children 130 (1976): 716-723.

Schrire, Carmel & Steiger, William Lee, "A Matter of Life and Death: An Investigation into the Practice of Female Infanticide in the Arctic," Man: The Journal of the Royal Anthropological Institute 9 (1974): 161-184.

Schwartz, Emanuel K., "Child Murder Today," Human Context, 4 (1972): 360-361.

Scott, P. D., "Parents Who Kill Their Children," Medicine, Science & the Law 13 (1973): 120-126.

Scott, P. D., "Fatal Battered Baby Cases," Medicine, Science & the Law 13 (1973): 197-206.

Scott, P. D. "The Psychiatrist's Viewpoint," The Maltreatment of Children, edit. Selwyn M. Smith, Baltimore: University Park Press, 1978, 175-204.

Scrimshaw, Susan C. M., "Infant Mortality and Behavior in the Regulation of Family Size," Population & Development Review 4 (1978): 383-403.

Scrimshaw, Susan C. M., "Infanticide in Human Populations: Societal & Individual Concerns," Infanticide, Comparative & Evolutionary Perspectives, edit. Glenn Hausfater & Sarah Blaffer Hrdy, New York: Aldine Publishing Co., 1984, 439-462.

Sensuke, Suga, "Gappo and his Daughter Tsuji," transl. Faubion Bowers, Joseph and Potiphar's Wife, edit. John D. Yohannan, New York: A New Directions Book, 1968, 247-258.

Shalinsky, Audrey, & Glascock, Anthony, "Killing Infants and the Aged in Nonindustrial Societies: Removing the Liminal," The Social Science Journal 25 (1988): 277-287.

Shapley, Deborah, "Anthropologist Fired: Stanford Plays Its China Card," Nature 302 (March 24, 1983): 280-281.

Shepler, Lynn T., "The Law of Abortion and Contraception – Past and Present,"

Psychiatric Aspects of Abortion, edit. Nada L. Stotland, Washington, D.C.: American Psychiatric Press, (1991): 51-73.

Shimkin, Demitri B., "Eastern Shoshone," Handbook of North American Indians, edit. William C. Sturtevant, Great Basin, edit. Warren L. D'Azevedo, Washington, D.C.: Smithsonian Institution, 1986, 308-335.

Shiono, Hiroshi, Maya, Atoyo, Tabata, Noriko, Fujiwara, Masataka, Azumi, Jun-ich, & Morita, Mashahiko, "Medicolegal Aspects of Infanticide in Hokkaido District, Japan," American Journal of Forensic Medicine & Pathology 7 (1986): 104-106.

Silverman, Robert A., & Kennedy, Leslie W., "Women Who Kill Their Children," Violence & Victims 3 (1988): 113-127.

Silverman, William A., "Mismatched Attitudes About Neonatal Death," Hastings Center Report 11(6)(December 1981): 12-16.

Sjovall, Hjalmar, "History of Abortion and Infanticide in Sweden," International Symposium on Society, Medicine and Law, edit. H. Karplus, Amsterdam: Elsevier Scientific Publishing Company, (1973): 173-179.

Small, Elisabeth C., "Contraception: Use and Failure," Psychiatric Aspects of Abortion, edit. Nada L. Stotland,Washington, D.C.: American Psychiatric Press, 1991, 89-103.

Smith, Charles R., "Tubatulabal," Handbook of North American Indians, edit. William C. Sturtevant, California, edit. Robert F. Heizer, Washington, D.C.: Smithsonian Institution, 1978, 437-445.

Smith, Eric Alden & Smith, S. Abigail, "Inuit Sex-ratio Variation: Population Control, Ethnographic Error, or Parental Manipulation?," Current Anthropology 35 (1994): 595-624.

Smith, James G. E., "Western Woods Cree," Handbook of North American Indians, edit. William C. Sturtevant, Subarctic, edit. June Helm, Washington, D.C.: Smithsonian Institution, 1981, 256-270.

Smith, James G. E., "Chipewyan," Handbook of North American Indians, edit. William C. Sturtevant, Subarctic, edit. June Helm, Washington, D.C.: Smithsonian Institution, 1981, 270-284.

Smout, Christopher, "Aspects of Sexual Behaviour in Nineteenth-Century Scotland," Bastardy and its Comparative History, edit. Peter Laslett, Karla Oosterveen & Richard M. Smith, Cambridge: Harvard University Press, 1980, 192-216.

Solomon, Theo, "History and Demography of Child Abuse," Pediatrics 51 (Supplement 4)(1973): 773-776.

Somander, L. K., & Rammer, L. M., "Intra- and Extrafamilial Child Homicide in Sweden 1971-1980," Child Abuse & Neglect 15 (1991): 45-55.

Speirs, Randall H., "Nambe Pueblo," Handbook of North American Indians, edit. William C. Sturtevant, Southwest, edit. Alfonso Ortiz, Washington, D.C.: Smithsonian Institution, 1979, 317-323.

Stager, Lawrence E. & Wolff, Samuel R., "Child Sacrifice at Carthage – Religious Rite or Population Control?," Biblical Archeology Review 10 (1984): 31-51.

Stannard, David E., "Recounting the Fables of Savagery: Native Infanticide and the Function of Political Myth," Journal of American Studies 25 (1991): 381-417.

Steele, Brandt F., "Psychology of Infanticide Resulting From Maltreatment," Infanticide and the Value of Life, edit. Marvin Kohl, Buffalo: Prometheus Books, 1978, 76-85.

Steele, Brandt, "Psychodynamic Factors in Child Abuse," The Battered Child, edit. Ray E. Helfer & Ruth S. Kempe, Chicago: University of Chicago Press, 1987, 81-114.

Steinbock, Bonnie, "Infanticide," Moral Issues in Mental Retardation, edit. R. S. Laura and A. F. Ashman, London: Croom Helm, 1985, 101-128.

Steinmetz, S. K., & Strauss, M. A., "The Family as Cradle of Violence," Society 10 (1973): 50-56.

Stern, Edward, "The Medea Complex: The Mother's Homicidal Wishes To Her Child," Journal of Mental Science 94 (1948): 321-331.

Straus, Murray A., & Kantor, Glenda Kaufman, "Stress and Child Abuse," The Battered Child, edit. Ray E. Helfer & Ruth S. Kempe, Chicago: University of Chicago Press, 1987, 42-59.

Strauss, R. P., "Culture, Rehabilitation, and Facial Birth Defects: International Case Studies," Cleft Palate Journal 22 (1985): 56-62.

Strickland, Charles, "A Transcendentalist Father: The Child Rearing Practices of Bronson Alcott," History of Childhood Quarterly: Journal of Psychohistory 1 (1973): 4-51.

Summit, Roland & Kryso, JoAnn, "Sexual Abuse of Children: A Clinical Spectrum," American Journal of Orthopsychiatry 48 (1978): 237-251.

Sutton, John R., "Stubborn Children: Law & the Socialization of Deviance in the Puritan Colonies," Family Law Quarterly 15 (1981): 31-64.

Taylor, L. & Newberger, E. H., "Child Abuse in the International Year of the Child," New England Journal of Medicine 301 (1979): 1205-1212.

Tefft, Sheila, "A Rush to Rob the Cradle – of Girls," Christian Science Monitor (August 2, 1995): 1.

Thearle, M. John & Gregory, Helen, "Child Abuse in Nineteenth Century Queensland," Child Abuse & Neglect 12 (1988): 91-101.

Thomas, David Hurst, Pendleton, Lorann S.A., & Cappannari, Stephen C., "Western Shoshone," Handbook of North American Indians, edit. William C. Sturtevant, Great Basin, edit. Warren L. D'Azevedo, Washington, D.C.: Smithsonian Institution, 1986, 262-283.

Thomas, Mason P., "Child Abuse & Neglect, Part I: Historical Overview, Legal Matrix, & Social Perspectives," North Carolina Law Review 50 (1972): 293-349.

Thomson, Ann, "Editorial, Why are Potential Women Being Killed?," Midwifery 9 (1993): 181-182.

Tien, H. Yuan, Tianlu, Zhang, Yu, Ping, Jingneng, Li & Zhongtang, Liang, "China's Demographic Dilemmas," Population Bulletin 47 (1992): 2-41.

Townsend, Patricia K., "Infant Mortality in the Saniyo-Hiyowe Population, Ambunti District, East Sepik Province," Papua New Guinea Medical Journal 28 (1985): 177-182.

Trexler, Richard C., "Infanticide in Florence: New Sources & First Results," History of Childhood Quarterly: Journal of Psychohistory 1 (1973): 98-116.

Turnbull III, H. Rutherford, "Incidence of Infanticide in America: Public and Professional Attitudes," Issues in Law & Medicine 1 (1986): 363-389.

Ulbricht, Otto, "The Debate About Foundling Hospitals in Enlightenment Germany: Infanticide, Illegitimacy, and Infant Mortality Rates," Central European History 18 (1985): 211-256.

Underwood, Nora, "Choosing Baby's Gender," Maclean's 100 (1987): 66.

van de Walle, Ettienne, "Illegitimacy in France During The Nineteenth Century," Bastardy and its Comparative History, edit. Peter Laslett, Karla Oosterveen & Richard M. Smith, Cambridge: Harvard University Press, 1980, 264-277.

Vanezis, Peter, "Women, Violent Crime and the Menstrual Cycle: A Review," Medicine, Science and the Law 31 (1991): 11-14.

Van Hook, LaRue, "The Exposure of Infants At Athens," Transactions of the American Philogical Society 51 (1920): 134-145.
Van N. Viljoen, G., "Plato and Aristotle on the Exposure of Infants at Athens," Acta Classica 2 (1959): 58-69.
Varga, Andrew C., "The Ethics of Infant Euthanasia," Thought 57 (1982): 438-448.
Viljoen, G. Van N., "Plato and Aristotle on the Exposure of Infants at Athens," Acta Classica 2 (1959): 62.
Wagatsuma, Hiroshi, "Child Abandonment and Infanticide: A Japanese Case," Child Abuse and Neglect: Cross-Cultural Perspectives, edit. Jill Korbin, Berkeley: University of California Press, 1981, 120-138.
Wagley, Charles, "Cultural Influences on Population: A Comparison of Two Tupi Tribes," Environment & Cultural Behavior, edit. Andrew P. Vayda, New York: The Natural History Press, 1969, 268-280.
Walraven, Ed, "Evidence for a Developing Variant of `La Llorona'," Western Folklore 50 (1991): 208-217.
Warkany, Josef, "Congenital Malformations in the Past," Journal of Chronic Disease 10 (1959): 84-96.
Weber, Leonard J., "In Defense of the Legal Prohibition of Infanticide," Infanticide & the Value of Life, edit. Marvin Kohl, Buffalo: Prometheus Books, 1978, 130-136.
Weisheit, R., "When Mothers Kill Their Children," Social Science Journal 23 (1986): 439-448.
Weisskopy, Michael, "China's Birth Control Policy Drives Some to Kill Baby Girls," Washington Post (Jan. 8, 1985): A1.
Wells, Robert V., "Illegitimacy and Bridal Pregnancy in Colonial America," Bastardy and its Comparative History, edit. Peter Laslett, Karla Oosterveen & Richard M. Smith, Cambridge: Harvard University Press, 1980, 349-361.
Wertz, Dorothy C. & Fletcher, John C., "Fatal Knowledge? Prenatal Diagnosis and Sex Selection," Hastings Center Report (May/June 1989): 21-27.
Wheeley, Shirley, "Looks That Kill the Capacity for Thought," Journal of Analytic Psychology 37 (1992): 187-210.
Wilczynski, Ania & Morri, Allison, "Parents Who Kill Their Children," Criminal Law Review January (1993): 31-36.
Wilkey, Ian, Pearn, John, Petrie, Gwynneth, & Nixon, James, Neonaticide, Infanticide and Child Homicide, Medicine Science & Law, 22:31-34, 1982.
Williams, Gertrude, "Introduction," Traumatic Abuse and Neglect of Children at Home, edit. Gertrude Williams & John Money, Baltimore: Johns Hopkins University Press, 1980, 9-13.
Williams, Gertrude, "Cruelty and Kindness to Children," Traumatic Abuse and Neglect of Children at Home, edit. Gertrude Williams & John Money, Baltimore: Johns Hopkins University Press, 1980, 68-88.
Williams, Glanville, "The Legal Evaluation of Infanticide," Infanticide & The Value Of Life, edit. Marvin Kohl, Buffalo: Prometheus Books, 1978, 115-129.
Williamson, Laila, "Infanticide: An Anthropological Analysis," Infanticide & The Value of Life, edit. Marvin Kohl, New York: Prometheus Books, 1978, 61-75.
Wilson, Stephen, "Infanticide, Child Abandonment, and Female Honour in Nineteenth-Century Corsica," Comparative Studies in Society and History 30 (1988): 762-83.
Winthrop, John, "A Heretic Bears a Monster," America Begins, edit. Richard M. Dorson, Bloomington: Indiana University Press, 1971, 121.
Wu, David, "Child Abuse in Taiwan," Child Abuse and Neglect: Cross-Cultural

Perspectives, edit. Jill Korbin, Berkeley: University of California Press, 1981, 139-165.

WuDunn, Sheryl, "In Japan, A Ritual of Mourning for Abortions," New York Times (January 25, 1996): A1.

Yengoyan, Aram A., "Biological & Demographic Components in Aboriginal Australian Socio-Economic Organization," Oceania 43 (1972): 85-95.

Yuan, H. Tien, Tianlu, Zhang, Yu, Ping, Jingneng, Li & Zhongtang, Liang, "China's Demographic Dilemmas," Population Bulletin 47 (1992): 11.

Zigmond, Maurice L., "Kawaiisu," Handbook of North American Indians, edit. William C. Sturtevant, Great Basin, edit. Warren L. D'Azevedo, Washington, D.C.: Smithsonian Institution, 1986, 398-411.

Zilboorg, Gregory, "Depressive Reactions Related to Parenthood," American Journal of Psychiatry 10 (1931): 927-962.

BOOKS

Abbo, John A. & Hannan, Jerome D., The Sacred Canons, St. Louis: B. Herder Book Co., 1960.

Abrahams, Roger D., African Folktales, New York: Pantheon Books, 1983.

Acts of the Apostles, The Anchor Bible, transl. Johannes Munck, Garden City, New York: Doubleday & Company, Inc., 1967.

Addison, Joseph, The Spectator, edit. Donald F. Bond, Oxford: The Clarendon Press, 1965.

Aeschylus, Agamemnon, transl. Richard Lattimore, Chicago: University of Chicago Press, 1953.

Aeschylus, Eumenides, transl. Philip Vellacott, Baltimore: Penguin Books, 1956.

The Age of Calamity, Alexandria: Time-Life Books, 1989.

The Age of God-Kings, Alexandria: Time-Life Books, 1987.

Albee, Edward, The American Dream, Coward, McCann & Geoghegan, Inc., New York, 1961.

Ancient Egypt, edit. David P. Silverman, New York: Oxford University Press, 1997.

Ancient Near Eastern Texts, edit. James B. Pritchard, Princeton: Princeton University Press, 1969.

Andersen, Johannes C., Myths & Legends of the Polynesians, London: George G. Harrap & Co., Ltd., 1928.

Anderson, G. L., Masterpieces of the Orient, W.W. Norton & Co., New York, 1961.

Anderson, Maxwell, The Wingless Victory, Washington, D.C.: Anderson House, 1936.

Anouilh, Jean, Medea, transl. Luce & Arthur Klein, Plays, New York: Hill & Wang, A Mermaid Dramabook, Volume III, 1967.

Apollodorus, The Library, transl. James George Frazer, London: William Heinemann, The Loeb Classical Library, 1921.

Aptekar, Herbert, Anjea: Infanticide, Abortion & Contraception in Savage Society, New York: William Godwin, Inc., 1931.

Apuleius, The Golden Ass, transl. W. Adlington, revised S. Gaselee, Cambridge: Harvard University Press, 1965.

Aquinas, St. Thomas, Summa Theologica,Great Books of the Western World, Chicago: William Benton, Volume 20, 1989.

Aristophanes, The Clouds, transl. Alan H. Sommerstein, New York: Penguin Books, 1981.

Aristophanes, Frogs, translated by Benjamin Bickley Rogers, Harvard University Press, Cambridge, Volume II, 1982.

Aristophanes, Thesmophoriazusae, transl. Benjamin Bickley Rogers, Cambridge: Harvard University Press, 1982.

Aristotle, Nicomachean Ethics, The Works of Aristotle, Chicago: William Benton, Encyclopedia Britannica, 1955.

Aristotle, Politics, The Basic Works of Aristotle, edit. Richard McKeon, New York: Random House, 1941.

Arnold, Matthew, Poetical Works, edit. C. B. Tinker & H. F. Lowry, London: Oxford University Press, 1966.

Arnold, Matthew, On the Classical Tradition, edit. R. H. Super, Ann Arbor: The University of Michigan Press, 1960.

Assyrian Laws, transl. G. R. Driver & John C. Miles, Oxford: Clarendon Press, 1935.

Athenagoras, Embassy For The Christians, transl. Joseph Hugh Crehan, Westminister: The Newman Press, 1956.

Atkinson, Dorothy, Dallin, Alexander & Lapidus, Gail Warshofsky, Women in Russia, Stanford: Stanford University Press, 1977.

Augustine, St., Against Julian, transl. Matthew A. Schumacher, New York: Fathers of the Church, Inc., 1957.

Augustine, St., The City of God, transl. John Healey, London: J. M. Dent & Sons, Ltd., 1973.

Augustine, St., Confessions, Basic Writings of St. Augustine, edit. Whitney J. Oates, New York: Random House, Volume I, 1948.

Augustine, St., The Works of Aurelius Augustine, edit. Rev. Marcus Dods, Edinburgh: T & T Clark, 1871.

Austen, Jane, Pride and Prejudice, New York: Washington Square Press, 1970.

Avebury, Lord, Pre-Historic Times, London: Williams & Northgate, 1900.

Avebury, Lord, The Origin of Civilization & the Primitive Condition of Man, London: Longmans, Green & Co., 1912.

Avery, Catherine B., The New Century Classical Handbook, New York: Appleton-Century-Crofts, Inc., 1962.

Baba Kamma, The Babylonian Talmud, transl. E. W. Kirzner, edit. I. Epstein, London: The Soncino Press, 1964.

Bacon, Roger, Opus Majus, transl. Robert Belle Burke, New York: Russell & Russell, Inc., 1962.

Badinter, Elisabeth, Mother Love, Myth and Reality, New York: Macmillan Publishing Co., Inc., 1981.

Baitsell, George Alfred, The Evolution of Man, New Haven: Yale University Press, 1923.

Balsdon, J. P. V. D., Life and Leisure in Ancient Rome, New York: McGraw-Hill Book Co., 1969.

Balsdon, J. P. V. D., Roman Women, New York: John Day Co., 1963.

Barbarian Tides, Alexandria: Time-Life Books, 1987.

Barclay, George W., Techniques of Population Analysis, New York: John Wiley & Sons, 1958.

Bardis, Panos D., History of Thanatology, New York: University Press of America, 1981.

Barnabas, Barnabas, Hermar and the Didache, transl. J. Armitage Robinson, New York: The MacMillan Co., 1920.

Barnstone, Willis, The Other Bible, San Francisco: HarperSanFrancisco, 1984.
Basden, G. T., Niger Ibos, New York: Barnes & Noble, Inc., 1966.
Battin, M. Pabst & Mayo, David J., Suicide: The Philosophical Issues, New York: St. Martin's Press, 1980.
Beane, Wendell C. & Doty, William G., Myths, Rites, Symbols: A Mircea Eliade Reader, New York: Harper & Row, 1975.
Beaumarchais, The Marriage of Figaro, transl. Anthony R. Pugh, London: MacMillan, 1968.
Beauvoir, Simone de, The Second Sex, New York: Vintage Books, 1974.
Bergamini, David, The Land & Wildlife of Australia, New York: Time-Life Books, 1972.
Bernatzik, Hugo Adolf, Akha and Miao: Problems of Applied Ethnography in Farther India, transl. Alois Nagler, New Haven: Human Relations Area Files, 1970.
Berndt, Ronald M. & Berndt, Catherine H., The World of the First Australians, Chicago: University of Chicago Press, 1964.
Best, Elsdon, The Maori, Wellington, New Zealand: Harry H. Tombs, 1924.
Biale, Rochel, Women and Jewish Law, New York: Schocken Books, 1984.
Bishop, Cecil, Women and Crime, London: Chatto & Windus, 1931.
Blackstone, Sir William, Commentaries on the Laws of England, edit. William Draper Lewis, Philadelphia: Rees Welsh & Co., 1898.
Blackwood, Beatrice, Both Sides of Buka Passage, Oxford: Clarendon Press, 1935.
Bloch, Dorothy, So The Witch Won't Eat Me, Boston: Houghton Mifflin Co., 1978.
Boccaccio, Giovanni, The Decameron, transl. Richard Aldington, New York: Dell Publishing Co., Inc., 1974.
Book of Mormon, Salt Lake City: The Church of Jesus Christ of Latter-Day Saints, 1990.
Boos, Claire, Scandinavian Folk & Fairy Tales, New York: Avenel Books, 1984.
Boswell, John, The Kindness of Strangers, New York: Vintage Books, 1988.
Bouscaren, T. Lincoln & Ellis, Adam C., Canon Law: A Text & Commentary, Milwaukee: Bruce Publishing Co., 1949.
Bremner, Robert H., Children & Youth in America, A Documentary History, Cambridge: Harvard University Press, 1970.
Briffault, Robert, The Mothers, New York: The Macmillan Co., 1927.
Briggs, Katharine, M., A Dictionary of British Folk-Tales, Bloomington: Indiana University Press, 1970.
Brockelmann, Carl, History of the Islamic Peoples, transl. Joel Carmichael & Moshe Perlmann, New York: Capricorn Books, 1960.
Brome, M. S., Abraham and Isaac, Everyman and Medieval Miracle Plays, edit. A. C. Cawley, New York: E. P. Dutton & Co., Inc., 1959.
Bronson, B.H., The Traditional Tunes of the Child Ballads, Princeton: Princeton University Press, 1959.
Buck, Pearl, The Good Earth, New York: Thomas Y. Crowell, 1977.
Buck, Pearl, Satan Never Sleeps, New York: Pocket Books, Inc., 1962.
Buettner-Janusch, John, Origins of Man, New York: John Wiley & Sons, Inc., 1967.
Bulfinch, Thomas, Mythology, New York: Avenel Books, 1979.
Bulgakov, Mikhail Afanasievich, The Master and Margarite, transl. Mirra Ginsburg, New York: Grove Press, Inc., 1967.
Bushnaq, Inea, Arab Folktales, New York: Pantheon Books, 1986.
Cadet, J. M., The Ramakien, Tokyo: Kodansha International, Ltd., 1971.

Calvin, John, Commentaries, transl. Joseph Haroutunian, The Library of Christian Classics, Philadelphia: The Westminster Press, 1958.
Calvin, John, Institutes of the Christian Religion, transl. Henry Beveridge, Grand Rapids: Wm. B. Eerdmans Publishing Co., 1957.
Calvin, John, Theological Treatises, transl. J. K. S. Reid, The Library of Christian Classics, Philadelphia: The Westminster Press, 1954.
Calvino, Italo, Italian Folk Tales, New York: Harcourt Brace Jovanovich, 1980.
Cameron, Averil & Kuhrt, Amelie, Images of Women in Antiquity, Wayne State University Press, 1983.
Campbell, Joseph, The Mythic Image, Princeton: Princeton University Press, 1974.
Cavendish, Richard, Legends of the World, New York: Schocken Books, 1982.
The Celestina, transl. Lesley Byrd Simpson, Berkeley: University of California Press, 1966.
Chaucer, Geoffrey, The Canterbury Tales, edit. Michael Murphy, Lanham: University Press of America, 1991.
2 Chronicles, The Anchor Bible, transl. Jacob M. Myers, Garden City: Doubleday & Company, Inc., 1965.
Chrysostom, S. John, The Homilies of S. John Chrysostom, Archbishop of Constantinople, transl. J. B. Morris, edit. John Henry Parker, London: F. & J. Rivington, 1848.
Cicero, De Inventione, transl. H. M. Hubbell, Cambridge: Harvard University Press, 1949.
Cicero, De Natura Deorum, transl. H. Rackham, Cambridge: Harvard University Press, 1956.
Cicero, De Officiis, transl. Walter Miller, Cambridge: Harvard University Press, 1956.
Cicero, De Re Publica, transl. Clinton Walker Keyes, London: William Heinemann, 1928.
Cicero, On Friendship, transl. Frank O. Copley, Ann Arbor: University of Michigan Press, 1967.
Cipolla, Carlo M., The Middle Ages, The Fontana Economic History of Europe, Harvester Press, 1976.
Clark, Grahame, & Piggott, Stuart, Prehistoric Societies, New York: Alfred A. Knopf, 1969.
Claudian, The Rape of Proserpine, transl. Maurice Platnauer, Cambridge: Harvard University Press, 1963.
Clement of Alexandria, Writings, transl. William Wilson, Edinburgh: T. & T. Clark, Edinburgh, 1867.
Clement of Rome, Epistles, transl. James A. Kleist, Westminster, Maryland: The Newman Bookshop, 1946.
The Code of Hammurabi, King of Babylon, transl. Robert Francis Harper, Chicago: University of Chicago Press, 1904.
Code of Jewish Law, transl. Rabbi Solomon Ganzfried, New York: Hebrew Publishing Co., 1961.
Colum, Padraic, A Treasury of Irish Folklore, New York: Crown Publishers, Inc., 1954.
Congreve, William, Love for Love, Lincoln: University of Nebraska Press, 1966.
Connery, John, Abortion: The Development of the Roman Catholic Perspective, Chicago: Loyola University Press, 1977.
Conrad, Joseph, Heart of Darkness, New York: New American Library.
Cook, James, Captain Cook's Journal During His First Voyage Round the World, edit. W. J. L. Wharton, London: Elliot Stock, 1893.

Copleston, Frederick, A History of Philosophy, Volume I, Part II, Greece and Rome, Garden City, New York: Image Books, 1962.
Costa, Joseph J. & Nelson, Gordon K., Child Abuse & Neglect: Legislation, Reporting & Prevention, Lexington: Lexington Books, C.C. Heath & Co., 1978.
Cotlow, Lewis, The Twilight of the Primitive, New York: The Macmillan Co., 1971.
Coulton, G. G., Life in the Middle Ages, Cambridge: University Press, 1967.
Covenant Book of Worship, Chicago: Covenant Press, 1981.
Crawford, D., Thinking Black: 22 Years Without a Break in the Long Grass of Central Africa, London: Morgan & Scott, Ltd., 1912.
Creekmore, Hubert, Lyrics of the Middle Ages, New York: Grove Press, Inc., 1959.
Croll, Elisabeth, Feminism & Socialism in China, London: Routledge & Kegan Paul, 1978.
Dante, The Divine Comedy, transl. Charles S. Singleton, Princeton: Princeton University Press, 1970.
Dante, The Divine Comedy, transl. John D. Sinclair, New York: Oxford University Press, 1972.
Dante, The Purgatorio, transl. John Ciardi, New York: New American Library, 1961.
Darwin, Charles, The Descent of Man, Chicago: Encyclopedia Britannica Great Books, 1971.
Darwin, Charles, The Descent of Man, and Selection in Relation to Sex, Princeton: Princeton University Press, 1981.
Darwin, Charles, The Origin of Species, New York: Collier Books, 1962.
Davies, Nigel, Human Sacrifice, New York: William Morrow & Company, Inc., 1981.
DeFrain, John, Taylor, Jacque, & Ernst, Linda, Coping with Sudden Infant Death, Lexington: Lexington Books, 1982.
Delarue, Paul, The Borzoi Book of French Folk Tales, transl. Austin E. Fife, New York: Alfred A. Knopf, 1956.
deMause, Lloyd, The History of Childhood, New York: The Psychohistory Press, 1974.
Dennis, Andrew, Foote, Peter, & Perkins, Richard, Laws of Early Iceland, Winnepeg: University of Manitoba Press, 1980.
Deuteronomy, The Anchor Bible, transl. Moshe Weinfeld, New York: Doubleday, 1991.
Devine, Philip E., The Ethics of Homicide, Ithaca: Cornell University Press, 1978.
Dibble, Sheldon, History & General Views of the Sandwich Islands Mission, New York: Taylor & Dodd, 1839.
Dickens, Charles, Great Expectations, Garden City, New York: Nelson Doubleday, Inc.
Dickens, Charles, Oliver Twist, London: Thomas Nelson & Sons, Ltd.
Dickens, Charles, A Tale of Two Cities, New York: Washington Square Press, Inc., 1967.
Dickson, John, Waving at Trains, Winnetka, Illinois: Thorntree Press, Inc., 1986.
Didache, Barnabas, Hermar and the Didache, transl. J. Armitage Robinson, New York: The MacMillan Co., 1920.
Diderot, Denis, D'Alembert's Dream, in Rameaus's Nephew and Other Works, translated by Jacques Barzun and Ralph H. Bowen, Bobbs-Merrill Company, Inc., Indianapolis, New York, 1956.
Dillon, Myles, Early Irish Literature, Chicago: The University of Chicago Press, 1958.
Dio Chrysostom, Discourses, transl. J. W. Cohoon, Cambridge: Harvard University Press, 1939.
Diodorus of Sicily, The Library of History, transl. C. H. Oldfather, London: William Heinemann, Ltd., 1933.

Diogenes Laertius, Lives of Eminent Philosophers, transl. R. D. Hicks, London: William Heinemann, Ltd., 1972.
Dionysius of Halicarnassus, Roman Antiquities, transl. Earnest Cary, Cambridge: Harvard University Press, 1948.
Disraeli, Benjamin, Sybil, Middlesex: Penguin Books, 1985.
The Documents of Vatican II, America Press, 1966.
Dorson, Richard M., Peasant Customs & Savage Myths, Chicago: University of Chicago Press, 1968.
Dorson, Richard M., America Begins, Bloomington: Indiana University Press, 1971.
Dunn, Charles W., The Foundling and the Werewolf, Toronto: University of Toronto Press, 1960.
Durant, Will, Our Oriental Heritage, New York: Simon and Schuster, 1954.
Eastman, Lloyd E., Family, Fields & Ancestors, New York: Oxford University Press, 1988.
Edmonds, Margot & Clark, Ell E., Voices of the Winds, New York: Facts On File, Inc., 1989.
Edmunds, Lowell, Oedipus, The Ancient legend and Its Later Analogues, Baltimore, The Johns Hopkins University Press, 1985.
Eggenton, Joyce, From Cradle to Grave, New York: William Morrow & Co., 1989.
Eliot, George, Adam Bede, New York: Everyman's Library, Dutton, 1978.
Ellis, William, Polynesian Researches, Rutland, Vermont: Charles E. Tuttle Co., 1969.
El-Shamy, Hasan M., Folktales of Egypt, Chicago: University of Chicago Press, 1980.
Elworthy, Frederick Thomas, The Evil Eye, New York: The Julian Press, Inc., 1958.
Emmison, F.G., Elizabethan Life: Disorder, Chelmsford, Essex County Council, 1970.
Empires Besieged, Alexandria, Virginia: Time-Life Books, 1987.
Encyclopedia Britannica, New York: Charles Scribner's Sons, 1879.
Encyclopedia Britannica, New York: Charles Scribner's Sons, 1881.
Encyclopedia Britannica, Chicago: William Benton, 1973.
Engelhardt, H. Tristam, The Foundations of Bioethics, Oxford University Press, New York, Oxford, 1986.
Epictetus, The Discourses, transl. W. A. Oldfather, London: William Heinemann, 1926.
Epiricus, Sextus, Outlines of Pyrrhonism, transl. R. G. Bury, London: William Heinemann, Ltd., 1933.
Erasmus, Colloquies, transl. Craig R. Thompson, Chicago: University of Chicago Press, 1965.
Erasmus, Handbook of the Militant Christian, transl. John P. Dolan, Notre Dame: Fides Publishers, Inc., 1962.
Erdoes, Richard, & Ortiz, Afonso, American Indian Myths & Legends, New York: Pantheon Books, 1984.
Ethiopic Didascalia, transl. J. M. Harden, New York: The MacMillan Co., 1920.
Euripides, Andromache, transl. John Frederick Nims, Chicago: University of Chicago Press, 1958.
Euripides, Bacchanals, transl. Arthur S Way, Cambridge: Harvard University Press, 1979.
Euripides, Hippolytus, translated by David Grene, in Euripides I, The University of Chicago Press, Chicago, London, 1955.
Euripides, Ion, Complete Greek Tragedies: Euripides III, edit. David Grene & Richard Lattimore, transl. Ronald Frederick Willetts, Chicago: University of Chicago Press, 1958.
Euripides, Iphigenia in Taurus, Euripides II, transl. Witter Bynner, Chicago: The University of Chicago Press, 1956.

Euripides, The Madness of Hercules, transl. Arthur S. Way, Cambridge: Harvard University Press, 1979.
Euripides, Medea, transl. Rex Warner, Euripides I, edit. David Grene & Richmond Lattimore, Chicago: The University of Chicago Press, 1955.
Euripides, Rhesus, transl. Arthus S. Way, Cambridge: Harvard University Press, 1966.
Eversley, Law of the Domestic Relations, edit. Alexander Cairns, London: Sweet & Maxwell, Ltd., 1926.
Ezekiel, The Anchor Bible, transl. Moshe Greenberg, Garden City, New York: Doubleday & Company, Inc., 1983.
Fairbank, John K. & Reischauer, Edwin O., China, Tradition & Transformation, Boston: Houghton Mifflin Company, 1989. Fairchild, Henry Pratt, People, The Quantity & Quality of Population, New York: Henry Holt & Co., 1939.
Falk, Avner, A Psychoanalytic History of the Jews, Cranbury, New Jersey: Associated University Presses, 1996.
Faulkner, William, Light in August, New York: The Modern Library, 1950.
Fei, Hsiao-Tung, Peasant Life in China: A Field Study of Country Life in the Yangtze Valley, London: George Routledge & Sons, Ltd., 1939.
Feldman, David, Birth Control in Jewish Law, New York: New York University Press, 1968.
Feldman, David M., Marital Relations, Birth Control & Abortion in Jewish Law, New York: Shocken Books, 1974.
Ferdowsi, Shah-nama, The Epic of the Kings, transl. Reuben Levy, Chicago: The University of Chicago Press, 1967.
Fielding, Henry, The History of Tom Jones, A Foundling, New York: Random House, 1964.
Fielding, Henry, Joseph Andrews, New York: Holt, Rinehart and Winston, 1967.
Fildes, Valerie A., Breasts, Bottles & Babies, Edinburgh: Edinburgh University Press, 1986.
Finucane, Ronald C., Soldiers of the Faith, New York: St. Martin's Press, 1983.
Firth, Raymond, Primitive Polynesian Economy, London: George Routledge & Sons, Ltd., 1939.
Firth, Raymond, We, The Tikopia, Boston: Beacon Press, 1957.
Fison, Lorimer, & Howitt, A. W., Kamilaroi & Kurnai, Oosterhourt, Netherlands: Anthropological Publications, 1967.
Fitzgerald, C. P., A Concise History of East Asia, Middlesex: Penguin Books, 1978.
Flaceliere, Robert, Daily Life in Greece at the Time of Pericles, transl. Peter Green, New York: MacMillan Co., 1965.
Flaubert, Gustave, Salammbo, transl. J. C. Chartres, London: Everymans Library, Dent, 1963.
The Fourth Book of Maccabees, edit. & transl. Moses Hadas, New York: Harper & Brothers, 1953.
France, Anatole, The Gods Will Have Blood, transl. Frederick Davies, Middlesex: Penguin Books, 1979.
Frankel, Ellen, The Classic Tales, London: Jason Aronson, Inc., 1989.
Frazer, James George, The Dying God, New York: Macmillan & Co., 1963.
Frazer, James George, The Golden Bough, New York: The Macmillan Co., 1935.
Frazer, James George, The Golden Bough, Aftermath, New York: The Macmillan Co., 1937.
Frazer, J. G., Totemism & Exogamy, London: Macmillan & Co., Ltd., 1910.

Freud, Sigmund, The Interpretation of Dreams, transl. James Strachey, The Complete Psychological Works of Sigmund Freud, New York: Basic Books, Inc., Volume IV, 1955.

Froissart, Jean, The Chronicles, transl. Lord Berners, Carbondale: Southern Illinois University Press, 1963.

Fromm, Erich, Man For Himself, New York: Rinehart & Co., Inc., 1947.

Fromm, Erich, You Shall be as Gods, New York: Holt, Rinehart and Winston, 1966.

Funk & Wagnalls, New Comprehensive International Dictionary of the English Language, New York: The Publishers Guild Press, 1973.

Fury of the Northmen, Alexandria: Time-Life Books, 1987.

Galdos, Benito Perez, Dona Perfecta, Great Neck, New York: Barron's Educational Series, Inc., 1960.

Gallagher, Hugh Gregory, By Trust Betrayed, New York: Henry Holt and Co., 1990.

Gardner, Jane F., Women in Roman Law & Society, Bloomington: Indiana University Press, 1986.

Gaubert, Henri, Abraham, Loved by God, transl. Lancelot Sheppard, New York: Hastings House, 1968.

Genesis, The Anchor Bible, transl. E. A. Speiser, Garden City, New York: Doubleday & Company, Inc., 1964.

Gibbon, Edward, The Decline and Fall of the Roman Empire, New York: Modern Library, 1946.

Gill, W. Wyatt, Jottings from the Pacific, New York: American Tract Society, 1885.

Ginzberg, Louis, On Jewish Law and Lore, Philadelphia: The Jewish Publication of America, 1955.

Goethe, Faust, transl. Charles E. Passage, Indianapolis: Bobbs -Merrill Educational Publishing, 1965.

Golden, Mark, Children and Childhood in Classical Athens, Baltimore: Johns Hopkins University Press, 1990.

Goldman, Irving, Ancient Polynesian Society, Chicago: University of Chicago Press, 1970.

Gorer, Geoffrey, Himalayan Village: An Account of the Lepchas of Sikkim, London: Michael Joseph Ltd., 1938.

Gorion, Micha Joseph Bin, Mimekor Yisrael Classical Jewish Folk Tales, transl. I. M. Lask, Bloomington: Indiana University Press, 1976.

Graves, Robert, The White Goddess, New York: Farrar, Straus and Giroux, 1966.

The Great Ages of Western Philosophy, Boston: Houghton, Mifflin Co., 1962.

Gribbin, John & Gribbin, Mary, Children of the Ice, Oxford: Basil Blackwell, Ltd., 1990.

Grillparzer, Franz, Medea, transl. Arthur Burkhard, Yarmouthport, Massachusetts: The Register Press, 1956.

Grimm's Fairy Tales, transl. E. V. Lucas, Lucy Crane & Marian Edwardes, New York: Grosset & Dunlap.

Grubb, W. Barbrooke, A Church in the Wilds, London: Seeley, Service & Co., Ltd., 1914.

Guerber, H.A., Legends of the Rhine, New York: A. S. Barnes & Co., 1905.

Guisso, Richard W. & Johannesen, Stanley, Women in China, Youngstown: Philo Press, 1981.

Guppy, H. B., The Solomon Islands and Their Natives, London: Swan Sonnenschein, Lowrey & Co., 1887.

Gurgani, Fakhr Ud-Din, Vis and Ramin, transl. George Morrison, New York: Columbia University Press, 1972.

Haaland, E. Sidney, Primitive Law, New York: Harper & Row, 1924.

Hackin, J., Huart, Clement, Linossier, Raymonde, Wilman-Grabowska, H. De, Marchal, Charles-Henri, Maspero, Henri, & Eliseev, Serge, Asiatic Mythology, New York: Thomas Y. Crowell Co., 1963.

Hale, William Harlan, The Horizon Book of Ancient Greece, New York: American Heritage Publishing Co., 1965.

Halsbury's Laws of England, London: Butterworths, 1976.

Hamilton, Edith, Mythology, New York: The New American Library, 1955.

Hamsun, Knut, Growth of the Soil, transl. W. W. Worster, New York: Vintage Books, 1972.

Hanawalt, Barbara A., The Ties That Bound, Oxford: Oxford University Press, 1986.

Handy, E. S. Craighill, & Pukui, Mary Kawena, The Polynesian Family System in Ka-'U, Hawaii, New Plymouth, New Zealand: Avery Press Ltd., 1958.

Hankoff, L. D., & Einsidler, Bernice, Suicide, Theory & Clinical Aspects, Littleton, Massachusetts: PSG Publishing Co., Inc., 1979.

Hardin, Garrett, Exploring New Ethics for Survival, New York: Viking Press, 1972.

Hardin, Garrett, Population, Evolution, and Birth Control, San Francisco: W. H. Freeman and Company, 1969.

Hardy, Thomas, Jude the Obscure, New York: The New American Library, 1961.

Hardy, Thomas, The Return of the Native, New York: The New American Library, 1959.

Harpers Dictionary of Classical Literature & Antiquities, edit. Harry Thurston Peck, New York: Cooper Square Publishers, Inc., 1962.

Harris, Marvin, Cannibals & Kings, The Origins of Cultures, New York: Random House, 1977.

Harrison, A. R. W., The Law of Athens, Oxford: Clarendon Press, 1968.

Harrisson, Tom, Savage Civilization, New York: Alfred A. Knopf, 1937.

Hartley, Shirley Foster, Illegitimacy, Berkeley: University of California Press, 1975.

Hastings, James, Encyclopedia of Religion & Ethics, New York: Charles Scribner's Sons, 1955.

Hauptmann, Gerhart, Dramatic Works, edit. Ludwig Lewisohn, New York: Viking Press, 1927.

Hauptmann, Gerhart, Teutonic Literature in English Translation, edit. James E. Miller Jr., Robert O'Neal, & Helen M. McDonnell, Glenview: Scott, Foresman and Company, 1970.

Hausfater, Glenn & Hrdy, Sarah Blaffer, Infanticide, Comparative & Evolutionary Perspectives, New York: Aldine Publishing Co., 1984.

Havard, J. D. J., The Detection of Secret Homicide, London: MacMillan & Co., Ltd., 1960.

Hearn, William Edward, The Aryan Household, London: Longmans, Green, & Co., 1879.

Hegel, Georg Wilhelm Friedrich, The Philosophy of History, transl. J. Sibree, New York: Dover Publications, Inc., 1956.

Helfer, Ray E. & Kempe, Ruth S., The Battered Child, Chicago: University of Chicago Press, 1987.

Heliodorus, An Ethiopian Romance, transl. Moses Hadas, Ann Arbor: University of Michigan Press, 1957.

Henry, Thomas R., Wilderness Messiah, New York: Bonanza Books, 1960.
Herodotus, The History, transl. D. Godley, Cambridge: Harvard University Press, The Loeb Classical Library, 1971.
Hesiod, Theogony, transl. Apostolas N. Athanassakis, Baltimore: Johns Hopkins University Press, 1983.
Hesiod, Works & Days, transl. Richmond Lattimore, Ann Arbor: University of Michigan Press, 1978.
Heyerdahl, Thor, American Indians in the Pacific, Chicago: Rand McNally & Co., 1953.
Hilton, Bruce, Callahan, Daniel, Harris, Maureen, Condliffe, Peter, & Berkley, Burton, Ethical Issues in Human Genetics, New York: Plenum Press, 1973.
Hines, Donald M., The Forgotten Tribes, Oral Tales of the Teninos and Adjacent Mid-Columbia River Indian Nations, Issaquah, Washington: Great Eagle Publishing, Inc., 1991.
Hinnells, John R., Persian Mythology, New York: Peter Bedrick Books, 1985.
The Hittite Laws, transl. Albrecht Goetze, Ancient Near Eastern Texts, edit. James B. Pritchard, Princeton: Princeton University Press, 1969.
Hobbes, Thomas, The Elements of Law, edit. Ferdinand Tonnies, Cambridge: University Press, 1928.
Hobbes, Thomas, Leviathan, London: Penguin Books, 1987.
Hoebel, E. Adamson, The Law of Primitive Man, Cambridge: Harvard University Press, 1961.
Hoffer, Peter & Hull, N. E. H., Murdering Mothers: Infanticide in England and New England 1558-1803, New York: New York University Press, 1981.
Hogg, Garry, Cannibalism & Human Sacrifice, New York: Citadel Press, 1966.
Holub, Eil, Seven Years in South Africa: Travels, Researches, and Hunting Adventures, Betweeen the Diamond-Fields and the Zambesi, Boston: Houghton, Mifflin & Co., 1881.
The Holy Scriptures, Chicago: The Menorah Press, 1957.
Homans, George C., The Human Group, New York: Harcourt, Brace & World, Inc., 1950.
Homeric Hymns, transl. Charles Boer, Chicago: Swallow Press, 1970.
Hoover, J. E., Uniform Crime Reports – 1966, Washington, D.C.: Government Printing Office, 1966.
Horace, Odes and Epodes, transl. Joseph P. Clancy, Chicago: University of Chicago Press, 1960.
Horan, Dennis J.,& Delahoyde, Melinda, Infanticide & the Handicapped Newborn, edit. Dennis J. Horan & Melinda Delahoyde, Provo, Utah: Brigham Young Press, 1982.
Horwitz, Robert M., & Davidson, Howard A., Legal Rights of Children, New York: McGraw-Hill, 1984.
Howarth, David, The Voyage of the Armada, London: Penguin Books, 1982.
Howells, William D., A Modern Instance, Boston: Houghton Mifflin Company, 1957.
Howitt, A. W., The Native Tribes of South-East Australia, London: Macmillan & Co., Ltd., 1904.
Hugo, Victor, The Works of Victor Hugo, Roslyn, New York: Black's Readers Service Company, 1928.
Hugo, Victor, Ninety Three, New York: Bantam Books, 1962.
Hume, David, Essays Moral, Political & Literary, edit. Eugene F. Miller, Indianapolis: Liberty Classics, 1987.

Hunt, David, Parents & Children in History, New York: Basic Books, Inc., 1970.

Hunter, William, Roman Law, London: William Maxwell & Son, 1876.

Huxley, Francis, Affable Savages, Rupert Hart-Davis, London, 1956.

Huxley, Julian, Man in the Modern World, New York: Mentor Books, 1948.

Infant Mortality: Its Causes and Remedies, Committee for Amending the Law in Points Wherein it is Injurious to Women, Manchester: A. Ireland & Co., 1871.

Inglis, Ruth, Sins of the Fathers, New York: St. Martin's Press, 1978.

Isaiah, The Anchor Bible, transl. John L. McKenzie, Garden City, New York: Doubleday & Company, Inc., 1968.

Isocrates, Panathenaicus, transl. George Norlin, London: William Heinemann, Ltd., 1968.

Jacobovits, Immanuel, Jewish Medical Ethics, New York: Bloch Publishing Co., 1975.

James, E. O., Primitive Ritual and Belief: An Anthropological Essay, London: Methuen & Co., Ltd., 1917.

Jeremiah, The Anchor Bible, transl. John Bright, Garden City, New York: Doubleday & Company, Inc., 1965.

Johnson, Samuel, Rasselas, Great Neck, New York: Barron's Educational Series, Inc., 1962.

Jones, Ann, Women Who Kill, New York: Holt, Rinehart & Winston, 1980.

Jordan, Paul, The Face of the Past, New York: Universe Books, 1985.

Josephus, Against Apion, transl. J. Thackeray, Cambridge: Harvard University Press, 1976.

Josephus, The Works of Flavius Josephus, transl. William Whitson, New York: American Publishers Corp., 1888.

Joyce, James, Ulysses, New York: Vintage Books, 1961.

Judges, The Anchor Bible, transl. Robert G. Boling, Garden City, New York: Doubleday & Company, Inc., 1969.

Jung, C. G., Civilization in Transition, transl. R. F. C. Hull, New York: Pantheon Books, 1964.

Junod, Henri A., The Life of a South African Tribe, New Hyde Park, New York: University Books, Inc., 1962.

Justinian, The Code of Justinian, transl. S. P. Scott, Cincinnati:The Central Trust Co., 1932.

Justinian, Digest, transl. Alan Watson, Philadelphia: University of Pennsylvania Press, 1985.

Justinian, Institutes, transl. J. B. Moyle, Oxford: Clarendon Press, 1955.

Juvenal, Satires, London: D. Browne, 1739.

Juvenal, The Satires of Juvenal, transl. Hubert Creekmore, New York: The New American Library, 1963.

Kalidasa, Shakuntala and Other Writings, New York: E. P. Dutton & Co., Inc., 1959.

Kaplan, Harold I., & Sadock, Benjamin J., Comprehensive Textbook of Psychiatry IV, Baltimore: Williams & Wilkins, 1989.

Kaplan, Harold I., & Sadock, Benjamin J., Comprehensive Textbook of Psychiatry VI, Baltimore: Williams & Wilkins, 1995.

Karplus, H., International Symposium on Society, Medicine and Law, Amsterdam: Elsevier Scientific Publishing Company, 1973.

Kempe, C. Henry, Franklin, Alfred White & Cooper, Christine, The Abused Child in the Family and in the Community, Oxford: Pergammon Press, 1980.

Kenyon, Theda, Witches Still Live, New York: Ives Washburn, 1929.

Kethuboth, The Babylonian Talmud, transl. Samuel Daiches & Israel W. Slotki, London: The Soncino Press, 1971.

Keye, William R., The Premenstrual Syndrome, Philadelphia: W. B. Saunders Company, 1988.

Khaldun, Ibn, The Muqaddimah, transl. Franz Rosenthal, Princeton: Princeton University Press, 1969.

Kiddushin, The Babylonian Talmud, transl. H. Freedman, edit. I. Epstein, London: The Soncino Press, 1966.

Kierkegaard, Soren, Fear and Trembling, transl. Walter Lowrie, Princeton: Princeton University Press, 1954.

2 Kings, The Anchor Bible, transl. Mordechai Cogan & Hayim Tadmor, Garden City: Doubleday & Company, Inc., 1988.

Kittredge, George Lyman, Witchcraft in Old and New England, Cambridge: Harvard University Press, 1929.

Kluge, Eike-Henner W., The Ethics of Deliberate Death, Port Washington, New York: Kennikat Press, 1981.

Knibbs, S. G. C., The Savage Solomons, London: Seeley, Service & Co., 1929.

Kohl, Marvin, Infanticide & The Value of Life, Buffalo: Prometheus Books, 1978.

Koran, transl. J. M. Rodwell, London: Everymans Library, 1968.

Korbin, Jill, Child Abuse and Neglect: Cross-Cultural Perspectives, Berkeley: University of California Press, 1981.

Krige, E. Jensen & Krige, J. D., The Realm of a Rain-Queen, London: Oxford University Press, 1956.

Kuhse, Helga & Singer, Peter, Should the Baby Live?, Oxford: Oxford University Press, 1985.

Lacey, W. K., The Family in Classical Greece, London: Thames and Hudson, 1968.

Lactantius, The Divine Institutes, Fathers of the Church, transl. Sister Mary Francis McDonald, Washington, D.C.: Catholic University of America Press, 1964.

Lamentation, The Anchor Bible, transl. Delbert R. Hillers, Garden City: Doubleday & Company, Inc., 1972.

Lammers, Stephen E. & Verhey, Allen, On Moral Medicine, Grand Rapids: William B. Eerdmans Publishing Co., 1987.

Laslett, Peter, Oosterveen, Karla, & Smith, Richard M., Bastardy & Its Comparative History, London: Edward Arnold, Ltd., 1980.

Laubscher, B. J. F., Sex, Custom & Psychopathology, New York: Robert M. McBride & Co., 1938.

Laura, R. S. & A. F. Ashman, Moral Issues in Mental Retardation, London: Croom Helm, 1985.

The Law Code of Gortyn, transl. Ronald F. Willetts, Berlin: Walter De Gruyter & Co., 1967.

Lawrence, D. H., The Rainbow, Middlesex: Penguin Books, 1974.

Lea, Henry Charles, History of Auricular Confession and Indulgences in the Latin Church, Philadelphia: Lea Brothers & Co., 1896.

Leavitt, Jerome E., The Battered Child, General Learning Corporation, 1974.

Lectionary for Mass, New York: Catholic Book Publishing Co., 1970.

Lee, Richard B. & DeVore, Irven, Man The Hunter, Chicago: Aldine Publishing Co., 1986.

Lee Yao, Esther S., Chinese Women: Past & Present, Mesquite: Ide House, Inc., 1983.

Leeuwen, Simon Van, Commentaries on Roman-Dutch Law, transl. John G. Kotze, London: Sweet & Maxwell, Ltd., 1923.

The Letters of Abelard and Heloise, transl. Betty Radice, Middlesex: Penguin Books, 1986.

Levenson, Jon D., The Death and Resurrection of the Beloved Son, New Haven: Yale University Press, 1993.

Levi-Strauss, Claude, The Elementary Structures of Kinship, transl. James Harle Bell & John Richard von Sturmer, Boston: Beacon Press, 1969.

Levy-Bruhl, Lucien, Primitive Mentality, London: George Allen & Unwin Ltd., 1923.

Lichtheim, Miriam, Ancient Egyptian Literature, Berkeley: University of California Press, 1975.

Light in the East, Alexandria: Time-Life Books, 1987.

Lindsay, Jack, The Ancient World, London, 1968.

Livy, History of Rome, transl. B. O. Foster, Cambridge: Harvard University Press, 1967.

Lobingier, Charles Sumner, The Evolution of the Roman Law, Omaha: C. S. Lobingier, 1923.

Locke, John, Two Treatises of Government, Cambridge: Cambridge University Press, 1988.

Lombroso, Caesar, & Ferrero, William, Female Offenders, New York: Philosophical Library, 1958.

London, Jack, Call of the Wild, New York: Bantam Books, 1963.

Longus, Daphnis and Chloe, transl. Paul Turner, Middlesex: Penguin Books, 1956.

Loudon, Nancy, Handbook of Family Planning, Edinburgh: Churchill Livingstone, 1985.

Lowie, Robert H., Primitive Society, New York: Boni & Liveright, 1920.

Lubbock, John, Pre-Historic Times, London: Frederic Norgate, 1878.

Lucan, Pharsalia, transl. Robert Graves, Baltimore: Penguin Books, 1957.

Lucian, The Works of Lucian of Samosata, transl. H. W. Fowler & F. G. Fowler, Oxford: Clarendon Press, 1905.

Lumholtz, Carl, Among Cannibals, transl. Rasmus B. Anderson, New York: Charles Scribner's Sons, 1889.

Lutheran Book of Worship, edit. Philip H. Pfatteicher & Carlos R. Messerli, Minneapolis: Augsburg Publishing House, 1979.

Lynn, David B., Daughters and Parents, Monterey, California: Brooks/Cole Publishing Co., 1979.

The Mabinogion, translated by Gwyn Jones & Thomas Jones, Everyman's Library, J.M. Dent & Sons Ltd., London, 1975.

MacDowell, Douglas M., The Law in Classical Athens, Ithaca: Cornell University Press, 1978.

Maimonides, The Book of Women, New Haven: Yale University Press, 1972.

Maimonides, The Book of Asservations, The Code of Maimonides, transl. B. D. Klein, New Haven: Yale University Press, 1962.

Maimonides, The Book of Holiness, The Code of Maimonides, transl. Louis I. Rabinowitz & Philip Grossman, New Haven: Yale University Press, Volume XVI, 1965.

Maimonides, The Code of Maimonides, transl. Abraham M. Hershman, New Haven: Yale University Press, 1949.

Maimonides, Moses, The Guide of the Perplexed, transl. Oram Shlomo Pines, Chicago: University of Chicago Press, 1963.

Malinowski, B., The Family Among the Australian Aborigines, New York: Schocken Books, 1963.

Malthus, Thomas Robert, On Population, edit. Gertrude Himmelfarb, New York: The Modern Library, 1960.
March of Islam, Alexandria: Time-Life Books, 1987.
Marcus, Jacob R., The Jew in the Medieval World, Cincinnati: The Sinai Press, 1938.
Marinatos, Spyridon, Crete & Mycenae, New York: Harry N. Abrams, Inc., 1960.
Markby, William, An Introduction to Hindu & Mahommedan Law, Oxford: Clarendon Press, 1906.
Marlowe, Christopher, The Jew of Malta, Five Plays, edit. Havelock Ellis, New York: Hill and Want, Inc., 1956.
Marlowe, Christopher, Tamburlaine, Part Two, edit. J. B. Steane, Middlesex: Penguin Books, 1971.
Martin, J. P., Violence and the Family, New York: John Wiley & Sons, Ltd., 1978.
Martinson, Floyd M., Growing Up in Norway, 800 to 1990, Carbondale: Southern Illinois University Press, 1992.
Martyr, St. Justin, Writings, transl. Thomas B. Falls, New York: Christian Heritage, Inc., 1948.
Martyr, Justin, The Writings of Justin Martyr & Athenagoras, transl. Rudolph Arbesmann, Sister Emily Joseph Daly & Edwin A. Quain, Edinburgh: T & T Clark, 1867.
Masson, Jeffrey Moussaieff, The Assault on Truth, Freud's Suppression of the Seduction Theory, New York: Farrar, Straus and Giroux, 1984.
Mathews, Jay & Mathews, Linda, One Billion, A China Chronicle, New York: Random House, 1983.
Matthews, Victor H., & Benjamin, Don C., Old Testament Parallels, New York: Paulist Press, 1991.
Maugham, R. C. F., Portuguese East Africa: The History, Scenery & Great Game of Manica and Sofala, New York: E. P. Dutton & Co., 1906.
Maugham, W. Somerset, The Complete Short Stories, Garden City, New York: Doubleday & Co., Inc., 1952.
Mayer, Ann Elizabeth, Islam & Human Rights, Boulder: Westview Press, 1991.
McClure, Ruth K., Coram's Children, New Haven: Yale University Press, 1981.
McMillan, Richard C., Engelhardt, H. Tristram & Spicker, Stuart F., Euthanasia and the Newborn: Approaches of the Ancient World, Dordrecht, Holland: D. Reidel Publishing Co., 1987.
McNeill, John T., & Gamer, Helena M., Medieval Handbooks of Penance, New York: Columbia University Press, 1938.
Mead, Margaret, Cooperation & Competition Among Primitive Peoples, Boston: Beacon Press, 1937.
Mead, Margaret, Male & Female, New York: William Morrow & Co., 1963.
Mead, Margaret, Sex & Temperament in 3 Primitive Societies, New York: Morrow Quill Paperbacks, 1963.
Meerloo, Joost, A. M., Suicide and Mass Suicide, New York: E. P. Dutton & Co., Inc., 1968.
Mekilita de-Rabbi Ishmael, transl. Jacob Z. Lauterbach, Philadelphia: The Jewish Publication Society of America, 1949.
Menander, The Arbitration, The Complete Greek Drama, edit. Whitney J. Oates & Eugene O'Neill, Jr., New York: Random House, 1938.
Menander, The Girl From Samos, The Complete Greek Drama, edit. Whitney J. Oates & Eugene O'Neill, Jr., New York: Random House, 1938.

The Middle Assyrian Laws, transl. Theophile J. Meek, Ancient Near Eastern Texts, edit. James B. Pritchard, Princeton: Princeton University Press, 1969.
Mill, John Stuart, On Liberty, Chicago: Henry Regnery Company, 1955.
Miller, Barbara D., The Endangered Sex, Neglect of Female Children in Rural North India, Ithaca, New York: Cornell University Press, 1981.
Miller, James E. Jr., O'Neal, Robert, & McDonnell, Helen M., Teutonic Literature in English Translation, Glenview, Illinois: Scott, Foresman and Company, 1970.
Miller, Nathan, The Child in Primitive Society, New York: Brentano's, 1928.
Millman, Laurence, A Kayak Full of Ghosts, Santa Barbara: Capra Press, 1987.
Milton, John, Paradise Lost, London: Longman Group Limited, 1971.
Minturn, Leigh & Hitchcock, John T., The Rajputs of Khalapur, India, New York: John Wiley & Sons, Inc., 1966.
Minucius, Marcus Felix, The Octavius, transl. G. W. Clarke, New York: Newman Press, 1974.
The Mishnah, transl. Herbert Danby, London: Oxford University Press, 1933.
M'Lennan, John F., Primitive Marriage, Edinburgh: Adam & Charles Black, 1865.
M'Lennan, John Ferguson, Studies in Ancient History, The Second Series, New York: Macmillan & Co., Ltd., 1886.
The Mongol Conquests, Alexandria: Time-Life Books, 1987.
Montagu, Ashley, Man: His First Million Years, New York: The New American Library, 1958.
Montaigne, Michel de, Essays, transl. J. M. Cohen, Middlesex: Penguin Books, 1970.
Moor, Edward, Hindu Infanticide, An Account of Measures Adopted for Suppressing the Practice of the Systematic Murder by Their Parents of Female Infants; With Incidental Remarks on Other Customs Peculair to the Natives of India, London: J. Johnson & Co., 1811.
Moore, George, Esther Waters, Boston: Houghton Mifflin Company, 1963.
Moorhead, Hugh S., The Meaning of Life, Chicago: Chicago Review Press, 1988.
More, Sir Thomas, Utopia, transl. Peter K. Marshall, New York: Washington Square Press, New York, 1970.
Morford, Mark P. O. & Lenardon, Robert J., Classical Mythology, London: Longman, 1977.
Morrison, Toni, Beloved, New York: New American Library, 1988.
Mukherjee, Bharati, Jasmine, New York: Ballantine Books, 1991.
Murdock, George Peter, Our Primitive Contemporaries, New York: MacMillan Co., 1971.
Murray, Thomas H. & Caplan, Arthur L., Which Babies Shall Live?, Clifton, New Jersey: Humana Press, 1985.
Mylonas, George E., Mycenae & the Mycenaean Age, Princeton: Princeton University Press, 1966.
Nansen, Fridtjof, Eskimo Life, London: Longmans, Green & Co., 1894.
Narayan, R. K., The Financial Expert, New York: Time Incorporated, 1966.
Netanyahu, B., The Marranos of Spain, New York: American Academy for Jewish Research, 1966.
New Century Classical Handbook, edit. Catherine B. Avery, New York: Appleton-Century-Crofts, Inc., 1962.
Newman, Horatio Hackett, Multiple Human Births, New York: Doubleday, Doran & Co., Inc., 1940.
Njal's Saga, transl. Magnus Magnusson & Hermann Palsson, Middlesex: Penguin Books, 1975.

Numbers, The Anchor Bible, transl. Baruch A. Levine, Garden City, New York: Doubleday, 1993.
Numbers, The Torah, A Modern Commentary IV, commentary W. Gunther Plaut, transl. Jewish Publication Society, New York: The Union of American Hebrew Congregations, 1979.
Oates, Kim, Child Abuse and Neglect, New York: Brunner/Mazel, 1986.
O'Connor, Anne, Child Murderess and Dead Child Traditions, A Comparative Study, Helsinki: Academia Scientiarum Fennica, 1991.
O'Connor, Frank, The Fountain of Magic, New York: Macmillan & Co., Ltd., 1939.
Of The Judgment of Homicide, London: Publications of the Selden Society, Bernard Quaritch, 1895.
O'Leary, De Lacy, Arabia Before Muhammad, London: Kegan Paul, Trench, Trubner & Co., Ltd., 1927.
Oliver, Douglas L., Ancient Tahitian Society, Honolulu: University Press of Hawaii, 1974.
Oliver, Douglas L., A Solomon Island Society: Kinship and Leadership Among the Siuai of Bougainville, Cambridge: Harvard University Press, 1955.
Oliver, Douglas L., The Pacific Islands, Honolulu: University Press of Hawaii, 1961.
O'Neill, Eugene, Desire Under the Elms, Three Plays, New York: Vintage Books.
Origen, The Fathers of the Church, transl. Ronald Heine, Washington, D.C.: The Catholic University of America Press, 1981.
Orleans, Leo A., Every Fifth Child: The Population of China, Stanford: Stanford University Press, 1972.
Orosius, Paulus, The Seven Books of History Against the Pagans, transl. Roy J. Deferrari, Washington, D.C.: Catholic University of America Press, 1964.
The Other Bible, edit. Willis Barnstone, San Francisco: HarperSanFrancisco, 1984.
Ovid, Amores, transl. Peter Green, Middlesex: Penguin Books, 1982.
Ovid, Fast I, transl. James George Frazer, Cambridge: Harvard University Press, 1951.
Ovid, Heroides, transl. Grant Showerman, Cambridge: Harvard University Press, 1958.
Ovid, Metamorphoses, transl. Rolfe Humphries, Bloomington: Indiana University Press, 1955.
Ovid, Tristia, transl. Arthur Leslie Wheeler, Cambridge: Harvard University Press, 1959.
Oxford English Dictionary, Oxford: Clarendon Press, 1961.
Paine, Thomas, The Age of Reason, New York: G. P. Putnam's Sons, 1924.
Pakrasi, Kanti B., Female Infanticide in India, Calcutta: Editions Indian, 1970.
Panigrahi, Lalita, British Social Policy and Female Infanticidein India, New Delhi: Munshiram Manoharlal, 1972.
Paredes, Americo, Folktales of Mexico, Chicago: University of Chicago Press, 1970.
Pascal, Blaise, Pensees, transl. A. J. Krailsheimer, New York: Penguin Books, 1980.
Pasternack, Boris, Doctor Zhivago, transl. Max Hayward & Manya Harari, New York: Ballantine Books, 1989.
Pausanias, Description of Greece, transl. W. H. S. Jones, Cambridge: Harvard University Press, 1969.
Pedroso, Consiglieri, Portugese Folktales, transl. Henriqueta Monteiro, New York: Benjamin Blom, Inc., 1969.
Pesahim, The Babylonian Talmud, transl. H. Freedman, London: The Soncino Press, London, 1967.
Petronius, Satyricon of Titus Petronius Arbiter, transl. Michael Heseltine, Cambridge: Harvard University Press, 1961.

Petrovitch, Woislav M., Hero Tales & Legends of the Serbians, London: George G. Harrap & Co., 1914.
Philalethes, Baptismon Didache or Scriptural Studies on Baptisms, Especially Christian Baptism, London: Bemrose & Sons, Ltd., 1907.
Philanthropus, The Institution of Marriage in the United Kingdom, London: Effingham Wilson, Royal Exchange, 1879.
Philo, Loeb Classical Library, transl. F. H. Colson & G. H. Whitaker, London: William Heinemann, Ltd., 1929.
Philo, The Special Laws, transl. F. H. Colson, Cambridge: Harvard University Press, 1950.
Philo, The Works of Philo, transl. C. D. Yonge, Peabody, Massachusetts: Hendrickson Publishers, 1993.
Philo of Byblos, The Phoenician History, transl. Harold W. Attridge & Robert A. Oden, Jr., Washington, D.C.: The Catholic Biblical Association of America, 1981.
Picard, Gilbert, Carthage, transl. Miriam & Lionel Kochan, London: Elek Books, 1956.
Piers, Maria W., Infanticide, New York: W. W. Norton & Co., 1978.
Place, Francis, Illustrations & Proofs of the Principle of Population, London: George Allen & Unwin Ltd., 1930.
Plato, Laws, transl. R. G. Bury, Cambridge: Harvard University Press, 1984.
Plato, The Republic, transl. Allan Bloom, New York: Basic Books, Inc., 1968.
Plato, Theaetetus, transl. B. Jowett, The Dialogues of Plato, New York: Random House, 1937.
Plautus, Truculentus, transl. George E. Duckworth, The Complete Roman Drama, New York: Random House, 1942.
Pliny, Letters & Panegyricus, transl. Betty Radice, Cambridge: Harvard University Press, 1969.
Pliny, Letters of Gaius Plinius Caecilius Secundus, transl. William Melmoth, New York: Harvard Classics, P. F. Collier & Son Corp., 1961.
Plutarch, Lives, Cambridge: Harvard University Press, The Loeb Classical Library, 1982.
Plutarch, Moralia, Cambridge: Harvard University Press, The Loeb Classical Library, 1971.
Poetry of the Orient, edit. Eunice Tietjens, New York: Alfred A. Knopf, 1934.
Polack, J. S., Manners & Customs of the New Zealanders, London: James Madden & Co., 1840.
Pollak, Otto, The Criminality of Women, Philadelphia: University of Pennsylvania Press, 1950.
Pollock, Linda A., Forgotten Children, Cambridge: Cambridge University Press, 1983.
Polo, Marco, The Travels, transl. Ronald Latham, Middlesex: Penguin Books, 1965.
Polybius, The Histories, transl. W. R. Paton, London: William Heinemann Ltd., 1927.
Pope, Alexander, Selected Poetry, edit. Martin price, New York: The New American Library, 1970.
Pritchard, James B., Ancient Near Eastern Texts, Princeton: Princeton University Press, 1969.
Propertius, The Elegies, transl. H. E. Butler, Cambridge: Harvard University Press, 1958.
Protocol for Determining if an Injury is a Result of Child Abuse or Neglect, Illinois Department of Children and Family Services, 1987.
Proverbs, The Anchor Bible, transl. R. B. Y. Scott, Garden City: Doubleday & Company, Inc., 1965.

Prudentius, The Poems of Prudentius, transl. Sister M. Clement Eagan, Washington, D.C.: Catholic University of America Press, 1962.
Pseudo-Phycylides, The Sentences of Pseudo-Phycylides, transl. P. W. Van Der Horst, Leiden: E. J. Brill, 1978.
Quennell Marjorie, & Quennell, C. H. B., Everyday Life in Prehistoric Times, New York: G. P. Putnam's Sons, 1959.
Quintilian, Institutio Oratio, transl. H. E. Butler, London: William Heinemann, 1922.
Qur'an, transl. M. H. Shakir, Elmhurst: Tahrike Tarsile Qur'an, Inc., 1991.
Racine, Jean, Athaliah, transl. John Cairncross, Middlesex: Penguin Books, 1972.
Racine, Jean, Iphigenia, transl. John Cairncross, Middlesex: Penguin Books, 1972.
Racine, Jean, Phaedra, The Best Plays of Racine, transl. Lacy Lockert, Princeton: Princeton University Press, 1966.
Radzinowicz, L. & Turner, J. W. C., The Modern Approach to Criminal Law, London: Macmillan & Co., Ltd., 1945.
Ramayana, transl. Aubrey Menen, New York: Charles Scribner's Sons, 1954.
Ramsey, Paul, Ethics at the Edges of Life, New Haven: Yale University Press, 1978.
Ransel, David L., Mothers of Misery, Princeton: Princeton University Press, 1988.
Raring, Richard H., Crib Death, Hicksville, New York: Exposition Press, 1975.
Rawson, Beryl, The Family in Ancient Rome, Ithaca: Cornell University Press, 1986.
Rees, Alwyn, & Rees, Brinley, Celtic Heritage: Ancient Tradition in Ireland and Wales, London: Thames & Hudson, 1961.
Reichel, Oswald J., A Complete Manual of Canon Law, London: John Hodges, 1896.
Reid, John Phillip, A Law of Blood, New York: New York University Press, 1970.
Riga, Peter, Sin & Penance: Insights Into the Mystery of Salvation, Milwaukee: Bruce Publishing Co., 1962.
Ritchie, Jane & Ritchie, James, Growing Up in Polynesia, Sydney: George Allen & Unwin, 1979.
Rivers, W. H. R., The Todas, London: Macmillan & Co., Ltd., 1906.
Robins, Joseph, The Lost Children, Dublin: Institute of Public Administration, 1980.
Roheim, Geza, Children of the Desert: The Western Tribes of Central Australia, New York: Basic Books, Inc., 1974.
Roscoe, John, The Baganda: An Account of Their Native Customs and Beliefs, London: Frank Cass & Co., Ltd., 1965.
Rose, Lionel, The Massacre of the Innocents: Infanticide in Britain 1800-1939, London: Ructledge & Kegan Paul, 1986.
Rosner, Fred, Studies in Torah Judaism: Modern Medicine and Jewish Law, Brooklyn: Yeshiva University Press, 1972.
Ross, James Bruce & McLaughlin, Mary Martin, The Portable Medieval Reader, New York: The Viking Press, 1949.
Roth, H. Ling, The Aborigines of Tasmania, Halifax: F. King & Sons, 1899.
Roth, H. Ling, Great Benin: Its Customs, Art and Horrors, Northbrook, Illinois: Metro Books, Inc., 1972.
Rousseau, Jean Jacques, Confessions, transl. W. Conyngham Mallory, Albert & Charles Boni, 1928.
Rousseau, Jean Jacques, Emile, transl. Barbara Foxley, London: Everyman's Library, Dent & Sons, Ltd., 1911.
Rousseau, Jean Jacques, The Social Contract, transl. Maurice Cranston, Middlesex: Penguin Books, 1985.
Routledge, W. Scoresby & Routledge, Katherine, With a Prehistoric People, London: Frank Cass & Co. Ltd., 1968.

Roux, Georges, Ancient Iraq, Middlesex: Penguin Books, 1977.
Ruhrah, John, Pediatrics of the Past, New York: Paul B. Hoeber, Inc., 1925.
Rule, Ann, Small Sacrifices, New York: Signet Book, 1988.
Russian Fairy Tales, New York: Pantheon Books, 1965.
Sagan, Eli, Cannibalism: Human Aggression and Cultural Form, New York: Harper & Row, 1974.
1 Samuel, The Anchor Bible, transl. P. Kyle McCarter Jr., Garden City, New York: The Anchor Bible, Doubleday & Company, Inc., 1980.
Sanhedrin, The Babylonian Talmud, transl. Jacob Schachter & H. Freedman, London: The Soncino Press, 1969.
Sartre, Jean-Paul, No Exit, transl. Stuard Gilbert, New York: Alfred A. Knopf, 1952.
Schaeffer, Francis A., & Koop, C. Everett, Whatever Happened to the Human Race, Old Tappan, New Jersey: Fleming H. Revell Co., 1979.
Schapera, I., A Handbook of Tswana Law and Custom, London: Oxford University Press, 1955.
Scheper-Hughes, Nancy, Death Without Weeping, The Violence of Everyday Life in Brazil, Berkeley: University of California Press, 1992.
Schiller, Friedrich von, The Poems of Schiller, transl. Edgar Alfred Bowring, Chicago: The Henneberry Company.
Schopenhauer, Arthur, On Human Nature, transl. Thomas Barley Saunders, London: George Allen & Unwin Ltd., 1957.
Scott, Sir Walter, The Heart of Mid-Lothian, Boston: Riverside Press, 1966.
Seder Nezikin, The Babylonian Talmud, transl. I. Epstein, London: The Soncino Press, 1935.
Seneca, Ad Lucilium Epistulae Morales, transl. Richard M. Gummere, Cambridge: Harvard University Press, 1953.
Seneca, Moral Essays, transl. John W. Basore, London: William Heinemann Ltd., 1928.
Seneca, Agamemnon, transl. Frank Justus Miller, The Complete Roman Drama, edit. George E. Duckworth, New York: Random House, New York, 1942.
Seneca, Mad Hercules, transl. Frank Justus Miller, The Complete Roman Drama, edit. George E. Duckworth, New York: Random House, 1942.
Seneca, Medea, transl. The Complete Roman Drama, edit. George E. Duckworth, New York: Random House, 1942.
Seneca, Oedipus, transl. Frank Justus Miller, The Complete Roman Drama, edit. George E. Duckworth, New York: Random House, 1942.
Seneca, Phaedra, transl. Frank Justus Miller, The Complete Roman Drama, edit. George E. Duckworth, New York: Random House, 1942.
Seneca, Thyestes, transl. Ella Isabel Harris, The Complete Roman Drama, edit. George E. Duckworth, New York: Random House, 1942.
Shabbath, The Babylonian Talmud, transl. H. Freedman, London: The Soncino Press, 1972.
Shahar, Shulamith, Childhood in the Middle Ages, London: Routledge, 1990.
Shakespeare, William, A Midsummer Night's Dream, New York: The Pocket Library, 1958.
Shakespeare, William, Henry the Fourth, Part One, New York: Bantam Books, 1988.
Shakespeare, William, The Life of Henry V, New York: New American Library, 1965.
Shakespeare, William, Macbeth, New York: Bantam Books, 1988.
Shakespeare, William, Much Ado About Nothing, New York: Bantam Books, 1988.

Shakespeare, William, The Tragedy of Titus Andronicus, New Haven: Yale University Press, 1926.
Shakespeare, William, The Comedy of Errors, New York: Bantam Books, 1988.
Shakespeare, William, The Winter's Tale, New York: Bantam Books, 1988.
Shelp, Earl E., Born to Die? Deciding the Fate of Critically Ill Newborns, New York: The Free Press, 1986.
Shepard, Sam, Buried Child, Seven Plays, New York: Bantam Books, 1981.
Shorter, Edward, The Making of the Modern Family, New York: Basic Books, Inc., 1975.
Shostak, Marjorie, Nisa, The Life and Words of a !Kung Woman, New York: Vintage Books, 1983.
Sibylline Oracles, transl. Milton S. Terry, New York: AMS Press, 1973.
Simon, Henry W., 100 Great Operas and Their Stories, Garden City, New York: Doubleday & Co., Inc., 1960.
Smith, Adam, The Wealth of Nations, Books I-III, Middlesex: Penguin Books, 1986.
Smith, Russell E., Concerning Human Life, Braintree, Massachusetts: Pope John Center, 1989.
Smith, Selwyn M., The Maltreatment of Children, Baltimore: University Park Press, 1978.
Smith, Thomas C., Nakahara, Stanford: Stanford University Press, 1977.
Smith, W. Robertson, Kinship & Marriage in Early Arabia, London: Adam & Charles Block, 1903.
Smyth, R. Brough, The Aborigines of Victoria, London: John Ferres, 1878.
Soga, John Henderson, The Ama-Xosa: Life and Customs, Lovedale, South Africa: Lovedale Press, 1931.
Song of Roland, transl. Dorothy L. Sayers, Baltimore: Penguin Books, 1963.
Sophocles, Electra, transl. E. F. Watling, London: Penguin Books, 1953.
Sophocles, Oedipus the King, transl. David Grene, Chicago: The University of Chicago Press, 1954.
Sophocles, Oedipus Rex, transl. Dudley Fitts & Robert Fitzgerald, New York: Harcourt Brace Jovanovich, 1977.
Soranus, Gynecology, transl. Owsei Temkin, Baltimore: The Johns Hopkins University Press, 1956.
Spence, Jonathan D., The Memory Palace of Matteo Ricci, New York: Penguin Books, 1985.
Spencer, Baldwin, & Gillen, F. J., The Northern Tribes of Central Australia, London: Macmillan & Co., Ltd., 1904.
Spencer, Baldwin & Gillen, F. J., The Arunta, London: MacMillan & Co., Ltd., 1927.
Spiegel, Shalom, The Last Trial, transl. Judah Goldin, New York: Pantheon Books, 1967.
Stacey, Judith, Patriarchy and Socialist Revolution in China, Berkeley: University of California Press, 1983.
Statutes of the Apostles or Canones Ecclesiastici, transl. G. Horner, London: Williams & Norgate, 1904.
Steinmetz, Suzanne K., The Cycle of Violence, New York: Praeger Publishers, 1977.
Steinmetz, Suzanne K., & Straus, Murray A., Violence in the Family, New York: Dodd, Mead & Co., 1974.
Stigand, C. H., To Abyssinia Through an Unknown Land, London: Seeley & Co., Ltd., 1910.

Stone, Lawrence, The Family, Sex, and Marriage, in England 1500-1800, New York: Harper & Row, 1979.

Storr, Anthony, Human Aggression, New York: Atheneum, 1968.

Stotland, Nada L., Psychiatric Aspects of Abortion, Washington, D.C.: American Psychiatric Press, 1991.

Stowe, Harriet Beecher, Uncle Tom's Cabin, New York: Literary Classics of the United States, Inc., 1982.

Strabo, The Geography, transl. Horace Leonard Jones, Cambridge: Harvard University Press, 1967.

Stuard, Susan Mosher, Women in Medieval Society, University of Pennsylvania Press, Inc., 1976.

Sturtevant, William C., Handbook of American Indians, Washington, D.C.: Smithsonian Institution, 1983.

Suetonius, The Lives of the Twelve Caesars, transl. Philemon Holland, New York: The Heritage Press, 1965.

Sumner, William, Folkways, Boston: Ginn & Co., 1911.

Swift, Jonathan, Satires and Personal Writings, edit. William Alfred Eddy, London: Oxford University Press, 1956.

Swift, Jonathan, Gulliver's Travels & Other Writings, edit. Ricardo Quintana, New York: Modern Library, 1958.

Tacitus, Annals, transl. Alfred John Church & William Jackson Brodribb, New York: Modern Library, 1942.

Tacitus, The Histories, transl. Clifford H. Moore, London: William Heinemann, 1931.

Talmudic Anthology, edit. Louis I. Newman, New York: Behrman House, Inc., 1947.

Tatius, Achilles, Clitophon and Leucippe, transl. S. Gaselee, Westport, Connecticut: Greenwood Press, 1976.

Tedlock, Dennis, Finding the Center, Narrative Poetry of the Zuni Indians, New York: The Dial Press, 1972.

Terence, The Lady of Andros, transl. John Sargeaunt, London: William Heinemann, 1926.

Terence, The Mother in Law, The Comedies of Terence, edit. Robert Graves, New York: Frederick Ungar Publishing Co., 1968.

Tertullian, Apologetical Works, The Fathers of the Church, transl. Rudolph Arbesmann, Emily Joseph Daly, & Edwin A. Quain, Washington, D.C.: The Catholic University of America Press, 1950.

Theodosian Code, transl. Clyde Pharr, Princeton: Princeton University Press, 1952.

Tien, H. Yuan, China's Strategic Demographic Initiative, New York: Praeger, 1991.

Tietjens, Eunice, Poetry of the Orient, New York: Alfred A. Knopf, 1934.

Tindale, Norman B., Aboriginal Tribes of Australia, Berkeley: University of California Press, 1974.

Todd, Arthur James, The Primitive Family as an Educational Agency, New York: G. P. Putnam's Sons, 1913.

Tohoroth, The Babylonian Talmud, transl. Herbert Danby, London: Oxford University Press, 1933.

Tolstoy, Leo, On Life & Essays on Religion, transl. Aylmer Maude, London: Oxford University Press, 1959.

Tolstoy, Leo, The Portable Tolstoy, transl. John Bagley, New York: Penguin Press, 1978.

Tooker, Elisabeth, An Iroquois Source Book, New York: Garland Publishing, Inc., 1985.

Totman, J., The Murderess: A Psychological Study of Criminal Homicide, San Francisco: R. & E. Research Associates, 1978.

Turville-Petre, E. O. G., Myth & Religion of the North, The Religion of Ancient Scandinavia, New York: Holt, Rinehart & Winston, 1964.

Ullmann, Walter, Law & Jurisdiction in the Middle Ages, London: Variorum Reprints, 1980.

Upanishads, transl. F. Max Muller, New York: Dover Publications, Inc., 1962.

Valerian, Saint, Homilies, transl. George E. Ganss, Washington, D.C.: Catholic University of America Press, 1965.

Van Buitenen, J. A. B., Tales of Ancient India, Chicago: University of Chicago Press, 1959.

Vaux, Kenneth, Birth Ethics, New York: Crossroad, 1989.

Virgil, Aenead, transl. Allen Mandelbaum, Berkeley: University of California Press, 1982.

Virgil, Virgil's Works, transl. J. W. Mackail, New York: The Modern Library, 1950.

Voyages of Discovery, Alexandria: Time-Life Books, 1988.

Waddy, Charis, Women in Muslim History, London: Longman, 1980.

Waley, Arthur, Translations From the Chinese, New York: Alfred A. Knopf, 1941.

Wallace, Alfred Russel, A Narrative on the Travels of the Amazon and Rio Negro, London: Wark, Lock & Co., 1889.

Weinreich, Beatrice Silverman, Yiddish Folktales, transl. Leonard Wolf, New York: Pantheon Books, 1988.

Weir, Robert F., Selective Nontreatment of Handicapped Newborns: Moral Dilemmas in Neonatal Medicine, Oxford: Oxford University Press, 1984.

Werner, Oscar Helmuth, The Unmarried Mother in German Literature New York: Columbia University Press, 1917.

Westermarck, Edward, The Origin and Development of the Moral Ideas, London: Macmillan & Co., Ltd., 1906.

Westermarck, Edward, The History of Human Marriage, London: Macmillan & Co., Ltd., 1921.

Westermarck, Edward, The Future of Marriage in Western Civilization, New York: The Macmillan Co., 1937.

Westermarck, Edward, A Short History of Marriage, New York: Humanities Press, 1968.

Westrup, C. W., Introduction to Early Roman Law, London: Oxford University Press, 1944.

Weyland, John, The Principles of Population and Production, as They are Affected by the Progress of Society; With a View to Moral & Political Consequences, London: Baldwin, Cradock & Joy, 1816.

White, Theodore H., In Search of History, New York: Warner Books, 1978.

Wiedemann, Thomas, Adults and Children in the Roman Empire, New Haven: Yale University Press, 1989.

Wiesel, Elie, Messengers of God, transl. Marion Wiesel, New York: Random House, 1976.

Williams, Gertrude & Money, John, Traumatic Abuse and Neglect of Children at Home, Baltimore: Johns Hopkins University Press, 1980.

Williams, Glanville, The Sanctity of Life & the Criminal Law, New York: Alfred H. Knopf, 1968.

Williams, Howard, The Superstitions of Witchcraft, London: Longman, Roberts & Green, 1865.

Wilson, Jerry B., Death by Decision, Philadelphia: Westminster Press, 1975.
The Wisdom of Solomon, transl. David Winston, The Anchor Bible, Garden City, New York: Doubleday & Company, Inc., 1979.
Wolff, Larry, Postcards From the End of the World, New York: Macmillan Publishing Co., 1988.
Wollman-Tsamir, Pinchas, The Graphic History of the Jewish Heritage, New York: Shengold Publishers, Inc., 1963.
World Almanac & Book of Facts, New York: World Almanac, 1993.
Wrigley, E. A., Population & History, New York: McGraw-Hill Book Co., 1979.
Xenophon, Anabasis, transl. Carleton L. Brownson, Cambridge: Harvard University Press, 1961.
Xenophon, Memorabilia, transl. E. C. Marchant, Cambridge: Harvard University Press, 1968.
Yao, Esther S. Lee, Chinese Women: Past & Present, Mesquite: Ide House, Inc., 1983.
Yohannan, John D., Joseph and Potiphar's Wife, New York: A New Directions Book, 1968.
Young, Marilyn B., Women in China, Ann Arbor: Center for Chinese Studies at the University of Michigan, 1973.
Yu-Lan, Fung, A History of Chinese Philosophy, transl. Derk Bodde, Princeton: Princeton University Press, 1952.
Yutang, Lin, The Wisdom of China and India, New York: Random House, 1942.
Zenkovsky, Serge A., Medieval Russia's Epics, Chronicles and Tales, New York: E. P. Dutton & Co., 1963.
Zohar, transl. Daniel Chanan Matt, New York: Paulist Press, 1983.
Zola, Emile, L'Assommoir, transl. Atwood H. Townsend, New York: The New American Library, 1962.

BIBLE

Acts 7:19,21; 11:16; 19:4; 26:5
II Chronicles 21:4; 25:4; 28:1-3,5; 33:6
I Corinthians 7:6,9; 10:21; 11:3,7,9; 14:34-36
Deuteronomy 4:24; 5:17; 6:5; 12:31; 13:5-7; 18:10; 19:21; 21:18-21,30-31; 22:18,21,22,23; 23:2,17; 24:16; 28:53; 31:2,9.
Ecclesiastes 12:13,14
Ephesians 5:23,24; 6:5-7
Exodus 1:16,22; 2:3-5; 13:1,2,13; 20:1,5; 21:7,15,17,22,23; 22:29; 32:9, 33:5,29; 34:9,20
Ezekiel 16:5-7,20,21,36-38; 18:13,20; 20:23-26,31; 23:37,39
Galatians 4:30,31
Genesis 1:26,27; 2:7,18,21-23; 3:16; 9:1,5-7; 16:1-3;18:10,20,23, 24,25; 19:5,8,10,32, 37,38;21:3,6,10,12,13,15,18;22:2,6,7,8,11,12; 35:11; 37:35; 38:24,28
Hebrews 6:16; 9:22,26; 10:4,12-14; 11:19,23
Isaiah 49:1,5,15; 57:5
James 2:22; 3:9
Jeremiah 1:1-3,5; 2:5,17; 7:31; 19:4-6,9; 20:17,18; 32:35
Job 3:11,13,16,17,23; 21:19
John 1:6,26,31; 3:5,16; 6:30,31,35,53-55
1 John 1:7
Joshua 16:26

Judges 9:53,54; 11:31,35,36
I Kings 3:19,20,25,27; 11:7,11-13; 16:18,34; 19:18; 21:21; 21:29
II Kings 3:27; 6:28,29,30; 10:6; 15:16; 16:3; 17:3,6,12,16,17,30, 31,40,41; 21:6; 23:4,10
Lamentation 4:10
Leviticus 1:2,3; 18:21; 20:2,9; 24:17,19,20; 26:29; 27:6
Luke 1:35; 3:3,16; 9:24; 12:4,5,52,53; 14:26; 18:15-17
Mark 8:35; 13:12; 16:16
Matthew 1:18-21; 2:16; 3:13-17; 10:21,34-37; 17:18; 19:24,29; 27:4,5
Micah 6:7,8
Nehemiah 5:2-3,5
Numbers 3:4,11-13; 8:13,17; 18:14-16; 35:12,30,31,33
1 Peter 1:18,19
Proverbs 5:21; 13:1,24; 17:25; 19:18; 20:20,30; 22:15; 29:15,17,
Psalms 106:38; 127:3; 139:13
Revelation 2:7
Romans 1:20; 4:16,20; 6:3; 8:4,7,32; 11:4
I Samuel 1:11,20,28; 2:11; 14:24,29,39,44,45; 15:22; 31:4
II Samuel 12:14; 17:23
I Timothy 2:10-14

LEGAL CASES

American Academy of Pediatrics v. Bowen, 795 F2d 211 (DC Cir 1986).
American Academy of Pediatrics v. Heckler, 561 F.Supp. 395 (D.D.C. 1983).
American Hosp. Ass'n v. Heckler, 585 F.Supp. 541, aff'd 694 F2d 676 (1984).
Bowen v. American Hospital Assn. 476 US 610, 106 SCT 2101 (plurality opinion, 1986).
Campbell v. People, 159 Ill 9, 42 NE 123, (1895).
Commonwealth v. Cass, 392 Mass 799, 467 NE2d 1324 (1984).
Fletcher et al v. The People, 52 Ill 395 (1869).
Ingraham v. Wright, 97 SC 1401, 430 US 651 (1977).
In the Matter of BABY K., 832 F.Supp. 1022 (E.D.Va. 1993), affm'd 16 F3d 590 (4th Cir 1994)
In the Matter of Baby K., 16 F3d 590 (4th Cir 1994).
Keeler v. Superior Court of Amador County, 87 CalRptr 481, 470 P2d 617 (1970).
Lynam v. People, 65 IllApp 687 (1895).
Matthews v. State, 240 Mis 189, 126 So.2d 245 (1961).
Parham v. J.R., 442 US 584, 99 SCt 2493 (1979).
People v. Greer, 79 Ill2d 103, 402 NE2d 203, (1980).
People v. Hayner, 90 NE2d 23, 300 NY 171 (Crt Appeals, 1949).
People v. Ryan, 138 NE2d 516, 9 Ill2d 467, (1956).
People v. Shum, 117 Ill2d 317, 512 NE2d 1183, (1987)
People v. Skeoch 408 Ill 276, 96 NE2d 473 (1951).
Prince v. Commonwealth of Massachusetts, 321 US 158, 166, 64 SCt 438, 442 (1944).
Quilloin v. Woolcott, 434 US 246, 255 (1978).
Repouille v. United States, 165 F2d 152 (CA2 1947).
Rex v. Brain, 6 Carr. & P. 349, 172 Eng.Rep. 1272 (1834).
Rex v. Enoch, 5 Carr. & P. 539, 172 Eng.Rep. 1089 (1833).
Rex v. Poulton, 5 Carr. & P. 329, 172 Eng.Rep. 997 (1832).

Roe v. Wade, 410 US 113, 93 SCt 705, (1973).
State v. Horne, 282 SoC 444, 319 SE2d 703 (1984).
State v. Jones, 95 NC 588, (1886).
State v. Osmus, 73 Wyo 47, 276 P2d 469 (1954).
State v. Perricone, 37 NJ 463, 181 A.2d 751, cert. den. 371 US 890 (1962).
State v. Winthrop, 43 Iowa 519 (1876).
State Ex Rel. Atkinson v. Wilson, 332 SE2d 807 (WVa 1984).
U.S. v. Spencer, 839 F.2d 1341 (9th Cir.), cert. den. 487 U.S. 1238, 108 SCt 2908 (1988).
United States v. University Hospital, State Univ of N.Y. at Stony Brook 575 F. Supp. 607 (EDNY 1984).
U.S. v. University Hosp., State U. of New York, 729 F2d 144 (2nd Cir 1984).
Weber v. Stony Brook Hospital, 60 NY2d 208, 456 NE2d 1186 (per curiam) (1983).

NEWSPAPERS

ACP Observer, December, 1997, Volume 17, pg 3.
American Medical News, April 20, 1992, pg 3, 42, 43.
American Medical News, November 28, 1994, pg 1.
American Medical News, November 20, 1995, pg 15.
American Medical News, March 25, 1996, pg 47.
American Medical News, July 29, 1996, 55.
Chicago Tribune, Nov 22, 1990, section 2, pg 20.
Chicago Tribune, April 23, 1991, section 2, pg 1.
Chicago Tribune, August 8, 1991, section 2, pg 1.
Chicago Tribune, November 15, 1991, section 2, pg 2.
Chicago Tribune, January 30, 1992, section 2, pg 4.
Chicago Tribune, February 16, 1992, section 1, pg 4.
Chicago Tribune, June 24, 1992, section 1, pg 8.
Chicago Tribune, August 21, 1992, section 2, pg 1.
Chicago Tribune, November 24, 1992, section 1, pg 1.
Chicago Tribune, December 12, 1992, section 1, pg 10.
Chicago Tribune, February 26, 1993, section 1, pg 3.
Chicago Tribune, April 7, 1993, section 1, pg 1.
Chicago Tribune, June 6, 1993, section 4, pg 1.
Chicago Tribune, June 22, 1993, section 1, pg 6.
Chicago Tribune, September 10, 1993, section 1, pg 1.
Chicago Tribune, September 10, 1993, section 1, pg 16.
Chicago Tribune, November 30, 1993, section 1, pg 4.
Chicago Tribune, April 1, 1994, section 1, pg 15.
Chicago Tribune, May 20, 1996, section 1, pg 10.
Chicago Tribune, September 27, 1997, section 1, pg 5.
Chicago Tribune, January 16, 1999, section 1, pg 9.
New York Times, November 18, 1990, section 1, pg 1.
New York Times, November 5, 1991, Science Times, pg C1.
New York Times, September 11, 1994, section L, pg 36.

Index

L

M

N

T

U

V

W

X

Y

Z